Contributions to Economics

For further volumes:
http://www.springer.com/series/1262

Marcel van Marion

International Trade Policy and European Industry

The Case of the Electronics Business

Springer

Marcel van Marion
Eindhoven
Netherlands

ISSN 1431-1933
ISBN 978-3-319-00391-7 ISBN 978-3-319-00392-4 (eBook)
DOI 10.1007/978-3-319-00392-4
Springer Cham Heidelberg New York Dordrecht London

Library of Congress Control Number: 2013941991

Printed on acid-free paper

Springer is part of Springer Science+Business Media (www.springer.com)

Preface

The writing of this book was initiated by the understanding that many developments in the electronics business have remained unexplained or will be forgotten. An account of practical experience related to trade policy and trade policy rules may also be lost. Some sectors of European business have disappeared. That would not be a disaster if ignoring some facts would not cause repeated catastrophes. According to the rules of probability, such disasters do not occur twice at the same spot. This may be correct.

Almost 25 years of practice in the electronics business, with Philips Electronics, and in the boards of industry associations plus an additional period as a private trade policy counsellor rendered me experience in the use of trade policy instruments. This book is a report on my experiences in this domain. Often it describes adventures that have gone astray in the jungle of rules and politics. It describes victories and defeats in the arena of international economic relations. Defeats have truncated the industry and reduced the need for trade policy representation.

I thank many people at Philips for giving me the opportunity to be at the centre of many events of international relations. Members of the board of Philips Electronics entrusted me with some interesting, even fascinating tasks.

Extremely important were those amazingly few members of the staff of Philips' Bureau for International Economic Relations who contributed to some of the episodes sketched on the pages hereafter. I would like to mention Karine Hustinx, Diny Janssen, Casper Garos, Wicko van Haalen, Frank Smits and André Rhoen, brilliant and dedicated people, who made a formidable contribution to the advancement of the international relations of Philips and the industry.

Companion in arms, Henri Anus, former délégué général of the French Simavelec, offered his friendship and fine cooperation in the many years that I worked on behalf of the European electronics industry and provided me with some supplementary documents used in this book.

I am grateful to Edwin Vermulst, this worthy opponent in various anti-dumping cases, gifted with an exceptional knowledge – causing envy – of international trade law, for his encouraging remarks and particularly for the intellectually stimulating discussions over the years, although we often found ourselves on different sides of the fence.

Frits Bolkestein earns my lasting gratitude for his friendship and encouragement during important stages of my career.

Showing her intellectual grasp of the matters described in the book and thanks to her quick mind and efficiency, Maegan McCann has made an invaluable contribution by editing and polishing texts that needed improvement. I thank her for it.

And last but not least, and in contrast to the Windhundverfahren in export licensing – first come, first served, as described in Sect. 3.3 of this book – I express my gratitude to my dear wife Anja, who gave a solid base to the project and has patiently waited until the completion of this book, encouraging me and requesting to be prudent in the texts, probably knowing that she asked for the impossible.

June 2013 Marcel van Marion

Abbreviations

ADA	Anti-Dumping Agreement, Agreement on Implementation of Article VI of the General Agreement on Tariffs and Trade 1994
ALARM	Association for Legal Auto Radio Measures, Temporary European Association of Car Audio Producers
ANIE	Associazone Nazionale Italiano dell' Industrie Elettrotecniche ed Elettroniche, Italian Electro Technical and Electronics Association
BCG	Boston Consulting Group
Benelux	Belgium Netherlands and Luxemburg (Economic Union)
BREMA	British Radio and Electronic Equipment Manufacturers' Association
BTS	Broadcast Television Systems (a Bosch Philips Joint Ventrue)
CAP	Common Agricultural Policy
CCC	Community Customs Code
CCC	Customs Cooperation Council, predecessor of the WCO
CFL-i	Compact Fluorescence Lamps Integrated (Electronic)
CIAJ	Communications Industry Association of Japan; now: Communications and Information Network Association of Japan
CIF	Seller Must Pay the Costs, Insurance and Freight to Bring the Goods to the Port of Destination.
CN	Combined Nomenclature: Codes and Product Definitions for Common Customs Tariff and of the External Trade Statistics
COP	Cost of Production
EACEM	European Association of Consumer Electronics Manufacturerts
ECSC	European Coals and Steel Community
EEC	European Economic Community
EECA	European Electronic Components Manufacturers' Association
EFTA	European Free Trade Area
EIAJ	Electronics Industry Association of Japan
EPR	Effective Rate of Protection
ESL	Energy Saving Lamp

Fabrimetal	Belgian Federation of Metal and Electrical Industry, Since 2000 Agoria
FME	Federation of Metal and Electrical Industry (in the Netherlands)
FOB	Free on Board: The Seller Must Load the Goods on Board the Vessel Nominated by the Buyer and Bear Costs Including Loading
GATT	General Agreement on Tariffs and Trade
GEC	General Electric Company Ltd, A UK Electronics Company
HDTV	High Definition Television Broadcasting System
HiFi	High Fidelity, Originally Meeting the Standard of Deutsche Industrie Normierung (DIN) 45500
HS	Harmonized System: International Code and Tariff Nomenclature
IC	Integrated Circuit
ITT	International Telephone & Telegraph Corp., later ITT Corp., Electronics Conglomerate Broken Up in 1995
JMEA	Japan Machinery Exporters' Association (Private Branch of METI)
JVC	Victor Corporation of Japan, a Subsidiary of Panasonic
LGE	LG Electronics, Formerly Lucky GoldStar
LoT	Level of Trade Adjustment (the Addition to the CIF Value of Imported Products for Calculation of Resale Price)
MES	Market Economy Status
MET	Market Economy Treatment
METI	Ministry of Economy, Trade and Industry of Japan, Previously MITI
MITI	Ministry of International Trade and Industry (of Japan). In 2001: Ministry of Economy, Trade and Industry (METI)
NEC	Nippon Denki Kabushiki Gaisha, Nippon Electric Company, Limited
NEDC	National Economic Development Council (Advisory Council for Industry Development) (Neddy)
NHK	Nippon Hoso Kyokai, Japan Broadcasting Corporation
NME	Non-Market Economy
NTSC	National Television System Committee (of the USA)
NTT	Nippon Telephone and Telegraph Company
OCT	Ordinary Course of Trade
OECD	Organisation for Economic Co-operation and Development
OEM	Original Equipment Manufacturers, Traders with Own Production in the Sector
OMA	Orderly Market Agreement
PAL	Phase Alternating Line
PCB	Printed Circuit Board
PCN	Product Code Number (Code for a Product with the Specific Characteristics)

PDO	Philips DuPont Optical, a Joint Venture for Optical Media, (CD, DVD, Magneto-Optical Discs)
POETIC	Producers of European Televisions in Cooperation, Temporary Association of Television Producers
PPF	Plain Paper Fax
QR	Quantitative Restriction (Quota)
RCA	Radio Corporation of America
RIC	Radio Industry Council, a British Industry Platform
RTC	la Radiotechnique Compélec, Frenchpart of Philips Components Division
SCAN	Society of Coherent Anti-dumping Norms, Temporary European Association of CTV Producers
SCART	Syndicat des Constructeurs d'Appareils Radiorécepteurs et Téléviseur, Later SIMAVELEC
SEL	Standard Elektrik Lorenz AG, since 1979 Part of ITT, Which was in 1988 Sold to NOKIA
SIMAVELEC	le syndicat des industries de matériels audiovisuels électroniques
SWP	Sector Working Party (of NEDC)
TCE	Thomson Consumer Electronics, previously Thomson Grand Public
TMM	Thomson Multi Media, Successor to TCE
TSP	Thermo Sensitive Paper
TT	Thermo Transfer
VCR	Video Cassette Recorders
VCR-TV	Combinations of Video Cassette Recorders and Television
VER	Voluntary Export Restraint
VHS	Video Home System, Video Cassette Format Introduced by JVC
VRA	Voluntary Restraint Agreement
WCO	World Customs Organisation, Successor of the CCC
WTO	World Trade Organisation
ZVEI	Zentralverband Elektrotechnik- und Elektronikindustrie, Central Association of Electrotechnical and Electronic Industry

Contents

List of Graphs

List of Diagrams

List of Pictures

List of Tables

Chapter 1
Introduction

Abstract International trade policy is a tool of business rather than of solemn statements. Some examples of industrial allocation policy issues and formal statements about international trade rounds show the discrepancy between the two. Knowledge of trade rules may prevent serious errors in settlement of industrial activities, of which some cases are presented. However, trade rounds offer serious opportunities for active input by industry for tangible results from trade negotiations, of which some examples are given.

"International Trade Policy and European Industry, The Case of the Electronics Business" is, of course, about trade policy: the rules, the economics of the law and the practical problems encountered the by European electronics business, and the outcome of the solutions it created or invoked. Trade policy is frequently, but incorrectly, conceived as the domain of governmental and international organisations. Cohorts of professional travellers from business urging governments to act vigorously might have created this idea. They have accompanied opening conferences of trade rounds with solemn declarations, suggesting that their presence at such conferences as in Punta del Este of the Uruguay Round and the many ministerial meetings in Doha, Cancún and Hong Kong of the Doha Development Round was of vital importance for both their enterprises and the success of the international negotiations. It is not. Ministerial meetings are mostly a start of actual negotiations and a signal for industry to do its homework. Business must take stock of its direct interests, make practical contributions and pay attention to whether there is a need to adjust to new conditions of competition.

Trade policy is definitely not restricted to governmental affairs. If they are used as tool of business management, companies can improve their competitive environment. Of course, they may and sometimes must adjust to outcomes of the trade policy decision-making processes, but they also may join the game and influence rules and outcomes. They can take existing rules for granted, or bend them. They may provide input into trade negotiations by influencing or even by specifying concessions. Knowledge of trade rules is required in any case. Rules and their

M. van Marion, *International Trade Policy and European Industry*,
Contributions to Economics, DOI 10.1007/978-3-319-00392-4_1,

applications are not immutable. They are multi-interpretable and alterable. And they can be implemented divergently. Corporate lawyers tend to explain the rules, and their explanations generally suggest that these rules do not leave room for executives to shape a trade environment to serve their interests. The opposite is the illusion that by trade measures, all management problems can be solved.

At Philips, for instance, some management wanted a panacea; they envisaged all of their industrial problems to be solved by trade policy, generally by protectionist measures. An example of this attitude was the rash establishment of a video recorder assembly factory in Hungary. Soon after the Iron Curtain was raised, in 1989 the management of the Philips video recording division in its headquarters in Vienna, Austria, concluded in an entrepreneurial dash and sufficient blindness that they "had to be there", i.e. in East Europe. A big factory was hurriedly built in the west Hungarian town of Szekesfehervar, where VCRs were assembled from kits and subassemblies made in Vienna. Austria was not yet a member of the European Community, but of the European Free Trade Area (EFTA). According to the origin rules in the preferential trade agreement between the European Economic Community (EEC) and EFTA, VCRs from Austria had duty-free access if wholly made in Austria or with sufficient components from Austria or other EFTA members or from the European Community. Before the transfer of assembly to Hungary, all Austrian made recorders had duty-free access to EFTA and the European Community. According to origin rules in the preferential trade agreement between the European Community and Hungary, all VCRs with sufficient combined Hungarian and EEC value and components had duty-free access to the European Community. VCRs made in Hungary from mainly Austrian components did not qualify for 0 % customs duty access to the EEC. The management of the VCR business found out that VCRs exported from Hungary to the European Community were unexpectedly hit with a customs duty of 14 %. This shows the importance of knowledge of origin rules. Management of the VCR division was furious, although not about the mistakes. They felt that the existing rules were radically wrong and they should immediately be changed; Philips experts and lobbyists should adopt a "street fighters" mentality and should change these unjustifiable rules. Efforts were made to change the rules and a change was on the verge of realisation when Austria joined the European Community in 1995. Due to Austria's accession, the problem of Hungarian assembly and origin was solved. Emergency brakes had to be applied immediately in order to avoid that the new rules would be implemented and become advantageous to others.

Fortunately, the factory in Hungary had perforce started production of VCR-TV combinations. Before this accidental VCR investment in Hungary, nobody within Philips had ever shown any interest in the production or marketing of these combinations. It was generally assumed that they were a useless and unprofitable product. Only Koreans and a few Japanese had the ambition to manufacture and market this worthless product. With a cathode ray tube from the European Community (made by Philips in Barcelona, Spain) this equipment had sufficient European Community content for duty-free access to the European Community after processing in Hungary. The 14 % EEC was therefore avoided. That was a sufficient reason for filling the capacity of the Hungarian factory, and the VCR-TV combi amazingly appeared a successful and highly profitable product that nobody had considered worth a glimpse.

External trade rules were considered the cause of the troubles actually attributable to Philips' own ignorance and carelessness. Blaming the rules was more suitable than admitting mistakes. Such a case, in which external trade policy measures had to solve problems attributable to internal mistakes, was not uncommon. Reshaping the world was increasingly preferred to solutions of relatively small internal problems. Internal discussions about trade policy became endemic within Philips. Rather than dealing with production, products and marketing, executives discussed grand proposals for new European Community trade rules. For a long time directors of business units in bad shape pronounced a trendy view that only products with 60 % European content should be allowed free European Community circulation. They seemed to think that all products not fulfilling this requirement should and could go into a destructor. This was notwithstanding the availability of trade instruments, requiring more efforts than simply a global reform of trade rules.

Although the possibility of adapting the rules to suit the specific needs of private enterprises may be overrated, the restriction of policy objectives under the General Agreement on Tariffs and Trade (GATT) or its successor the World Trade Organization (WTO), in which the benefits of free trade are only applauded, is the opposite extreme and equally ineffective.[1] Apart from the fact that the practice of companies often contradicts their statements, belief in such phrases may bereave companies from valuable actions in the field of trade, including contributions to liberalisation of trade. Of course, trade rounds are salutary to the global economy. There is no need to underline such a truism with empty and riskless statements. Trade rounds should foster trade and welfare, and strengthen the legal basis for participants in trade. That does not rule out the possibility of economic actors to use concessions offered in negotiations between the governmental actors or to offer concessions themselves in exchange for certain advantages.

This book gives an account of use of trade policy tools in practice, while paying respect to trade rules, and explains the economic rationale of such rules. It is also a history of the adventures of European electronics industry from the trade policy annals. Battles between competitors are sketched, but not merely as a narrative. Frequently the book discusses trade policy events, underlying trade rules and

[1] A letter by the International Chamber of Commerce (ICC) to the Financial Times of 8 November 2005 is of striking triviality: "We underline our conviction that a successful Doha Round is vital to enable business to continue to play a leading role in the eradication of poverty and the raising of global living standards." And: "The need is for strong political leadership. And the time for it is now!" Politicians were probably not flattered by businessmen's incitement for strong leadership. Proudly, the ICC announced in its leaflet "What ICC achieved for business in 2005": "ICC obtained the support of more than 60 chairmen and CEOs of leading companies from around the world who signed a letter to the Financial Times published on 8 November 2005 calling on governments to redouble their efforts to ensure the success of the Doha Round." It did not help.

related economic theory. Topics presented from trade practice are largely those in the electronics industry. Trade policy has often been a weapon in the skirmishes among rivals in the market. Trade rules can be used in two directions: for the creation of impediments to competitors and for the improvement of one's own market position both in domestic and export market. Trade instruments used are described and explained and their legal and economic backgrounds expounded.

Those interested in the history of European electronics industry and decline may find new facts and background information. Management can use the book as practical and theoretical guide. Lawyers will find many examples from trade policy practice and can also take some notice of the economic theoretical background of rules, events and policies. Economists are often confronted with theory without practice. They will find some of both.

A selection from European trade policy history in the electronics sector is presented, including some anecdotes. A narration on too many hilarious episodes would distract the reader from serious issues this book tries to tackle. It deals with historical events and acts that failed to prevent the disappearance of many producers and production areas. It tells what occurred in television markets and in VCR and Compact Disc business. It gives historical reports on what occurred in anti-dumping cases concerning fax equipment, television camera systems and energy saving lamps. These cases are described on the basis of practical experience. The book offers some information about such proceedings, both internal business aspects and the procedural matters.

In various chapters, the method of WTO tariff negotiations is clarified. Tariff protection and how effective protection is calculated is another subject. Disadvantages and advantages of protection are shown with computations. Outward processing is a trade tool, the essentials of which are demonstrated with numerical example from practice. Legal matters are touched upon when dumping cases and other trade policy matters and trade fraud are discussed, and certain precautions and warnings are given. Excellent books on anti-dumping law are available that deal in detail with legal issues. This book closes with a methodological guide on anti-dumping proceedings and methods of calculation of dumping and injury on the basis of practical data allowing both a legal and economic and practical insight.

Examples provide readers with technical tools and background, and the businessman gets a lead into the world of trade, which is not necessarily soporific. The use of these instruments did not prevent the European industry from seriously suffering. Descriptions of the fate of the electronics industry and especially the consumer electronics industry, which has finally disappeared, go hand in hand with the description of trade and trade policy.

Chapter 2
Limitations of Voluntary Restraints

Abstract The consumer electronics industry in the Benelux and the United Kingdom sought protection against Japan. Both governments pursued Voluntary Restraint Agreements (VRA). Scrutiny of the agreements shows that they failed to protect and even injured the industry involved. In the United Kingdom their effect favoured the Japanese industry, offering cheap and uncomplicated access to the European market. Imposition of a highly innovative protective measure by France, and massive dumping of video recorder imports from Japan endangering survival of a European VCR format, necessitated intervention by the European Commission. The result was a VRA, the details of which are presented below. This restraint implied discontinuation of both Sony's Betamax and European Video 2000 formats. It took some time before European Community authorities became aware of the catastrophic effect of this VRA. The VCR case was the first signal of the decline of the European electronics industry.

2.1 VRA Fashion

Voluntary export restraints (VERs), restraint agreements (VRAs) or orderly market agreements (OMAs) are the most characteristic settlements for Japan's export trade with importing countries in trouble. Criticism of such agreements is frequent.[1] Agreements on export self-restraint were not seen as alternatives to import restrictions, but as new forms of protectionism. VRAs and OMAs were considered a special type of protection against imports, especially from Japan. The issue of VER or OMA characteristics and their relationship with Japan is discussed in next chapter.

[1] McClenahan (1991) blames the Americans; Hindley (1986) belongs to a circuit of professional criticasters of both VERs and the Community trade policy in general. He generally confines his criticism to importing countries.

M. van Marion, *International Trade Policy and European Industry*, Contributions to Economics, DOI 10.1007/978-3-319-00392-4_2,

2.2 Benefits and Luxury of a Benelux Agreement

In the second half of the 1970s, the former director of the Canadian Philips organisation returned to corporate centre in Eindhoven, the Netherlands, with serious concerns about the Japanese threat to non-Japanese consumer electronics. His concerns stemmed from negative experiences with the Japanese presence in the North-American region; the organisation had lost market share and he personally held the Japanese responsible for the loss, while others within the company held him responsible. He may have been correct, however. In the United States the audio and television industry was practically destroyed by the Japanese and TV audio industry. In his opinion, Japan posed a serious threat to Europe. European producers might technologically have been able to compete in North America, but they focused on the European domestic market: an expensive mistake. United States resistance against Japanese penetration came, although restricted to the legal front and not very successfully, from Zenith.

Prior to the introduction of CTV in Japan, RCA licensed its technology in 1962[2] and Japanese producers began manufacturing sets and exporting them, in limited quantities, to the United States. The Japanese broadcasting organization NHK prepared itself for introduction of colour television – while Japanese television manufacturers introduced their products to the United States market, a network of colour television broadcasting was set up in Japan, allowing for reception in practically every Japanese household. Together, the wide availability of reception, the Japanese wage system with its large bonus share, Japanese consumer eagerness for new products, and the high level of Japanese savings stimulated sales of luxury goods and a fast penetration of CTV. Within 5 years, more than 75 % of Japanese households had a colour television set.[3]

The formidable initial production capacity of Japanese industry for mainly small sets with a diagonal screen size of 20 in. (20″ or about 51 cm) or less made exports imperative. In contrast to the United States and European markets, the Japanese market started with small-screen sets, offering pictures with resolution more suitable for tiny rooms in small houses. When reception improved, sets with larger screen sizes were sold. In North America and Europe small screen sets were sold as second sets, i.e. after sufficient penetration of large-screen sets took place. Until 1975, not one single set larger than 21 in. was shipped to the Japanese market. Because of protective devices, such as the distribution structure – dealt with in Chap. 7 –, and technical approval procedures serving as trade barriers, competitive imports into Japan never took place. The first Japanese sets of 22 in. and above were marketed in 1975 and initially achieved a market share of only 1.6 %. Although the United States industry specialised in large screen sets, its imports into Japan remained absent. The argument that the market would not pick up large screen

[2] Prestowitz (1988, p. 201).

[3] Electronics Industry Association of Japan: "Electronics Industries in Japan, 1979–1980".

Table 2.1 Share of 22-in. sets and above in Japan's CTV market

1974	1975	1978	1984	1985	1990
0 %	1.6 %	3.8 %	3.5 %	7.3 %	45 %

sets would have been valid if sales and share of 22 in. sets and above had not increased in a series of shocks, as Table 2.1 shows.[4]

Under conditions of liberal market-access, foreign supplies imported by Japanese traders could have filled the gap between Japanese market demand and domestic supply. That did not occur. Due to booming demand and absence of imports, Japanese manufacturers could make huge wind-fall profits. In 1974, the deceleration of growth in demand in Japan came as a shock. Japan then doubled its imports into the United States between 1975 and 1976, which was mirrored by declining sales in Japan.[5]

Japan's export success crushed the United States consumer electronics industry. In 1967, Japan's TV exports to the United States totalled about 320,000 units only, but the following year exports more than doubled to 680,000 units. In June of the same year, an anti-dumping suit was filed with the Commerce Department, which launched an investigation that lasted for several years but was abruptly terminated. The Japanese import share in the US market rose from just 11 % to more than 17 % in 1970. The findings of the U.S. Tariff Commission, later the International Trade Commission, in response to the first anti-dumping complaint lodged by the Electronics Industries Association was that American industry suffered serious injury in 1971.

Only drastic undercutting of United States producers' prices could attain such a drastic increase in exports. One of the methods to accomplish such an achievement was selling under stencil brands to mass retailers and producing competitors. The products were sold under the brand of the customer rather than under the producer's own brand. Mass sales under the brand of the customer is the alternative to sales under the producer's own brand, which require costly creation of distribution reach and advertising. Another commercial concept is the Original Equipment Manufacturers (OEM) supplies. The customer, generally a manufacturer of similar products or products in the same industrial sector, draws up certain specifications and the foreign producer produces and sells these products at prices far below the costs the purchasing manufacturer would incur if it produced them itself. One of the basic features of OEM or stencil brand supplies is that the supplier offers at prices undercutting those of other potential sources, be it alternative producers or the customers' own potential or existing production.

Rather than let industry make use of legal means available, United States government agencies pre-empted legal actions and measures, thereby depriving United States industry from its legal instruments. Instead the United States came to

[4] Source: Electronics Industry of Japan (EIAJ) Survey.

[5] Data from EIAJ and Japan Tariffs Association.

terms with the Japanese Ministry of International Trade and Industry (MITI) in 1977, which involved an orderly marketing arrangement. The Japanese "restraint" limited exports of CTVs to 1.75 million units annually from 1977 to 1980. The agreement hardly protected the United States' domestic industry. Japanese companies responded by investing in assembly operations in the United States. By the end of the 1980s, only Zenith, a United States-owned television manufacturer, had survived. The President of Zenith, John Nevin depicted the collapse of the American colour television industry ably and fervently.[6] His report gives a cynical, if not humorous impression of United States trade policy toward Japan. The outcome of this colour television OMA agreement, which was concluded in 1977, was a total collapse of the United States American television industry. This unfortunate result became apparent after Philips had started a campaign in the Benelux, which, after all, would finally have almost as derisory results, but less widely known, as Nevin's attempts. Before Philips started its trade policy actions, it had analysed the rather fragmentary European trade policy situation.

Until the creation of the Single Market in 1992 France and Italy – and also Spain, when it was not part yet of the EC, but related to the Community in a preferential trade agreement – maintained quantitative restrictions toward a variety of Far Eastern countries. The quotas were exceptions to most-favoured nation, or non-discriminatory, treatment in the General Agreement on Tariff and Trade (GATT, the predecessor of the World Trade Organisation, WTO) and accepted as conditions for accession of these countries to GATT. France, Italy and Spain introduced these quotas as a condition for recognition of Japan as full member of the General Agreement on Tariffs and Trade; they made a general reservation on the application of the General Agreement on Tariffs and Trade to Japan when Japan acceded to the Agreement in September 1955 (invocation of Article XXXV concerning "non-application of the agreement between particular parties"). Acceptance of Japan's accession and some other Asian countries to the General Agreement on Tariffs and Trade, for instance, was considered a one-sided concession by some countries.[7] The terms of Japan's accession prompted other countries to impose quantitative restrictions or to demand a special bilateral trade agreement with Japan. After Japan's acceptance of residual restrictions and a special safeguard clause, most the rules of GATT applied to Japan from 1964. Various residual quantitative restrictions of EEC countries remained in place until 1992.

Effectiveness of quantitative restrictions (QRs), and avoidance of deflection of trade required appropriate origin rules with minimum standards for processing of parts and components from the countries under QR. The general origin rules had been laid down in Regulation 802/68. QRs required specific origin rules in order to be effective. According to Article 24 of the Community Customs Code of 1992, a codification of various rules since the customs Regulation 802/68 of 1968, goods

---

[6] Nevin (1978) gives an account of his adventures in attempts to stem the tide.

[7] "Report on the Accession of Japan" adopted by an ad hoc Committee on agenda and intersessional business on 13 February 1953 (GATT, L/76).

whose production involved more than one country shall be deemed to originate in the country where they underwent their last, substantial, economically justified processing or working in an undertaking equipped for that purpose and resulting in the manufacture of a new product or representing an important stage of manufacture.

The essential issue is the definition of "last, substantial, and economically justified processing". The European Community specifically defined the phrase with regard to television sets and audio tuners (radio).[8] Under the specific definition, "last, substantial, and economically justified processing" refers to 45 % of the ex-works price added during the last processing or 35 % of the materials value. By buying a tube in Europe, which represented about 30–45 % of the materials value ex-works, it was not difficult for Japanese CTV producers established in the United Kingdom to bypass the quota and to get access to the French and Italian market. For Japanese producers, the possibility of the circumvention of quotas was one of the motives for assembly in the European Community. The requirements of origin

[8] The original television origin rule (and an identical one for radio and audio tape decks) was a specification with criteria for sufficient processing of the European Community's general origin rule of Regulation 802/68 of 1968. This television rule was laid down in Commission Regulation (EEC) No 2632/70 of 23 December 1970, which has been replaced by Commission Regulation (EEC) No 2454/93 of 2 July 1993, containing provisions for the implementation of Council Regulation (EEC) Council Regulation (EEC) No 2913/92 of 12 October 1992 establishing the Community Customs Code, OJ L 253, 11.10.1993 pp. 1–533, Article 39 of 2454/93: In the case of products obtained which are listed in Annex 11, the working or processing referred to in column 3 of the Annex shall be regarded as a process or operation conferring origin under Article 24 of the Code. Annex 11 to 2454/93 (part concerning CTV) describes the following processing in column (3) conferring origin to the product in column (2):

(1)	(2)	(3)
ex 8528	Television receivers, (excluding video tuners, television projection equipment and video monitors), whether or not combined, in the same housing, with radio-broadcast receivers or sound recording or reproducing apparatus, bur not with video recording or reproducing apparatus	Manufacture where the increase in value acquired as a result of assembly operations and, if applicable the incorporation of parts originating in the country of assembly represents at least 45 % of the ex-works price of the products When she 45 % rule is not met, the apparatus shall be treated as originating in the country of origin of parts whose ex-works price represents more than 35 % of the ex-works price of the apparatus When the 35 % rule is met in two countries, the apparatus shall be treated as originating in the country of origin of parts representing the greater percentage value

To radios with tuners and car radios, the same rule applied. Accordingly, only tuners in audio racks are restricted, but amplifiers, loudspeakers, record players and tape decks (the latter with the same origin rule, but there were no quantitative restrictions on the product) were not. The rule initiated some tuner assembly in the European Community, like Pioneer's assembly in Antwerp, and some assembly in France.

implied a certain level of non-Japanese content of the television sets assembled in Europe. Export limitations undertaken by an exporter were, however, of a different category than quotas with their supplementary origin rules. The origin rule is discussed in more detail below in this Chapter and in Chaps. 11 and 12.

Philips did not envisage a common European Community policy toward Japan's disruptive imports that would replace a patchwork of French and Italian restrictions, relatively liberal trade regimes of other member states and the special arrangements of the United Kingdom, which are detailed below. Germany was expected to oppose further European Community import restrictions toward Japan. Consequently, Philips had for its actions not taken stock of opportunities in the future, but based itself on the past. Certain disadvantages inherent to European-wide actions, due to historical data, were rather decisive indicators for choices between the options.

The Benelux, a trade and customs and economic cooperation union among Belgium, the Netherlands and Luxemburg founded during the World War II, concluded a bilateral treaty with Japan as condition for acceptance of Japan's accession to GATT.[9] In October 1964 the general non-application of the GATT was exchanged for approval of Japan's accession and bilateral agreement with Japan. In the bilateral agreement with Japan, a provision was included enabling measures against market disruption. Formally, the Benelux was the trade policy authority for the three countries in those cases in which the European Community had not yet received the mandate, i.e. bilateral relations between member states and Eastern Europe and Japan. However, if formal import restrictions were to be imposed, approval of the European Commission for measures against deflections of trade was required. That was a bad omen for any Benelux measure, an omen that was, neglected by Philips. The director of the Philips Canada organisation, later the

[9] The Agreement on Commerce among Japan and the Kingdom of the Netherlands and the Belgo-Luxemburg Economic Union, which was signed on 8 October 1960; the Protocol Concerning Trade Relations between the Kingdom of the Netherlands and the Belgo-Luxemburg Economic Union on the one hand and Japan on the other hand, 30-04-1963:

1. If, in the view of either Contracting Party, there is reasonable evidence that, as a result of unforeseen developments, any product of the other Contracting Party is being imported into its territory under such conditions as to cause or threaten serious injury to its domestic producers of like or directly competitive products and that certain action is required to prevent or remedy such injury, it shall give to the other Contracting Party written notice to this effect with a reasonable explanation of the circumstances. The Contracting Parties shall, upon such notice, enter into consultations immediately for the purpose of finding a mutually satisfactory solution.
2. If the consultations referred to above do not result within a reasonable period of time in a mutually satisfactory solution, the importing Contracting Party may, in respect of the product in question, apply quantitative import restrictions to the extent and for such time as may be necessary to prevent or remedy the injury referred to in paragraph 1 above.
3. In critical circumstances where delay would cause damage which it would be difficult to repair, action under paragraph 2 above may be taken provisionally after the notice mentioned in paragraph 1 above has been given or before the consultations referred to in that paragraph are completed, provided that such consultations shall be continued in an endeavour to find a mutually satisfactory solution.

head of Philips' Bureau for International Economic Relations, had limited confidence in the route via the European Community. While in Canada he became solidly convinced, based on United States press, that the European Community and European Community's executive, the Commission, were lame ducks. Mistrust towards European solutions was also attributable to an analysis of existing European trade policy regulations, which did not provide a ready solution for the future. Territorial and product scope of protection sought were, consequently, rather limited; Japanese imports of audio and television into Benelux competed with Philips' products in Belgium and the Netherlands, the location of Philips' highest market shares and main production sites.

Philips started a mix of extensive and intensive lobbying, wining and dining and political pressure, in pursuit of protection against market disruption by Japanese competition. Some within the company detested the action as interfering with liberal principles, to which they either adhered or which they pretended to in order to be able to challenge the competence of the former director of the Canadian organisation, later the head of Philips' Bureau for International Economic Relations at headquarters. For various reasons, some within the company hoped that the efforts were futile, fearing Japanese retaliation. Philips exerted pressure on the governments of Belgium and the Netherlands as main authorities in the Benelux with competency –as the European Community had not yet effectively taken over this domain – for bilateral trade policy instruments with Japan. Philips' pressure resulted in the recommendation by the Dutch government, not too overtly supported by the Belgians, that Dutch and Belgian associations of metal and electrical industry would send a mission to Japan in order to negotiate an OMA with the Electronic Industry Association of Japan (EIAJ). As final threat, the use of a safeguard clause in the bilateral Benelux trade agreement with Japan by the Benelux was suggested. In high spirits, a small delegation chaired by the dynamic director of the Dutch federation of metal and electrical industry (FME), along with his Belgian companion of the Fabrimetal association, went to Japan.

Negotiations did not go well. The Benelux industry federations' leader was an energetic negotiator, but his energy was useless in discussions with tenacious, reluctant Japanese negotiators. The Japanese negotiators' tenacity, induced by the Benelux industry negotiators' indecisiveness or unwillingness about concessions, deflated the spirits of the Benelux industry negotiators. The EIAJ knew the liberal attitude of the Dutch government quite well and was confident that measures could be avoided. The Belgian partners in Benelux were often ridiculed by the Dutch because of their "protectionist" behaviour, and for Belgian concentration on industry, especially the steel and car industry and crystal and production of Philips consumer electronics, which contrasted sharply with Dutch trade interests and verbal concentration on Ricardian principles.[10] They also knew that the Benelux

[10] Dutch policies were characterised by deriding French trade policy, which was contemptuously coined "Colbertism". French policy was not as protectionist as the Dutch and others assumed. The French have an inclination to demand an extremely well balanced "tit for tat" or, in trade policy

could not undertake action against Japan without the approval or cooperation of the European Commission. Since 1968, the European Community was supposed to implement a common trade policy on behalf of the member-states. Consequently, Benelux's application of a bilateral safeguard clause was unfeasible without prior European Community permission. The Dutch, more than the Belgians, feared the possible repercussions of actions against imports from Japan. Any protective move could be met with retaliation by the Japanese, either by phyto-sanitary measures against Dutch agricultural exports, or by choice for another port than Rotterdam, as was regularly the Japanese threat. Dutch support for protective measures could create a liability to the French in terms of "protection equivalence". The French would demand, the Dutch feared, that Benelux support French protection in return for European Community support – what the French understood to be French approval and support of Benelux measures. The French could, for instance, ask for Dutch support of restrictions on Japanese cars, which coincided with a Belgian interest.[11] Another complication was that privately negotiated export limitations were formally considered a violation of European competition rules. Article 85 of the Rome Treaty prohibited agreements limiting trade between member states. A limitation of exports from Japan to the Benelux would automatically result in limitation of trade in Japanese products between member states and violate competition rules in the Rome Treaty.[12] Preference for private negotiations was explicable: private parties would run the risk of violation of Community rules and the Dutch government could wash its hands in innocence.

Not surprisingly the delegation of industry associations returned empty-handed. The Japanese had evaluated the situation quite well. Philips, under the inspiring leadership of its director for International Economic Relations with his American/Canadian approach to matters, turned to the Benelux governments and increased its pressure. Helicopters were flown to Brussels to bring Belgian government representatives to Eindhoven for informative sessions, wining and dining. The pressure on The Hague increased as well, but in accordance with Dutch tradition, more soberly. The Benelux officials surrendered: a delegation of the three Benelux countries' officials paid a visit to Japan. Negotiations were expectedly unsuccessful; no progress whatsoever was made. The leader of the Benelux delegation announced that his delegation would not leave the room until he received a

language, "quid pro quo". Indignation about perceived trade barriers elsewhere are often the motivation for French trade actions.

[11] It is often forgotten that Belgium has been a major car assembling country. Car assembly in Dutch-speaking towns in Belgium comprised assembly of Renault Vilvoorde, General Motors in Antwerp and Ford in Genk and Volvo in Gand. Belgian Walloon crystal producer Val Saint-Lambert needed regularly protection. Dutch Philips had concentrated television production in the Flemish towns Bruges (television), in Louvain (tuners and amplifiers) and Hasselt (record players and cassette recorders) and in Dendermonde (loudspeakers), but there was hesitation to support this company in trade policy matters. The management of the Philips organisation in Belgium was predominantly French speaking. This inhibited the representation of Philips' interests in Belgium.

[12] Article 85 became Article 81 of the Consolidated Text after Maastricht and is Article 101 of the Treaty Establishing the European Community in Official Journal C 83/47 of 30.3.2010.

satisfactory response and both delegations, from Benelux and MITI. The negotiators spent one night in MITI, opposite each other at the negotiation table, but completely in silence. Sanitary needs required an interruption of the session. In the washing room, some civil servants agreed that the situation had become untenable. After some internal consultation in the Benelux delegation, the meeting was adjourned and after a subsequent meeting, the adjournment seemed eternal. The Benelux delegates returned depressed to their respective capitals.

To appease Philips, the biggest private employer in both the Netherlands and Belgium, the Benelux governments felt compelled to act. A second meeting at governmental level took place. Expectations of success were as low as the level of Benelux officials in attendance. But a miracle occurred. A Dutch official of lower rank who had claimed striking success in earlier negotiations headed the second Benelux delegation. Nobody had ever taken the trouble to verify his alleged successes. This time the delegation returned home with a wonder: a great success again. This chairman of the delegation announced that the Benelux had successfully concluded a "tacit voluntary self-restraint gentlemen's agreement" with MITI. The tacit and the gentleman-like nature of the agreement put it beyond all doubt; nobody could possibly discuss either its existence or its content. The advantage of the tacit nature of the agreement was that, as long as it remained tacit, the European Commission could not take action against it. Not even the threat of using the safeguard clause in the bilateral agreement between the Benelux with Japan was used.

The tacit agreement could not be subject of open discussion; therefore, everybody seemed content. Philips' pressure on the Dutch government ceased with the agreement, which satisfied the Dutch government. A tacit agreement seemed satisfactory to the European Commission. As long as it remained tacit, it was not an official barrier to internal trade in the European Community, and therefore it did not interfere with the Commission's competency in trade policy affairs. Since Philips thought it had an arrangement and now everybody in the company could return to work, Philips was also content. The Philips executive of international economic relations was extremely content. He needed some success after his stay in Canada. Because they had new ammunition for new animosity and for destruction of his position, his enemies at Philips were content. One of his assistants was so content that he jubilantly reported his triumph to his contacts at Philips in national sales organisations in member states of the European Community. A contact in the United Kingdom asked him to send – in view of their confidentiality – such highly sensitive reports to his home address. The assistant at Philips headquarters obeyed. A few months later it was found out that this careful recipient in the United Kingdom had joined Sony and thus Sony acquired information on Philips' interpretation of this "agreement". The Japanese were highly satisfied both on the fact that no tangible restrictions were agreed and about Sony's acquisition of information. As it turned out, there was not any negative effect on Japanese business and they could in several ways take advantage of such a "tacit gentlemen's agreement".

The Dutch civil servant triumphantly claiming success as chairman of the second Benelux governmental mission exploited the situation to its fullest. The fact that his colleagues did not know the content of the tacit arrangements did not impair, but rather strengthened his role. When his Belgian colleagues were asked for information about the agreement, they did not have the slightest notion what it entailed. Visits by Philips representatives to The Hague became a regular Canossa. The allegedly existing tacit voluntary gentlemen's export restraint required regular information for discussions with the Japanese embassy about imports into the Benelux and Japanese market share. Generally, such issues are discussed at the level of the economic attaché, who is the representative of the ministry of economic affairs of Japan, but the Dutch civil servant elevated the issues to a more suitable level – so he declared –, between him and the ambassador. Philips' audio and video product divisions and the Dutch Philips sales organization collected semi-annual market data. They had always been extremely careful not to reveal such data in view of Philips' market position that it was considered highly secret. Under the "tacit agreement", however, the details of Philips' and Japanese market shares were supplied to the Dutch civil servant, who subsequently provided them to the Japanese for discussions. On the basis of the figures provided, the civil servant declared the agreement highly effective. The figures on imports and market shares did not show a change in imports from Japan, but that phenomenon had no relationship with an agreement, regardless of whether it existed.

The Japanese market shares in the Benelux appeared similar to comparable countries. Japanese per segment audio market shares in the Benelux were equal to other open European economies, like the United Kingdom, Germany, Sweden and Denmark. Shares in the television markets were also similar. The latter phenomenon was related to the particular nature of the European television market, to which the Philips' external relations executive paid no attention.

The above matter requires an explanation. As explained before, France, also protected by its SECAM television system, and Italy, maintained quotas toward Japan and some other Far Eastern countries. Another reason was due to trade restrictive Phase Alternating Line (PAL) licences. The PAL television broadcasting and reception system was the main standard in use in Europe. Telefunken claimed the system as an invention, the patent holder of which was Telefunken's Dr. Bruch. The Interessengemeinschaft für Rundfunkschutzrechte (IGR) was created as a German industry platform for support to the system and for support in negotiations with potential licensees on conditions. With a view to possible exports to the United States as the most important part of the world market, Japan adopted the American TV system, called NTSC after the American National Television System Committee. It offered an inferior picture (therefore aliased Never Twice the Same Colour) with only 525 scan lines, as compared with the 625 lines of the PAL system, which contained improvements on NTSC, but NTSC offered an excellent export market to the Japanese. Telefunken imposed limitations on the licenses it granted to the Japanese. One condition of the license was an allowance to sell abroad a quantity of sets with a diagonal screen of 20 in. and above equal to the volume they sold in a domestic market. Japanese companies, of course, sold NTSC and not PAL sets on the domestic market. As a consequence, Japanese companies could not export large PAL screen sets to Europe. In the CTV introduction period Europe's main market, at least in Northern Europe, consisted mainly of sets of 20 in. and above, i.e. medium and large screen sets, and in France and Italy there were the QRs. Consequently, Japanese small PAL sets were the only colour television export article to Europe and their market share in television was limited to only a few per cent. The restrictions on Japanese exports in terms of screen sizes expired in 1981. For the Japanese this was too long a period. Industrial strategies of government and industry in the United Kingdom would be of great assistance, as Sect. 2.3 will show in more detail. The main consequence of these limitations was that if there were any restriction on Japan's exports to the Benelux by a voluntary restraint, its effect was not different from the situation in the United Kingdom, Germany, Denmark or Sweden, i.e. nil: quantities were naturally constrained by PAL licenses.

Trends in the audio business were quite different. Radios, allegedly covered by the Japanese restraint on exports to Benelux, had become old fashioned. Audio racks with separate components for reception – tuners –, amplifiers, record players and cassette decks accompanied by stereo loudspeaker boxes had replaced them. As a result, sales of radios dropped. It was not difficult for the Dutch civil servant to prove the success of his tacit agreement by a significant drop in imports of Japanese radios. Imports of portable radios and radio recorders from Japan had decreased, which he proudly attributed to effectiveness of the agreement. Cheap portable radios were no longer produced in Japan; rather, they were assembled by newly established Japanese subsidiaries in South East Asia not covered by any tacit agreement. During one of the Philips visits to the ministry – without the former director of the Canadian organisation, who had to find another job due to the success of his opponents in undermining his position – the civil servant recommended that the Board of Management of Philips write a letter to his minister expressing satisfaction about his handling of the matter. After reception of such a communication to his minister he would also, of course, maintain contact with the Japanese ambassador and keep the agreement effective at the prevailing appropriately high, satisfactory level.

That letter was never written. Philips' board of management could, of course, not write about tacit agreements. The "agreement", moreover, created some commercial complications. Philips' intention to import some up-market HiFi audio equipment from a relatively small Japanese producer of audio components and audio in Japan, Foster Electric Company, met some resistance. The producer mentioned "some voluntary restraint toward the Benelux" impeding exports to Philips. The equipment could easily have been shipped from Japan to Germany and re-exported to the Benelux, but Philips' advice to its purchasing officers was that only sales to those others than Philips could disrupt the Benelux market. The export limitation did not apply to products purchased by Philips. Since the agreement was tacit and its content was unknown, the interpretation was not open to discussion. The interpretation was accepted and the contract concluded. Philips' interpretation of the "tacit agreement" appeared the best approach, as test of its existence and content. The lack of response from Japan was a satisfactory aid to conclusions.

After one of the final visits to the ministry of economic affairs, as far as the subject of the tacit agreement was concerned, a discussion was arranged with the director of the pivotal civil servant. This director looked troubled and disappointed when he learned of doubts regarding the agreement. He showed some delight when he was informed that data on Japanese Benelux market shares were not different from other countries. He disclosed that he was generally satisfied with the state of affairs. He hoped that there would not be a ripple in the pond. He summarised the events: A civil servant discussed something in the corner of a meeting room in Tokyo. Irregularly, he allegedly phoned the Japanese ambassador regarding something about which nobody exactly knew. It was a formidable construction: a gentlemen's agreement about which nobody is supposed to speak, even if it did not exist. These were "The Emperor's New Clothes".

The "gentlemen's agreement" did not die, but quietly faded away. Whatever its status, it had become apparent that such a fragmented geographical approach in the European Community would not have any effect. European Community measures adopted on behalf of the entire European Community, based on the rule of law and formally published in the Official Journal of the European Community, and in this respect based especially on what were Articles 113–115 of the Rome Treaty, in the consolidated EC treaty of 2002 Articles 131–134 (now Article 207 of the European Union Treaty) were the only acceptable course. A serious roadblock, or rather, watershed, posed by the United Kingdom to a European-wide approach, was that it had engineered its own solution. That was an impediment to a solution attractive enough for the French and Italians to abandon their QRs in exchange for a European solution.

2.3 Voluntary Agreement on Suicide: Euthanasia of United Kingdom Consumer Electronics Industry

Partly due to trade limitations in Telefunken's PAL licenses, the fate of the European Community television industry was less gloomy than the United States'. Restrictions on exports in the PAL license required investments in production and domestic sales in a country with a PAL system.[13] The question for the Japanese was where to make such investments. Sony was quick in its decision and chose the United Kingdom, with Matsushita and other Japanese producers following soon afterwards. Already in 1972 the platform of the radio and television industry, Radio Industry Council (RIC), complained about imports from Japan. The Secretary of State for Trade and Industry advised business-to-business discussions between RIC and the Electronics Industry Association of Japan (EIAJ). These discussions

[13] Although informed about the need for Japanese investments as the consequence of the PAL licenses, some authors obstinately explained these investments by high customs duties (14 %) and voluntary restraint agreements (called "tariff jumping"). Tariff and VRAs did not represent a barrier at all, as is explained in this and some subsequent chapters. According to the data on Japanese domestic prices and dumping, in Chaps. 7 and 8, the Japanese were not superior in efficiency.

resulted in agreements, which allowed the Japanese the quantity of exports that they would have obtained without an agreement, i.e. 10 % of the market, which were all small screen sets.

The Labour Government of 1974–1979 appeared to help the Japanese by setting up a National Economic Development Council (NEDC), a sort of corporatist institution nicknamed NEDDY. It was a tri-lateral council in which industrialists, trade unions and government officials developed ideas about the future structure of the economy. A so-called NEDC Sector Working Party (SWP) on consumer electronics had a firm hand in the design of the United Kingdom television industry's extinction and served as the architect of a Trojan horse for Japanese consumer electronics in Europe. The SWP was tasked with the development of a strategy for competitiveness of the United Kingdom television industry. The chairman of the SWP and chairman of the British Radio Industry Council (RIC) and of the British Radio and Electronic Equipment Manufacturers' Association (BREMA) was the director of a formerly owned British company acquired by Philips, Pye of Cambridge Ltd. He held contempt for the new ownership and views other than British. He visited the Philips consumer electronics headquarters in Eindhoven, the Netherlands, certain he could convince Philips directors of the superiority of the British views by mere presence and speech. During a 4 h lunch with Philips directors in a restaurant near Philips' headquarters, he failed to convince the directors that the British views were superior. "You have not got a strategy," he stated and – as the lunch progressed – his tone became louder and the voice of British industry weaker.

The SWP adopted a recommendation by the Boston Consulting Group (BCG) of a minimum production volume of half a million CTVs, instead of the actual 100,000, for sustainability. The critical level of 500,000 units proposed by BCG might have helped, but – as the Japanese demonstrated – it was certainly neither a necessary nor sufficient condition for survival. It was based on the existing British production process. This minimum volume was applied to integrated production, including research and development, design of chassis and stuffing of printed circuit boards in the factory. Outsourcing of production – like stuffing of printed circuit boards, which could even have been organised collectively[14] – could improve cost effectiveness, but such a solution was too simple for the strategists, who did not want to abandon old established methods. With the exception of Sony, Japanese producers did not need to achieve BCG's minimum volume. Sony installed its own Trinitron colour tube factory in Wales, which required a scale of production, as recommended by the BCG, which investments were – in the framework of industrial conversion of coal mining areas in a European Community policy scheme – subsidised by the European Coals and Steel Community ECSC).[15]

[14] A condition for BREMA membership was that manufacturers stuffed boards in their production premises.

[15] The United Kingdom government was furious when the Netherlands, after an unexpected intervention from Philips at the Permanent Representation in Brussels, made a reservation – without prior

The SWP also signed the death warrant of United Kingdom industry by its recommendation that the "kernel of this strategy lies in improvements in the quality and supply of UK manufactured components."[16] The SWP's proposal was to promote an inflow of Japanese investments in order to improve quality of components. The theory was that since the Japanese set high standards of quality through their specifications, the quality of British components would thereby increase. The other idea of the SWP was for Japanese investors to replace existing capacity, rather replace it, with the exception for, of course, Sony and Matsushita, which had already established their subsidiaries.

Possibly ignorant of the peculiarities of the Japanese economic system – the subject of Chaps. 7 and 8 – and of Japanese interests, the SWP rendered extremely valuable services to Japanese manufacturers. The recommendation "*that* [United Kingdom] *companies should use their ownership of distribution channels as a positive force to accelerate the growth of new product markets while supporting UK production*" was of great help to eager Japanese producers. The distribution system was indeed characteristic of the British consumer electronics industry. Both the bad quality of consumer electronics manufactured in the United Kingdom, as admitted by the Sector Working Party of the NEDC, vicissitudes in the market as consequence of a recurrent "stop-go policy" of the British Government and consequential economic cycles with fluctuations of the Pound Sterling were main factors why this rental market developed in the United Kingdom. Consumption of rented television sets and other electronics gave stability in a cyclical market and consumers did not have to worry about service problems. Rentals soothed trade cycles, thereby diminishing dependence on income sensitive sales.[17] Cooperation with British industry through joint ventures offered the Japanese two windows of opportunity. They could overcome the PAL restrictions, and they got access to mass consumer rentals. Integrated production using European components was certainly not Japanese producers' objective, as the SWP hoped, as such a move did not offer a cost advantage. The Japanese were clearly going for production in the United Kingdom, but not on the same footing as British producers. Their main target was to overcome the PAL restrictions, not to incur additional costs by production integration instead of shipping key modules from Japan. The British government,

---

instruction from the Ministry in The Hague – for granting subsidies to Sony in Wales and requested postponement of the decision. The director of the EEC unit in the Ministry of Economic Affairs lamented that the British ambassador even visited the Ministry. He admitted that it was the first visit of the ambassador. Thanks to this intervention by Philips, the Ministry gained importance The approval for the subsidy was finally given: Assent No 33/81 given by the Council, pursuant to Article 56 (2) (a) of the ECSC Treaty, to enable the Commission to grant a conversion loan of £3.7 million (±6.11 million ECU), for redundant ECSC workers, to Sony (UK) Ltd., United Kingdom for a project in Bridgend, South Wales.

[16] National Economic Development Council: "Industrial Strategy: Electronics Consumer Goods Sector Working Party; Summary Note by the Chairman"; NEDC, 1 March 1979.

[17] Apart from the lack of technical reliability of their products, the stop-go policy of the United Kingdom government had as a corollary that fluctuations of the Pound Sterling prevented British producers from exporting to the continent.

embarking on a course of fatal trade policy moves, offered collateral help to the Japanese.

In 1977 the Labour Government unilaterally imposed quotas on monochrome – black and white – television sets from Taiwan. Since Taiwan had been outlawed in international trade by removal from the GATT as an observer after the People's Republic of China was admitted to the United Nations, unilaterally imposed quotas had become legally possible.[18] The Republic of Korea was also hit by a quantitative restriction to 35,000 sets per year during 1977 and 1978 – a move that the European Community defended in the GATT, but was generally criticised and condemned by a great number of GATT members and, consequently, had to be abandoned.[19] Restriction of imports of monochrome televisions was not exactly an act by which vital interests of British industry were served, but this signal endorsed further negotiations on industry-to-industry level. The RIC subsequently concluded VERs on colour television with these countries, Japan and tried to do so with Singapore. As it appeared, by their presence in the United Kingdom, Japanese manufacturers first and foremost benefited from these deals.

Sony and Matsushita established themselves in Wales in 1974 and 1976, while a number of other Japanese manufacturers followed shortly thereafter, using opportunities offered by the United Kingdom industry of joint ventures recommended by SWP strategists. Their new home market, the United Kingdom, offered protection against low wage CTV imports from Taiwan and Korea, to which the VERs with the industry of these countries negotiated by the RIC contributed. The RIC rendered also services to the Japanese during negotiations on VRAs by providing them with forecasts for the United Kingdom market. The restriction of Japanese exporters to 10 % of the United Kingdom market was not a sacrifice. It was in accordance with normal small screen exports to any country in the European Community, except France and Italy. For additional and larger screen sales in the United Kingdom and exports to other countries, including PAL countries, they needed production facilities in the United Kingdom. Consequently, the Japanese received highly beneficial treatment. The RIC both supplied market forecasts and protection of the United Kingdom CTV market – a highly attractive business climate for Japanese investors – enhanced by the United Kingdom industry's eagerness for joint ventures. The government subsidized Japanese investments. The NEDC suggested that new investment only be allowed if old capacity was replaced. The Japanese industry cleverly understood this brilliant recommendation.

---

[18] The observer status of the Republic of China (Taiwan) ended in November 1971.

[19] The Council of GATT discussed the in March 1978 concerning the EEC's invocation of Article XIX with respect to the imposition of import restrictions on monochrome television sets imported into the United Kingdom from Korea. All contracting parties condemned the move. GATT document C/M/124 p. 19. The 1978 Secretariat Note on "Modalities of Application of Article XIX" states "This case is the only one in the history of the GATT in which Article XIX action has unilaterally been taken on a discriminatory basis with regard to a single source of supply in a transparent manner." (L/4679, p.14). The EEC action was revoked after conclusion of a voluntary export restraint arrangement as from 22 June 1979; C/M/134, L/4613/Add.1.

Toshiba started a (30 %) joint venture (of £10 million, subsidized by the United Kingdom Government to the tune of 1.9 million pounds) with Rank (70 %, with brands Rank Arena, Bush and Murphy), and Hitachi set up a 50/50 joint with GEC. With these agreements, both Japanese companies gained access to the unrestricted PAL licenses of their partners and to their distribution networks – the Rank rental network was a strong asset. Once the Japanese obtained access to the United Kingdom market, the United Kingdom partners were no longer needed. Soon Toshiba and Rank experienced differences of opinion about, inter alia, the supply and especially quality and supply prices of certain components from Japan, which Rank wanted partly to purchase in the United Kingdom (the new 110° 30 AX tube from Philips' subsidiary Mullard) in accordance with SWP strategy. Buying European components in accordance with its partner's wishes was clearly not in Toshiba's components interests. Because technical management was contractually designated to Toshiba, the Japanese side made designs demanding Japanese components. This was against the intentions of the European partner. The situation soon became intolerable and Rank left the joint venture.[20] Toshiba subsequently closed three factories and reduced the workforce from 2,600 to 300 people, pointing at mere assembly rather than integrated United Kingdom production. The rationalisation reduced manufacturing to final assembly of simple modules shipped from Japan, while European-produced tubes supplied by Mullard/Phillips were used in order to achieve sufficient European content for compliance with the origin rules for access to the French and Italian markets.

The situation between Hitachi and GEC, another joint venture formed in 1978 subsidised by the United Kingdom government, was not very different. The Japanese engineers at the joint venture wanted at least 1 year's notice in the event GEC desired a European component. Moreover, the factory incurred losses, whereas Hitachi made a profit on components used in the joint venture and imported from its factories in Japan and South East Asia. Mitsubishi made the cheapest capital investment. It took over Norwegian Tandberg's factory in Haddington, East Lothian in Scotland, including the PAL license. Despite the assumptions by the Boston Consulting Group on minimum requirements for volume of production, Hitachi and Mitsubishi produced no more than 350,000 sets. In 1979 Hitachi announced it would consider colour television tube manufacturing in the United Kingdom. Philips' components subsidiary in the United Kingdom, Mullard, panicked. Its director Jack Akerman hired a parliamentarian consultancy group, which he joined immediately after his impending retirement, for lobbying in the House of Commons against this danger. In view of Hitachi's maximum television production attained in the United Kingdom, it was highly improbable that it ever envisaged making this investment. Hitachi planners must have known Thorn's sad experience with tube production. Due to the "Trinitron" tube technology, Sony needed tube investments and created a capacity of 500,000 sets and a picture tube capacity of

[20] Geddes (1991) has sketched this story of the demise of British industry, but presented it as a victory of strategy.

700,000 units in Wales. Sony's sales in Europe were about 800,000 in 1988.[21] To fulfil European origin rules, other Japanese producers purchased European tubes, mainly from Philips. Matsushita acquired the tube factory of SEL/ITT from NOKIA when this company stopped its consumer electronics activities in Finland, Germany, Spain and France in 1996, concentrating completely on mobile telephones. It also acquired some of the television production capacity from Nokia, which increased its total production in the European Community to a more impressive level of more than 1.2 million units in total. The purchase of the tube assets from Nokia did not produce much benefit. Within less than 10 years, flat screens replaced cathode ray tubes.

Component sourcing by Japanese manufacturers, naturally, remained a constant source of dispute between the RIC, which was practically formed by BREMA, and the EIAJ during their annual talks. According to the Japanese, European components inadequate in quality. Even in 1988, the low level of components sourcing by Japanese manufacturers was a source of discontent. In addition to prices, quality was again alleged to be the main problem. There was only one colour picture tube factory in the United Kingdom (Philips' subsidiary Mullard) and the Japanese claimed Mullard's prices were too high and tube quality too low; they added that they wanted to see an alternative local source. In 1991, only 15 % of total Japanese electronic components demand – not limited to colour television sets – was supplied by British industry.

The disadvantage of local European supplies to Japanese producers was self-evident. It did not contribute to cost advantage by volume of production. The market share of the Japanese in the United Kingdom peaked at 47 % in 1996. In 2001, the level of Japanese market share in the United Kingdom, including imports from South East Asia and Japan and United Kingdom production, dropped to 24 %.[22] The devastative behaviour by Turkey that caused this fall is discussed in Chap. 11.

In any case, the SWP was wrong in its expectation that the new joint ventures and other production of the Japanese should and would exceed half a million units in order to be viable. Table 2.2 shows that there was only 1 year in which Toshiba's manufacturing exceeded a production quantity of 0.5 million that was deemed the vital minimum. Others in the United Kingdom, except of course Sony, remained below the critical production volume. A necessary minimum volume was fully dependent on the production structure. If all major components were imported as

[21] The Japanese estimate of their production in the EEC was about 3.19 million colour television sets in 1989, or about 15 % of the European market (together with imports the total approaches 30 % of the market). Sony U.K. was supposed to produce 0.63 million (1989 figures; sources: data made available by Mr. Henri Anus, Directeur-Général Délegué of the French consumer electronics association Simavelec, partly from press cuttings); Matsushita (U.K.) 0.48 million, Hitachi (U.K.) 0.18 million, Mitsubishi (U.K.) 0.23 million, Toshiba (U.K.) 0.39 million, Sanyo (U.K.) 0.18 million. With the exception of Sony, production runs remained far below the critical level of the British Sector Working Party.

[22] From the market research company GfK (survey on October /November 1999).

Table 2.2 European production of CTVs by Japanese producers, compared with three Europeans

Years 1990–2000	Maximum units × 1,000	Year of maximum	Minimum units × 1,000	Year of minimum
Hitachi UK	360	1995	279	1992
Mitsubishi UK	378	1991	262	1992
Matsushita[a]	1,210	1996	432	1992
Sony[b]	3,525	1997	1,645	1992
JVC UK	385	1998	131	1992
Sanyo (Spain)	540	1991	263	1996
Sharp (Spain)	985	1998	324	1993
Toshiba UK	631	1998	480	1992
Total Japanese production in Europe	8,014		3,816	
Grundig	2,921	1991	2,155	1996
Philips	3,797	1991	2,544	1998
Thomson	1,968	1991	1,053	1998
Total production in community	21,308	1995	15,871	1992
Japanese share in production	38 %		24 %	
Three Europeans' share	41 %		36 %	

[a]Various factories in the United Kingdom, Germany and later Czech Republic
[b]Various factories in the United Kingdom, Spain and later in Slovakia

chassis and kits – modules that can be assembled with little added value –, the maximum quantity can be substantially lower. Proof of this is the presence of Tatung in the United Kingdom. After the Radio Industry Council's VER with Taiwan, Tatung moved to the United Kingdom. Its production was between 100,000 and 200,000. The NEDC's SWP clearly used a wrong starting point of unchanged production technology, which was in accordance with the Boston Consulting Group that had based its recommendation on past deplorable experience in the United Kingdom. The vicissitudes of interest rates and Pound Sterling and adherence to obsolete manufacturing methods were the main handicaps of the United Kingdom industry.

French and Italian QRs, combined with the special origin rules for television, PAL conditions and the existence of preferential trade agreements between EEC and EFTA, with their preferential origin rules, were obstacles to Japan's direct exports to Europe and were stimulus for investments in the United Kingdom rather than a 14 % customs tariff and Japan's voluntary export restraint. Preferential access to EFTA (Portugal until 1986; Austria, Sweden and Finland until 1995; Norway, Iceland, Switzerland and Liechtenstein) with preferential origin rules requiring a European added value of 60 % was an additional reason for investment in Europe.[23] The issue of origin rules is discussed in Chap. 12.

[23] Some authors explained Japanese investments in the United Kingdom by United Kingdom protection and the high 14 % customs duty. This is evidently incorrect. Although informed about

In 1979 Philips, Hitachi and Sony in Singapore were summoned by the RIC to reduce their competition with Japanese and remaining producers in the United Kingdom by a voluntary limitation of their small screen or tiny vision CTV exports. After several threats of quantitative restrictions, BREMA forced the Singapore association of manufacturers to discuss the matter at the negotiation table with the more formal RIC. A problem for Philips was that, in order to avoid quantitative restrictions in South Europe toward Taiwan, it had moved its production of small screen sets to Singapore. No Southern European countries imposed quotas on exports from Singapore subsequent to gaining independence. From Singapore, Philips supplied the European Community market, including the United Kingdom. Other Singapore producers, Hitachi and Sony, both producing small screen sets and tubes for the European market, were not inclined to limit their exports because it required them to reduce capacity in Singapore and increase in the United Kingdom. Bernard Lap, the president of Philips' Singapore organisation, wondered how he could thwart BREMA initiatives. The Philips headquarters concluded that the United Kingdom solutions were detrimental to its industry and to European industry in general and that the Japanese in the United Kingdom were the only party to benefit from these restraints. Frustration of the United Kingdom scheme was inevitable. The solution was rather simple:

1. Since the United Kingdom's objective was a gentlemen's agreement, it was practical to send Chinese citizens of Singapore to the meeting to ask for information about what comprised a "gentlemen's agreement". British disdain would be a sufficient impediment to treating the Chinese as peers and gentlemen.
2. The Singapore side should stress that the basic interest of the industry was not limitation, but production and export, and that it did not have the authority to limit exports.
3. If, however, an agreement should be concluded, its terms must be indisputable so that discussions about interpretations would be ruled out.
4. In order to make the gentlemen's agreement watertight, it should be written and signed.

The last point was decisive for frustration of a "gentlemen's agreement" or an agreement in general. The limitation of exports to the European market was a violation of the anti-cartel policies of the European Community. The Commission published a warning that such agreements, by which inter-state trade was impeded, were in violation of European Community legislation. A written agreement would offer evidence on violation of European Community policy. In BREMA's minutes of the meeting, a supercilious remark was made that the Singapore side was unable to understand gentlemen's agreements, therefore, also unable to conclude such an

these backgrounds of Japanese investments, Belderbos (1994), for instance, stuck to this explanation for tariff jumping because it fit his theory that "tariff jumping" was the explanation for these investments. In the meanwhile he inevitably assumed – it was merely an assumption without evidence – that Japanese producers were more efficient than European producers. Section 8.10 of Chap. 8, the Tosoh, shows that this assumption is misleading.

agreement, apart from the lack of representativeness. Subsequently, BREMA put pressure on the Philips United Kingdom to insist on moderation of imports from Singapore. Philips United Kingdom accepted the self-restraint on the condition that any reduction of imports from Singapore would result in a commensurate decrease of a total Singapore export ceiling. The objective was to prevent other Singapore producers abusing the reduction. In the meantime, Philips commenced small screen television production in Bruges, Belgium. Philips United Kingdom could simply comply with the wishes of BREMA. The Philips gesture was void and made BREMA aware that a national road towards a trade policy solution was unsuccessful.

After inward investments and failed Japanese-United Kingdom joint ventures, Japanese production of about 2.8 million sets had crushed all indigenous manufacturing. Rank, GEC, Rediffusion and Fidelity disappeared very quickly. A few years later, Thomson of France acquired Ferguson from Thorn EMI and closed the factory near London and abandoned its brand after a drastic brand rationalisation. All VERs and attraction of inward investments resulted in the replacement of local production with United Kingdom R&D, and chassis design by mere assembly by Japanese manufacturers. New entries, inter alia, of Sinclair for pocketsize colour television sets, failed. Spectra, not a member of the BREMA, because of criteria for membership that the producer crams printed circuit boards with components from the United Kingdom, disappeared. Its last convulsion was a very weird policy of importing Chinese workers during their "holidays", letting them assemble CTVs in the United Kingdom for a month, and to then replace them with other Chinese workers.

The United Kingdom industry hoped to improve its position at the cost of continental producers by a "grand" strategy, which proved irrational. It became clear that the European Community had the trade policy competence. The European Electronic Components Manufacturers Association (EECA) took initiative and made a demarche with the European Commission, warning of Japanese inroads. Commissioner Étienne Davignon did not want discussions with tube producers without the presence of their customers, the television industry. He summoned a common platform of the industry. Since the television industry might easily perceive tube actions against Japan as actions against interests of European industry, such a common platform would be indispensable. For the same reason an anti-dumping case against Japan was rejected by tube producers. Standard Electric Lorenz (SEL, subsidiary of ITT) imported glass parts – screens and necks or panels and funnels – from Nippon Electric Glass (NEG, a subsidiary of NEC), for its tube production in Esslingen (Germany). Price information offered evidence for a dumping complaint. The EECA, however, decided that it was not proper to attempt a dumping complaint, which would frighten the television industry. The CTV and tube industry started a lobby with the European Community authorities. The foundation of the European Association of Consumer Electronics Manufacturers (EACEM) in 1978 was supported by BREMA. The Japanese in the United Kingdom preferred BREMA's participation in an association at the European level. It would offer BREMA the possibility of insight of events in Europe. The chairman of BREMA, Ferguson's director Richard E. Norman, was honoured with the impossible task of subtly balancing Ferguson's interest of survival and BREMA's majority membership, i.e. the Japanese interest, which was the blocking of anti-Japanese measures. Richard Norman both succeeded and failed. Several measures were taken, but he did not play an active role.

2.4 Video Recorders: Informal Peace to a Format War

Not long after worldwide acceptance and introduction of its compact audiocassette format, which it freely licensed and which received worldwide acceptance as audiotape format, Philips announced its invention of the Video Cassette Recorder (VCR). This invention was made public in 1964. This was too early and long before introduction of colour television in Europe and long before CTV penetration was sufficient for mass sales of VCRs.[24] The early announcement and display of the product offered an opportunity for copying the product and developing it. Just as with the audiocassette recorder, Philips hoped to establish a global format for VCRs. The international climate had changed, however. The advantage of Philips over competitors decreased with passage of time that was spent with attempts to persuade competitors to accept Philips or common format. Sony profitably started to sell recorders for professional use. Sony was aware that its position in the Japanese consumer market and abroad was insufficient for setting of a standard for consumer purposes. It tried to convince its Japanese competitors, Matsushita and its daughter JVC, Victor Corporation of Japan, as early as 1974, to adopt its product as the standard. In a conversation in 1993, a chief economic journalist of Nihon Keizai Shimbun revealed that, in order to create a Japanese VCR format, MITI had in 1976 organised a conference of bureaucrats, industrialists and invitees, inter alia from the press, with the objective of establishing one single Japanese VCR format that should by its massive support force foreigners, including Philips, to accept the Japanese standard. Since Sony's Betamax, both for reasons of technical quality and of its stage of commercialisation, offered prospects superior to those of the JVC/Matsushita's Video Home System (VHS) format, the proposal was to push Betamax. Of course, Matsushita and its daughter, JVC, patent holder of VHS, opposed the proposal.[25] Matsushita's superiority to Sony both in the Japanese consumer market power and in presence in the United States convinced Japan's biggest consumer electronics producer that its format would win a battle, provided that other Japanese majors would support the VHS format. Toshiba – belonging to

---

[24] Philips Annual Report on 1964.

[25] Matsushita (http://www.fundinguniverse.com/company-histories/Matsushita-Electric-Industrial-Co-Ltd-Company-History.html) claimed that Sony was not prepared to share its Betamax technology with others: "Sony refused to share its Betamax VCR technology with other manufacturers. But Matsushita knew that despite its VCR monopoly, Sony had a limited VCR production capacity."

the powerful Mitsui grouping of companies, keiretsu, and the biggest and oldest of the major electronic groups – felt compromised in its general industrial leadership and, consequently, obstructed the government initiative. It gave preference to the VHS system; thereby tipping the scale in favour of Matsushita. Primacy of Sony's Betamax system as a standard, pushed by MITI, would upset Japan's industrial hierarchy.[26] It would give Sony, with its lead in VCR production, an undue industrial advantage over its rivals that were substantially stronger in the Japanese consumer electrical appliances market (see Chap. 7). MITI's efforts to establish a common Japanese standard on the basis of Betamax clearly failed, for JVC showed that "*it had formed alliances with major manufacturers ... and, very humbly, trotted out its political allies: Matsushita, Hitachi, Mitsubishi, and Sharp...*"[27] This intervention by MITI aiming at elimination of Philips failed because finally both Philips' format and Betamax would be eliminated due to certain market circumstances explained below and in Chaps. 7 and 8.

How differently acted the European Commission in 1977! It prohibited a standardisation agreement on Video 2000 (V2000) standardisation between Philips and Blaupunkt, Bosch-Siemens, Grundig, Loewe Opta, Nordmende, and SABA. The grounds under which it prohibited the standardisation agreement were that Philips' market share was too large and alternative videocassettes and recorders and participants would not make competitive formats available to consumers:[28]

> *Philips has a pre-eminent position in the European market for videocassette recorders. Its market share is considerably larger than that of Sony, its nearest competitor. The two together account for more than 70 % of total sales in the common market. Since this is a relatively new product, there are no official production and sales statistics available for the European Communities. Estimated sales of videocassette recorders in the EEC totalled 34 500 in 1974, 41 000 in 1975, and the upward trend continued in 1976.*
>
> *Moreover consumers were not allowed a fair share of the resulting benefits. For the agreement denied them the opportunity to buy videocassettes or videocassette recorders of a different system from any of the parties.*

Thus, ignorant of developments elsewhere, the European Commission sentenced the V2000 format on basis of lack of data and on assumptions, and contributed to destruction of the format. A decade later consumers did not have a choice at all, partly due to this decision and to trade policy events reported below, but mainly because of lack of competition in the market of the exporters in Japan – as Chaps. 7 and 8 show. Restriction of competition abroad had the opposite effect of what the European Commission wanted: "to buy videocassettes or videocassette recorder of a different system".

---

[26] Nayak, and Ketteringham (1986, pp. 36–37).

[27] Nayak and Ketteringham (1986, p. 43).

[28] European Commission Decision of 20 December 1977 relating to a proceeding under Article 85 of the EEC Treaty (IV/29.151 – videocassette recorder, OJ L 047, 18/02/1978, 42–47).

In 1975, Sony launched its Betamax consumer video recorder application, first mainly in Japan, later in the United States and Europe. Its total number of sets produced in that first year was 119,000,[29] almost four times total sales by all producers in the European Community. The picture was of reasonable quality and it sold well in the three markets, but Sony's potential was too small compared with the marketing power of its big and powerful Japanese rivals. Production volume, supported by destructive dumped export prices, finally appeared decisive when the alliance of the big producers had agreed on adoption of VHS and gained the upper hand with their overwhelming domestic position in the consumer market. The major rivals to Sony held a natural share in the Japanese market of 85 %; of which Matsushita represented 25 % (see Chap. 7). When the attractiveness of video recorders to consumers in Japan's domestic market became apparent, Sony lost the battle domestically. Its major Japanese opponents finalised Sony's role both domestically and abroad by distribution clout and dumping abroad.

Some economists and journalists depict the outcome of the format war, the dumping complaint lodged by European industry and the ensuing voluntary restraint agreement as either a weakness or a trick of European industry to deprive consumers of their money. The VCR format war in the 1980s was certainly the opposite of a victorious outcome of normal industrial competition.[30] Kenichi Ohmae referred to the result of this conflict as an example of keen, strategic marketing, using the Triad or three main markets, by the winner, Matsushita Electrical Industrial (in 2008 re-baptised Panasonic) with its daughter JVC.[31] It was essentially a fight, however, decided in Japan, about a standard achieved not through co-operation or consultation but by a trade war, in which distribution power in Japan and the destructive weapon of dumping were decisive. The defence against the assaults was not a consumer-hostile trick of European industry, nor was it policy considerations of the European Community, nor even a purely commercial triad that was decisive in this game: instead, decisions about the outcome of the struggle were made in Japan and were attributable to special conditions in Japan. The concept of Triad is biased, and based on the conviction that the three main markets are equally accessible. They are not, as Chap. 7 makes clear.[32]

Two incidents in 1982, often referred to since, manifested themselves as the first overt and fundamental conflict in electronics trade between the European Community and Japan. The first was Poitiers, often denounced or recommended as a most imaginative trade barrier, which at least aroused some admiration on the part of Mr. Akio Morita, Chief Executive Officer and Chairman of Sony.[33] The second incident, which immediately followed Poitiers, was the draft and submission of a

[29] Japan's Bureau of Statistics.

[30] Particularly Brian Hindley has been active to prove it, even to calculate the losses to the consumer in Greenaway and Hindley (1985) and Hindley (1986).

[31] Ohmae (1985, pp. 58–59).

[32] That they are not is generally eliminated from considerations.

[33] Morita (1986), p. 261.

dumping complaint by two European producers of VCRs of the Video 2000 format, Grundig and Philips.

French policy caused the first incident. After its establishment in 1981, the socialist government in France formulated a new electronics policy in the "Plan d'Action Filière Electronique", published in March 1982. Since 1981, the policy was to re-launch the French consumer electronics industry.[34] There was clearly no collective view on the strategy. The boss of Thomson Grand Public (later called Thomson Consumer Electronics, TCE) Jacques Fayard, was a particularly fierce adversary of Philips and wanted Thomson Grand Public to acquire its own technology, independently from TCE's Dutch competitor. Fayard detested the Dutch company and particularly its strength in France, where it had obtained a share of about 50 % in the television market, which, in order to avoid too evident a market omnipresence, required use of three brands: Philips, Schneider and Radiola. Fayard repeatedly expressed his dislike of the successful chairman of Philips France, Jurazinski, by imitating the accent of this Philips executive of Polish descent during meetings of the European Association of Consumer Electronics Manufacturers, over which he presided for a few years. Fayard's rival in Thomson Brandt, Abel Farnoux, the long-time director of Thomson's Videocolor television tubes manufacturing division in Italian Anagni, who left Thomson in 1980 and was author of the electronics industry policy (Filière Electronique) plan, adhered strongly to European cooperation, which implied collaboration with Philips. The boss of Philips France, Jurazinski, had in vain tried to persuade Thomson to industrial cooperation. Although he masterminded the general policy framework, Farnoux could not force Thomson into the direction of cooperation by TCE with Philips and Grundig.[35] One year later, nationalisation of Thomson took place. It was Thomson's plan to join the venture between VHS patent holder and Matsushita Panasonic daughter JVC with Thorn EMI, the parent of CTV producer Ferguson, and German Telefunken. This joint venture, called J2T, started production in New Haven and Berlin. Later, Thomson joined it and became the single partner of JVC, after having taken over Telefunken and Thorn EMI's Ferguson with state finances. After reunification of Germany, the special financial assistance to production in Berlin was discontinued and Thomson left Berlin and its partner JVC and moved to Singapore for VCR production with Toshiba.

On 22 October 1982, the new French government of Mitterand announced the imposition of a luxury tax of Ff 471 (about €72) per unit. Customs clearance of imported VCRs was to take place in the town of Poitiers. Date and place were derived from history. The Moors had moved northeast across the Pyrenees Mountains but were defeated by the Frank king, Charles Martel, in the Battle of Poitiers in 732 A.D. The Customs Cooperation country code for Japan is 732 and the decision was made 1250 years after the battle and victory at Poitiers. Three issues induced the customs clearance and tax collection measure. The first, and least

[34] Commission of the European Communities, 21-4-1985, TF-2, p. 49.

[35] Quatrepoint (1984, pp. 31–41).

important, was the deficit on the budget of the French state, which amounted Ff 93 billion. Consequently, the luxury tax was about 0.3 % of this deficit and hardly offered solace. A second reason was that France was annoyed by the lack of the European Community's trade policy toward Japan.[36] The third issue concerned industrial policy. About 550,000 (85 % of total sales in the country) Japanese VCRs were sold in 1982 in France, an influx – as the French government feared – that thwarted France's ambition of hosting a video recorder industry. Philips had a site in Le Mans, where VCRs were assembled from key components made in Austria. Thomson was aware that VCR offered new opportunities in the market and had ambition to become a video producer. By forcing cooperation with the Japanese owner of the VHS license, it could become a European VCR player. Imports from Japan would also, although marginally, increase France's €14 billion foreign trade deficit.

The Council of Ministers frequently and extensively discussed which trade policy the EEC should conduct towards Japan. Northern countries – such as Germany, the Netherlands and Denmark – refused to take action both against imports from Japan and against non-tariff barriers in Japan. The French felt, apart from own industry strategies, the need for a European Community posture and action towards Japan. And it thought that by its one-sided action it might lure those other European Community member states into a common European approach toward Japan. Trade minister Michel Jobert suggested establishing the customs clearance on the Puy de Dôme, but Finance and Economics minister Laurent Fabius did not consult Jobert and highhandedly designated Poitiers as customs clearance site. The public appreciated the minister's move. In France history education is an important part of civil life and culture. The place of customs clearance with its symbolic fringe raised Fabius' popularity. It is remarkable that not the Minister of Finance, but French External Trade Minister announced the customs clearance and a tax collection through Poitiers. Finance Minister Fabius had invented the move, but Jobert's ambition and the wish to make the tax collection a trade policy signal became decisive.

The order had its intended effect: more than 60,000 video recorders were now backed up awaiting customs clearance, and only 22,000 of the 200,000 recorders ordered for the holiday season were expected to make it in time to store shelves. Imports of VCRs, a total of 550,000 in total 1982 fell to about 300 a day, or 110,000 on an annual basis.[37] Tokyo initially expressed "regret" only, but its reaction created worries for the European Commission.

The European Commission's Internal Market and Industry Commissioner Étienne Viscount Davignon responded quickly and assumed responsibility for a way out of the embarrassing situation. His colleague of External Relations should

[36] Precise description has been given by Klousen (1986), based on data from Trade Minister, Michel Jobert.

[37] Agence Européenne d'Informations: "EEC – Japan – United States: World Traders in Conflict"; Brussels: 1983, p. 122.

have solved the inconsistency of the collection of taxes in Poitiers and designation of this town as customs clearance point with the General Agreement on Tariffs and Trade (GATT). Japan announced a protest in the GATT against this nullification or impairment (Article XXIII of GATT[38]) against the creation of customs point of entry with too small capacity of handling the imports, a violation of Article IX of GATT (concerning customs treatment of imports). According to the Japanese, imports into France fell from 53,013 sets during the month of August, according to French statistics to 14,500 sets during the period 22 October – 7 November, and to 900 sets during the period 8 November – 30 November 30 (the latter two figures are Japanese statistics). Although Wilhelm Haferkamp, as Commissioner for External Relations, had the competence to deal internationally with the matter, he lacked the stature to tackle the issue.

European Commission vice-president Davignon, responsible for internal market and consequently for the solution of the internal market inconsistency of Poitiers' designation as customs point with the free common market (Article 30 of the Rome Treaty; 28 of the European Union Treaty), saw a chance both to tackle the problem of the Poitiers internal trade barrier and to establish a common European Community trade policy, latter of which was Haferkamp's domain. The need for a common policy was self-evident in view of individual member states' efforts to wipe their own street. German Minister Graf Lambsdorf, for instance, arranged a tacit gentlemen's "agreement" with the Japanese on export restraints of passenger cars.[39] Since every member state arranged its own affairs, the European Community as a whole remained powerless. Commission vice-president Davignon phoned the president of Philips Electronics and asked him whether Philips could lodge an anti-dumping complaint against Japanese VCRs. Philips could. Without informing anybody that they would visit Brussels, a representative of Philips and the young, new President of Grundig, Horst Rosenbaum, and Director Beseler of the anti-dumping division, held a meeting in the Berlaymont Commission building. During this session, the Japanese ambassador to the EEC phoned and asked what the industry representatives, Messrs Rosenbaum and the Philips representative, whose name he also mentioned, had decided. The Brussels offices of the Japan Association of Machinery Exporters (JMEA), a private branch of MITI, in the Rue Copernic offered a direct and clear view on Mr. Beseler's room in the Berlaymont building. Within a week a dumping complaint was finalised and lodged by an association specially created for the occasion, Association of Firms with a Common Interest in Video 2000, actually Grundig and Philips. The complaint was lodged on

[38] On 21 December 1982, it launched its protest against the practice in GATT (L/5427) "European Economic Communities – Import Restrictive Measures on video tape recorders Recourse to Article XXIII:1 by Japan"; practically simultaneously the Community opened an anti-dumping investigation against Japanese video recorders.

[39] This became apparent during discussions with the minister about a proposed increased of customs duty on CD players, but must also have been known by Viscount Davignon, who dealt with French anger on such betrayal.

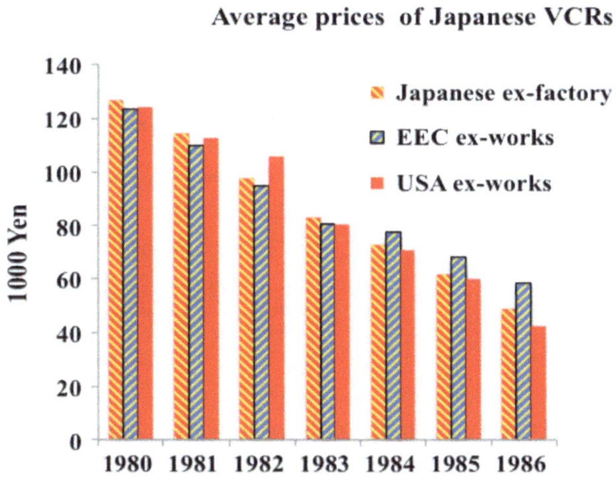

Graph 2.1 Average VCR shipment prices (in 1,000 Yen) (*Sources*: Japan Tariff Association (JTA). Brian Hindley (1986) used similar figures, comparing United States and European average prices only, concluding that after 1982 Europe had a welfare loss because prices rose compared with the United States. Hindley doubts whether there was dumping. How he would explain price differences between Japan and the United States and between Japan and the EEC prior to 1982 is difficult to guess; Japan Tariff Association; Statistics Bureau; Electronic Industry Association of Japan (EIAJ))

5 December 1982 and before Christmas it was published in the Official Journal of the European Economic Community. That was the second incident.

There was solid ground for an anti-dumping complaint. Striking commercial events had taken place in 1982. Average cost of manufacturing of VCRs in Japan was higher than the export price, as data in Graph 2.1 show. Dumping was evident. In 1980 and 1981 average manufacturing costs – that means ex-factory costs without cost of sales and without general and administrative costs and profit – were higher than export prices including these costs to the United States and Europe. Because Japanese ex-works prices were structurally higher in that period than export prices, it could be concluded that Japanese dumping – defined as sales of similar or like products in export markets at a lower price level than normal value, which is generally the price in the domestic market – has taken place in the United States. The same applied to export to the EEC until 1982.[40] But the definition of dumping is not associated with average prices. A comparison should be made between normal value and export price on a product-by-product basis. The picture shows that, prima facie, the United States consumer was better off than the Japanese consumer, while the European consumer superficially seems to have suffered from higher prices after 1983, for which phenomenon an easy explanation is given below. In any case European prices were – ex-works including overheads and selling costs – substantially lower than the ex-factory prices without selling,

[40] According to the definition in Article VI of the General Agreement on Tariffs and Trade.

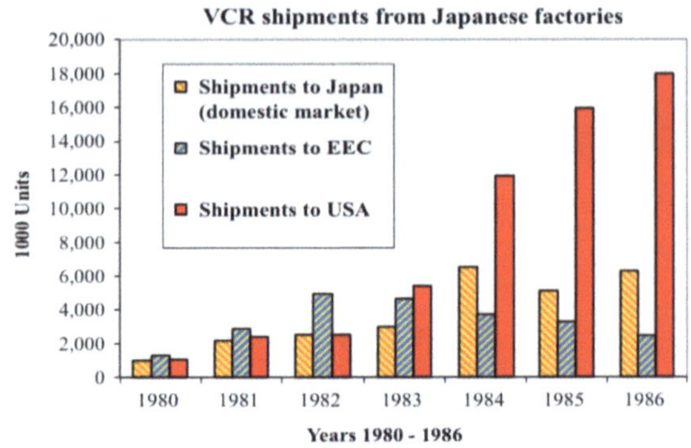

Graph 2.2 First a blow in Europe (*Sources:* EIAJ, Japan Tariff Association)

general and administrative costs for deliveries within Japan, which amount normally between 15 % and 25 % on top of the ex-factory costs.

Graph 2.1 requires an explanation. It shows per year in the left column the average *ex-factory price* of Japanese production, the middle column is FOB export price to the EEC including manufacturing costs, cost of sales and general costs normally borne by an exporter (*ex-works price*). Per year the right hand column shows the FOB export price to the United States on the same basis. That means that average cost of manufacturing, i.e. the left column, which excludes sales, general and administrative cost and profits, is higher than the average export price including such selling, general and administrative costs, to Europe in the period 1980–1983 (included) and to the United States for the whole period covered in Graph 2.1. Cost of manufacturing for 3 years was higher than export sales price to the EEC and continuously to the United States. This implies that sales at a loss on exports and – since the Japanese majors made profits – at very high prices in Japan took place. Various Japanese must have incurred severe losses on their sales abroad.

In 1982, both Japanese and European prices were below the United States level. In 1983, the export prices to the United States were for the first time above manufacturing cost. In view of the concentration of the VHS group on the elimination of the V2000 format and of Betamax in Europe, this trend was logical. In the following year, the price level of exports to the United States fell drastically. Betamax had to be eliminated and supplies to the United States geared up volume – Betamax still held about 20 %, in 1982. In 1983, the share declined to 10 %. Sony's share in the United States market dropped to 7 % in the following year.[41] As a complementary element, the quantitative aspect is revealing, as appears from Graph 2.2. The sales to the European Community dropped, but these were exports of ready-made VCRs in the high price range. The simple machines were assembled in the European Community. This story is told below.

The impression the data gives in Graph 2.1 is that low prices were reserved for the elimination of resistance by V2000 in Europe, and the European Community was given priority, both in terms of prices and, as Graph 2.2 shows, of quantity.

[41] Television Digest, 18 March 1985.

Picture 2.1 The Sanyo Betamax VTC 5000 top loader in Sanyo's offer to Grundig

Elimination of the V2000 and Sony's Betamax by both price undercutting and quantitative strategies, or simply by dumping, was the path followed by Japan's heavyweights, headed by Matsushita, assisted by other majors.

In the year 1982 price decreases by 30 % and 60 % took place in the EEC VCR market. European producers thought that a lack of competitiveness caused this havoc. Sanyo, still uncertain as to which format would win, produced both Betamax and VHS format recorders. The company wanted Grundig to switch from Video 2000 format production to Betamax import and distribution. Whether Sony urged Sanyo is unclear, but Sanyo offered two Betamax VCR sets to Grundig at devastating prices. The up loader, the VTC 5000, shown in Picture 2.1, was offered at a price of 500 German marks (€255.65 or ¥50,000). Sanyo offered the front loader at DM 550 (€281.21 or ¥55,000).[42] Sanyo offered both types as Original Equipment Manufacturers' (OEM) equipment.[43] Grundig's sales to trade price of Video 2000 VCRs was 50 % higher than Sanyo's offer price. If the intention of the Japanese manufacturer was to convince European producers of the hopelessness of own production, it was based on a misapprehension of Max Grundig's personality and temper. The man became furious and wanted prompt action. Consequently, the telephone call from Philips to Grundig resulted in a shouted and angry reply that Grundig would participate in a hunt for the Japanese. Sanyo's tender also offered basic evidence for an anti-dumping complaint.[44] The presentation of dumping was not based on Sanyo's offer, which was considered too confidential, but on a comparison of Sanyo's popular model sold in the Japanese market and a similar model sold in retail trade in the European Community, VTC 5000. In both cases,

[42] This offer of the high specification machine was even less than 50 % of the average ex-factory price in Japan (in Graph 2.1).

[43] With the brand name of the European customer on it, in this case the producer involved, Grundig.

[44] The Association of Firms with a Common Interest in Video 2000: "Anti-Dumping Complaint Concerning Video Tape Recorders Originating in Japan" lodged the complaint on 5 December 1982 and the announcement of opening of an investigation was published before Christmas 1982, the quickest opening ever.

Table 2.3 Dumping calculation on a Sanyo Betamax VCR

Normal value (Japanese domestic price to trade)		
Sanyo VTC-G1 top loader (model sold in Japan)		Yen
Recommended, listed retail price		¥118,000
Usual rebate	6 %	6,679.25
Net price ex-retailer		111,320.75
Retailer's margin	20 %	18,553.46
Price to retailer		92,767.30
Wholesaler's margin	10 %	8,433.39
Price to trade		84,333.91
Commodity tax	10 %	7,666.72
Price to trade ex-manufacturer		¥76,667.19
At the exchange rate 100 Yen = DM 1		DM 766.67
Export price (Selling price in the EC)		
Sanyo VTC-5000 (model similar to VTC-G1)		
Average retail price		DM 1,198.00
Value Added Tax	13 %	199.67
Net retail price		998.33
Dealer's margin	20 %	166.39
Price to retail trade		831.94
Agent's fee	10 %	75.63
5 % GEMA (author's rights)	5 %	36.01
Landed price		720.30
Customs Duty	8 %	53.36
CIF Price		666.94
Insurance, Freight	2 %	13.08
FOB Price (offer price to Grundig was DM 500)		DM 653.87
Dumping		
Normal value		DM 766.67
Export price		653.87
Dumping margin		112.80
As % of CIF value		**16.9 %**

selling, general and accounting costs, and the margins to trade and taxes were taken into account.[45] The calculations are presented in Table 2.3.

The percentages of trade margins in Table 2.3 were common in European trade in 1982. The retailer's net margin in Japan is lower than presented in the calculation. In Japan, wholesalers and retailers are tied to the manufacturer, which means that a substantial part of the trade margins in Japan is ploughed back to the producer

[45] Non-confidential file of the Association of Firms with a Common Interest in Video 2000. The Association made some errors in its calculations, for which the author was responsible, which have been revised here. The Association found a dumping margin of 27 % of the CIF value. Recalculation by the author results in a lower dumping margin. It should also be noted that the retail margins in VCR trade were at that time considerably higher than today. Nevertheless, a trade margin of 30 % has been calculated. The confidential offer of the Japanese producer would show a dumping margin of more than 40 %.

as profit.[46] The Sanyo price in Japan is derived from the recommended retail price with deductions of all taxes and margins as usual in the Japanese market, while the European price is the actual retail price of retailer TeVi-Markt in Nuremberg on 12 December 1982. A page with this calculation instead of the Sanyo offer was added to the file after submission of the draft. Because of the tremendous uncertainty in European retail and wholesale trade about the winning format, the margins were substantially higher than the 20 % and 10 % allocated as respective retail and wholesale margins in Table 2.3. In addition, the margin must have been higher than 20 % because of the remarkable price decreases, which made the retailer very susceptible to stock depreciation. The retail price of a comparable successor Sanyo set of the VTC 5000, the VTC 5300, decreased by 50.1 % in 8 months. All brand prices, except V2000 models, decreased by more than 40 % in the same period. At that time, therefore, a dealer margin of about 40 % was a better approximation of reality.[47]

The average ex-factory production price of VCRs in Japan, as given in Graph 2.1, was DM 955, a comfortable price for V2000 producers. This level does not include general, selling and administrative costs and profits. The average production, ex-factory, value was 3 % higher than the average price to the European Community including selling costs and profit, i.e. manufacturing value plus domestic transport cost in Japan, plus selling, administrative and general (SG&A) expenditures for export to the export destination plus profit, if any.[48] The ex-factory value as apparent from the calculation in Table 2.3 was DM 653. Compared with the average cost the dumping was 45 %. The offer price of Sanyo's VTC 5000 top loader to Grundig was DM 500. Compared with the Japanese ex-works domestic selling value derived from the Japanese retail price compared with this price to Grundig represented a dumping of 52 %. Consequently, it was clear from all sides that substantial dumping had taken place.

The complaint by the Association with a Common Interest in Video 2000 was made in an extremely short period – a few days only – and in due time. The complaint was the material that Vice President of the Commission and Commissioner for Industry and Internal Market Étienne Davignon needed as basis for action. As indicated, on behalf of the European Community, the European Commission had to deal with Japan's complaint with GATT in the framework of Article

[46] See Chap. 7 on forward integrated or captive trade in Japan.

[47] Source: retail prices GfK. Margin of retail trade: non-confidential file "Anti-Dumping Complaint Concerning Video Tape Recorders Originating in Japan", Brussels: Irelco, December 1982.

[48] The sources of Graph 2.1 are from EIAJ statistics and the Japanese Tariff Committee.

XXIII[49] – Nullification or Impairment of Concessions by the EEC.[50] Because it presented an internal EEC trade barrier,[51] which was probably difficult to reconcile with Article VIII of GATT regarding customs formalities,[52] the European Commission had to deal with issue of point of levy of the French luxury tax on VCRs in Poitiers.

In addition to the restoration of its position regarding the internal market of the European Community, firm establishment of competence in trade policy matters, underlying the Poitiers measures, was also a vital issue. The objective of Commission vice-president Davignon was to settle both problems in one strike and, as a consequence, to establish his supremacy in the European Commission. In some respects he succeeded. The anti-dumping complaint lodged by the Association of Firms with a Common Interest in the Video 2000 System resulted in a notice of investigation in December 1982, published in the Official Journal of the Community, a phenomenal achievement by the European Community services. In February 1983, Commissioners Davignon (Internal Market and Industry) and Haferkamp (External Relations) came to an agreement with MITI. The Agreement was not a "tacit gentlemen's agreement" but a "Weather Forecast", and it seems absurd that this non-agreement was written on a non-paper, the content of which is reproduced in this Chapter (Picture 2.2). The Association of Firms with a Common Interest in the Video 2000 System was essentially compelled to withdraw its complaint and the French Government found another method of collecting its luxury tax other than solely in Poitiers or in factories. The French government sensibly seemed to dislike the outcome.

Viscount Davignon staged his discussions with the Japanese with backing from a very few, cleverly selected contacts in European Community industry, who were unaware of trade policy practices and effects of certain agreements. The directly commercially responsible in the companies concerned did not have the slightest idea of the consequences of their approval of certain details. Davignon phoned from Japan in the European night, which made consultations in Europe about his discussions with the Japanese impossible. The Weather Forecast, backed by only a few persons in European industry during nightly consultations and agreed to the Japanese, would spell doom to Video 2000 and Betamax.

[49] Recourse to Article XXIII:1 by Japan, document L/5472, 21 December 1982, see footnote 39. The retaliation of the Community was a complaint concerning the general barriers to imports caused by the distribution system (see Chap. 7), in the document: "Nullification of benefits and impediment to the attainment of GATT objectives", L/5479. Neither matter was pursued.

[50] According to Article 113, the European Commission will submit proposals to the Council and conduct negotiations (at present Article 133 of Consolidated Text of the Treaty and Article 207 of Treaty on the Functioning of the European Union, OJ C 83/47 of 30.3.2010).

[51] The point of entry prescription has the equivalent effect to a quantitative restriction and is not permitted by Article 31 of the Rome Treaty, which was Article 28 in the Consolidated Text of the Treaty establishing the European Community and Article 34 of the Treaty on the Functioning of the European Union, OJ C 83/47 of 30.3.2010.

[52] "Concerning Fees and Formalities connected with Importation and Exportation".

SUBJECT: Undertaking on VTRs

1. The Japanese side will exercise export moderation for VTRs towards the Community for two years. Export moderation will be implemented by a weather forecast. This weather forecast takes into account the following four elements:

(1) The export floor price system established by the Japanese authorities

(2) The European industry (see footnote) will be in a position to produce and sell at least 1.3 million VTRs within the Community in 1984.

(3) Chassis kits will be supplied to companies which contribute substantially to EC-Japan industrial cooperation by satisfying the following criteria, without being subject to the weather forecast in 1984.

(A) A considerable level of European value in the first half of 1984;

(B) The target of increasing substantially the European value of this production in the course of 1984 and 1985;

(C) Location in Europe of major tools;

(D) Total level of investments in manufacturing company should not be less than three million US dollars.

(4) Total Japanese export of VTRs, including chassis kits, but excluding those defined above, will not exceed 3.95 million units in 1984.

footnote: Including production by Community companies in Austria

2. The content of the weather forecast for 1985 will be the subject of consultation at the end of 1984.

It is understood that one-quarter-inch VTRs, professional VTR installations and VTRs for re-export outside the Community are not covered by the weather forecast. The Japanese side will implement a control system which will ensure that only clearly identified re-exports are credited against the forecast. Administrative guidance will be given to the effect that no re-routing into the Community market takes place.

Picture 2.2 Copy of the "Weather Forecast" (part of it)

One of the decisive factors was the market situation in the United Kingdom. The strategy of the United Kingdom and industry did not prevent, but rather accelerated destruction of the United Kingdom television industry, and certainly contributed to the precipitant decline of the European V2000 and the Betamax VCR format. In this destruction, Thorn EMI was principal party. Thorn EMI believed so strongly in the superiority of Matsushita that it introduced VHS recorders into its rental system with the companies DER, Radio Rentals and Rumbelows. This rental support was crucial. As shown above in this Chapter, the United Kingdom industry planned to offer these rentals as an asset in the acquisition, for survival, of television technology. They neither obtained the technology nor the survival, but the Japanese got access to United Kingdom distribution. The control of United Kingdom distribution channels, after the take-overs by Japanese producers as sketched above, substantially helped the Japanese firms Hitachi, Toshiba and Mitsubishi. Due to this particular property of the United Kingdom market, consumers avoided risks and were susceptible to new products. In the case of VCRs, they avoided the risk of choosing equipment of the wrong format. Fortunately for VHS producers, major

Japanese producers with access to distribution opted for VHS production. This is one of the explanations for why the United Kingdom market was ahead of the continent and even of the United States in videocassette recorder consumption. In 1982 the United Kingdom VCR market consisted of more than 2.8 million sets, compared with three million in continental EEC and 2.5 million in the United States.[53]

The lack of technological capability and urge for technology for survival tempted Thorn EMI – one of the last independent United Kingdom manufacturers and the greatest in the rental market – to market VHS and VHS film software on cassettes in return for VHS technology. EMI was an important producer and distributor both of music and films. Thorn EMI became very important as video software supplier. With support from Thorn EMI, the VHS format group was able to supply pre-taped software as a support to its sales of VHS machines via the same rentals, which had considerable impact on the position of VHS in the United Kingdom and later, in the rest of Europe. Through this, the VCR was promoted from a time shifter – recording of television programmes that could be viewed later –[54] to a Video Home System (VHS) that was supported by software supply, so that the VCR was both a time shifter and a home cinema. This was the marketing concept that particularly helped this system in Europe.[55] But the Weather Forecast would entail the decisive blow.

In return for this material software advantage, Thorn was able to start a joint VCR production facility in New Haven with JVC. Just as the television sector working party of the NEDC hoped to acquire television technology from Japan by means of stimulation of inward investments and by offering distribution channels to the Japanese – just what the Japanese needed – Thorn got its joint venture for VCR production. As shown, this policy did not help very much in colour television. VHS conquered with one blow, through Thorn's and other rentals, a huge share of the United Kingdom market – about 90 % –, which was of decisive importance for the European Community at large. Thorn also opted for JVC's capacitative disc system, Very High Density (VHD) rather than the laser optical disc systems, i.e. LaserVision, and for Audio High Density (AHD) instead of laser Compact Disc. By this latter move it came late with software on the CD market and missed

[53] Sources: "Television Digest", Vol 30, No. 34, 20 August 1990, p. 12, Simavelec and Euromonitor Market Research.

[54] Morita (1986, p. 208) considered it a time shifter.

[55] The market situation in the United States differed substantially. Its development was delayed because it hardly offered anything in addition to the huge number of television channels and pay television. The attractiveness of the machine came with availability of software.

Table 2.4 Brand policies and the VHS group

OEM supplies in Europe by the VHS group			
Customer	Brand	Country	Japanese supplier
Thorn EMI (later Thomson)	Ferguson	UK	JVC
Telefunken (later Thomson)	Telefunken	Germany	JVC
Bosch	Blaupunkt	Germany	Matsushita
Granada TV rental	Granada/Bush/Murphy	UK	Matsushita
Rank	Rank	UK	Toshiba
Thomson	Brandt, Continental Edison, Pathé Marconi, Teleavia, Saba, Nordmende	France	JVC
Thomson	Nordmende, Saba	Germany	JVC
Schneider	Schneider (Germany)	Schneider	Matsushita
ITT	Graetz, Standard Elektrik, ITT	Germany	Matsushita

substantial profits. Due to its acceptance of and preparation for AHD it was unable to start CD audio equipment production in due time.[56]

In addition to Thorn were Telefunken's strong television brand and distribution position in the German (second to Grundig), Italian and Spanish markets and its technologically frail position, which was attractive to JVC. Telefunken joined the club: J2T. Although production intentions are not always representative of effective output, total production announced by JVC and its allies in Europe, Thorn and Telefunken, was assembly of about 480,000 units in 1983, a substantial amount.[57] The consequence of these relations was that VHS built a strong production basis in the European Community in terms of assembly of VCR in the European Community. The survey of the brand relations is given in Table 2.4.

The volume policy of both Japanese VHS and Betamax (Sony less, Sanyo more) manufacturers on export markets can be deduced from their OEM deliveries. The great bulk of sales took place via United States and European manufacturers under their brand names at prices that discouraged even an intention of production by Sony and Sanyo. The following customers of VHS producers, mainly Matsushita

[56] The source is the memory of the author about a conversation with the managing director of Ferguson. The importance of both Thorn and Telefunken to JVC as a partner was also in the audio sphere. JVC had developed a digital audio system, Audio High Density, derived from Video High Density (VHD). It needed software support from Thorn EMI and Telefunken, which had a soft software pillar.

[57] Commission of the European Communities: "The European Consumer Electronics Industry"; TF-2, April 1985, p. 21.

and its daughter company JVC, were well-known brand names of television set manufacturers with developed distribution networks.[58]

Some European (and United States) traders and OEM customers later changed their sourcing to other manufacturers, some of which were Koreans.

2.5 European Trade Policy of Foreign Make: Japanese Self-Restraint

Picture 2.2 is a copy of part of the Weather Forecast. An agreement written on "non-paper" that contained a quantitative Weather Forecast: undertakings by MITI as to the value added of production by Japanese VCR assembly factories in the European Community and a commitment to set of floor prices.

> *"Export floor prices will be established by the Japanese authorities. The European industry (footnote: including production by Community companies in Austria) will be in a position to produce and sell at least 1.2 million VCRs within the Community in 1983"* and *"total Japanese exports of VCRs including chassis kits will not exceed 4.55 million units in 1983"*,

according to the non-paper, which also included Weather Forecasts for colour receiver picture tubes, colour television sets and some other items. In one stroke, all issues were at first glance settled.

A colour receiver picture tube part –in the forecast – enabled the EECA to have consultations resulting in understandings about Japanese export quantities between the European Commission and MITI.[59]

> *It was understood that France's customs clearance procedures would be normalised as soon as possible, and that the anti-dumping procedure initiated by European VCR manufacturers would be dropped.*[60]

The Weather Forecast on VCRs was a one-page "non-paper", which is produced in Table 2.5. It spelled out some details agreed upon. Some parts had to be specified in a later stage. This implied that all sorts of meetings would be arranged: between MITI and the European Commission, between the European Commission and European industry, which required internal meetings between various departments of the European Commission and also between industry leaders. Thomson started the arrangement of regular meetings between European industrialists and MITI

[58] Kenichi Ohmae (1985, pp. 35–37); Metze (1991, pp. 45–46); Nayak and Ketteringham (1986, pp. 24–49); Kostecki (1991, p. 92).

[59] Colour television and tubes were part of the Weather Forecast. As the number of tube users was rather small, the negotiations were not very complicated. The demand for "free", i.e. non-captive, tubes was highly predictable. For the delegations these discussions were attractive, for they offered the possibility of trips to picturesque sites.

[60] "News and Views from Japan", Japanese Mission to the European Communities, 24 February 1983.

Table 2.5 The VCR "Weather Forecast"

Video Tape Recorder Quota Arrangement between EC and Japan		(thousand sets)
	1983	1984
Finished Products	3,950	3,950
Kits (SKD)	600	Est. 1,100 Free, If European Value 25% or above
European	1,200	1,300 Assured Free, If European 55% or above
Total	5,750	6,350

officials, some of whom in the JMEA, the Club de Cagnard, named after the splendid hotel where the first meeting took place. Thomson hoped to influence the negotiations in two ways: one via the governmental tables and one directly with MITI. During such lobby activities, and also directly, hard and bitter negotiations took place between Thomson and Philips about ceilings of Japanese exports of completely assembled VCRs and of chassis kits. Thomson wanted as many kits as possible, whereas Philips tried to reduce it because these kits were all VHS format machines. All negotiations took place with the objective to influence the content of the VCR Weather Forecast, as given in Table 2.5.

The non-written quantitative agreement, of Table 2.5, resulted in the detailed Table 2.6.

A second element in the agreement was the undertaking by MITI that Japanese firms would increase the local value of their production in the European Community. Since this was practically unfeasible, it was never properly checked. Initially, assembly remained restricted to the unpacking of mechanical decks and printed circuit boards stuffed with components, soldering them, putting them on the frame and packing them in the housing or cabinet purchased in Europe. Some Japanese manufacturers since added the assembly of mechanical decks, due to some

Table 2.6 Details of "Weather Forecast" consequences

	Agreement and reality	1983	1984
A	Finished products ex-Japan	3,950,000	3,950,000
B	Kits and subassemblies for Japanese assembly in EEC	600,000	1,100,000
C	European sales (including Austrian production)	1,200,000	1,300,000
D	Total sales forecast	5,750,000	6,350,000
E	VCR imports into the EEC (Eurostat)[a]	4,581,138	3,677,712

Sources: Nihon Keizai Shimbun, 20 August and 25 August 1983; Het Financieele Dagblad, 11 November 1983; Eurostat import statistics
[a]Excluding deflections of trade via Hong Kong, etc.

manoeuvres sketched in Sects. 5.4 and 6.2. The sets made in Europe were simple models. It is therefore not amazing that the average price of VCR shipments to Europe did not decrease as much as those to the United States. The share of complex, more up-market models in Japanese exports to the EEC increased.

The third element was a scheme of minimum prices based on a system of points, indicative of the value of certain features in the models.[61] Features specific to Video 2000, relating to length of playing time and noiseless still picture, were, of course, allotted the highest number of points. Minimum export prices of ¥70,000 for simple models, ¥85,000 for more sophisticated models and ¥100,000 for luxury models were proposed by MITI and accepted. Categories were defined in such a way that V2000 models were automatically in the highest range and Japanese prices could always undercut them. Or, if Europeans aligned their prices to Japanese levels, the Japanese could accuse Europeans of price disruption and excuse themselves. Although it was maintained that "price rises of up to 50 % characterised VER-restricted exports of Japanese video tape recorders to the EEC in the mid-80s. . ."[62] statements for which no tenable evidence was forwarded, the average Japanese export price to the EEC in 1983 was ¥80,610, which was not very different from the price of the products sent to the United States, ¥80,570. Consequently, the minimum price, which should have especially served the interests of Sony, because its products were generally higher priced, had hardly any effect. In subsequent years, the average export price of Japanese sets went up, but this did not imply a price rise in the European Community. In the first place, simple and cheap models were assembled in Europe. Second, prices in the statistics are partly inter-company prices. The export price may have been relatively high, but the resale price was be compensated by financial transactions with the European subsidiary.

Normally a VRA concerns quantities only. An additional price clause might raise questions concerning the need for such a part. However, the format struggle elicited quantitative competition for acceptance of one single standard. Volume competition is hardly possible without a price fight. Low prices would imply severe injury to at least one party, the adherents to Sony's Betamax format, which was the

[61] British Radio and Electronic Equipment Manufacturer's Association, March 1983.
[62] Kostecki (1991, pp. 87–99).

weakest inside Japan and, European V2000 interests aside, was harshly hurt by dumping outside Japan. Consequently, a price minimum was imperative in order to avoid decision on formats at the cost of losses. The price chapter in the Weather Forecast did not have the effect as often alleged. Products with the lowest ¥70,000 floor price were assembled in Europe and this price became irrelevant as export floor price – excluding the products exported to the European Community by means of deflection of trade via other countries. Prices of models assembled in Europe appeared much lower. More expensive models were produced in Japan. Compliance with the minimum price clause in the Weather Forecast was tested by a check of average prices rather than on the basis of a model-by-model inspection.[63]

Sony's interests were, apparently, not longer of primary importance to MITI. As sketched in the second paragraph about standardisation of Sect. 2.4, when Sony's system offered the best perspective, it was different. After the failed efforts in setting the VCR format in the 1970s, MITI had reluctantly given up its preponderant role in the VCR standard scene. It was clear that there was a victorious format. MITI was glad to take the lead again and to play a role in international trade, thereby strengthening its own authority.[64] The minimum price was in the interest of Sony, which had the smallest market share in Japan and could not benefit as much from the high domestic selling prices of video recorders as the VHS producers. Under the agreement on floor prices, Sony's sales in the European Community should have been more profitable. The minimum prices were, however, decreased a year later as proposed by MITI. Perhaps MITI had become aware that Sony could not be saved by the agreement. In view of the fear about protests from consumers, the European Commission could hardly refuse to agree. A differentiation was again made according to features. The minimum remained ¥70,000 for a "leader model". The other minima were ¥75,000 for a standard model, ¥80,000 for a top model and ¥87,000 for a stereo model. But the calculated FOB price derived from European shop prices and all costs incurred between shipment and sales in the shop was inferior to the agreed FOB minima, taking the currency movements between moment of shipping and sales taken into consideration.[65] The average price of a "leader" VHS model was DM 170 (€86.92) below the price actually expected in the retail shop, i.e. a lower price had been quoted than the one agreed. It may be

[63] Brian Hindley (1986) conceded the necessity of the check on the basis of model-by-model, but did not take the trouble or did not have or did not know sources for such inspection.

[64] It seems that measures were legally based on the same law as the Trade in Semiconductors Agreement in force since November 1986 – also a voluntary restraint agreement – with the United States, i.e. the Foreign Exchange and Foreign Trade Control Law, which was introduced for the purpose of COCOM enforcement, i.e. controls on strategic exports to Communist countries.

[65] It would take too much space to make the analysis here, but depending on the EEC country in which the distribution takes place and specific costs incurred, the calculation can be made from the shop backwards to FOB (with deduction of Value Added Tax, trade margins, selling expenses, costs of inland storage and freight, costs of importation, duty, insurance and freight costs) and those prices can be compared with the minima. The calculations had been made from data in Videomarkt in Germany and Institut Français de Recherche.

assumed that independent traders were not prepared to incur losses. Supply prices were considerably lower than could be expected on basis of agreed minima. A standard model cost DM 136 less than it should, and the top and stereo models DM 140 (€71.58) and DM 123 (€62.89) respectively. In France, the differences were more than Ff 85 (€12.96).[66] The European OEM customers, Thorn, Telefunken, Thomson of VHS imported either from JVC or assembled in the joint ventures (J2T). Bosch purchased from Matsushita or got sets from MB Video. Since the Japanese respected minimum prices in supplies to their European partners, but did themselves sell at lower prices under own brands, these Europeans loathed the minimum price system. This Japanese practice of dual pricing had its effect in on the future attitude towards arrangements proposed by the Japanese, discussed in Chap. 4.

The VCR arrangement was not only a compromise between the EEC and Japan. It was also a compromise among Japanese – Betamax and VHS – interests and among Europeans – producers of V2000 and assemblers in the joint ventures. Since limits on Japanese exports and hypothetical European sales clearly exceeded quantities of market demand, on which market European industry had presented pretty reliable forecasts to European Commission negotiators, disappointments were inevitable. The agreement did not improve the position of European producers at all. Since the German government demanded that sufficient kits for assembly by joint-ventures, of Telefunken with JVC and Bosch with Matsushita in MB Video (35 % owned by Bosch and 65 % by Matsushita) become available and the United Kingdom demanded sufficient kits for the joint-venture factory of Thorn and JVC in New Haven, the arrangement did not offer any certainty to those producers who needed relief from the injury by dumping.[67] As for the compromise in Japan, minimum prices served the Betamax format group (mainly Sony and Sanyo), needing profit on its sales abroad. The quantitative part was in the interest of VHS with its many production footholds in the European Community. It soon became clear that, while the price side of the agreement was ineffective, the quantitative element was decisive. The quantitative element of the agreement was the deathblow to European production, as Table 2.6 shows. Investments by

[66] Sources: Estimates circulated by the Commission of the European Communities; Nihon Keizai Shimbun, 11 July 1987; Dempa 27 January 1983; Simavelec (the French consumer electronics association). The retail prices come from GfK.

[67] Hindley (1986) alleged that Germany was silent about the self-restraint arrangement because Grundig and Philips produced in that country. It was the opposite. Frau Helga Steeg, Director General for Foreign Trade of the Federal Ministry of Economic Affairs, fervently opposed the agreement if it meant that Telefunken would not get its kits and components for production in Berlin. "You are killing our joint-ventures," she exclaimed to Vice-President of the Commission Davignon in a meeting of the trade policy advisory committee, Committee 113 (thereafter 133 and now Article 207 of the Treaty on the functioning of the European Union, OJ C83/47 of 30.3.2010), when the practical implementation of the Weather Forecast was discussed. The lobby of Telefunken's boss Josef Stoffels from Berlin and Blaupunks's chief Herbert Thum on behalf of a sufficiency of imported kits from Japan was stronger than the voice of Bavarian entrepreneur and Stoffels' former boss, Max Grundig.

Japanese VHS companies and co-operation between JVC and Thorn Ferguson, Telefunken and later with Thomson of France, which would take over Telefunken and Ferguson, and in a later stage between Matsushita and Bosch, gave a distinct advantage to the VHS system: export licenses of VCRs were allocated according to historical performance, the quota of kits according to requirements in Europe. The historical performance of VHS dramatically improved in 1982 and, consequently, the agreement by MITI and the managing of the export quota resulted in the victimizing of Sony and its Betamax format. Furthermore, the minimum prices for the leader models had no significance because the simple models were assembled in the European Community. Moreover, minimum prices for the medium class, above the simple models, decreased, which was to the disadvantage of more up-market Sony.

In one night, or 1 day in Japan, the results of Poitiers and the anti-dumping complaint had been thrown away, and Betamax and V2000 sentenced as Table 2.7 shows. The market was overstated and the sales of V2000 were accordingly assessed or guessed too high: a market share of 21 % in 1983 that would increase to 32 %, whereas the reality was a fall from 16 % to 12 %. Distribution by MITI of export licenses according to historical performance appeared lethal to Sony's Betamax and, as a corollary, to Video 2000. Estimates of Betamax and VHS market shares in Europe in 1982 were V2000 11 %, Betamax about 23 % and VHS 66 %.[68] The kits and sub-assemblies were practically only for VHS production in Europe. About 850,000 units were supposed to be assembled by VHS and only 80,000 by Sanyo and Sony.[69] The conclusion from the survey, which is presented in Table 2.7, that the MITI had opted for the powerful, Matsushita and its allies, seems self-evident. MITI checked the export quantities and, at a certain moment, acted as though it was able to check the destination of quantities. Massive transhipments, however, appeared to take place, which MITI must have noticed. After all, it appeared that the situation as consequence of these transhipment, was even better for VHS and worse for Betamax and V2000. Prices could not be checked; if they could, MITI would have found disrespect of the non-written agreement.

Immediately after the industry, Philips at the least, obtained information about details of the Weather Forecast a table was drawn presenting the figures and conclusions about the consequences of the arrangement, which were alarming. The interpretation of the data presented in the Weather Forecast, as spelled out in Table 2.7, was that a victory of and a switch to VHS were unavoidable. This outcome was predictable as early as March 1983. The overwhelming market share of 67 % held by VHS in 1983 and more in subsequent years as the consequence of the VRA meant that V2000 and Betamax would have insufficient market share and would not be capable of attracting sufficient software support. This rather poignant experience may have been – as already mentioned – the reason for the

[68] Commission of the European Communities: "The European Consumer Electronics Industry", 1985.

[69] Dempa, 1 January 1983.

Table 2.7 Alarming prediction: doom for Betamax and Video 2000 (units × 1,000)

					Share in actual market (% of D)		
		1983	1984	1985	1983	1984	1985
	VHS assembly in EEC[a]	695	909	1,400	12 %	16 %	23 %
	Weather Forecast: VHS imports[b]	3,061.25	3,061.25	3,061.25	55 %	53 %	49 %
A	**Total VHS**	3,756.25	3,970.25	4,461.25	67 %	68 %	72 %
	Betamax assembly in EEC[a]	60	60	120	1 %	1 %	2 %
	Weather Forecast: Betamax imports[b]	888.75	888.75	888.75	16 %	15 %	14 %
B	**Total Betamax**	948.75	948.75	1,008.75	17 %	16 %	16 %
C	**Weather Forecast: Video 2000 sales**	1,200	1,300	2,000	21 %	22 %	32 %
	Weather Forecast market	5,750	6,350	6,400			
D = A + B + C	**Weather Forecast and actual**	5,905	6,219	7,470	105 %	107 %	120 %
E	**Actual demand (market research)**	5,600	5,800	6,200	100 %	100 %	100 %
F = D − E	**Actually remaining for V2000**	895	881	730	16 %	15 %	12 %
	Percent V 2000 of Weather Forecast	75 %	68 %	37 %			

Source: paper circulated by the Commission of the European Communities; Nihon Keizai Shimbun, 11 July 1987; Dempa 27 January 1983; Simavelec; transhipments: Census & Statistics Department, Hong Kong: Hong Kong Trade Statistics
[a]Based on market research and information from sources below
[b]The Weather Forecast imports are the Weather Forecast exports divided over VHS and Betamax according to their exports in 1982

take-overs by Sony in a later stage of music and picture companies CBS and Columbia, a strategic move that might also have been prompted by the successful introduction of the Compact Disc standard with support of the software industry led by Philips' music division Polygram as well as the failure of introduction of a standard for the Rotary-Digital Audio Tape Recorder (R-DAT).[70] Because a removal of the export restraint might have resulted in legal steps against Japanese manufacturers on dumping, MITI announced, although nobody asked for it, that Japan maintain its voluntary restraints.[71] The real reason for this announcement was fear of anti-dumping actions against the leading Japanese producers. MITI hoped that it could protect the majors from dumping charges and to discipline certain

[70] Financial Times, 16 December 1991.

[71] Nikkan Kotyo, 20 November 1985.

newcomers in Japan that wanted to export VCRs at low prices, much to the dislike of the major Japanese. Sections 10.1, 10.2, 10.3, and 10.4 deal with this issue.

In March 1983 – a fortnight after the agreement – everyone within the company did not welcome the conclusion from Tables 2.6 and 2.7 that a switch by Philips from Video 2000 to VHS was inevitable. It was in the first place an indication of a mistaken judgment of the communication with Davignon during his negotiations, but also against declared internal policy. The grain of the message fell on rocky ground and resulted in animosity towards the messenger. Nevertheless, the switch actually took place in 1984. Sony formally abandoned its format in 1988 and started production and sales of VHS alongside Betamax. Philips increased its equity stake in Grundig, after Thomson tried in vain to acquire in 1984 – with French state funds – this German number one company. Thomson had already acquired too many German producers and Philips refused to sell its minority stake so that Thomson did not obtain competition authorities' approval for a take-over. Hermanus Koning from Philips became the first Chief Executive Officer of the new owned company. In the video sector, Grundig became a multi-system supplier, producing VHS systems alongside Video 2000 recorders. What Philips did not know, when it agreed on the acquisition price, was that it paid heavily for stocks of Video 2000 recorders at Grundig, valued at market price, but actually worthless. The stock clearance contributed to some revival of V2000 sales, but aggravated the price fall in the European Community VCR market in general.

Together with their joint ventures Japanese VHS producers obtained a majority of production in the European Community.[72] The Betamax group total sales worldwide declined from 28.3 % to 16.9 % in the second half of 1984. In 1985 the two VHS founders, JVC and mother Matsushita produced 13.4 million sets worldwide; Hitachi, Mitsubishi, Toshiba, NEC and Sharp together added another 14 million.[73] In 1987, the Betamax market share in Japan was reduced to only 5 %, which in view of its distribution position was Sony's normal market share in Japan.[74] Sony made another strategic mistake, discussed in Chap. 10. Instead of accepting VHS, not as a technically superior system, but as a political and commercial hegemony of the grouping supporting the standard, it tried to win the Koreans over to its system. That had destructive effects and created problems Europeans had to solve for the Japanese. Formally, Sony dropped its system a few years later. Formal abandonment by Sony in 1988 of its Betamax system,

[72] Joint ventures are Thomson and JVC) with a mechanical deck production in Tonnerre (Burgundy, France) and VCR production in Berlin (Germany) and Matsushita-Bosch Video in Ostenrode (Germany). The production of J2T – at first a joint venture between JVC and Thorn and Telefunken, both latter acquired by the state-owned company Thomson – had a maximum level of about one million. After a few years, Thorn's factory in New Haven closed for VCR production. Later, Thomson created a joint venture with Toshiba in Singapore and an increasing part of its production was shifted to East Asia. The Berlin factory was abandoned in 1990 after the reunification of Germany and the discontinuation of the Berlinhilfe, aid for producers in Berlin.

[73] Dempa, 31 October 1985.

[74] Sony surrendered in 1988. The Japan Times, 6 August 1988.

technically the best Japanese system, came just a few years after surrender by V2000, which was considered technically the best system of all. Betamax flopped for the same reason as V2000. Often it has been alleged by Philips management that the availability of hard pornography software on cassettes was the main driver of VHS. That is only a part of the explanation. One of the major points was that Japanese VHS producers had a dominant share on the Japanese market and dumped their exports to Europe and also to the United States, reducing unit cost and improving profitability in the Japanese market and in the meantime predatorily establishing their video format. Chapter 7 shows the nature of Matsushita's position allowing high market share and domestic sales at high prices in the Japanese market. Chapter 8 explains the consequences of that market system.

Another serious consequence of the VCR case was that transition to the VHS absorbed investments and R&D intended for development of related products. Development of video camera recorder production had to be postponed. Dumping and turbulence in VCR market were not the only cause of a failure to produce camcorders. Destruction of the European photo camera and consumer film camera industry by Japanese imports caused a crippled European mass film lens and fine mechanical motors industry. The technological basis for a launch of video camera recorders was weak, but dumping and transition to VHS implied the end to the offspring of this new development, which was in progress. It would finally have its effect on the professional television camera industry. Thomson was not interested in consumer camera recorders; it would purchase them. It was only interested in – highly needed – profits on VCRs and, consequently, in VHS. It later even blocked an action in favour of domestic European video camera recorder production. It paid for this behaviour, discussed in Chap. 5.

2.6 Voluntary Restraints as Trade Policy Instrument: Preliminary Remarks

The lesson from the case of VCR is similar to those from other voluntary restraint agreements. These lessons are dealt with in the next chapter. It is clear from the examples that any arrangement not built on legal proceedings and measures without a legal basis are unsuitable as trade policy instruments. Because it makes their lives more interesting and their role more important, officials prefer "voluntary" arrangements. It gives them some discretionary power, and commercial parties become dependent and must show gratitude. The same applies to inter-industry arrangements, as displayed in the case of the RIC's arrangements. Delegations' members try to acquire good relations with the other party and gradually prefer to emphasise the benefit of such good relations. Finally, good relations acquired priority over firm arrangements and results for the industry generally came in at second place. The following quote about GEC's CEO Lord Arnold Weinstock opinion might serve as an example:

Talks were held several times a year and are widely regarded as having been remarkably successful, given the two industries' very real conflict of interests. Indeed, in about 1980 the Government advised the Machine Tool industry's trade association to visit BREMA in order to learn how to set up similar talks. Not everyone takes such a favourable view of the RIC/EIAJ talks, however; Lord Weinstock likens them to a deer talking to a tiger and considers the simile to have been borne out by events.[75]

Actually, self-restraint agreements have effects that border on corruption. A legally based measure closes the proceeding and parties can dedicate their time to activities they are normally supposed to perform. No repeated sign of gratitude or subservience toward a party at the negotiation table by another party is required. The next chapter deals with voluntary restraints in greater detail.

References

Belderbos R (1994) Strategic trade policy and multinational enterprises: essays on trade and investment by Japanese electronics firms. Thesis Publishers, Amsterdam

Geddes K (1991) Setmakers: a history of the radio and television industry. BREMA, London

Greenaway D, Hindley B (1985) What Britain pays for voluntary export restraints, Thames essays. Trade Policy Research Centre, London

Hindley B (1986) EC imports of VCRs from Japan, a costly precedent. J World Trade Law 20(2):168–184

Klousen P (1986) L'affaire du Dédouanement des Magnétoscopes à Poitiers. Université des Sciences Sociales, Toulouse

Kostecki M (1991) Marketing strategies and voluntary export restraints. J World Trade 25(4):87–99

McClenahan W (1991) The growth of voluntary export restraints and American foreign economic policy, business and economic history, 2 (20). In: Proceeding of Bus. Hist Conference: 1956–1969

Metze M (1991) Kortsluiting. Uitgeverij Sun, Nijmegen

Morita A (1986) Made in Japan, Akio Morita and Sony. Dutton, New York

Nayak P, Ketteringham J (1986) Breakthroughs! How leadership and drive created commercial innovations that swept the world. Rawson Associates, New York

Nevin JJ (1978) Can U.S. Business survive our Japanese trade policy? Harv Bus Rev 56(5):165–177. doi:10.1002/tie.5060210112

Ohmae K (1985) Triad power: the coming shape of global competition. Mc Kinsey and Company. The Free Press, New York

Prestowitz CV (1988) Trading places: how we allowed Japan to take the lead. Basic Books, New York

Quatrepoint JM (1984) Un échec exemplaire: l'affaire Grundig. Rev Econ Ind 27(1):31–41

[75] Lord Arnold Weinstock was the CEO of GEC, the company that had the joint venture with Hitachi, which collapsed; Geddes (1991), p. 386.

Chapter 3
Follies of Voluntary Restraints: Politics and Economics

Abstract Voluntary Restraint Agreements (VRAs) have both practical and theoretical peculiar properties. They have a history that is closely related with certain economic structures, in particular the Japanese system of economic groupings. This system's origins are in the Japanese Meiji Restoration and its program of rapid national industrialisation. VRAs favour big and strong exporters and disadvantage smaller exporters, newcomers and importers. Two usual models, one on quantitative restrictions and the other VRAs, show the differences between these two different forms of trade policy measures. Economically, VRAs are beneficial to exporters and negative for the importing country. This was the case with the VCR agreement. The special case of video recorders gave the Japanese Ministry of International Trade and Industry (MITI) substantial power, which two newcomers undermined. MITI later punished these two renegades by Japan's approval of an anti-dumping proceeding by the European Community, *inter alia* against them.

3.1 Some Characteristics of Voluntary Export Restraints in General

The highly political nature of VRAs or Voluntary Export Restraints (VERs) and the amusing and sad aspects of such trade policy solutions may be clear from Chap. 2. Unlike import tariffs or quotas, VRAs lack a sound legal basis. To politicians, import restrictions appear a trade policy instrument to be avoided. There are rules for application of such instruments and those who impose them can be held accountable. Import quotas do not allow arbitrariness. Export restraints are, therefore, considered more attractive. Politicians who agree on restraints with exporters rarely concede their mistakes when the agreements appear flawed. They might blame the exporting country, but the exporting country is not accountable in the importing country. Since nobody can take exact stock of their outcome, VRAs are always depicted as successful. At least two parties inevitably and incessantly keep discussing and disagreeing about the content of the VRA: quantities agreed upon

M. van Marion, *International Trade Policy and European Industry*, Contributions to Economics, DOI 10.1007/978-3-319-00392-4_3,

and shipped and, as in the case of the VRA on VCRs, prices. Surveillance and administration of VRAs create serious problems. Quantities and prices of exports are not necessarily equal to those of imports. Import figures might include transhipments, whereas the exporting country may only keep track of licences requested and granted for products destined for the importing country. As a consequence, it appears that in the case of VCRs, units entered the European Community via Hong Kong and Switzerland. The importing country can investigate whether the provenance of a product is also the origin. The exporting country is not able to check whether the destination indicated on a license request is indeed the final destination of the goods. That may result in conflicts between the "restraining exporting" and the importing country, if the latter indeed makes serious objections to a sudden proliferation of provenance of imports of VHS VCRs. In the case of the VRA on VCRs, the European Commission neither noticed the sudden change in pattern of trade, nor wanted to accept any defects in the agreement, and considered criticism on the agreement a sign of ingratitude of European industry.

The case above is not theoretical. In a dumping investigation, a directorate general of the European Commission other than the Directorate General of Internal Market and Industry who conducted discussions about the VRA, the Directorate General of External Relations, now of Trade, found export destinations in two Japanese companies' accounts, which were clearly transhipments.[1]

> *The Commission's investigation showed that the two Japanese exporters had incorrectly declared a large proportion of their exports as having been sold to third countries. However, from the customer names and the technical specifications of the VCRs, the Commission concluded that these exports were destined for consumption in the Community and they were, therefore, included in the provisional calculations.*

The discovery of irregularities was attributable to the availability of legal means to this department. The Anti-dumping Regulation was the internationally accepted legal base. In the view of the Internal Market and Industry (Davignon's) Directorate General, the Japanese applied the "Weather Forecast" strictly, and circumventions were inexistent or negligible. The Directorate General of External Relations however, found striking quantities[2]:

> *The combined exports of Funai and Orion amounted to 293 000 units in 1984, 466 000 units in 1985, 991 000 units in 1986 .... Funai started exporting VCRs to the Community in 1984 and Orion in 1982. Their joint market share developed from 5,1 % in 1984 to 7,6 % in 1985, to 13,9 % in 1986 ....* [Circumvention was the cause] ... *why the precise quantity of exports destined for Community consumption and actually imported is difficult to establish. For this assessment the Commission evaluated data on destinations and technical specifications from the exporters concerned and from other sources.*

---

[1] Commission Regulation (EEC) No 2684/88 of 26 August 1988 imposing a provisional anti-dumping duty on certain imports of video cassette recorders originating in Japan and the Republic of Korea, Official Journal L 240, 31/08/1988 pp. 5–17, recital 28.

[2] Regulation quoted in footnote 1, recital 49.

Although the experience was embarrassing, one European Community producer knew the route of circumvention quite well. It purchased VCRs with the tuner and recorder in separated housings from a well-established Japanese company. The portable recorder part could be linked to a camera. The purchase was ordered before February 1983, but the shipment took place in March. Since these extraordinary supplies would be charged against the supplier's export quota based on historical performance, the Japanese supplier created difficulties. Consequently, the Japanese subsidiary of the European company made the purchase and shipped the product to Hong Kong, where it was transhipped into other containers destined for Italy. However, the tuner part was a television receiver and covered by an Italian QR for television. Therefore, a volume of recorder separates was unloaded in Genoa, and tuner parts went to Rotterdam, where the corresponding volume was put on lorries destined for Italy. This was conducted in the hope that the Italian government did not request approval for application of Article 115 concerning internal EEC border controls permitting quantitative restrictions on imports from European Community member states. In the Italian town of Chiasso near the Swiss border, the lorry with tuners was stolen. The recorder parts in Genoa had become useless. The whole manoeuvre, concerning only 0.2 % of the Japanese export ceiling for that year, had been in vain.

Such transhipments were directly ascribable to the VRA. Proper administration of a VRA and prevention of abuse appeared legally and practically unfeasible. Apart from all other disadvantages, for proper surveillance of goods movements and prices a VRA requires a strict dual administration in order to be effective. Because the agreement did not have legal status, there was no possibility to examine the exporter's compliance with the VRA for VCRs. There was no certainty that Japanese exporters would respect the agreement. Any doubt expressed in meetings with the European Commission about insufficient effectiveness was considered offensive. It appeared that transhipments as far as only two companies were concerned – those detected in a legal anti-dumping investigation – represented 7 % in 1983 and 12 % in 1984 of Japanese maximum export ceilings undertaken in the Weather Forecast. The total excess of average imports in the 2 years covered by the VRA into the European Community over the agreed volume of 3.95 million (in each year 1983 and 1984 it was 3.95 million) was 45 % of the quantity generously allocated to European production in those years. Instead of an average quantity of 1.250 million units in 1983 and 1984, only 0.691 million was left to European producers or 55 % of the volume assigned to them. Consequently, the VRA was highly unreliable instrument. It did not offer what it promised, and was susceptible to fraud. In any case, the VRA did not have the effect some authors imputed to it (Hindley 1986; Turner and Tuveri 1984).

Quotas and customs duties or tariffs offer some certainty both to exporters and to the protected industry, which VRAs generally lack. The imposition of quotas and tariffs normally occur in accordance with the rules of the General Agreement on

Tariffs and Trade (GATT).[3] For import restrictions, compensation must be given to the exporting by the importing country, which of course prefers a VER because it avoids the compensation requirement. The arrangement itself, however, is to the advantage of the exporter, as shown in this Chapter. The start of export restraint agreements lies in trade with Japan. Before, but particularly after, the Pacific War the Japanese initially offered VERs mainly to the United States, which in turn supported Japanese accession to the GATT in 1955.[4] The VERs had to appease the United States and United States foreign secretary of the Eisenhower Administration, Allen Dulles, who preferred discussion on high level with the Japanese to the application of trade rules. Because they are voluntary, VRAs or VERs require cooperation of exporting country and exporters in that country. Commitments by the exporting country, Japan, coincided with interests of established exporters. Export licenses are distributed according to past performance. If exporters change the destination of the goods, there is not much that an importing country can do about it, unless the importing country has introduced an administrative surveillance system. That phenomenon existed during the textile agreements (first bilateral voluntary restraints, but when the bilateral agreements spread like a wildfire, as Short-Term and then the Long-Term Cotton Textile Arrangement. This arrangement was succeeded by a multilateral man-made fibre agreement in the GATT). These agreements necessitated administrative systems both on the export and on the import side and implied a huge bureaucratic burden. All ceilings for all products from all participating countries had to be checked twice. The VERs proliferated quickly to other exporting countries and other products, but the main products were been textiles and steel. Introduction of VERs was easy; they were convenient instruments, generally not under supervision of United States legislative bodies. They were considered a panacea by the United States administration for trade problems, even if VRAs (or VERs) did not offer any relief to the United States industry.

An example a VRA was the Orderly Marketing Agreement (OMA) concerning television sets between Japan and the United States, concluded on 24 June 1977, limiting Japanese CTV exports to 1.56 million annually, an amount that demonstrated that the OMA offered sufficient protection, according to US officials. According to an unappreciative United States industry, however, the OMA was not effective at all and should have been exchanged for a legal anti-dumping proceeding. The United States television industry had become at the mercy of the Japanese and indeed, the United States industry disappeared. The agreement was concluded after filing of a complaint on dumping in 1968 and a subsequent finding of dumping in 1971. In 1979, it appeared that the United States negotiator, Robert Strauss, agreed with all sorts of concessions in secret side letters. One of the agreed

[3] The example of the discriminatory United Kingdom monochrome television restriction toward Korea shows that such restrictions must meet certain condition based on GATT rules, such as those in Article XIX of the Agreement.

[4] McClenahan (1991, p. 182).

concessions was that a lawsuit would be repealed by the United States administration, smothering a USD 400 million suit won by United States CTV producer Zenith.[5]

More or less the same situation as with the OMA described above occurred in Europe with the Weather Forecast on VCR, which also included obscure clauses with an understanding on exports of colour television sets and tubes. The essentials of the understandings, however, remained obscure, even to industry insiders, and apparently also to European Community officials and representatives from the European Community's member states.

3.2 History of Voluntary Restraints

The history of voluntary restraint covers a few decades. A relatively short period of industrialisation of Japan and especially Japan's industrial development policy mark its features. After foreign intervention in Japan by United States Admiral Perry, forcing the Japanese to open their economy to foreign trade, the Japanese became aware of serious economic problems that, in the view of the elite, others apparently solved by means of colonies. Political, administrative and social change took place: the Meiji (restoration of imperial rule) restoration in 1868. Lack of resources became a main theme in Japanese thinking and fundamental to its economic organisation and policy. While shortages, of course, existed before the Meiji restoration, there was now a sudden awareness that the elite were threatened by the superiority of foreign powers.[6] Japan then faced a dilemma. Japan needed Western technologies and institutional models. Yet, the Japanese wanted to avoid political concessions to the Western powers. "Wakon Yosai", or Japanese Wisdom and Western Technology – the slogan that had even become popular in the West – expressed both the needs of the Japanese and their mentality: the ideology of a nation feeling itself superior in talents, yet inferior in terms of gifts of nature, as far as natural and technological resources are concerned.[7] Japan's history from 1868 was marked by the granting of benefits to big groups of corporations on behalf of national policy goals. Since the Meiji restoration, Japan's industrial development policy was outward oriented. National favourites were designated, which received preferential treatment in dealings with foreign suppliers and customers. Big trading corporations, such as Mitsui, Mitsubishi, Sumitomo and Yasuda, were regarded as carriers of a Japanese industrial development policy independent from other countries and preventing waste of scarce foreign exchange. Trading companies were licensed and financed to supply Japan with raw materials and subsequently

[5] Nevin (1978) gives an account of the sad developments under which United States politicians trapped United States business.

[6] Fukutake (1974, p. 14).

[7] Tsurumi (1976, pp. 5–6).

export processed products manufactured from these raw materials.[8] Manufacturers related to these trading companies were involved in the processing of the imported materials. The trading corporations own shipping companies took care of transport. Big companies received many advantages and concessions, particularly in the period up to 1920.[9]

> *Throughout the 1920s, a rising clique of nationalists was fomenting discontent and fostering militarism in Japan, while arousing public sentiment against business in general and the largest zaibatsu in particular. Mitsui, of course, was a frequent target of both the speeches and actions of these fanatics.*

Thus Mitsui disappointedly described its own role in the decade prior to the Pacific War.[10] The fanatics preferred to bestow benefits on groupings other than Mitsui and Mitsubishi.

The allocation of the role of saviours to big commercial entities was a novelty in Japan, compared with pre-Meiji history and with other countries. Before the Meiji restoration, business did not have the glamour, part of which was lost in the late 1920s, which it has today. The feudal clans of the Tokugawa period were replaced by big companies and some of these were founded on the ashes of colonies that Japan acquired and exploited in the twentieth century, i.e. Korea and Manchuria. Examples of the latter type are Nissan and Hitachi, which were both active in exploitation of overseas territories, the very areas in which war crimes were committed.[11] While the feudal system was appropriate for stability and independence of the power élite in Tokugawa Japan, business clans played the same role after the Meiji Restoration, with large companies representing power and glory.

During United States' occupation of Japan, the most important zaibatsu, including Mitsui, Mitsubishi, Sumitomo and Yasuda were dissolved. In 1950, 27 former Mitsui companies joined to form the Monday Club, a weekly working lunch "*during which executives of these 27 companies compared notes and organised co-operative activities*".[12] In 1955, the presidents of the former group formed the Mitsui Group Presidents' Voluntary Society, which in 1961 became the Second Thursday Club (Nimoku-kai). It "*... provides the necessary contacts among senior executives of Mitsui Group members that smoothes co-operation among the companies which have returned to the Mitsui fold.*"[13] Mitsui group members – a bank (formerly Mitsui, now Sumitomo Mitsui Bank), Mitsui trading company, a car producer (Toyota), Mitsui Chemicals, fibre producer Toray Industries, electronics producer Toshiba and its own shipping company, Mitsui O.S.K. Lines – together explored their mutual and group advantages and opportunities.

---

[8] This role of the big groups has been described by Tsurumi (1976).

[9] Storry (1982, pp. 123–124).

[10] The Mainichi Newspapers, "Mitsui" (1978, p. 27).

[11] Van Wolferen (1989, p. 382); Johnson (1982, p. 131).

[12] Mainichi Daily News: "Mitsui" (1978, p. 35).

[13] Mainichi Daily News: "Mitsui" (1978, pp. 31–32).

Other groupings also convened as economic cooperation units. Nine major economic groupings like Mitsui formed after the Pacific War – each with in-house financing, and a sogo shosha or trading house dominating trade on behalf of the group within and with Japan, and many with their own shipping corporation. These groupings operated according to the one-set principle, by which only one company from each industry sector could be a group member, and only one from the group made investments in a certain product sector. The general trading company looked after the import of raw materials, such as wool and cotton (each grouping has its man-made fibre industry) and the export of the finished product. If the volume of final product becomes substantial, thereby requiring specialised advertising and after-sales service, then the industrial company itself generally took over the export. Mitsui, for instance, often started exports of Toshiba's television sets to new markets. Sumitomo Corp. handled Matsushita exports to marginally developed markets. After a certain level of sales was achieved, the manufacturer took over the distribution.

Because of the scarcity of foreign exchange, purchases of technology and raw materials and components from the West should have preferably been reserved to those companies within an economic grouping expected to add the highest value to imported raw materials and efficiently export a substantial part of the production involved. This system prevented waste of financial means (foreign exchange). Finances for imports and proceeds from exports were allocated to banks in the midst of large Japanese groupings of traders and industry. Toray Industries, for instance, was the textiles manufacturing unit within the Mitsui grouping and Mitsui Trading imported its wool and cotton requirements. Mitsui Group member Toray received as member of the grouping permission from the Ministry of International Trade and Industry (MITI) to import the technology. Toray's grouping ally Mitsui Trading exported final products. It was natural that, in case of export restraints, export licenses were granted to companies with historical performance, i.e. already involved in the trade and the natural exporter on behalf of a grouping. Discrimination against smaller or newcomer enterprises was regular practice. The practice of a simultaneous start of production that had priority in the industrial strategy by members of groupings implied that huge production capacity was built, and massive exports from this simultaneously created capacity caused market disruption abroad. It forced foreign governments to take measures against unexpected, flooding imports. Instead of imposing measures in accordance with international trade rules of the GATT, they were tempted or convinced by Japan to circumvent these rules and to come to terms with the exporting country Japan. Agreements on self-restriction suited Japan better than GATT conformity of safeguard measures against market disruption, import quotas, in which import licenses are distributed by the authorities of the importing country, or increased tariffs. Voluntary restraint agreements strengthened the position of the MITI bureaucracy as partner of established groupings, and the role of the economic groupings was not disturbed. The system was discriminatory towards newcomers in Japan.

For several decades, this Japanese type of trade management was the main characteristic of trade in cotton textiles and man-made fibres. The textile agreements were followed by steel self-limitations and restraints in many other product fields where concentrated massive market disruptions took place. The commercial and legal consequences of export restraints are many. The GATT tried to get grip on the phenomenon and in the past, the textile agreements were formalised in GATT. The Trade Negotiations Committee in the Uruguay Round had adopted a notification obligation on 15 December 1993 and 14 April 1994.

3.3 Commercial and Legal Consequences of VRAs

As for those commercial and legal consequences not discussed in Sect. 3.1, import quotas and tariffs in conformity with the GATT are the proper instruments for temporary defence of domestic industry against market disruption. A main characteristic of a GATT compliant quantitative restriction is that it limits imports but does not, in principle, distort import trade patterns. Depending on the system of granting of import licenses, either on first-come-first-served basis or, in German terminology, "Windhundverfahren", i.e. grey hound procedure, on the basis of auction of licenses by the importing state, or on basis of historical performance. The first system is the most fair to newcomers; the effect on competitive positions is relatively neutral. Quotas or tariffs neither, in principle, adversely affect nor improve the competitive position of the exporters. VRAs as tools of commerce, however, can be manipulated by exporting countries and exporters. VRAs strengthen the position of exporters, resulting in cartelisation by granting licenses to vested interests with historical performance. They diminish the competition among exporters.

As stated before, in the case of a VRA the exporting country has the hand in the distribution of export licenses and it can squeeze out historical and established importers abroad, in short managing the direction of trade. The fate of the Betamax format, which might have collapsed anyway, is to some extent attributable to the Weather Forecast or the VRA that left the export licensing to the Japanese, which based it on the export performance in 1982. In 1982, however, the VHS group made huge inroads, and obtained its pre-eminent position in the format war, due to dumping and market disruption. The licensing system thus benefited the cause of havoc on trade. Had the European Community taken anti-dumping measures, the Betamax group, as well as V2000, might have survived. Betamax's position in the Japanese market did not allow Sony and Sanyo to dump their products at the same level as those with a huge share of the Japanese market, Matsushita, Hitachi, Mitsubishi and Toshiba.

MITI's attitude toward two small dumping VHS producers, Orion and Funai, now relatively big producers after Funai's take over of the Philips brand in the United States, reinforced doubts about the desirability of voluntary arrangements. The VCR VRA or Weather Forecast enabled exporters to squeeze out their OEM customers. After the OEM customers helped the VHS producers to achieve scale of production and to win the battle of the formats, they lost their attractiveness to

Diagram 3.1 Effect of a quantitative restriction (QR)

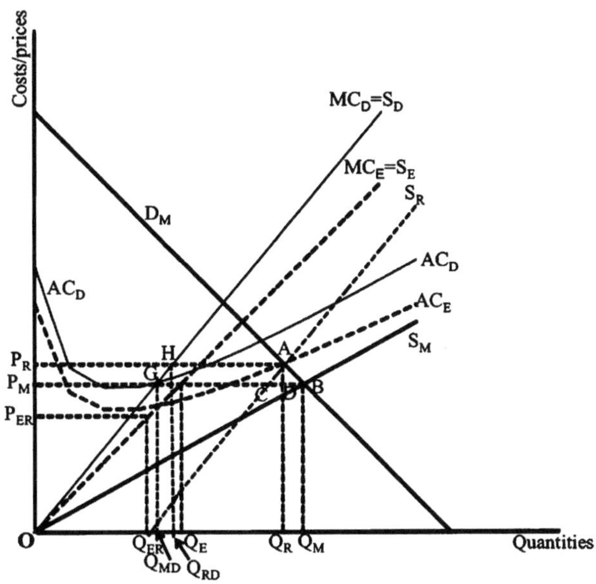

established Japanese VHS. Prices for European brand customers increased more than Japanese prices because the Japanese, referring to the VRA, told European customers that minimum prices should be respected. The Japanese themselves respected the FOB minimum prices of their shipments to their own subsidiaries in the European Community rather easily. It was a question of transfer pricing and financial compensations.

3.4 VRA and Economic Theory

A few diagrams illustrate some characteristics of QRs compared with VRAs. Diagram 3.1 shows the effect of a QR. Diagram 3.2 demonstrates the effect of a VRA: that the advantages of this trade policy instrument go to the exporting economy and to exporters.

In Diagram 3.1 a domestic (D) and exporting (E) producer together serve a market. The domestic producer's marginal cost curve, which represents incremental increase in total cost caused by a very small addition to production, is its supply curve. This is explained as follows: at a each given price on the vertical axis the producer adds to its production until a surplus of the price over the additional cost of a small additional quantity of product disappears. The marginal cost and supply of the domestic (European Community) producer, is the line from $MC_D = S_D$ from origin O. As a concession to the usual prejudice, the domestic producer's marginal cost is assumed to be higher than the exporter's (Japanese) supply, which is line $MC_E = S_E$ from origin O. At each price level, each producer is prepared to offer a

Diagram 3.2 Effect of a voluntary export restraint

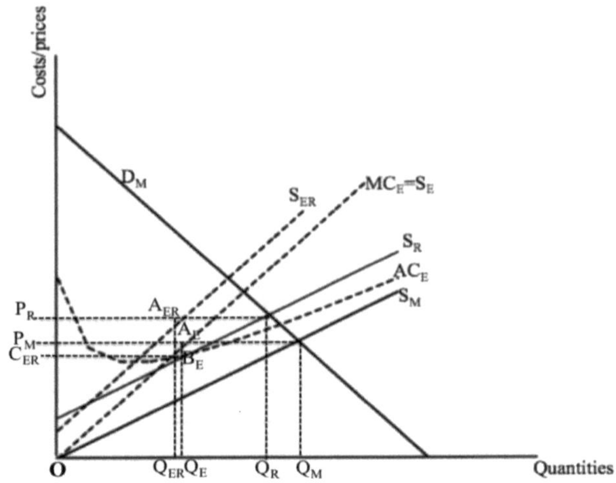

certain quantity. This is where the price equals marginal cost of each. The sum of quantities they offer at a given price represents combined supply, i.e. line OS_M from origin O. Take, for instance, price OP_M. At this price, the domestic producer offers quantity OQ_{MD}. The exporter offers OQ_E. The total supply at price OP_M is $OQ_{MD} + OQ_E = OQ_M$. The quantities at price OP_M are not incidental. Price P_M has been chosen as example because it is the price at which total demand represented by line D_M intersects total supply, i.e. the level of market clearance or equilibrium of demand and supply. At price $P_{M,}$ the market quantity demanded Q_M is established.

The QR imposed in Diagram 3.1 reduces demand for the exporter's product from OQ_E to OQ_{ER}. The QR artificially limits demand for the import product. It leaves total demand for the product unaffected. The restriction of demand for the imported quantity is the quantity $OQ_E - OQ_{ER}$. If the quantity of import demand is reduced to OQ_{ER}, the exporter offers at a lower price, i.e. P_{ER}. Line OS_M represents total supply prior to the QR. The imposition of the QR reduces total supply to dotted line $Q_{ER}S_R$, i.e. fixed restricted quantity OQ_{ER} plus the supply curve of the domestic industry. This decrease in quantity of the exporter results in a total market clearance price increase from OP_M to OP_R, which benefits the domestic producer, whereas the exporter is confronted with a decrease in its price from OP_M to OP_{ER}. The domestic producer, consequently, produces and sells a higher quantity, which increase is from OQ_{MD} to OQ_{RD} and at a higher price, i.e. to OP_R instead of OP_M.

Thus total supply does not drop equally with the reduction of imports. The decrease of the quantity imported is more than the decrease in total supply: $O_{QE} - O_{ER} > Q_M - Q_R$. The loss in consumer surplus is the triangle ABD and the gain in the domestic producer surplus is ACD. Before the imposition of the quantitative restriction, the exporter made a considerable profit; the average market price PM is far above his average cost ACE at exported quantity QE. The profit of the domestic producer is very meagre in Diagram 3.1 because the line PMG is hardly above the domestic producer's average cost curve ACD. Under the quota, $O_{QE}-O_{ER}$, which reduces foreign supply more than total supply. The restriction of total supply results in a more profitable price, P_R. The profitability of the domestic producer increases; the new price level, P_R and the line P_RH, is far above the average cost level of AC_D. The QR results in a loss to the exporter. Its marginal cost at the quantity of OQ_{ER} is below average cost. The price the exporter receives due to decreased demand for his product is P_{ER}, which lies below the lowest point of A_{CE}, the average cost curve of the exporter. The new market price, however, now lies substantially above the average cost AC_D of the domestic producer, and also above the market price the exporter receives P_{ER}. The difference between the market price P_R and the price to the exporter P_{ER} is the margin to the importer. The quota results in a considerable increase in the profit of importers. If an importer is a party related to the exporter, the profit indirectly goes to the exporter. Importers have clearly an interest in a QR, which improves their profit margin.

The effect of a tariff is similar to the effect of a quantitative restriction in that the advantages and disadvantages of a tariff are similar to those of a quantitative restriction. An advantage of a tariff over a quantitative restriction is that that customs procedures are simpler and do not imply a system of licensing.

The situation of a VER or VRA is completely different. Diagram 3.2 depicts the economic effect of a VER. The supply curve of the exporter remains the curve $M_{CE} = S_E$, but now up to the point of Q_{ER}. The exporter will not supply a quantity to the right of Q_{ER}. This implies that the supply function becomes a vertical straight line at Q_{ER}. In the case of normal market circumstances, the profit per unit at the exporter's quantity level of Q_E, which is the normal market export/import quantity, is the surplus of price P_M over the average cost curve AC_E, which is the difference between A_E and B_E. The difference between A_E (at the price level of P_M) and B_E (the average cost at the quantity of the exporter AC_E at quantity Q_E) is inferior to the profit per unit of P_R minus C_{ER}. The latter is the average cost at the quantity of the ceiling of the VRA, which in Diagram 3.2, is quantity Q_{ER}. The solution is attractive to both exporters (the Japanese) and to European Community (domestic) industry. From the point of view of the consumer and the importing economy, it is not an attractive solution at all. From the point of view of importers – major clients of JVC's VHS machines, Thomson, Telefunken and Thorn were and Bosch of Matsushita's machines – it is highly negative. Their profit margins are squeezed. Under a QR, the importers would have benefited from an additional margin. The export price would have been driven down by a restriction of import demand, the domestic European Community price would have gone up, and their margin would have increased. In the case of the VER or Weather Forecast for VCR, the price went up for both exporters and domestic European Community producers and the VRA dented into the margin of traders. Since the arrangement concerned export prices, the invoice prices of which were relevant, non-related importing firms were especially disadvantaged, except when they were daughter companies of Japanese exporters.

From the national economy's point of view, most of the benefits of a QR (shown in Diagram 3.1) go to the importing economy. Although the consumer is worse off, the treasury benefits from higher profit tax, both from importers and producers. The exporting country's finances are worse off under import restrictions (shown in Diagram 3.2) because profits on exports are reduced or turn even into losses, while as the consequence of decreasing prices in the domestic market of the exporter due to excess capacity, corporate tax income decrease. In the case of a VRA, the exporting economy benefits.

3.5 Politics and Economics of the VRA on VCRs

Did Commissioner Étienne Viscount, Stevie Davignon, conclude an imprudent arrangement and, if so, why? He established his fame as diplomat and although his education is primarily in law, he also had an education in economics. He was likely acquainted with the economic theory that explains the shortcomings of VRAs for the importing economy, in this case, the European Community. Economists might wonder why Davignon's agreement contained so many clauses: quantitative export ceilings, indication of sales by European producers, supply of kits to the European Community and finally, a set of minimum prices. It is probable that economic problems were only secondary to him. Political problems had to be solved: customs clearance at Poitiers as an infringement of European Community rules and of the GATT, authority on trade policy matters and confirmation by member states that trade policy belonged to Brussels' (the Commission and Council of Ministers), rather than to individual member states. Davignon was not a modest person. If he made an arrangement, it was impossible for him to be blamed for its failure. This implied that the agreement should have so many clauses that nobody could check whether it was ineffective or weak. He also cleverly arranged himself as the authoritative pivot in relations with the Japanese. Another reason why Commissioner Davignon introduced so many clauses in his Weather Forecast was because nobody knew the shape of demand and supply curves. It was completely unclear what the reactions of demand and supply would be to simpler solutions. There was a complete absence of knowledge about demand for and supply of VCR, cost curves and all other factors that are indispensable for a sound judgment.[14] The complexity of the situation was the main issue, underestimated in literature.

[14] The author derived the Japanese average cost from total VCR production values and quantities based on information published by the Electronics Industry Association of Japan (EIAJ). Export statistics of Japan gave units and values of export from Japan in general as well to the European Community and the United States. Average export price to the European Community was taken as European Community market prices, from which the demand curve was derived. For the average cost, 3 years were used as parameters for calculation of a marginal cost. Data on European Community sales were used and added to Japanese sales quantities. In this way, supplies have been calculated. The calculations serve as a demonstration of principles at work. The calculations

The agreement served many purposes, but did not solve the main problem. If its objective was to save European VCR production in the European Community, it failed. Production of the European V2000 format was doomed by the arrangement. The Commission became aware of this fact and circumstance served future industry objectives. At Philips, the conclusion was confirmed again that unpublished measures not based on existing legislation should be avoided.

According to various authors, Japanese export prices of VCRs to the European Community went up. This was unavoidable, not as the consequence of the VER, but because of the shift in the export range from simple sets, which were increasingly assembled in Europe, to more advanced machines. Indeed, normally a price increase would have been corollary of a VER. That such a conclusion is self-evident from a theoretical exposition in this Chapter does not imply that the agreement actually resulted in higher prices. Hindley (1986) tried to prove it, but his assumptions were simplifications that did not demonstrate anything but his own belief that VERs necessarily result in price increases. He also forgot the possibility of the circumvention of measures by the Japanese producers at low prices. Theoretically, the outcome of anti-dumping measures is that prices should increase, but neither easy transfer of the final assembly in Europe of simple sets nor circumvention were assumed.

All evidence points at one single conclusion, that VERs, VRAs and the like should be avoided and preferably be banned. The Weather Forecast proved a monstrosity, which helped the exact exporters that instigated the problems by their rush for market share. In the case of VCR, the market share was decisive for the establishment of the format, in this case VHS. The results appeared opposite to objectives. The business lesson from the voluntary restraint experience was that it was a trap that seriously damaged European industry, and should be avoided in the future. The problem is that collective amnesia prevents non-recurrence of such occurrences.

References

Fukutake T (1974) Japanese society today. University of Tokyo Press, Tokyo

Hindley B (1986) EC imports of VCRs from Japan, a costly precedent. J World Trade Law 20 (2):168–184

are not presented as "actual true picture" of the situation. Nobody could possibly know the shape of supply and demand curves when the discussions about the dumping and about an agreement took place. Between 1976 and 1987, Japanese cost of production decreased annually by 12.2 %, whereas production of VCRs increased by 80.6 % annually. The correlation between percent production increases and cost decreases is −0.34929. Consequently, many assumptions must be made for any presentation of data in form of an economic model. At that point in time, Commissioner Davignon was unacquainted with most of the relevant data. So were economists criticising the Commissioner: they did not know the shape of the curves and thus they guessed.

Johnson C (1982) MITI and the Japanese miracle: the growth of industrial policy, 1925–1975. Stanford University Press, Stanford, CA
McClenahan W (1991) The growth of voluntary export restraints and American foreign economic policy. Business and Economic History 2 (20). In: Proceedings of the bussiness history conference, 1956–1969. Stanford, CA
Nevin JJ (1978) Can U.S. Business survive our Japanese Trade Policy? Harv Bus Rev 21:165–179. doi:10.1002/tie.5060210112
Storry R (1982) A history of modern Japan. Penguin, Hammondsworth/Middlesex
Tsurumi Y (1976) The Japanese are coming, a multinational interaction of firms and politics. Balinger Publishing, Cambridge, Mass
Turner P, Tuveri JP (1984) Some effects of export restraints on Japanese trading behaviour. OECD Econ Stud 2(1), Paris
Van Wolferen K (1989) The enigma of Japanese power, people and politics in a powerless state. Alfred A Knopf, New York

Chapter 4
CD Players: Laser Light at the End of the Tunnel

Abstract The Compact Disc player, even more than VCR, was a complex product to standardise; it needed international support for acceptance of a format of both player and discs. This acceptance implied that the strongest business opponents had to join hands. Since the threat of market disruption was tangible, trade policy measures were considered. Increase in customs duties in accordance with rules of the General Agreement on Tariffs and Trade (GATT) in the WTO must fulfil special conditions. The final solution was complex, but in compliance with customs rules and the GATT. Although Japan previously introduced similar measures, a combination of customs legislation and trade policy instruments, the case of CD players was an innovation and took a route that closed afterwards. Chapter 4 reveals the background of the increase in duty on CD players and the various industrial, commercial, general economic, legal and political. Reactions from Japanese and European business communities were inevitably divergent.

4.1 Emergency Call: Fear of Failure

In January 1982, the director of Philips' business unit of CD players expressed fear in a telephone call that the European Community customs tariff on CD players – the bound most-favoured nations customs tariff on record players was 9.5 %[1] – was insufficient to meet Japanese competition in the European market for CDs players that were to be produced in the near future and to be launched in 1984. This was a rather disappointing signal. A tariff of at least double the level of 9.5 % was

[1] Most-favoured nation according to Article 1 of the GATT means that the tariff is applied to all contracting parties of the GATT, with the exception of lower tariff in case of free trade areas, customs unions or preferential treatment of developing countries. Bound (Article II GATT) means that the tariff is contractually laid down in a schedule of tariff concessions and that the measure cannot be changed unless compensations are granted under specified circumstances and according to specified procedures.

M. van Marion, *International Trade Policy and European Industry*, Contributions to Economics, DOI 10.1007/978-3-319-00392-4_4,

required: an alarming confession. In the past lies the cause of this cry for help. During the 1970s, Philips lost much of its position in the global and even in the European audio market. The Japanese had conquered about 95 % of the global audio HiFi market and 70 % of the European market. Actors such actors Akai, Kenwood, Pioneer, Sony, and Yamaha – with a modest position in Japan – were buoyant in the European market. The biggest Japanese producer, Matsushita Panasonic, ranking number one in Japan in all consumer electronics with its Technics brand specially developed for HiFi, fought with Sony for the first place in European and American audio markets. The contest between these two made them unreliable partners for relative outsiders, like Philips. The circumstances in Japan were difficult to judge, but had a serious impact on the world market developments, as might be concluded from the VCR case. A coalition with one could elicit unexpected moves from the other induced by competitive relations, not necessarily in Europe, but also – and this was essential – in Japan.

Condescending behaviour put Philips in the rear in the HiFi audio market. Instead of recognising that Japanese producers had taken the upper hand in the international audio market and trying to analyse its causes, its focus was on pretexts for lack of performance and on European sales. It was alleged that, because of non-compliance with German (from the Deutsches Institut für Normung, DIN) HiFi connector norms, which inter alia prescribed a special plug, Japanese products were not of HiFi quality. At least the DIN 41529 loudspeaker connector norm should be applied. According to this argumentation, the management at Philips audio declared Philips still number one in the HiFi product range, redefined to suitable proportions. Such argumentation may have served acceleration of personal careers within the company, but Philips' market position certainly suffered. When reality forced recognition of facts, the reality caused panic, but did not elicit a profound change of policy. That would have compelled analysis of underlying causes of the loss of market and such an analysis would have dreaded consequences. One recommendation – based on price data in Japan and Europe – was to lodge a dumping complaint. This was rejected. The – false, see Chaps. 7 and 8 – argumentation was that, since they earned profits, Japanese producers did not dump. The other line of reasoning was that anti-dumping was a difficult proceeding. Although this was correct, it was not a reason for not advancing this route. The third was that dumping might be conceived as an anti-Japanese act. Since people were uncertain as to how to behave towards certain Japanese companies, particularly Matsushita, any act that might hurt the Japanese was dreaded as being interpreted as anti-Japanese, regardless the behaviour of the Japanese themselves and regardless the fact that the Japanese themselves were rather hostile in their policies toward foreign producers.

An anti-dumping complaint was complex but feasible and even critical, and was obvious as concluded from a price and injury analysis. Such a proceeding would, of course, not solve the problem of distortion of competition in the launch of a new product, like CD players. CD players did not exist yet and, therefore, could not be dumped yet. An anti-dumping proceeding could have mitigated effects on imports of other equipment with which the CD player might be a complementary component in HiFi chains, however. Such a proceeding was, however, already rejected in 1979 before introduction of CD players was even considered. Fear of the Japanese gradually came to mark every step of Philips' audio management. The deficiencies relentlessly surfaced. Philips' and other European producers' market shares were too small to create a competitive industrial infrastructure required to launch a completely new product with completely new specifications and new components requirements. Such awareness was partly provoked by experiences with VCR. First, it was feared that the Japanese would not join the CD standard, a decision that would result in the loss of Philips' massive investments in research and development. It was also feared that if the Japanese accepted the standard, they would kill their competitors. Market disruption was quite well expectable and feared. If market disruption took place, it would imply that Philips' position in the launch of a new product it invented would fail. It would not only imply an industrial and commercial failure, but also a serious blow to its image with a negative commercial impact.

As the inventor of the CD system, Philips should have had a relative advantage over competitors in manufacturing the product. The need for a widely accepted standard, however, was a cause of delay and consequently, weakness. There were some competing systems in the industrial showroom. Matsushita daughter Victor Corporation of Japan (JVC) had two systems competing with the Philips laser system. Philips' Laser Vision disc system, which was an analogue system, and digital CD system, had counterparts developed by JVC. JVC's capacitance based Video High Density (VHD) and Audio High Density (AHD) systems were not equivalent alternatives to the laser, but fear was that the mother of JVC, Matsushita, would push these systems in spite of their inferiority, and that other Japanese producers would support such a system. In Europe there was also opposition. Thorn EMI had great confidence in Japanese technological input and hoped or expected to launch JVC's systems with its software and to produce the players in a joint venture of Thorn's hardware producer Ferguson with JVC in New Haven. Telefunken had another competing system, in which a mechanical pickup stylus traces digital information contained in the spiral groove.[2] Because Telefunken was a pioneer in technology, the German press considered its system promising. Telefunken's system could rely on software support from its record brand Teldec, but it soon became apparent that Telefunken's system had insufficient manufacturers' and software support to pose a threat to both alternatives. The CD laser system might technically have been superior, but this did not imply that it would become winning format. If Philips and Sony, which was the first ally of Philips in the CD project, would have acquired a striking technological leading position, others might have switched to a competing system in order to prevent too much profit from accruing to competitors. These considerations caused inhibitions in the tooling up of production. The technological advantage of an invention did not automatically result in industrial primacy. There was a compelling need to license the technology to potentially interested companies in order to obtain international acceptance of the product. For each player sold, the licensee paid a fee of 2 %, 1.5 %

[2] New Scientist, 8 January 1981, p. 77.

of which went to Philips. Creation of the standard did imply creation of competitors.

Matsushita was the most redoubtable opponent and main worry. For a long period, since 1952, Philips and Matsushita had warm and initially tender ties, even when Matsushita benefited from Philips' technology. A cross license enabled both companies to mutually utilise patents. Creation of a joint venture, Matsushita Electronics Corporation (MEC) producing active components, including picture tubes, strengthened ties between companies. MEC was a tremendous source of income to Philips, which had a minority 35 % share in the joint venture company and initially provided technology, while Matsushita lead manufacturing and sales. Philips developed an inclination not to affront Matsushita because of this relationship, in spite of Matsushita's clear intentions to crush Philips, an objective it achieved in consumer electronics. The relationship was more complex to Philips than to Matsushita. Had Matsushita not had access to Video 2000 and CD technology because of its cross-license with Philips, the possibility to confuse others about its intentions would have been less ample. The cross-license offered Matsushita an opportunity to hide its objectives. Would it switch to the JVC's VHD and AHD technology and thus thwart the CD project, or would it select the CD format? This was not so much the choice for a special sort of product, but a major technological choice. The question was whether magnetic or laser technology would have the upper hand in the future.

4.2 Industrial Concerns of a Big Corporation

Apart from these technological and commercial strategic considerations, other factors played a role. Japanese destruction of the European photo and film industry seriously affected European industrial infrastructure. Mass production of optics was moved to Japan. Lenses and prisms were estimated to amount to 13 % of the cost of materials of the CD player. The remaining and main optics supplier was high quality producer Rodenstock. Rodenstock's competitive position in mass optics production was inferior to major Japanese lens and other glass components manufacturers, like Asahi and Nikon. Rodenstock's products were considerably more expensive than its competitors'. Motors made by the Philips factory in Dordrecht, Johan de Witt, were technologically outstanding, of high quality and cost effective, but the initial series – a few hundred thousand – was inferior to the quantities Japanese manufacturers produced. The cost position in motors was feeble. Initially the motor represented about 4 % of the materials cost. Philips' electronics components and materials division, Elcoma, made the lasers and other integrated circuits (ICs). The initial cost of the laser and other ICs was 49 % of materials and decreased quickly. The speed of decrease was highly dependent on quantity produced. A doubling of quantity of production halved the cost per unit. That meant that the competitive position of the CD producer relied on the quantities to be produced by components producers. For Philips it meant that it needed CD

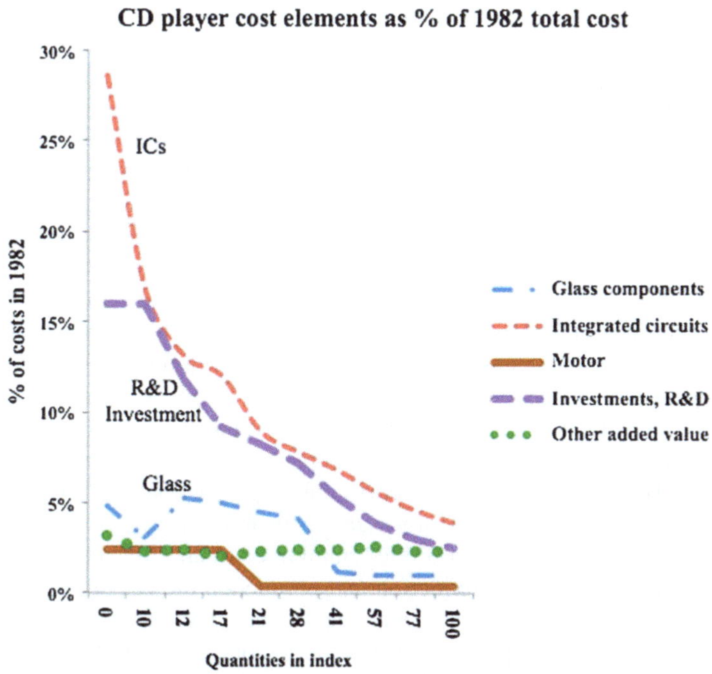

Graph 4.1 Cost and volume of production of CD players: projection 1982–1991

player producers in Europe. The higher the volume of components sales, the better the cost position of Philips itself. This condition would preferably be met by breaking the catch-22, obtained by temporary protection.

The relation between cost of production and volume is exhibited by Graph 4.1, which shows a projection of volumes and cost of production over a period of 10 years.[3] In order to protect company sensitive information and to reflect relative magnitudes, data have been indexed on the basis of 1982. As is apparent from Graph 4.1, initial volume of production had a considerable impact on the competitive relations. Obviously a higher volume brings cost advantages and improvements in a company's relative competitive position. In view of the impossibility of sales in Japan, a European producer had a natural disadvantage, which needed compensation elsewhere. Through careful marketing, Sony had built a considerable market share outside Japan. This position was always contested by giant Matsushita, a company with the nickname "Manishita," or copycat, by undercutting with a cost advantage due to a dominant market position in Japan, but more likely by dumping. The latter strategy both caused injury to non-Japanese producers and to Sony and other smaller exporting Japanese producers.

[3] It is impossible to separate effects of volume from time; they are corresponding phenomena.

Obviously Philips attached great importance to acceptance by other European Community companies of its CD standard and to a vow by Europeans that they would commence production. Thomson Brandt's (consumer electronics part of Thomson) CEO Jacques Fayard's resentment towards Philips dominated the main competitor in Europe, Thomson. Fayard envisaged that Thomson would become the number two in Europe in audio independent from any Philips technology. Killing the CD project would be an improvement to Thomson's position, he thought. His preference was JVC's VHD and AHD system, which was a course independent from Philips. The Havana cigar-smoking CEO of Thomson, socialist Alain Gomez, appointed by the French socialist Mitterand government after nationalisation of Thomson, confirmed and perpetuated Fayard's policy. In 1981, Thomson still did not want to participate in the joint ventures of Thorn and Telefunken in J2T. As soon as pro-European and pro-cooperation opponent Abel Farnoux left and the company was nationalised by the French government, however, Fayard moved quickly in the direction of cooperation with J2T. By cooperation with JVC, and with Thorn, Thomson and Telefunken were supposed to obtain production of VHD and AHD equipment in New Haven, video recorders in Berlin and camera recorders and HiFi in Moulins in France. Therefore, a limited number of small allies in the industrial battlefield for the CD player introduction and production did remain with Philips. Later, after the acquisition of the Dual record player company by Thomson, Thomson started CD player production, but the factory in the Black Forest never became a viable producer of CD equipment. An escape to Malaysia did not offer a refuge from misery. Even if Thomson would have started cooperation in the field of CD production, it might be assumed that such cooperation would not have offered any advantage to other European producers. Thomson had financial support from the French government, and its management would certainly not opt for an approach that was advantageous to other European producers.

The question, then, was why the inventing company did not start the activities alone. In 1980 and 1981, the Philips system was introduced in the Digital Audio Disc conference. Philips and Sony began to "join hands in CD development".[4] The failure of the VCR standardisation taught that licensing of audio technology was inevitable. Philips licensed all qualified producers of audio products. The licensees had to report their sales per model and had to pay a license fee of 2 % of the net sales value.[5] The acceptance of a record player without sufficient carriers of suitable software, the discs, was of course unimaginable. Acceptation of the new carrier standard would not take place without sufficient availability of CD players. Thirty-nine producers, mainly in Japan and a few in Korea, of audio hardware accepted the CD standard. Production by European producers was not very promising. Grundig

[4] Leaflet of Electronics Industry Association of Japan (EIAJ), Tokyo, widely distributed in Europe in 1983: "Compact Disc. Why Double the Import Tariff Now".

[5] Companies had to report their sales specified according to model number and markets. In Chaps. 9 and 13 this reporting appears as source of highly convincing evidence.

would start some production and Bang and Olufsen was interested, but the effect on the industrial infrastructure was meagre.

4.3 Hard Work on Software

The music industry's acceptance of the CD as software carrier was another cumbersome task. Philips made vigorous efforts to get the software carrier standard, the CD, accepted. Software producers had to be convinced to switch from vinyl to CD, which required substantial investments, both in production of discs and commercial costs of distribution. Production of the two elements of the new system required a delicate balance in introduction of CD player equipment and discs. Consequently, Philips' responsibility was quite more substantial than its competitors'; It was not just investment in capacity for production by some factories of players and discs, but in the success of a mutually supporting software and hardware industry. Polygram, the music subsidiary of Philips, along with renowned brands like Deutsche Grammofon Gesellschaft (DGG), Decca and Philips accepted the format. Highly important producers of software as CBS and MCA were also convinced. As described above, in the beginning EMI did not join the club. This would prove to be a costly omission. In any case, the necessity of convincing software producers automatically implied that a sufficient number of competitors in CD set manufacturing had to be created as a condition for software acceptance.

Convincing software producers was another cause of delay. Due to declining sales of records, the music industry should have been easily convinced to switch from cheaper vinyl to this new carrier. Any hesitation of the software suppliers implied that it was impossible to go for mass production of players, until this hazardous switch was made. It was evident that there needed to be a balance of development of marketing of both players and carriers. Japanese CD player production candidates showed no interest in steady development of the two as a condition to success, but rather paid attention to their own competitive position in CD players, which depended on market share.

4.4 Market Perceptions and Market Realities: Fear of Distortion

This discrepancy caused differences in expectations on the required or possible level of production. Newly revived consciousness of Philips' relatively low market share necessitated a review of competitive positions. Japanese forecasts of CD production and the CD market especially necessitated this review. Initial prognoses by the Electronic Industry Association of Japan (EIAJ) and Philips clearly, substantially and alarmingly diverged, creating worry that market disruption was the outcome of Japanese expectations. The Japanese were always tempted to overestimate foreign markets, which resulted in havoc. Such an overestimation implied excess capacity,

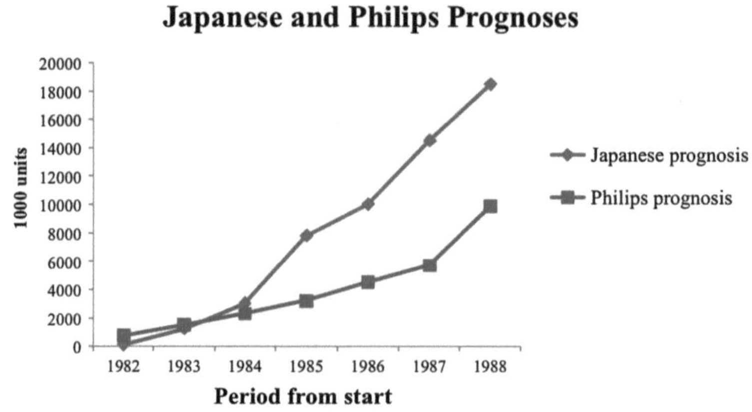

Graph 4.2 Prognoses on CD market by Japanese producers and Philips

dumping and severe market disruption. The problem with the Japanese forecasts was that they were self-fulfilling prophecies: market disruption. With forward pricing, the Japanese themselves would bring about market demand, which is by definition unexpected and dumped. Philips was convinced that market developments, both of hardware and software, required balanced and parallel growth. The Japanese did not care about stability of markets so far as the markets outside Japan were concerned.

The plan was that the product would be introduced in Japan in January 1984 at special request of Japanese producers, and in Europe in March 1984. As apparent from Graph 4.2, Philips' sales forecast was considerably lower than the Japanese. Philips' estimate was an outcome of its own market research. Japan's industry (EIAJ's) projection was a result of common deliberations of Japanese industry, and had been published. EIAJ might have published this material with the objective of misleading non-Japanese producers. In view of the habit of Japanese producers to declare foreign markets and market shares higher than reality, this was a dark omen. In terms of HiFi market penetration Japan, had the highest degree of saturation. That meant that the Japanese market potential of the CD, in addition to HiFi equipment already sold and placed in homes, was impressive. The captive distribution system guaranteed a share of Japanese producers in the global market and offered a high volume, market share and opportunity of dumping. In Chaps. 7 and 8 the Japanese market structure and consequences thereof are dealt with. Under the captive distribution system, Matsushita had a guaranteed 25 % or greater market share in the domestic market.[6] This dominating home market position with related high and

[6] Chapters 7 and 8 deal with the issues of captive distribution systems and consequences for trade. Van Marion (1993) described the system. Bartlett (2008, p. 8) also elucidated: "*Capitalizing on its broad line of 5,000 products (Sony produced 80), the company opened 25,000 domestic retail outlets. With more than six times the outlets of rival Sony, the ubiquitous "National Shops" represented 40% of appliance stores in Japan in the late 1960s. These not only provided assured sales volume, but also gave the company direct access to market trends and consumer reaction.*"

stable trade prices was a formidable starting point for any export drive. If Japanese's production capacity was commensurate with its overestimation of the market, market disruption abroad would inevitably take place.

4.5 Trade Policy Innovation for a Novel Product

An expectation of dumping a product that has not yet been produced and exported cannot possibly be the basis for an anti-dumping proceeding. There was not any trade in the product, prices were inexistent and repetition of the past and injury were dreaded. Consequently, anti-dumping measures were not yet an available remedy. It would probably take some years before anti-dumping measures could or would be taken. Quantitative restrictions (QRs) were also ruled out. In the first place, only market disruption allows application of Article XIX of the GATT. At that time, there was only an expectation of market disruption. The inventor's conviction of future market disruption is an insufficient condition for measures under Article XIX of the GATT. Additionally, a QR could create a barrier to acceptance of the CD format and introduction of the technology. The only acceptable instrument, both for economic and strategic, was some tariff device.

This starting point required deliberations about acceptable legal constructions. It was obvious that only a trade policy device in accordance with existing rules was acceptable to the European Community's member states, especially the most legal-oriented and liberal member states, the Netherlands, Germany and Denmark. The absence of trade in CDs precluded an anti-dumping proceeding, but enhanced the feasibility of tariff measures. If there were no trade, an increase in a tariff would not create a barrier to trade. According to the Customs Cooperation Council's (CCC, at present the World Customs Organization, WCO) tariff definitions and customs practice, CD players would normally be classified under the heading of record players. The European Community GATT bound tariff for record players was 9.5 % and there were substantial imports of this product from Japan. The solution to the problem was a new customs definition for the product "CD player" and a new classification, in which CD players would be in a distinct and separate line. Everything in the GATT is directed at the decrease of duties and protection of tariff concessions made in the past, not to their increase. Therefore, a simple increase in duty was excluded as an option. Record players were defined by the WCO's predecessor CCC as using a needle or a stylus as pick-up element for the reproduction of sound. The CD player uses a laser optical reading system. Consequently, by classification of CD players under a separate heading with a distinct definition, no harm would be done to the logic of the CCC, to traditional trade in record players and to GATT rules. With the new definition and reclassification, the tariff on the product was deconsolidated and modified – in this case increased – in accordance with Article XXVIII of the GATT *Modification of Schedules*.

Such modification is only allowed on the condition that principal suppliers are compensated for their loss of trade value attributable to the trade barrier increase. The compensation is negotiable, and retaliation by means of withdrawal of concessions is a potential drawback. The amount of compensation was uncertain, however, because trade in the product was unknown and inexistent. Japan's opportunity for retaliation was rather small. Europe's exports to Japan did not compete with domestic production, but with other third countries. Since retaliation by the Japanese would, because of the requirement of most-favoured nation treatment or non-discrimination, affect all exporters of those goods covered by measures in reprisal, international opposition likely impeded retaliatory measures. Since there was no trade in the product, a deconsolidation and increase in duty would, formally, not hurt the interest of principal suppliers. The idea was to increase the duty to 25 %. The argumentation was twofold. The first was that 25 % was a very easy percentage. One could multiply the import value by 25 % or divide it by 4. The autonomous duty of the European Community, not the contractual GATT duty, on the customs line of record players was 19 %. It was assumed that if the idea of the increase in duty was accepted, 19 % would be the only acceptable duty. The second was more complex. The second argument for 25 % was that CD players were a "sui generis" product and the heading for record players could not be starting point of reasoning. Therefore, a "sui generis" new tariff of 25 % must be applied. Since the European Community defended its agricultural system with its variable levies and restitutions in GATT as "sui generis", there was strong opposition within the European Community institutions against this idea of "sui generis" treatment for CD. Since it was assumed that no member state would accept a lasting increase in duties, the idea was also that it would be temporary relief with allowing the construction of an industrial infrastructure. It would temporarily offset the disadvantages of disruption of the European audio market in the past and resulting superior Japanese market share. The infant industry argument was used: due to Japanese dominance of the audio market by disruption in the past, there was a need to safeguard new production with temporary measures.

The first test of this idea was its proposal to the civil servants at the Ministry of Economic Affairs in The Hague. The Hague's Directorate-General for Foreign Economic Relations was one of the most free trade oriented group of civil servants in the European Community.[7] Directors-General conducted their own policy without much information to or interference by their Ministers. This case, however, was a special one. The Directorate General conceived the idea fully in line with the rules of the GATT and believed that it could perhaps stop some of the Japanese practices of abusing GATT rules. Some parts of the Directorate-General for Industry saw a good chance to regain some territory in international trade affairs, which it had lost by the catastrophe of industrial policy disaster inflicted by failing massive financial support to and unstoppable bankruptcy of the major Dutch shipyard industry RSV, which finally succumbed in 1983. Industrial policy was considered a failure, and other departments tried to roll back the influence of the industry department in the Ministry of Economic Affairs. This department, however, saw a new opportunity to

[7] By their principled approach of trade questions, firmly opposing "protectionism" of the French, who were accused of "mercantilism", the Dutch were called Ricardists.

take the lead in support of industry with a product of truly European dimensions. Chips and motor came from the Netherlands, optics from Germany, other parts from France and final assembly with other materials in Belgium. In view of probable compliance with GATT rules, the financial costs to the department were nil, which was an asset. One of the most dedicated and meticulously rule-obeying civil servants radiated with joy and declared with delight that he would have this experience before retirement. Some officials of the Foreign Economic Relations department saw a chance to hinder their highest boss, who was chosen for his convictions in free trade and especially for Dutch distribution interests, mainly airports and seaports, road transportation and, consequently, for traffic jams.

This positive response was an incentive to propose the matter to the European Commission. Problems in trade with Japan held the European Community member states in a deadly embrace of conflicting views and interests. The member states generally felt that the European Community should act.

The European Commission wanted support by European consumer electronics industry as a whole before embarking on this course. Thomson CE's CEO Jacques Fayard was Chairman of the European Association of Consumer Electronics Manufacturers (EACEM). Since he hoped that this policy might in the long run extend to other products, Fayard accepted the idea of a tariff increase on CD players. He was not interested in the legal subtleties of this case, the special role of CCC definitions and Article XXVIII of GATT. This disinterest was later a disadvantage to Thomson, as Chap. 5 clarifies. The EACEM could be convinced not to withhold its support to a duty increase. That hurdle overcome, the European Commission accepted the proposal and made a formal proposal to Committee 113, the Advisory Committee for Trade Policy (now Committee 207).

It took time and travel to convince European Community member states. A model (the CD 100, see Picture 4.1) was demonstrated in order to enlighten member states officials. Denmark especially proved to be an obstacle. Although Bang & Olufsen intended and prepared to launch CD players and had firmly lobbied in Copenhagen, the Danish government opposed measures towards Japan and very firmly expressed a negative position. It took some time to find out that the Japanese had advised Denmark that since Sweden had taken measures against Danish meat in relation with prevailing foot and mouth disease in Denmark, the Danish government could not possibly expect that Japan would warmheartedly import bovine meat from Denmark if Japanese CD players were not welcome in Denmark. As soon as other member states were aware that the Danes were blackmailed, determination to take measures increased. On 10 February 1983 the Council of Ministers approved a mandate to the European Commission for negotiations. On 24 February 1983, just when Commissioners Haferkamp and Davignon were in Tokyo for trade negotiations, inter alia on the VCRs (explained in Chap. 2), the European Community notified

Picture 4.1 Philips' CD 100 top loader

the request concerning the modification of the tariff on CD players.[8] No negotiations were formally held. But the Japanese were highly active in lobbying.

Akio Morita of Sony urgently invited Vice-president Van der Klugt, at that time Vice President of the board of Philips, for "friendly" discussions in Hotel Okura Tokyo to be held in the beginning of May 1982. Van der Klugt first went to Mr. Max Grundig's birthday party on 7 May 1982 in the old tycoon's villa in Baden-Baden and subsequently flew to Tokyo. In case the Japanese wanted to negotiate minimum prices, Van der Klugt had negotiation papers with two sets of minimum prices in his briefcase. In Tokyo Okura, all major leaders of Japanese consumer electronics industry were present: Matsushita's Akio Tanii, Toshiba's Shoichi Saba and, of course, Akio Morita as their intermediary. Minimum prices of CD players immediately became the main subject. Since the long flight in a Philips Mystère company aircraft to Japan via the Aleutian Islands had tired Van der Klugt, an understanding was quickly reached. This understanding was, however, about the lowest acceptable minimum price: he presented the fallback position instead of a set of higher negotiating prices. It did not matter what had been agreed upon, however. After his return to Philips headquarters, he wondered whether the minimum price indications given in Tokyo would create problems or provoke serious objections. This was the very bottleneck. An understanding with the Japanese had never been the intention. Such deals at private level were forbidden by European Community competition law (Article 85 of the Rome Treaty and 101 of the present Treaty on the Functioning of the European Union) and would spoil actions for more serious and tangible measures. The first signs of non-compliance by the Japanese with the undertaking on VCRs had been discovered: any other trade policy route than a tariff would be unacceptable to most in the business, and a private undertaking would be unacceptable to anti-cartel authorities in the European Community.

A telex to member companies and associations of the EACEM was phrased vaguely enough to suggest that the Japanese proposed that they would respect the minimum prices in exchange for a peace on the tariff front. Expectedly, within a few minutes the German Cartel Office received a copy of the telex. It was unanticipated, however, that already within half an hour the German Ministry of Economic Affairs wanted to be informed whether the author of the telex did not know that such an agreement was not acceptable to the German Bundeskartellamt (BKA), and

[8] GATT Document Secret/296 + Add contains the request for or rather announcement of the intention to increase the duty.

even illegal. It was made clear that an agreement did not exist, that there was not slightest intention to conclude one and that the tariff increase would be the only legally, but also economically, acceptable option. That helped convince the German ministry of economic affairs. It steadily supported further proceedings that would result in a tariff measure.

During discussions in the Netherlands about support to the European CD player producers, one of the ministers wondered whether it was preferable to let the Japanese CD merchandise, as the Dutch expression for accidents with freight transfer reads, "drop from the tows" in the port of Rotterdam rather than increase duties. The response of the Director-General of Foreign Economic Relations was that this understandable but striking move might harm the reputation of the port of Rotterdam. An EEC customs duty was preferred over the bad name of the Dutch port of Rotterdam. The decision of the ministry was positive. Philips sent a letter to the Minister of Economic Affairs and a draft-response to the same letter to some of his civil servants. After a long period of time, the minister sent this draft as his own letter. It appeared that the minister had gone on holidays and had not had time for a signature. When the response letter finally arrived, there were rust stains from the staple on the paper. One of the sentences started with the phrase: "In view of the urgent nature of this case, I have already requested my staff to start necessary preparations..." He had left the letter unsigned on his desk until after his holiday. His successor, Bolkestein, was a staunch adherent to liberal trade principles, but not dogmatic and his principles were accompanied by a high degree of scepticism about Japanese trade practices.[9] He was well aware that he might expose the position of the Dutch to too much pressure from Belgians and French. The Belgians were not as active as the Belgian CD player production interest in the town of Hasselt might suggest. When the Belgians requested the support of their Benelux partners to take measures against Japanese car imports, the Dutch did not show any temptation to support such a move. Now, the Belgians were careful not to show too much appetite for measures for CD players. Dutch action for CD players could later be exchanged for support for Belgian demands in other fields, the Belgians unjustifiably hoped. The Belgians were inclined to support an initiative, provided it could be presented as a Dutch interest. Later, this attitude became expensive for the Belgians. When some other Belgian interests required Dutch support, they left the initiative again to the Dutch, a tactic that resulted in closure of various Philips factories in Belgium.

The question whether tariff concessions should be offered to the Japanese as compensation for an increase of the duty on CD players was a serious issue for some member states. Although the change in product definition and the reclassification of the tariff heading formally secured that trade in a product not yet in existence or traded would not demonstrably be impeded, the European Community pretended to wish to offer tangible compensation. A maelstrom of efforts to find a source of

[9] Before a trip to Japan, he accused the Japanese of "scorched earth trade policy", a phrase not welcomed by more timid civil servants in his department. Especially those who accompanied him on the trip feared that the visit would not have the relaxed character they naturally hoped for.

payment by lowering protection for products at the cost of others started. Some wanted to offer record players, but the industry concerned – mainly the United Kingdom's industry – did not accept such a manoeuvre, although the products were supposed to disappear in the long run.[10] People in some ministries intended to offer CD discs as tariff compensation, an idea heavily opposed by the record industry, the biggest player of which was Polygram, a subsidiary of Philips. Thorn EMI opposed this idea because it thought that any deal to Philips' benefit would be to Thorn's disadvantage. The issue of compensation had already been examined: an inexpensive and acceptable solution had been found; the offer should be a tariff reduction on reel-to-reel audio tape recorders. There was no European Community production of the product. Reel-to-reel recorders were fashionable consumer products in the 1970s, but later became confined to professional products. Studer Revox in Switzerland produced such professional recorder equipment for studio purposes. This company was not situated in the European Community, was not harmed by a concession on consumer products and in any case, Switzerland could not block a tariff concession.

One month prior to the decision on the increase from 9.5 % to 19 %, Philips audio division's director expressed his worries and asked whether this increase in duty could be done quietly and silently. "Please, do it carefully," he insisted. He did not like the answer, which was that carefulness was impossible: The new duty would be published in the Official Journal of the European Community. Philips' components division, Elcoma, appeared incapable of producing the unrivalled laser semiconductor, the essential part of the CD machine, designed in Philips' superb research laboratory. For laser IC supplies, Philips had become fully dependent on Japanese Sharp. This company made covert threats. It wondered how, given behaviour as hostile as an increase in duties, Philips could possibly expect an undisrupted supply of lasers. The Philips audio director acquiesced, encouraged to keep quiet. If Sharp refused to supply, Philips could take action against abuse by Sharp of a dominant market position. Sharp did reliably supply and did not blackmail Philips. The company was known as a keen and firm competitor but also as a reliable business partner, and would not run the risk of damaging its reputation. Or so Philips hoped.

In December 1983, the European Council had to decide on the matter of the increase of the duty. The Philips organisation had a matrix structure. Divisions had responsibility in product management and coordination, national organisations had commercial and industrial authority and took care of relations with governments. Philips organisations had contacts with national delegations in the Council of Ministers. Parallel to discussions in the Council, Philips representatives had telephone conferences in which the moods in the delegations of the European Council of Ministers were discussed. When necessary, it was discussed and decided how to approach the delegations in the European Council of Minister's debate on the proposal of the European Commission on the tariff increase. This fine-tuning

[10] Nobody expected, of course, that the record player would return for disco applications.

resulted in an affirmative vote by the European Council of Ministers. The duty would be increased by 1 January 1984.

4.6 Japan's Conduct and the Trade Environment

Some facts from Japan's own rich history of the creation of trade barriers facilitated decision-making. Japan had an impressive record of imaginative trade policy actions. It tried to increase tariffs on record players with 33 (and 16) revolutions per minute (r.p.m.) under the pretext that these products were clearly totally different from 45 to 78 rpm turn tables. Allegedly in order to protect the Burakumin, descendants of outcast communities of the feudal era that had been involved in "impure" meat and leather production, Japan imposed a QR for leather. Allegedly to protect the Burakumin in the leather shoe industry, a duty of 28 % was imposed on synthetic shoes, with GATT Article XXVIII as a ground. As compensation, Japan offered *inter alia* rear mirrors for cars, as if this was a product that could compensate the loss of sales by North Italian ski shoe producers. This manoeuvre took place in 1974. The Burakumin might have expected that they could continue production of leather ski boots. Big Japanese companies started manufacturing of synthetic ski boots, however, and Burakumin leather ski boots disappeared. The history of these cases, both concerning "new" products, did not stimulate Japanese popularity in the trade arena. Compared with these cases, the case of the CD was really a novelty. The product definition by the CCC for an existing similar product, record players, was completely different from the new product and introduced before the new product was marketed. The new methodology complied with the rules. A story on the Burakumin returns in Chap. 5.

4.7 New Products and Innovation of GATT Rule

In view of its own policy in the past, rather audaciously Japan tried to close the gap in GATT provisions. It made a representation on the subject. Future manoeuvres of introduction of a new customs should be prevented[11]:

> *The preemptive raising of tariff rates by invoking Article XXVIII on new products such as digital audio discs whose trade is expected to expand in the future raises serious problems in the light of the basic objective of the GATT to expand trade.*

Contracting Parties of GATT agreed with Japan. Article XXVIII of the GATT, incorporated in the body of rules and agreements of the WTO, refers to the case.[12]

---

[11] General Agreement on Tariffs and Trade Application of Article XXVIII to new products, L/5522 11 July 1983, communication from the Permanent Mission of Japan, dated 7 July 1983.

[12] Understanding on the Interpretation of Article XXVIII of the General Agreement on Tariffs and Trade 1994.

4. When a tariff concession is modified or withdrawn on a new product (i.e. a product for which three years' trade statistics are not available) the Member possessing initial negotiating rights on the tariff line where the product is or was formerly classified shall be deemed to have an initial negotiating right in the concession in question. The determination of principal supplying and substantial interests and the calculation of compensation shall take into account, inter alia, production capacity and investment in the affected product in the exporting Member and estimates of export growth, as well as forecasts of demand for the product in the importing Member. For the purposes of this paragraph, 'new product' is understood to include a tariff item created by means of a breakout from an existing tariff line.

That clause creates the impression that Article XXVIII could not be used as an instrument of defence. Sufficient possibilities remain for actions in conformity with GATT rules, however, including Article XXVIII. It requires some inventiveness.

4.8 The Aftermath

At Philips some people heaved a sigh of relief, mainly those with direct bottom-line responsibility. But success also creates internal animosity, and the trade policy success was not everybody's triumph. A director of Philips' industrial coordination department set up a working group of three highly qualified people from his own department, available for an investigation into desirability of such a duty increase. He had already instructed what inevitable conclusions of the report should be. The conclusions of the report were somewhat contradictory. The conviction was that the duty increase weakened Philips. But if a duty had to be imposed, it should have been 25 % instead of 19 %. There was no awareness of discussions with the European Community about this rate. Duties of 19 % for 3 years, from 1 January 1984 until 31 December 1986, and reductions to 16.5, 13.5 and 9.5 in the subsequent years, the latest of which in 1989, covered too small a period for a creation of a sound industry and, consequently were insufficient. The conclusion boiled down to the statement that any result other than an imaginary result involving the industrial coordination department was wrong. But an increase of the duty to 25 % would not have given much solace either. The expectation of Philips about future price developments was, from the point of view of European Community producers, more optimistic than realistic. In spite of the higher customs duty, price developments were far below Philips' expectation, as Graph 4.3 shows.

An additional 6 % increase of the duty from 19 % to 25 %, as suggested by the people in the spectators' box, Philips' industrial coordination department, would not help restore prices to the level originally expected and desired. The conclusions about the duty increase had the value of internal politics, discrediting those involved in this trade policy case.

Some Philips audio directors were educated at business universities. During meetings about consumer behaviour and consumer expectations, they firmly announced without sound consumer research, backing or any special knowledge, that the CD player would replace the vinyl record player. Since the record player was a top loader, its replacement should also be a top loader. Thus, proudly the first

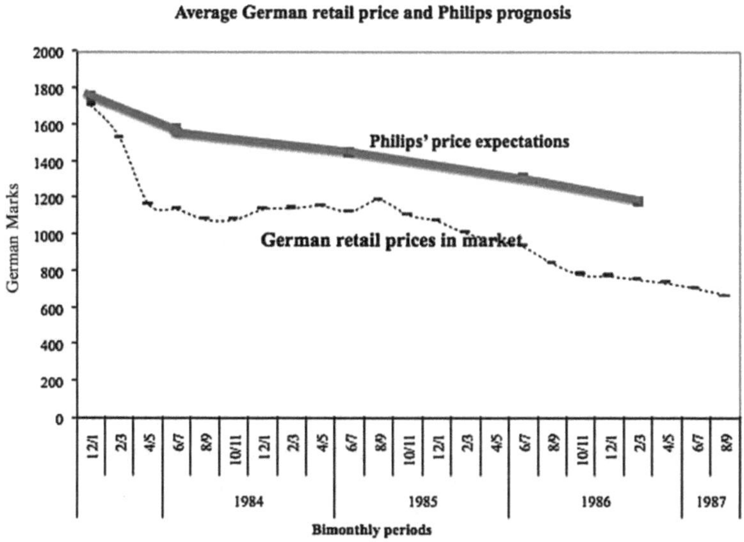

Graph 4.3 Development of retail price (*Source*: Geselschaft für Konsumforschung (GfK) on retail markets in period 1983–1987) and Philips' prognosis

player was introduced: the CD 100 top loader, see Picture 4.1. It was technically a splendid machine. The motor, supplied by the Dutch Johan de Witt factory, was inaudible. The Philips CD player was the only product with a swing arm guided by a semiconductor with correction. The error correction was magnificent but the machine was a top loader and not very useful as part of an audio chain, in which the old record player was positioned on top. The blunders were immediately covered or blamed on those no longer present or not responsible at all.

The product was of superior quality but consumers kept their records and record players, and the CD player was initially an addition to the audio HiFi chain. The bright marketers were panic-stricken once it became apparent that most Japanese producers had introduced a front loader, on top of which the old familiar record player could be placed. The Sony CDP 101 had a magnificent horizontal front loader mechanism. Hitachi's DA-1000 had a vertical front loader. A new design, a front loader, had to hurriedly be made. Unfortunately, the driving mechanism was part of the loading tray. It was a huge, heavy and rather expensive construction, as Picture 4.2 shows. Turnover and business results of initial CD player sales were not very encouraging.

Although, apparently, some Philips people involved in internal politics had diverging views, the increase of the duty was considered a success. The Japanese gave the impression that they were stupefied by a demonstration of Community willingness to action on behalf of its industry. Japanese industry seemed to estimate Philips at the centre of decision-making. Sony's Akio Morita sensed the changes and proposed an annual round table on consumer electronics, in which to discuss future technical developments and cooperation. Morita had a relatively inferior

Picture 4.2 Result of panic: CD 303 with front loader (including motor with driving mechanism)

position in the Japanese hierarchy. He was neither chairman of the Electronics Industry Association of Japan nor of the federation of Japanese industries, Keidanren. He presided over a foreign investment committee of Keidanren. Philips selected the European delegation. All sorts of organisations and persons vied to occupy a seat. For example, when Mr. Carlo De Benedetti of Olivetti was invited, it was indicated by Philips Italy that, in view of the Jewish background of De Benedetti, it was inevitable that high-ranking Italian Christian Democrat, Mr. Lamberto Mazza of Zanussi, would also be invited to be a member of the European delegation. "We do not need whitesmiths in our delegation", was the rather haughty response from Philips' board of management to this suggestion, referring to the refrigerator speciality of Zanussi. When Mazza finally received an invitation, he sent his substitute Riccardo Viziale, Zanussi's TV executive and a long-standing leader in Italian CTV manufacturing. Karlheinz Kaske, CEO of Siemens, restricted his presence in the delegation to only one meeting. Siemens was hardly present in consumer electronics, and such a spectacular theatre with a Philips man in the chair did not please him. Carlo De Benedetti did not feel his presence was necessary either. Riccardo Viziale continuously replaced Mr. Mazza.

Sony's Akio Morita and Philips President Wisse Dekker presided the first round table discussion. It was held under the supervision of the European Commission and the Japanese Ministry of International Trade and Industry. The first session in Brussels was held in October 1983. Mr. Max Grundig felt compelled to complain loudly about the market behaviour of the Japanese because of the marks left and still felt on the financial position of European Community producers. He exclaimed that Japanese practices had cost him a lot of money because he had to pay salaries and social security, slapping his hip pocket where his, then empty, purse was supposed to be. Indeed, Japanese behaviour in the domain of VCR and CD were the start of his company's demise and had cost this great entrepreneur a lot of money, but problems were not limited to these products and to the Japanese. The round table conferences continued for about a decade and were subsequently taken over by EIAJ and EACEM in 1991, disappearing soon thereafter once there were hardly grounds for the Japanese to continue discussions. The Japanese lost some battles, and the final victory in the war was in sight. In 1984, the European electronics industry was jubilant about the CD player tariff.

As for the CD tariff increase itself, after a few years it became evident that the Japanese simply jumped over the higher tariff and that market disruption was a part of normal practice. This phenomenon is dealt with in Chaps. 7, 8, and 9.

References

Bartlett CA (2008) Philips versus Matsushita: a new century a new round. Harvard Business School, Boston, Mass., Rev. January 17, 2008

Van Marion MF (1993) Japan and international trade, the incompatibility issue. Physica-Verlag, Heidelberg

Chapter 5
Meeting the Challenge: Blind Alley of New Protection

Abstract After the increase of the customs duty on CD players, the European Community electronics industry went for protection of some essential products. French state-owned Thomson demanded support for such actions in exchange for its alleged cooperation in CD duty increase. The reasons for protective action diverged among company strategies. Major European producers tried to hide their interests. Legally, the basis for safeguard measures sought for video recorders and audio equipment was insufficient. Therefore, other methods were devised. The customs tariff on VCR – and DVD –increased in accordance with the General Agreement on Tariffs and Trade (GATT) rules, which are explained. Through a new interpretation of a customs rule on VCR mechanisms, these mecadecks were temporarily protected with a higher duty. In accordance with formal GATT rules for trade negotiations and with tariff reduction formulae, the European industry succeeded in excluding some vital products from general tariff reductions. A re-classification and a higher tariff on camera recorders failed due to betrayal of agreed policies. An effort to use the enlargement of the European Community under a new interpretation of the GATT rules for higher audio duties failed. This implied the end of mass audio production and closure of factories in Europe by major producers, and it marked a start of decline of the industry in general.

5.1 Revival of European Industry?

After the setback of the VCR VRA, the victory of the CD customs tariff increase rose the spirits of the European industry and formed the nucleus of its thinking. At Philips, evaluation of the CD duty increase was mixed. Some reactions of well-versed internal politicians have already been described. The major internal reaction within Philips was that it demonstrated some power. What is important – one of the Philips leaders said – is not what we can, but what the Japanese think we can. Unfortunately, not only the Japanese were misguided. Philips and European industry were also moving into the dark, in spite of the light spotted at the end of the tunnel.

M. van Marion, *International Trade Policy and European Industry*, Contributions to Economics, DOI 10.1007/978-3-319-00392-4_5,

Thomson's vice-president for external relations, Jean Caillot, wrote a letter to Philips France's director for external affairs Claude Bonnet, chairman of Simavelec, the successor to the SCART (of the famous plug[1]), presenting Thomson's demands to be fulfilled in exchange for Thomson's alleged contribution to the positive outcome of the CD tariff case. Thomson wanted an increase in customs tariffs on video cameras, high-resolution colour television tubes and other screens, on home interactive systems, VCRs, satellite receivers and audio equipment. Thomson was more modest than ever! As understood at Philips, these demands would never be accepted, but Thomson would not tolerate a more moderate selection.

The victory of the CD duty, as a clear and firm trade policy measure, caused a feeling that industrial revival was approaching the verge. The victory of VHS, by means of dumping, and the voluntary restraint had caused serious frustration, but now the electronics industry saw daybreak or light at the end of the tunnel! In March 1984, a delegation from electronics industry, led by Philips President Wisse Dekker, held a meeting with European Commission officials hosted by Commissioner Davignon. Max Grundig, boss of Grundig, stricken by setbacks was present, but, and this frustrated him, he could not take the lead. As the only founder of an industrial corporation among the business leaders, he felt he was the single entrepreneur in this ensemble of industrial and governmental officialdom. He did not speak English, and this was a strong barrier to greater responsiveness to his entrepreneurial ideas. Alain Gomez of French state-owned Thomson did not speak at all, but kept to smoking his Havana cigars. He had developed intrinsic resentment about the inferior position of Thomson in this theatre. Afterwards, he frequently ostentatiously showed this antipathy by irregular but striking absence from meetings. His deputy, vice-president and specially appointed for relations with the European Commission, Jean Caillot, was thereby placed in a difficult position. The major task forced upon him was, with the help of the French state, to obtain competitive advantages from the European Community, which if possible were disadvantageous to Philips. The CEO of Thorn EMI, Peter Laister, was present at the March 1984 delegation. Director of Thorn's audio and video producer Ferguson Richard E. Norman, CBE, Chairman of the British Radio and Electronic Equipment Manufacturers Association (BREMA) and leading Thorn's ailing consumer electronics branch Ferguson had a secondary role, which he tried to change. Vagn Andersen of Bang & Olufsen and Dr. Hans Lutz Merkle of Bosch (and Blaupunkt) also joined the group of business leaders.

[1] This 21-pin SCART plug or Euroconnector – a means of connection of the television with peripheral equipment – was mandatory and imposed in France in 1980. According to information from French electronics industry, initial intention was that its compulsorily introduction would take place in 1978. No television set without this connector could be sold in France. Max Grundig heavily protested – both in France and at Philips' headquarters, which latter did not have a hand in this tactic – against this French ploy to stop unwelcome competition, but nevertheless hastily introduced televisions with SCART facility into trade, taking back sets without SCART connection. When it appeared that Thomson and Philips France had substantial stocks of sets without SCART plug, the introduction was delayed by more than one year. Consequently, Grundig and others ran into serious costs because of this scheme.

Commissioner Davignon was the host in the Berlaymont Palace, headquarters of the European Commission. Commissioner for External Relations Vice-President Wilhelm Haferkamp was travelling again, but both the External Relations (DG-I) and the Internal Market and Industry (DG-III) departments were well represented by directors-general Lesley Fielding and Fernand Braun and their staff.

This group of men discussed the future of European Community electronics industry on the basis of a paper drafted and submitted by Philips titled "Meeting the Challenge". This paper voiced the idea that the European Community should enable European electronics industry to recapture market share by tariff relief using the methodology applied in the case of CD players. The discussion soon went into the direction of protection of European audio and video industry and the question whether tariff protection would enable the European Community industry to survive Asian competition. Part of the paper gave Mr. Max Grundig the opportunity for a lengthy exposition, in German, on the relation between cost and volume of production and his "EURO plan". This plan was a proposal for a complex cartel. The plan proposed that the European Community industry should combine its distribution in an exclusive trade and distribution organisation, from which non-Europeans would be barred. Sales in the trade should be made on an exclusive basis. If traders purchased from Asia, then participants of the cartel, not unlike the Japanese system, should exclude traders from access to their supplies. Cost reductions would be attained by both standardisation of components and a combination of European after-sales services. Max Grundig's secretary, Heinlein, distributed papers with complex schemes and organisation diagrams. Max Grundig did not receive many responses to his proposal. Some group members did not understand the complex schemes, others members pretended not to understand them because competition authorities might reject the ideas or because Grundig's communication was in German only. After the industry responded affirmatively to Davignon's question whether the industry thought itself capable of revival and survival if ideas in the paper "Meeting the Challenge" became a reality. From this affirmative response, Davignon concluded that industry should be capable of guaranteeing European Community-wide consumer electronics industry support for the paper "Meeting the Challenge". He also insisted on documentary evidence of such general support.

This assignment was practically unattainable. Davignon's conclusion was shrewd. He knew more about the organisation of consumer electronics industry than industrial leaders of Philips and Grundig, who had delegated such matters to their industrial company "officials". The European Association of Consumer Electronics Manufacturers (EACEM) was a federation of national associations with some company delegates as board members. To its membership belonged divergent associations, such as the French organisation Simavelec, free trade oriented ZVEI (Zentralverband der Elektrotechnik- und Elektronikindustrie, Central Association of Electrotechnical and Electronic Industry), Italian ANIE with its membership of small Italian producers and big majors, and the British Radio and Electronic Equipment Manufacturers' Association (BREMA) with practically wholly Japanese membership, except of Thorn Ferguson. BREMA would never support the provocative paper "Meeting the Challenge" with its anti-Japanese tone and proposals for tariff harmonisations, or

Table 5.1 Protection of radio or modules by customs duties

	Value structure	Protection if integrated part of radio by tariff 14 %	In form of separate modules protection
Tuner/receiver	34	14 % of 34 = 4.76	14 % of 34 = 4.76
Amplifier	40	14 % of 34 = 5.60	4.9 % of 34 = 1.96
Loudspeaker boxes	26	14 % of 34 = 3.64	4.9 % of 34 = 1.27
Total	**100**	**14.00**	**8.00**

rather, custom duty increases. If the Japanese in BREMA accepted the paper, however, the powerful major Japanese companies would support it and Davignon would encounter relatively little opposition from the Japanese Ministry of International Trade and Industry (MITI) against this "duty harmonisation". Richard E. Norman of Thorn Ferguson would, as he was aware or hoped, play a pivotal role in negotiations about an industry position.

The term "harmonisation", unlike increase of tariffs, does not have the cynical connotation that might be suspected. HiFi audio and television had become increasingly modular. Separate modules of tuner, amplifier, record player, cassette deck, and loudspeaker boxes replaced radios with integrated tuner, amplifier, record player and cassette recorder and loudspeakers. These separate modules were in use as professional products, the customs tariff of which was unimportant. The professional supplier-customer relation was more important than a customs duty. International trade in the products was rare. This professional equipment was for systems at stations, stadiums, theatres and other mass indoor and outdoor occasions.

During various GATT tariff rounds, inter alia the Tokyo Round of tariff negotiations, the tariffs on professional products decreased substantially (generally from 8 % to 4.9 %, with VCR as an exception; see Chap. 2). The decrease of protection on the constituents of an audio system, for instance, compared with the complete piece of equipment, the integrated HiFi radio combination, might be clear from Table 5.1. Through importation of radios transformed in racks or chains of separate modules, the protection became 8 % instead of 14 % on the complete sets. The decrease in protection was due to the fact that in the past amplifiers and loudspeakers were professional products and, according to the philosophy on protection, such products did not need much tariff defence. Video recorders were also considered professional products but just before the end of the Tokyo Round, Philips intervened and convinced the European Commission that the exemption of VCRs from the tariff reductions (from 8 % to 4.9 %) would not have any negative effect on the European Community's tariff offer to Japan. There was not any trade in the product in the statistically relevant years (see inter alia the discussion on Table 5.4) and the product would become very important in the future. Of course, other products were also exempted, but Philips and other companies had already overplayed their hand by claiming exceptions for "sensitive", i.e. old products.[2] Table 5.1 summarises the situation.

The difference between the 14 % on integrated HiFi equipment and a rack of audio components (tariff 4.9 % with exception of the 14 % on the tuner/receiver) is 6 % with respect to competition with the Japanese was, as far as Philips and Grundig were concerned, the difference between profit and loss.

Thomson had also started HiFi operations and had made its feasibility calculations at the end of the 1970s when HiFi equipment were still integrated radios with tuners and amplifiers and loudspeakers. Its acquisition of German record player producer Dual in 1982 was a part of this strategy. Unfortunately for Thomson, Dual was a record player company and did not produce CD players before 1985 (CD40) and Thomson had to import from Hitachi.[3] With a duty of 19 %, to be set at 9.5 % after 5 years and with 4.9 % on other modules, except tuners (which had the 14 % duty of radios), Thomson hardly benefited from the duty imposition and could not manage its CD business profitably, neither in Europe nor, later, in Asia. In the Philips operations in Belgium, in Hasselt for CD players (9.5 % and temporarily 19 %) and cassette decks (duty 4.9 %), in Louvain for tuners (14 %) and amplifiers (4.9 % tariff) and in Dendermonde for loudspeaker boxes (4.9 %), heavy investments were made. Philips' operations were in extreme difficulties, both as the consequence of likely dumped imports of the Japanese, and by the Thomson's launch of HiFi production. But, as calculations demonstrated, Philips could manage under a tariff regime of 14 % on all components of audio chains, even under conditions of systematic dumping. Consequently, both Thomson and Philips were interested in "harmonisation" of the tariff on audio equipment to a level of 14 %. But for products like home interactive systems, VCRs and satellite receivers such harmonisation should also have been introduced, according to Thomson. It was doubtful that general consent could be obtained for such comprehensive changes in tariffs and that any legal basis could be found for such a move with approval of BREMA's Japanese membership. The common interest of Europeans and the Japanese with production in Europe was only a 14 % customs duty on VCRs. The reason for the common interest is explained below.

The paper "Meeting the Challenge" did, of course, not receive full support. Richard Norman, chairman of BREMA insisted, as BREMA's Japanese membership demanded, on a drastic change of text and wanted almost all products eliminated from the list of "tariff harmonisation". Even the title had to be changed. Norman disliked and did not appreciate the suggestion to change the title into "Challenge the Meeting", meeting referring to the meeting of industry leaders with

[2] This was rather a stupid strategy. Customs duties on monochrome televisions and picture tubes were exempted, while the products with a big market potential in the future were decreased. It would have been better to decrease the tariff on monochrome television and radio to "save" the duty on several other items, like amplifiers, loudspeakers and other important audio and video equipment as separate components and some video equipment.

[3] In 1987, the company DUAL in the Black Forest was reduced to a small factory and in 1987 Thomson sold it again.

the European Commission. He might not have understood why the opposition to a change in title was so firm. The title remained the same as the original, which opened some other opportunities. If textual changes were made to the content, they should not change the layout. The content of statistics, but not their structure could be changed. During one of the meetings with the European Commission, the new paper comprising the result of the negotiations with the delegates of Japanese interests in BREMA was circulated. Industry representatives recognised the agreed paper, but European Commission officials assumed that because of the same appearance, they received the old text. The new copy was sent by mail with the formal EACEM heading. Nobody at the Commission noticed the change. After some time, only Thomson became aware of the methodology applied in the presentation of the text.

The tariff on CD players could temporarily, as long as this scheme was tolerated, in accordance with GATT rules[4] be increased without much compensation on account of a new product definition and simultaneous customs reclassification of CD players. A temporary tariff decrease on reel-to-reel recorders from 8 % to 0 % did not have much effect on industrial well being in the European Community. Now the endeavour was apparently to stretch the limits of trade rules.

Under instruction from Thomson – and, under force from Thomson, also Philips in France – the French association Simavelec came up with a range of new, but often stupefying definitions of consumer electronic products. For instance, audio-frequency electric amplifiers with one channel were distinguished from "others". The others were the stereo amplifiers, the duties of which were to be increased from 4.9 % to 14 %. Loudspeakers sets were divided into those with single loudspeakers and those with more loudspeakers in the enclosure. A new customs classification system was proposed that made a distinction between audio equipment and professional applications. More precise definitions were made for various products and new names were proposed for the products. The European Commission services were bewildered by the imaginative definitions, the meanings of which they did not understand. Thomson also wanted mechanical decks, the mechanical cassette loading system with the writing and reading drum or scanner with the video and audio heads mounted into them, added to the list. Grundig agreed. Both companies had difficult negotiations with JVC and Matsushita. The situation is explained in Sect. 5.4. Both Thomson and Grundig had special relations with Japanese producers in Europe, and needed a high duty on the mechanical decks.

[4] The Permanent Mission of Japan pre-empted such new initiatives at GATT by an intervention on 7 July 1983. See below.

5.2 Beaten Tracks of Trade Policy Again?

It was all a bit too fanciful for the European Commission officials of DG-III (Directorate General for Internal Market and Industry). The officials created the impression of strong determination to support the new trade policy initiatives, but strongly advised industry to obtain also support from Directorate General for External Affairs (DG-I, now DG Trade). DG-I could be persuaded, they suggested, by a demonstration of market disruption by Japanese producers of the products concerned, and measures could thereafter be taken. Thus they were off the hook for some time. They did not inform industry about the chance of a proceeding implicating Article XIX of the GATT concerning market disruption. A GATT proceeding would require comprehensive files with strong and irrefutable evidence concerning market disruption. Philips, which had already done most of its homework, knew the immensity of such a job. Thomson, however, still had to move on the learning curve. Thomson thought that lobbying accompanied with excellent restaurant meals and some support from the French government would be sufficient. Thomson was unaware of the fact that the protection of concessions was one of the major accomplishments of the GATT achieved in rounds of eliminations of trade barriers.[5] Trade concessions may be modified on certain conditions. For instance, in the case of safeguards against market disruption (Article XIX, *Emergency Action on Imports of Particular Products*):

> *If, as a result of unforeseen developments and of the effect of the obligations incurred by a contracting party under this Agreement, including tariff concessions, any product is being imported into the territory of that contracting party in such increased quantities and under such conditions as to cause or threaten serious injury to domestic producers in that territory of like or directly competitive products, the contracting party shall be free…*

The suggestion by the DG-III officials was tantamount to transfer of the issue of dealing with trade measures – listed in the first "Meeting the Challenge" paper – to the Directorate General of External Affairs. Thomson's lack of interest in the subtleties the CD case was heavily felt.[6] Not only had the Japanese already brought the issue of CD players before the GATT, it was rather naïve to think that the European Community was prepared to risk a clash with the GATT and Japan a second time. Thomson did not restrict its demand of an increase of tariffs on one new and one non-traded product. Rather, it wanted to increase duties by changing names

[5] Mark 1993: "*Tariff concessions granted in negotiations with one member are automatically extended to all GATT members. Once a tariff concession is made on a particular item, that item is "bound" against any increase above the agreed level. A contracting party is committed not to impose duties or other charges that would tend to undercut such concessions.*"

[6] CEO of Thomson's consumer electronics division, Jacques Fayard, was uninterested, and Thomson's vice-president for external relations, who came from France's diplomatic service, was not acquainted with trade rules concerned.

of various products that represented a considerable value of trade.[7] Consequently, the tactic of DG-III to refer the matter to DG-I was sensible and clever.

A competent official of DG-I explained requirements for safeguard proceedings based on Article XIX of the GATT: safeguards are intended for situations in which a European Industry is affected by an unforeseen, sharp and sudden increase of imports. Very unfortunately for and unknown by Thomson, these requirements are rather hefty. It was obvious that the European Commission official did not expect eminent results of such a demanding exercise. In the original VCR case, resulting in the VRA, safeguard measures might have been taken. However, dumping and injury caused by that dumping was clearly demonstrated in a file. When dumping is evident and injury caused by the dumping is demonstrated, clear and specified proceedings may result in measures without further interference of GATT.[8] Safeguard measures are subject to the supervision of GATT, now the World Trade Organization (WTO), and subject to negotiations. Although dumping of VCRs could have probably been demonstrated, the injury disappeared by Japanese investments in assembly subsidiaries. Anti-dumping measures were therefore ruled out. If injury according to the rules governing anti-dumping is absent, however, safeguard measures are also discarded. Dumping of HiFi from Japan could also have possibly been demonstrated. In the case of HiFi, the injury issue was the bottleneck. Growth in market share had been achieved at the end of the 1970s, but, with exception of CD players, there was no growth in imports. Injury is also the urgent issue in a safeguard case. None of the member states, perhaps with the exception of the shareholder of Thomson, the French Republic, would support safeguard measures on the basis of data of an ambiguous injury. Nevertheless, Thomson wanted to move ahead. Thomson's vice-president for external relations thought it was smart to invent a division of tasks. He proposed that Thomson prepare the VCR file, and delegate the HiFi safeguard clause file to Philips, a flawed move.

Since data on VCR were well known and already made available from Philips to the European Commission and by the Commission to industry, Thomson correctly held the opinion that preparation of a file on this product required minimal efforts. However, demonstration of market disruption by the Japanese was a greater challenge than Thomson was aware of. As shown in Chap. 2, mainly due to Japanese assembly in the European Community and to the joint ventures of Matsushita and JVC respectively with Bosch-Blaupunkt and with Thomson, Thorn and Telefunken, European Community production increased and imports from Japan decreased. Such data did not exactly constitute a sound basis for a convincing file on market disruption. As for audio HiFi, Thomson insisted that Philips accept the task of demonstrating market disruption by Japanese imports in a convincing file. Possibly Thomson insisted in hope that Philips would not have a

[7] General Agreement on Tariffs and Trade Application of Article XXVIII to new products, L/5522 11 July 1983, communication from the Permanent Mission of Japan, dated 7 July 1983.

[8] Measures must be reported to GATT.

notion of European industry's, and especially Thomson's sales in the European Community. Thomson apparently hoped that Philips would not discover its role in the European market.

Philips' audio division and Philips headquarters worked on the HiFi file. Market disruption by Thomson, backed by French state finance, was well known and evident, but it was also clear that Thomson made a dent in both Japanese and competing European industry's shares in the European Community market. Although it was not part of the file on market disruption, evidence on dumping could be found. The problem, however, was that the Japanese inflicted the heavy injury prior to the 1980s. The introduction of Thomson's HiFi line caused a price decay and injury to all parties. Because various Japanese producers tried to bypass the quantitative restrictions of France and Italy by assembly in the European Community, data about injury in the field of audio tuners, amplifiers, cassette decks, loudspeakers, radios in all sorts of combinations – with or without CD player and cassette deck – did not offer hope of a satisfactory safeguard proceeding against Japan on the basis of Article XIX of GATT. Thomson had gained market share at the financial cost of the shareholder, i.e. the French state and taxpayers, and at the cost of competitors' market volume and bottom-line.

The European Commission official responsible for accepting files with requests for safeguard measures was a bright French civil servant with civil courage. Had he been English or German, he might have been accused of anti-French prejudice. Thomson's vice president for external relations gave him the result of Thomson's efforts on the VCR file, a copy of which he did not give to Philips. Knowing what the content of the file would be, there was hardly ground for a serious protest by Philips against such treatment. After examination of the file, the official's conclusion was rather simple: the file came too late. It should have been submitted 2 years earlier when the Video 2000 group lodged the anti-dumping complaint. Subsequently, he received the HiFi file, whereupon the Thomson representative in a lofty tone demanded a copy of this file. The European Commission official retorted that the file clearly contained confidential company material. He studied the file, lit a big cigar of the type that Thomson's boss Alain Gomez cherished so much, and smoked for more than an hour while reading. When his cigar was as small as the hope he could offer, he concluded, almost contented, that the file did not demonstrate injury inflicted by unexpected imports and that it was not the consequence of trade concessions made to Japan in the framework of GATT, but that the injury was self-inflicted, in particular by Thomson. These remarks not only reduced Thomson's ambitions for safeguard measures, but also its aspiration to continue HiFi production in Europe. Not long thereafter, Thomson abandoned the idea of continued audio production in the European Community. This created unexpected and disastrous consequences for Philips' audio position in Belgium. Philips already had an alternative trade policy in mind, which still required detailed elaboration. The idea was to use GATT Article XXIII, on the formation of customs unions and free-trade areas, rather than Article XIX (safeguards), in combination with Article XXVIII (modification of schedules) for a tariff solution for the audio industry in the European Community (see Sect. 5.7).

Table 5.2 VCR imports and market share of Korea (1985–1987)

VCR imports from Korea	1985	1986	1987
Units	75,000	425,000	1,224,000
Market share	1.2 %	6.1 %	15.3 %

Table 5.3 VCR imports from two rebellious Japanese producers

	1984	1985	1986
VCR from Funai and Orion	293,000	466,000	991,000
Market share	5.1 %	7.6 %	13.9 %

Consequently, the list of products identified as eligible for duty increase, an imitation of the CD case, was reduced considerably. Only VCR remained. It was decided that an Article XXVIII-5 procedure, by which the Contracting Party – the EEC – can modify the tariff, but other parties have the right of compensations, would be chosen. Therefore, a list of products to offer as compensation had to be drafted. As a principal supplier Japan, had the right of compensation. By its investments in VCR assembly in the European Community, Japan had acquired a vested interest in imposition of duties on imports. The format was of secondary interest; Matsushita had won the format battle. A fundamentally different problem had arisen. In order to save Betamax, Sony licensed Koreans to produce Betamax. Matsushita had followed the example. Its licensing contract included export restrictions until 1985. As the Japanese feared, the Koreans were serious competitors. Akio Morita admitted Sony's mistake in 1987 during a lunch meeting of Keidanren with European Round Table (ERT) business leaders in Rome. He suggested necessity of a policy toward Korea similar to the Coordinating Committee for Multilateral Export Controls (CoCom), which stood for restriction of technology transfer to the Communist block under the auspice of the Organisation of Economic Cooperation and Development. Japanese worries about the Koreans were not surprising in view of Korean advance in the European Community market, so clearly demonstrated in Table 5.2; the Japanese needed improvement of profitability after the format fight and dumping.

Korea was not the only problem, as Table 5.3 shows. For implementation of the Weather Forecast and a restriction of exports, MITI introduced a surveillance and licensing system for VCR exports to the European Community. Two companies clearly fouled and their permits indicated destination Hong Kong, Singapore, Switzerland and Finland – the latter not yet a member of the European Community. From these countries, the two countries' products were shipped to the European Community. The quantities involved were substantial.[9]

All imports by circumvention were of VHS format. In 1983, Matsushita might have welcomed these covert imports into the European Community. The share of VHS, as fixed by the Japanese implementation of the Weather Forecast on the basis of historical performance of a market as stated in the Weather Forecast plus VHS assembly, was 65 %. If the circumventions are added, it was 71 %. The conclusion

[9] COM REGULATION (EEC) No 2684/88 of 26 August 1988 imposing a provisional anti-dumping duty on certain imports of video cassette recorders originating in Japan and the Republic of Korea; OJ L 240, 31.8.1988, pp. 5–17.

of Philips to stop production of the V2000 because the Weather Forecast spelled doom appeared correct. The circumvention had contributed to establishment of VHS. The assistance of the two sinners was not required any longer. On the contrary, their prices hurt the profitability of the major Japanese companies.

The Japanese did not oppose the idea of an increase in duty on VCR. The increase twice served their interest. The first interest served was protection of their investments. The second was that they received compensation for this increase by means of tariff reductions on products of interest to Japan. Not all of these products were of direct interest to Japan's exports, but exports of Japanese, and also of European companies' subsidiaries in South-East Asia, benefited from the envisaged tariff cuts. On 27 June 1985, the European Commission requested directives from the Council of Ministers for negotiations on adjustments of certain tariffs by means of a proposal.[10] The final increase occurred on 1 January 1986. The intention of an increase was notified in August to GATT and the amount of trade involved as notified to GATT for negotiations was €3,044 million.[11]

The list of products for compensation – as an example of the methodology the final list negotiated with the Japanese is given in Table 5.4 – was drafted with some discord among the industry. The Portuguese association ANIMEE, for instance, could not agree with a concession on monochrome television. Philips had concentrated its remaining European production of black & white television production in the Portuguese town of Ovár. This activity neared collapse. The Portuguese industry association ANIMEE's protests were disregarded as rearguard action of a haystack industry. The camera industry was, of course, not part of the consumer electronics industry and several countries objected to concessions on this product. A majority of member states considered this industry sector lost to the Japanese.

The fiercest opposition came from the European Electronic Components manufacturers Association, EECA. The customs tariff on semiconductors was extremely high, 17 %. The European computer industry association ECMA, chaired by Bruno Lamborghini of Olivetti, passionately attacked the level of the 17 % customs duty on chips. The argument of the computer industry about the high cost of semiconductors due to the high tariff was, though in practice irrational, accepted as theoretically sound. But irrational factors are often decisive. The high tariff had only some impact if a computer's materials bill were important. This might be the case if a computer was not state of the art. The theoretical economic argument that a 17 % duty on semiconductors affects effective protection of a final product with an import duty of only 4.4 % was also kept in mind and is theoretically correct, as Chap. 6 shows. Some officials in member states probably knew of the theory exposed in Chap. 6. In the internal debate at Philips, some had the expectation that this high tariff level was not tenable in the long run. Powerful companies such as IBM with their own chips production and worldwide production would

---

[10] Com (85) 349 final, Brussels, 27 June 1985.

[11] 6 August 1985, Secret/312 + addendum.

Table 5.4 Compensation for the VCR duty increase (values in €1,000,000)

Products	Duty 1985	Reduced duty	1982–1985 Average value of Japanese imports	Compensation	Products	Duty 1985	Increased duty	Value VCR imports	Incidence of duty increase
Semiconductor	17 %	14 %	€344	€10	VCR	8 %	14 %	€1,519	€91.1
Photo camera	7.7 %	1 %	324	€22					
Magnetic tape	5 %	0 %	436	€22					
Pocket calculator	12 %	0 %	82	€10					
Portable cassette player	7 %	0 %	120	€8					
Clock radio	14 %	0 %	4	€1					
Monochrome television	14 %	0 %	12	€2					
Portable radio	14 %	0 %	133	€19					
Total			**€1,455**	**€92.9**	**Total**			**€1,519**	**€91.1**

undoubtedly take care of United States pressure on the European Community to get rid of this duty.

However, within Philips and Thomson and some other chips makers the high duty was sacrosanct. Philips' components division was lead by a sensible director who preferred decisions on the basis of calculations to firm viewpoints based on opinion. He asked for a calculation of the effect of a duty increase for VCRs on European VCR manufacturing and the consequence for sales of semiconductors to the VCR industry. These effects had to be compared with the negative effect on European industry's margins of a tariff cut on semiconductors. The positive cash effect of their own imports from Philips' United States semiconductor subsidiary Signetics was also taken into account. Furthermore, a calculation was made on advantages and disadvantages of a duty decrease, compared with the existing situation, on cash basis. A 3 % points concession on chips yielded a reasonable amount of compensation for the VCR increase. The Information Technology Agreement (ITA) concluded in the framework of the WTO (the comprehensive successor to GATT) in 1996 resulted in the complete abolition of duties on semiconductors. Table 5.4 shows that sacrifices were partly made in sectors other than the consumer electronics industry. Had the semiconductor industry agreed with more drastic steps and had it made a tangible concession, at the level that it would lose anyway later as occurred under the ITA, the burden on other sectors would have been less.

The value of imports of VCRs – as reported to the GATT– was higher. According to the European Community document submitted to the GATT for Article XXVIII consultations, European Community imports were €3,044 million over 3 years.[12] The average presented in the Table 5.4 above was the average as presented by the European Commission to industry. An inexplicable gap existed between the figures presented to various parties. Some products were exempted from the tariff reduction, like monochrome television, but were used afterwards for some other purposes, i.e. the GATT Uruguay Round of trade negotiations, where they were compensations for the exclusion of tariff reductions on other products.

5.3 Japanese Shoe Repair

In order to safeguard the position of the factory of portable radio cassette and CD player combinations (ghetto blasters) in Althofen, Austria, it was agreed with a competent official in the Directorate General for Industry of the Commission that the single customs heading of portable radio would be split into two distinct categories just before the end of the year and before the tariff changes would be announced in the Official Journal of the European Community. At that time, the heading included both portable radio and combinations of radio with cassette and/or

[12] The document, Secret/317 + Add.1, submitted on 12 August 1985, indicated imports of ECU 3,044,106.

CD player. A reduction on portable radio from 14 % to 0 % was offered as compensation. Since European (Eurostat) import statistics did not distinguish between these groups of portable audio, nobody could prove the amount of imports from Japan of portable radio only, without cassette or CD player, and that the compensation on portable radio only instead of on portable combinations was insufficient. However, the French official was transferred just before the final publication of the measures was drafted and he did not transfer this part of his work to a successor. It may also be that his cordial relations with Thomson and the latter's decision to abandon European production caused this negligence. His relations with the Japanese also caused suspicion.[13] In any case, the customs duty on VCRs was raised. However, the duty increase also concerned other equipment for recording and reproduction of television pictures, an implication unknown to the major part of the European industry. DVD players and hard disc recorders, which were already in the laboratory stage in some companies, were also covered.

The publication in the Official Journal of 1 January 1986 created upheaval at Philips. The customs heading of portable radio had not been split. All tariffs on portable radio, including CD and cassette player, was reduced from 14 % to 0 %. The closure of the Philips portable combination factory in Althofen, Austria, which not member of the European Community, was the corollary. Since nobody within Philips was supposed to make mistakes, the question whether the increase of the duty on VCRs and other video reproducers was salutary for the total business result was irrelevant. A mistake is worse than an advantage obtained. Fortunately, the kind permanent representative of the Netherlands at GATT, Joop Fey, was not the greatest taciturn person in the history of officialdom. On a beautiful summer day of 1985 at the border of Lake Geneva, at a lunch of little fried fish, "brochet et féra du Léman", accompanied by tasty Swiss white wine, he fully deployed his loquacity, which became unstoppable. He told about the problems with Japan, in particular with the secret Japanese quantitative restrictions on shoes. Japan secretly applied restrictions on imports of shoes, allegedly again on behalf of the Burakumin. When this became known, Japan tried to maintain these secret quotas under the pretext that special historical, cultural and socio-economic circumstances of the Burakumin required this policy. A GATT panel rejected these circumstances.[14] Japan continued its measures, however, not for leather in general but for shoes. When the disaster of the 0-duty rate on portable radio became apparent, officials of the European Commission's DG-III were informed about some of the errors. They did not know what to do about it. When it was suggested that the solution of the problem was to give the Japanese some time to sort out their shoe problem, the European Commission's DG-III readily agreed and the matter was settled with Japan. Japan replaced the secret quota by a tariff quota (a high tariff as soon as a

[13] He moved to another directorate-general and was suspected to have leaked information on the anti-dumping file on CD players.

[14] The 1984 GATT "Panel on Japanese Measures on Imports of Leather", (L/5623 – 31S/94) adopted on 15/16 May 1984.

certain quantity of imports was attained) in April 1986.[15] The tariff on shoes above the quota became 27 % and on leather between 15 % and 20 %.[16] In a confidential letter, the Japanese promised to gradually increase these quotas, but they did not. The shoes had repaired the situation: The duty on portable radio CD and cassette combinations was restored in March 1986. The leather case could have been used for a settlement of the VCR duty increase without any compensation to the Japanese. Politically, this was unacceptable. That the compensations had been given was deplorable, however, for in the meantime the GATT Uruguay Round negotiations required attention and interventions by the consumer electronics industry in order to safeguard its interests. The compensations for the VCR duty increase could have been used for the Uruguay Round.

5.4 The Uruguay Round and Tariff Reductions

The objectives of the Uruguay Round were ambitious. Many barriers to trade were to be eliminated, and tariffs reduced by 30 %. The problem for the consumer electronics industry was that any tariff reduction would have a unilateral effect. The level of non-tariff barriers in the shape of restrictions by all sorts of technical approval licensing restrictions and distribution cartelisation in some countries made tariff reductions by some exporting countries void. A tariff reduction by the European Community effectively entailed a liberalising effect. It was simply impossible, of course, to claim an exception from the 30 % target tariff reduction in the Uruguay Round. The only alternative was a proposal for reductions beyond the general rate of tariff reduction on products that were statistically relevant but economically less important. Tariff cuts higher than the average could be given in order to compensate exceptions from the general reduction rate. In the same way as in Table 5.4, the chairman of the statistical committee, the director of the French association Simavelec, Henri Anus, and the chairman of the trade policy committee of the EACEM sorted out which products might be made available for tariff concessions exceeding the target and which exceptions should be claimed. Products to be sacrificed were considered sensitive products by some producers, but did not have much of a future.

Table 5.5 provides a second methodology example of negotiations about tariff cuts. On the left hand side are the products sacrificed for a tariff cut deeper than the

---

[15] The leather trade row between Japan and the European Union surfaced again in 1996, when the European Commission began to exert pressure on Japan to increase imports from Europe by modifying the tariff quota system. The European Union apparently made the move at the prodding of such major leather-exporting union members as France, Italy and Spain. This was especially pressing because Japan attacked continuously the European Community as Fortress Europe because of the intention of the European Community to create one single market by 1992 lifted the residual quotas maintained by member states toward Japan, whereas Japan rigorously maintained its residual restrictions.

[16] Belassa and Noland 1988, p. 54.

Table 5.5 Products used as credit for exclusion from EEC tariff reductions in GATT

Product "sacrificed"	Duty was	Duty after Uruguay Round	Product "saved"	Duty after Uruguay Round
Record players/ turntables	9.5 %	2 %	CTV	14 %
Styli; diamonds, sapphires	4.9 %	Free	Car radio with cassette	10 %
Black and white TV	14 %	2 %	Pocket digital radio cassette players	14 %
Black and white tubes	14 %	7.5 %	VCR, DVD players	14 %
Car radio without cassette or CD	14 %	2 %	Car radio with CD player	14 %

generally agreed average tariff reduction and on the right hand side are products excluded from the tariff cuts, to which a lower percentage was applied. The list of products sacrificed still had a considerable trade weight in terms of import value, but that would not last long, for the products were at the end of their life cycle. Because of the trade involved, they were formally – according to the negotiating rules – acceptable as a tariff offer. This list was agreed with EEC tariff negotiators in Geneva, without prior approval by EEC officials in Brussels.

Anxious that some member states might attempt to interfere and use such negotiation lists for national interests or worse, to obstruct efforts to exempt some duties, industry representatives did not inform them. It was understood that especially in the Netherlands, where liberalisation was seemingly necessary for the free-trade image, there was the intention to sacrifice industrial interests unilaterally. The idea was that destruction of the European industry would foster additional imports via the port of Rotterdam and this would be in the Dutch interest.

An official within the Commission's Directorate General for Internal Market and Industry (III) was suspected of representing Japanese interests and of special keenness for the importance of his own position. Out of fear that he might try to frustrate their results, the consumer electronics industry representatives negotiating on behalf of the European industry on the GATT tariff cuts took care not to inform this official about the agreed exceptions from GATT tariff reductions. Thomson CE's CEO Pierre Garcin decided that there was not any future in European audio and small screen television manufacturing.[17] He decided that this state-owned company would move to Asia. The decision might have been expected to be made on the basis of calculations, including customs duty costs. But this did not seem to be the case. Consequently, Thomson wanted decreases in tariffs rather than maintaining the present level. That other exporters to the European Community would also take advantage of such tariff cuts was immaterial to Garcin, who had inherited from his predecessor the aversion to Philips as tunnel vision. One of the

[17] Industriemagazin, Munich, September 1987, 59–67.

Thomson public relations officers asked the official of DG-III whether information about a tariff deal of industry with negotiators of the EEC in Geneva was correct and whether this deal was feasible. The official was furious that he had not been the centre in balancing the interests, and tried to undo the arrangement. These efforts resulted in a conflict between his department and the Directorate General for External Relations (Trade). Relations between him and part of the industry, the European consumer electronics producers, became bitter. His interventions did not spoil the deal.

Gradually, however, the number of perils to such industry actions increased. Unity in the industry was waning. Japanese producers increasingly dominated European Community decision-making, either in the professional associations or in their lobby with the European Commission. Some member states did not accept "innovations" in the use of trade policy instruments to any further extent. But there still remained some possibilities.

5.5 Customs Classification as a Trade Policy Tool: Mechanical Decks

The initial objectives of an alignment of duties on several products to a level of 14 % were not achieved. Grundig and Thomson still struggled with their Japanese partners about the price of mechanical decks for VCRs and they wanted, still or again, an increase though a XXVIII proceeding. Cooperation agreements influenced interests behind such an increase of the tariff. Initially, when it wanted the joint venture with JVC in Berlin to use the mechanical decks made in Tonnerre (Burgundy), Thomson showed interest in an increase of effective protection on mechanical VCR decks, mecadecks. Subsequently, abandoning the site of joint production with JVC in Berlin after the reunification of Germany and the abolition of Berlin production subsidies, it wanted an outward processing advantage for its production in a joint production with Toshiba in Singapore, to which a tariff increase on decks would contribute.

Grundig held the opinion that the manufacturing of scanners containing magnetic heads was a key technology and wanted to keep production of drums or scanners with heads for recording and playing in Nuremberg. These were to be incorporated in the mechanical decks made by Matsushita for its own production in the Matsushita-Bosch Video Werke in Peine (Germany) and for Grundig's VCR production. Matsushita always preferred to import mechanical decks directly from its factories in Japan and regularly put pressure on Grundig, considering Grundig's scanner prices, of course, to be too high. Grundig hoped that this discussion would stop if a 14 % tariff on mecadecks was imposed. Philips' mechanical deck production was not for supply to a third party, but for its own VCR production. Although it did not have supply interests for mecadecks, Philips preferred that competitors incur higher costs on these key components, through which cooperation with Phillips on mecadecks would become more attractive. Another argument was that some Korean producers would experience difficulties because of the increase of the duty on mechanical decks, which they imported from their home country.[18] The economic interests and effects of certain trade and customs regimes are presented in Chap. 6.

Since the route of increasing the duties was barred, Grundig promptly accepted another path pointed out to it by Philips. Thomson also embraced the idea. If a tariff on the product could not be increased, then the customs definition of the product should, under the prevailing poor trade policy conditions, be changed. The effect of the change would make the mechanical deck and its duty identical to the product with the higher duty, the VCR, because the deck had the "essential characteristics" of the VCR. The argument was that the mecadeck was essentially a VCR and therefore, should be considered a VCR, incidentally bearing a duty of 14 % rather than the 5.8 % duty of VCR components. The VCR classified under the heading 8521 10 39 (now 8521 10 30) of the Combined Nomenclature (CN)[19] of the European Community was subject to the European Community customs duty at a rate of 14 %, whereas the deck was classified under the heading 8522 90 99 (now 8522 90 59) was subject to customs duty at a rate of 5.8 % (now 4 %). Grundig's Karl-Heinz Kotter, a courageous and dynamic person, succeeded in convincing the European Commission that the mechanical deck or mecadeck had all basic characteristics of a VCR and actually was a VCR. Philips also made various presentations and with Thomson's help in France, the European Community's Nomenclature Committee finally agreed with to include the mecadeck into the VCR category because the mecadeck "*presented the essential characteristics of a video recording or reproducing apparatus*".[20] According to Article 2 of the "General rules for the interpretation of the Combined Nomenclature", the incomplete or unfinished article shall be treated as the finished article if it has the essential character of the complete or finished article. This interpretation implied a duty on mechanical decks of 14 % instead of 5.8 %.

The Japanese government and industry were, of course, furious. They promptly brought the case before the Customs Cooperation Council (CCC), presently the World Customs Organisation. WCO decision-making occurs by simple majority, in contrast with the GATT, where interested parties discuss discords and panels of

[18] Judgment of the Court (First Chamber) of 13 December 1994. GoldStar Europe GmbH v Hauptzollamt Ludwigshafen, Case C-401/93.

[19] In the period in which the discussion took place, the Combined Nomenclature of the European Community was not based yet on the Harmonised System of the Customs Cooperation Council, which entered into force on 1 January 1988. When the issue of mechanical decks was discussed, the heading for VCRs was 92.11 B. Discussions in the Customs Directorate of the European Commission usually took place in French, discussion about a product with the heading "quatre-vingt-douze onze" is not easy for non-French speakers (is it 4-20-12-11 or 80-12-11 or 92-11?).

[20] Commission Regulation (EEC) No 2275/88 of 25 July 1988 concerning the classification of certain goods in the combined nomenclature, Official Journal L 200, 26/07/1988 pp. 10–12: "Mechanical assembly for a video recording or reproducing apparatus of CN code 8521, equipped with recording and reproducing heads (Mecadeck). // 8521 10 39 // Classification is determined by the provisions of general rules 1, 2 (a) and 6 and the texts of CN codes 8521, 8521 10 and 8521 10 39. This mechanical assembly presents the essential characteristics of a video recording or reproducing apparatus."

experts decide on the matter. The Japanese lobbied heavily among African and Asian countries and bribed, as suspected by some European industry officials, a few representatives of these countries in the CCC. The majority of the CCC finally shared the Japanese view and on 7 April 1991, it issued an opinion to the effect that mecadecks should be classified under subheading 8522 90 as "parts" of video recorders. The European Commission withdrew the reclassification on 23 October 1991.[21]

Thomson for some time enjoyed advantages from this nomenclature device in two respects. Deck production in Tonnerre obtained higher protection, and part of the profit margin was shifted from Berlin (VCRs) to deck production (Tonnerre). After re-unification of Germany and discontinuation of the "Berlin Hilfe" (aid by production subsidies), Thomson left its partner JVC in VCR production in Berlin and switched to a joint venture with Toshiba in Singapore. It saved on its imports of VCRs from Singapore by the deduction of duties on components exported from the Community to Singapore in the framework of the outward processing regime of the European Community. The increase in the deck duty increased the deductible amount in the processing relief. Chapter 6 shows methodologies of calculation of increased protection and of a higher margin in outward processing.

Grundig continued its supplies of scanners to the MB-Video Werke and received mechanical decks in return, and the temporary change in classification of the mechanical decks also brought Grundig temporary relief from the continuous and oppressive discussions with Matsushita. When Grundig finally joined a VCR joint venture with iR3, together with its parent Philips, the issue of deck supplies to Matsushita was solved.

5.6 Camera Recorder Customs Heading: "Essential Characteristics", Buying or Making

The change in nomenclature and classification is certainly not a usual instrument for improving a competitive position. Another customs interpretation, which could have impact on the duty, was raised almost simultaneously with the issue of the mecadeck. The launch of the video camera recorder, a combination of a video camera with a recorder part, raised the issue which part of this combination of camera and video recorder should be considered decisive for customs definition and customs heading. The duty on cameras was 4.9 % and on recorders 14 %. When these products arrived from Japan at the European Community frontier, the importers' customs declaration was, of course, as cameras. The European industry with ambition of its own of camcorder production considered the correctness of this classification questionable. They preferred a higher duty, but they had good arguments for treatment of the camcorder as video recorder. In this view, the

[21] By Commission Regulation (EEC) No 3085/91 of 21 October 1991 amending Commission Regulation (EEC) No 2275/88 of 25 July 1988.

function of the camera part was secondary to the recorder part. According European Community industry with intentions of European production, the camera recorder was a recorder with a sensor and a lens in front of the recorder. It was comparable with the normal VCR, in which the tuner was integrated or not. Since the video recorder with a tuner was not classified as a television receiver, there was not a good argument in favour of the treatment of a camera recorder as camera. As for the VCR, the recorder part recorded the television signal received by the reception part. In the camcorder, the camera part had the same function as the tuner in VCR: reception of the picture, which was recorded by the recorder part. As for the cost of the video camera recorder, the recorder part was the most expensive. Additionally, some camcorders also contained a tuner device. The European Community's "General rules for the interpretation of the Combined Nomenclature" Article 3(c) and of the former CCC, prescribe that if goods cannot be classified by the specific descript and if reference to essential character does not provide a classification, "*the product shall be classified under the heading which occurs last in numerical order among those which equally merit consideration*". In the case of the camera recorder, the recorder part, with the expensive tiny recording mechanism was the most expensive part. Finally, the argument was that the heading for video recorders was – at that time – in Chap. 92, heading 9211 12, whereas the camera was in Chap. 85. Consequently, according to the rules for interpretation the camera recorder could (or should) have been classified as video recorders, bearing the customs duty of 14 %. If the situation were to be dealt with at present, the conclusion would be the opposite. The video recorder has now combined nomenclature heading CN and Harmonised System (HS) heading 8521 10 30, whereas the sensor television camera CN has heading 8525 30 90. However, the European Commission decided that the camera recorder should have the same duty as the camera (now defined as camera recorder with CN 8525 40 91) with a duty of 4.9 %. The camcorder with a tuner (CN 8521 10 30) would be classified as having 14 %. This distinction still exists: video camera recorders only able to record sound and images taken by the television camera are classified as 8525 40 91 with the duty of 4.9 % and other are classified as 8525 40 99 with a duty of 14 %. In 1991, the Harmonised System Committee of the WCO decided that all camera recorders should not be considered VCRs but be headed as television cameras. In 1991, the European industry had, however, lost its interest in the issue: there was no industry in Europe manufacturing the product and intentions to do so had been abandoned.

The issue caused a lasting friction in the industry association EACEM. It was agreed that all consumer electronics tariffs should be harmonised at 14 %. In the past, Thomson voiced its resolve to produce camcorders and insisted on an increase in duty for camcorders but suddenly, and without any notification to European colleagues and competitors, it changed its mind and had decided to abandon this plan and to import camcorders, of course at the lowest possible duty. The EACEM's chairman, also chairman of BREMA and on Thomson's wage list because of the acquisition of Ferguson, when asked by the European Commission, gave an opinion on the subject totally opposite to the agreed position. As indicated, the EACEM chairman also chaired the British Radio and Electronic Equipment Manufacturers

Association (BREMA) with Japanese dominance. He did not seem to have another option than to voice incorrectly as the opinion of European industry that it considered camcorders essentially cameras bearing a duty of 4.9 %. Besides, according to him there was no European Community production interest. This act of subversion, as some considered it, was a heavy blow to cooperation within the European industry. Philips was involved in serious negotiations about camcorder standards and about production of such equipment in Vienna. The calculations indicated that at 4.9 % import duty it had to abandon its efforts. Gradually, it became apparent that the European consumer electronics industry moved into different directions, all to the abyss.

5.7 EC's Enlargement as a Tool: The Customs Union Tariff Harmonisation

The final attempt to "harmonise tariffs" to the level of 14 % in accordance with the rules and in conformity with the GATT and CCC was the endeavour to draw on accession of Spain and Portugal to the European Community in 1986 and the higher duties that these countries both generally maintained, but specifically in the domain of consumer electronics compared with the duties of the European Community. The termination of preferential access and the reduction of Spanish and Portuguese tariffs to the European Community level would increase pressure on European Community industry regarding disruptive imports from Japan and some other Asian exporters. In general, the level of protection against imports from third countries of the 10 European Community member states and the two new members would decrease through adjustment of Spanish and Portuguese customs duties to the European Community level. GATT Article XXIV on customs unions and free-trade areas requires that protection after the creation of the customs union is not greater than before. The accession implied the creation of a new customs union of the 10 old and the two new members. The European Community of 12 members would have less protection than 10 + 2, suggesting that a "credit" from net liberalisation could be used for tariff harmonisation in some specific cases. It was suggested to "harmonise" the customs duties on some HiFi products. If there was a net liberalisation, Article XXVIII of the GATT concerning modification of duties could be used in order to "harmonise" the duties upward. In any case, the net result for the European Community's trading partners would be positive.

The European Commission accepted this recommendation and made a proposal accordingly. Customs tariffs of the European Commission of 12 were increased by roughly 2 %, which was the net liberalisation, and subsequently these higher duties were presented as new bound duties, but the increased duties were suspended and the European Union customs of the European Communities of 10 were actually or autonomously applied by the EC-12.[22] The "credit", the difference between the import-weighted customs duties of the 10 and the import-weighted duties of Portugal and Spain, was supposed to be negotiated in GATT in Article XXIV:6 negotiations. Spain and Portugal's accession required an assessment in Article XXIV negotiations by GATT contracting parties. Under this Article, negotiations with principal suppliers should be held, and member states should approve proposals concerning modification of duties in the framework of Article XXVIII. This Article was also used on behalf of the CD duty increase described in Chap. 4 and the VCR duty arrangement described above in this Chapter.

European Community approval on such negotiations must be given in accordance with article 113 of the Rome Treaty, later Article 133 and now Article 207. Expecting and fearing a rearrangement of duties on HiFi equipment, the Japanese government exerted heavy pressure on member states, urging them under various threats not to approve such proposals. Various member states were, to use an understatement, not eager to take the initiative. Most unexpected and highly disappointing was that France did not want to push the matter. Since Thomson Consumer Electronics had redefined its position in HiFi and had decided to abandon European production and to transfer this production to Asia, France did not have an interest in an increase of audio duties. Apart from the fact that France regretted that Philips rather than Thomson was still the leading producer in the European Community, the French authorities also had some antipathy toward Philips, attributable to Thomson's habit to depict any Philips step as anti-Thomson, treacherous and anti-French. The German ministry of economic affairs expressed its intention to support the case on the condition of Dutch sponsorship. Although all HiFi factories of Philips were located in Belgium, the Belgians waited for Dutch initiative.

The Dutch Director General of Foreign Economic Relations withheld his support. His boss, a Christian Democrat trade minister, was not supposed to have an opinion or other opinion other than the Director General's. The Dutch Director General held the view that enlargement of the European Community should contribute to free trade rather than his support to European Community industry. A Japanese offer to the European Community for decrease of duties on tomato purée, allegedly a Spanish interest, and cork, produced in Portugal, appeared highly acceptable to him. Since the Japanese do not use tomato purée and cork is not transported that distance, the offers were empty. After Japan's concession, the proposal appeared to represent less than €7 million of exports. Tomato purée export was worth only about €20,000. An attempt to get the support of Dutch ministers other than the trade minister failed by some misunderstandings.

The damage was huge. HiFi production in Belgium had to be abandoned and factories closed. Manufacturing of audio was transferred to Singapore and China. Unlike the executives in the late 1990s and in the third millennium, those in the 1980s and early 1990s cared about continuity of business and employment rather

[22] By Council Regulation (EEC) No 3330/85 of 5 December 1985 amending Regulation (EEC) No 950/68 on the Common Customs Tariff, Official Journal L330/1 of 9 December 1985.

than about their bonuses, the latter of which hardly existed in that period. The factory in Louvain, with its considerable labour force, had to be closed. Management of Philips Belgium looked for alternative employment for the HiFi factory in Louvain. Some crook succeeded in convincing management of Philips Belgium to assume production of slot machines for video rentals company Superclub. Soon finances of Superclub appeared in disorder. Philips participated in Superclub. That became a disaster. Later the founder of Superclub went to jail for another case of fraud. The collapse of the HiFi activities and the Superclub adventures severely reduced the Belgian Philips organisation to a group of shambling factories. Heavy losses were incurred both on HiFi and on the adventures with the Belgian master felon. The Louvain factory also finally closed.

5.8 Blind Alley of Mere Protection

When it appeared that the Dutch government's trade policy rejected any other trade policy than complete liberalisation and all other policies as French and, consequently, Mercantilist, it was clear that a European Community trade policy, which would have to use the complex proceedings of European Community decision making on normal trade policy matters, was a blind alley. It was obvious that the way of decision-making via the Committee Article 113 – Committee Article 133 in the European Community Treaty and in the Committee Article 207 in the Treaty on the Functioning of the European Union[23] – was a blind alley. European Community trade policy is conducted without democratic control, in the backrooms of ministries and in some Brussels hotel lobbies and dinner tables. The director-general in the German Ministry of Economic Affairs, Lorenz Schomerus, indicated that he did not digest tariff increase actions longer. Germany would stop its support to tariff protection attempts. The German government had changed its policy. If the industry was able to demonstrate dumping, Germany would certainly support such cases. This was a challenge and an invitation. Such promises have a short life, certainly when governments and bureaucratic machineries are their source. It lasted some time until this lesson was learned.

It was supposed that if anti-dumping actions were supported by the most important member states, then the European Community industry had a case. The principal fact encountered in trade relations was that competition with Japanese was asymmetrical. Philips had a history of technological and product superiority over Japanese producers. The Japanese, headed by Matsushita, hunted for licences from Philips. But, nevertheless, Philips as all other Western competitors was utterly unsuccessful on the Japanese market, with exception of a few products. Its successes, shavers and coffee makers, were quickly imitated. Philips taught housewives the advantages of coffee and how to make coffee. Matsushita and others sold

[23] OJ C83/47 of 30.3.2010.

the copies of coffee makers. Shavers and coffee makers hardly require specialised sales knowledge and after sales service. They need not be sold in specialised retail distribution, but can be sold as luxury items in department stores. There was a possibility to sell outside the normal electrical distribution determined their success: the shaver, which remains a success. The Philips shaver is hardly imitable. Its shaving head construction is unique and its production cost must be inferior to those of any other producer. The Philips shaver production was about twice the production of the second-ranking Braun and three times the production of Matsushita Panasonic or of Hitachi. However, in Japan Panasonic and Hitachi easily survived any foreign competition despite the fact that export prices were substantially lower than their prices. An investigation of the causes of this phenomenon was indispensible and was undertaken. Theoretical summaries of cases presented before are presented in subsequent chapters.

References

Belassa BA, Noland MI (1988) Japan in the world economy. Institute for International Economics, Washington, DC

Mark C (1993) CD dictionary & CD glossary, the language of international trade: a handbook of concepts & terms. Institute for Trade and Commercial Diplomacy, www.commercial-diplomacy.org/dictionaries

Chapter 6
Trade Rules and Struggle for Margin

Abstract Protection is often simply understood as a high trade barrier. If tariffs on inputs or the components are also high, high tariffs on final products may not offer much protection. The notion of "effective protection", the protection of added value, is more useful. The increase of duty on mechanical decks affects the effective protection on VCRs negatively. The effective protection of various duties is presented. The benefits and disadvantages of higher tariffs on VCRs and mechanical decks are visualised in computation. They were made in order to analyse the interests of competitors in trade policy actions. The outward processing legislation and its advantages are explained. It appears that Thomson had some relative advantages as a consequence of the higher duty on mechanical decks directly related to this outward protection. Both effective protection and outward processing benefits are computed from actual cost compositions.

6.1 Computing Competitors' Advantages

Before it supported Grundig and Thomson's wish to increase the duty on mechanical decks by a customs redefinition to 14 % instead of the duty on components of 5.8 %, Philips calculated the effects on the competitiveness of these both companies. The calculations by Philips concerned changes in the competitors' profitability by changes in the rate of the competitors' effective protection and by additional outward processing advantages. It is uncertain whether other companies in the sector made similar computations. For a proper judgment on the outcome of certain trade policy actions, such quantitative estimates on competitors' advantages are indispensable.

M. van Marion, *International Trade Policy and European Industry*, Contributions to Economics, DOI 10.1007/978-3-319-00392-4_6,

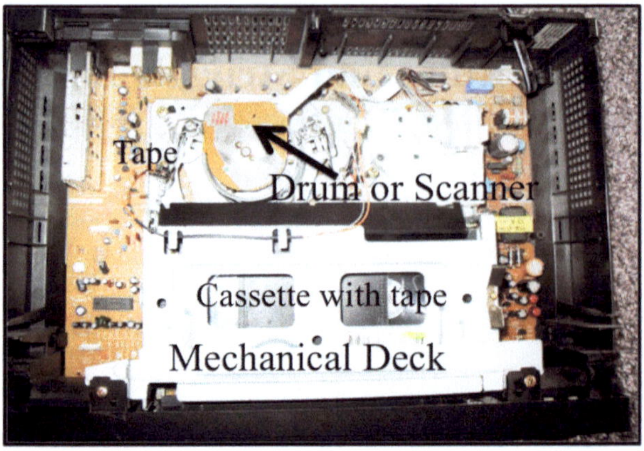

Picture 6.1 Content of VCR: mechanical deck with drum or scanner

6.2 Effective Rate of Protection: VCR and Mechanical Deck

Protection as such is a meaningless notion. A 100 % import duty on a final product and of 90 % on its components, results in an effective protection, i.e. the protection of the added value, of less than a 25 % duty on finished product and 10 % on the components. Economically relevant is the protection of added value, i.e. of the value added to imported or importable components. It is assumed that a customs duty raises a price above the world market price by the percentage of the duty.

Before the issue of protection is addressed, some insight into the content of a VCR is worthwhile.

Picture 6.1 shows a mechanical deck or mecadeck with its cassette loading system, drum and other components in an open cabinet. The mecadeck is the major part or subassembly of the video recorder and its share is about 33 % of the materials value of the VCR. The mechanical deck was the subject of a struggle between producers for more margin or added value in their production.

The effective rate of protection (EPR) is based on the protection of added value. The added value $\boldsymbol{V_j}$ in the finished product is the unit value of the finished product at world market price $\boldsymbol{P_J}$ minus the price of the inputs at world market price $\boldsymbol{C_j}$. The share of the components in the value of the final product is $\boldsymbol{a_{ij}}$. The added value, $\boldsymbol{V_j}$, is also equal to $\boldsymbol{P_J}$ times the difference between the price of the total and this share of components in total:

$$V_j = P_j - C_j = P_j.(1 - a_{ij}) \tag{6.1}$$

If tariffs on the output (t_j) and input (t_i) are imposed, there is a new added value, $\boldsymbol{V'_j}$, which amounts to:

$$V'_j = P_j.[(1 + t_j) - a_{ij}.(1 + t_i)] \tag{6.2}$$

The EPR, g_j, is the relative increase in added value due to tariff protection:

$$g_j = \frac{V'_j - V_j}{V_j} = \frac{t_j - a_{ij}.t_i}{1 - a_{ij}} \tag{6.3}$$

If several inputs play a role, the formula is:

$$g_j = \frac{t_j - \sum_{i=1}^{n} a_{ij}.t_i}{1 - \sum_{i=1}^{n} a_{ij}} \tag{6.4}$$

As stated before, the notion of effective protection is based on the assumption that a duty increases the domestic price of a product above world market level. If the world market price of a finished product (the VCR) is 100, a tariff on the finished product of 8 % increases the price of the domestic product to 108.[1] The increased domestic price, as well as all other monetary values that appear in this chapter, is in Euros. In the hypothetical case of a VCR, the following values are used, summarised in Table 6.1.

- The world market price of the VCR is assumed 100 and of the components is taken 87.
- Consequently, addition of value to components is 100 − 87 = 13, which is 15 % over the value of components (13: 87 = 14.9 %).
- The initial European Community duty of 8 % on VCR results in a price on the European Community market of 108, i.e. 8 % over the world market price of 100. The duty on components (including mecadeck) initially was 5.8 %. A distinction is made between mecadecks and other components. The mecadeck is assumed at 33.0 % of the components value of 87.

Table 6.2 reports various combinations or relevant duties and related effective protection:

The duty on assembled video recorders was initially 8 %. The discrepancy in protection between the VCR with a duty of 8 % on the assembled product and with a lower 5.8 % on its inputs, the components, results in an effective rate of protection of 23 % (row 15 of Table 6.2). In the formula the effective rate of protection is at duties of respectively 8 % and 5.8 %:

[1] For the sake of simplicity, the value of a VCR is set at 100 rather than a more appropriate 180.

Table 6.1 Values of VCR and components at world market prices

Products and composition	Value	%
Value VCR	100.00	
Components VCR	87.00	
Added value VCR and as % of components	13.00	14.9
Value mecadeck (part VCR) and as % of components VCR	28.71	33.0
Value other components VCR and as % components of VCR	58.29	67.0
Added value mecadeck over components of mecadeck	4.31	18
Components mecadeck and as % of mecadeck value	24.40	85
Value scanner (part mecadeck) and as per cent of components mecadeck	10.05	41
Other components mecadeck	14.36	59

$$
\begin{aligned}
EPR_{VCR1} &= \frac{(1+8\%)\times 100 - [(1+5.8\%)\times 33\%\times 87 + (1+5.8\%)\times 67\%\times 87]}{100-87} \\
&= \frac{108-92.5}{13} = 23\%
\end{aligned}
\tag{6.5}
$$

The increase in duty on VCR as described in Chap. 5 results in a substantial increase of the effective protection (row 20 in Table 6.3). Whereas the previous rate of effective protection $\boldsymbol{EPR_{VCR1}}$ was 23 %, under the duty of 14 % instead of 8 % the $\boldsymbol{EPR_{VCR2}}$ is 69 %.

$$
\begin{aligned}
EPR_{VCR2} &= \frac{(1+14\%)\times 100 - [(1+5.8\%)\times 33\%\times 87 + (1+5.8\%)\times 67\%\times 87]}{100-87} \\
&= \frac{114-92.5}{13} = 69\%
\end{aligned}
\tag{6.6}
$$

The increase of the duty on mecadecks from 5.8 % to 14 % resulted in an increase of the cost or value of the input of mechanical decks, which represent 33 % of the components of the VCR. The formula for the effective protection rate $\boldsymbol{EPR_{VCR3}}$ after this increase – caused by the reclassification of the mecadecks – of the duty on the mecadeck is:

$$
\begin{aligned}
EPR_{VCR3} &= \frac{(1+14\%)\times 100 - [(1+14\%)\times 33\%\times 87 + (1+5.8\%)\times 67\%\times 87]}{100-87} \\
&= \frac{114-94.40}{13} = 51\%
\end{aligned}
\tag{6.7}
$$

This implied that Philips was not bothered by this increase of the mecadeck duty, for the competitive position of Thomson and Grundig as producers of VCRs did not effectively improve by the increase of the duty on the mecadeck (or the reclassification).

Table 6.2 Value of VCR and components with added value and effective protection

	Product and duty	Finished product	Components	Added values	Eff. protection
	VCR without protection	**Duty 0 %**	**Duty 0 %**		
1	Mecadeck 33 % of 87 (at 0 %)		28.71		
2	Other components (at 0 %)		58.29		
3	Values world market	100.00	87.00	13.00	
4	Protected values and added value at 0 %	100.00	87.00	13.00	
5	**Added value and effective protection**	13.00	−13.00	= 0.00	(0 ÷ 13.00=) **0 %**
	VCR with protection 1	**8.00 %**	**0.0 %**		
6	Mecadeck		28.71		
7	Other components		58.29		
8	Value world market	100.00	87.00	13.00	
9	Protected values and added value	108	87.00	21.00	
10	**Added value and effective protection**	21.00	−13.00	= 8.00	(8.00 ÷ 13.00=) 62 %
	VCR with protection 2	**Duty 8 %**	**Duty 5.8 %**		
11	Mecadeck		30.38		
12	Other components		61.67		
13	Values world market	100.00	87.00	13.00	
14	Protected values and added value	108.00	92.05	15.95	
15	**Added value and effective protection**	15.95	−13.00	= 2.95	(2.95 ÷ 13.00=) **23 %**
	VCR with protection 3	**Duty 14 %**	**Duty 5.8 %**		
16	Mecadeck (5.8 %)		30.38		
17	Other components (5.8 %)		61.67		
18	Values world market	100.00	87.00	13.00	
19	Protected values and added value	114.00	92.05	21.95	
20	**Added value and effective protection**	21.95	−13.00	= 8.95	(8.95 ÷ 13.00=) **69 %**
	VCR with protection 4	**Duty 14 %**	**Duty 14 % (mecadeck) and 5.8 % (other)**		
21	Mecadeck **(14 %)**		32.73		
22	Other components **(5.8 %)**		61.67		
23	Values world market	100.00	87.00	13.00	
24	Protected values and added value	114.00	94.40	19.60	
25	**Added value and effective protection**	19.60	−13.00	= 6.60	(6.60 ÷ 13.00=) **51 %**

Table 6.3 Consequence of reclassification of mechanical decks and effective protection

Finished product	Finished	Components	Added values	Eff. protection
Mecadeck old situation	**Mecadeck**	**Scanner and other**		
Mecadeck and components tariff	**5.8 %**	**5.8 %**		
Scanner		10.63		
Other components mecadeck		15.19		
Values world market	28.71	24.40	4.31	
Protected values and added value	30.38	25.82	4.56	
Added value and effective protection	4.56	−4.31	= 0.25	(0.25 ÷ 4.31=) **5.8 %**
Mecadeck new situation	**Mecadeck**	**Scanner and other**		
Mecadeck and components tariff	**14 %**	**5.8 %**		
Scanner		10.63		
Other components mecadeck		15.19		
Values world market	28.71	24.40	4.31	
Protected values and added value	32.73	25.82	6.91	
Added value and effective protection	6.91	−4.31	= 2.60	(2.60 ÷ 4.31=) **60 %**

Other VCR producers importing mechanical decks would be disadvantaged. There was also a shift of margin from VCR assembly to deck supplier. This caused MITI's anger, because interests of both JVC and Matsushita as VCR assemblers and other Japanese in Europe as importers of decks were harmed.

A similar calculation can be made for the producer's benefit from scanners of the increase of the mechanical deck duty under reclassification into the heading of the deck and classifying it as VCR. For the producers of mechanical decks the change in heading had an advantage. Using the data in Table 6.1, the change in effective protection of mechanical decks production as the consequence of the change in heading from components to finished product is computed in Table 6.3.

The protection of the added value was simply the 5.8 % duty on finished mechanical deck and its inputs before the heading changed because of the new views. By changing the heading, the protection of the added value in mechanical deck production (effective protection of mecadeck production) increased to 60 %. The increase in effective protection of mechanical deck production by 54.2 % points caused a decrease of effective protection of VCR by 18 % points to take place. This clearly shows why MITI was furious. Although it may be doubtful that the ministry made a detailed calculation, it must have been aware that the change in heading redistributed the margins between various producers mainly in favour of some Europeans and without approval of MITI.

Consequently, the issue was not restricted to protection of European Community industry. In the case of JVC/Thomson (J2T Video), with scanner and deck production in Tonnerre, in the French Burgundy area, and VCR production in Berlin, it was a struggle for margin. The price of 114, the world market price of 100 plus 14 % customs duty, might have been the competitive price, allowing J2T in Berlin a profit of, say, 4.00 (3.51 % over the price). By the increase of the margin of mechanical decks made by in Tonnerre by 2.35, the cost for J2T in Berlin went up by 2.35 and the profit margin decreased from 4.00 % to 1.65 % or 1.47 % over the price. It offered a shift of profits from the VCR production to the mecadeck factory in Tonnerre.

The increase of the duty on, or re-baptising of, mechanical decks from 5.8 % to 14 % had another consequence. It facilitated a switch in Thomson's alliance from JVC in Berlin to Toshiba in Singapore. In 1989, imports of VCRs into the European Community were 390,400 and went up to 662,476 in 1990 and 765,518 in 1991. Mechanical decks were shipped from Tonnerre to Singapore and VCRs were shipped from Singapore to the European Community. The facilitation of this switch arose from improvement of Thomson's outward processing position.

6.3 Outward Processing and Duty on Exported Components

Outward processing relief allows a European Community producer to deduct the value of exported inputs, including the import duties payable on those inputs, from the customs value of the final product, including the import duties payable. The exporting Community producer and producer processing these and other inputs, are supposed to be related. The duty value of an input, part or component (mecadeck) produced in the European Community and processed outside the European Community (into a VCR) may be subtracted from the value of the finished product (the VCR) at EEC customs. The customs value is the ex-Community value of the inputs at the percentage prevailing as customs duty for the input (mechanical deck). This method is called the duty differential method.

Table 6.4 shows the issue. It is assumed that the cost of the mechanical deck made in Europe is at the level of the world market price plus the protection by 5.8 %, i.e. 30.38 instead of the world market price of 28.71, which was the starting point for the calculation of effective protection. The value of the other components is assumed to be the same as the world market price without protection in Table 6.3. The cost of the mechanical deck exported from France to Singapore is 30.38. When the deck arrives, the cost of insurance and transport of 0.61 has been added. The total cost is 30.98. The deck is incorporated in the VCR. With other components and a value added of respectively 58.29 and 13.39, the cost of the VCR when the product leaves the factor is 102.66. It is loaded aboard and adding the cost of insurance and freight of 2.05, the CIF value before customs is 104.72. The customs duty of 14 % must be paid. That is 14 % $\times$ 104.72 $=$ 14.66. The outward processing relief results in the subtraction of 5.8 % $\times$ 30.38 $=$ 1.76. The net payment of duty is, therefore, at a duty on decks of 5.8 % and the duty on VCR in total 12.90. The relief results in a duty of 12.32 % instead of 14 % on the VCR. The relief is 1.68 %

Table 6.4 Outward processing benefit by mecadeck duty increase

(I&F) and added value	Item	Values	Duties	Duty value
	Value Mecadeck when exported	30.38	5.8 %	1.76
I&F 2 %	Transport cost	0.61		
	Deck cost Singapore	30.98		
	Other components	58.29		
	Total components of VCR	89.27		
Added value 15 %	Added value in VCR to components	13.39		
	FOB production cost VCR	102.66		
2 %	Cost of I&F (insurance and freight)	2.05		
Incl. I&F	CIF VCR value import EEC	104.72	14 %	14.66
			Duty-drawback	1.76
			Net payment of duty	12.90
			Duty saving	1.76
			Duty saving as % CIF	1.68 %
	Item		**Duties**	
	Value Mecadeck when exported	30.38	14 %	4.25
I&F 2 %	Transport cost	0.61		
	Deck cost Singapore	30.98		
	FOB production cost	102.66		
I&F 2 %	Cost of I&F (insurance and freight)	2.05		
Incl. I&F	CIF VCR value	104.72	14 %	14.66
			Duty-drawback	4.25
			Net payable	10.41
			Duty saving as % CIF	4.25
	Saving by increased duty drawback			2.49
	Additional duty saving due to increase in deck duty			2.42 %

If the duty on that input (mecadeck) rises from 5.8 % to 14 %, the benefit also increases. The duty on the VCR is still 14.66, but the subtraction is 14 % × 30.38 = 4.25. The net payable duty is 10.41, resulting in a total duty payment of 9.9 % instead of 12.32 % payable when the duty on the deck was 5.8 %. As presented in the second last row of Table 6.4, the advantage is 2.42 %. The increase of duty from 5.8 % to 14 % results in an additional benefit of the outward processing regime of 2.70, as can concluded from Table 6.4, where I&F are costs of insurance and freight.

A formula reflecting the duty payable in the case of outward processing can present the benefits of outward processing. $\boldsymbol{D_O}$ is the duty amount payable, $\boldsymbol{t_j}$ is the tariff (14 %) on the final product (104.72), $\boldsymbol{i}$ is the percentage (2 %) of freight and insurance cost. $\boldsymbol{P_j}$ (102.66) is the free on board price of the finished product and $\boldsymbol{C_i}$ (30.38) is the free on board cost of the input exported and processed in a third country. The duty $\boldsymbol{t_i}$ is the duty on the input if treated as imported. Transport cost in the country of the component exporter and in the country of the finished product producer have been neglected.

$$D_O = t_j \times (1 + i) \times P_j - t_i \times C_i \tag{6.8}$$

The interest of Thomson in increase of a duty on mecadecks from 5.8 % to 14 % (or in reclassification resulting in the same) may also be concluded from the two Eq. 6.9 and 6.10 on duty payable in the case of the duty on mechanical decks of 5.8 % and 14 % respectively.

$$D_{O1} = 14\% \times (1 + 2\%) \times 104.72 - 5.8\% \times 30.38) = 12.90 \tag{6.9}$$

$$D_{O2} = 14\% \times (1 + 2\%) \times 104.72 - 14\% \times 30.38) = 10.41 \tag{6.10}$$

By the increase of the duty on mecadecks from 5.8 % to 14 %, the duty payable decreased from 2.49 % or by 2.4 %. In relation to total imports this is a considerable amount. The average price of a VCR was about 180. In cash the total advantage was about two million a year. Thomson wanted, of course, continuation of this higher duty on mecadecks for Singapore VCRs with decks from France. Other producers had lost their interest in mechanical decks duties and they did not want to fight for Thomson with its Singapore interests. When Japan tried to convince the Customs Cooperation Council (CCC) that mecadecks were not essentially VCRs, the European industry hardly reacted and did not defend interests of Thomson.

Chapter 7
Japan's Market Structure as International Trade Barrier

Abstract Scrutiny of Japan's market structure, with modifications also existent in Korea, results in the conclusion that it presents a serious obstruction to competition, both from abroad and from domestic newcomers. The economic system explains the behaviour of Japanese producers on foreign markets. Restrictions on competition were decisive for the infallibly strong position of Panasonic and ultimate victory of its video recorder system. The restrictions also resulted in exclusively Japanese trade flows of Japan with Asia. A computation of Customs Duty Equivalence is an effort to quantify the import barrier effect of the distribution system. The protective effect of the distribution system does not only affect foreign exporters but is also a barrier to domestic innovation. The effect of the system equals a prohibitive import tariff of about 40 %. It also has some disruptive effects on export markets. Additionally, this distribution causes a sclerotic economy, where small innovative initiatives are suffocated. This contributes to Japan's continuous economic depression.

7.1 In Search of Evidence

The conclusion at the end of Chap. 5 that member states would not support tariff manoeuvres and other protective devices, but that they would back anti-dumping on condition of sufficient evidence, presented a challenge. Evidence of dumping generally requires knowledge about the market of the dumping exporter and prices in that market. Fortunately, evidence on experience with the Japanese market was available. A Philips executive admitted he had been unsuccessful in Japan. He had made an analysis of causes of this failure. It was a courageous report. In the first place, he admitted to failing in Japan, and failure was a sin at Philips. He endangered not only his own career but also implicated his bosses in Japan who had moved to Philips' board of management. The report was immediately suppressed. However, Philips' Bureau of International Economic Relations used one copy for further analysis. The Bureau also used the study for information to the

M. van Marion, *International Trade Policy and European Industry*, Contributions to Economics, DOI 10.1007/978-3-319-00392-4_7,

European Commission and member states of the European Community. The description of trade practices and of the distribution made clear that Japan's non-tariff barriers were of a special nature and a grave impediment to imports. Various facts reported to the European Commission were grounds for an action in the framework of the General Agreement on Tariffs and Trade (GATT) Article XXIII by the European Community against Japan on Japan's impairment of its concessions made under the GATT.[1] As for the Japanese market, the Commission stated:

> *(iii) [T]he marked concentration and interlinking of the structure of production, finance and distribution in Japan, which makes it difficult for foreign suppliers to establish Japanese distribution channels.*

The European GATT Article XXIII action did not achieve tangible results. The Japanese underlined progress in the elimination and adjustment of technical barriers. Distribution barriers were not discussed. The representative of Chili remarked on this approach in the Council of GATT, in which the matter was discussed.[2] He remarked that the European Commission

> *...referred to one of its [GATT' s] objectives. This was unprecedented and he wondered, for example, whether his delegation, using the same rationale, could then ask for a working party to examine the EEC' s Common Agricultural Policy in the light of the objectives of the GATT. Such problems and precedents could arise if such loose terms for a working party were accepted.*

This was a perilous enough threat to stop action against Japan on the basis of Article XXIII.

It was wondered why Japanese prices were so high domestically and so low abroad where competitors had been destroyed. Further analysis of Japanese market mechanisms appeared necessary. What were causes of impenetrability of the Japanese markets and why did this have consequences for world trade?

7.2 Japan's Captive Distribution

Domestic prices in Japan appeared structurally higher than export prices. The difference was on the average about 30 %.[3] Major Japanese producers prided themselves in coherent and exclusive distribution networks. "*Business practices which place a high value on human relationships tend to raise entry costs. This*

[1] Article XXIII concerns nullification or impairment of concessions made in the past. The complaint was made by a communication, L/5479 dated 8 April 1983: Japan – Nullification or Impairment of the Benefits accruing to the EEC under the General Agreement and impediment to the attainment of GATT objectives.

[2] GATT C/M/167, 6 May 1983, Minutes of Meeting, Held in the Centre William Rappard on 20 April 1983.

[3] The 30 % figure, found for electronics, was also found in an investigation on behalf of the European car industry into dumping of cars from Japan that took place during the early 1990s. It appeared that the same applied to the passenger car industry.

Diagram 7.1 Structure of distribution in Japan

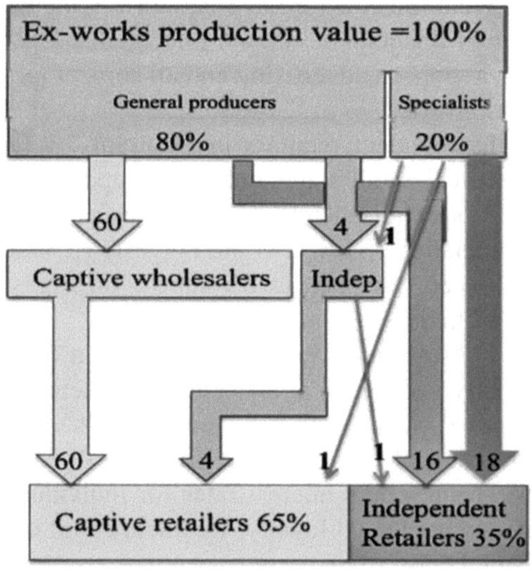

applies equally, however, to Japanese and foreign companies trying to enter the market".[4] This statement confirms the explanation for Philips' lack of success in Japan.[5] "*In defending the keiretsu shops, Matsushita vice-president Shoji Sakuma said the home appliance retail industry's practices are not exclusive because they are inherited sales methods established collectively by the Japanese industry.*"[6] Matsushita inherited these sales methods, however, from Matsushita, for this manufacturer created them in the 1960s: "*Capitalizing on its broad line of 5,000 products the company opened 25,000 retail outlets. With more than six times the outlets of rival Sony, the ubiquitous "National Shops" represented 40% of the appliance stores in Japan in the late 1960s. These not only provided assured sales volume, but also gave the company direct access to market trends and consumer reaction.*"[7] Diagram 7.1 presents the structure of Japanese distribution as it was, quantitatively, in the beginning of the 1990s and still exists in its structural form.[8]

---

[4] Japan Chamber of Commerce: "Distribution System and Market Access in Japan, 1989, for Promoting Better Mutual Understanding"; Tokyo: The Japan Chamber of Commerce and Industry; June 1989, p. 18.

[5] It was practically impossible to sell the idea that Philips was not successful in Japan. Various Philips executives claimed extraordinary accomplishment, often referring to the income from the joint venture with Matsushita. Former bosses of Philips Japan pretended to be extremely effective in the Japanese market, but only shavers appeared to be sold in Japan. This is explained in this chapter.

[6] The Japan Economic Journal, June 2 1990.

[7] Bartlett (2008), p. 8.

[8] Source: UNICE, External Relations Department: "Main Obstacles to Imports in Japan. Working Paper"; Brussels, February 1985. An updating has been composed from various marketing data, MITI statistics, miscellaneous newspaper articles, such as ACE, Vol. 11 No. 9; Electronic Industry Association of Japan Statistics. According to recent literature, the situation has not changed very much.

What the structure in Diagram 7.1 shows is created by cementation of distribution by financial ties (lower interest loans than obtainable for independent retailers), sales support, advertising and all sorts of rebates, and, finally threat with disruption of deliveries.

Independent retailers in Diagram 7.1 represent 35 % of total electronic and electrical retail trade turnover. Supermarkets represent 8 %, department stores 2 %, specialised retailers' purchasing organisations (Nippon Electric Big-stores Association (NEBA) is the biggest) 15 % and others 10 %. In this 35 %, the big producers' supplies have a share of 64 %, resulting in a total market share in sales to retail trade of 81 %.

Matsushita created 77 captive of in total 79 wholesalers, to which it assigned strictly geographical areas and commercial tasks.[9] One of the means of fostering captive loyalty is the financing mechanism. Bank loans to big companies in a grouping of companies, in the case of Matsushita, the Sumitomo group, tend to be cheaper than interest rates for individual small retailers. Low interest loans to trade guaranteed loyalty. Retailers could not possibly settle debts with reasonable bank loans.

Other means of fostering dependability were special rebate conditions, such as relatively high end-of-year bonuses. Matsushita's 77 Japanese wholesalers, later reduced to 31, supplied 25,000 Matsushita branded shops, exclusively selling Matsushita products, with the danger of discontinuation of credit and of supplies in case of sales of "hostile products". Matsushita had a capital share in its distributors, between 25 % and 100 %. The distributors' activities included those that are normally those of sales departments of a Western manufacturer. The tasks of the sales departments of the manufacturer in Japan were limited to assistance to distributors by advertising and general support, but did not include active sales. Part of the operational results of the manufacturers was obtained from the distributors' and retailers' profits. The distributors of professional products were similarly organised. Matsushita had, for instance, 59 related and exclusive distributors with geographical territories and special, but not normal and independent distribution, functions assigned in the professional sector such as printers, fax machines and copiers.[10] Matsushita Panasonic tried to protect this system by the prevention of low priced sales in alternative channels. Trade-in discounts, rebates granted for the return of old products, prevent price decay. Normally, imports of refurbished or second-hand products from third countries take place in a competitive market. Japanese producers denied that these trade-in costs should be taken as selling cost in the domestic market sales. It appears that 90 % of the discounts granted by Matsushita to its related professional products sales companies corresponded to the

[9] Matsushita Electric Industrial versus Council of Ministers, Case C104/90-1a, No. 362762, 1990, and Defence of the Council, 11 July 1990.

[10] Opinion of Mr. Advocate General Mischo delivered on 13 December 1990. – Matsushita Electric Industrial Co. Ltd and Matsushita Electric Trading Co. Ltd v Council of the European Communities. – Anti-dumping duties on plain paper photocopiers originating in Japan. – Case C-175/87, paragraph 9.

trading-in of used machines.[11] Such schemes create a system of price maintenance. In 2001, the Fair Trade Commission warned Matsushita against urging wholesalers and retailers not to sell its products to discount stores.[12] Matsushita received the warning, but did not pay attention.

Sony has tried to supplement its electronics product range with domestic appliances by cooperation with United States and European domestic appliances makers. The cooperation with Whirlpool, Oster Inc. (United States) and Robert Krups (Germany) was not successful. One of the causes of failure was imitation by Japanese competitors of the products launched by Sony.[13] "*Japanese manufacturers may not have any morals for international business*," Sony Trading president Tetsuro Yotsumoto stated. *"They are always imitating - it's a very bad point.*"[14] Akio Morita, Sony's president, blamed Western manufacturers, however.[15] Sharp started cooperation with Swedish Electrolux covering import of major domestic appliances,[16] and expressed the situation eloquently: "their [Sharp's] efforts to increase imports have met with limited success because there are few such products that Japanese consumers cannot buy from domestic companies."[17] The greatest problem for the cooperation was that the structure of the Japanese market requires higher speed of changes in models that is usual in the West. In order to give their captive trade more volume and income, some Japanese producers tried to import certain electrical household appliances as complement to their own product range. The example of Sony has been given.

Small producers of audio like Akai, Kenwood, Pioneer, TEAC, and Yamaha, small CTV and special lighting and domestic appliances producers supply to the independent specialist retailers, as do importers. Newcomers may distribute products not needing after-sales service, like halogen lamps, electric shavers, bread toasters and some other small domestic appliances, into the distribution line of department stores. As already indicated, electric shavers sold well as luxury items in department stores. Therefore, Braun and Philips shavers were present. Danish high-end manufacturer Bang & Olufsen found cooperation with a chain of luxury furniture shops for its audio equipment and colour television sets and

---

[11] Opinion of Mr. Advocate General Mischo, 13 December 1990, recital 23.

[12] Japan Times, Saturday, 30 June 2001.

[13] Wall Street Journal, 6 January 1982: "Imitators Thwart Sony Unit, Exporting Is Easier Than Importing in Japan": Sony imported Whirlpool refrigerators, small domestic appliances made by Oster Inc. (United States) and Robert Krups (Germany), but these products were then imitated. "'Japanese manufacturers may not have any morals for international business,' says Sony Trading president Tetsuro Yotsumoto. 'They are always imitating – it's a very bad point.'"

[14] Wall Street Journal, 6 January 1982: "Imitators Thwart Sony Unit, Exporting Is Easier Than Importing in Japan".

[15] Morita (1986, pp. 77–78).

[16] Wall Street Journal, 31 August 1989: "Electrolux Forms Alliance With Sharp to Sell in Japan". Electrolux's Mr. Johansson, who conceded that quick revenue was not expected, is quoted as saying: "This is an experiment in opening up the Japanese distribution system."

[17] Japan Economic Journal, 7 October 1989.

Table 7.1 Japanese distribution with captive retail shops

	Matsushita	Toshiba	Hitachi	Mitsubishi	Sharp	NEC	Sanyo	Sony
Number of captive retail shops	25,000	12,500	10,000	5,000	4,000	2,000	6,000	3,000
Domestic turnover billion Yen	8,617	7,651	8,067	5,580	1,447	5,313	1,587	1,189
Domestic sales' share in their turnover	63 %	71 %	63 %	71 %	38 %	66 %	38 %	31 %

Sources: Keizai Koho Center: "Japan 1988, an International Comparison", Tokyo, 1988; MITI Statistics; "Export Magazine", Economische Export Bevorderingsdienst, The Hague, 20 May 1989; Japan Economic Journal, 2 June 1990; Tokyo Business Today, September 1990, p. 27. Dodwell Marketing (1988); Nikkei News, 21 November 1990

Marantz, which was acquired by Philips, initially took charge of distribution. The Beo concept stores fit well in the Japanese system of exclusive trade. Although Nihon Keizai Koho Centre has heralded successful efforts to find alternative channels, such innovative sales are minimal and insignificant in volume. When after-sales-service is required, dedicated distribution is needed and access to that distribution appeared highly limited.

Japan's electrical appliances distribution structure has rendered tremendous protection to well established major producers. It is discriminatory towards newcomers, new and smaller producers in and exporters to Japan. The market share of the Japanese majors has been commensurate to their distribution networks, as Table 7.1 illustrates.[18] Of the producers with the accent on consumer products, Matsushita Panasonic, Sharp, Sanyo and Sony, the correlation between number of shops and domestic sales shares in total sales is 0.986. If the other four companies are included, the correlation drops to 0.378. The correlation of the domestic turnover of the four companies mainly in consumer electronics and their domestic turnover is 0.997, and when the others are included is 0.7.

Because they started their activities after the Pacific War and focused on consumer electronics instead of a broad range of electrical consumer appliances, efforts by Sony and Sanyo to build trade keiretsu of a size similar to the well-established majors had limited success. By the acquisition of Sanyo by Matsushita Panasonic in 2009, Panasonic consolidated its power position in Japan. It may be concluded that the biggest companies on the domestic market are also large-scale exporters. Although Matsushita or National Panasonic exported only 37 % of its turnover against Sony's 69 %, Panasonic's exports were almost twice the value of

[18] Keizai Koho Center: "Japan, An International Comparison", 1991. Nikkei News, 26 June 1990: "Toshiba Corp. overtook Sharp Corp. for second place in domestic colour television shipments in 1989, scoring 15 % against its rival's 14.5 %. This was attributed to Toshiba's success with large-screen TVs. Matsushita Electric Industrial Co. expanded its range of large screen TVs and retained top spot with 24 %. Domestic shipments of colour TV sets in 1989 numbered 9,485,000, down 0.2 % from previous year. At least in 1987." TV Digest, 13 July 1987. The television market was, according to the Japanese electronics and information industry association JEITA, in 2002 not much different (9.6 million units of cathode ray TV).

Sony's. A small presence in domestic retail trade and small home market shares imply greater reliance on export markets.

Companies specialising in audio products like companies as Pioneer, Crown, Kenwood, Yamaha and, in the past, Akai, as well as certain others (a broad range of firms like Accuphase, Denon, Luxman, Nakamichi, Onkyo or TEAC) are domestically of marginal importance and dependent on the small free part of the market and on exports. They are highly dependent on a high price level in the domestic market and the slightest head wind in export markets endangers their existence. The export price behaviour of the majors is essential for their survival. These kinds of relatively newcomer companies consider it easier to export than to market its products domestically.[19] A comparable situation seems to exist in the car sector.[20]

"Electronic firms aim to keep keiretsu", the Japan Economic Journal reported.[21]

> *Japanese home appliance manufacturers did not come to world-wide dominance by dint of innovative technology and high quality alone. They also got a big boost from a nurturing domestic market. For industry leader Matsushita Electric Industrial Co., for example, its 25% share in the domestic refrigerator market is supported by its 24,000 "National" shops that sell nothing but its National and Panasonic products. In exchange for special rebates and other remunerations, these keiretsu shop proprietors also promise to sell Matsushita goods at the manufacturer's suggested prices. Other leading manufacturers, such as Hitachi Ltd. and Toshiba Corp., maintain similar keiretsu distribution networks in the 6.25-trillion-yen home appliance market. Useful as the outlets have proved to be in ensuring domestic profit margins and market shares, they are now facing affronts from several quarters.*

Matsushita's 24–25 % market share reflected the number of 25,000 shops, which number was at its peak in 1960 at 40,000 with 106 sales companies and 210 distributors or wholesalers[22]; now the number of shops is about 19,000. Sony's share is higher due to a higher proportion of its sales via independent wholesalers and retailers. The correlation between number of captive shops of the companies in Table 7.2 and market share is 0.94 for CTV and 0.95 for VCR.

This system's protection results in a pecking order. Between 1990 and 2004, Matsushita's number of exclusive shops dropped to 19,000, which handle only 50 % of Matsushita's domestic turnover, while 30,000 stores handled 90 % after completion of the network in the 1950s. It would be suicide for Sony or Sharp to start a price fight against Matsushita for one product. If a price fight took place, it should be done for the sake of market share for the whole distribution group. The outcome would be highly uncertain for the weaker party and is inevitably self-destructive.

Japanese propaganda has tried to create disbelief about impenetrability of this market by presenting some success stories. Businessmen concealing their own

---

[19] Prestowitz (1988), p. 77. Relatively young companies like Sony and Sanyo also had a higher share of overseas production in total output, according to McMillan (1985), p. 36.

[20] Nester (1991), p. 109.

[21] Japan Economic Journal, 2 June 1990, reports a few thousand less than in Table 7.1.

[22] Shimotani (1995), p. 65.

Table 7.2 Domestic market share of Japanese major producers in consumer electronics

	Matsushita (%)	Toshiba (%)	Hitachi (%)	Sharp (%)	Sony (%)
CTV	24	15	11	15	11
VCR	25	11.5	13	11	8

failures in Japan or boasting success, as well as civil servants outside Japan, considering their own bureaucratic performance superior to their national businessmen and creating suspicion about others' laziness and inflexibility, readily share these disseminated ideas. Restrictive business practices as applied in Japan, copied by Korea, are forbidden in the United States and Europe. A few cases of exemptions from general anti-trust policy exist as, for instance, Bang & Olufsen. These exemptions have provided their distributors with special products and, due to the limited number of specialised outlets, are allowed to keep an eye on strict pricing policies. For outsiders, competitive pricing is often a sufficient condition for sales on the United States and European market. That is clearly different from Japanese. Foreigners hardly have a chance to launch a product in Japan. This applies also to Japanese newcomers. The result is a sclerotic economy. This issue is, however, not the scope of the present study.

A Japanese distributor does not differ much from a foreign distributor; both are dependent on purchases and sales of products for their livelihood. However, an industry outside Japan is generally not allowed to punish a distributor with non-delivery if it purchases and sells cheaper products from imports or sells below the domestic manufacturer's "recommended" or prescribed price minus a rebate permitted by the manufacturer. Disobedience and non-disciplinary behaviour threaten Japanese distributors' existence. The discontinuation of supply is the immediate retaliation. Sometimes such a manufacturer intervenes in the market and buys back products too cheaply sold. Manufacturers even mark their products with hidden codes for detection of unwelcome trade practices. Relative competitiveness with one or a few imported products is of no importance on the Japanese market. Products needing installation and after-sales service require handling through dedicated trade chains. These are not available unless the importer offers distributors some income guarantee. In Sect. 7.5 equivalence of this captive distribution system to a very high, even prohibitive tariff or a quantitative restriction will be demonstrated.

But some, like Higashi and Lauter (1987, p. 39), advise simply to accept such barriers that undo elimination of formal barriers in the GATT:

> *It is difficult to penetrate but equally for the Japanese government to change. However unusual and irritating this logic [of the system] may be, the distribution system is a reflection of the historical evolution of the Japanese society and economy. Consequently, it is erroneous to decry the system as a non-tariff barrier that must be speedily dismantled. Such demands are unrealistic and cannot be met within the foreseeable future, if ever. Instead of asking the Japanese government to intervene, foreign companies should learn to function within the system, and help change it from the inside as market conditions and consumer behaviour allow and promote changer over time.*

The thesis is that accepting the difficulty of a government to implement the obligations under liberalised trade is tantamount to acceptance of nullification of trade concessions under the GATT. Section 7.6 shows that the system is a trade barrier in which the tariff equivalence is substantially higher than any tariff applied by the United States or Europe. The statement of Higashi implies that it is unrealistic for Japan to introduce an anti-cartel policy similar to United States practice, and the law introduced in Europe by means of a treaty (EEC treaty of Rome). The authors have not recognised the impact of the Japanese system on export markets, which is the subject of Chap. 8.

7.3 Market Structure: Ancillary Suppliers

Similar to a structure of related and captive wholesalers and retailers at the front door of the factory from where final products are shipped, a galaxy of ancillary suppliers deliver just in time components and materials as inputs of the majors' manufacturing. Matsushita's pyramid-like structure of 340 subsidiary suppliers of mainly non-electronic parts, like wires, small metal parts, cabinets, etc., is an example.[23] For a main producer, the creation of a relation of monopsonist with these suppliers, which must be forced into a position of price takers (as if it were perfectly competitive market), is essential.

A system of dependent ancillary suppliers is not necessarily an advantage. Lifetime employment and a supply keiretsu are a burden in the slum. For the continuity of a business, it must maintain its activities. It is the responsibility of the major producer to keep this dependent party alive. That is why Japanese consumer electronics companies "Keep up with the Joneses". In order for major producers to fulfil the obligations of lifetime employment and to maintain their suppliers, which they often also finance, they produce a wider variety of products than United States and European producers. Forced by price competition, the latter are inclined to a higher degree of product specialisation. Those products that are complementary to a product range and not essential to the technological position are purchased from third parties.

7.4 Market Structure: Restriction of Competition

No industry's range is as multiproduct as Japan's consumer electrical producers. Very big producers, like Matsushita Panasonic, Toshiba, Hitachi and Sanyo, produce bread machines, rice cookers, lamps, vacuum cleaners, electric flat irons, refrigerators, washing machines, audio, television sets, VCRs and microwave

---

[23] Japan Economic Journal, 10 February 1990.

ovens, electric shavers, hair care sets, etc. If it were only their distribution chains that had to be loaded, this could also be done by imports from independent producers in third countries. In some, highly limited cases this has occurred. Toshiba, for instance, imported cheap, simple, low-end microwave ovens from Korea. Generally, however, the existence of the supply chain keiretsu or grouping requires that products be produced within Japan and are distributed in Toshiba's captive chains. Both captive suppliers and sellers have to be fed with production and products.

There are three serious consequences of the Japanese market structure:

- A Japanese market of, for instance, about ten million CTVs and seven million VCRs, was impenetrable to foreigners that were not a subsidiary of one of the majors in Japan.
- Producers like Matsushita, Toshiba and Hitachi had an advantage of undisrupted domestic sales of respectively 2.5 million, 1.5 and 1.1 million CTVs and of 1.75 million, 0.8 and 0.9 million VCRs sold at highly profitable prices. That is a fine starting point for exports.
- The combination of these factors has had a devastating effect on foreign markets, as Chap. 8 shows.

Japan's industry was able to conduct a Triad policy of selling in three main markets,[24] and others could not. In defence of Japan's liberal trade policy, Japan's authorities referred to rising imports of industrial products from Asia, but this increase clearly correlates to Japanese foreign direct investment. Correlation between Japanese overseas assembly units and the value of imports of CTVs in 1990 was 0.98, i.e. high. Japanese producers' low cost equipment assembled in South East Asia and China is distributed via their exclusive networks in Japan. In the springtime of 2011, Sony had to postpone the summer introduction of a new home theatre system assembled in Malaysia because supply of components from Japan was not stable.[25]

These imports are resold at high prices and profits in Japan. A corollary may be that exports from these subsidiaries to Europe and the United States are sold at dumped prices. The next chapter demonstrates the structurally compelling relation of the Japanese system and dumping from Japan. It is a perfect basis for exports of the major producers. But it may also imply that the products from the subsidiaries are dumped into Europe. In 1995, the imports of colour television sets from Asia exceeded domestic Japanese production[26]:

> *Until now Japanese manufacturers have supported domestic production by shifting production at their domestic plants to new wide-screen TV sets (with a vertical-horizontal screen ratio of 9:16). Since earlier this year, however, many manufacturers have turned to*

[24] Ohmae (1985).

[25] Asahi Shimbun, 20 April 2011: "Delayed electronics releases lead to bleak summer outlook".

[26] Information Bulletin No. 29, 25 August 1995, Japan Web, http://web-japan.org/trends95/29.html

Table 7.3 Foreign country's shares in CTV, VCR and DVD player imports into Japan (year 2000)

	CTV (%)	VCR (%)	DVD (%)
R Korea	5	5	17
China	29	25	53
Thailand	16	4	0
Singapore	3	0	1
Malaysia	48	53	29

overseas production and reimports even for these products, thereby giving an added spur to the import of color TVs.

Rather than from independent producers, television imports come from countries where the Japanese invested, as Table 7.3 shows for the year 2000.

Investments by Japanese major companies in the Republic of Korea are rare. Only 4 % of all 320 assembly sites established by Japanese electronics multinationals in South East and East Asia is situated in Korea.[27] It may be concluded from Table 7.3 that Japan's market is of a selectively closed nature. Microwave ovens offer a striking example of the situation. Japan and Korea were involved in an anti-dumping complaint in the middle of the 1980s. Philips prepared a complaint on behalf of CECED (Conseil Européen de la Construction d'Appareils (Électro-) Domestiques). There was insufficient awareness that the Koreans were so much more efficient than the Japanese that they apparently did not dump. It was assumed that the two countries did not differ much in efficiency, but Korea seemed to have been the most efficient producer. Table 7.4 compares cost of a Samsung magnetron oven with General Electric's (GE) oven.[28]

The Japanese dumped and sold at marginal cost but the Koreans, however, appeared more efficient. GE discussed supply of microwaves by Matsushita, but finally decided to purchase from Samsung. The purchases were very profitable to GE.[29] Matsushita declined a joint production with GE in the United States. It needed sales volume in the United States market for survival.[30] Nevertheless, as Graph 7.1 shows, the GE price in Table 7.4 and Japanese export prices did not differ very much. Korean prices were far below those of Japan. Korea's average import prices into the United States were, indeed, in accordance with the level of Table 7.4.

Japanese producers' ovens became competitive again by use of subsidiaries overseas. Japan shifted its low end production of cheap ovens to third countries and was able to compete, as Graph 7.1 shows.

A low interest and high Yen rate allowed and stimulated Japanese investments and assembly in Malaysia, China and Thailand. Although the products represented all sorts of models, Korean prices of all ranges remained below Malaysian level for products at the lower end of the range. Korea had a 99 % import market share of

[27] Marukawa (2004).

[28] Magaziner and Patinkin (1989).

[29] Magaziner and Patinking (2004), p. 65. See also Sect. 8.2 of Chap. 8 about the role of export volume.

[30] Magaziner and Patinking (2004), p. 64.

Table 7.4 Microwave oven cost comparison General Electric and Samsung

	Per microwave oven	
Cost category	GE cost	Samsung cost
Assembly labour	$8.00	$0.63
Overhead labour	$30.00	$0.73
Material handling	$4.00	$0.12
Line and central management	$10.00	$0.02
Cost of labour total	$52.00	$1.50
Cost of materials	$166.00	$153.50
Total	$218.00	$155.00

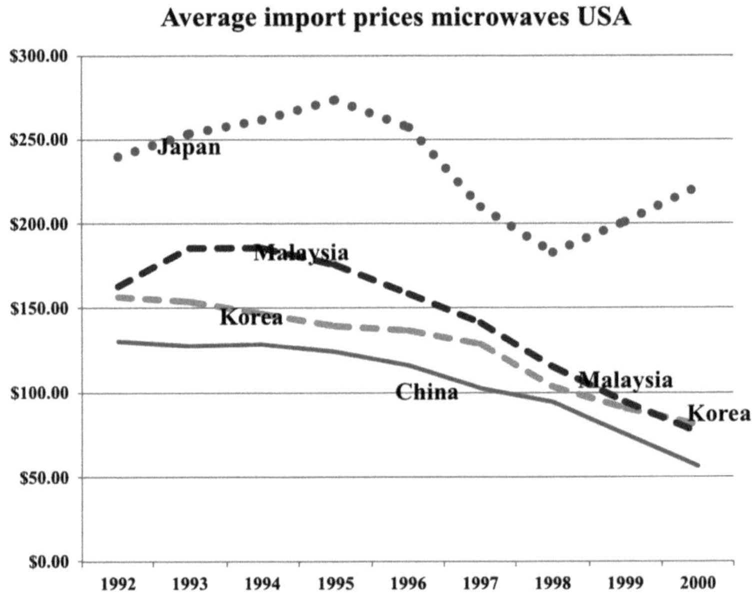

Graph 7.1 Korea's competitiveness in microwaves

microwave ovens in Japan in 1990, which reduced to 11 % by 2000. Imports from independent producers in Korea had been replaced by imports from subsidiaries in China, Malaysia, Singapore and Thailand. With the exception of Malaysia, all average import prices were higher than those from Korea.[31] In 2001, the situation was marked by even more biased purchasing. Although the average price of the Korean was 2 % lower than the Chinese equipment in 2002, imports from Korea had fallen by 17 % compared with the preceding year and imports from China had risen by 48 %. In 2008, imports from Korea into Japan stopped, even though the

[31] It is not well possible to judge whether the prices of Japanese supplies from subsidiaries in ASEAN countries are relatively cheap, because profits have to be made in Japan. Striking aspect of Japanese imports is that imports prices are extremely low compared with those from the same countries into the United States. It may be a matter of inter-company prices.

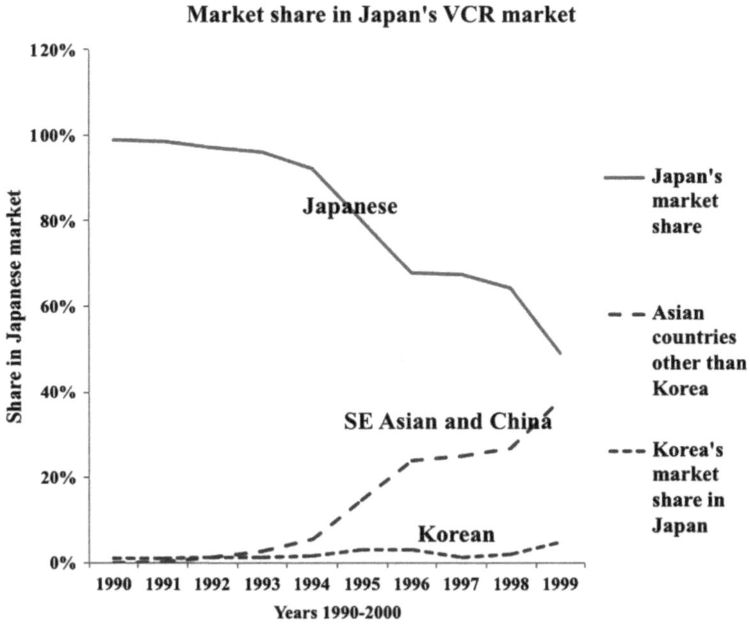

Graph 7.2 VCR market shares of Korean and Japanese and their "related" subsidiaries

price level of Korean microwaves was equal to or below the price level of Chinese imports. In 2008, the Korean price was 21 % below the Chinese average. The Japanese apparently preferred imports from their own subsidiaries.

A similar phenomenon was noticeable in VCR trade. The average import price of Korean VCRs in 1990 was 50 % of the Japanese export price. This did not imply that Korea would become major supplier of non-Japanese VCRs in Japan. Imports from Japan's "industrial colonies", subsidiaries in China and South East Asia, mirrored Japan's decline in production of VCRs. Independent imports from Korea did not obtain a place in the distribution in Japan (Graph 7.2).

From 1990 to 1993, the prices of Korean imports into Japan were below those of others. This was not a reason for Japanese importers to increase their imports of VCRs from Korea. They preferred imports from other Asian countries, i.e. from China, Malaysia, Thailand and Singapore, where they had their subsidiaries. Imports into Japan are strongly related to offshore production of Japanese producers, as is shown by the trends in domestic and offshore production.[32] Domestic production of colour television and VCRs showed a mirror image of production in third countries, as Graph 7.3, also derived from Electronic Industry Association of Japan (EIAJ) data, shows. The highly efficient Koreans did not have a chance in the Japanese market, their neighbours, whereas they outperformed their

[32] Electronics Industry Association of Japan (EIAJ) and trade statistics of the Ministry of Finance of Japan.

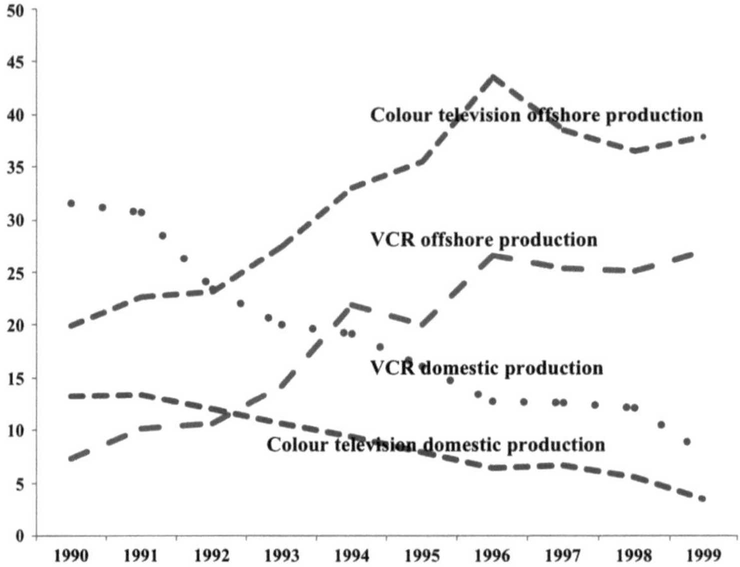

Graph 7.3 Relation between domestic and offshore production of Japanese firms (EIAJ)

Japanese competitors on foreign markets. This is also an explanation why the Koreans, with Samsung as a leading company, demonstrate such a formidable performance in electronics.

The correlation between a decrease in domestic Japanese production and set-up of production abroad and imports is significant. It was −0.90 for television and −0.94 for VCR. Free trade into Japan is selective. Graph 7.3 shows how rising imports of television sets and VCRs mirrored the decline of Japanese production of these items.

Japan is caught by its economic system in a way similar to the way the European Union has been ambushed by its agricultural system. Only outside pressure seems capable of changing it. Politicians outside Japan have neglected systemic differences between Japan and Western economies. The legal system in Japan happens to serve the big and strong.[33] Where the new entrepreneur has reasonably fair chances in the United States and Europe, the Japanese system supports vested interests. New companies, as have risen in the United States and Europe, are rare in Japan. The patents of newcomers are very often legally challenged by the majors or

[33] Van Wolferen (1989), describes these weird practices. It has resulted in an economy hampered by its own success. The big companies appear a brake on progress. Having become leading in various industry sectors, their ability to copy other producers has lost its effect, but their problem is how to innovate in an economy without the stimulus of competition with foreigners and without competition in Japanese market, where newcomers are crushed and, often, their innovations are appropriated by the big. Van Wolferen saw Japanese behaviour as a conspiracy. It is not. It is a Catch 22.

simply infringed. However, the subject here is market structure and dumping. The distribution system in Japan does not provide for expansion of sales turnover by price cuts. Price fighting endangers the system and the market parties. In a system in which competition is not in prices, competition must take another shape. In this case, competition is in a wide range of quickly changing product models and in product change. This was the cause of failure in cooperation between Sony and foreign household appliances manufacturers. Often innovations are merely an addition of features to existing equipment. If business developments are dissatisfactory and measures must be taken, the way is rather specific for the Japanese economy: "*strategic alliances are necessary to differentiate products and secure profits amid the rapid digitization of electronics devices*", as Sharp and Pioneer explain their tie-up.[34] Product differentiation is costly. Sales abroad reduce fixed costs.

Product differentiation, in which products are changed, is not identical to innovation. If innovation is measured in terms of the number of patents a country generates per million people, Japan considers itself number one in innovation. However, patenting an innovation can be a defensive practice. "*Because Japan's population is only 42 per cent of that of the U.S., its ratio of patents per million population is 3.5 times higher than the United States—and indeed the highest such ratio of all,*" is a claim by the Japanese Ministry of Economy, Trade and Industry (METI). This does not imply innovative power, but an inclination to apply for patents and to grant them. Registered patents of foreigners in Japan are 15 % and are 50 % of total registrations in the United States.[35]

7.5 Captive Distribution as a Import Barrier

The failures of Philips, successful in several countries, but unsuccessful in distribution in Japan, cannot exclusively be attributed to incompetence. The reason for a joint venture with Matsushita in the 1950s (Matsushita Electronics Corporation for active components, which had a 35 % minority share of Philips that it later sold to Matsushita) was that it was impossible to put Philips products on the Japanese market without a joint venture with a Japanese company, even in product fields in which Philips was superior.

A major effect of captive distribution or trade keiretsu is that market shares are hardly influenced by prices. The distribution system is rigid, and so are market shares for individual products. Some products may be highly successful and a company may temporarily gain a higher share in the "free market segment", such as Philips and Braun shavers. The "free" part consists of department stores and

[34] Japan Times, Friday, 21 September 2007: "Sharp and Pioneer to form alliance."

[35] Japan Patent Office, annual report 2011, published in Keizai Koho Center, "Japan 2012, an International Comparison".

specialised shops as in Akihabara and Nihon Bashi districts in Tokyo. Original equipment manufacturers (OEM) supplies, i.e. of products, with the brand name and sometimes with specifications suggested or demanded by the customer (trader or producer) are generally absent in Japan. In the United States and Europe, Japanese producers started mass sales by selling under the brand of mass distributors as customers and subsequently they introduced their equipment under their own brand. The exception was Sony, which only sold under its own brand. In Japan, this phenomenon of export sales by third parties to Japanese brands is unknown.

7.6 Captive Distribution: Customs Duty Equivalence

Captive trade implies that wholesalers and retailers do not decide on sales of a single product. They earn their income from a wide range of products from one single supplier rather from cheaper single products purchased from various producers. It they switch to competitors, a boycott is imminent. Therefore, wholesalers and retailers need sufficient turnover and a risk premium above the normal income that they obtain from the sales of products from their captive producer. Let us assume that an exporter can supply one product $\boldsymbol{m}$, for instance a CTV sets, far below the price of a Japanese television set. The introduction of $\boldsymbol{m}$ is not based on the price of that single television set, however, but on the ability of the exporter to provide an income to traders, i.e. by turnover plus a risk premium.

The trade barrier presented by the distribution keiretsu or oligopolistic cementation of the market can be expressed in a customs tariff equivalence. The tariff equivalence can be defined as the sum of costs incurred by the exporter because he must provide a full income plus some risk premium to traders rather than offer a profit by a single cheaper product. The tariff incidence equivalence is the sum of costs incurred for marketing of a full product range by which he provides traders with an income plus some risk premium for perilously abandoning a trade keiretsu. These additional costs imputed to the single more competitive export product can be considered the customs duty equivalence.

Before it is able to sell its product to the consumer, an exporter must at least respect normal wholesales and retail margins. The average wholesale margin is $\boldsymbol{w}$ and the average retail margin is $\boldsymbol{r}$; generally the percentages of the wholesale and average retail margin are about 5 % and 25 %, respectively, in the consumer electronics market. These percentages will be applied as initial margins. The price, $\boldsymbol{P_{KPK}}$, of the producer is expressed in the price of the retailer and the margins is:

$$P_{KPK} = \frac{P_{KR}}{(1+w).(1+r)} \tag{7.1}$$

Where $\boldsymbol{P_{KR}}$ is the retail price of a product distributed by a domestic retailer belonging to a captive distribution network, and $\boldsymbol{P_{KPK}}$ is the average price the Japanese (keiretsu) producer receives. Normally, an exporter should sell in a foreign market if one single product, for this instance television sets, ***m***, is sufficiently cheaper than television sets produced domestically. In order to attract purchases an exporter must normally grant a higher margin to wholesalers and retailers than the usual ***w*** (the 5 %) and ***r*** (25 %) for product ***m*** and other products in the market.[36] In the case of captive trade, the benefit from one product only is not sufficient. The exporter must offer an income in accordance with distribution practice: it must offer a standard range of products usual in these distribution channels. It must partly copy Sony's efforts to complement its product range and offer the full package of products normally traded.

Additional income must convince wholesale traders that defection is attractive, i.e. in an increase in wholesale margin ***w*** by $\boldsymbol{g_W}$. The wholesaler requires at least the same turnover as before, offering it an adequate covering of costs and normal income, and $\boldsymbol{g_W}$ comes in addition as premium on defection. Similarly, retail traders want some risk premium or loyalty bonus for defection from a domestic producer, whose normal retaliation consists of halting supplies and revoking credits. This risk premium, including financing costs, is $\boldsymbol{g_r}$ in addition to the turnover at prevailing price to retail trade. Therefore, the price $\boldsymbol{P_{FP}}$ received by the exporter is the retail price $\boldsymbol{P_{KR}}$ without the margins to trade, as keiretsu suppliers receive, and without the risk premiums $\boldsymbol{g_W}$ and $\boldsymbol{g_r}$:

$$P_{FP} = \frac{P_{KR}}{(1+g_c).(1+w).(1+g_W).(1+r).(1+g_r)} \tag{7.2}$$

The difference between domestic producers' and exporter's price is the loss in price attributable to the necessity to gain runaways from the keiretsu and to join the exporter's wholesale and retail group. Turnover has to be, at least, the same. The product composition of total market sales of consumer electronic products i (= 1..n) is assumed to be optimal and representing demand. The margins to trade are not additional costs, but defection allowances $\boldsymbol{g_W}$ and $\boldsymbol{g_r}$ are.

The exporter with ambitions on the Japanese market can offer product ***m***, CTV sets, at a substantially lower price, for instance at a price of ¥30,995, which is 75 % of the prevailing domestic Japanese price of ¥41,327. The exporter aims for a market share of 1 %. It must invest in brand awareness by advertising and pre-sale selling cost, like salesmen's cost for convincing wholesalers and retailers and consumers to switch to his products. Although such outlays may seem spectacular in amount, every exporter has to make such efforts and to spend certain amounts. This amount is a fixed amount $\boldsymbol{A_O}$, which is, as an assumption, one-fifth of the total sum of 1 % of the producer's value of the television sales proceeds at a share in the

[36] Distribution trade happens to apply just a certain per cent gross margin, irrespective of the product involved. Products with a high turnover are, of course, pushed by such a system.

market of 1 %. Traders want turnover for their wholesale company and retailers for their shops.

The exporter's loss of margin $\boldsymbol{L_F}$ is the annual lump sum investment $\boldsymbol{A_O}$ plus the additional margins to be given to consumers, retailers and wholesalers over the whole range of all products usually traded in the captive trade at the market share that must be obtained, in accordance with the market share $\boldsymbol{S_F}$ also applicable to the target market share for television sets. The initial investment, $\boldsymbol{A_O}$, however, is a normal outlay to be paid by any initial exporter wishing to bring products under own brand. However, if an exporter wants only to export television sets, there is no need for such investments. The rebate of 25 % to trade should normally be sufficient. The loss of margin can be expressed in terms of turnover of the captive retail keiretsu of all products in the sector, $\sum_{i=1}^{n} Q_{jK}.P_{iKR}$ at retail basis:

$$L_F = A_O + \frac{(1+g_c).(1+g_W).(1+g_r).S_F.\sum_{i=1}^{n} Q_{iK}.P_{iKR} - S_F.\sum_{i=1}^{n} Q_{iK}.P_{iKR}}{(1+g_c).(1+w).(1+g_W).(1+r).(1+g_r)} \tag{7.3}$$

The profitable quantity for the exporter of the exportable product, in this case television sets, is $\boldsymbol{Q_{Fm}}$, which represents a share of $\boldsymbol{S_{Fm}}$ in the Japanese market. The quantity sold by the foreigner of product $\boldsymbol{m}$ is $\boldsymbol{Q_{Fm}}$ or $\boldsymbol{S_{Fm}} \times \boldsymbol{Q_m}$. In order to sell $\boldsymbol{Q_{Fm}}$, the exporter will have to sell $\boldsymbol{i_{Fm}} \times \boldsymbol{Q_i}$ (i = 1..n) at the prevailing market prices $\boldsymbol{P_i}$, which in the case of retail prices are domestic Japanese producers' prices plus wholesale margin $\boldsymbol{m}$ plus retail margin $\boldsymbol{r}$. The total market turnover is at retail prices $\sum \boldsymbol{P_{iKR}}.\boldsymbol{Q_i}$. If the exporter was not be confronted with such a system it would just offer $\boldsymbol{Q_{Fm}} = \boldsymbol{S_{Fm}} \times \boldsymbol{Q_m} \times \boldsymbol{P_{Fm}}$, but now it has to offer $\boldsymbol{S_F} \times \boldsymbol{Q_i}$, where $\boldsymbol{S_F}$ equals $\boldsymbol{S_{Fm}}$, at prices $\boldsymbol{P_{iKR}}$ and receives as proceeds these retail prices minus the margins to trade and price reductions to consumers, which are in its case, higher as the consequence of the need to convince trade to defect from the trade keiretsu and to join his own chain.

On the basis of Eq. 7.3, a calculation of the tariff effect (***T***) of the captive trade Keiretsu may be expressed as a percentage of the television imports at the competitive price, $\boldsymbol{i_{Fm}} \times \boldsymbol{P_m}$, of the foreign exporter:

$$T = \frac{L_F}{i_{Fm}.Q_{Km}.P_{Km}} \tag{7.4}$$

The Japanese market of CTVs and other consumer electronics in Table 7.5 can serve as the start of the example. It is assumed that Table 7.5 represents the whole product package as a means of the existence of trade. It is assumed that the Japanese market of the product in question CTV, ***m***, is 9.8 million units and the average price ex-works (ex-works or price to trade) of a television set is ¥41,327. The exporter aims at an overall market share of 1 % only. The exporter must, therefore, sell 98,000 television sets. Because of the exporter's competitive edge in CTVs, while

Table 7.5 Market of consumer electronics in Japan in 2003 in million Yen (excl. tax)

Product	Ex-factory value (1)	Wholesale margin 5 % (2)	Value to shop (1) + (2) = (3)	Gross shop margin 25 % (4)	Retail value (3) + (4) = (5)
CTV	¥405,000	¥20,250	¥425,250	¥106,313	¥531,563
VCR	350,000	17,500	367,500	91,875	459,375
Stereo	228,245	11,412	239,657	59,914	299,572
Radio	62,555	3,128	65,683	16,421	82,103
Tape recorder	228,327	11,416	239,743	59,936	299,679
Car stereo	62,356	3,118	65,474	16,368	81,842
Other	589,253	29,463	618,716	154,679	773,394
Total	¥1,925,736	¥66,824	¥1,403,307	¥350,827	¥2,527,528

other products must be sold at least at the same price as the Japanese made products in the retail market minus a price rebate, these 98,000 units have to bear the burden of full market penetration of other products. If the import price of the exporter, after customs clearance, is 75 % of the selling price of CTVs of the domestic Japanese industry, this price is ¥30,995 instead of the domestic prevailing price of ¥41,327. Sales in the Japanese market are, according to an estimate based on data of the Japanese industry association, given in Table 7.5.[37] The value of trade in this Table 7.5 is a small part, only 30 %, of the amount reported by Japan Economic Journal, 2 June 1990 (see: footnote 22).

To offer the income to traders, the exporter to Japan must sell consumer electronics in a composition in accordance with the market, estimated in Table 7.5. If the exporter aims at a market share of 1 %, its retail turnover must be equal to ¥25,275 million, the retail turnover of the Japanese. However, the exporter must give a rebate to consumers. This rebate may vary. How much the rebate actually should be is not relevant for the principle at stake. The only question is what the level of protection is if rebates must be granted on all products in the standard marketable range of ¥25,275 million.

Wholesale and retail trade margins of $\boldsymbol{w} = 5\ \%$ and $\boldsymbol{r} = 25\ \%$, respectively, are basic margins. The right hand column of Table 7.5 gives the retail prices. These percentages of 5 % and 25 % are close to margins in reality both in Japan and in the European Community.[38] The income to European and United States traders is generally higher because of higher turnover per worker, partly attributable to stiff

[37] The estimate is derived from production figures from the EIAJ, presently the Japan Electronics and Information Technology Industry Association (JEITA) in 2003. The calculation is supported by trade statistics of Japan of the Ministry of Finance. The figures used are an example and the case does not depend on microscopic presentation of real figures.

[38] In Chap. 2, Sect. 2.2, Table 2.3 the example of VCR dumping, the Sanyo VTC G1 was given with a retail margin of 20 %. Twenty-five per cent is normally a more appropriate percentage, but it depends on the market situation of the product.

Table 7.6 Turnover at 1 % market share of exporter and 1 % rebate and bonuses (million Yen)

	Retail turnover	Sales to retail	To wholesale	Level of Japanese
Market share:	1%	By wholesale	By exporter	Market share: 1%
Rebate to consumer/retailer/ wholesaler	1%	1%		
Gross margin	25%	5%		
Product				
CTV	¥5,263	¥4,169	¥3,931	¥4,050
VCR	4,548	3,603	3,397	3,500
Stereo	2,966	2,349	2,215	2,282
Radio	813	644	607	626
Tape recorder	2,967	2,350	2,216	2,283
Car stereo	810	642	605	624
Other	7,657	6,065	5,719	5,893
Total	¥25,025	¥19,822	¥18,**691**	**¥19,257**

competition attributable to the independence of wholesalers and retailers in Europe and the United States, resulting in efficiency.

If the exporter is able to offer at ¥30,995 instead of the Japanese price of ¥41,327 average per set, this is insufficient. The exporter cannot limit its sales to televisions, but must sell a range of products with a brand, providing an income to trade that is dependent on it. Knowing that it would not be able to sell under the brand of a potential customer, the exporter must invest in brand awareness and initial sales cost, trying to win over wholesalers by a higher margin. A relatively small amount for initial advertising equal to 1 year of television sales at a market share of 1 % (98,000 units in a market of 9.8 million units) or an absolute amount of (¥30,995 × 98,000) / 5 = ¥608 million, the depreciation in 5 years of an amount equal to the turnover on imports of television sets in 1 year, is spent. The exporter has to offer consumers a lower price, for instance a rebate of 1 % (or more). It also has to guarantee the maverick wholesalers and retailers an additional margin, which is an increase in income to wholesalers' margin by, for instance, $\boldsymbol{g_W} = 1$ % or more, and the increase in retailers' margin by, for instance $\boldsymbol{g_R} = 1$% or more. Table 7.6 shows the issue if the exporter aims at 1 % market share and all products that must be available in the shops are supplied in the same product composition as the market demand:

The difference between the exporter's proceeds with these bonuses or higher margins to trade of 1 % only and the normal proceeds, incurred if it were an established producer in Japan, is between ¥19,257 million and ¥18,691 million. This difference amounts to ¥566 million. On top of the turnover on 98,000 CTVs at an average price of ¥30,995, this is a duty equivalent of 18.6 %, if the amount of the initial investment is not included. The amount plus one-fifth of total commercial investment in the launching of its products, which is ¥608 a year, has to be borne by the sales of television sets (98,000 units at the price of ¥30,995) or by ¥3,038

Table 7.7 The tariff effect of varying market shares and trade margins: price of and for fear

Marketing = ¥608 million	Market share (%)	Consumer price rebate (%)	Retail bonus (%)	Wholesale bonus (%)	Turnover of producers Keiretsu	Exporter	Duty effect (%)
Duty effect; no marketing	1	1	1	1	19,257	18,691	18.6
Duty effect with marketing	1	1	1	1	19,257	18,691	38.7
Duty effect with marketing	1	2	2	2	19,257	18,147	56.6
Duty effect with marketing	1	3	3	3	19,257	17,623	73.8
Duty effect with marketing	1	4	4	4	19,257	17,120	90.0
Duty effect with marketing	2	4	4	4	38,515	34,239	160.8

million. The additional burden of penetration of the market has the tariff equivalence of 39 %. If the bonuses are higher than 5 %, the tariff equivalence increases to 106 %. If the market share increases from 1 % to 2 %, the tariff effect, of course, decreases. In this case it becomes 29 %, which is still prohibitive as duty equivalence. If the rebate to consumers and the margins to trade is 2 % rather than 1 %, the duty effect becomes 57 % at 1 % market share. Table 7.7 presents some of the combinations of percentages market share and of rebates and bonuses:

Captive trade is evidently a barrier to trade, as the price of and for fear of trade for retaliation, with a phenomenal impact on ability to penetrate the market of Japan and, consequently, on pricing in Japan. The consequence of the system is high prices with the biggest company with the largest trade network as the price leader.

References

Bartlett CA (2008) Philips versus Matsushita: a new century a new round. Harvard Business School, Boston, Mass., Rev. January 17, 2008

Higashi C, Lauter GP (1987) The internationalization of the Japanese economy. Kluwer Academic, Boston

Magaziner I, Patinkin M (1989) The silent war: inside the global business battle shaping America's business future. Random House, New York

Magaziner I, Patinkin M (2004) Korea: winning with microwaves. In: Yin RK (ed) The case study anthology. Sage, Thousand Oaks

Marukawa T (2004) Towards a strategic realignment of production networks: Japanese electronics companies in China. In: Haak R, Tachiki DS (eds) Regional strategies in a global economy multinational corporations in East Asia. Iudicium Verlag, Munich

McMillan CJ (1985) The Japanese industrial system. Walter de Gruyter, Berlin

Morita A (1986) Made in Japan, Akio Morita and Sony. Dutton, New York

Nester WR (1991) Japanese industrial targeting: the neomercantilist path to economic superpower. Macmillan, Basingstoke

Ohmae K (1985) Triad power: the coming shape of global competition. The Free Press, New York

Prestowitz CV (1988) Trading places: how we allowed Japan to take the lead. Basic Books, New York

Shimotani M (1995) The formation of distribution Keiretsu: the case of Matsushita electric. Bus Hist 37(2):54–69

Van Wolferen K (1989) The enigma of Japanese power, people and politics in a powerless state. Alfred A. Knopf, New York

Chapter 8
Market Structure and Dumping

Abstract Differences between markets result in dumping. Two models are opposed in order to explain dumping from a cooperative oligopoly into a market of competitive oligopoly, the Bertrand versus Cournot model: price maintenance on one hand and volume of production increase on the other. Definitions of dumping in economic literature appear insufficient. Dumping appears an extremely rational phenomenon, resulting from market circumstances, in which producers have an often-disregarded active and influential role. It appears that dumping can add to profitability. It is also demonstrated that dumping is, in principle, predatory. The business case of Tosoh shows how a Japanese producer takes a high domestic price and a low export price as given fact. Feasibility calculations for a joint venture project have been based on assumption of completely different prices: a proposal for a joint venture with apparent objective of eliminating the Western competitor by offer of Original Equipment Manufacturers (OEM) supply of dumped magneto optical discs and by using the Westerner's technology.

8.1 Assumptions in Models of Dumping

After the analysis of the Japanese market and its restrictive nature, a second issue needs an answer. The issue is that restrictions on price competition can possibly generate devastative effects on export markets. Outcome of research on individual markets was that in electronics, selling prices in Japan were about 30 % higher than export prices. A further exploration for an explanation appeared inevitable.

The general assumption underlying economic models of dumping is that the nature of competition in two countries, the domestic market country and in the export market country, is either identical or that the restriction of competition in a domestic market does have no other consequence than that the export price is lower, if more competition on that export market prevails. It may also be a question of different demand characteristics. There may, according to most theories, be barriers to (re-) imports in the exporting country. The general assumption may in some cases

M. van Marion, *International Trade Policy and European Industry*,
Contributions to Economics, DOI 10.1007/978-3-319-00392-4_8,

be correct, but it is rather naïve to make it under all circumstances. If one country has a distribution system allowing restrictive practices, an assumption of equal market access is, to use an understatement, not appropriate. If a structure of captive distribution exists, such assumption makes the economic models appear void.[1] Denial of the differences between economic structures may have the advantage of elegant economic models, but the models have a limited explanatory value. The problem is that quantitative evidence on trade barriers, such as captive distribution, is rare and difficult to supply.[2] The existence of such trade has been found in anti–dumping cases, in which the structure of distribution was detected and the cost of sales and profits are known, but kept confidential in accordance with procedural rules. Japanese exporters and the Japanese government have, however, strongly criticised findings concerning Japanese distribution practices and measures based on them, and have challenged the veracity of data found and presented.

Therefore, this Chapter is an illustration of what occurs. To those who deny existence of captive distribution, which is even admitted by Japanese sources, this Chapter showing the consequences of such distribution on export pricing does not have much meaning, for it is not in accordance with the beliefs and assumptions. To others, it may offer a background or even an explanation.

8.2 Domestic Competition and Exports: Bertrand and Cournot Models

A Japanese producer is not able to sell domestically much more than his distribution reach allows. If it tries to sell more by price increases, this would have a devastative effect on the price edifice and be perilous. Before the takeover of Sanyo was finalised in 2009,[3] Panasonic's market share was 25–30 %, and commensurate to its distribution reach or trade keiretsu. Domestic competitors defend their distribution keiretsu by all means and in respect to the whole product range. Matsushita

[1] The majority of theory is based either on reciprocal access to markets with differing demand characteristics. Brander and Krugman (1983) present a theory of "reciprocal dumping", included in almost all their textbooks. Assumption of such access is, of course, justified as starting point for a model, but not if this assumption is imposed as a truth and as a guideline for trade policy. In the latter case, it becomes prejudice with a political connotation. Another assumption is that one country has some restrictions on competition and re-import, but there is not special stimulus for dumping.

[2] Various studies have been made, which use Japanese statistics on distribution, such as Maruyama (1993) and Rawwas et al. (2008), pp. 104–115. However, the details on the distribution system as presented in the previous Chapter are generally not accepted or neglected by economists, since these are data contradicting available aggregate and official data.

[3] In 2009, the white good (refrigerators and washing machines etc.) business of Sanyo was sold to the Chinese company Haier, which thought it obtained access to the Japanese market, but this access had the disadvantage of supply in Japan of only a few products. The distribution of Sanyo had already been incorporated into the Matsushita Panasonic keiretsu.

Panasonic, the biggest, will not endanger its relatively comfortable domestic position by price competition. Domestic competition takes shape mainly in short feature sequences, making products more attractive by product differentiation. A sufficient load of its distribution in terms of products and product range is key strategy. Exports can additionally enhance competitiveness. An expansion in volume by exports results in a decrease of the average cost of production. Consequently, exports are almost a compelling necessity.

Two economic models can be used to sketch situations of limited competition. Augustin Cournot pioneered and was first to present a case of a duopoly of two water producers in 1838. They had fixed cost only and, consequently, a straight marginal cost or supply line.[4] For maximisation of their profit, both producers vary their quantities produced and sold. If one producer does not produce at all, the other produces at its maximum. The opposite may also be the case. Bertrand critiqued this model in 1883. He postulated that in the case of a duopoly, competitors maximise profits by setting prices rather than quantities. The question is not whether one of these economists is more correct than the other. It is more useful to establish under which circumstances a model is suitable. First, the model most suitable as sketch of the domestic market in Japan, the Bertrand model, is presented. This model is depicted in Diagram 8.1.

The assumption in Bertrand's model in Diagram 8.1 is that two producers have equal cost functions. They both independently set a price. There are two logical minimum and maximum possibilities. The first is where the price is set at perfect competition level, i.e. where MC = P. Where marginal cost equals price is at the lowest extreme. Where marginal cost equals marginal revenue, the highest extreme at the monopoly price level is attained.

The explanation why a monopolist can set its quantity at the level where marginal cost equals marginal revenue and that this price is the highest is given in footnote 4 and in greater detail in Sect. 8.4. Line $\boldsymbol{R_1(P_2)}$ is the price–setting reaction ($\boldsymbol{R_1}$) by party 1 at each conjecture on the price–setting ($\boldsymbol{P_2}$) by party 2. If producer 2 puts its price at the level of his marginal cost $\boldsymbol{P_2 = MC}$, which is the price at the level of perfect competition, producer 1 must, in order to avoid losses of sales, also respect this price. If producer 2 sells at a price above marginal cost, producer 1 can sell at a slightly lower price, i.e. where price equals his marginal cost, $\boldsymbol{P_1 = MC}$, and gain all sales. If producer 2 sells at monopoly price, producer 1 may sell below monopoly price and gain all sales. If both players

[4] Marginal cost (**MC**) is the additional cost resulting from an additional unit product produced and sold. Marginal revenue (**MR**) is the additional turnover resulting from an additional unit product sold. If proceeds from one extra unit product sold is equal to the additional cost of that one unit product sold, no additional profit can be made, or additional profit is zero, and that means that the profit is at its maximum. When the demand (quantity demanded as relation to a price) is, for instance, $\boldsymbol{Q = 12\text{–}0.2.P}$ or $\boldsymbol{P = 60\text{–}5.Q}$, the turnover or revenue is $\boldsymbol{Q.P = 60.Q\text{–}5.Q^2}$. In the case of a monopolist, an increase in revenue due to a small increase in Q (or marginal revenue) is $\boldsymbol{MR = d(Q.P)/dQ = 60\text{–}10.Q}$. The quantity where marginal cost equals marginal revenue is lower than where marginal cost equals price. The resulting price is also lower than where $\boldsymbol{MC = P}$.

Diagram 8.1 The Bertrand duopolistic price competition model

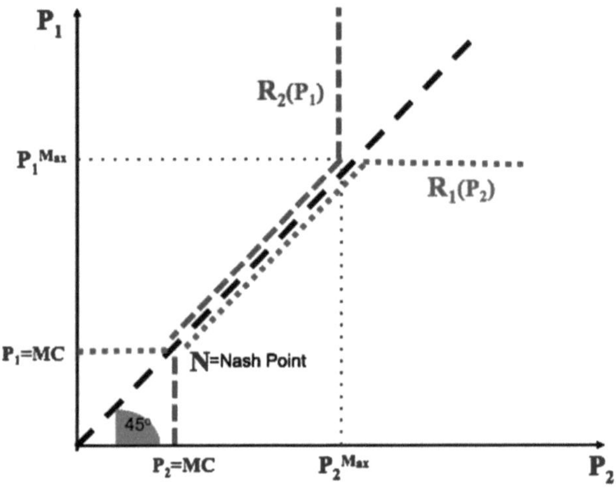

play at monopoly price, they share the sales equally, but as soon as one undercuts this price, he will get all sales, whereas the other loses all sales. According to general economic theory, normal competition results in the lowest and equilibrium price, i.e. where $MC = P_1 = P_2$. This point is called Nash equilibrium (*N*). The natural situation is a situation in which a player loses all sales if his price exceeds another's. In a market where all producers meet the quantitative boundary of their distribution system, however, price decreases do not work. In such a market, the monopoly price, the cooperative price, is dictated by the price of the biggest producer, which is perceived as having the most advantageous position in terms of cost of production. The cooperative equilibrium is the monopolistic price, which is the natural and respected price. This price level is where $P_1^{Max} = P_2^{Max}$. In Japan's distribution system, a cooperative or monopoly price is self–evident since the price leader, the biggest producer, sets it. More complex and stricter models may explain the situation, but the Bertrand model gives a reasonable sketch of what occurs in a market such as Japan's with its distribution borderlines.

Characteristic for Japan is that one producer, Matsushita Panasonic, has had a superior position in power and amplitude of distribution since the 1950s and, therefore, generally in cost curve resulting in a high, cooperative price in Diagram 8.1, which is P^{Max}, where the superscript ^{Max} stands for Matsushita and maximum. Japan is a characteristic phenomenon of a Bertrand cooperative price system, which is naturally respected. Clyde V. Prestowitz described meetings of Japanese electronics industry in Tokyo's Okura Hotel.[5] Indeed, the chapters on the VCR and CD cases indicate that such meetings were regularly held in Okura. In a convention of Japanese major producers in May 1983 in Tokyo Okura, a price

[5] Prestowitz (1988), presented it as if the Japanese were plotting the extermination of foreign competitors. Collusion may have taken place for the sake of peace keeping, but abroad all Japanese are fierce competitors among themselves and with others.

agreement on CD players with vice president of Philips' board Van der Klugt, Sony's president Akio Morita acted as an intermediary in negotiations with the Philips executive and the agreement was soon reached, although it has never been put into practice.

The Japanese presented an elaborate list of features and their values for minimum or target prices to be fixed in the framework of the VCR Weather Forecast or VRA, the voluntary restraint agreed with the European Community in March 1983. Such readiness and ease to settle minimum prices, based on commonly selected specifications, would have been impossible in Europe. Although it takes time, the assemblage of a list as such is not too difficult. Disagreement within the European industry would have been a decisive barrier to its adoption. Japanese had an accepted list, which implied an agreement on prices and features related to them, possibly favoured by natural price leader, Panasonic. These meetings in Okura have been called conspiratorial with the intention of elimination of foreign competitors. Conspiracy meetings aiming at the destruction of foreign competitors have probably been rare. Chapter 13 mentions one case, the television cameras systems, in which Japanese export conduct may have been a concerted action. Japanese firms' export policies normally appear to have been uncoordinated and the export drive has been relentless, both towards foreign and Japanese competitors abroad.

The opposite of the Bertrand model is that Japan's exports are volume oriented. If domestic price competition is suicidal and quantitative expansion on the domestic market unfeasible, an expansion of the volume of production and decrease of costs by exports is inevitable. It is a necessary condition for domestic competitiveness and profit, as admitted (see below) by Matsushita. The Cournot duopoly or oligopoly model comes into the fore. The exporting producer behaves as oligopolist or, in the model presented here, as duopolist in the export market, selling a volume deemed appropriate, but profitability on the export market is not essential. The expansion of volume and domestic profit are sufficient and crucial.

In Cournot's duopoly model, profit Π_i of each party (***i*** is either party 1 or party 2, i.e. the exporter and the firm producing in the country of import) is the result of setting a certain quantity in the market by each, while assuming a quantity set by the other. A party's own quantity and the conjectured quantity of the other result in a market price, which is the function of the quantities put onto the market by the two parties together, i.e. this price is determined by demand function $P(Q_1 + Q_2)$: price as a function of both quantities Q_1 and Q_2 sold by each party. The profit of each is the quantity sold by each firm times the price, which is determined by supply of the two together, minus cost of each of both producers. This is expressed in Eq. 8.1.

$$\Pi_i = Q_1 . P(Q_1 + Q_2) - C_i Q_1 \tag{8.1}$$

Each producer tries to maximise own profit independently by considering the production of the other as datum for his optimum quantity setting. Consequently, each producer maximises profit (Π in response to its own and to the other's quantities ($\boldsymbol{Q_1}$ and $\boldsymbol{Q_2}$ made and sold, respectively), and the cost underlying such

Diagram 8.2 Cournot reaction functions and reciprocal equilibrium

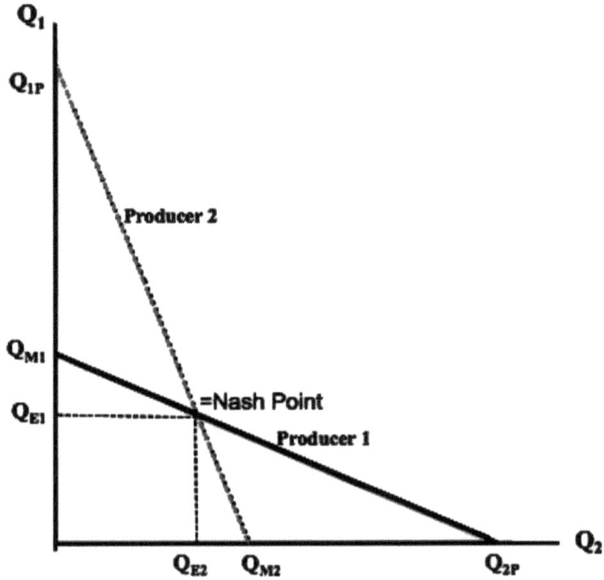

production C_i). Applying rules of partial differentiation, the formalisation of profit maximisation is expressed as:

$$\frac{\partial \Pi_i}{\partial Q_i} = \frac{\partial P(Q_1 + Q_2)}{\partial Q_i} . Q_i + P(Q_1 + Q_2) - \frac{\partial C_i(Q_i)}{\partial Q_i} = 0 \tag{8.2}$$

Diagram 8.2 depicts the reactions of both firms. If Producer 1 does not sell at all, Producer 2 sells a quantity Q_{M2} of Q_2. That is the maximum, monopolistic quantity, i.e. where ***MC*** = ***MR***. If Producer 1 produces 1 unit, the total market available to Producer 2 is the demand curve minus 1, in which it puts a quantity where ***MC*** = ***MR*** on the market. That market, first at Producer 1's zero production and subsequently at Producer's 1 unit and finally at 100 % of the market produced and sold by Producer 1, is the residual market remaining for Producer 2. At each step, it establishes the maximum profit and connected maximum in the residual market. When Producer 1 produces 100 % of the market, the residual market for Producer 2 is zero. That latter is at Producer 1's quantity level Q_{1P}. Similarly, the quantities of Producer 1 are derived from residual markets left to it by Producer 2. Line Q_{1P}–Q_{M2} reflect the processes of mutual reactions for Producer 2 and line Q_{2P}–Q_{M1} for Producer 1. At one point, Q_{E1}–Q_{E2}, is equilibrium, the Nash point. P_1 (=MC) – N = P_2 (=MC) – N in Diagram 8.1 is the equilibrium Nash point for the Bertrand model.

Table 8.1 Various outcomes of duopolistic behaviour compared (monopoly = 100)

Cases of duopolistic equilibriums	Price	Quantity	Sales	Average cost	Total cost	Profit
1 Monopolistic price formation (Bertrand's $\boldsymbol{P}^{MAX}$)[a]	100	100	100	92	92	108
2 Cournot (Nash equilibrium) (Q_{E1}, Q_{E2})	71	71	50	121	85	16
3 Bertrand (Nash minimum) ($P = MC$)	49	171	84	92	157	15

[a]The cooperative Bertrand price setting is the monopoly price where marginal revenue equals marginal cost

In order to give an impression of the levels of the cooperative equilibrium values and of the Cournot and Bertrand Nash equilibriums, Table 8.1 has been compiled.[6] For the sake of comparability, the index of quantities, prices and sales, each separately, at monopoly level have been put at 100.

Cooperative equilibrium (row 1 in Table 8.1) in the Bertrand model is, understandably, the most profitable solution. Under normal circumstances this would not be the equilibrium situation. The Japanese case is simple, however. One leading firm with the greatest market share is leading in cost effectiveness and in pricing, while the others do not put their position in the domestic market at risk. Why would a Japanese producer view the export market as mainly quantitatively determined, like in the Cournot case of Diagram 8.2 or row 2 in Table 8.1? In the first place, the foreign market is unknown to the exporter and its quantitative planning is the only certain instrument, provided that its price is below the existing foreign price, the price of his foreign competitors. The only question is whether the price is low enough to meet the quantitative target.[7] If it determines a quantity that should be exported, the only risk it runs is that his price is not low enough to sell that quantity. Another reason for quantitatively oriented exports is that the domestic cost position is improved or defended by sales abroad of an additional quantity. The additional quantity improves the cost per unit. The more each Japanese producer expands foreign sales, the more its profit at home is improved. This is especially the case when fixed cost is relatively high because Japanese production is capital intensive, which is due to artificially low interest rate, and labour is considered a fixed cost (see Sect. 8.10). Section 8.4 shows that dumping is advantageous, but first, attention is paid to the definition and explanation of dumping.

[6] The total demand function applied is $P = 60 - 2.5 \times Q$, the total cost used is $TC = 60 + Q^2$. That means that marginal cost is $MC = 2.Q$ and average cost is $AC = 60/Q + Q$.

[7] Arthur Karl, director of the Dutch Japan Trade Association DUJAT and former director of the Dutch company importing Mitsubishi cars, explained during a lunch in early 1993 that import plans of Mitsubishi cars into the Netherlands contained a quantitative target, whereas the price, to meet this target, was set in accordance with the quantitative target. This could be called Cournot behaviour.

8.3 Conflicting Market Perceptions

That export volume is essential for Japanese producers may be clear from the following anecdote. In 1982, General Electric (GE) contacted Matsushita regarding the formation of a joint venture in the United States for microwave oven production. Matsushita declined and the GE executive, Enders, was surprised. The Matsushita executive explained that Matsushita could not agree, because "*it would mean losing some of the American market to GE. In Japan, he explained, foreign market share is a key priority*." He continued, speaking to GE executive Enders:

> *'Enders–san', he said, 'you have to understand. In Japan it's our destiny to export. If we don't export we don't survive'.*[8]

He did not discuss the level of export prices. Export volume appeared undeniably essential to the profit of Matsushita, as it is to other Japanese producers, and price is of subordinate importance. The establishment of a domestic market keiretsu was a condition for such export steps, however. In 1992, as it would be repeated in 2002, the Japanese Fair Trade Commission concluded that companies operated unfair trading practices by proposing "estimated market prices" which large retailers were "requested" to adopt. Shimotani (1995) implicitly stated a link between domestic Bertrand cooperative keiretsu and export performance via Cournot:

> *Warnings to stop such practices were issued, but the fact that such a 'request' could be made by the large non-keiretsu retailers demonstrates both the tenacity and desperation of the distribution keiretsu networks. Before emerging as successful international competitors, Japanese companies had to establish themselves as indigenous concerns. The development of organisational capability in marketing was, like the more well-known instances of improved supply-side and production organisation, an important component of overall competitive achievement.*[9]

An alternative to the Cournot strategy on the export market is a non–cooperative Bertrand price where $\boldsymbol{P_1} = \boldsymbol{P}_2 = \boldsymbol{MC}$ in Diagram 8.1 or row 3 in Table 8.1, or even below that price. The strategy of a price lower than the Bertrand minimum duopoly equilibrium, i.e. below the perfect competition level, results in the exporter's acquisition of the total sales volume in the export market. If there are several exporters from the exporting country respecting the domestic Bertrand cooperative strategy, they may be inclined to adopt a Cournot policy, having in mind certain quantities they want to bring on the export market. It will be shown that this it is exactly the intention of major producers with a large trade keiretsu to improve their competitive stance by increase in volume.

The issue is also what the perception of competitors in the European, and the United States, which is not very different, of the market is. It happens to be a Bertrand view. At Philips, for instance, the "*market minus*" principle has been

[8] Magaziner and Patinking (2004, p. 64).

[9] Shimotani (1995, p. 69).

applied. The expectation on the market price in the future determined a normative cost of production and the quantity to be produced. The methodology is comparable with the dumping calculation of a Sanyo Betamax VCR in Table 2.3. From the expectable retail market price taxes, margins to trade and selling and distribution costs and profit are subtracted in order to obtain the necessary cost of manufacturing. This adjustment of production to the price is a Bertrand situation. It was certainly not a cooperative Bertrand situation. Discussions about price agreements or price accommodation were not only forbidden, they were useless. In fact, European industry moved continuously from an oligopolistic cooperative price, in the initial period of a product, when it was scarce, to the uncooperative price and, when dumped imports took place, even below the uncooperative price.

8.4 Dumping Defined and Explained

Dumping and anti–dumping policies arouse emotions. Outstanding authors on international economic relations limit their scrutiny of dumping to a rejection of anti–dumping policies, as for instance, Bhagwati, et al., even though they have their own idea about the nature of dumping[10]:

> *Finally, the most popular policy instrument of the protectionists today needs to be mentioned. This is the time–honored remedy against "unfair" trade: the tool of antidumping actions.*
>
> *In theory, the argument against dumping is that it is predatory, eliminating an efficient (domestic) producer and replacing it with an inefficient (foreign) producer.... Showing that such predatory pricing occurs would naturally be difficult, since the analyst would have to show that without governmental subsidy a firm should be able to price a more competitive firm out of the market by predatory pricing...*

Such a rejection of an ill described phenomenon rather than a definition, description or explanation of dumping shows emotions instead of analysis. The authors appear incorrectly informed, however. Dumping is not a question of government subsidy. Government subsidy is not the subject of dumping proceedings, but of countervailing actions. A government subsidy is a special category covered by special agreements and legislation. Dumping is another issue. Price discrimination, a lower export price than normal value, which is normally the domestic price of an exporter, not government intervention by financial support, is the essential characteristic of dumping. In the case of dumping, a price difference is attributable to producers' behaviour.

To Kindleberger (1973, p. 173) dumping is simply "*charging different prices in different markets*": two markets, assumed separated by a trade barrier preventing re–importation of a product of originating in the exporting country. Demand on the

[10] Bhagwati et al. (1983, p. 235).

export market is assumed more elastic than on the home market.[11] Since the exporter equates marginal cost and marginal revenue in respective markets, this results in a lower price in the country of import, which has a higher elasticity of demand than in the originating country. The definition creates the impression that markets are a datum to market parties and that dumping is caused by incidental difference in elasticities. Producers do apparently not play an active role in creation of market conditions and structures. Diverging demand elasticities are presented as natural phenomena.

Freeman (1971, pp. 165–168) similarly presents a model in which an exporter equates marginal cost and marginal revenue both on domestic and export market. Segmented markets are the first condition for dumping and the other one is that "*the two markets must have different demand elasticities.*" Such a view creates the impression that economic structures do not matter but that demand differs, and that competition policies do not matter. Demand is apparently understood to be the relevant factor, apart from market segmentation. The possibility has been neglected that dumping may take place in spite of equal demand elasticities. Demand elasticity in the export market may even be higher. What is decisive is whether the elasticity of marginal revenue in the country of the exporter is less than in the export market.

A definition by Helpman and Krugman (1989, p. 134) similarly seems to disregard some essentials of dumping: "*Dumping is simply price discrimination.*" They add: "*It takes place when the demand abroad is more elastic than the demand at home and arises only because of the monopolistic element in the home market.*" In case of a monopolistic element, demand does not appear to be the main issue. If there is a monopolistic element, marginal revenue is decisive. If a product is sold at a lower export price than in the domestic market, it may be that demand elasticity is identical, but that the level of competition results in different marginal revenue curves. If marginal revenue is higher in the domestic market than abroad, the producer maintains a higher price at home than abroad. A second issue Helpman and Krugman neglect is that exports may contribute to a different cost position of the exporter.

Helpman and Krugman (1989, p. 134) refer also to active behaviour of the exporter. On segments markets: "*Firms segment their markets, restricting deliveries to the domestic market in order to keep the price high while selling more aggressively abroad.*" Although the Japanese restriction was induced by distribution reach, the remark allows for an active role in shaping market conditions. In their phrasing, the authors introduce a psychological notion of "aggressiveness". They do not give a reason for aggressiveness or dumping and,

[11] Elasticity of demand is the percentage of demanded quantity in response to a percentage price decrease. If a company offers a product at a price decreased by 1 % and the quantity demanded (sold) increases by more than 1 % demand is elastic. If it decreases by less than 1 % demand is inelastic. The more elastic demand, the less steep the demand curve. Differences in demand elasticity result in different price levels, provided that supply conditions are the same.

therefore, do not offer an explanation for dumping. It is either chance (elasticity) or mood (aggressiveness).

The definitions presented above do not refer to injury caused by dumping. Pricing more "aggressively" should be understood as pricing in the export market below the domestic market price. A necessary condition for dumping, however, is that a producer in the import country demonstrates that dumping causes injury; the dumped product must, of course, be sold on the export market and unless the exporter is a monopolist on al markets, exports are always at the expense of others. Bhagwati et al. (1983) correctly, but unfortunately in the wrong context, point at the injury phenomenon. If market share, selling price level and profitability of an industry and other economic indicators do not have a relation with the fact of dumping, then price discrimination by an exporter between a higher domestic market and the export market, i.e. dumping, neither deserves attention nor measures against imports. If a company maintains high prices in the domestic market and has had a stable share in an export market for many years, its price discrimination has no relevance for analysis, or is at least, by virtue of international agreements, ineligible for trade actions.[12] Consequently, it is not vital that the export pricing is more aggressive, but that it causes injury. Dumping is neglected if the dumping margin is 2 % of the export price on the basis of CIF value. It is considered not to have inflicted injury if the market share is less than 3 %, unless it is more than 7 % in combination with other dumped imports. Therefore, a high price in the country of the origin of the exported goods and lower abroad is, in practice, not necessarily considered dumping.[13]

Economic theory and most countries' legislation primarily assume that products are dumped if the export price to the country of export is less than a comparable price for the like product as established, in the ordinary course of trade, for sales in the domestic market, i.e. in the exporting country, if the exporting country is a market economy.[14] In practice, however, dumping can also be established in cases of:

1. Sales in the domestic market of less than 5 % of export volume.
2. Sales below cost in the domestic market (and in the export market).
3. Sales made domestically, but in a country not considered a market economy (for instance China and Vietnam) and therefore and by definition, not made in the normal course of trade.

---

[12] World Trade Organisation Agreement on Implementation of Article VI of the General Agreement on Tariffs and Trade 1994 (the Anti–Dumping Agreement, ADA) Article 3 concerning the Determination of Injury defines the injury.

[13] Article 5.8 of the ADA lays down these thresholds of dumping and injury.

[14] Council Regulation (EC) No 384/96 of 22 December 1995 on protection against dumped imports from countries not members of the European Community No 384/96 on protection against dumped imports from countries not members of the European Community mentions this as definition, Article 1 Principles, paragraph 2.

These three cases cannot easily be described in terms of economic models and are, therefore, generally neglected or rejected as acceptable calculations of dumping. Economic models describing them are practically absent. In the practice of anti–dumping policy, normal value is, in such cases, not the domestic selling price but a constructed price, including General, Selling and Administrative costs and some profit. In the case of non-market economies (case 3 above), the normal value is the representative market price in a third domestic market, often called the analogue or reference market or surrogate country. In this Chapter, these three cases are omitted. In our case of the investigation of the Japanese situation, however, these deliberations are not important. However, in many recent anti-dumping cases, the question of market conformity has become highly relevant. Some of them are also dealt with in the present book.

8.5 Domestic Competition and: Dumped. Exports

The observation has been made that Japanese producers undercut prices of Western competitors on Western markets. Often this price undercutting has been conceived as a sign of superior competitiveness. Such a conclusion is based on the assumption that competition in the country of exports is stiffer than abroad or at least at an equal level. That is a circular argumentation and, therefore politically biased: Lower export prices are explained as manifestation of competitiveness because the export price is lower than the industry's prices of the importing economy. Convinced by Japanese propaganda or other statements rather than by facts, various authors assume that Japan's industry is more competitive than others and base their theories on such superior competitiveness.[15] If made without demonstration of correctness of assumptions, allegations on the reality of superior Japanese efficiency as a starting point for trade models are void and have a political nature, i.e. are based on bias.

Diagram 8.3, borrowed from Caves et al. (2007, p. 216), may clarify the case of dumping. Their presentation is criticised in a textbook by Krugman and Obstfeld (2006, p. 133) as being "*an extreme version of a wider class of situations in which firms have an incentive to sell exports for a lower price than the price they charge domestic customers*". The model is not as extreme as suggested and rather fits a model the criticising authors presented themselves. Diagram 8.3 shows the effects of restriction in domestic competition and unrestricted exports, which happen to represent dumping. Demand in two countries is, in this presentation of the case, identical and the competition circumstances are also identical, except the issue of market access. Two firms have a monopoly in their domestic market.

[15] Belderbos (1994), imputed superiority to Japanese competitiveness because, without much clarification, of the superior management methods of Japanese executives. Although it is essential to the relevance of his writings, he has never supplied any evidence on competitive superiority of Japanese firms, which, the author shows, is a myth.

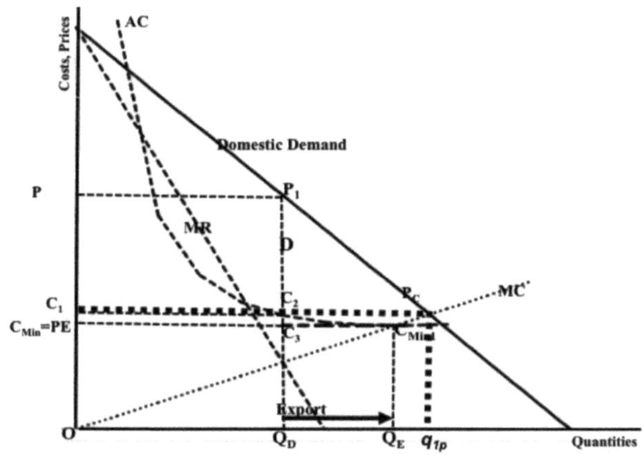

Diagram 8.3 Domestic and foreign demand; costs, profits and dumping margin

Market segmentation is assumed with asymmetrical access to markets. One market, country F (for Foreign) offers ample access to imports and the other, E for exporter, has barriers to access, by which it is a segmented market, for instance a "wholesale and retail keiretsu" discussed in previous Chapter.

The dumping producer in Diagram 8.3, because the producer in country E, the exporting country, is assumed to be involved in an anti–dumping procedure and henceforth sometimes a Defendant, is not a price taker, but restricts its sales volumes domestically as to maximise profits. This is the case of a producer with a distribution keiretsu, which impedes domestic sales beyond distribution reach. The producer is a monopolist in its distribution keiretsu. On the domestic market, it maximises income by adjusting sales volume in such a way that incremental income ***MR*** and incremental cost ***MC*** balance.[16] All quantities sold at and below this level are profitable and the quantity that equates ***MR*** with ***MC*** maximises profit, which is at quantity Q_D, a quantity resulting in the highest domestic profit without exports and in accordance with the quantity that can be absorbed by his market, the trade keiretsu. Demand for this quantity results in a corresponding price of ***P***, and the average cost of this quantity is C_1. The unit profit is ***P*** minus C_1. The total profit is the rectangle $P\ P_1\ C_2\ C_1$. In this case, the average cost at the quantity where $MR = MC$ is higher than the minimum average cost at $\mathbf{C_{min1}}$. The minimum average cost C_{Min} is obtained at quantity Q_E. Under conditions of perfect competition, the marginal cost equals the price. The quantity produced would be higher than OQ_E. The price would be slightly above C_1 and if the situation were the same in the country of export, there would not be the slightest reason for a producer of E to export. The point where ***MC*** intersects demand, i.e. the competitive price at point P_C in Diagram 8.3, which is the point of perfect competition, which in Diagram 8.1 is where $P_1 = P_2 = MC$, is the minimum equilibrium in the Bertrand model.

[16] The case can also be presented for an oligopoly, but it does not essentially change the argument. The oligopolist with a trade keiretsu is a monopolist within this keiretsu, which is its market.

The Defendant, the producer in E, starts exporting and knowing that its domestic price is an oligopolistic price of the Bertrand cooperative type, or monopolistic price as far as his captive trade network is concerned, it necessarily puts its price at a level below $\boldsymbol{P}$ or $\boldsymbol{P_1}$ in Diagram 8.3 or below the level of $\boldsymbol{P_1^{MAX}}$ and $\boldsymbol{P_2^{MAX}}$ in Diagram 8.1, the latter of which is the monopolistic or cooperative price. If the Defendant producer does not sell below this price, it may not expect to sell anything in country F. Equally, the Defendant necessarily puts the export price below the foreign competitor's price (and assuming that Complainant, producer in country F, has the same demand curve, marginal revenue and cost curve as the producer in E) and below its own domestic market price. Selling at a higher price in the domestic market than the export price in the ordinary course of trade is the general definition of dumping. Disregarding transport and insurance costs, the dumping margin is the normal value minus the export price, which is in Diagram 8.3 $\boldsymbol{P - PE}$ (or $\boldsymbol{P - C_{min}}$). Commonly, the dumping margin is expressed as percentage of CIF value. Injury is caused by a lower price, and resulting higher volume of sales, than the price quoted by producers in the country of import, of the Complainant.

The export price $\boldsymbol{PE}$, here at the level where average cost is minimal, i.e. where marginal cost equates average cost, contributes to Defendant's profit. Exports increase the quantity required for a decrease in average cost of production sold domestically. If that quantity produced, for both the domestic market and for export, is $\boldsymbol{Q_E}$, where $\boldsymbol{MC = AC}$, then the average cost is minimised. Defendant's profit on domestic sales increases from $\boldsymbol{P\,P_1\,C_2\,C_1}$ to $\boldsymbol{P\,P_1\,C_3\,C_{Min}}$. Defendant can export, of course, at such low prices and as much as can be offset by increase in profit incurred domestically due to the decrease of overall average cost, which in this case, is somewhere between $\boldsymbol{C_M}$ and $\boldsymbol{C_1}$. The exporter might also see the foreign market as an oligopoly market and it might sell on the export market either at or below the Bertrand uncooperative price $\boldsymbol{P_1 = P_2 = MC}$ in Diagram 8.1, or sell the Cournot equilibrium level quantity or above the Cournot equilibrium level (more than $\boldsymbol{Q_{E1}}$ in Diagram 8.2). There are, however, no a priori reasons to do so. If the cost is below $\boldsymbol{PE}$, there is still profit on exports in spite of dumping and an increase in profit on the domestic market due to the improvement of the cost position.

It is demonstrated here that dumping is advantageous to the dumper. It is not necessary that the dumper is selling at a loss, as some decision makers in Philips audio headquarters assumed. Intentions need not be "aggressive" – as suggested by Krugman and Obstfeld – or to monopolise markets by dumping, which is called "predatory dumping". Section 8.10 presents a business case from practice showing how even loss-making exports can improve profitability. It is also demonstrated that dumping in the case of producers with the same demand and cost curves is predatory by definition.

According to Krugman (1990, pp. 242–243) the model of Caves et al. in Diagram 8.3 omit to mention possible reasons for a Defendant to start dumping. Krugman makes three remarks on the Cave presentation:

> *The first is that while for simplicity it has been assumed that* **PE** [in Diagram 8.3, vM] *is given, this is not essential. What is important is that the firm perceives itself as facing a higher elasticity of demand on exports than on domestic sales. That is, dumping is simply international price discrimination.*

Second, the figure illustrates a case in which a price taking domestic firm would not export – in the usual sense of the term, the domestic industry has neither a comparative advantage nor a comparative disadvantage. Yet the firm does in fact export. Clearly we could have an industry that has at least some comparative disadvantage and yet dumps in the export market. In other words, dumping can make trade run "uphill" against conventional determinants of its direction.

Third, the difference between the domestic and foreign markets remains unexplained. Why should the domestic firm be a price setter at home, a price taker abroad (or more generally, face more elastic demand for exports)? We would like to have a model in which this asymmetry is derived, rather than built in by assumption. In the new I–O trade literature, such models have finally emerged.

It may be wondered why a firm would perceive itself as facing a higher elasticity of demand in the export market. Such an assumed perception does not add to explanation of dumping. Helpman and Krugman introduced *perceived marginal revenue* of exports. The issue, however, is what induced this perception. When marginal revenue is merely perceived, an exporter is, if real and perceived marginal revenue differ, a price taker of his exports. The perception of marginal revenue on the export market may be that it is more elastic because at home it is known to be inelastic. A firm starts exports for an increase in income and the mechanisms underlying the decision to export are relevant. The firm knows its own market and if restrictions on the domestic market result in a high price, it will inevitably have to quote a lower export price. The firm necessarily exports at a dumping price. The perception of a relatively elastic marginal revenue abroad and dumping is an implication of domestic restrictions, which induce certain perceptions of elasticity. If a cooperative Bertrand equilibrium exists in the domestic market, then an export market without an own trade keiretsu in the export market inevitably has a lower price level. Besides, an export volume contributes to the profitability of sales on the home market. We refer here again to the statement, previously quoted, by the Matsushita Panasonic director: "*foreign market share is a key priority*". The business case in Sect. 8.10 of Tosoh confirms this statement.

If an exporter wants to sell a certain volume, it has to accept or take a price that is lower than the price prevailing in F. The exporter is always price taker of a certain quantity it sells. That is the fate of initial exports. If the price is not lower than the existing price in F, the exporter does not sell. Additionally, any export at a price below the domestic level in E contributes to an increment of profit of the producer in E, provided that the firm in country E produced at a level where marginal cost is lower than the average cost before exportation commenced, i.e. to the left of the point where the quantity in Diagram 8.3 determines C_{MIN}. The exporter's perception of demand or elasticity of demand or of marginal revenue is less important than the perception of its increase in total revenue. The exporter increases income by exports and can take the foreign price for granted. Moreover, the criticism on Cave's presentation damages allegations by the authors themselves. Their own model of "reciprocal dumping" presents oligopolists in "Cournot" duopoly as price takers for given quantities put on the market. The Cournot model is a model of price takers, in which prices result from quantities put onto the market. Their criticism of Caves et al. appears void.

Most authors neglect the difference between elasticity of demand and elasticity of marginal revenue. The steeper a producer's marginal revenue compared with the demand curve, the higher the difference between the actual market price and the theoretical competitive price (in Diagram 8.3 between ***P*** and the price that is the result of ***MC* = *D*** or equality of marginal cost and demand, the line C_1–C). Monopolistic producers in a market without a policy tackling monopoly profits can perceive a less elastic domestic demand. More important, however, is that the revenue curve is less elastic than when policy surveillance on market conditions results in more competitive prices. Demand should not necessarily be different, but the marginal revenue should be. Helpman and Krugman (1989, p. 107) introduced this point. If economic grounds are not given for such a perception and if dumping did not offer any advantage, a statement on "*perception of marginal revenue*" on export markets does not make dumping much more understandable.

The final result of dumping, whether intended or not, is the elimination of the producer in the country of import. On the basis of Diagrams 8.3 and 8.4, dumping is predatory by definition. This implies, with some exceptions dealt with at a later stage, that as a general case, dumping is predatory dumping. "*Pricing below marginal costs*", as assumed by Tharakan (1997, p. 6), is not a necessary condition. He defines predatory dumping as dumping with the objective of eliminating the opponent in the export market, resulting in a monopoly. Pricing below marginal cost can occur, but it is certainly not a necessary condition. Diagram 8.4 demonstrates why dumping is predatory without Tharakan's conditions.

In Diagram 8.4 the exporter, Defendant, is inevitably a "Predator". The Defendant, which is a monopolistic or oligopolistic producer in country E, enjoys a profit on its domestic market due to market segmentation and domination of its part of the market. Exports increase the Defendant's profits by dumping, as shown in Diagram 8.3. Diagram 8.4 sketches the situation of the party facing dumped imports. Due to a price below the price $\boldsymbol{P_M}$ in country F, the Victim, producer in country F, must adjust. The Victim is never able to reach a point where **MC = AC,** or average cost at its lowest point. The demand for the Victim's products shifts to the left by the full volume of imports. The dumper or Predator can be considered price taker for this quantity.[17] The demand remaining for the Victim or Complainant is called residual demand, denoted as $\boldsymbol{D_R}$. Forced by this quantitative shift of demand to the residual demand, the Victim adjusts its quantity to the remaining most profitable level, which is where marginal cost equals his marginal revenue. This is the Cournot response in a market it considered a Bertrand model market. The quantity sold decreases from $\boldsymbol{Q_M}$ to $\boldsymbol{Q_R}$. Profit decreases for three reasons:

- The quantity sold has decreased.
- The selling price has decreased.
- The cost per unit has increased.

---

[17] Any price below the prevailing price in F is sufficient, provided that it is not below average cost of the Predator. Even a loss in market F is acceptable, provided that the increase in profit in E is not exceeded by the loss in F. Consequently, the Predator, formally, is a price–taker.

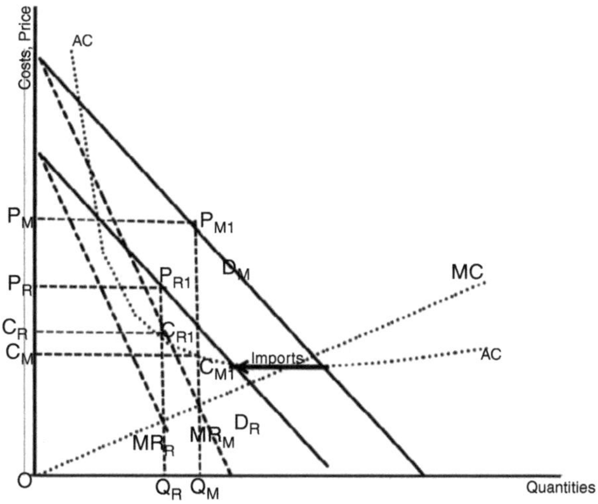

Diagram 8.4 The Predator's victim and its reactions

Consequently, profit decreases from the assumed initial monopoly profit in Diagram 8.4 from rectangle $\boldsymbol{P_M\ P_{M1}\ C_{M1}\ C_M}$ to $\boldsymbol{P_R\ P_{R1}\ C_{R1}\ C_R}$. The only option open to the Victim is dumping in country E, in the way Brander and Krugman (1983) have suggested, i.e. by reciprocal dumping. In this case, asymmetry in market access prevents reciprocal dumping and avoidance of predation.

The margin of dumping in Diagram 8.3 is $\boldsymbol{P-PE}$ (or $\boldsymbol{P-C_{min}}$). The Commission of the European Community uses the difference between the weighted average selling price of the Complainant to the first independent customer and the export price of the Defendant on CIF basis plus a trade margin between CIF value and the same trade level as Complainant's sales to independent trade as measuring rod for injury (see Chap. 16, Sect. 16.13). In Diagram 8.4, this measure of injury, the undercutting, is the difference between $\boldsymbol{P_M}$ and $\boldsymbol{P_R}$. As is clear from Diagram 8.4, the injury exceeds the difference between these two. The injury is more than the undercutting: the loss of volume results in a cost increase, which is not taken away by a duty at the level of $\boldsymbol{P_M-P_R}$.

The Complainant is trapped. The exporter, Predator by definition, may increase its export price above the minimum of its average cost, may earn additional profit and increase its quantity for exports that it sells below the average cost of the Victim, which is higher than the Predator's average cost. Finally, predation leads to a monopoly of one player in two markets. The Predator conquers the market at prices that increase its profit and not, necessarily, below marginal or average cost. Often it is assumed that the predator intends to establish a monopoly to reap the benefits of a monopoly. Such vicious intentions are rarely the basis of dumping and if they are, such intentions are not verifiable.

Competition authorities are entitled to investigate abuse of market domination, but not whether this is the result of predatory dumping. Anti–dumping proceedings do not, and are not supposed to, investigate the intentions of dumping parties and in some case, allegations of predatory behaviour are profoundly false.[18] The case of predatory dumping might extend over such a long duration that new, more competitive, but possibly also dumping parties enter the market. By this fact, the monopoly of the first predatory dumper is not established. This was the case in video recorders, where Korean producers outmanoeuvred Japanese competitors and in television, where the Koreans overtook the Japanese and the Chinese even sold below cost and Turkish producers established an oligopoly The Japanese did not attain the stage of reaping the monopoly or oligopoly benefits from predation, but on the road to this phase, they reaped benefits from dumping both on the domestic market and possibly abroad.

8.6 Costs and Benefits of Dumping and Anti–Dumping Measures

Calculations of cost to consumers in the country of import of anti–dumping duties on dumped products usually report such cost as $\boldsymbol{P_M} \times \boldsymbol{Q_M} - \boldsymbol{P_R} \times \boldsymbol{Q_R}$.[19] As long as damages caused by dumping in terms of losses inflicted to employment and skills are unknown and the price of payment for exports for dumped imports is unknown, economists dealing with these issues should show restraint in their criticism. Workers can attribute a higher value to employment than to low video recorder prices. This preference cannot be compared with consumer preferences for cheap video recorders. Worker preferences are, therefore, generally discarded as irrelevant. The injury to consumers from products exported for payment of dumped imports is also extremely difficult to measure. It is even an illusion that acceptable cost calculations can be made. Most efforts to show the disadvantages of measures against dumping are based on the assumption that dumping in fact represents subsidies from the dumper to consumers in the importing economy. Some authors try to prove on basis of this assumption that anti–dumping measures are injurious to consumers. Dumping also brings about costs, even if there are no anti–dumping duties. Among these costs is, in the first place, the increase in costs and possibly losses of the domestic producer in the import country. Other costs, i.e. those for exports as payment for dumped imports, are less spectacular. They represent

[18] The European Council of Ministers refers in "*Recordable Compact Disks from Taiwan*", Council Regulation (EC) 1050/2002 of 13 June 2002, recital 31, to "*a very predatory form of dumping*". These sales below cost of production are apparently considered "predatory". Sales below cost are, however, not necessarily a sign of predation. In the proceeding sampling of exporters had to be applied, which by definition, implies many competitors in the domestic market and therefore, improbability of predation.

[19] Blonigen and Prusa (2003) give an extensive list with literature on the subject.

exports necessary as payment for import of the dumped product, considered a product that subsidises the consumer in the importing country. This issue is discussed in this Section.

The issue is illustrated here. Two products Q_1 and Q_2 are produced in variable quantities in two economies of the same size, E and F. It is assumed that both countries have the same stock of capital and labour, which are fully employed in perfectly competitive markets. Production technology is identical. At full utilisation of both economies' capacity, an increase in production of product Q_1 must necessarily result in a decrease in production of product Q_2 and vice versa. For the manufacturing of product Q_1, varying units of capital, K_1, and labour, L_1, are used as variable inputs resulting in varying quantities of Q_1 of product 1 (as in Eq. 8.3).

$$Q_1 = {K_1}^{\alpha}.{L_1}^{1-\alpha} \tag{8.3}$$

This applies both to Country **E** and **F**. This is a so–called homogeneous production function of the Cobb–Douglas form (where $\alpha + (1 - \alpha) = 1$).[20] For the production of the product Q_2 another composition of capital and labour is required:

$$Q_2 = {K_2}^{\beta}.{L_2}^{1-\beta} \tag{8.4}$$

However, since the economy only has a given level of fully utilised capital K_o and of completely employed labour L_o, the production function of Q_2 can be expressed in terms of K_1 and given K_o and L_1 and given L_o: Indirectly via K and L Eq. 8.4 is expressed in terms of 8.3, resulting in 8.5 below:

$$Q_2 = (K_0 - K_1)^{\beta}.(L_0 - L_1)^{1-\beta} \tag{8.5}$$

Consequently, production of Q_1 and Q_2 are inversely related. With each variation of K_1 and L_1 a production quantity of Q_1 and consequently, of Q_2 is obtained. Final quantities of Q_1 and Q_2 are determined by demand and by the production functions presented above. It is assumed that demand in countries E and F is identical. The curve representing all possible combinations of Q_1 and Q_2 is given in Diagram 8.5 as ***PPF***. The ***PPF*** curve is the possible combination of goods produced if all factors of production are used under condition of perfect competition. The technical derivation of the curve representing a locus of combinations of Q_1 and Q_2 at full use of the production factors is disregarded. ***PPF*** represents production combinations of Q_1 and Q_2, while both $K_1 + K_2 = K_o$ and $L_1 + L_2 = L_o$ and $dK_1/dL_1 = dK_2/dL_1$ (a small change in the relationship between capital and labour in production of the two products).

[20] The reader should not panic. A homogenous production function means that there are constant returns to scale. If factors of production capital and labour (K and L) are both doubled, the product doubles.

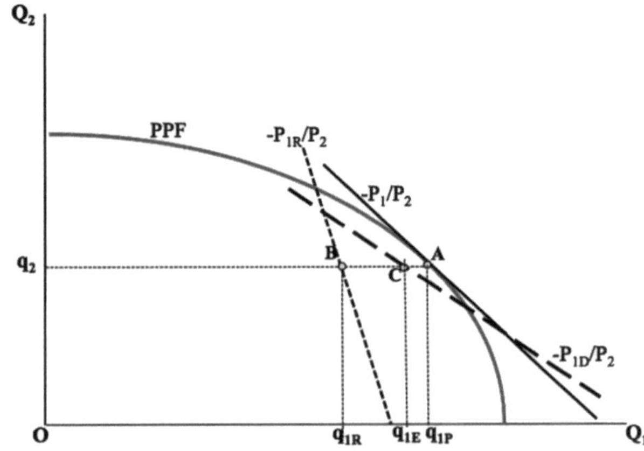

Diagram 8.5 Production possibility frontier, restriction of competition and dumping

The situation changes when a restriction of competition in product Q_1 takes place. The restriction of competition in Q_1, i.e. in trade and consequently, in production, in economy **E** implies that one or more of the production factors, capital and labour, are not fully utilised for the production of Q_1 in the domestic market. More capital and labour for the production of Q_2 would normally become available in this situation than in the case of perfect competition in production of Q_1.

The restriction of competition for product Q_1 results in relative overproduction in economy **E** of the other product Q_2, for which more capital and labour have become available. The price of Q_2 in economy E becomes lower than in the case of perfect competition on all markets, as still is the situation in economy F. If there were no trade barriers, economy **E** would export product Q_2 to economy **F** and, because the price level is relatively higher, economy **E** would import Q_1 from economy **F**. The imports would nullify the restriction within economy **E**. If, however, economy **E** has a barrier to wholesale and retail trade, it does not import Q_1. Instead, it exports, in accordance with Diagram 8.3, the product Q_1 and it imports Q_2, which is the payment for Q_1. Economy **F** must export a quantity of – relatively cheaper – Q_2 to economy **E** as payment for the imported dumped product Q_1 dumped by economy **E**. The consumers of Q_2 in economy **F** are disadvantaged.

Diagram 8.5 illustrates the case. It was assumed that both economies have the same size and same preferences, and produce under the condition of perfect competition, i.e. production is at PPF, which is the transformation curve or production possibility frontier, i.e. the locus of combinations of products Q_1 and Q_2 produced by means of production at full employment, i.e. full use of capital and labour.

Let demand in **E** and **F** determine production at point **A** on the ***PPF***. The line (−) (P_1/P_2) represents the relation between the prices of Q_1 and Q_2 at point **A**, where the level of consumption of both consumers of **E** and **F** is: Oq_{1P} of Q_1 and Oq_2 of Q_2. Restricting competition in **E** brings about a restriction of the volume of production of Q_1 from q_{1P} to q_{1R}. Since it is normally assumed that all factors of production are used, the factors of production K and L set free by the production restriction of

$\boldsymbol{Q_1}$ would normally move to the industry of product $\boldsymbol{Q_2}$, resulting in an increase of $\boldsymbol{Q_2}$ and an increase in the price relation between $\boldsymbol{Q_1}$ and $\boldsymbol{Q_2}$. Diagram 8.3 shows, however, that capacity remains for the production of $\boldsymbol{Q_1}$, the quantity $\boldsymbol{Oq_{1E} - Oq_{1R}}$ of which is exported to **F**. Therefore, the level of production of economy **E** that would have moved from **A** to **B**, for instance (with less of $\boldsymbol{Q_1}$ and more of $\boldsymbol{Q_2}$ under the assumption of full allocation of means of production), moves to **C**. There are now two price relations between $\boldsymbol{Q_1}$ and $\boldsymbol{Q_2}$. One is $(-)(\boldsymbol{P_{1R}/P_2})$, which is steeper than $(-)(\boldsymbol{P_1/P_2})$. That price relationship is the domestic price relation in **E**. The other price relationship is between the dumping export price of $\boldsymbol{Q_1}$ and the price of $\boldsymbol{Q_2}$. This price relationship is $(-)\boldsymbol{P_{1D}/P_2}$. **E**'s production, at level ***C***, is still less than the efficient production on the border of the ***PPF***.

Exports of $\boldsymbol{Q_1}$ at the level of $\boldsymbol{Oq_{1P} - Oq_{1R}}$ take place from **E** to **F**. The corresponding production point at **A** is below efficient use of means of production, i.e. below ***PPF***. If **E** stretches its exports to the minimum of average cost, a quasi–perfect competition situation is created. Point **A** will be reached. The price formation is not a single line $(-)(\boldsymbol{P_1/P_2})$, but in violation of the usual assumptions of perfect competition there are two price relations, one a domestic price relation of **E**, $(-)(\boldsymbol{P_{1R}/P_2})$, and an export price relation of **E**, $(-)(\boldsymbol{P_{1D}/P_2})$, where $\boldsymbol{P_{1D}/P_2}$ (domestic restricted competition) $> \boldsymbol{P_1/P_2}$ (perfectly competitive) $> \boldsymbol{P_{1D}/P_2}$ (export). The allegation that dumping is a subsidy to the consumer of the dumped product in economy **F** and is advantageous to economy **F** is an illusion. The logic of that allegation is that anti-dumping measures take benefits away from consumers in **F** and damage economy **F**. Consumers of $\boldsymbol{Q_1}$ in economy **F** are understood to be better off in the country of importation, in economy **F**. However, consumers of $\boldsymbol{Q_1}$ in economy **E** and consumers of $\boldsymbol{Q_2}$ in Economy **F** are both worse off. The value of imports into economy **F** is necessarily balanced by exports of $\boldsymbol{Q_2}$ by economy **F** as payment of imports of dumped $\boldsymbol{Q_1}$. The consumers of economy **E** subsidise the consumers of $\boldsymbol{Q_1}$ in **F** because of the distortion created in economy **E**. The shift from $\boldsymbol{q_{1p}}$ to $\boldsymbol{q_{1R}}$ is paid for by consumers of $\boldsymbol{Q_1}$ in economy **E**. Consumers of $\boldsymbol{Q_2}$ in economy **F** pay for the imports of $\boldsymbol{Q_1}$. Thereby the arguments in defence of dumping as a subsidy by economy **E** to the consumers in economy **F** appear void. Are economists allowed to decide whether economy **F** is better off if this economy does not counter the dumping? Whether the low price of the dumped products $\boldsymbol{Q_1}$ should be balanced in **F** by consumers of $\boldsymbol{Q_2}$ by their payment in terms of higher $\boldsymbol{Q_2}$ prices for the dumping of $\boldsymbol{Q_1}$ is a political decision. Allegations by some economists on the undesirability of anti-dumping measures appear statements by politicians disguised as economists. The final equilibrium in the exchange of the two products depends on price relations and consumer preferences. Quantities of exports are indicated as $\boldsymbol{Oq_{1ED} - Oq_{1R}}$. An essential point here is whether politicians are aware that indirect subsidies take place. Since the volume and total value of imports of $\boldsymbol{Q_1}$ is known when an anti–dumping proceeding takes place, but the value of $\boldsymbol{Q_2}$ escapes attention, there is an inclination to consider the measures against dumping of $\boldsymbol{Q_1}$ to be bad.

Apart from paying a higher price for $\boldsymbol{Q_2}$, economy **F** must also adjust by redundancies caused by dumping of $\boldsymbol{Q_1}$ and invest in additional production in sector $\boldsymbol{Q_2}$.

Dumping implies a transfer of income to producers of Q_1 in economy **E**. All costs of adjustment are borne by economy **F**. It is often assumed that markets of inputs, labour and capital are completely flexible and costs of adjustment are nil. They are clearly not zero. Costs of adjustment might in the case of dumping be borne by the economy that is more efficient. One economy has to adjust because of the inefficiencies and lack of competition policy in another economy. An anti–dumping duty eliminating the difference between (perfectly competitive) P_1 and (export) P_{1D} prevents the transfer of income in **F** from consumers of Q_2 to consumers of Q_1 and reduces the problem posed by restrictive business practices to economy **F** by **E**.

Article 21 of the Basic (Anti-Dumping) Regulation, a rule under the European Community's anti-dumping legislation, requires a test of the effect of measures on European Community interest. The argumentation or theoretical evidence above shows that the test of European Community interest in the European Community anti–dumping legislation is untenable.[21] The European Community interest test focuses exclusively on the product concerned, in this case Q_1. If duties are imposed on imports of a product concerned, the effect on users or final consumers of Q_1 is investigated. The effect of dumping for products other than the product concerned, in this case Q_2, is important but neglected. The effect of the elimination of dumping on all products exported to the dumping country should be measured against the disadvantage of not doing so. Such a balancing test is, of course, practically unfeasible. Economic literature has not paid much attention to this simple issue. A calculation of the cost of dumping has been limited to lower prices of only one dumped product without attention for higher prices that result from exports of products exported as payment for dumped imports. Indeed, such a calculation is infeasible, but that does not imply that only the simplest of exercises, the effect of the duty on the use of the dumped product, is acceptable. By an anti–dumping levy the balance can be restored; the consumers of Q_1 and Q_2 get what they got before the influence of the distortion of competition. If the exporting economy adjusts and restores competition, consumers in economies **E** and **F** both benefit.

Generally, assumptions in theories on international trade are made about condition of markets. Either both markets are restricted, as Krugman and Baldwin (1990) assume, or both markets are perfectly competitive, so that there is always an adjustment to shocks and the market reintegrates all labour that has lost its job by dumping is into the economy. There is no reason for such assumption. The second assumption is especially useless, because as Keynes already stated, there is no time

[21] Article 21 Community interest, of Council Regulation (EC) No 461/2004 of 8 March 2004 amending Regulation (EC) No 384/96 on protection against dumped imports from countries not members of the European Community and Regulation (EC) No 2026/97 on protection against subsidised imports from countries not members of the European Community Official Journal of the European Community 13.3.2004, L 77/12, and the basic regulation Council Regulation (EC) No 384/96 of 22 December 1995 on protection against dumped imports from countries not members of the European Community (Council Regulation (EC) No 1225/2009 of 30 November 2009, codified AD OJ L 343/51 of 22.12.2009).

for all markets to adjust to a theoretical long-term equilibrium level. Rather than making assumptions on perfect conditions or balanced imperfect conditions, assumptions that are attractive in theory, it was necessary to find an explanation for the fact that Japan had such a high domestic price level, both to trade and to the consumer and such low export prices. In any case, the findings concerning the Japanese distribution sector and the consequences for international trade were sufficient for Philips to investigate the situation in various product markets. It appeared that dumping was an endemic, chronic trade practice. Section 8.10 provides an example of a company, Tosoh, making recommendations for a joint venture for the production in Japan of magneto–optical discs with a European partner. A feasibility study, in which the feasibility was fully dependent on high domestic Japanese prices and low export prices, accompanied the proposal.

8.7 Methodology of Finding Dumping and Injury and Differences in Causes of Dumping

The definition in the General Agreement on Tariffs and Trade (GATT) and various national legislations of dumping is that the export price to the export country is less than a comparable price for the like product as established, in the ordinary course of trade, for sales in the domestic market, i.e. in the exporting country. Chapter 16 presents a survey how dumping, dumping margin and injury margin are established and what criteria for ordinary course of trade are. As stated before, injury in an anti–dumping case is essential. In order to be actionable, a dumping complaint should not only demonstrate dumping but should also demonstrate injury and the causal relation between dumping and injury.

This Chapter dealt with differences in degree of competition in various markets as cause of dumping, in particular in relation with consequences of a special type of trade barrier, captive distribution. Since differences in protection result, in case of exports by the protected companies, in differences in the level of competition and price differences and the cost of production relations are distorted, in the final analysis it is a form of predatory dumping. Dumping producers may not attain the stage of reaping all the benefits of their predation by imposing prices at the point where marginal cost equals marginal revenue, at the level of the monopoly price. The cause is that new predators enter the market and also dump and take their part of that market at the cost of earlier dumping. Predatory dumping is often considered a special, even exceptional, case of dumping. As seen above, in principle it is not. The sequence of new entries of dumping exporters finally destroys the industry in the country of imports. Various subsequent chapters show that new predators enter the market and reap the benefits of eliminating competitors away from their predecessors. There is more to predation than establishing a final oligopoly of the first dumpers. Producers in import markets may be destroyed, but this does not imply that the competition on these markets stopped. If the exporting predators are a single company, the harvest might take place. If there are more dumping producers, however, discriminatory pricing may continue. In one economy, the restriction of competition may continue and the Bertrand cooperative model is applicable, whereas the competition in the importing market, even among producers of one exporting country, may continue. In some market segments, it superficially seems that the benefits of predation are reaped. The European video and electronic camera market is practically entirely Japanese and the recommended retail price seems compulsory. Camera retailers are punished with non-delivery in case of price stunting, i.e. the Japanese system. This is not an issue of anti–dumping but has become one for anti-monopoly authorities in Europe.

8.8 Korean Distribution and Imports

Korean distribution is like Japanese distribution. Cross–ownership, however, as it exists in Japan, where banks, insurance companies and other companies own shares in one another, is absent. The big Korean conglomerates are privately founded companies of relatively recent origin, i.e. after the Korean War. The trade structure, however, is also rigid. Apart from the wholesale and retail distribution, which copies the Japanese system, some department stores are related to big conglomerates. Daewoo has its own department stores, Masan. Cases of anti–dumping investigations in Korea concerning imported shavers and flat irons have taken place in the past. The relations of department stores to major producers played a comical role in some Korean anti–dumping measures against foreign imports. Until the late 1990s Samsung, for instance, owned Shinsegae department stores. Samsung did not consider shaver production worthwhile. For some time, Shinsegae sold shavers of the Kaiser brand made by Korean producer Woolim. It became clear that other department stores sold more profitably imported shavers of a superior quality. Shinsegae also switched to imported products.[22] As compensation, the trade policy department of Samsung Electronics engineered an anti–dumping complaint for Woolim (or Ulim) of the same quality as Ulim's shavers

In spite of the similarities between the Japanese domestic market and Korean domestic market, Koreans had to cope on third markets with domestic producers and with competition by dumping by Japanese. Its operating basis, the domestic

[22] Because they supplied Korean department stores with products that were superior to a Korean product, three shaver producers Braun, Panasonic and Philips were accused of dumping. Since the Woolim (or Ulim) product was relatively cheap but qualitatively inferior, the price undercutting was based on highly artificial comparisons, which put the imports always on unequal footing, resulting in undercutting. The shaver case of Korea towards the EEC (Braun and Philips) and Japan (Hitachi and Matsushita) took place in 1996 and ended in price undertakings, under which the exporters respected a price, which were higher and even more profitable than before. It did not save the Kaiser brand of Woolim.

Korean market, was smaller. As they had to compete with the Japanese for export markets, such companies as Samsung, Daewoo and Lucky Goldstar (LGE) had to be more efficient than the Japanese. Although dumping took place, the dumping margins were often lower than those of the Japanese or in some cases, such as microwave ovens, even inexistent.

8.9 Distribution and International Trade Rules

Japanese and Korean distribution systems are a non–tariff barrier to trade, jeopardising international trade by their effect on foreign markets. Indeed, Matsushita Panasonic was correct by declaring hat "*foreign market share is a key priority.*" It is vital for competitiveness both in the domestic and world market. The founding fathers of the GATT did not know these structures and could not expect turmoil and destruction on foreign markets as a consequence of such structures. The GATT's fundamental basis is the idea that import restrictions take the shape of governmental and mostly legal measures, such as quantitative restrictions or tariffs. Formal measures are Western practice. That practice is based on liberal ideology: imports are free, unless restricted by formal law or legally backed measures. In the domain of the elimination of formal governmental barriers, the GATT and its successor, the WTO, are extremely successful. In the domain it does not cover, including non–official barriers as cartels and other restrictive practices, it is hardly victorious. This resulted in many conflicts in the GATT, which are now part of the past. Japan's system has eliminated many competitors in key sectors and is now hampering its own growth. New rivals also cause worries, although of a different nature.

As long as Japanese companies had a clear view on the product fields in which they wanted to be leading, they could embark on improving their competitive position by obtaining foreign market share. The economic system of cemented ancillary suppliers and captive wholesale and retail, however, is sclerotic and a barrier to new entrants, i.e. a barrier to innovation and development. Due to a lack of new products or product imitation, destructive trade practices have become less spectacular. Those who consider competition from China and market destruction by Chinese companies similar to or a repetition of Japanese practices are wrong. The case of China is clearly different. It is discussed in Chap. 15.

8.10 Business Case: Tosoh's Dumping of MODs in a Proposal for a Joint Venture

In 1996, the Japanese chemical company Tosoh made a proposal to European producer PDO Media for the common production of Magneto–Optical Discs, a data storage device, in Japan. PDO was the owner of an essential (Philips) patent on

Table 8.2 Tosoh's royalty statement (1995): Japan and dumping in the United States

Models and destination	Units sold	Average price	Dumping margin	Dumping as % CIF
TODC–3A50 3.5″ Japan	32,716	$15.78		
TODC–3A50 3.5″ United States	25,300	10.21	$5.57	53.5
TODC–3D50 3.5″ Japan	33,232	25.48		
TODC–3D50 3.5″ United States	23,060	13.06	$12.42	93.2

Table 8.3 Mitsui chemical supplying evidence on dumping

Type and destination	Units	Price in Yen	Dumping margin	Dumping as % CIF
5.25 MO Oct. 92–Sept. 93 Japan 1	7,302	¥15,434		
5.25 MO Oct. 92–Sept. 93 Japan 2	28,282	10,193		
Average all Japan	35,584	11,268		
5.25 MO Oct. 92–Sept. 93 United States	16,712	8,554	¥2,714	31.1
5.25 MO Oct. 92–Sept. 93 Europe	20	9,687	1,581	16.0

this product, of which Tosoh was a licensee, for which royalties were due. The license required regular reporting of information on sales volumes and prices to Tosoh's customers in royalty statements.[23] Table 8.2 shows part of such a statement.

Tosoh's domestic Japanese prices were far above export level. At 2 % costs of insurance and freight, they were as high as 53.5 % and 93.2 %. Tosoh's prices were ex-works prices. They did not differ much from similar discs sold by Japanese competitors. Other Japanese producers of MO Discs, Hitachi Maxell, Sony, Teijin, Mitsubishi Kasei Corp. and Mitsui Chemical, were considerably heavier rivals. Table 8.3 shows that Tosoh is not alone in dumping.

Dumping is a salient feature again. Tables 8.2 and 8.3 present ex-works selling prices. Price differences are not attributable to computation of margins attributed to some complex distribution system in Japan or some "artificial" establishment of data by anti–dumping authorities, which so infuriated Japanese authorities. Exporters themselves reported the domestic and export prices in accordance with royalty payment obligations and consequently, they provided the evidence on dumping directly. To save royalty payments, it was in their interest to report low price levels.

[23] This is information obtained from PDO in Germany in 1995 during the preparation of a dumping complaint, which for undisclosed reasons was never lodged.

Table 8.4 Persistent price gap: Japan's dumping of magneto optical discs

3.5″ average disc prices US$				
	1992	1993	1994	1995
Japan	$58.75	$19.36	$23.09	$20.67
United States	21.95	16.17	15.13	11.57
Europe	21.50	16.18	18.82	13.42
Dumping from Japan into USA as % of CIF (2 %)	164 %	19 %	52 %	77 %
Dumping from Japan into EU as % of CIF (2 %)	170 %	19 %	22 %	53 %
5.25″ average disc prices: US$				
	1992	1993	1994	1995
Japan	$153.77	$68.71	$103.70	$79.84
United States	60.00	53.56	49.69	34.60
Europe	57.23	46.78	54.01	42.60
Dumping from Japan into USA as % of CIF (2 %)	153 %	28 %	107 %	128 %
Dumping from Japan into EU as % of CIF (2 %)	165 %	46 %	90 %	86 %

Table 8.4 is compiled from market research. It demonstrates the market trend and the persistent gap between Japanese domestic market prices and export prices.[24]

The dumping margins in Table 8.4 are overwhelming, but a caveat is that prices are averages. Dumping should be established at the level of identical or similar products. Tables 8.2 and 8.3 present irrefutable evidence on dumping. Since quality differences can impossibly cause price differences of such dimensions of some dozens of per cent, Table 8.4 appears, however, also a reliable indicator of the persistent nature of tremendous dumping.

Tosoh convincingly confirmed the dumping already evidenced by Japanese producers' royalty statements. Tosoh proposed to PDO Media a joint venture for common production in Japan of more advanced discs than those actually produced by Tosoh. Tosoh presented feasibility calculations of common production and sales. Table 8.5 shows data underlying Tosoh's joint-venture proposal. It revealed *inter alia* the intention of OEM production for PDO, which could convince PDO it would be better to completely stop its production of 400,000 units and switch to supplies from the new joint venture. The inherent ambition demonstrated in this proposal was to boost production substantially by the addition of PDO's OEM purchases. Tosoh only revealed very low export selling prices to PDO, irreconcilable with an average 24.25 % target profit for the project. PDO found out that, if it would produce and sell the same volumes at the same selling prices as Tosoh proposed, but at the cost of PDO at such volumes, PDO would make a considerable profit of 19.9 %, instead of its actual loss, whereas Tosoh would incur a loss of 13.2 % over cost of production.

What is remarkable is that labour cost (in row 10 of Table 8.5) is considered fixed rather than variable cost. Jackson (1989) pointed out that this is an "interface

[24] Market price data from Fujiwara-Rothchild Ltd., market analysis reports.

Table 8.5 Basic data of a Tosoh's proposed joint venture

(1)	Production 5.25″	255,000
(2)	Production 3.5 ″	1,302,000
(3)	**Total production**	1,557,000
(4)	Sales revenue 5.25″	¥1,035,000,000
(5)	Sales revenue 3.5 ″	¥1,436,000,000
(6)	**Total sales revenue**	¥2,471,000,000
(7)	**Variable production cost/unit** 5.25″	¥1,289.00
(8)	**Variable production cost/unit** 3.5 ″	¥437.00
(9)	**Fixed costs** of which	**¥1,657,000,000**
(10)	Labour cost	539,000,000
(11)	Depreciation	479,000,000
(12)	Royalty payments	85,000,000
(13)	Other	554,000,000
(14)	**SG&A cost** of which	**¥291,000,000**
(15)	Sales	125,000,000
(16)	R&D	141,000,000
(17)	General expense	25,000,000
(18)	**Total revenue** (6)	¥2,471,000,000
(19)	**Total cost** (1) × (7) + (2) × (8) + (9) + (14)	¥2,845,669,000
(20)	**Results of above**	−¥374,669,000
(21)	As per cent over cost	−13 %
(22)	**Profit objective:** average in years 1997–1999	24.25 %

problem".[25] Japanese "lifetime employment" implies that labour cannot be dismissed. Consequently, the labour cost is fixed, while in the West labour cost is variable and labour can be discharged. Profit objective is 24.25 % over cost of production (row 22), although the cost survey shows a result of minus 13 % over cost of production (row 21). Nevertheless, Tosoh had a profit objective of 24.25 %.

Data from Table 8.5 can be used for a Table 8.6. This table was the nucleus of Tosoh's proposal. At its own cost level but at Tosoh's quantities, PDO would be highly profitable compared with the actual situation of 150,000 sales of 5.25″ and 250,000 of 3.5″ MODs, in practice resulting in awful losses.

If some adjustments are made to Tosoh's data, the outcome would be totally different:

1. If sales were restricted to Japan and if labour cost were treated as variable cost instead of fixed, the results would improve.
2. If export sales are added to Tosoh's domestic sales, the situation for Tosoh improves substantially.
3. If PDO's sales quantities (400,000 units) are added to Tosoh's exports as OEM sales, overall profitability is attained.

[25] According to Jackson (1989, pp. 218–223), dumping was a consequence of different systems of employment. Dumping by Japan was due to the fact that labour was considered fixed cost and this should be tolerated. He did not explain why Western labour should be dismissed for the sake of maintenance of employment in Japan.

Table 8.6 Basic data of a Tosoh's proposed joint venture applied to Tosoh and PDO media

	Tosoh proposal		PDO media (actual volume)		PDO media (Tosoh volume)	
	5.25″	3.5″	5.25″	3.5″	5.25″	3.5″
Variable cost	¥1,289	¥437	¥1,353	¥634	¥1,353	¥634
Fixed cost	1,064	1,064 }				
SGA cost	123	123	5,073	1,668	1,303	428
Total costs	2,540	1,688	6,427	2,302	2,657	1,062
Price per unit	4,059	1,103	4,059	1,103	4,059	1,103
Result per unit	1,519	−585	−2,368	−1,195	1,402	41
Result per unit (%)	59.8 %	−34.7 %	−36.8 %	−52.1 %	52.8 %	3.8 %
Total result %	−13.2 %		−42.5 %		19.9 %	

Table 8.7 Fixed and variable cost; domestic sales, exports and results: stimulus to dumping

	Level of fixed cost	Fixed cost per unit	Variable cost	Total cost	Target profit price	Result
Only domestic sales	High fixed cost 5.25″	¥2,918	¥1,289	¥4,207	¥3,156	−¥1,051
60,578 units 5.25″	High fixed cost 3.5″	2,918	437	3,355	2,098	−1,258
606,933 units 3.5″	Low fixed cost 5.25″	2,111	1,755	3,866	3,156	−709
	Low fixed cost 3.5″	2,111	903	3,014	2,098	−916
Domestic plus own exports	High fixed cost 5.25″	1,684	1,289	2,973	3,156	184
105,000 units 5.25″	High fixed cost 3.5″	1,684	437	2,121	2,098	−23
1,052,000 units 3.5″	Low fixed cost 5.25″	1,218	1,755	2,973	3,156	184
	Low fixed cost 3.5″	1,218	903	2,121	2,098	−23
Domestic plus OEM (PDO)	High fixed cost 5.25″	1,251	1,289	2,540	3,156	616
255,000 units 5.25″	High fixed cost 3.5″	1,251	437	1,688	2,098	409
1,302,000 units 3.5″	Low fixed cost 5.25″	905	1,635	2,540	3,156	616
	Low fixed cost 3.5″	905	783	1,688	2,098	409

Tosoh intended that PDO would stop production. Accordingly, Tosoh could have increased its exports by 400,000 units. That addition would have brought Tosoh to profitability level. The more exports, even at extremely low prices, the better the profitability as Table 8.7 teaches. If labour is a variable cost, losses incurred by absence of exports are, of course, lower than if the fixed cost is high.

Table 8.8 Tosoh's profitable domestic market and export sales: dumping

	Disc type	Units	Fixed cost	Variable cost	Total cost	Price	Results
Domestic sales	5.25″	147,118	¥1,251	¥1,289	¥2,540	¥12,945	¥10,405
	3.5″	751,166	1,251	437	1,688	1,970	282
Export sales	5.25″	107,882	¥1,251	¥1,289	¥2,540	¥4,059	¥1,519
(incl. OEM)	3.5″	550,834	1,251	437	1,688	1,103	585
Dumping margins	5.25″					¥8,886	= 215 %
	3.5″					¥867	= 77 %

High fixed costs, mainly as consequence of the inclusion of labour cost, are an additional stimulus for dumping. Dumping by Tosoh and additional export sales improve profitability.

The question indicated above, what the differences would be between domestic and export prices if profits were allocated equally over the two products, 5.25″ and 3.5″, can be tackled by the assumption of the sales quantities in Table 8.7.

Tosoh was not efficient. Low export prices did not reflect competitiveness but rather indicated weakness. Japanese domestic sales prices and export volume should have restored profitability. The equalisation of low export prices with competitive advantage is clearly a circular argument. Under the same conditions as Tosoh, PDO suffered no losses. According to the law of comparative advantage, shown in Diagram 8.5, relatively low costs result in the division of trade. The Tosoh case shows the opposite. Dumping appeared a *sine qua non* for survival, which drove more competitive producers, such as PDO, out of business. The domestic economic system of Japan in which Tosoh operated, caused the destruction of the sound by the inefficient (Table 8.8).

References

Belderbos R (1994) Strategic trade policy and multinational enterprises: essays on trade and investment by Japanese electronics firms. Thesis publishers, Amsterdam

Bhagwati JN, Panagariya A, Srinavasan TN (1983) Lectures on international trade. The MIT Press, Cambridge

Blonigen BA, Prusa TJ (2003) The cost of antidumping: the devil is in the details. J Policy Reform 6(4):233–245

Brander J, Krugman P (1983) A reciprocal dumping model of international trade. J Int Econ 15:313–321

Caves RE, Frankel JE, Jones RW (2007) World trade and payments. Pearson Addison Wesley, Boston

Freeman AM (1971) International trade: an introduction to method and theory. Harper and Row, New York

Helpman E, Krugman P (1989) Trade policy and market structure. The MIT Press, Cambridge

Jackson JH (1989) The world trading system: law and policy of international economic relations. The MIT Press, Cambridge

Kindleberger CP (1973) International economics. Richard D. Irwin, Homewood

Krugman PR (1990) Rethinking international trade. MIT Press, Cambridge
Krugman PR, Baldwin RE (1990) Market access and international competition: a simulation of 16K random access memories. In: Krugman PR (ed) Rethinking international trade. MIT Press, Cambridge
Krugman PR, Obstfeld M (2006) International economics, theory and policy. Pearson, Boston
Magaziner I, Patinkin M (2004) Korea: winning with microwaves. In: Yin RK (ed) The case study anthology. Sage, Thousand Oaks
Maruyama M (1993) A study of the distribution system in Japan, No 136, OECD Economics Department working papers. OECD Publishing, Paris
Prestowitz CV (1988) Trading places: how we allowed Japan to take the lead. Basic Books, New York
Rawwas MYA, Konishi K, Kamise S, Al–Khatib J (2008) Japanese distribution system: the impact of newly designed collaborations on wholesalers' performance. Ind Mark Manag 37:104–115
Shimotani M (1995) The formation of distribution Keiretsu: the case of Matsushita electric. Bus Hist 37(2):54–69
Tharakan PKM (1997) The Japan-EC DRAMs anti-dumping undertaking: was it justified? What purpose did it serve? De Economist 145(1):1–28

Chapter 9
Myth of Japanese Efficiency: Dumping of Compact Disc Players

Abstract Japanese CD player producers themselves submitted evidence of dumping. In their royalty statements on CD player sales, tremendous differences between domestic and export prices for identical models became apparent. On the basis of this data, a calculation reveals they were actually inefficient and that without dumping they did not stand a chance on world markets. If Philips operated under the same conditions, it would have been profitable, in spite of the distress and serious havoc caused by colossal dumping. The length of the anti-dumping procedure, which reflected the lenient attitude of the European Commission toward the trespassers, allowed the dumping practices to continue for a long time and relocation to other countries. Finally, it appeared inevitable that production in Europe would be abandoned and transferred to Asia. Continuation would have meant the complete annihilation of manufacturing by European producers of CD players.

9.1 Discovery of Massive Dumping

The findings on relation between economic structure and dumping became subject of discussion and resoluteness about the course to be taken. First, presentations about the Japanese market had resulted in unsuccessful actions by the European Community in the General Agreement on Tariffs and Trade (GATT) concerning "Nullification or Impairment" (Article XXIII). However, the conclusion that the anti-competitive structure of Japanese distribution was the cause of dumping led to a firm policy, for a time, within Philips that dumping would be tackled.

Spectacular evidence on a lack of ubiquitously acclaimed Japanese superiority in the cost of production and presence of dumping was obtained during a CD market tempest in 1987. Like producers of the Magneto Optical Discs described in the previous Chapter, the producers of CD players were obliged to report their sales in respective markets in regular royalty statements. In the case of MOD, the license fee was a fixed amount per disc and for CD players it was 2 % (1½ % to Philips and ½ % to Sony) over the net selling value. Since it shared the patent rights, Sony was

M. van Marion, *International Trade Policy and European Industry*, Contributions to Economics, DOI 10.1007/978-3-319-00392-4_9,

exempted from reporting obligations. Other exceptions were companies that had cross-licenses with Philips, such as Matsushita. The reporting concerned the sales value and units sold, specified per territory of sales. The accounting departments of licensees sent these royalty statements to Philips' accounting department. As long as the licensees paid their fees, nobody paid attention to the royalty statements.

In 1987, increased Japanese and Korean undercutting of European Community producers' prices became even more ominous. Inventories at Philips' production centre in Hasselt, Belgium, were alarming. B&O and Grundig were also in distress. The cause of bad results was initially ascribed to their own production inefficiency. A comparison of material content and cheapest possible production methods with an analysis of CD players of competitors gave no clues of flaws in their own capabilities. It took several months of serious examination during a period of continuous severe industrial and commercial damage before a hypothesis of dumping was considered. Philips' headquarters requested national sales organisations in Japan and Korea to supply documentary evidence on selling prices in these markets and on trade margins and other costs. When the information arrived, dumping was manifest from comparisons with European Union data. There was a gap of 30–60 % between domestic prices and the prices to the same levels of trade in the European Union.

By incidence, existence of royalty statements was mentioned and an inspection of these royalty statements yielded highly spectacular results. Japanese and Korean had submitted irrefutable evidence on heavy price discrimination between domestic and export sales. The royalty statements confirmed that the differences between domestic prices and export prices of about 30–60 %. The data allowed calculation of Philips' theoretical results if conditions were similar to those of a Japanese producer. Sanyo was taken as example. Sanyo's circumstances were assumed applicable to Philips. The assumptions were:

- Thirty-eight percent of Philips' sales would have been made at prices as prevailing in Japan, i.e. domestic sales prices were 31 % above the export price.
- Philips sold its products in the European Community at the same level as Sanyo.
- Philips' actual costs were applicable, i.e. actual costs as they were under the prevailing bad conditions.

If Philips were in the position of Sanyo and could have practiced the same level of dumping, it would have made a profit instead of incur heavy losses. If turnover is ***TO*** and the total cost is ***C***, the following expression is applicable:

$$\frac{38\% \times (1 + 31\%) \times TO + (1 - 38\%).TO - C}{TO} > 3.6\% \tag{9.1}$$

Although, due to dumping, Philips incurred high costs by loss of market share, it would make a profit if it could operate under the same circumstances as Sanyo with 38 % of its sales at prices as in Japan. At a dumping margin of 27.82 % determined by the European Commission (Table 9.3), the domestic price applied to 38 % of the sales would have yielded a profit of 2.4 % instead of an actual loss on turnover by 7.8 %. The picture is like the Tosoh case in the previous Chapter. Philips'

Table 9.1 An example: dumping of CD players by Kenwood

Kenwood 7020 (made in Japan)			
Listed retail price		Yen	37,055
Rebates, trade margins			14,469
Net wholesale price			22,586
Consumption tax	3 %		658
Ex-works price Yen 1,000 =	5.9326	ECU	130.09
Netherlands Kenwood 1030 (made in Japan)			
Actual retail price		D Gld	399.00
VAT and dealer's margin	32.6 %		82.78
Price to trade (landed price)			253.93
Import duty	9.5 %		22.03
Shipment costs	2 %		4.55
Ex-works price			227.35
D Guilder =	0.43	ECU	97.76
Normal value		ECU	130.09
Export price		ECU	97.76
Dumping margin		ECU	32.33
CIF value		ECU	99.72
As % of CIF price			32.4 %

production capacity utilisation dropped to 40 % in 1987. This affected cost of production heavily. Without distortions caused by massive dumping, which reduced Philips volume of production and increased its costs, Philips appeared highly efficient and decidedly profitable, if compared with Sanyo's situation. If the parameters of Matsushita were applied, the picture obviously became even more favourable. Due to the fact that Philips incurred losses and lodged a dumping complaint, its image was tarnished because of "weakness and protectionism", although actually the Japanese companies were the weaker.

Since the royalty statements were confidential material, company lawyers feared the use of this reliable information as evidence in an anti-dumping complaint. It was used as confidential back up for the European Commission, which tried to neglect it. The information did not allow for the freedom of manipulation the European Commission seemed to need. Discriminatory and insufficient measures were the outcome of this policy. The royalty statements were used as test and generally confirmed the documentary information about domestic markets of Japan and Korea and correctness of dumping calculations. Table 9.1 on the dumping by Kenwood gives an example of such a calculation.

Kenwood's actual export price reported in the royalty statement was lower than the listed retail price minus tax and usual trade margins. It reported a domestic price ex-works of ¥21,928. The recommended retail price found by Philips Nihon was ¥55,000. Application of the usual margins yielded a normal value of ¥32,547 instead of the ¥21,928 reported by Kenwood in the royalty statements. If the ¥55,000 would have been starting point of calculations, the dumping margin would have been 135 % instead of the 32.4 % presented in Table 9.1, based on Kenwood's own reporting in the license statement.

Philips asked whether Grundig and Bang and Olufsen were prepared to participate and they were.[1] During a meeting of some European electronics industry representatives and officials of the Japan Machinery Importers' Association belonging to the Ministry of International Trade and Industry (MITI), Thomson was approached with the question of whether it was prepared to participate in the complaint. As reported in Chap. 5, however, Thomson had lost interest in European production. Only if the anti-dumping duties would be quickly imposed and would amount to at least 60 %, was Thomson prepared to participate. Of course, such guarantees were impossible. Thomson actually planned to move to Malaysia in accordance with the doctrine of Thomson's CEO, Pierre Garcin. The complaint was lodged without any pre-warning to any party.

For fear of leakages, nobody within the Philips organisation or within the European Commission received information about a pending dumping complaint. The day after copies of a file for inspection and the confidential file had unexpectedly and suddenly been submitted in the offices of the European Commission's anti-dumping division, the chairman of the Japanese Philips organisation was summoned to the Ministry of Trade and Industry. Apparently there was a serious leakage at the European Commission. The Japanese authorities declared the complaint a hostile act. Since the complaint had been kept secret, the poor Philips director did not have any information, but he courageously resisted Japanese threats of tax investigations. Indeed, not long afterwards tax authorities staged a raid and Philips Nihon's premises were closed and sealed for some time. The director of the Korean organisation, whose telephone was tapped even more intensely than before, felt that this required provocative statements over the phone. He was courageous and, not knowing that anti-dumping was an instrument that could not randomly or politically be used as retaliatory policy instrument, he warned the Ministry of Trade and Industry of Korea that the frequency of use of such trade policy weapons would increase if the Korean market remained as closed as it was.

Of course, the Japanese industry was also upset. Efforts to appease the European Community industry, such as the Japanese European Round Table on Consumer Electronics, seemed fruitless. Relations between the industrialists were excellent, but such relations did not imply a free card for distortion of competition. Sony also actively chose its own way during the proceeding. Sony's president Akio Morita tried to convince Philips' Vice-President Cor van der Klugt and several European Commission officials he knew from the Round Table on Consumer Electronics conferences of its innocence. He also sent a confidential report, in which it was emphasised that whatever the others might have done, Sony had not dumped and in any case had not undercut Philips' prices. Philips was neither supposed to distribute this highly confidential report nor discuss it with others, according to Morita. Sony itself widely distributed the paper in the European Community on the same condition of confidentiality. Although Sony, like a few other Japanese companies like Pioneer, Kenwood, Sansui, Teac or Yamaha, was also partly victim of

[1] The complaint was made on behalf of the association Committee of Mechoptronics Producers and Allied Technologies (COMPACT), in which Bang & Olufsen, Grundig and Philips were participants.

disruptive export prices, it benefited from high domestic prices and participated in dumping. Since they could afford it because of their position on the domestic Japanese market, as explained in Chaps. 7 and 8, Matsushita, Toshiba, Sharp, Hitachi and Sanyo had been very "aggressive", volume oriented, in their exports. Their dumping margins were higher and they undercut the prices both of European and of several other Japanese companies with less prominent market share in Japan extremely intense. The majors clearly went for volume of production in accordance with the strategies sketched in Chap. 8.

The European Community rarely received such convincing and detailed evidence on dumping and on injury directly attributable to that dumping. Never before had producers themselves provided such ample and convincing evidence. It appeared that allegations about Japanese, and Korean, production efficiency superiority was bogus, mainly derived from claims by exporting countries and exporters themselves and some of the admirers. Nevertheless, the European Commission did not use the information, although various exporters did not cooperate in the proceeding. The European Commission neglected information provided by Kenwood and other Japanese producers in their royalty statements. It established a dumping margin for Kenwood of 20.05 % and imposed a duty of 19.3 %. The provisional duty was lower because it was based on the injury margin (i.e. the undercutting, which is the difference between the sales price of European Community producers and Kenwood's price in the European Community market; see methodological Chap. 16). This margin was slightly less than the dumping margin. Kenwood had bad luck that the necessary profit allocated to European industry raised by 2 % points between imposition of provisional and definitive duties. This increased its anti-dumping duty. Had information from Kenwood in the royalty statements been used, both dumping and injury would have been superior to the level that the European Commission found after an intolerably long investigation. The duty did not hurt Kenwood very much. Thanks to the length of the investigation, it moved its final CD player assembly for the European market to Singapore before the duties were imposed. Similarly, Sharp's royalty statements indicated a dumping margin of 60 %. Sharp did not cooperate in the proceeding and 60 % should have been the residual duty. In case of non-cooperation, the best evidence available should be used. Nevertheless, the European Commission applied a duty of 32 %. Again, the information from Sharp was neglected.

9.2 Strategies and Tactics in the Anti-Dumping Proceeding

Normally an anti-dumping duty is based on the dumping margin or on level of price undercutting.[2] The injury, represented by price undercutting attributable to dumping must be eliminated. For the calculation of the injury margin, the price of the

[2] For those curious how proceedings occur in practice, Chap. 16, the methodological chapter, shows the details of calculations of dumping and injury margin (undercutting and underselling) and several complexities and technical, economic and legal issues.

injured industry may be adjusted by eliminating losses and by adding some target profit, which is the profit attained under normal circumstances, i.e. a situation with no dumping. If such adjustments are made, the methodology is called a calculation of "underselling". Profit allocated to European producers for the calculation of the injury inflicted to them is not based on the profits that exporters make. In the case of CD players, the losses attributable to the loss of the market inflicted by dumping parties were not compensated. Only the price injury margin, the underselling, is eliminated in the future, but the damage already inflicted, *inter alia* by cost increases and losses, remains unrepaired. In Chap. 8, Sect. 8.5, the deficiencies of such a method are explained.

For a calculation of dumping and price undercutting, margins comparisons should be made between similar products. This implies for CD players and other consumer electronics comparisons on a model-by-model basis. As already indicated in Chap. 7, Japanese domestic competition is not in price, but rather in features. Japanese products have as a consequence often more and different, not infrequently useless, features than European products. In the case of CD players, variation in the models was ample. Varying loading mechanism, display, programming possibilities, and various HiFi norms cause comparability problems. Comparability of products is an urgent issue. Before lodging the complaint, the European industry compiled a list of features with values attached to them meant for use in the investigation proceeding. If the prices of Japanese models are lower than the prices of similar European models, there is price undercutting. Some Japanese producers stated in their propaganda prior to the opening of the proceeding that Philips' products were inferior to theirs and that this was the cause of Japanese success on the European market. If their players were superior, they did not need to export at extremely low prices undercutting the prices of Philips' inferior equipment.

Sony's and various other exporters' lawyer, Jean-François Bellis, must have seen the danger of these claims. Sony seemed to fear that Philips would overrate in the proposed feature list certain features characteristic for Sony sets. That would make Sony's price-performance ratio low and consequently, Sony's export prices low in relation to the offered features. Sony fiercely rejected Philips' valuation list submission and urged the appointment of an independent expert. Sony insisted on the appointment of an editor of a Dutch HiFi audio magazine as model comparison expert, expecting that if the expert were Dutch, Philips could not possibly reject him. The editor was a well-known admirer, voluntarily or on financial grounds, of Sony's products. In his magazine he jubilantly reviewed some Sony's CD players as superior to other machines. The danger of such delighted reviews for Sony was that its models would be considered cheap compared with its performance and with European products. Another risk was that this expert would just apply a list handed over by Sony for the valuation of features. Finally, Sony's recommendation was accepted by the Complainant, under the European Commission's pressure.

Another important topic is the determination of the dumping level, i.e. establishment of normal value of export price and of comparison between the two.

The Japanese industry clearly feared that its captive trade system as a main factor for artificially high domestic prices resulting in dumping would be disclosed by the proceeding. Many major producers refused to cooperate in the proceeding. Official Japanese support for this attitude was given in the GATT. Japan was of the opinion that the European Community was not allowed to take the special situation of captive trade into account.

> *Japan noted that since the early 1980s there had been a sharp increase in the number of anti-dumping investigations opened by the EEC of imports from Japan. In applying its anti-dumping legislation, the EEC had developed new methodologies which, when applied to the structures and trading patterns of Japanese companies, created artificial dumping margins.*[3]

The Japanese authorities were wrong: European legislation had not changed. Philips made European institutions aware of captive distribution and the difference between the role of Japanese company's sales departments and their Western competitors. Awareness of certain characteristics of captive distribution and higher domestic prices in Japan and dumping abroad as consequence of the restrictive distribution resulted in scrutiny of price levels at various levels of distribution in Japan.

The Japanese government was aware of distinction between "*structures and trading patterns of Japanese companies*" and structure and patterns elsewhere. Methods were developed to hide these structures and patterns. Domestic market leader, Matsushita, tried during the proceeding, but revealed some structures in a lawsuit contesting findings of the European Commission before the Court of Justice. According to Japan, the European Community should disregard the special nature of Japanese distribution and treat, as if the relationship did not exist, the transfer price to wholly or partly owned distributors, performing tasks normally performed by sales departments of companies, as normal value.[4] All other profits accruing to the mother company from tied trade and resulting high profits should, therefore, also be disregarded. Thereby Japan declared its trade restrictions a normal business that other countries should accept. All major Japanese producers refused to inform the European Community investigators about prices and trade structures of business in Japan. Sony pretended to cooperate and received special

---

[3] EEC – Regulation on Imports of Parts and Components, Report by the Panel adopted on 16 May 1990, (L/6657 – 37S/132). Japan stated in a footnote: "*Japan referred in this respect to the methodology used by the EEC in the comparison of normal values with export prices based on an asymmetrical deduction of costs, the determination of constructed values including unrealistic profits and the calculation of dumping margins based on a comparison between a weighted average of domestic prices with export prices established on a transaction-by-transaction basis.*"

[4] Information from "Opinion of Mr Advocate General Mischo", delivered on 13 December 1990. Matsushita Electric Industrial Co. Ltd and Matsushita Electric Trading Co. Ltd v Council of the European Communities. Anti-dumping duties on plain paper photocopiers originating in Japan. Case C-175/87; Judgment of the Court (Sixth Chamber), 13 October 1993; Matsushita Electric Industrial v Council, "Opinion of Advocate General Van Gerven", delivered on 29 April 1993.

Picture 9.1 Administrative burden: verification visit at Matsushita's

treatment by the European Commission. Matsushita Panasonic found ways to provide false information. It did not provide transaction-by-transaction information and impeded the verification of invoices.[5]

> *The Commission was therefore unable to follow its normal verification procedures during the on-the-spot investigation and consequently the Commission estimated the discounts on the basis of the facts available.*

A lack of enthusiasm on the part of Matsushita about verification may be obvious from Picture 9.1, taken during a European Commission's verification visit to Matsushita's premises in Osaka in another case on plain paper copiers. A verification visit does not seem to be an exciting affair. It takes a few days and is cumbersome for those involved. Verification visits require an accurate preparation of evidence underlying responses to questionnaires, in which the European Commission asks for detailed information on purchases, manufacturing, selling, general and administrative cost items and volumes and prices on a transaction-by-transaction basis concerning generally a recent year (the period of investigation). Cooperating parties in a proceeding, both exporters and European Community producers, must support their responses with documents, like copies of invoices and payment documents. This applies both to complaining producers and to exporters. It is a substantial administrative burden, which causes some producers to refrain from dumping complaints and from support to anti-dumping proceedings. It also explains why some exporters do not cooperate, especially when they have dumped substantially and hope to get lower duties than they encounter if their own conduct and data were investigated. For investigators, verification visits are

[5] Commission Regulation (EEC) No 2140/89 of 12 July 1989 imposing a provisional anti-dumping duty on imports of certain compact disc players originating in Japan and South Korea, Official Journal L 205, 18/07/1989, recital (24).

Table 9.2 Aversion from cooperation by Japan's exporters

Recital[a] and exporter	
(16) Matsushita	Response to questionnaire for Italy contradict internal documents
(24) Matsushita	No transaction-by-transaction listing of sales in Japan
(63) Sharp	Refused response to questionnaire
(64) Chuo-Denki	Replied in part only
(65) NEC	Denied opportunity of investigation
(66) Toshiba	Denied opportunity of investigation
(67) Hitachi	No information on SG&A and prices of related distributors (60 % of sales)
Mitsubishi	Did not react at all

[a]Commission regulation (EEC) No 2140/89 of 12 July 1989 imposing a provisional anti-dumping duty on imports of certain compact disc players originating in Japan and South Korea, official journal L 205, 8/07/1989 pp. 5–21

definitively demanding.[6] Apart from simple non-cooperation, some exporters are creative in shadow or false accounting. In some cases, export transactions are presented as domestic sales, by which the normal value is decreased.

In addition this obstinate behaviour impeding proper investigation, Matsushita's sales companies in the European Community provided false information. Nevertheless, the provisional duty was decreased from 33.9 % to a definitive duty of 26.3 %. Why dumping margins and dumping duties were reduced remains in the dark. The European Commission decided on the reduction in spite of clearly misleading information. In the GATT, the Japanese authorities "*objected to the application of a residual duty to imports from companies which had not been investigated*", to which companies belonged the majors like Hitachi, Toshiba, Sharp and of which some refused to provide information and others gave false information. The residual duty was too high, for "*it was desirable that the amount of the duty be less than the full margin of dumping if such lesser duty was adequate to remove injury*".[7] Japan thus wanted the European Commission to favour non-cooperation. According to Japan, the European Commission should guess a lower injury margin for non-cooperating exporters and the European Commission bowed to Japanese pressure.

In view of the duties finally imposed on CD players, the reasonably fair dumping calculations in the dumping complaint were unwise. Exporters abstaining from or obstructing cooperation, like Matsushita, demonstrated strategic prudence. The European Commission rewarded them. Table 9.2 gives a survey of non-cooperation by exporters and the nature of their non-cooperation. The major companies did not allow scrutiny of their captive distribution or, like Mitsubishi, did not react at all. None of

[6] Verification visits are definitively demanding unless investigators know that the Commissioner will discontinue a case. The example is colour picture tubes. Investigators knew that Commissioner Mandelson had read a newspaper article on tubes and LCDs in the Financial Times of 20 January 2006 and would discontinue the case, so after an ultra-short inspection of documents they visited a tourist attraction. On 15 November 2006 the Commission indeed terminated the case because of "an investigation" of "other factors", reported in the newspaper. Chapter 15 mentions the case in footnote 38.

[7] Committee on Anti-Dumping Practices, Minutes of the meeting held on 23 April 1990, ADP/M/28, 21 September 1990.

Table 9.3 Provisional and definitive dumping margins and duties: dumping or injury as basis?

	Provisional			Definitive		
Countries and companies	Dumping Margin	Dumping Duty	Lowest Dumping=D Injury=U M=De minimis	Dumping Margin	Dumping Duty	Lowest Dumping=D Injury=U M=De minimis
Japan						
Nippon Columbia/Denon	17.59%	17.5%	D	17.02%	17.0%	D
Funai Electric	8.49%	8.4%	D	8.95%	8.9%	D
Kenwood	20.05%	19.3%	U	23.3%	23.3%	D
Lux Corporation/Alpine	1.54%		M	1.54%	M	M
Marantz	2.29%		M	2.29%	M	M
Matsushita	42.61%	33.9%	U	26.3%	26.3%	D
Onkyo	8.57%	8.5%	D	8.57%	8.3%	U
Pioneer	34.56%	28.8%	U	26.32%	26.3%	D
Sanyo Electric	27.82%	27.8%	D	26.6%	26.5%	D
Sony	15.97%	15.9%	D	10.17%	10.1%	D
Teac	18.34%	6.4%	U	18.34%	12.7%	U
Victor Company of Japan (JVC)	20.98%	20.9%	D	17.99%	17.9%	D
Nippon Gakki /Yamaha	45.57%	23.7%	U	27.58%	27.5%	D
Sharp Corporation }		Not established		32.0%	32.0%	D
Toshiba Corporation }		Not established		31.0%	31.0%	D
Chou-Denki				17.82%	17.8%	D
Residual (Undercutting/dumping Matsushita)		33.9%	U	32.0%	32.0%	D
Korea						
Inkel	20.1%	20.1%	D	14.49%	14.4%	D
Goldstar	32.56%	32.5%	D	26.11%	26.1%	D
Samsung	23.07%	23.%	D	10.73%	10.7%	D
Haitai	21.34%	21.3%	D	19.24%	19.4%	D
Residual (Dumping Goldstar)		32.5%	D	26.11%	26.1%	D

the majors fully cooperated. Thus, they prevented detection of the details of the distribution system. They also hid transfer of final assembly to countries in South East Asia. Mainly smaller companies, players like Pioneer, Kenwood, Nippon Gakki (Yamaha), Teac and Lux (Alpine), but even and also Sony and Sanyo were companies with relatively less significant captive trade and they cooperated. Matsushita, the biggest of them, refused full cooperation, and challenged findings of the European Commission before the Court of Justice, flanked by the Japanese government in other actions on the same question in various institutions.

9.3 Politics and Proceeding

Although many producers did not cooperate, which Table 9.2 demonstrates, uncertainty at the European Commission and Japanese political pressure caused the proceeding to last for more than 2 years, giving ample opportunity for the continuation of damage to Europeans and for transfer of assembly.

Normally, non-cooperation is disadvantageous. In case in which evidence of dumping and injury was overwhelming, however, non-cooperation was profitable. The proceeding was protracted, allowing dumping and injury to continue. Matsushita did not allow proper verification and a dumping margin of 42.61 % was provisionally found. The injury margin was lower, 33.9 % (see Table 9.3) and

Matsushita's provisional duties were based on the injury. Although Matsushita obstructed establishment of normal value, the European Commission decreased the dumping margin by 16 % points to 26.3 %. From the evidence presented on Toshiba and Sharp, the lowest dumping margins were selected. The documentary evidence from the royalty statements was not chosen; rather, the more lenient calculations were applied. European industry was continuously disadvantaged and damaged.

Reasons for a decrease of duties for producers that did not cooperate, like Matsushita, Toshiba, Sharp, Chuo-Denki and all other non-cooperating producers were absent. The best information available was the information based on the license statements of Kenwood, the evidence of dumping given in Table 9.1 and similar data provided by other companies. Nevertheless, the duties were adjusted downward, as Table 9.3 shows. Furthermore, they were adjusted downward to a level below the level of the injury provisionally established for Matsushita. There was, however, not the slightest reason for such a revision, except for interference by the Japanese government and consequently, politics, which hugely delayed the investigations.

Sony managed to change the way in which the European Commission treated captive distribution. Sony claimed that the few independent regional distributors should be made a yardstick of total normal value. No information was given on Sony's regional distribution organisation and what the share of the independent distributors was in total sales. Inherent to the distribution system is that strictly geographically separate sales areas and separate sales are allocated to distributors, some of which appeared to be independent. That does not imply that some of the independent distributors were representative of all trade. A sharp geographical delineation in activities implies that Sony's captive distributors, constituting the majority of Sony's turnover, did not experience competition from prices of independent distributors and, consequently, establishment of average normal value on basis of sales to a few distributors was not acceptable for all of Sony's sales. The special beneficial treatment resulted in a decrease for Sony in the normal value by about 5–8 %. Such a discriminatory treatment was not only highly unfair to the complainant, but also to the rest of the exporters. Sony's export prices were certainly not superior to other exporters, like Matsushita's, for which the European Commission found an undercutting of 33.9 %. Consequently, the damage caused by Sony was substantial and the European Commission seemingly based its low anti-dumping duties on an arbitrary judgement. Matsushita's captive trade was regarded differently from Sony's and its sales to two independent distributors out of 79, of which 77 were captive traders with a strictly regional task, were naturally not considered as decisive for normal value.[8] Although the number of Sony's captive wholesalers and retailers was inferior to Matsushita's, this was not a reason to exclude data on its captive sales from the determination of normal value.

[8] Judgment of the Court (Sixth Chamber) of 13 October 1993: "Matsushita Electric Industrial Co. Ltd v Council of the European Communities", Case C-104/90.

Table 9.4 Sony's dumping margins and anti-dumping duties

Sony's dumping margins	%	Sony's AD duties	%
Dumping margin provisional	15.97	AD duty provisional	15.9
Dumping margin definitive	10.17	AD duty definitive	10.1

The European Commission's treatment of Sony discriminated against Japanese exporters other than the majors. Some of them lacked Sony's massive distribution power. Among them were Kenwood, Teac, Yamaha and various other smaller exporters. Instead of using all relevant sales of related distributors to trade and prices to independent distributors as the normal value, the European Commission selected only prices to independent distributors and this resulted in the establishment of normal value that must have been about 20 % below the level of smaller producers with only limited captive outlets.

The Commission also accepted that domestic sales to distributors was the most appropriate level of trade for comparison with export sales and that, accordingly, the normal value for this exporter should be established selectively on the basis of the weighted average domestic prices of its sales to independent distributors.[9]

This proved that Sony's political lobby was effective and that it received indefensibly preferential treatment. This may be apparent from the dumping margins found and the duties applied as given in Table 9.4, which, without justification, was again adjusted downward.

Sony's effort to influence the model comparison, and consequently undercutting, by the appointment of a Sony-friendly expert, appeared superfluous. Sony arranged an exception from the ordinary treatment of resale prices for determination of normal value in a distribution system with captive trade resulting in a lower normal value. It was an exception from the usual normal value determination so heavily contested by Japan and the Japanese industry.

However, all Japanese exporters, including non-cooperating, were treated more leniently than the evidence available suggests. If the European Commission had selected higher normal values and lower export prices (those declared by the Japanese in their royalty statements), the duties would have undoubtedly been higher, provided the European Commission did not see the CD player as a "political" case. For companies that did not co-operate at all, the final duty was 32 %, which was far below the level on which evidence existed, but which was discretionally put at the same level as the level reported in the complaint for Kenwood, as given in Table 9.1. For companies that showed some co-operation, but either tried to hide essential information or tried to fool the European Commission, the duties were lower. What was striking was that the European Commission accepted the false information supplied by exporters. Instead of using the information available, the reports by the producers themselves, which indicated much

[9] Recital (31) of Commission Regulation (EEC) No 2140/89 of 12.7.1989 (provisional), OJ L 205, 18/07/1989, pp. 5–21.

Graph 9.1 Imports of CD players into the European Community

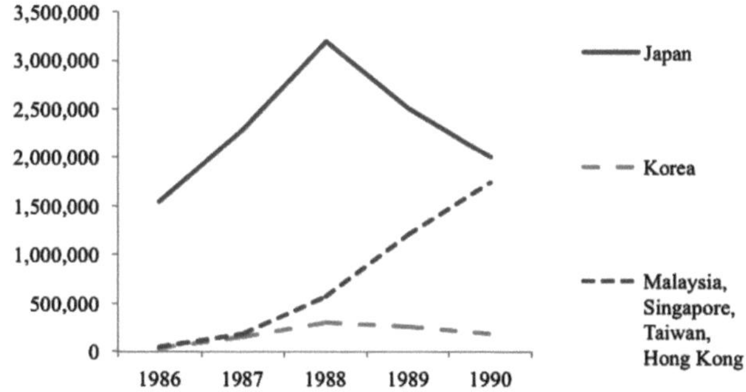

higher dumping and undercutting margins, the European Commission adjusted false figures supplied by the exporters and resulting in better outcomes for the Japanese, in the meantime protracting the proceeding.

Another striking feature was the duration of the investigation. In spite of the unique and ample evidence available, it took the European Commission more than 2 years to investigate the matter. During the investigation, the losses increased by 133 %. The outstanding Philips Centre for Quantitative Methods, now Consultants in Quantitative Methods, used statistical methods for demonstration of injury. This injury was demonstrated on the basis of price developments before the excessive and massive dumping started and during the year of investigation. By profit and loss developments of Philips, a similar degree of injury was demonstrated. The head of the investigating team looked at the elaborate injury submission of the complainant and wondered: "*Now what is all this*?" The evidence was too convincing and the head of the investigation team disliked what he saw. The length of the proceeding gave the Japanese ample occasion to transfer production to sites in other countries, especially in East and South East Asia. Graphs 9.1 and 9.2 show what happened. The losses accumulated by Philips in that period were 230 % times the loss incurred in the investigation period.

Strategically, the dumping was a serious setback for Philips. The Philips CD players operated with a swing arm; the Asian CD players had an axial or radial mechanism, both shown in Picture 9.2. Philips calculated that the cost of production would decrease as the amount of mechanical parts used decreased. The swing arm mechanism used chips for correcting the location of the one beam light pen (containing the laser). After a shock, the arm was fixed to the previous position with correction for the time played. The Japanese and the Koreans had adopted a different approach. The more robust radial system contained more mechanical parts. The light pen moved over a radial rail. It was a three-beam linear tracking system. The latter system was simpler in construction and offered no opportunity for correction of errors, but it needed less corrections. Since Philips was the only producer of the swing arm and supplied this essential part in Europe only, it was strategically imperative that European producers' production be saved from collapse. Production and sales of major parts could not fall below an acceptable level.

Graph 9.2 Development of turnover and results of Philips CD production in Europe (*indices*)

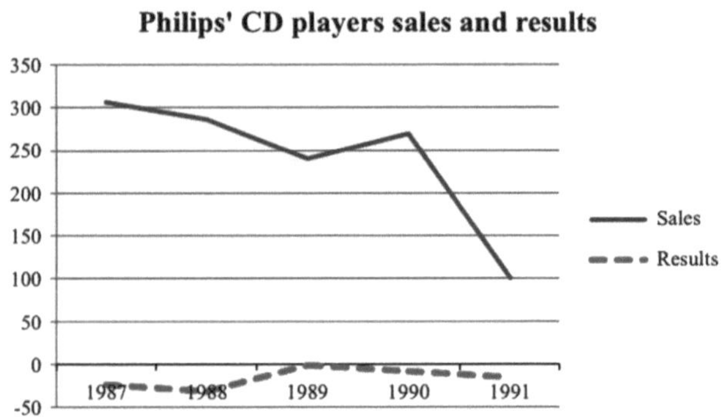

Picture 9.2 Technological discrepancies: CD mechanisms ((**a**) Swing arm, (**b**) Radial or axial system)

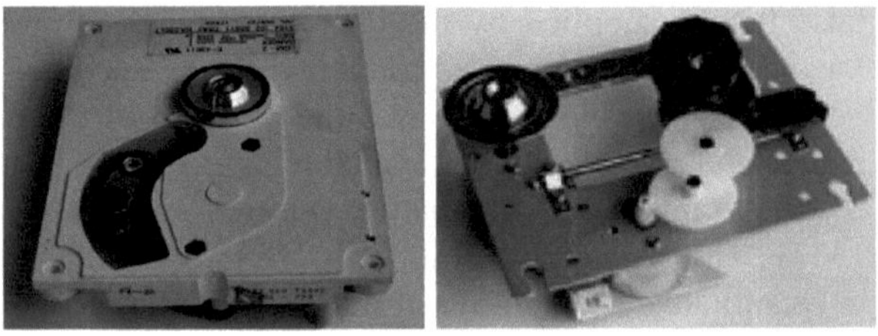

At Philips, the information on dumping and intentional injury was so ample and substantiated that a private law suit against exporters, with the objective of forcing a court to acknowledge that the GATT condemns dumping and that indemnification was imperative, was considered.[10] The implementation of GATT rules in European Community legislation enables the European Community to find a breach of trade rules. The infringement of these rules caused injury to Philips and there was a case for compensation for inflicted injury. Duties as such do not offer compensation for past injury, but seek the elimination of future injury. The duties imposed by the European Commission could never compensate the accumulation of losses. Recovery from injury would have required another increase of duties as compensation for losses that impeded regain in market share. Although the evidence on intentional dumping was overwhelming, private law action was finally abandoned. Decisive was the worry that the Japanese government would increase and extend its retaliation beyond fiscal investigations, closing offices for longer periods than the raid on offices immediately after the lodging of the CD complaint. Another reason was that such an increase would not help very much. Major Japanese exporters had already found their way and an increase in duty would only hurt smaller companies without such opportunities.

[10] The author did not share this view. The intentional injury was consequence of the system and market behaviour, but evidence of the intention to inflict injury was insufficient for a lawsuit. Lawyers at Philips, nevertheless enjoyed spending hours of useless theoretical deliberations about such a proceeding. It did not result in action.

9.4 Much Ado About Nothing: Mishit

During the investigation, several Japanese producers transferred final assembly to neighbouring countries like Singapore, Malaysia and Taiwan. Only one producer, Sony, thought that it was wise to invest in Europe. In order to save his theory that anti-dumping duties resulted in tariff jumping, Belderbos (1994, p. 31) provided misinformation, without reference to sources, claiming knowledge that:

> *eleven CD player plants in the EC were established just before or after the antidumping investigations started.*

Only one single Japanese CD player factory in the European Community was established, however. Sony was the only Japanese producer with an assembly facility in the European Community in Alsace (France). Sony's production fulfilled requirements allowing it to escape from European Community measures against circumvention of duties.[11] In the development laboratory of the Philips CD factory in Hasselt, Belgium, a Sony CD player, model CDP-M 49, made by Sony in Japan, imported into the European Community before duties were imposed, was analysed and compared with a product with the same model code manufactured in Alsace in France after duties were imposed. The construction of Sony's model contained exactly sufficient European content, i.e. more than 50 % of components and materials, by which it could avoid anti-circumvention measures. The outside appearance of both models was identical, but the construction inside (the chassis) was completely different. Clearly Sony's usual law office Van Bael & Bellis had advised the company about the composition of the CD player. "*A very inventive but expensive solution*", one of the experts at Philips in Hasselt observed. For this reason no complaint was ever intended against Japanese subsidiaries in Europe. There was only one Japanese company that spent great sums of money for the avoidance of measures against its assembly activities. Others found a cheaper way, for which no anti-circumvention rules existed

The effect of dumping from Japan seemed to have continued at the same or even higher level, in spite of anti-dumping duties. Prices at resale stage in Europe remained at the same low level. A second complaint, proving that the anti-dumping duties were absorbed and that the dumping increased, was therefore prepared and lodged, but withdrawn as soon as other information arrived. It was not the intention to punish small independent companies that did not have much chance to avoid the duties. A company like Accuphase, with a price to trade of about €1,700, was not to

[11] This highly challenged and finally rejected rule, "Council Regulation (EEC) No 1761/87 of 22 June 1987 amending Regulation (EEC) No 2176/84 on protection against dumped or subsidized imports from countries not members of the European Economic Community" made it possible to impose anti-dumping duties on products put into free circulation in the European Community by a related party of an exporter covered by an anti-dumping duty if the value of the components of that product from the country of origin exceeded the value of the components from other sources by 50 %. This was the case when more than 60 % of the components came from the country to which the duty was applied.

be punished. Such small companies did not have the opportunity to evade the duties. The intention was not to focus on Asahi, which supplied models, as the royalty statements revealed at a price of €80–90, to Braun in Europe, which resold them – a lesson in marketing – at a price of about €700. The complaint concerning the absorption of duties, made on the basis of the information in the royalty statements and additional trade information, was withdrawn. The royalty statements indicated an increasing gap between prices of sales in Japan and export prices. For instance, the dumping margin of Kenwood had gone up from 23.3 % as found by the European Commission in the earlier proceeding to 135.3 %. Onkyo had increased its dumping margin from 8.3 % as found in the proceeding to 162.23 %. For Matsushita, no evidence existed in the form of royalty statements, but on the basis of all trade data it appeared to have widened the gap from 26.3 % to 136.4 %. The losses by Philips amounted 7.8 % over sales during the initial proceeding, which had decreased after the measures, but soon increased again, this time to 15 %.

The direct cause of the withdrawal of the request for an absorption review and start of a complaint toward Malaysia, Singapore and Taiwan was a survey on CD players in the English consumer paper "Which?" with origin indications of tested players. A complaint concerning absorption of duties appeared useless. It was not absorption of duties that caused a continuation of dumping, undercutting and other heavy injury; rather, it was a transfer of final assembly from Japan to three countries in Asia. The royalty statements of the companies concerned did not reveal this shift in location of final assembly. The Japanese had changed their reporting in the royalty statements. The British consumer paper "Which?" revealed their provenance. With the exception of Sony's products, assembled in France, all the products came from subsidiaries in other countries, especially the three Asian countries. This was in the meantime confirmed by Eurostat statistics on importation into the European Community, as shown in Graph 9.1.

Graph 9.1 shows a shift of provenance of imports into the European Community from Japan to three other Asian countries, which started in 1987 and accelerated in subsequent years. NEC did not cooperate with the investigation, and had shifted its production to Malaysia. Akai, Sanyo and Pioneer had joined NEC. Thomson joined the club and had exchanged Dual's production site in the Black Forest in Germany for Malaysia. Singapore was overcrowded with transplants from Aiwa, Funai, Kenwood, Matsushita, Sanyo, Hitachi and Asahi. Sansui and Akai found their refuge in Taiwan. It was clear that some producers used their factories already present in the countries for either redirecting Japanese products to the European Community without or without much processing, i.e. by fraud, or with some minor assembly.

A new complaint against dumping from these three countries was made and submitted. It required a substantial amount of work to find evidence on prices in the domestic markets of these countries. Prices of identical models in Japan were well known from the royalty statements, but prices in the countries of circumvention required new research, which was finally also traced in royalty statements. The European Commission opened the case and started its investigations. Indeed, although the findings were not published, it quickly became clear that dumping was taking place. This dumping was even worse than the previous case against Japan.

While investigations by the European Commission on CD player dumping from Singapore, Taiwan and Malaysia progressed, a sensible managing director of Philips' CD player business wondered what would occur when Japanese producers would shift assembly to China. The final answer was dumping and suffering, depicted in Graph 9.2, would continue and losses would accumulate. This would imply that Philips would never be off the hook. The managing director of Philips' CD player business decided that there was only one way to stop the erosion of results in Europe and to seek refuge in a place where he could use product and production superiority at a low enough cost so that Philips could possibly and continuously meet the dumping by Japanese and Koreans on the European market. He concluded that the continuation of the anti-dumping policy was a waste of time, of efforts and of finance. The first step towards full-scale production in China would be a production start-up in Singapore, which would be the springboard for manufacturing in China. It was decided to consult Grundig and B&O. These two, although committed to production in Europe, agreed. The European Commission was informed about the intention to withdraw the complaint and a request for the discontinuation of the duties toward Japan and Korea. It was clear that anti-dumping would not stop serious erosion of CD players' production in the European Community. The only possibility for regaining market share was cheaper production than the Japanese export price on a more cost effective location. That would be China.

This decision could have been implemented without a request for discontinuing the investigation toward Malaysia, Singapore and Taiwan and without a request for eliminating existing measures towards Japan and Korea. Maintaining the existing measures could create preferential access for Philips' own imports from a future investment in Singapore and, when measures toward Singapore were imposed, later from China. Continuing the duties was considered both unfair to smaller Japanese competitors that suffered from dumping by major Japanese producers, and insensible. A continuation of the measures would mainly benefit those companies that could move their production relatively easily, like Sony in France, to South-East Asia. Disadvantages to smaller companies would also upset competition in Japan itself. One day after the European industry expressed its consideration of these requests to the European Commission, Jean-François Bellis, representing Sony's and some other Japanese exporters' legal interests, phoned and communicated an opinion that withdrawing the existing measures would be bad for Philips. If what he heard were correct, Philips would move to Singapore, but maintain a preferential position for its products from Singapore or later China by the maintenance of the duties toward Japan. During a visit to his Brussels office in the Avenue Louise, it became apparent that it was in Sony's assembly interest in Europe that duties toward Japan be maintained. Philips proposed to Sony that it write a letter to Philips with the request that Philips abstain from applying for the discontinuation of the measures. This was, of course, rejected. Bellis pleaded again for a continuation of measures. It may be wondered how he reconciled this plea on behalf of Sony's interests in Europe with the interests of other Japanese exporters he represented in the proceedings. The final response to Bellis was that Philips was very interested to learn how Sony would cope with a situation of production in Europe while meeting dumping from Japan. Furthermore, it would be fascinating to learn how Sony would cope with the social problems related to the closure of a factory in Europe.

The French government was extremely annoyed by this move of the European Community industry, by which Sony's CD production in France was exposed. However, the French authorities were not acquainted with the surprise Thomson's activities in Malaysia could offer if the proceeding had been completed. To the European Commission, the withdrawal meant a serious defeat. It prompted awareness that without a proper instrument countering the circumvention of anti-dumping duties and deflection of trade, the European Community industry would remain a target of dumping, especially by the Japanese who could easily afford assembly operations abroad. This occurrence was a major contribution to the introduction of the present anti-circumvention clause in European Community legislation, implementing the Anti-Dumping Agreement in the framework of the Uruguay Round. In this respect, it should be emphasised that the Japanese especially could rather easily circumvent anti-dumping measures. Their production had a high capital intensiveness in the last stage of production. The great number of ancillary suppliers required modular product constellation. The last stage of production is a relatively simple operation that can easily be transferred. The low cost of capital, attributable to the high savings rate in a rigidly closed capital market, enabled transfer of machinery for the final assembly. Koreans, for instance, had more integrated production, which was initially labour intensive. The design of products was based on labour intensive manufacturing. That made the transfer of the last stage of production very cumbersome, as they would experience after measures for video recorders and final assembly of VCRs in the United Kingdom (Samsung and Daewoo) and Germany (Goldstar, LG).

The whole story is, therefore, completely different from the delusion sketched by Belderbos (1994, p. 43), who presented a peculiar, but inventive picture of the case:

> *The results of the two 1992 cases indeed indicate that Japanese investments are finally changing the balance in antidumping cases. In July 1993 the CD player case against imports from Taiwan, Singapore, and Malaysia was cancelled as well as the 1991 review of the antidumping case concerning CD player imports from Japan. The reason for this was remarkable. Philips and Thomson withdrew both complaints because they planned to stop all production of CD players in the EC and transfer production to South-East Asia by the end of 1993. There was no 'Community industry' left to protect against injurious imports.*

Thomson had never been complainant in a CD case. The complainants were Bang & Olufsen, Grundig and Philips. Thomson played a role, but it was another and a sad one, i.e. as an exporter from Malaysia. It abandoned a factory in the Black Forest in Germany where it started CD player production in the formerly independent record player producer Dual's factory. As reported before, Thomson was requested to participate as a complainant, but asked for unrealistic guarantees. In accordance with the "Garcin doctrine", Thomson decided to move to Malaysia. During the investigation in the proceeding towards Malaysia, it became apparent that losses incurred by Thomson on this production in Malaysia were about 17 % on turnover on CD players shipped from Malaysia. Had the proceeding been continued, the scandal of Thomson's transfer of production to a location in Malaysia, where it incurred a severe loss, would probably not have been kept quiet. Consequently, the French government could have been more grateful about this withdrawal of the complaint than blaming Philips for Sony's problems in France.

The cause of withdrawal of the two cases after the initial one was awareness that anti-dumping measures did not offer a solution for CD player operations in Europe. Dumping would continue from other countries as long as circumvention could take place. The long duration and the lenient attitude toward the Japanese had made the case completely useless. Another anti-dumping case against again another country would imply a delay for so many years that the CD player business of Philips would have completely perished. For the French government, the discontinuation of the investigation toward Malaysia, Singapore and Taiwan was a blessing in disguise in view of the losses incurred by Thomson. French taxpayers would undoubtedly strongly protest against such a waste of state finance in a Southeast Asian country. A similar phenomenon would also take place in a case concerning colour televisions from Asia, in which Thomson was involved as complainant and as exporter from Thailand.

Some economists have assumed that Japanese producers were so superior in cost of production efficiency that they overcame trade policy measures by means of "tariff jumping" by investments in the countries taking the measures.[12] Superior cost efficiency is a necessary condition for tariff jumping. By some additional investment, the producer can overcome the barrier to trade and continue sales in the market, which was previously an export market. If the assumption of superiority in efficiency is incorrect, and in the case of CD players it was demonstrably incorrect, a library of articles, books and theses has been written to no avail. Another point, which has been forgone by "tariff jumping" theorists, is that cost superiority is not a necessary condition and certainly not a sufficient condition. If dumping continues, but the product's final, often a very simple, assembly is transferred to a country other than the home market where sales at superior prices take place, the exporter and new investor is not superior in costs. Rather, the lower price is a continuation of the dumping by a producer with an oligopolistic domestic market. In the case of CD players, the evidence obviously demonstrated that this occurred. Shipping driving mechanisms and printed circuit boards from Japan, and processing these items abroad in a local assembly in a locally purchased cabinet, which might even be cheaper than in Japan, is not very different from local production in Japan. Additional shipping and handling costs and some transferred

[12] Belderbos (1994) made efforts to demonstrate that protective measures had induced Japanese consumer electronics investments in Europe, by which their superior competitiveness in direct exports was replaced by investments, also characterised by superior efficiency, in the European Community. He did not present evidence on alleged superiority of Japanese management.

wage and machine costs are required for final assembly. The domestic Japanese prices remain high. The texts on "tariff jumping" appear to be based on quicksand.

Protests by Japan against the now abandoned European Community legislation concerning screwdriver operations in the European Community creating the possibility of measures against assembly operations within the European Community,[13] and against the present anti-circumvention provisions, are very understandable. Although the advantages of dumping of products assembled outside Japan still remain, the benefits of dumping from subsidiaries abroad are, because of leakage of such advantages due to additional costs, clearly inferior. Therefore, at long last anti-circumvention actions have impact and appear sometimes useful.

The most important finding in the CD player case, however, was that it was based on evidence provided by Japanese exporters themselves that they were not more, but less efficient, in spite of unsupported allegations by Japanese sources and some European adepts, than their European competitors. If Europeans had been able to sell a similar share of their products, in accordance with the Japanese share of domestic sales in total sales, at prices prevailing in Japan and could dump their exports, they would be profitable and be at least as efficient as or even more than the Japanese. If appropriations were made for the effects of market disruption and market share gain by Japanese and Korean exporters and, the mirror effect, loss by Europeans would be allowed, the Europeans would appear even superior. The situations of Diagrams 8.4 and 8.5 in Chap. 8 appear relevant. The global division of labour is distorted. The world is worse off by dumping. The more cost efficient producer is eliminated.

Reference

Belderbos R (1994) Strategic trade policy and multinational enterprises: essays on trade and investment by Japanese electronics firms, vol 68, Tinbergen research institute series. Thesis Publication, Rotterdam

---

[13] Council Regulation (EEC) No 1761/87 of 22 June 1987 amending Regulation (EEC) No 2176/84 on protection against dumped or subsidized imports from countries not members of the European Economic Community, the "assembly regulation".

Chapter 10
Aftermath of VCRs: The Politicised End to a Continuing Story

Abstract After VHS had won the format dumping war and subsequent intervention, an aftershock threatened all parties. The Korean invasion of the European market, accompanied by illicit imports from Japan, threatened a deceptive peace. By supporting an anti-dumping action, the Japanese government and industry agreed with the actions against Koreans and apostate Japanese VCR producers, which due to internal European Community industry politics coincided with the television and microwave oven cases. Finally, these cases resulted in measures that gave European production some breathing space. Philips and Grundig used the results for the reconstruction of their VCR business and became number one in European production. Copying of an alien commercial policy, Original Equipment Manufacturers (OEM) supplies, bolstered the leading position. Opposite to an export OEM policy, the application of this copy in the domestic European market requires, in order to prevent defections, price discipline among customers not accepted by some competitors. Efforts to correct the situation by an anti-dumping case failed. The Korean transfer of production to the European Community and collapse of Thomson's VCR sales, foreshadow of an expectable final breakdown of this company, caused the failure of the proceeding.

10.1 New Troubles in the VCR Market

In the beginning of 1986, some European Community industry officials, especially from Japanese European joint ventures, told alarming stories about Korean videocassette recorder producers and hidden moves of Japanese producers mentioned in Chap. 5, Sect. 5.2. It gradually became apparent that the Weather Forecast had not prompted the state of affairs envisaged by the European Commission and, what was worse, by the Japanese Ministry of International Trade and Industry (MITI; presently the Ministry of Economy, Trade and Industry (METI) since 2001). The state of affairs envisaged by MITI was peace in the European market and an established position of the Japanese major companies in Europe. Additionally, there were rumours that two

M. van Marion, *International Trade Policy and European Industry*, Contributions to Economics, DOI 10.1007/978-3-319-00392-4_10,

Table 10.1 Shares in the European Community VCR market: Koreans and Japanese (1984–1987)

	1984 (%)	1985 (%)	1986 (%)	1987 (%)
Koreans	0.0	1.2	5.6	15.3
Two Japanese newcomers (Orion and Funai)	5.0	7.2	13.1	14.3
Total Koreans and two Japanese	5.0	8.3	18.7	29.6
Official imports from Japan	64.2	49.9	32.0	29.8
Euro-Nips production[a] and Japanese assembly	20.0	31.7	40.7	32.4
Total Japanese supplies of kits and VCRs, majors	84.3	81.7	72.8	62.3
Other	10.7	10.0	8.6	8.1

[a]Joint ventures of Europeans and Japanese (see Chaps. 2 and 3)

Japanese producers, Orion and Funai, hardly known until the beginning of 1986, exported extremely low-priced VCRs by means of transhipments. Table 10.1 sketches the situation.

Until the middle of 1985, additional supplies of VCRs in kits and subassemblies seemed able to compensate the reduction of Japanese imports and MITI's strategy successful. In 1986, however, it became apparent that two threats disturbed the scheme. Koreans suddenly took the market share that MITI thought was reserved for Japanese majors. Additionally the Japanese outsiders disturbing order and peace, posed a problem.

10.2 Japanese Affection for Koreans

European industrialists with ties to Japanese VCR producers, representatives of J2T partner Ferguson and from Thomson and from MB Video's Blaupunkt, warned of the disaster the Koreans inflicted on European producers. Retail prices of Korean VCRs of one hundred or more Euros below the going retail price of both European and Japanese manufacturers and their European OEM' clients and Japanese-European joint ventures appeared highly destructive. It was rumoured that even some Europeans were guilty of business with the Koreans. It was alleged that the Koreans supplied ITT/Graetz (Nokia). The Korean producers delivered to egregious brands such as Anitech, Bondstech,[1] Clatronic, Condor and Teletech, but also to established trade brands such as SEG Schmidt, Schneider and Tensai and many other trade brands and potential OEM clients, even though the equipment to OEMs did not differ from their branded products, apart from the brand names and some superficial appearances.

Sony's efforts to save its Betamax by a license to the Koreans are mentioned in an earlier chapter.[2] Under contracts, the Koreans could not start exporting VHS

[1] The company Bondstech allegedly even received an investment subsidy from the Dutch government under the pretext of job creation in the assembly of VCRs. The company would soon disappear.

[2] Section 5.2 of Chap. 5 mentions the opinion of Mr. Morita of Sony in a meeting of Keidanren with the European Round Table of Industrialists in Rome in springtime of 1990 about the need to apply a COCOM, as applied toward Communist countries, to the Koreans.

Table 10.2 Average price of Korean electronics for export and domestic market in 2000 (US$)

	Microwave ovens	CTV	VCR	Disc recorder
Production value average	$74.37	$132.27	$88.27	$120.31
Domestic selling price reported by EIAK	$70.36	$147.84	$153.79	$233.28
Selling, general and administrative cost added: 15 %	$80.92	$170.02	$176.86	$268.27
Export average price	$77.59	$104.54	$56.57	$100.74
Difference between domestic (plus SG&A) and export price	$3.32	$65.48	$120.29	$167.53
Dumping margin of CIF (I&F 2 %)	4.2 %	61.4 %	208.4 %	163.0 %

VCRs before March 1985. The Korean share in the European Community market soon rose from 1 % in 1985 when they commenced exportation, to 6 % in 1986 and about 15.3 % in 1987.[3] Korean prices in the EEC clearly undercut those of European producers and of Japanese assembly units in the EEC and, of course, the more expensive models imported from Japan. After some analysis of evidence on the Korean market, dumping appeared undeniable.

As in Japan, the Korean domestic distribution characteristics allowed for domestic sales at high prices and exports at lower prices. Korean efficiency was higher and dumping margins appeared lower. Lower dumping margins for colour television and for VCRs than Japanese exporters' margins were found. Table 10.2 shows the gap between the average domestic and export prices.[4] Microwave ovens were a test: the outcome of the European Community anti-dumping investigations was that there had been no dumping. The assumption that Korean producers were dumping, but not much less than Japanese, appeared wrong. Table 10.2 shows firm dumping on other products, however.

Dumping should be established on model-by-model comparison of equipment sold domestically and abroad. The dumping gap between the domestic market price and export price by percentages such as 61.4 % for CTV, 208.4 % for video recorders and 163.0 % for disc recorders cannot possibly be explained by differences in consumer taste or in quality and features of equipment. In any case, with the exception of microwave ovens all products like CTV were exported at prices far below the domestic value.

In Graph 7.1 (Chap. 7), the average United States import price of microwave ovens from Korea was $84.74 in 2000. Dumping must have been absent. From Japan,

[3] Many of the data are from market statistics that were made available by the French association Simavelec. Import statistics and export statistics are from Eurostat, Korean, Japanese, Hong Kong and Singapore official statistics.

[4] Source: Electronic Industry Association of Korea (EIAK), 2001 Statistics for Electronic Industries.

the United States imported at an average price of $222 and from China at $56.44. The latter probably represented exports from Japanese subsidiaries. The United States import price of VCRs from Korea in 2000 was $80.88. That was far below the Korean production value per unit. The Korean average export price at $65.48 to all destinations was also below cost of manufacturing. That may have been a serious level of price dumping. It implied that Korean consumers were, when not cooking with their microwave ovens, worse off compared to foreigners. The Koreans clearly posed a serious threat to the Japanese. For the VCR, this problem already started in the mid 1980s. Korea had become Japan's VCR apprentice.

In 1986, Koreans appeared able to supply more than 15 % of the United States VCR market in direct competition with and at the expense of Japan's historical presence. The Koreans' market share in Europe rose amazingly to 15 % in 2½ years. Their average prices were substantially lower than the Japanese, although apparently not low enough to penetrate the Japanese market by more than 2 %. The Japanese clearly wanted this phenomenon of disruption in their market in Europe halted.

10.3 MITI's Discipline Problem

Japan, therefore, rather readily accepted a European customs duty increase from 8 % to 14 % on VCRs, sketched in Chap. 5. Japan's investment interests in Europe would be better protected against new inroads into Europe, this time from Korea. This duty increase, of course, discriminated against Japanese newcomers and Koreans exporting to the European Community. This apparently did not bother Japan and Japanese major companies. However, the level of this higher duty of 14 % appeared hardly a barrier to the Koreans and the two Japanese companies. It did not appear sufficient. That was why some European industrialists of the European Japanese joint ventures (Euronips) tried so eagerly to convince others, Philips and Grundig, of the necessity of an anti-dumping action. The formal submission was finally made in March 1987.[5] The reason why Philips prepared the case was that it wanted to prevent the case from going in the wrong direction. Some of the manufacturers that were a member of European Association Consumer Electronics Manufacturers (EACEM) imported Korean sets under their own brand name. They complained about the behaviour of the two Japanese producers. These were also target of the Euronips, but these could not voice their views openly. When the complaint concerning Korean VCRs was extended to those companies, it was also supported by the joint ventures of JVC (J2T with Thomson) and Matsushita (MB Video with Bosch).[6]

---

[5] Complaint made by the European Association of Consumer Electronics Manufacturers (EACEM) Against Imports of Video Cassette Recorders from Korea and Japan.

[6] This is according to the non-confidential file submitted by the European Association of Consumer Electronics (EACEM).

It was alleged that the market shares of Orion and Funai were made possible by cooperation, *inter alia*, with ISP, a German company, and Alan Sugar's Amstrad. The latter pretended to establish a production facility in 1984, but it was mainly a veil for hiding circumventions and Funai's share in the evasions. Similarly, Orion and the Koreans had also hastily set up operations where some cursory assembly took place. Some "solid" European producers had also imported products, which had been shipped from Japan to other destinations than the European Community and subsequently re-exported to the European Community. The two Japanese companies, Orion and Funai had commenced production in 1983, stealthily exporting about 300,000 VCRs in 1984 to more than a million in 1987. The exportation was clandestine, hiding the origin of the export by transhipment via Hong Kong, Singapore, Switzerland and Finland, which allegedly escaped the attention of MITI.[7] Orion, Funai and Shintom had sold no or negligible small volumes in Japan. The greatest problem they posed to Japanese majors was their disruption of the European market. Afterwards it became apparent that their products were substantially cheaper than their Japanese major competitors. Their competitiveness was superior and this advantage would be taxed away by anti-dumping duties. Their production, selling and overhead costs were extremely low. Lack of domestic distribution opportunities prevented sales and profits in Japan and they had to rely on exports. In Europe, they sold mainly to traders under the stencil brands of the traders or to European electronics manufacturers of other equipment than VCRs, called OEM manufacturers that were actually VCR traders. They caused nuisance to established Japanese producers assembling in Europe or exporting under MITI's export control regime. They also affected MITI's authority. The situation had become embarrassing to MITI and the ministry's foreign representation via the Japan Machinery Exporters' Association (JMEA), therefore, readily yet silently in bilateral contacts agreed with a proceeding that would end the dire state of affairs and would also, fortunately, deal with Korean imports.

Japanese newcomers in VCR trade did not have a comfortable position, as Chap. 7 indicates is the general situation in Japan. These newcomers generally do not have a chance in the Japanese market. Additionally, since they had no historical performance and no possibility to export, they did not obtain export licenses. Their big brothers assembled VCRs in Europe from dumped VCR parts and, under the MITI licensing system, were able to export complementary VCR volumes in accordance with their export performance in 1982. The only chance newcomers had was transhipment via third countries that had PAL television systems and were not covered by the system of export licenses, for instance, Hong Kong, Finland and Switzerland.

[7] Statistics of the Ministry of Finance of Japan, Eurostat, Import and Export Statistics and Transit statistics of Hong Kong and Singapore.

10.4 Company Politics and Trade Law

The organisation of support for the dumping complaint was highly political. Industrial importers of Korean sets demanded actions against the two Japanese companies. They rejected a limitation of a complaint to Korea. Including only two Japanese exporters was discriminatory. Normally such discrimination is unacceptable. Table 10.1 implies that, if a non-discriminatory complaint were lodged against Japan, dumping but not injury would probably be found. To the former Video 2000 parties, Grundig and Philips, a limitation in the complaint to two Japanese exporters did not seem appropriate. Analysis of their machines, in combination with the circumstance that the two companies did not have local sales in Japan, resulted in the conclusion that these companies were just more cost-effective than their Japanese competitors. Including these two producers should imply a general case toward Japan, which would have been contrary to the statistics in Table 10.1 that indicated a decreasing share of Japanese imports in the European Community market. The statistics are repeated in Table 10.3 below as imports of Japanese VCRs as share of the European Community market.

It is apparent from Table 10.3 that if major Japanese exporters were excluded from the proceeding, a dumping complaint could be lodged on behalf of European industry against Japan. If the complaint was not discriminatory, Japanese VCR import market share would have decreased and injury by decrease of European market share could not have been demonstrated, unless the data were limited to 1986 and 1987. Grundig and Philips could have lodged a complaint without the others. They could have extended the scope of the "product concerned" to essential parts of video recorders as mechanical decks and scanners. In this way, both the issue of sufficient support for the complaint and the issue of injury could have been solved. All Japanese and joint ventures could have been excluded. Since Grundig and Philips were the only producers also making the decks and the scanners, they represented more than 50 % of producers not importing VCRs and not importing these decks and scanners from the countries concerned. If the injury was restricted to the product VCR, then including Japanese exporters other than the two mentioned above would have been possible only if the Koreans were added and the injury limited to data on the last 2 years, i.e. 1986 and 1987. Discrimination between the Japanese was both procedurally and politically preferable. Article 9.5 of the present Basic Regulation, the European Community anti-dumping legislation prohibits discrimination and prescribes:

> *An anti-dumping duty shall be imposed in the appropriate amounts in each case, on a non-discriminatory basis on imports of a product from all sources found to be dumped and causing injury...*[8]

---

[8] Council Regulation (EC) No 384/96 of 22 December 1995 on protection against dumped imports from countries not members of the European Community (OJ L 56, 6.3.1996, p. 1) Amended by: the following Regulations No 2331/96 of 2 December 1996, OJ L 317 of 6.12.1996; No 905/98 of 27 April 1998, OJ L 128 of 30.4.1998; No 2238/2000 of 9 October 2000, OJ L 257 of 11.10.2000; No 1972/2002 of 5 November 2002, OJ L 305 of 7.11.2002; No 461/2004 of 8 March 2004, OJ L 77 of 13.3.2004; and No 2117/2005 of 21 December 2005, OJ L 340 of 23.12.2005.

Table 10.3 Total market share of VCR imports from Japan

	1984 (%)	1985 (%)	1986 (%)	1987 (%)
Orion and Funai	5.0	7.2	13.1	14.3
Japanese plus Orion and Funai	69.3	57.1	45.1	44.1
Koreans added to Japanese	69.3	58.3	50.7	59.4

The Basic Regulation applicable on the case states something more vague:

Where a product is imported into the Community from more than one country, duty shall be levied at an appropriate amount on a non-discriminatory basis on all imports of such product found to be dumped or subsidized and causing injury, other than imports from those sources in respect of which undertakings have been accepted. [9]

Europeans besides Grundig and Philips feared that if a dumping complaint were lodged without their consent and participation, it might implicate all Japanese exporters and anti-dumping measures might hit their imports. They were not aware that declining imports made injury difficult to find. The fear was that the Japanese, including the joint ventures of J2T and MB Video, would be excluded from the definition of "Community industry" as companies related to dumping exporters.[10] This would have resulted in a case against their interests. They did not know that there should be a clear demonstration of injury, which was absent. Due to pressure on the Europeans from their Japanese allies, the complaint was limited to Korea and the two Japanese outsiders.[11]

The Commission decision to initiate the present investigation against exporters in South Korea and against Funai and Orion only was based on the complaint which was expressly limited to Korea and the two Japanese firms and which did not contain any evidence of dumping or injury from any other source. At this time there was no other evidence available to the Commission, which would have indicated that other imports from Japan or other countries were dumped, or that they were causing injury. Under these conditions the Commission did not in any way behave in a discriminatory manner.

Certainly, however, all Japanese, perhaps with the exception of Funai and Orion, dumped. Dumping is endemic in Japanese export behaviour, as described in Chaps. 7 and 8. The European Commission may have behaved in a non-discriminatory way, but European and joint venture industry did not. Some European industrialists did not have the slightest notion of what dumping was about and how the procedural requirements had to be fulfilled. They just formulated demands. One demand was that they and their partners should be safeguarded from anti-dumping. The data on dumping by Japanese major producers had to be suppressed. Part of the European Industry instigated the discrimination by the European Commission.

[9] The texts of the Basic Regulations of 1984 and 1988 had this reference to discrimination.

[10] Chapters 15 and 16 dedicate ample attention to the issue of "Community industry".

[11] Commission Regulation (EEC) No 2684/88 of 26 August 1988 imposing a provisional anti-dumping duty on certain imports of video cassette recorders originating in Japan and the Republic of Korea (OJ L 240, 31.8.1988, pp. 5–17), recital (8).

Orion and Funai later, correctly, protested against the discrimination between them and other Japanese producers. In the proceeding, the European Commission rejected this protest, alleging that the complainant did not include other producers or find dumping by others. However, the complainant could have easily found dumping by other Japanese companies; there was a chronic price difference between Japan and Europe, or dumping of 30 %. This was more than the dumping by Orion and Funai, as constructed by the European Commission. The European partners of the Japanese were horrified by the prospect of Japanese retaliation. The case against Orion and Funai was exceptional, and was the consequence of Japanese and their related European partners' pressure, to which Grundig and Philips finally yielded and dropped the idea of extending the product scope to VCR plus basic components to prove injury and exclude the European-Japanese joint ventures.

Certain developments suited some parties within Philips well. If there was not a case against Japan and the Japanese were safeguarded against anti-dumping with regard to VCR, other options were open. The internal politics at Philips required three dumping complaints to be made almost simultaneously. The director of the VCR unit did not like to admit that technologically inferior Koreans posed problems. Besides, he did not want to expose his business unit as the unprofitable driving force behind anti-dumping procedures. The accounting system at Philips enabled him to shift losses to the factories as "target profit" shortfall, i.e. a mistake of the factory that did not meet the target cost. The director of the television business unit demanded in a high tone that his problems, which were according to him attributable to external factors like the Koreans, were immediately solved. In the segment of 14-in. (36 cm, tiny vision) sets, Korea, and later China and Hong Kong, started exports, which spoiled this market. He did not want to be alone as responsible for anti-dumping actions at Philips. The Swedish Philips factory of microwave ovens was in difficulty because of an increasing market share of Japanese and Korean ovens in the European Community market. Consequently, at the request of the Division of Major Domestic Appliances in Italy, Philips' department for International Economic Relations prepared a microwave complaint. Three dumping complaints on behalf of the industry had been compiled. One, for microwave ovens, was made on behalf of the European domestic appliances industry European Committee of Manufacturers of Electrical Domestic Equipment (CECED). In 1987, Sweden was not part of the European Community. The complaint was against Japan and its subsidiaries in Singapore and against Korea. The idea was that MITI's anger could be mitigated if the VCR case was handled to the advantage of the Japanese majors, some of which were implicated in the microwave oven case. This supposition appeared correct. This time, it was not MITI that reacted, at least as far as VCR was concerned. The other two complaints were made on behalf of the EACEM.

The first reaction and action of Japanese industry after opening of the microwave proceeding was an effort to prove that Philips dumped its products from Sweden. Most striking, the Japanese microwave oven industry had accurate information on Philips' production on the basis of a collection of data on the number of magnetrons supplied by Japanese companies to Philips. Normally, components manufacturers keep information on their customers to themselves. But the Japanese did not have such inhibitions, as was already clear when MITI asked for information from the Japanese industry about the production volume of Philips in the European Community for the sake of negotiations about the Weather Forecast. The Japanese effort to extend the dumping action to Philips Sweden was futile, however. The evidence on Philips' prices in Sweden and the European Community was incorrect. CECED's complaint appeared also mistaken. The Japanese, although heavily dumping microwave ovens, had lost market share in Europe to the Koreans, who did either not or only marginally dump. This appears in accordance with the data in Table 10.2. Consequently, the complaint had to be withdrawn.[12] Table 10.2 shows that microwave ovens were, indeed, an exception to the rule.

In 1990, an occasion arose to start a similar case for VCR again, but now against one single Japanese company, Shintom, a relatively small Japanese firm that was able to conquer about 6 % of the European market under miscellaneous European known and exotic brand names. This company was also supplier of mecadecks to Funai, which switched its production to China in 1993 and discontinued Shintom's deck supplies, and to Sony for low-end mecadeck requirements. This company had incurred losses on its sales and therefore a dumping complaint was possible. It is doubtful whether MITI officials would have protested this time, provided that the "majors" would not be involved. It was not worthwhile to repeat such an action, however. J2T, incited by its ally Thorn, seemed eager to go ahead with such a case because Shintom had reasonable sales in the United Kingdom. The European Commission considered the case highly unattractive and made this clear to the Thorn/Ferguson industrialists.

10.5 Reshuffle of the European Theatre

The Korean VCR producers were found guilty of dumping at margins of between 17 % and 24 %, while the dumping margins of the two Japanese firms, Orion and Funai, were between 11 % and 13 %.[13] The three exporters from Korea and Funai offered price undertakings, which were accepted. In the case of the Koreans, it was found that their prices undercut the prices of European producers, including two Euronips, European-Nipponian combinations J2T and MB Video, by more than the dumping margins. The conclusion could be drawn that the Koreans, although their dumping margins were substantial but more moderate than margins that Philips had calculated for Japanese majors before the file had been transferred to EACEM, were slightly more efficient than their major Japanese counterparts. In view of their relatively high prices in the

[12] Commission Decision of 12 December 1988 terminating the anti-dumping proceeding on imports of microwave ovens originating in Japan, the Republic of Singapore and the Republic of Korea (88/622/EEC).

[13] Probably based on artificial normal value as discussed in Sect. 16.10 (Chap. 16), taking cost of production plus the selling, general and administrative costs (SG&A) incurred by the majors in Japan as yardstick for normal value; an extremely unfair approach, supported by the Court of Justice.

Korean market, dumping and a finding of dumping was inevitable. The Koreans conducted a policy similar, explained in Chap. 8, to the Japanese. The similarity explains Korean OEM and stencil brand export supplies to Currys (Matsui), Dixons, Tandy (Memorex), Quelle (Universum), Carrefour (Blue Sky), Vendet, Molenaar (Frontech), ITT, Innohit and so forth. Their eagerness to pass the Japanese encouraged them to win market share. It was not surprising that they were dumping, but it was unforeseen that they would outrival Japanese exporters. The great Korean enterprises or chaebol, comparable with the pre-war Japanese zaibatsu, now gurupu, had established captive distribution networks similar to those in Japan so that dumping had the same background as the Japanese. However, Korea's population is smaller than Japan's, and purchasing power was inferior. The Korean domestic market served as a springboard for exports, but both domestic and export prices were lower than those of Japanese competitors. Dumping margins officially established were generally smaller, as was also the case with Compact Disc Players, than the Japanese dumping margins. A dumping margin of 11.5 % for Funai and 13.0 % for Orion, the latter margin higher because of Orion's non-cooperation, was not high compared with the margins found for the Japanese majors in other cases, which generally were above 20 %.

The difference was in the first place attributable to absence of domestic sales by these two companies.[14] Secondly, the special treatment of the OEM by the European Commission also resulted in lower duties. The two Japanese exporters moved production from Japan to other locations and exported VCRs to Europe from the other locations. It appears that they were more efficient than their big compatriots. Chapter 16, Sect. 16.11 discusses the position of manufacturers of OEM equipment without domestic sales and tries to show that the imposition of anti-dumping duties in this case was a serious error in principle. By relocating production, the two both escaped from the duties and the undertaking and from the efforts by MITI to supervise and direct some of their activities. The most important aspect of this case was that although Japanese producers and authorities pretended that they had a peace agreement with the European Community, the Weather Forecast, the deal was completely ineffective. Therefore, anti-dumping measures, although much time would have passed before they would have effectively applied, would have been more correct and would have had the required impact, provided that the proceeding was not as protracted as the CD player case.

A Deputy Director General of the European Commission's External Affairs Directorate General had not demonstrated much interest in anti-dumping, but suddenly and unexpectedly intervened shortly before retiring, and tried to appease the Koreans. He advised them and Funai to offer an agreement to the European Commission, committing themselves to minimum prices and to a certain minimum domestic content for assembly in Europe. The Koreans plucked courage from this interference and started negotiations with delegations of European industry associations. EIAK negotiated with the EACEM and with the CECED. After a

[14] Funai produced mecadecks and made VCRs for domestic Japanese producers.

minimum price promise by EIAK, CECED withdrew its complaint: "*On 26 September 1988 the Commission was informed by the complainant that it was withdrawing the complaint because of profound changes in the market place*".[15] The Japanese had dumped but had not inflicted injury, due to loss of market share to the Koreans; whereas the Koreans inflicted injury but had not dumped.

Since EACEM was involved in two procedures, the Koreans expected to make a deal on both VCRs and small screen colour television sets. However, the Philips director of colour television, who insisted on participating in the negotiations, appeared incapable of making up his mind whether he would accept self-restriction by the Koreans on colour television or opt for a more risky outcome of an anti-dumping duty, about which all Koreans, except perhaps the Koreans in EIAK, were in the dark. He was a risk-avoiding person and he manoeuvred so that others could be blamed for failures. Eager to conclude a deal for colour television, he hoped that a concession on VCR might serve a deal for colour televisions. Such a benefit for his television business would be at the cost of his VCR colleagues. Other Philips delegates were able, however, to thwart these efforts. As a consequence the negotiations collapsed. The benefit was that official Community measures would be taken, rather than, again a voluntary restraint by the Koreans. The representative of Thorn Ferguson was highly disappointed, imagining a resumption of past practice of annual negotiations and travelling as in the times of the voluntary restraint discussions of the British Radio Industry Council. Instead, anti-dumping would be imposed for small screen CTV. Although he was served well by appropriate anti-dumping duties on small screen CTV from Korea (Chap. 11), from then onwards the Philips television director blamed everyone else for bad results in colour television. He grumbled about Korean competitors, the Japanese, the alleged Finland route for duty-free picture tube imports, price erosion by competitors and the lack of prompt service by Philips headquarter executives to solve his problems. He alleged, for instance, that television sets were produced in Finland containing duty-free Hitachi tubes. He demanded strong measures against the circumvention of trade. An investigation into the Finland issue resulted in the conclusion that the colour television sets he had referred at were Nokia and Salora sets containing European Philips tubes. A salient result from Philips' responses to the inquiry by the European Commission on the cost of production per model was that he had not been able to withstand the claims of Philips national sales organisations that television should be specified according to unidentified national consumer taste in their countries. The result was a chaotic number of different versions per model.

[15] Commission Decision of 12 December 1988 terminating the anti-dumping proceeding on imports of microwave ovens originating in Japan, the Republic of Singapore and the Republic of Korea (88/622/EEC).

A cost explosion was the consequence.[16] That information had to be suppressed, but measures to streamline the number of models were taken.

An undertaking on minimum prices for both exported and assembled Korean (and Funai) VCRs in the European Community, and assurance to the European Commission of 45 % European content in assembly operations in the European Community proved, against all expectations, extremely disadvantageous to the Koreans. Unlike Japanese producers, they could not easily transfer production, let alone to industrialised countries with high wage rates. Japanese assembly was, due to low capital costs, capital intensive, highly mechanised and relatively independent from the country of the production location. Some additional machinery could solve the problem of final assembly for circumvention of duties at relatively small labour cost. The design of Korean VCRs was based on low wage rates in Korea, relatively high motivation of the workforce and, consequently, low labour cost. The labour intensiveness of production required by the design of their products created an impediment to transfer to Europe. Goldstar in Worms and Samsung and Daewoo in the United Kingdom suffered serious complications in their operations in Europe. A vacuum in stencil brand and OEM supplies had suddenly arisen.

After VHS gained sufficient market share, Japanese producers abandoned supplies of products on OEM basis to European customers. Koreans and Funai and Orion filled this gap. They supplied traders, big department stores, mail order companies and manufacturers under theses distributors' brands. Since the assembly that the Koreans transferred to Europe stagnated, Philips increased its VCR production by acquiring the former customers of the Koreans and the two Japanese producers. The formation of a Grundig-Philips VCR joint venture, iR3, combined the VCR production of Grundig and Philips, and the new company became number one producer of VCRs in the European Community. It attracted the stencil brand and OEM customers that the Koreans could not serve because of their production problems. ITT/Nokia, Schneider, Blaupunkt, Quelle (the Universum brand), Goodmans, Siemens, Blaupunkt and some others, even Sony for a few models, switched to iR3. The production of iR3 increased from a few hundred thousand units before the dumping case against Koreans and Orion and Funai to 2.3 in 1991 and to 2.8 million units in 1994. This created substantial cost effectiveness. It also created serious problems.

Some new customers of the new joint venture had been obdurate price fighters. German mail order company Quelle with its Universum brand, for instance, was a fierce price fighter on the German market. Schneider-Rundfunkwerke AG, was a regular OEM or stencil brand customer of Japanese majors and of the Koreans in the initial period of VCR. The new Japanese in subsequent periods acquired fame by Schneider-Rundfunkwerke AG's disruption of the market. Low prices in the United Kingdom had given Goodmans a reputation. Other iR3 customers, like

[16] He also wanted price agreements and wanted the European Union to impose the High Definition Standard. He remained deaf to warnings that agreements on prices were forbidden, but also as history would demonstrate, that imposing a television system (HDTV) lacked a legal basis in the European Community and was an illusion.

Bang and Olufsen and Blaupunkt and Grundig, loathed such rough price practices. A major problem for the new VCR company iR3 was discipline among customers. From point of view of iR3 it was useless that each of the ten customers would try to obtain market share at the cost of any of the others. For the producer, there was no advantage in gain of market share by one distributor, like Schneider, at the cost of another, Blaupunkt, for instance. If one distributor lost market share, it might try to get a cheaper source than iR3 and switch to Koreans or Funai and Orion. This would destroy a carefully constructed edifice of market participation and volume of production, with its cost advantage. With some success, iR3 was capable of keeping peace among its customers. This phenomenon shows the difference between Japanese and Korean on one hand and European production for OEM on the other. The Japanese and the Koreans conducted an OEM policy on export markets, and volume of production was more essential than the price levels on export markets. European producers with OEM customers were stuck between the need to attain production volume and not to disturb the price level too much.[17] Although the volume decreased the cost of production and prices had generally gone down in accordance with cost cuts, European competition authorities would undoubtedly have tried to forbid such practices to keep volume high and cost of production low and to maintain some peace in pricing among the customers. They would have preferred that exporters take the market and dump their products in supplies to European OEM customers.

Japanese majors sold under their own brand names rather than to OEM customers and kept quiet on the price front. As far as pricing is concerned, they were used to peaceful coexistence in settled markets, especially when market shares were reasonably established. Two groups of producers did not embrace this serene market picture. Having lost considerable customer potential by their assembly production problems, the Koreans were eager to regain the ground. The other threat came from Thomson. Not satisfied by cooperation in the joint factory with JVC in Berlin, where subsidies were discontinued, it switched to production in Singapore together with Toshiba. For several reasons Thomson was again eager to obtain market share. The serious gap between Thomson's budgeted ambitions in an internal Thomson document and worldwide actual production revealed to competitors that serious problems were ahead. Annual production was to rise from 1.9 million units in 1994 to 3.8 million in 1995. World market share would rise from about 4 % to 7 %. This could never be achieved without serious market disruption. This was not a major problem to Thomson, however. Gaining market share before Thomson's privatisation was imperative. Inevitably, this boost should take place at the cost of competitors and of French taxpayers. In 1982, Thomson had become state-owned, but financial assistance by the French state to this company

[17] Price maintenance by producers is forbidden by what is now Article 101(1) of the Treaty on the Functioning of the European Union ("TFEU"). The existence of iR3 and the decrease in cost of production or relatively low cost were threatened by the prohibition. Dumping and price maintenance in the domestic market of dumpers and OEM is allowed, but the defence against that policy is forbidden.

Table 10.4 Actual VCR production of Thomson and ambitions

VCR (units × 1,000)	
End September 1994	1,903
End September 1995, budget	2,841
Actual 1995	2,658
Budget 1995	3,835

became too expensive and privatisation was close.[18] It became apparent that continuous state support would be prohibited at some moment. For Thomson's competitors this condemnation would come too late (Table 10.4).[19]

An increase in volume brought the cost of production down by about 5–10 %. Prices also decreased by 8 %. Damage to other producers was inevitable. In order to obtain this position and to lay a smokescreen over Thomson's moves, Pierre Darrot, previously boss of the microwave oven business in the Thomson Group since 1985, had drawn up a radical plan for a drastic repositioning of Thomson's brands, causing confusion among competitors, among consumers and finally disaster to Thomson itself.

10.6 Failed Attempt of Appeasement

iR3's OEM customers could, but the Koreans and Thomson could not be kept to a price peace. Philips' low margins also created problems as reseller of iR3 machines According to customers' complaints to iR3, Philips was extremely aggressive in the market. Philips' defence was its heavy competition with Thomson and the Koreans. Other iR3 customers' complaints about Philips' price policy amounted to threats to switch to Koreans for low prices and market share, which Philips took away from them. Table 10.5 shows the market behaviour of various iR3 customers. Table 10.5 shows the relation of average retail prices of some iR3 customers to the prices at which iR3 supplied to them.[20] The lower the factor, the lower (assuming wholesalers' and retailers' margins equal for all) the gross margin of iR3's customer. In internal calculations, companies generally assumed a necessary gross margin from the ex-factory to the consumer of 1.8 to 2.1. That means that the market behaviour of some companies in the Table 10.5 with a lower ratio may be identified as aggressive.[21]

The market behaviour of customers of iR3 clearly differs, as Table 10.5 shows. Table 10.6 confirms this difference and shows the relations with other producers'

[18] It took place in 1999.

[19] It was expected that at last the Commission of the EC wanted an end to these practices. Commission Decision of 1 October 1997 concerning aid granted by France to Thomson SA and Thomson Multimedia (98/183/EC), Official Journal L 67/31, 7.3.98.

[20] These are weighted selling prices by iR3 of various models supplied to OEM customers and compared with the prices of the same products of these customers in retail trade in Germany, as reported by GfK.

[21] Sources: iR3 and the Gesellschaft für Konsumforschung (GfK).

Table 10.5 Relation of VCR retail prices to iR3 supply prices of some iR3 customers (Germany)

Brand customers of iR3	Ratio retail price Germany (incl. VAT) to purchasing price from iR3	Market share in Germany (%)
Schneider	1.30	3
Philips	1.62	7
Sony	1.84	8
Siemens	1.86	1
Blaupunkt	1.91	4
Grundig	1.92	11
RFT	2.19	0.1

Table 10.6 iR3 customers' retail prices compared with Thomson and Korean VCRs

Supplier and OEM	Two head mono	Four head stereo
iR3 customers		
Schneider	469.06	928.51
Nokia	516.22	1,128.29
Siemens	561.96	1,152.97
Philips	599.93	1,239.17
Blaupunkt	603.88	1,516.53
Metz	626.14	1,558.46
Grundig	644.66	1,365.84
iR3 customers	590.80	1,347.33
Thomson		
Saba	574.70	965.87
Nordmende	659.03	1,473.61
Telefunken	674.53	1,250.41
Thomson	643.93	1,254.91
Trade brands	477.36	908.91
Korean brands		
Daewoo	513.68	897.00
LGE	482.04	
Samsung	454.23	800.25

market conduct. Some iR3 customers, headed by Schneider, buying also from some other suppliers, were more aggressive than others. Schneider was aggressive by habit, and keen to buy from the Koreans, in view of prices in Table 10.6. The policy of Philips was not understandable and a serious damage to the interests of its supplier and subsidiary, iR3. Since Grundig was related to Philips and had obtained a profit guarantee from Philips,[22] any action that would undercut Grundig's prices would cause price erosion and damage to the interests of the company Philips in general, especially because it was in a market where Grundig was relatively strong, the German market.

Korean resurrection caused serious headaches. Their assembly of simple VCRs with two and three-head drums and imported high-end products with HiFi and

[22] An agreement to guarantee Grundig its profits had been concluded as part of the take-over deal with Max Grundig.

Table 10.7 Market of VCRs in the European Community of 15 member states (1989–1994) (× 1,000)

	1989	1990	1991	1992	1993	1994[a]
Production of Nuremberg (iR3)	1,472	1,753	525	810	511	409
Production of Vienna (iR3)	713	760	1,797	1,551	1,982	2,381
Total VCR production (iR3)	2,185	2,513	2,322	2,361	2,493	2,790
Japanese assembly (in the Community)	5,040	5,751	6,433	4,765	3,975	3,390
Korean assembly (in the Community)	0	488	578	584	965	1,200
Korean imports (high-end products)	976	956	1,120	572	769	1,078
Imports from Singapore (Thomson)	390	663	766	869	1,079	2,091
Imports from Korea and Singapore	1,366	1,619	1,885	1,440	1,848	3,169
Imports from other countries	1,899	4,448	3,758	5,380	3,312	4,500
Total imports	3,265	6,067	5,643	6,820	5,159	7,669
Market (exports neglected)	10,490	14,819	14,976	14,530	12,592	15,049
Market share of iR3	20.8 %	17.0 %	15.5 %	16.2 %	19.8 %	18.5 %
Market share of Japanese assemblers	48.0 %	38.8 %	43.0 %	32.8 %	31.6 %	22.5 %
Market share of Korean assembly	0.0 %	3.3 %	3.9 %	4.0 %	7.7 %	8.0 %
Market share of production in EC	68.9 %	59.1 %	62.3 %	53.1 %	59.0 %	49.0 %
Market share of production in EC[b]	68.9 %	55.8 %	58.5 %	49.0 %	51.4 %	41.1 %
Market share of imports from Korea	9.3 %	6.5 %	7.5 %	3.9 %	6.1 %	7.2 %
Market share of Thomson	3.7 %	4.5 %	5.1 %	6.0 %	8.6 %	13.9 %
Market share of dumped imports	13.0 %	10.9 %	12.6 %	9.9 %	14.7 %	21.1 %
Market share of Koreans (total)	9.3 %	9.7 %	11.3 %	8.0 %	13.8 %	15.1 %

[a]1994 data were based on the trends in months available
[b]Market share of production in EC excluding the Korean assemblers

stereo (the four head machines) from Korea quickly regained market share. Table 10.7 shows the composition of the European Community market from 1989, when the Korean VCR undertaking became effective, to 1994.

As a consequence of aggressive pricing policies of Philips, the Koreans and Thomson, iR3's customers rebelled. The development of market share of both price-aggressive parties, Thomson and the Koreans, was alarming. Such developments resulted in iR3's and its customers' loss of market share, and affected cost positions and, consequently, results. Thomson was clearly not prepared to moderate imports from the joint venture with Toshiba in Singapore. Its imports were on schedule and an implementation of its plan, doubling of imports, was evident, as Table 10.7 shows. Thomson's gain in market share from 8.5 % to 14 % showed its ambitions before privatisation. The Koreans' market share had dropped from 15 % in 1987 to 4 % in 1992, but climbed again. The increase in imports of the Koreans was a response to surge in demand for more complex machines with more functions, which were still made in Korea.

Thomson reacted entirely hostile to complaints about its behaviour. It even rejected, not for reasons of EEC competition law, consultations. In order to survive as a private company without state aid, it was relentlessly going for market share, provisionally assisted by French governmental or Crédit Lyonnais (hidden governmental) finances.[23] Since there was not the slightest improvement in relations with the Koreans and Thomson, it was investigated whether dumping margins promised a sufficient scope for a dumping complaint. In the case of the Koreans, substantial dumping was found at a margin of more than 30 %. The dumping from Singapore was relatively moderate, about 17 %. The evidence about undercutting by the Koreans was not difficult to find, but Thomson's prices were on average rather near the level of Philips' selling prices. On a model-by-model basis there was, however, some undercutting and Philips' and some other iR3 customers' prices were certainly not profitable.

The detection of dumping was a minor problem compared with other obstacles. Obtaining status for a complaint, i.e. sufficient backing by producers, "*whose collective output of the products constitutes a major proportion of the total Community production*", which is more than 50 % of European Community production,[24] was essential and more cumbersome. In the old regulations (see footnote 24) a majority of production, from which producers related to the dumping exporters were excluded, should have supported the complaint. In the present Basic Regulation, more than 25 % of production is considered European Community industry, provided that less than 50 % of industry opposes the opening of an investigation.

Initially, iR3 tried a dumping complaint in 1994. The problem was that the German branch of iR3 only represented 8.3 % of European production. If Koreans were excluded from European production as parties related to dumping exporters, the share in production was only 10.9 % (in 1994). Excluding Korean assemblers as parties related to exporters from European industry was self-evident. However, the percentage of European production not rejecting a complaint should constitute at least 50 % of European Community production. It was practically impossible to lodge an acceptable complaint. The first draft-complaint in 1994 tried, therefore, to define the product as VCRs including their essential and indispensible component, the recording and replay drum or scanner with heads. With this combination, iR3 in Nuremberg represented 100 % of production. The European Commission did not take the risk of accepting this innovative product definition. The European Commission, demanding continuously small changes in the file, succeeded in delaying the formal submission of the complaint by more than a year until Austria had acceded to the European Community. Austria's accession increased iR3's production in the European Community substantially. The complaint could be lodged, now representing production of iR3 both in German and Austria. This production represented 41.5 % of European production. This was more than the minimum 25 % for a complaint. There still was not

[23] Later Trade Commissioner Pascal Lamy, who assumed a remarkable role in the television case (see Chaps. 11 and 12), was director of Crédit Lyonnais in this period.

[24] In 1994, Council Regulation (EEC) No 2176/84 of 23 July 1984 on protection against dumped or subsidized imports from countries not members of the European Economic Community, O J L 201, 30/07/1984 pp. 1–16 was applicable, with a similar text in its successor Council Regulation (EC) No 384/96 of 22 December 1995 on protection against dumped imports from countries not members of the European Community, which was replaced by the present.

a guarantee that more than 50 % would not oppose the complaint and that the Japanese would not oppose opening of the case. Mr. Mitsuru Osugi of Matsushita Brussels Liaison Office could now be convinced that objecting to the case was imprudent. His company's production in the European Community was slightly more than 730,000 and, after Thomson left the cooperation, JVC's production in Berlin was only about 300,000. Matsushita represented 8 % of European Community production, JVC 5 % and Sony, which was an additional 5 % could also be convinced to remain neutral. This implied that not more than 47 % could oppose an investigation into dumping. Calculations showing Japanese dumping margins on their exports to the European Community helped. The Japanese still exported their high-end models from Japan and the gap of 30 % between domestic price and export price was a constant characteristic. However, it was doubted whether the Japanese inflicted sufficient injury to iR3 and whether measures could be taken against them. They were not more efficient than iR3, and their exports did not undermine results of iR3.

French civil servants in the European Commission, of course, warned Thomson about a complaint waiting to be circulated among the anti-dumping committee, the advisory committee of member states to the European Commission. An impressive lobby started. Thomson ordered a study from BIS Mackintosh to demonstrate that iR3 did not have sufficient production to be a complainant. Neither Thomson nor BIS Mackintosh understood the issue. They certainly were not aware that the Japanese in Europe would not reject a case. Some officials at the European Commission's electronics department in the Industry Directorate General did the utmost to influence the other European Commission services against adopting of the complaint. Two of these officials had a record in leaking information to the Japanese and as a servant of French interests. According to one official, the BIS Mackintosh study demonstrated that the presentation of Japanese production figures in the European Community was wrong. This official refused, however, to supply evidence from the study. At the invitation of Philips this official had paid a visit to the VCR factory of iR3 in Vienna. He abused the knowledge acquired there by stating that the complaining producer incurred no injury because it did not have stocks. Since the logistical system implied production to order, his statement was correct, but it was irrelevant for the question of injury. Interference by some people in the Directorate General for Industry and the efforts to block the case were unprecedented, but futile.

The behaviour of some member states was remarkable. At least one member state sent a copy of the non-confidential file of the complaint to exporters. Two employees of Thomson demanded to pay a visit to Philips headquarters, the first that Thomson representatives voluntarily paid to Philips headquarters in nasty and humble Eindhoven in the Netherlands. Thomson's Vice of President Public Affairs, sanguineous with a tempestuous temper, the colour of his face similar to Thomson's business figures, and the anaemic Vice President for trade and customs, pale as the Thomson's future, both had a history of animosity toward Philips. During the conversation, both Thomson representatives foretold severe and dark perspectives for Philips. Their threat or prediction was that both complaining company and the author of the complaint would not long be able to present their cases in the

European Community. They demanded withdrawal of the complaint from the agenda of the Anti-Dumping Committee, the advisory committee of the member states.

They appeared uninformed about the demand of the Department of Trade and Industry (DTI) of the United Kingdom that the complaint should be discussed in the European Community's Anti-Dumping Committee. DTI had acted at the request of Thomson's representative in the United Kingdom and chairman of the United Kingdom producers' association BREMA. This association had some comments on the complaint, in spite of the fact that it could not possibly know its content. It particularly questioned, in accordance with the BIS Mackintosh report, the representativeness of the complainant, iR3, not knowing that the support had already been safeguarded. Threats from Thomson to Philips executives remained fruitless, and animosity increased.

10.7 Case Lost

Thomson's brand director, Pierre Darrot, was an enthusiastic person with bright ideas that lacked touch with Thomson's reality, however. Nobody seemed to know the situation Thomson was in. Its organisational structure was too chaotic. Darrot developed a brand policy without deliberating what the practical prospects of implementation were. In the newspaper La Tribune, a press article was published in September 1995 explaining his vision: the brand name Thomson had to stand for technological avant-garde (les "produits de rêve"). Telefunken was the brand for products for the fireside of the privileged, cherishing family values and wanting comfort. Saba was the product for those who wanted ease of use and low prices. The problem was that this change in market approach was neither clear to competitors nor was it communicated or clear to the public. Thomson omitted advertisements making consumers aware of the brand positions. A shift in composition of products, whereby simpler models were attributed to and sold under the Saba brand, resulted in a steep fall in sales. Price decreases by more than 40 % did not induce higher but rather lower sales. As for Nordmende, a repositioning of models resulted in a relatively modest fall in prices and quantities, but the overall decrease in sales was dramatic. Only the shift of Telefunken to the higher end of four heads HiFi sets resulted in improvement in prices and positive results, but overall sales were deplorable. The price instrument preceded communications to consumers about the characteristics of the different brands.[25]

This dramatic repositioning of Thomson's brands, with its disastrous effects, was as ill understood by iR3 as by consumers. Thomson Darrot's firm statement

[25] Darrot was gifted in confusing consumers. In Le Point of 4 May1996, he announced that design was essential and that he had made Philippe Starck designe for Thomson. The equipment did not sell and some went in stock clearance sales at prices even below those of more conventional Thomson equipment with identical specifications.

about brand policy had a disastrous effect. Thomson's pricing policy caused a collapse of sales and results. iR3 correctly interpreted the fall in Saba prices as an attempt to gain market share by high volumes as indeed was Thomson's internally documented declared objective. This interpretation was based on the budgeted sales of Table 10.4 and the import figures of Table 10.7. After the opening of the anti-dumping proceeding investigations, it became apparent that Thomson's attempts were serious failures. Thomson perished due to blindness to market events and grandiloquently announced new strategies abstracted from reality. Instead of efforts to independently find its way, its perspectives were mainly based on animosity toward competitors. Darrot's announcement that Thomson would reposition its brands, "*Les "produits de rêve" ne sont pas des gadgets ou la dernière toquade d'un désigner, mais figurent au cœur du dispositif guerrier mondiale qu'il se livre avec Sony et Philips*",[26] is clearly not based on Thomson's ability to deliver models that could take their place in the brand repositioning in competition with two of its main competitors. The company was not aware that it should have kept its supply of models in harmony with demand. Table 10.8 gives a survey on Thomson's sales between February/March 1994 and February/March 1995.[27]

Table 10.8 presents changes in market composition, changes in market price of segments and changes in Thomson's market share and prices. Between 1994 and 1995, the share of the two-head (simple) recorders segment in the total market increased 2.4 %. In spite of the fact that Thomson's prices decreased by 2.6 % more than the market average decreased, Thomson's market share of two-head machines decreased in this growing segment. The same applied to the high-end stereo sets. This segment occupied a growing share in sales, but Thomson did not supply the products in time. In order to keep up with the market in a declining segment (four head mono), Thomson had to exceed market price cuts considerably or gain a moderate increase in share by heavy price reductions (in three-head mono). Thomson hoped to reduce its costs by production in low cost areas. It had imitated other companies that had moved to low cost areas, but it was too late and the imitation had become disadvantageous.[28] The market for VCR had become relatively saturated and highly susceptible to changes in consumer taste, requiring swift reactions and short leading times. Time to market had become increasingly important. The distance between Europe and Singapore was too great. It took a few weeks to transport scanners and mechanical decks to Singapore and to ship VCRs back from Singapore to Europe. This caused delays. When a market

---

[26] La Tribune, September 1995. Darrot stated that the avant-garde products are not gadgets or whims of a designer, but are in the centre of the world war formation that takes place with Sony and Philips.

[27] Source: derived from the bimonthly retail reports of Gesellschaft für Konsumforschung (GfK).

[28] Industriemagazin, Sept. 1987, pp. 59–67: "Garcin is now having all other entertainment electronics equipment assembled in Thomson owned plants in the Far East (exception: video recorders manufactured in a joint venture with JVC in Berlin). His reasoning: 'Hi fi, audio, and small TV sets can no longer be produced in Europe at acceptable costs.'" Finally, the VCR activities also went to the Far East, a wrong decision in a market needing quick response to changes in taste or short time to market.

Table 10.8 Market change and Thomson in Singapore: low cost and long time to market

	Market segment change (%)	Market price changes (%)	Change in Thomson's market share (%)	Thomson price changes (%)
Two-head	2.4	−10.2	−8.7	−12.8
Three-head	−4.1	−16.4	−4.9	−22.2
Four-head mono	−3.8	−7.4	1.3	−15.8
Four-head stereo	6.4	−6.0	−2.8	−5.4

Table 10.9 Market share of VCR imports from Korea and Singapore

	Investigation period		
	1992 (%)	1993 (%)	1994 + 1st Q 1945 (%)
Korean imports	4.5	7.1	3.0
Singapore imports	6.8	9.9	8.5

Source: European Commission information during the investigation

segment showed growth, Thomson lost market share. When the market declined, Thomson had to cut its prices more than market average. By a change in composition of product models, Philips and Grundig were able to increase average prices (of two-head and four-head stereo sets), whereas Thomson showed a drop in average price by 47 %. Its turnover decreased substantially, while the turnover of the Philips and Grundig together increased. There was no injury. Thomson's huge price cuts, especially for the Saba brand, which should have become the price fighter's brand, by on average more than 50 %, caused serious damage to Thomson. More positive developments for the Nordmende and Telefunken brands could not soften the misery.

The Korean case was different. The Koreans expected a complaint and had transferred more production to the European Community. The consequence was that injury caused by Korean imports had decreased. The share of imports from the two countries, Singapore and Korea, fell instead of rose and injury was absent, as Table 10.9, based on finding during the investigation, shows.

The decrease of import market share of the Koreans represents accelerated transfer of production. The factories in Europe took over production of high-end models. Thomson's decreased market share is attributable to its marketing failure. Its plan to increase its market share before the state financing stopped failed and this was not attributable to a dumping complaint. As a consequence of Thomson's disaster the complainant, the Direct Remedy Against Unfair Merchandise (DRUM) Association, representing iR3, had to withdraw the complaint.

Those responsible at Thomson for the collapse in sales were not blamed. In Brussels, the lobbyists of Thomson blamed Philips for the negative results of Thomson. At Thomson, politicians had annexed the company. They formulated all sorts of brilliant business theories and destroyed a business that cost the French taxpayers billions. Had Thomson concentrated on production and marketing rather than on politics and on enemies, it is possible it would not have perished. It tried to use the French state and all sorts of trade policy tricks to attain its objectives, but this had been costly to the French state and the history of trade policy manoeuvres had hurt had other European producers. Politicians had headed this company and they concentrated on other companies and their strategies and on strategy presentations rather than on actual business. Their dislocations of production, continuous change in priorities and disruptive interference in trade policy matters had a devastating effect on Thomson itself as well on others.

State-owned Thomson contributed strongly to the distortion of competition in the European Community. Its destructive role on various occasions is sketched. Its efforts to expand in the television, audio and VCR markets at the cost of other industries and trying to use trade policy where it suited and frustrating the policy of others had a highly destructive effect. The role of Thomson in other fields of trade policy rendered another remarkable contribution to the demise of European industry, in particular its own failure. It was not alone, however. The following chapters give an account.

Chapter 11
Blurred Picture: Trade Policy and Television's Future in the Dark

Abstract Trade policy and subsidies played an overwhelming role in the demise of the colour television industry in Europe. Origin rules, created for the effectiveness of quotas, were blindly applied to situations for which the rules were not intended and even exporters' fraud was accepted for the sake of calculation of certain parameters in accordance with the rules. The deficiencies in interpretation of the origin rules are explained. During anti-dumping cases, the rules caused serious confusion and harm. Additionally, some European companies preferred short-term benefits from complex trade policy situations to advantages of long-term cooperative behaviour. Various trade policy issues, like definition of the product scope, origin rules, self-inflicted injury, target profit for elimination of profit and complications caused by state-ownership of a CTV producer, Thomson, are discussed in this Chapter. Chaotic, inappropriate and even biased application of the rules finally resulted in the demise of European colour television industry, to which personal interference by officials and European Commissioners strongly but calamitously contributed.

11.1 Quotas and the Origin of Origin Rules

If a product is produced in more than one country, the last substantial, economically justified processing confers origin. Chapter 2, Sect. 2.2, mentioned origin rules for television and radio in relation with quantitative restrictions (QRs) in European Community member states and footnote 8 of Chap. 2 presents details. The specific European origin rule intended to make QRs of France and Italy effective, a wish triggered by Japanese companies' circumvention of QRs via their subsidiaries in South East Asia. France's QR for televisions from Japan was, for instance, about 83,000 units. As soon as the level of quota of imports into France was attained, Japanese exporters could ship their CTVs to Rotterdam or Hamburg, clearing goods through customs there and transporting them in "free circulation" to France. The French government could request exclusion of CTVs from free European

M. van Marion, *International Trade Policy and European Industry*,
Contributions to Economics, DOI 10.1007/978-3-319-00392-4_11,

Table 11.1 Example of cost structure of television set for determination of Turkish origin

Items in manufacturing (ex-works) costs 14-in. set	Value	% of ex-works	% of materials
Tube (Malaysia)	€33.06	32.9	46.3
Tuner (country A)	3.21	3.2	4.5
Transformer (country A)	2.85	2.8	4.0
Integrated circuits (country A)	7.55		10.6
Other materials (from Turkey)	***24.79***	***24.7***	***34.7***
Of which: cabinet (from Turkey)	4.83		6.8
Of which: other encaging materials (from Turkey)	4.82		6.7
Of which: other (mainly electronics) (from Turkey)	11.87		16.6
Of which: wires and packing (from Turkey)	3.27		4.6
Total materials	**€71.46**	71.1	100
Direct labour (in Turkey)	***5.60***	***5.6***	
Depreciation (in Turkey)	***1.34***	***1.3***	
Processing costs (in Turkey)	***2.69***	***2.7***	
Other (in Turkey)	***1.08***	***1.1***	
Total manufacturing costs	**€82.17**	**81.8**	
Other (selling, indirect) (in Turkey)	***14.00***	***13.9***	
Total cost of production	€96.17	95.7	
Profit (in Turkey)	***€4.32***	***4.3***	
Added value non-materials excluding result (Turkey)	***€24.71***	***24.6***	
Total added value non-materials (Turkey)	***€29.03***	***28.9***	
Total added value in Turkey production/selling/materials	***€53.82***	***53.6***	***34.7***
Total domestic selling price, normal value (Turkey)	**€100.49**	**100**	

Country A any or arbitrary country except Malaysia or Turkey

Community circulation by application of Article 115 of the Treaty of Rome. If television sets were assembled outside Japan it remained unclear, however, whether the quotas applied to them. This loophole should have been closed by an effective, special origin rule for products covered by quotas. This rule of 1970 determined that television sets underwent their last, substantial, economically justified processing where 45 % of the ex-works value or 35 % of the value of the materials were obtained. Television sets assembled outside of Japan, for instance, would be considered originating in the country of assembly if the added value was 45 % or more or the components content in that country was 35 % or more. If not, the highest components value was originating. It was assumed that the highest value would be Japanese. As already stated, this definition caused serious complications for situations other than quotas.

For determining origin, Table 11.1 gives a survey of costs of a TV and composition of these costs. The cost composition is taken from information on the most efficient European Community producer.[1] The price of €100.94 is the domestic

[1] The situation of cathode ray tube rather than an LCD or plasma television set is presented for the sake of instructiveness. An LCD or plasma TV does not have such diversity of components as a cathode ray tube TV. LCD and plasma screens and their chips sets of are generally manufactured by the same suppliers and purchased as a whole. Issues are, however, not very different.

Table 11.2 Effect on origin of change in components sourcing: non-Turkish (Malaysian) origin

Items in manufacturing (ex-works) costs 14-in. set	Value	% of ex-works	% of materials
Tube (Malaysia)	€33.06	32.9	46.3
Electronic components (Country A) (unlike Table 11.1)	€25.48	58.3	35.7
Other materials (from Turkey) (unlike Table 11.1)	***12.92***	***12.9***	***18.1***
Of which: cabinet (from Turkey)	4.83		6.8
Of which: other encaging materials (from Turkey)	4.82		6.7
Of which: wires and packing (from Turkey)	3.27		4.6
Total materials	€72.86	71.0	100
Total manufacturing costs (as in Table 11.1)	**82.17**	**92.8**	
Total cost of production	€96.17	95.7	
Added value non-materials excluding result (Turkey)	***€24.71***	***24.6***	
Total added value non-materials (as in Table 11.1) ***(Turkey)***	***€29.03***	***28.9***	
Total added value in Turkey production/selling/ materials	***€40.90***	***40.7***	***18.1***
Total ex-works value	**€100.49**	**100**	

A any or arbitrary third country except Malaysia or Turkey

Turkish price, the normal value, derived from a disclosure on injury inflicted by Turkish producer Bekoteknik (Beko) in the last TV anti-dumping case.[2] Beko's export price in the disclosure was €80.33. The dumping margin disclosed was 25.1 % (for CTVs of Malaysian origin). Consequently, its normal value was €80.33 × (1 + 25.1 %) = €100.49. For the sake of context, the tube in Table 11.1 has Malaysian origin.

A small TV tube represents 46.3 % of materials cost. In Table 11.1, Turkish producer Beko had purchased (bold italic) €24.79 (24.7 % of ex-works) materials in Turkey and added €29.03 (28.9 %) value in manufacturing, sales, overheads and profit. Turkish value is €53.82 or 53.6 % of ex-works value, i.e. more than 45 % of ex-works value. The origin is Turkish. If Beko purchases €12.92 of materials in Turkey, the total added value decreases to €40.90 or 40.7 % of ex-works value. Table 11.2 shows this situation. Turkish materials in Table 11.1 are 34.7 % of materials cost, which is below 35 %.

In Table 11.2, it decreases to 18.1 %. Due to the low value of domestic materials, Turkish added value is less than 45 % and Turkish materials less than 35 %. The origin is the highest level of materials value, i.e. in this case the value of the tube, Malaysian. Although not one single characteristic of the television set is changed, dumping can alter the origin of the CTV, as Table 11.3 shows. The materials content is the same as in Table 11.1, but the Turkish exporter dumps. The dumping margin is 25.1 % (the difference between the domestic value and the export value as

[2] This normal value is extremely low as consequence of a mistaken application of Malaysia's normal value to Beko. If Beko's Turkish price were normal value, it would be about €135, equalling Vestel's normal value (see Chap. 12).

Table 11.3 Dumping from Turkey: non-Turkish (Malaysian) origin

Domestic value in Turkey last processing 14-in. set	Value	% of ex-works	% of materials
Cabinet from Turkey	€4.83	6.0	6.8
Other encaging materials from Turkey	€4.82	6.0	6.7
Wires and packing from Turkey	€11.87		16.6
Part of electronics from Turkey	€3.27	4.1	4.6
Total materials from Turkey	***€24.79***	30.9	34.7
Total materials (as in Table 11.1)	€71.46		100
Direct labour (in Turkey)	***5.60***	7.0	
Depreciation (in Turkey)	***1.34***	1.7	
Processing costs (in Turkey)	***2.69***	3.3	
Other (in Turkey)	***1.08***	1.3	
Total manufacturing costs	***82.17***		
Other (selling, indirect) (in Turkey)	***14.00***	17.4	
Total cost of production (in Turkey)	***96.17***		
Profit (in Turkey)	*−€15.84*	−19.7	
Total added value in Turkey	*€33.66*	41.9	
Ex-works price	*€80.33*		

per cent of CIF value; the dumping found for the Turkish company Beko as disclosed by the European Commission). The dumping does not change the cost of materials, but of non-materials. Table 11.3 depicts the situation. The starting point of calculation is Beko's export price of €80.33, calculated from a disclosure of the European Commission.[3] The total added value, i.e. materials and processing, in Turkey is €33.66 or 41.9 % of the ex-works export value, i.e. below 45 %. Turkish materials are below 35 % of the materials bill. The highest level of the materials other than from the country of last processing, Turkey, is the tube from Malaysia, which is 46.3 % of materials value. In this case the television set originates in Malaysia.

The manufacturing cost in Tables 11.3 and 11.1 are identical. The difference between the normal value and export price is in the value added to manufacturing cost. The dumping export price in Table 11.3 causes a different origin from the origin of the product at normal value. An issue in Chap. 8 is that exports volume might result in a lower cost of production. Here, it is assumed that such cost reductions have not yet been achieved. Under normal circumstances, a Turkish product selling abroad without dumping would have Turkish origin, i.e. if the cost composition were in accordance with Table 11.1. Dumped exports change origin from Turkish into Malaysian (Table 11.3).

Tables 11.1 and 11.2 appear suitable for origin in situations of QRs. If dumping takes place origin of Table 11.3 is different from origin in Table 11.1 and the existence of dumping causes an origin problem. Origin rules are supposed to

[3] Note on the Undercutting and Injury Margin Calculations, sent as annexe to a letter of 1 Augustus 2001, number 057867.

support effectiveness of trade policy measures.[4] They are in any case not intended to impair or influence establishment of dumping. The ludicrous result of application of the origin rule during establishment of dumping is that an authority could conclude that there is no dumping because there are no originating exports from the dumping country. The dumping changed the origin and, therefore, the dumping from the dumping country is nil. This idiosyncrasy was the gloom hovering over some anti-dumping proceedings for colour television sets from Asia and Turkey finally destroying European electronics industry. The situation is explained in an interlude in which dumping is examined.

11.2 Dumping and Origin Rule: Does the Origin Change the Nature of Dumping?

Tables 11.1, 11.2, and 11.3 concern essentially similar, even identical television sets. The issue is whether identical television sets with identical features and identical functions, while the source of some materials is the only difference, may be treated as dissimilar products, for which different dumping and injury margins can be established or even no dumping can be established because the origin of the components is different. Section 12.9 shows the case of a Bush television set. The origin of the television set was Chinese because of the Chinese tube, but if the tube were purchased in Europe, not from the Chinese company Irico in China, but from Korean producer Orion/Daewoo in France, would the principle of dumping and injury change because of a different source of these components only? Or if in Table 11.3 the tube was produced in the European Community instead of Malaysia, would this change the fact of the dumping and the injury? Dumping is[5]:

> *A product is to be considered as being dumped if its export price to the Community is less than a comparable price for the like product, in the ordinary course of trade, as established for the exporting country.*

In other words, dumping is the difference between the price in the last row to Table 11.1 (or the last row of Table 11.2) and the export price, last row in Table 11.3. That means that normally the export price would not be the price of

---

[4] Council Regulation (EEC) No 2913/92 of 12 October 1992 establishing the Community Customs Code Official Journal L 302, 19/10/1992, pp. 0001–0050, Article 22: "Articles 23 to 26 define the non-preferential origin of goods for the purposes of: (a) applying the Customs Tariff of the European Communities with the exception of the measures referred to in Article 20 (3) (d) and (e); (b) applying measures other than tariff measures established by Community provisions governing specific fields relating to trade in goods..." Clearly the origin rules are not intended for the sake of establishing the necessary measures or parameters before measures are taken.

[5] Article 2, 2.1 of the Agreement on Implementation of Article VI of the General Agreement on Tariffs and Trade 1994 (Anti-Dumping Agreement or the ADA).

the country that does not export the product concerned. In the case of Tables 11.2 and 11.3, the export price is not the price of Malaysia because Malaysia does not export the product in Tables 11.1, 11.2, and 11.3. Unfortunately, however, the second paragraph of the article on principles may cause and has caused confusion, at least with the European Community institutions[6]:

The exporting country shall normally be the country of origin. However, it may be an intermediate country, except where, for example, the products are merely transhipped through that country, or the products concerned are not produced in that country, or there is no comparable price for them in that country.

From the first sentence of the quote of Article 1.3, the conclusion can possibly be drawn that the exporting country is the country of origin of the product, but this can never be the case if the country of origin has not exported that product, but other, possibly similar, products. It may be wondered whether the paragraph of this article implies that the exporting country must be chosen as the country that is the country of origin, according to an origin rule, but which is actually the exporter of a dissimilar product, the tube. If in Tables 11.1, 11.2, and 11.3 the tube had been exported from the European Community, the country of export of the television is not the European Community, for it does not export television sets to itself; rather, the country of export is Turkey, whatever the origin may be according to an obscure television origin rule.

The Agreement on Implementation of Article VI of the General Agreement on Tariffs and Trade 1994 (ADA), on anti-dumping, of the World Trade Organization (WTO) states[7]:

In the case where products are not imported directly from the country of origin but are exported to the importing Member from an intermediate country, the price at which the products are sold from the country of export to the importing Member shall normally be compared with the comparable price in the country of export. However, comparison may be made with the price in the country of origin, if, for example, the products are merely transshipped through the country of export, or such products are not produced in the country of export, or there is no comparable price for them in the country of export.

The logic of the ADA is clear: the issue is that the export price is relevant, not the price in a country that exported a component and did not export the product in question. The television set in Tables 11.1, 11.2, and 11.3 is exported from Turkey and if Turkey were an intermediate country, it is exported from Turkey, unless it was transhipment, which it was not. The set exported from Turkey in Table 11.3 was not exported from Malaysia, although Malaysia may have exported and actually did export television sets that can be compared with similar Turkish and European Community television sets. The tube has been exported from Malaysia. A set exported from Malaysia may be a similar set, not because of the origin, but because of appearance and functions, but its own exports cannot be substituted by other sets nor themselves substitute sets exported by another country. It cannot

[6] Article 1 Principles, paragraph 3 of the ADA.

[7] In Article 2.5 of the ADA.

export sets from Turkey, which have been manufactured in Turkey and sold in Turkey and exported from Turkey and cannot be held accountable for exports from Turkey and certainly the quantities of sets from Turkey cannot be cumulated with the sets exported by Malaysia.

Would serious institutions like European Commission and Council of Ministers of the European Community indeed think that television sets, as those in Tables 11.1, 11.2, and 11.3, produced in Turkey and exported from Turkey, of which identical copies are also manufactured and sold in Turkey as made in Turkey and originating in Turkey – though at a price 25.1 % higher than the export price –, should be treated as having been exported from Malaysia, because the television set dumped at the price of Table 11.3 has – according to an origin rule – the origin of the tube producing country, although the set in Tables 11.1, 11.2, and 11.3 has not been exported from Malaysia? The astonishing answer is: "yes". The European Commission, for instance, thinks that a television set can impossibly have been dumped into the European Community if and because the tube for that television set has been exported from the European Community or another country not involved in the anti-dumping proceeding. The weird twist of mind has been that the European Community cannot apply an anti-dumping duty on a television set that has European Community origin, because the tube was exported from the European Community to a country that dumped this television set into the European Community with a European Community tube, which tube as the consequence of the dumping confers European Community origin to that dumped television set.[8] As we will see this idiosyncrasy has had the unconceivable consequence of total destruction of European industry.

This Chapter covers part of the economic consequences of application of this rule and of some other misfortunes of European television industry, among which the behaviour of a state backed producer. The next Chapter goes in greater detail into the consequences of the rule, which appear a violation of what the World Trade Organisation and its rules and agreements and normal human thinking stand for.

11.3 Grundig's Taiwanese Television Troubles and Mullard's Comfort by an Origin Rule

The television origin rule was a source of serious tensions, as predicted in previous Sections. In the 1970s this was because producers encountered restrictions due to QRs; after 1992, it was because the origin rule did not fit any trade policy situation. An example from historical practice is an experience of tempestuous manufacturer Max Grundig. Not all entrepreneurs knew the complications caused by the quotas in the European Community that prevailed until 1992, the year of completion of the

[8] This was the conviction of the director of the anti-dumping division, who had also negotiated the Customs Union Protocol between the EC and Turkey with its many deficiencies.

single European Community market, when individual member states' QRs were eliminated and television, sound recorder and radio origin rules lost their purpose. Autocratic Max Grundig did not always consult his customs experts, but made decisions blindly or based on a grand vision. He wanted also to be present in the Far East because Philips had established a tube factory in Taiwan in the 1970s. Grundig not only wanted to follow Philips' example, he wanted to show superiority. He made television sets in Taiwan using, unfortunately enough, Philips cathode ray tubes made in Taiwan. The operation started in 1977 in a southern Taiwanese export-processing zone. Grundig encountered serious difficulties in selling his products in Asia. Grundig lacked a sales infrastructure in the region and he assumed that the Grundig brand was sufficient to sell his products. In Asia, nobody had heard of Grundig. He was compelled to export his small screen television sets to Europe, where he met a serious problem.

Europe's South was originally the main market for small screen or tiny vision television. Ten years later the situation would be totally different. The small screen market would shift to Northern Europe as second set market. People that looked at small screens in small houses lived predominantly in Italy and France. These countries were precisely those applying QRs toward Japan, Korea, China and Taiwan. Grundig's Taiwanese TVs had Taiwanese origin and he could not import them freely into Southern Europe. Old Max Grundig was outrageous about such an injustice and he never stopped complaining about it. His anger peaked when he found out that Philips' small screen television sets containing Taiwanese tubes, manufactured in and exported from Singapore to Europe, had unlimited access to the European Community. South European quotas did not hit Malaysia and Singapore and components other than the picture tube apparently conferred Singapore origin.[9] Grundig's factory in Taiwan had to be closed again. Grundig guessed that Philips had devised the QRs and the origin rule. Habitually he complained with Philips' board of management about this nasty deception, disbelieving that producers other than Philips' national organisations in France and Italy had spurred the French and Italian governments. It was probable, however, that Philips organisations in these countries had joined this request for such devices.

The origin rule brought Jack Akerman, the chairman of Philips' components daughter in the United Kingdom, Mullard, to a more comfortable position. The introduction of the television origin rule, before the United Kingdom's accession to the EEC, implied that Japanese assembly operations outside Japan, including those in the United Kingdom, had in the country of assembly to add sufficient (45 %) value or to use non-Japanese components up to 35 % or more of the components value for television sets to be exported to France or Italy. If tubes were not European, sets assembled in the United Kingdom were considered Japanese and the producers might expect lengthy and costly investigations into the origin. By

[9] If further investigation had been conducted on the Singapore sets, perhaps more sets of Taiwanese origin would have been found. Many components came from other countries than Singapore and the value of the Taiwanese tube (more than 35 % of the value of materials) might have been decisive. On the other hand the Philips forwarding department was extremely well capable in customs matters.

purchasing a tube in Europe, Japanese manufacturers could circumvent the QRs and increase their popularity in the United Kingdom by "purchasing British goods". The Japanese companies settling in the United Kingdom gave Mullard, the only tube supplier in the country, a quiet life. The need for 35 % components content guaranteed that Japanese assembly units became Mullard's customers. An exception was Sony, requiring its Trinitron tubes that it manufactured in Wales. Suddenly in the middle of the 1970s, imports by Chunghwa, the tube-producing subsidiary of the Taiwanese television producer Tatung with an assembly of not more than 200,000 television sets in the United Kingdom only intended for the United Kingdom market, raised fear in Jack Akerman. Jack Akerman reacted strongly against the use of Taiwanese tubes in Taiwanese television sets assembled in the United Kingdom, but was accused of foul play: [10]

In the 1970s Akerman rallied furiously against imports of Taiwanese TV tubes – until, that is, he was caught importing and relabeling them to fill gaps in his own production.

The allegation was that tubes supplied by Philips Taiwan or by Matsushita Electronics Corporation (MEC), the joint venture between Matsushita and Philips that they established in 1952, were sold with false origin indication. Indeed, Philips sold small tubes in Europe from its factory in Taiwan and from MEC in Japan. Evidence of fraud was never produced. In 1980, Philips decided to start production of small screen tubes (14 and 16 in.) in Lebring, Austria, which started a new conflict with Grundig (described in Sect. 11.4).

The announcement in 1977 by Hitachi, only shortly after the revelation by Thorn in 1976 that it would close its 5-year old tube factory in Skelmersdale, of its intention to start CTV and tube greenfield production in northeast England is mentioned in Chap. 2. This announcement especially alarmed Jack Akerman, who panicked and hired a parliamentarian consultant company to lobby and create opposition to tube manufacturing by the Japanese. He feared that investments by Sony and Matsushita in CTV production in 1974 and 1976 would result in declining demand for Mullard tubes because of the history of the decline of his United Kingdom customers. Finally, Hitachi decided to discard the tube plan and create a television joint venture with GEC. According to Akerman, this success was attributable to his successful lobby, undertaken by a rather expensive parliamentarian consultants firm he hired. The threat by Hitachi was probably merely a strategic move. The start-up of a tube factory was a highly hazardous and costly affair. The investment of roughly £18 million would be too costly for an estimated 350,000 units of internal demand by Hitachi's European production.[11] The fundamental problem in the United Kingdom was overcapacity in tube production, partly as consequence of an overestimate of TV manufacturers' demand, as minister of Industry and Trade Gerald Kaufman revealed[12]:

[10] The Manufacturer, Leadership and Lean, October 2006.

[11] Geddes and Bussey (1991, pp. 392–393).

[12] The Minister of State, Department of Industry (Mr. Gerald Kaufman) in Commons Debates 22 January 1976 Orders of the Day [5th allotted day], Public Accounts.

The total capacity at existing factories of about 2.3 million has been less than half loaded and has resulted in uneconomic production. In 1976, total demand which could be met from our factories will be no more than last year. In 1977, it may be more but only at a level to half load capacity which would then be available.

The minister did not deplore the closure of Thorn Colour Tubes Limited very much, for it was not real British technology[13]:

The technology employed at the factory was drawn from RCA. The other tube manufacturer in the United Kingdom—Mullard—uses the technology of its parent company, Philips. There is no indigenous technology in this country for colour television tubes. So it should be recognised that, deeply regrettable though the closure of the factory at Skelmersdale is, this is not a case of abandoning a key United Kingdom technology. In this country we have had two foreign technologies.

Although the United Kingdom government was financially extremely hospitable to the Japanese, Hitachi ran a risk of severe losses on tubes. If Hitachi's operation after some initial financial government support ran into troubles, further assistance would remain absent. Its joint venture with ailing GEC and strangulation of that patient was cheaper than implementing a threat by Greenfield production of television tubes and sets. Mullard kept its position in a feeble market, but was continuously under threat of imports from Japan at lower prices. The origin rule of the EEC put Akerman at ease. As long as the Japanese producers did not start their own components operations, there was no reason for concern. For exports of non-Japanese origin to Southern Europe, the Japanese in the United Kingdom needed European tubes, which Akerman supplied.

11.4 Origin as Commercial Strategy: Grundig and Philips Struggle in Austria

Grundig was confronted as first and only European Community CTV producer in the Far East with misfortunes of wrong origin in connection with QRs, he also became the victim of origin problems in Europe. To most European Community producers, the origin question of television sets was irrelevant for their business. Japanese, Korean and Taiwanese TV producers became acquainted with it. Component makers were, of course, well aware of the opportunities offered by this rule. Most TV producers purchased their tubes within the European Community. Only a few producers had in-house cathode ray tube production, and until 1981 none of them made tiny vision tubes (small screen of 14 and 16 in.) in Europe. Philips was initially and for a long the only producer of small screen displays in the European Community. It had started production in the early 1980s after acquiring sufficient experience in production both in the joint venture with Matsushita and in Taiwan and demand for small screen sets and tubes attained sufficient volume.

[13] House of Commons Debate, 22 January 1976.

Austria was selected as the location of tubes manufacturing for the European market. The main reason for this location was that Grundig, after departing from Taiwan, had become the major small screen TV producer in Europe with 14 and 16 in. factory in Vienna. The Austrian government granted Grundig a secret suspension of the import duty on small tubes purchased from Korea.[14] That implied that Korean small tubes, mainly purchased from Orion, Daewoo's tube division, were duty-free. The customs duty on tubes in Austria was, as it was in the European Community, 15 %. By suspending the 15 % duty, the cost saving of €4.96 per tube at a price in Tables 11.1, 11.2, and 11.3 was obtained. With a 15 % duty, the tube cost rose to almost 50 % of materials cost and 36.1 % of ex-works value.

In order to bring an end to this suspension and to Grundig's relative cost advantage connected with 14- and 16-in. tube imports from Korea, the commercial director of Philips' tube division allocated production of small screen tubes to a Philips factory in Lebring, Austria. A condition for this production allocation was that Austria terminate the duty suspension. This Philips move and Austrian lenience incensed Max Grundig, and he threatened to relocate small screen television production from Austria to Portugal. The Austrian government appeased him by a subsidy on tubes used in the Vienna TV factory at an equivalent of the 15 % duty or about €5.00 per tube (or what is the same, per TV set). This was well known to Philips components sales people, who tried to abuse the situation by balancing their prices with Grundig's advantages. Austrian subsidies were even continued through 1994. For the tube division of Philips this result was, of course, satisfactory as long as Grundig procured Philips tubes. For Philips' television division it was an unattractive solution, about which its management of course complained a lot. When Grundig, in spite of the fact that it had become Philips daughter, started again in 1993 to purchase tubes from Daewoo/Orion in Asia, now located in Vietnam, the Philips Display Components Division wanted this practice to be terminated. Internal calculations on the advantages of additional tube supplies from Philips' Barcelona, Spain factory or a continuation of the subsidies stemmed the tide. Cost advantages on tubes and incremental profits from additional production and sales were inferior to Austrian subsidies.

In the case of Grundig television sets made in Austria not only the non-preferential origin rule was relevant, but also, and even more, the preferential origin rules. The 15 % duty increased the value of the tube to 36.1 % of the ex-works value and to 49.5 % of the materials value, instead of the percentages of 32.9 % and 46.3 % in Table 11.1.

For access without the barrier of French, Italian and Spanish quotas the non-preferential origin was applicable, and for duty-free access to the European Community and members of the European Free Trade Area (EFTA) the Grundig television sets at that time had to meet certain criteria of minimum processing:

[14] According to the agreement between Austria as member of the European Free Trade Association (EFTA) and the European Community, consultations should be held in case of duty suspension. This did not occur.

- The value of all non-originating materials used does not exceed 40 % of the ex-works price of the product, and
- The value of all the non-originating materials used does not exceed the value of all the originating materials used.

If prices of Korean tubes increased by 5 %, Grundig would lose its preferential Austrian origin and duty-free access to the European Community. The value of the tube would rise to 36.1 % of the ex-works value and to more than 50 % of the materials value. In that case, the value of non-originating materials would be more than 50 % and Grundig would have to pay a 14 % CTV duty on imports into the European Community and EFTA countries. Even without an increase in tube price, freedom would be lost. If Grundig purchased other materials from Asia, it would incur similar problems. The issue haunted the company until the accession of Austria to the European Community. Before the accession, Grundig had to meet another challenge. The closing of production in Creutzwald, France and transferring production to Vienna was attractive to Grundig because of the subsidies granted by Vienna at the level of $11 million. France did not welcome this, and the European Commission was soon informed about Vienna's subsidies.[15] In order to avoid the payment of a 14 % duty on imports into the European Community, which was the European Community's threat, Grundig refunded the major part of the subsidy. The successor in Creutzwald, Gooding, was heavily subsidised by the French state. The European Commission's action against this phenomenon was considerably less drastic. The internal debate within Philips about the admissibility of the subsidies thereby subsided.

11.5 CTV Dumping, Market and Tailored "Like Product" Definition

Determining the origin of a television is based on the cost structure and origin of components of a television set. As may be clear from Table 11.1, the origin does not have any relevance if all of the components are procured in the country of last processing, which normally is the country of provenance and by total procurement of materials and of complete processing also the country of origin. Countries with a policy of mercantilist attitudes of self-sufficient economic growth do not create a problem as far as establishment of origin of the products is concerned. They try to enhance integration of production so that the origin is almost automatically the country of last assembly. Countries as Korea, Japan and China conducted this policy in their initial stage of development.

---

[15] Rosenthal and Nicolaïdes (1997, p. 380); Council Regulation (EC) No 318/94 of 7 February 1994 repealing Regulation (EC) No 317/94 of withdrawing tariff concessions in accordance with the provisions of Articles 23 (2) and 27 (3) (a) of the Free Trade Agreement concluded between the Community and Austria (Grundig Austria GmbH), OJ No L 41/20, 12. 2. 94.

Spending much of his time on problems beyond his reach, the director of Philips' television business devoted ample energy to complaints about cheap dumped imports from Korea.[16] He neither had the time nor patience to postpone measures against these imports and to fit such action into a broader plan including a wider variety of dumping countries. Although imports from Korea rose very quickly, from 0.6 % market share in 1984 to 12.3 % in 1987 in quantities from 23,000 to 781,000, Korea was only one of the problems. The growth of imports from various other countries was substantial, and the first calculations proved that the increase represented dumping. Among the causes of these problems were subsidiaries of Japanese companies in South East Asia. Another problem was Chinese imports at prices far below cost of manufacturing. Such imports, if dumped, could be tackled in one single proceeding. If an action covered all dumped imports, it would have saved time and improved the image of Philips and others in the industry. The Philips television leader, however, preferred ill-considered short-term action to certain benefits that successive executives after him might derive from more deliberate action.

The result of this pressure was a complaint limited to Korea and restricted to small screen sets, which were sold at extremely cheap prices compared with the price level of Korean sets sold in the domestic market. If injury inflicted by Korean exports was expressed as share of the small screen market, the damage to European producers of small screen television sets was more impressive than damage inflicted to production of all television sets combined. Imports of Korean sets compared with the whole European market were less impressive. Not long thereafter, small sets from China and Hong Kong also caused injury. The problem posed by the selection of small screen was that, if large screen imports also caused troubles, the significance of only large screen sets in the total market would be smaller than if all screen sizes would have been involved, and they could hardly be recombined with the small screen sets (already excluded in a special case) as quantitative indication of injury. The concentration on small screen necessitated an argument as to why tiny vision television were different from television sets in general.

In the beginning of the 1970s, small sets were predominantly sold in Southern Europe, but this had changed. The argument for selecting small screen television sets as a "product concerned" in a complaint was now that the 14- and 16-in. sets were sets for children and bedroom. It was the second set in the household, and it was fully dependent on penetration of large screen television in households. That penetration was highest in Germany, the United Kingdom and in Benelux. The market had changed: Italy and France had moved to larger screens and in Northern Europe the small screens had become a booming second set market. The small screen market share of Korea had increased to 12.3 % in 1987, but the market share of all Korean sets in the total television market was only 5 % and insufficient for a

[16] In Sect. 10.5, reference is made to this case, which became part of negotiations between the Korean manufacturers' association EIAK and the European association EACEM.

satisfactory action against dumping. The fact that small screen sets and the small screen market could be defined as a special domain saved the case of the Philips director, who hardly cared about legal problems or issues that might arise later. Fortunately in its argumentation on behalf of measures, the European Commission supplied arguments why Korea could also become a target for measures concerning television sets of all sizes[17]:

Furthermore, it is considered that a threat exists of increased injury from Korean exports in the future, in view of the extremely large production capacity available to Korean industry. This capacity is known to be completely out of proportion to the domestic market: in basic model colour picture tubes the capacity of 25 million tubes per year corresponds to one-third of world consumption.

The European Commission did not report how it established Korean origin in the case of small screen television. Since Korean producers Samsung, Lucky Goldstar (now LGE) and Daewoo had their own tube production and internal tube supplies to domestic television factories in Korea, the European Commission probably assumed that the origin of all Korean television sets was Korean. That assumption was held in 1987 during the investigation period; it was correct, but wrong in more recent times. Later, only Daewoo/Orion produced small tubes in Korea and the origin of small screen sets from Korea exported by CTV producers other than Daewoo/Orion necessarily had an origin other than Korean. In subsequent review investigations, the European Commission did not investigate the origin of the Korean television sets, and this was obviously a mistake. Prior to the drafting of a complaint on small screen television sets by the European Association of Consumer Electronics (EACEM), Philips had analysed the content of the Korean television and the construction of the chassis. In order to learn from the Korean construction of the sets, cost calculations were made and the conclusion was that the chassis and materials content of Korean sets were extremely expensive. Many components, like the mechanical tuner, were old fashioned and the design was based on low labour cost. That implied that, differently from the Japanese, the probability of transfer of final assembly to Europe was small. In case of duties, the Koreans would probably move their assembly to low wage South-East Asia.

Proving of Korean dumping was easy. Margins to trade in both Korea and the European Community were well known from own, though scanty, sales in Korea and documentary evidence could be supplied on ex-works prices, similarly to the method of Table 2.3 in Chap. 2. The tiny vision television case toward Korea was submitted at the end of 1987, almost simultaneously with a complaint concerning VCRs and microwave ovens. The dumping margins for Korean colour televisions were much lower than those found in calculations for Japan. The complaint about Korean dumping presented margins of about 20 %. The European Commission found and finally applied half that level. This was partly due to the fact that the

[17] Commission Regulation (EEC) No 3232/89 of 24 October 1989 imposing a provisional anti-dumping duty on imports of small screen colour television receivers originating in the Republic of Korea OJ L 314, 28/10/1989 recital (48).

market domination of Samsung, LGE and Daewoo was smaller in tiny vision than in large screen sets. Many Korean competitors were busy in manufacturing and selling TVs with sizes below 14 in., which were not produced by the three majors. From later calculations, it became apparent that when the screens of television sets sold on the Korean market and exported became larger, the dumping margin increased. As reported in the previous Chapter in Sect. 10.5, the Koreans wanted an orderly marketing agreement for VCR and small screen televisions and microwave ovens. The negotiations were unsuccessful for the Koreans. They hoped for a package of VCR, microwave ovens and CTV in a comprehensive self-restraint agreement, but achieved a self-restraint for microwaves, a case the Europeans had already lost. The VCR undertaking with the European Commission was highly cumbersome.

11.6 Politics of Origin: Deceptions About Origin and Non-market Economy Normal Value

In view of what is discussed in Sects. 11.1 and 11.2, confusion about origin might have been expected. Unexpected, however, was that the political priorities resulted in manifest misapplication of the rules and Kafkaesque constructions. China's dumping differed completely from Korean or Japanese practice. The dumping from Japan and Korea was related to restrictions on domestic distribution. The Chinese case was the consequence of absence of a proper domestic market, of acceptable accounting and of export marketing. A complaint was prepared that demonstrated that Chinese manufacturers exported below the cost of materials. However, this discovery of an export price below international costs of materials was immaterial to the case. The cost of production and market price in China are not accepted as starting point for normal value, unless producers meet certain market economy status requirements, for which a special enquiry is made. That the value of the foreign exchange earned with exports clearly exceeded the value of the domestically purchased inputs, even at artificial prices, must have been the main cause of exports by Chinese producers.[18] EACEM submitted a case against China and, in view of the significance of Hong Kong (SCTV HK) as transit port, inevitably against Hong Kong.

The European Commission apparently disliked the inclusion of Hong Kong because it contravened United Kingdom induced European Community policy towards Hong Kong, which was that it should be treated differently than China.

[18] In 1993 in a meeting of the economic faculty association of the Free University Amsterdam, Aureus, this possibility was contested by a discussant: "Those Chinese are not crazy, are they?" Chinese people are, of course, not crazy, but the economic system was and is for several reasons. The first is that foreign cash earnings have more attractiveness than domestic Yuans. The other is the problem Chinese have with costing and pricing. See also Chap. 15.

It could not be expected, however, that the European Commission would infringe upon European Community legislation. First, the European Commission concluded[19]:

> *...it has not been possible for the Commission to verify the correctness or otherwise of the claimed origin during the course of the proceedings...*

An unusual confession contradicting the European Commission's own statement in recital (3) that it

> *verified all information it deemed to be necessary for the purposes of a preliminary determination and carried out investigations at the premises...*

Either the European Commission verified all information it deemed necessary, or it did not. If the European Commission was not able to verify the correctness of origin, the conclusion is that it did not deem the verification necessary or that the European Commission reported tales. The European Commission reported verification visits to six Hong Kong producers and three Sino-Japanese joint ventures, but not whether the verifications had taken place in premises of the Hong Kong firms producing in China, which was important because of:

> *the finding that most of the Hong Kong producer/exporters carried out a part or the whole of their assembly operations in facilities owned and managed by them over the border in China.*

The European Commission allegedly verified all information deemed necessary, but not the evidence that was necessary for implementation of European Community rule. The product was either wholly obtained or produced in China, in which case the origin was Chinese and the set was made in a non-market economy. None of the Hong Kong television sets could possibly have originated in Hong Kong:

> *it was found that there was no production in Hong Kong of the major components used in SCTV manufacturing, such as colour picture tubes, fly back transformers,* etc. *Components were imported from several sources, among which figured Korea principally, and to a lesser extent, Japan.*

This is the situation of Table 11.2, but with the ex-works price as in Table 11.3. None of the television sets shipped from Hong Kong originated in Hong Kong. If on the spot verifications, which should have been deemed necessary, in Hong Kong had taken place in the administration of the Hong Kong exporters, it was inevitable that the European Commission established the origin of assembly in Hong Kong from the accounts, if any assembly had taken place there. The purchasing accounts could show the origin of the tube. The only conclusion the European Commission could have drawn was that all Hong Kong producers had made false origin declarations. That is normally intolerable behaviour. This was not the case for the

---

[19] Commission Regulation (EEC) No 129/91 of 11 January 1991 imposing a provisional anti-dumping duty on imports of small-screen colour television receivers originating in Hong Kong and the people's Republic of China, Official Journal L 014, 19/01/1991, pp. 31–45, recital 10. Quotations below on this page are from the same source.

European Commission, however. False declarations were assumed to be correct; but assumed correct as: [20]

> *working assumption that the SCTVs investigated do have the origin that is declared to Community customs authorities,* i.e. *Hong Kong or Chinese origin.*

Thus, the European Commission regarded as correct what it knew were false origin declarations, or fraud,[21] and this "as working assumption". The reporting of false origin is fraud. The European Commission corroborated with fraud. This must have made a weird impression in Hong Kong and China: false information on origin is accepted as correct. In later, similar and even less obvious cases, the anti-fraud organisation of the European Community, OLAF, investigated the information to determine whether it was fraudulent or false. Parties involved in false information had to face consequences, and had to pay duties and fines. In the case of Hong Kong, fraud was considered non-existent and accepted as working assumption. Subsequently, an infringement of the anti-dumping regulation was pursued. The normal value of non-market economies, such as China, is determined by the normal value of an analogue country. The European Commission took the values of Hong Kong to establish the normal value, in spite of the fact that majority of the products had been made in China and in all cases were not of Hong Kong origin.

Under the European Commission's working hypothesis that obviously false origin declarations were treated as correct, and with the help of incorrect and even fraudulent data, the European Commission made calculations on normal value. Thereby the European Commission infringed European Community anti-dumping legislation:

> *In the case of imports from non-market economy countries, normal value shall be determined on the basis of the price or constructed value in a market economy third country, or the price from such a third country to other countries, including the Community, or where those are not possible, on any other reasonable basis, including the price actually paid or payable in the Community for the like product, duly adjusted if necessary to include a reasonable profit margin.*

The European Commission assumed that false origin was correct, declared the origin Hong Kong, even when products where wholly made in China. The value in Hong Kong with false, Chinese, origin was subsequently used for the determination of the normal value for China. The use of a Chinese value – directly or via this awkward detour – is an infringement upon the Community's anti-dumping legislation. This legislations requires the establishment of the normal value of a non-market economy as China on the basis of an analogue market economy and not to use the non-market values via a deception. The consequence of these assumptions and of the acceptance of false origin declarations was that the dumping margins of the Hong Kong owners of factories in China were absurdly low and

[20] Commission Regulation (EEC) No 129/91 of 11 January 1991 (provisional Hong Kong China), recital 10.

[21] Since QRs were still operative toward China in France, Italy and Spain, correct origin declaration made a difference and incorrect origin reporting was significant. It was fraud.

reflected the distortion of competition of a non-market, i.e. between 2.1 % and 4.8 % based on an artificially low non-market economy: Chinese prices of sales in Hong Kong of products made and originating in China. Export prices of Hong Kong producers undercut European prices practically as much as those of Chinese producers, i.e. between 14.52 % and a maximum of 31.59 %. Chinese undercutting was between 13.13 % and 25.03 %. The result of the inadmissible normal value was a Chinese dumping duty of 15.3 %. Although "*they did not operate fully on a market economy basis*", two companies in China, Fujian Hitachi Television Co., Ltd and Huaquiang Sanyo Electronics Co., Ltd, were treated as market economy. The duties applied to them were 13.1 % and 7.5 %. What is crucial is that in all subsequent cases, the European Commission treated export prices of television sets with a tube from another country as originating in that other country. It did not do so in the case of Hong Kong and China, where it just assumed Hong Kong origin even though it knew that the assumption of Hong Kong origin was completely incorrect, and applied extremely low duties. Consequently, the European Commission deliberately injured the European industry by accepting fraud as the norm and applying values in a dumping case based on fraud, arriving at a too low normal value for China.[22] A similar move was made, when Turkish origin was declared falsely, but considered correct and, as a consequence, of that decision no measures were taken.

In the cases of Korea and China, the European Commission found, after all not amazingly, low dumping margins and relatively high injury. The Philips television division's director was highly disappointed and blamed both the European Commission, not on false grounds, and those who lodged the complaint and conducted the proceeding on behalf of the industry for the bad results of his television business. He had high expectations of anti-dumping measures and felt cheated, which he was. It was not only impossible to explain in detail what the European Commission had done in the Hong Kong/China case, but also was it impossible to explain that a duty only eliminates the injury that might take place in the future and that the level of duty was not necessarily commensurate with the damage inflicted and in this case artificially low because of manoeuvres with normal value.

The partial and transitory approach of the dumping problem of CTVs, focused on small screens, created serious hindrances for the future. The dumping duties for Korea of about 10–13 % and of 15.3 % for most Chinese exporters presented some, but as far as China was concerned, negligible relief. At Philips, internal pressure for further trade measures against the Far East and for larger television screen sizes started. An essential problem had not been solved. The Japanese had their subsidiaries in Europe, a fact that could not be changed, and in South East Asia. From the latter countries they shipped assembled products to the European Community. The construction of Korean television sets required labour intensive

[22] The Commission repeated these disastrous and unworthy practices in the case of Turkey. See below. The European industry should have, of course, started a Court case against deception, but this would not result in higher duties. Such cases have never resulted in any positive result for a complainant.

production and duties resulted in a shift of final assembly to South East Asia rather than to Europe. A complaint against Asia should have also included the larger screen sizes from China and Korea, which were included in the next wave of imports from these countries. However, Philips also produced television sets in Singapore. These sets were identical, with the same type number, to small screen television sets made in Barcelona. The executive of the Philips television business did not want to run the risk of cutting off supplies from Singapore, fearing that CTV supplies from Barcelona were not safe. After lengthy discussions, he finally gave in when the Philips Bureau for International Economic Relations convinced him that if resale prices of Singapore were equal to those of Barcelona, chances of duties toward the imports from Philips would be minimal. Afterwards this prediction appeared wrong. Irregularities that would not have taken place in a disciplined organization appeared to have taken place.

11.7 Multinationals and Origin in CTV Dumping

The origin of Chinese and Korean televisions as such had not been major issues in the period of proceedings for small screen television sets. In 1987, both Korea and China used their own tubes for television set production. In addition to the highly questionable establishment of normal value for China via Hong Kong values, new complications developed. Korean and Japanese television producers had moved to South East Asia. This could, as far as Korea was concerned, be a deflection of trade and should have been investigated by UCLAF, the predecessor of the Organisation pour la Lutte Anti-Fraude (OLAF) of the European Community, as long as the tubes came from Korea. The situation, however, had increased in complexity. Some television tube producers had commenced tube production in new locations. Samsung and Chunghwa, subsidiary of Taiwanese Tatung, commenced manufacturing of tubes since the early 1990s in Malaysia. Hitachi had a tube-manufacturing unit in Singapore and Thai CRT Co., Ltd., part of Siam Cement (SCC), which was related to the royal family, was a domestic Thai producer in which producer Mitsubishi Electric Corporation (MELCO) had a minority share. Toshiba had also moved a plant to Thailand. Since Sony's Trinitron tube production in Singapore was for internal use only, this production was less relevant for trade policy considerations. Chinese exports of tubes were relatively limited at that time. Production was mainly destined for domestic television production. Daewoo's tube division Orion planned to move its small and medium screen (14 and 20 in.) to Vietnam, and LGE would open a plant in Indonesia for the same sizes in 1996.

The corollary of the television origin rule was that customs services of the European Community examine the origin of all small screen television sets as soon as anti-dumping measures made the rule relevant. If small television sets contained tubes from Korea, the origin was possibly Korean, in accordance with Tables 11.2 or 11.3. If they had not been declared as originating in Korea, the imported set evaded anti-dumping duties for Korea. It was unfeasible for customs to examine all small screen television sets. The self-evident conclusion was that if there were no implementation rules for inspection, the rule did not meet requirements. After tube factories were established in South East Asia, television sets made in that area might, if the European Community stuck to its weird interpretation of that rule, originate in the country of the tube. The situation was chaotic. Some television sets originated in Korea, but some sets with Korean brands could have also originated in Malaysia. Japanese branded sets might originate in Japan, but also in Thailand or Singapore.

The increasing influx of cheap dumped television sets from South East Asia inflicted serious injury. It was not an issue of cost differences because costs of television sets made in Europe and identical sets made in Singapore did not differ too much. It was a price issue. There was a remarkable difference between the levels in Asia and the European Community. The discrepancy allowed dumping. Both Philips and Thomson had production in that region. Philips' production in Singapore was mainly for sales in South East Asia and shipments of sets identical to those made in Barcelona were made to Europe. From selling price comparisons in respective markets, the conclusion was that substantial dumping took place. That was one of the reasons why the Philips Singapore organisation was highly dissatisfied with its supply of certain quantities to Europe rather than to the Asian region. Some other producers of the South East Asia region, the Japanese and Koreans, also sold in South East Asia, but shipped parts from these locations to their home country, where their distribution system allowed substantial profits, and to Europe.

Thomson's production location was a separate issue. The doctrine of its CEO Pierre Garcin was that mass small consumer electronics production should move to Asia. Thomson had done so, partly because Philips was established in that region and was imitated. The difference with Philips was that it sold in Asia and had also transferred production from Asia to Europe, such as small screen television production. Philips had flexibility, whereas Thomson's political top made the resolute decision, elevated to a doctrine, that Asia should be a production location. Thomson's allocation policy was mysterious. On the one hand it had acquired a factory with small screen tube production in Poland, on the other hand it closed its small screen television factories in France and Spain and moved to Singapore and later to Thailand. These transfers were not popular with French politicians. The problem was that Thomson incurred henceforth losses on its small screen tubes, for which it did not have internal demand as consequence of transfer of CTV production from Europe to Asia. As became apparent during an anti-dumping proceeding it also incurred heavy losses on its small screen TV production that it had transferred to Asia. The acquisition of the Polish tube factory caused tremendous European overcapacity, which was aggravated by the move from Thomson's small screen production to Asia.

11.8 Dictate by a Company of the State

When asked to join an anti-dumping complaint, Thomson refused to accept a complaint against Singapore or Turkey. An argument for its opposition remained absent. It did not discuss its production locations or plans. Thomson's ultimatum was that only Korea, China and Hong Kong should be involved. How such discrimination should be achieved was irrelevant. It just persisted that Turkey and 14-in. television sets from Singapore and Thailand should be excluded. It was an impossible ultimatum. Market share of the three countries to be included ranged from 1.8 % in 1987 to 7.4 % in 1990. Excluding Thailand, Singapore, and as a corollary the ASEAN country Malaysia, a market share of 7 % in 1987 up to 12 % in 1990 would be discarded. Philips was prepared to take the risk of exposing its exports from Singapore, which in case of duties could be compensated by additional production in the European Community. Thomson, however, had decided that it could not produce tiny vision television and audio equipment in Europe.

Thomson correctly feared that its production in Singapore and, after transfer, in Thailand might be found dumped. The importance of the French state in European Community decision-making and still impressive volume of production of Thomson made including it in the group of complaining producers appealing. Excluding Thomson as party related to a dumping exporter was an option, but Philips was also related to Philips in Singapore. It was held impossible at Philips that Thomson would incur losses on production in Asia and that it dumped. If Thomson would dump but did not inflict injury, this would safeguard Thomson for anti-dumping duties. Therefore, expectation of some minimum resale prices would keep Thomson safe from injury. These non-injurious prices were communicated to the trade expert of Thomson. But he left the company soon and his successor, who was later undeservedly blamed for subsequent disasters, was in the dark. During the proceedings, it became apparent that calamities would come from Thomson. Thomson's resale prices in the European Community were far lower than suggested as non-injurious minima.

Thomson did not want its agreement since 1990 with the Turkish Profilo Telra on production and sales of its Telefunken and Saba brands in Turkey, for which Thomson supplied the tubes, burdened with trade policy conflicts. Involving Turkish companies in huge fraud and dumping, to be discussed below, was immaterial to Thomson. Thomson's decisions seemed to have been made on the basis of impulses rather than calculations.

These excessive demands compelled Philips to confront Thomson with three options. Thomson could participate and have some influence on the outcome. The second option was, since there was insufficient knowledge about Thomson, this option was bluff, that Thomson's dumping would be demonstrated and Thomson would as related party be excluded from the definition of European Community industry. The third option was that Thomson as minority in European industry would object to the opening of an anti-dumping proceeding. Both the second and third options would give Thomson negative publicity. Opposing anti-dumping in combination with state funding would not increase Thomson's popularity in French politics. Thomson yielded, but this clearly appeared to have a negative outcome.

11.9 State Aid and Undercutting or Underselling: Doom for European Television Industry

Thomson's newly started production in Thailand was unprofitable. The Garcin doctrine did not work. For a state-owned company with multinational ambitions, it kept the French public and politicians in the dark about losses incurred in an operation in Asia, for which factories in Europe were closed. The losses on new cheap sites after transferring production were a political disaster. The company remained uncommunicative to other European producers participating in the complaint against China, Korea, Malaysia, Singapore and Thailand.[23] Initially, Thomson lobbied for the acceptance of a principle that it incurred start-up losses. This possibility was legally inexistent in the investigation period of the case (CTV Asia 1) 1 July 1991 to 30 June 1992, however. The ADA of the WTO[24] contained such a clause, but European Community legislation had not yet implemented it.[25] Without notification, the Thomson lobby took a new, surprising and ultimately destructive course. The law firm Thomson hired started a covert lobby to prevent anti-dumping measures toward its exports from Thailand, which spoiled Thomson's name. The rest of the industry wondered why the proceeding did not make progress and Thomson kept them ignorant.

Thomson tried to avoid at all cost its practice in Thailand from coming into the limelight.[26] Therefore, Thomson's lawyers and lobby propagated a view that the usual necessary target profit of 10 % on sales of European industry should not be applied. A target profit is profit normally incurred in a situation in absence of dumping. For the calculation of injury the undercutting of European prices, from which losses incurred due to dumping are eliminated and a target profit is added, by prices of the dumping exporters on the European market is taken. Undercutting of prices adjusted in this way is called "underselling". By taking only undercutting plus loss elimination instead of underselling, the anti-dumping duty on Thomson's exports from Thailand could be kept at 3 %, as appears from Table 11.4, instead of at least 13 %.

---

[23] Because the British Radio and Electronic Equipment Manufacturers' Association (BREMA) with its Japanese membership objected to this comprehensive complaint covering *inter alia* some Japanese subsidiaries in Asia, it was impossible for the European Association of Consumer Electronics Manufacturers (EACEM) to act a as complainant. The Society for Coherent Anti-Dumping Norms (SCAN) was formed outside EACEM and, at request of the majority of the producers supporting the complaint, an executive of the Philips trade policy department assumed management of the proceeding. Supporters were, apart from Thomson and Philips, Grundig, Nokia, Bang & Olufsen and Seleco, and some Italian producers expressed their sympathy with the complaint.

[24] Agreement on Implementation of Article VI of the General Agreement on Tariffs and Trade 1994 (the Anti-Dumping Agreement, ADA) Article 2, 2.2.1.1.

[25] Regulation (EC) No 384/96 on protection against dumped imports from countries not members of the European Community. It is doubtful whether Thomson was really still in a start-up stage.

[26] Initially, the European Commission found a dumping of about 28 %. The reduction of this margin to 14.7 is a miracle.

Table 11.4 CTV dumping margins, undercutting margins and anti-dumping measures: lesser duty

CTV definitive dumping margins	Dumping margin (%)	Undercutting Minimum (%)	Undercutting Maximum (%)	AD duty (%)	Lesser value
Malaysia					
Makonka	2.3	7.5	23.4	2.3	Dumping
Orion	13.5	10.1		10.1	Undercutting
Technol silver	25.1	7.5		7.5	Undercutting
Residual	25.1	23.4		23.4	Undercutting
Thai companies assembling CTVs of Malaysian origin					
GoldStar Mitr	19.6	7.5	23.4	19.6	Dumping
World electric	17.3	13.5		13.5	Undercutting
Thailand					
Thomson	14.7	3.02		3.0	Undercutting
Teletech	33.6	29.9		29.8	Undercutting
Samsung	29.7	12.1		12.1	Undercutting
Residual	33.6	29.9		29.8	Undercutting
People's Republic of China Residual	25.6	58.7		25.6	Dumping
Republic of Korea					
Daewoo	17.9	38.61	54.0	17.9	Dumping
GoldStar	13.4	38.61	54.0	13.4	Dumping
Samsung	13.7	38.61	54.0	13.7	Dumping
Residual	17.9	38.61	54.0	17.9	Dumping
Turkish companies assembling CTVs of Korean origin					
Profilo	0	38.61	54.0	0	Dumping
Bekoteknik	0	38.61	54.0	0	Dumping
Singapore					
Hitachi	16.3	0		0.0	Undercutting
Funai	0.0			0.0	De Minimis
Philips	24.6	2.8		2.8	Undercutting
Sanyo	14.4	4.3		4.3	Undercutting
Thomson	13.3	2.6		2.6	Undercutting
Residual (highest individual)	24.6			23.6	Dumping

Table 11.4 shows dumping and undercutting margins found and duties finally imposed (see methodological Chap. 16). The European Commission reported minima or maxima undercutting of margins as per cent of the CIF export price. Table 11.4 shows that the undercutting margins rather than the dumping margins were applied in the majority (11 out of 18) of individual duties. The residual duties of two countries were also based on undercutting. Applying a target profit of 10 % as usual and as applied in small screen television sets in Asia 1 would have produced radically different results. In a disclosure meeting, the European Commission stated that only in exceptional cases the 10 % profit inclusion would make a difference. This was deceptive information.

Table 11.5 Effect of undercutting or underselling for an anti-dumping duty

	Dumping margin (%)	AD duty (%)	Duty based on	Duty if target profit of 10 % (underselling) (%)	Lesser: underselling or dumping
Malaysia					
Orion	13.5	10.1	Undercutting	**13.5**	Dumping
Technol Silver	25.1	7.5	Undercutting	**20.2**	Underselling
Residual	25.1	23.4	Undercutting	**25.1**	Dumping
Thai of Malaysian origin					
World electric [is of Orion]	17.3	13.5	Undercutting	**17.3**	Dumping
Thailand					
Thomson	14.7	3.0	Undercutting	**14.7**	Dumping
Teletech	33.6	29.8	Undercutting	**33.6**	Dumping
Samsung	29.7	12.1	Undercutting	**25.2**	Underselling
Residual	33.6	29.8	Undercutting	**33.6**	Dumping
Singapore					
Hitachi	16.3	0	Undercutting	**11.9**	Underselling
Philips	24.6	2.8	Undercutting	**15.0**	Underselling
Sanyo	14.4	4.3	Undercutting	**14.4**	Dumping
Thomson	13.3	2.6	Undercutting	**13.3**	Dumping

A reconstruction of Table 11.4 into Table 11.5 shows the effect of injury margins with a profit level of 10 %.[27] The outcomes differing from Table 11.4 are presented only. Differences were huge and the Table shows that the European Commission and Thomson harmed European industry excessively.

The two right hand columns in Table 11.5 show the level of the injury margin with the inclusion of a 10 % target profit and whether the anti-dumping duty is based on dumping or underselling, whichever the lowest. Table 11.6 shows an amazing European Commission flexibility in application of a target profit.

The European Commission defended suppression of the target profit with arguments that were later supplemented[28]:

[27] Percentages of undercutting are given. The price of the European product has been put at 100. The undercutting as % CIF is 100 minus the CIF export price to which the level of trade (LoT) adjustment has been added. Since the level of trade adjustment is 19 % and the customs duty is zero, except for China, and the insurance and freight is 2 %, the export price can be found. Since the dumping margins are given, normal values can also be found. An increase of the LoT adjustment by 10% points results in a decrease of underselling by 1 %.

[28] Commission Regulation (EC) No 2376/94 of 27 September 1994 imposing a provisional anti-dumping duty on imports of colour television receivers originating in Malaysia, the people's Republic of China, the Republic of Korea, Singapore and Thailand Official Journal L 255, 01/10/1994, pp. 0050–0069, recital (141): "For the establishment of this amount the Commission's practice is to take account of specific circumstances of individual cases. In this case the Commission has considered it appropriate for the purposes of the preliminary determination to limit such amount to that sufficient to eliminate price undercutting."

Table 11.6 Politics of target profit allocation for CTVs

Case	Investigation period (IP)	Target profit (%)
SCTV Korea	1987	10
SCTV China/Hong Kong	1988	10
CTV Asia 1 (Thailand involved)	Half 1991 – half 1992	**0**
CTV Asia 2	1994 – 1st Quarter1995	10
CTV Asia 3 (Thailand involved)	1999	**0**

(i) *factors other than the dumped imports, specific to the Community CTV market,* ***appear*** *to have contributed to the injury to the Community industry;*
(ii) *on a world-wide basis this industry has for a number of years realized no or extremely low profits.*

No evidence was ever supplied. What the "other factors" under (i) were was never revealed. The only possibility was a temporary increase in the capacity of Grundig's factory in Creutzwald as a response to increased sales in East Germany after reunification. The European Commission guessed about factors, however[29]:

> *As far as the acute internal competition in the Community is concerned,* ***it cannot be ruled out*** *that newly established Community producers* ***may have exerted a certain price pressure*** *in order to enter the market. Similarly, the result of over-optimism on the part of the Community producers following German unification* ***may have had*** *a negative impact.* [Emphasis added in bold]

The European Commission did not and apparently could not supply information about those "*other factors*". According to the European Commission they "*may have*" had an influence. It must have been hearsay, the source of which was not difficult to find. At a meeting of temporary industry association Society for Coherent Anti-Dumping Norms (SCAN), the source of this information became apparent. Thomson's Vice-President for external relations showed Thomson's annoyance about Grundig's achievement in the East German market where Thomson had hoped to gain the upper hand with its Telefunken, Nordmende and Saba brands, and emphasised this point, also without factual evidence. This increase of production by 578,000 units in Creutzwald was substantially less than the shift of production by Thomson from Europe to Asia to an amount of up to 800,000 units.[30] Thomson had closed several factories in the European Community and discontinued small screen production, which it had transferred to Singapore and subsequently to Thailand. Thomson reported the capacity that had become idle because of this transfer as normal "idle" capacity. Consequently, the capacity increase of Grundig was depicted as overcapacity caused by over-optimism, but

[29] OJ 2376/94 of 27 September 1994, Recital 128.

[30] Press coverage on the closure of Creutzwald; Commission Decision of 16 November 1999 on aid granted by France to Gooding Consumer Electronics Ltd in connection with the purchase of the former Grundig plant at Creutzwald (notified under document number C (1999) 4230) Official Journal L 165, 06/07/2000, pp. 25–32. Imports from Thailand increased from 29,000 in 1988 to more than a million in 1991, which represented transfer of production from Europe.

Table 11.7 European production and other factors: political prejudice and over-optimism

Years	EU production	EC capacity	Total imports	Imports from countries in proceeding	EU CTV consumption
1987	100	100	100	100	100
1988	120	106	148	113	129
1989	124	108	127	211	125
1990	141	112	167	285	147

Grundig's capacity actually replaced Thomson's. Additionally, there was not the slightest reason why a target profit should have been reduced from, for instance, 10 to 0 %, instead of, for instance to 5 %.

The European Commission neglected both requests for evidence and the arguments presented by the complainant. The European Commission argumentation was untrue, as Table 11.7 shows.

Market growth exceeded European production increase. The increase in European production was attributable to a higher utilisation of capacity rather than to increased capacity. Between 1989 and 1999, European production volume fell by 38 %, attributable to continuation of dumping, which had not been sufficiently eliminated. Conclusions about over-optimism were political falsifications, aggravated by inclusion of Thomson's production capacity, the empty factories from which production was transferred to Asia that it no longer needed, i.e. idle capacity. The idle capacity of Thomson attributable both to the injury and to the transfer of production to Singapore was cumulated with the, according to Thomson's opinion, objectionable, increase of capacity by Grundig attributable to additional sales in East Europe. In its view of course, these sales should have been Thomson's.

In this respect, some amazing experiences with Thomson must be mentioned. Its acquisition in 1992 of a tube factory and investments of $100 million in Poland, where 1.1 million tubes, including small tubes, were produced, lost the major internal customer by its transfer of small screen production to Asia. Thomson demanded duty-free and unlimited access of the Polish tubes to the European Community, which came on top of the production of the Lithuanian producer Ekranas. This company had produced for Soviet CTV manufacturing, but that market had soon disappeared after the collapse of Communism. The production of 800,000 small tubes was directly competing with existing production of Philips and representing 25 % of total television production in which Thomson's share in European (small screen) television production practically disappeared. The argument Thomson had invented with respect to other factors to consider implied that no other company should have been allowed to create or utilise idle capacity that resulted from Thomson's transfer of production to Asia.

Table 11.8 A "mature product" growing by 5.8 % annually (1995–1999)

	1995	1996	1997	1998	1999	IP
Consumption *units*	24,727,803	24,492,961	27,748,574	31,021,098	30,706,970	32,470,213
Consumption *index*	*100*	*99*	*112*	*125*	*124*	*131*
EU production *units*	21,308,217	20,384,079	19,625,619	20,032,542	19,119,798	17,223,899
EU production *index*	*100*	*96*	*92*	*94*	*90*	*81*
Market share EU production	*86 %*	*83 %*	*71 %*	*65 %*	*62 %*	*53 %*
Turkish imports	839,724	1,012,597	2,810,453	4,214,040	4,581,515	5,301,118
Turkish market share	3 %	4 %	10 %	14 %	15 %	16 %

In 2002, the European Commission published results of a colour television anti-dumping review combined with a new dumping proceeding toward Turkey, the outcome of which would be complete destruction of European Community industry. Again, the target profit was reduced to zero. This time arguments were: [31]

(iii) "Maturity" of the product, which notion remained undefined. Evidence was not supplied.
(iv) Again, worldwide low profitability. Again factual evidence remained absent.

For the maturity argument, Thomson's history might have been the background. The notion of "maturity" can be found in European Commission Decision of 1 October 1997 concerning aid granted by France to Thomson SA and Thomson Multimedia.[32] The concept of maturity was not substantiated. When average annual volume growth is 5.8 %, as apparent from Table 11.8, there is no ground for an allegation of maturity of the product, at least not in relation to the past, which is the only basis for judgment in anti-dumping.[33]

As for profitability, Chap. 12 shows Vestel's selling price of 14 in. television sets in Turkey at €135.24, which is an extremely profitable price compared with the European price of €103.19. Profitability was not the worldwide low. Vestel made a profit on its 14 in. television set, the disclosure of which reported exact prices – of about 20 % in Turkey. Normally, the 14 in. was the product range with relatively the lowest profit rate. The European Commission must have known the data about

[31] Council Regulation (EC) No 1531/2002 of 14 August 2002 definitive CTVs China, Korea, Malaysia and Thailand, OJ L 231, 29/08/2002, pp. 1–28, recitals 231 and 232.

[32] Commission Decision of 1 October 1997 concerning aid granted by France to Thomson SA and Thomson Multimedia OJ L 67/32 of 7.3.98: "*Despite acknowledged technological know-how, the group suffered in the 1990s from inadequate industrial competitiveness, essentially because its production plants were widely scattered. At the same time its trading positions in Europe were being eroded. In a market that had reached maturity, on which the leading producers were engaged in a price war, the group's industrial and commercial fragility caused considerable losses, generally in excess of FRF 1 billion a year since 1992, and even higher in 1996.*"

[33] General Disclosure Document AD No 433, R No 232, 1 August 2001.

profit in Turkey. The European Commission, therefore, either did not know the facts or deliberately distorted them. In markets from where the dumping took place, profit appeared extremely high and far above the 10 %. Kafkaesque arbitrariness was a main characteristic of these proceedings, in which Thomson's failure was veiled by joint efforts of a few officials using unsubstantiated arguments and the European Commission's discretionary powers, which finally did not save Thomson, but were destructive for the rest of the industry. Thomson was firmly led to disaster by its French politicians in CEO-cloths. Thomson also firmly doomed the European Community industry at large, to which the European Commission added one final blow described in further detail.

11.10 Dissimilarity of Philips and Thomson: Industrial Flexibility Versus Political Theory

The distinction between private Philips and state-owned Thomson is especially clear in their responses to trouble. Some European Community sales organisations of Philips were supposed to sell small screen television sets from Singapore at the same price level as identical small screen sets made in the factory in Barcelona. When the anti-dumping complaint was prepared and drafted, prices of Singapore sets were identical to Philips' European Community sets. Although it was known that intercompany supply prices are not treated as selling or resale prices, it was not expected that difficulties would arise as a consequence of the behaviour of some Philips European sales organisations. Resale prices were based on expected market prices, a system of market minus cost budgeting, explained earlier, not on the provenance and purchasing costs of products.

However, in 1989 a newly appointed consumer electronics executive in Germany came from the music business and did not stay for long. He had been the managing director of the Philips' Polygram music company. It was his conviction that profits could be made on software rather than on simple television sets, and loudly voiced this view in the press. Unfortunately, his views were a self-fulfilling prophecy. The 14 in. set 1221 Philetta, leading model in the German market, was sold at a retail price of €234.48. The ex-factory price, however, was €187.87. It was clear that the sales occurred at a considerable loss of about 15 %. The price was 8 % below the level of Thomson's best selling Telefunken set, and below top sellers of Grundig and some other well-known brands, but far above the level of other exporters. Had he sold Spanish Philetta television sets, losses would also have been incurred, but these could have been presented as injury caused by foreign dumping. It would have been allocated to and accounted for as a European Community industry loss. He sold sets both from Spain and Singapore. The sets from Singapore were dumped by his low resale prices and they undercut prices of European Community industry. The sets from Spain were also sold at a loss, which contributed to injury figures. However, he also undercut the average of

Table 11.9 Options for Thomson: non-payment of duties or improvement of profitability

If	Units Thai imports (×1,000)	Avg price Thai imports Euro	Turnover of Thai CTVs (million)	Payable AD-duties (million)	Turnover Thomson's EU production (million)	Target profit (million)	Advantage Thomson (million)
Target profit 0 %; Thomson duty 3.1 %	800	€80.35	€64.3	**€1.9**	€507	€0	**€ 6.4**
Target profit 10 %; Thomson duty 13.1 %	800	€80.35	€64.3	**€8.4**	€507	€50.7	**€42.3**

Europe-wide Philips sales of sets from Barcelona and other Europeans. Another source of worry in Singapore was that Philips Singapore had to supply Philips Italy at low transfer prices in order to compensate for financial deficiencies caused by mismanagement in that organisation. This transfer pricing was uncommon, against the OECD guidelines for multinationals and highly deplored. These phenomena were unknown by the authors of the anti-dumping complaint.

Philips' Singaporean television sets were, accordingly, found dumped by 24.6 %. Due to the fact that the European Commission, prompted by Thomson and its lawyers, reduced the injury margin, the anti-dumping duty for Philips Singapore was only 2.8 %. The Philips Singapore organisation highly appreciated any discontinuation of low-priced deliveries and preferred more profitable sales henceforth in the Asian region where prices were more attractive than in Europe. Philips Singapore preferred higher injury margins and higher anti-dumping duties by the inclusion of normal target profit. Philips Europe had already decided to stop its imports of television sets from East Asia and the low duties were a blow to expectations.

In an effort to convince Thomson of the serious damage it would inflict on itself and European industry, Philips made various calculations about effects of duties on profitability. The consequences of various options for anti-dumping duties were calculated for both Thomson and other producers. The data of the complainant, SCAN, were used for calculation of Thomson's alternatives. The consequences for Thomson of anti-dumping duties, displayed in Table 11.9, were submitted to Thomson for discussions.

Two options were compared. The first was an absence of a target profit (or a 0 % target profit). The duty on Thomson's Thai sets would be 3.1 %. The amount of duty payable in that case is €1.9 million annually. At a target profit margin for European industry of 10 % (that was the second option), Thomson's duty on sets from Thailand would have been 13.1 % and this would cost Thomson an amount of €8.4 million annually. If the calculation is restricted to duties on Thai sets,

Thomson's advantage would be €6.5 million. If a 10 % target profit margin for European producers were included for elimination of injury, the maximum improvement would be 10 % of total turnover of Thomson's European-made televisions, or €50.7 million. The maximum advantage in case of a target profit of 10 % to Thomson was this amount minus the higher duties on Thai sets. The duties of 10 out of 16 exporters would increase by 10 % or less. Consequently, the advantage to Thomson would be less than €42.3 million, but in any case it would be more than the loss of duties on sets from Thailand.

By a 10 % target profit Complainants' turnover would, if the prices could increase by 10 %, rise by €250 million and total European Community industry's by another €262 million. Alternative lower percentages to a 10 % improvement of profits were presented, all of which would be substantial improvements for European producers. Both arguments and amounts, however, appeared unacceptable and irrelevant to Thomson Consumer Electronics. It was unacceptable because it would show that the "Garcin doctrine" of transfer to Asia was wrong. It was irrelevant in relation to Thomson's total annual losses since 1992 of €152 million, or 2.5 % of total turnover. Such amounts were considerably more impressive than some marginal improvements in results by less than one-third of this amount. Thomson's balance showed a deficit of €427 million in 1995.[34] The magnitude of Thomson's problems was disguised by French state aid, and a continuation of that aid had a higher priority than certain advantages that solid measures against dumping would offer. It was essential to Thomson that silence would be kept about its sales at a loss and dumping from Thailand after the closure of its factories in Europe. Data showing Thomson's interests in improved anti-dumping duties were not even rejected; they were just neglected, and covert actions continued. The French connection, French ministry of Finance and Economics and European Commission officials helped conceal Thomson's real position and implied disaster to European industry and finally, to Thomson, which would disappear. Improving the European industry's bottom line was certainly not Thomson's main preoccupation.

11.11 Appearances of Privileged Treatment and the Damage to European Industry

Because China was treated as non-market economy, Chinese authorities regularly complained about discrimination against their country. Non-market economy treatment implies that normal value is established on the basis of data of a representative, analogue market economy. In the United States jargon this is called a surrogate country. Chapter 16 shows that in some cases this treatment has favoured Chinese exporters. In the case of small screen televisions, China was favoured by an

[34] Commission Decision of 1 October 1997 concerning aid granted by France to Thomson SA and Thomson Multimedia OJ L 67/32 of 7.3.98.

application of the Hong Kong normal value, which factually was the distorted value of Chinese products and was extremely low for China.

In the first comprehensive case (CTV Asia 1) towards Asia, the complainant, SCAN, suggested Singapore as the representative market economy in order to establish the normal value for China, which was accepted. For colour televisions, the Chinese exporters wanted a low normal value so that their dumping margin would be small[35]:

> *Given the relatively large number of models exported from the People's Republic of China, the suggestion that the country with the lowest normal value be used could not be followed as no country could be found which had lower normal values for the totality or a very large majority of models.*

It might be expected that the normal value finally established for China would be at a similar level as Singapore's. On the contrary! The normal value for China was 13 % below the lowest normal value found for Singapore and 22 % below the average normal value of the Singapore exporters. These data are derived at from Table 11.4. The normal value can be found via the undercutting margins in combination with data on dumping margins, similar to the method of construction of Table 11.5. The normal values of China were consistently lower than those of Singapore, and also lower than the normal values established for any other individual exporter or normal value that could be calculated from Table 11.4. The undercutting by the Chinese was 58.7 %. This meant that the export price was 53.28 (putting the European price at 100) and normal value should have been $53.28 \times (25.6\ \% \times 1.02 + 1) = 67.19$.[36] The normal value for Singapore for Philips, the Philips price, was 86.04 and lowest normal value in Singapore was Funai's, which was 77.52 according to the same calculation method. The European Commission never explained why it applied a normal value for China that was 22 % and 13 % lower than Philips' and Funai's, respectively. It probably was a political concession or effort to bring the normal value in line with the absurdly low Hong Kong value, which actually was an impermissible Chinese value. Again, this was a policy at the cost of European industry.

From the last investigation, Asia 3, the deathblow to the European Community television and consumer electronics industry, it became apparent that both Thomson and Vestel were involved in substantial fraud. From the final disclosure in Article 20.4[37] of the European Commission, fraud was apparent to complaining

---

[35] Commission Regulation (EC) No 2376/94 of 27 September 1994 imposing a provisional anti-dumping duty on imports of colour television receivers originating in Malaysia, the people's Republic of China, the Republic of Korea, Singapore and Thailand, OJ L 255, 01/10/1994, pp. 50–69, recital 68.

[36] Equations Dumping margin $= \frac{\text{Normal value - Export price}}{\text{CIF export price}}$ and Undercutting margin $= \frac{\text{European price minus export resale price}}{\text{CIF export price}}$ with a given level of trade percentage (the margin between CIF price and resale price or Level of Trade Adjustment) and CIF 2 % give the normal value.

[37] Basic Regulation Article 20.4: "Final disclosure shall be given in writing. It shall be made, due regard being had to the protection of confidential information, as soon as possible and, normally, not later than 1 month prior to a definitive decision". This information is not confidential.

industry. If fraud could only be concluded from confidential information, it meant that the European Commission was not supposed to reveal information from which fraud could be inferred. Reporting confidential information would inhibit cooperation in anti-dumping investigations. State-supported Thomson seemed to have enjoyed firm assistance and protection, however, from within the European Commission. Its former lawyer had become European Commission official and took over the review case on Asia and the case toward Turkey (R No 232 and AD No 433, which started in 2000 and ended in 2002) as head of the "injury department". As lawyer, the person had lobbied on behalf of Thomson during the first comprehensive CTV case (Asia 1) and propagated a zero target profit, which had been applied in all later cases in which Thomson Thailand was involved. Good practice in case of conflict of interest is withdrawal from a case. Instead, the person was extremely active during the case, except when reporting on fraud by Thomson was expected.[38] In this case, the arguments for zero target profit, mentioned as (iii) ("Maturity" of the product) and (iv) (worldwide low profitability), again served Thomson well. The European Commission once again did not base its arguments for a zero profit on factual evidence.[39]

The result of all the manoeuvres was a zero duty for Thomson for television sets, which were not as Thomson's origin declarations indicated, originating in Thailand, but in Korea and Malaysia. Thomson's customs clearance at the European Union border took place with Thai origin certificates, although the real origin was, because of the origin of the tubes, Korean and Malaysian. Chapter 12 shows the amounts involved in this fraud. The investigators of the European Commission were aware of fraud but did not report it to fraud authorities in the European Commission, OLAF. The information was not confidential and there was no reason to conceal it for other participants in the proceeding. In the complaint by the industry, reference was made to fraud, if the weird interpretation of the origin rule would prevail. Thomson's non-confidential replies to enquiry forms also contained evidence. Thomson's responses to the investigation were added to the files that other parties could inspect closely before the end of the proceeding. The Anti-Dumping Division of the European Commission did not do anything with or about the facts of fraud. Only 1 week before the publication of the decision, clear evidence popped up about Thomson's involvement in fraud. Sets from Thailand by Thomson Thailand (TTT) had contained and still contained tubes from Korea and Malaysia and Thomson complained on 28 August 2001: "*There was no discussion in 1993/1994 of separate individual margins for the CTVs manufactured by TTT and incorporating Malaysian or Korean tubes.*" Indeed, in 1993/1994 the European Commission did not take the trouble to investigate the matter fully. The investigation team of the European Commission did not do its work: "*Due to the limited information*

[38] Since the bosses of this person appreciated this pro-French behaviour, the career went into a rapid.

[39] None of the allegations resulting in the 0 % profit was supported by facts. Factual evidence submitted by the industry was neglected. See also Table 11.7: A "mature product" growing (1995–1999) by 24 %.

provided by one of the Thai producers, the origin of this company's exports to the Community was based on that declared to the Community customs authorities".[40] When the complainant found fraud, it was reported to OLAF. In the last case, Asia 3, the European Commission concluded that duties for Thomson with the Korean and Malaysian origin should be 0 %. The 0 % duty for Thomson was certainly a surprising, unjustifiable and unfounded outcome. The data collected in the investigation contradicted such beneficial treatment, which appeared to be groundless[41]:

> *A comparison of the prices of **Korean** CTVs as reported by Eurostat and by the cooperating Turkish and **Thai** exporting producers with those of the Community industry in the review IP per screen sizes shows that the prices of the CTVs originating in Korea **undercut** those of the Community industry between **11 %** and **36 %**.*
>
> *A comparison of the prices of **Malaysian** CTVs as reported by Eurostat and by the cooperating Turkish and **Thai** exporting producers with those of the Community industry in the IP per screen sizes shows that the prices of the CTVs originating in Malaysia **undercut** those of the Community industry between **17 %** and **21 %**.* [Emphasis added]

Thomson had clearly undercut European prices and inflicted injury, and if there was a dumping margin, there should have been an anti-dumping duty. The minimum undercutting was 11 % (Korea) and 17 % (Malaysia). A closer look at the prices reveals that there was not the slightest ground for Thomson's 0 % duty on the basis of injury margin, i.e. price undercutting: [42]

> *These prices (14 inches) amounted to EUR 90 for China, EUR 86 for imports originating in China and exported from Turkey, EUR 151 for Korea, EUR 93 for Malaysia, EUR 82 for imports originating in Malaysia and exported from Thailand and EUR 147 for Singapore.*

Never before had the European Community institutions so thoroughly manipulated evident facts, as when it granted Thomson the zero duty on the basis of absence of injury, which were clearly contradicted by facts presented by the European Commission itself. The European Commission concluded: [43]

> *For the same reasons, the same dumping margin of 25,1 % was attributed to Thomson Television Thailand, Thailand and Beko Elektronik AS, Turkey, which were found to export CTVs of Malaysian origin during the IP.*

Consequently, the dumping margin was 25.1 %. The undercutting was at between minimally 13 % and 17 %. The European Commission denied existence of injury and, consequently seemingly fooled the Council of Ministers and European industry. How did they come to a reduction of the undercutting to 0 %? This requires a separate calculation.

In the European Commission's disclosure on Beko, its resale price of exported 14-in. sets in the European Community was €88.00.[44] This resulted in an

[40] Commission Regulation (EC) No 2376/94 of 27 September 1994, OJ L 255, 01/10/1994, pp. 50–69, recital 30.

[41] Council Regulation (EC) No 1531/2002 of 14 August 2002 (CTV Asia 3), recital 180 and 189.

[42] Council Regulation (EC) No 1531/2002 of 14 August 2002 (CTV Asia 3), recital (124).

[43] Council Regulation (EC) No 1531/2002 of 14 August 2002 (CTV Asia 3), recital (79).

[44] Note on the Undercutting and Injury Margin Calculations, sent as annex to a letter of 1 August 2001, number 057867.

undercutting of the European price of €102.63 by 14.2 % and an injury margin of 18.2 % (the additional 4 % was not the profit allowed, but the elimination of losses from the European price). The European Commission disclosed the average (CIF) export price of Beko's exports, as given in Table 11.3, i.e. €80.33. That means that €88.00 − €80.33 = €7.67 costs had been incurred between CIF and resale price. The level of trade adjustment of €7.67 or 9.6 % over CIF value is applied to all exporters in the same way if the products were imported under the same circumstances. This 9.6 % reflects cases in which no customs duties are paid, as was the case with Turkish imports, which were covered by the customs union treatment according to the agreement between the EEC and Turkey. Since Thomson falsely reported the imports into the European Community as having Thai origin, it only had to pay an anti-dumping duty of 3 %. The average CIF price was €82. An addition of the duty results in a landed price of €84.46. Addition of 9.6 % for level of trade adjustment gives a resale price €92.53. The European price was €102.60 and the undercutting is consequently 9.8 % and the injury 13.8 %. Nevertheless, the European Commission arrived at an injury of 1.9 %, which is *de minimis*, because it was below 2 %.

The minimum undercutting found for television sets originating in Malaysia and revealed in the final Council Regulation was 11 % (recital 189 of the Regulation), not 1.9 %, and the reported minimum for Korea was 17 %. Although the Council of Ministers declared that the minimum undercutting was 11 %, the undercutting by Thomson was, without reasonable explanation, put at a level below 2 % (1.9 %), which is *de minimis* and consequently, put at 0 %. The only solution is that two calculations were made. One was without fraud by Thomson. If Thomson had paid the anti-dumping duties, the injury it inflicted would have been below 2 %. With fraud, it was the level of injury reported in the Council regulation. The French connection within the European Commission, assisted by Thomson's former lawyer in the injury department, had worked miracles.

It is uncertain whether the serious damage inflicted to the European Community industry by putting Turkish dumping and injury of origins other than of countries already the subject of anti-dumping measures at a zero level on the basis of a weird interpretation of an origin rule is the consequence of a lack of insight in the nature of dumping and purpose of origin rules, or of a friendly attitude towards the Turkish exporters. The French director in charge of the anti-dumping division in the case of Asia 3 had conducted the customs union agreement negotiations with Turkey. The result of these negotiations, the Decision, had so many deficiencies that both suspicions may concur.[45] In next Section, the details of the disaster are spelled out.

[45] Decision No 1/95 of the EC-Turkey Association Council of 22 December 1995 on implementing the final phase of the Customs Union, OJ L 035, 13/02/1996, pp. 1–47.

Table 11.10 Uninhibited Turkish dumping and undercutting at retail level (minus VAT)

	Turkish sales[a]		All brands			
Segment	Domestic price	Price in Germany	Price in Turkey	Price in Germany	Dumping as % export price	Undercutting as % all brands
14 in.	€202.84	€107.91	€204.20	€130.47	88.0	17.3
20 in.	€277.01	€149.98	€292.06	€165.29	84.7	9.3
21 in. mono	€271.37	€164.64	€300.10	€222.59	64.8	26.0
21 in. stereo	€337.05	€183.12	€339.51	€278.57	84.1	34.3
21–25 in. stereo	€421.69	€231.17	€490.41	€554.05	82.4	58.3
26–30 in. stereo	€477.19	€272.39	€526.99	€585.34	75.2	53.5
Super large	€935.29	€558.43	€537.02	€1,262.80	67.5	55.8
Wide screen	€786.63	€478.90	€513.36	€1,143.35	64.3	58.1
CTV and Dolby	€918.92	€453.11	€878.70	€1,018.18	102.8	55.5

[a]Sales in Turkey Koç (Beko and Arçelik) and Vestel and Shov; in Germany by Beko (and Crown) and Vestel (SEG)

11.12 Dark Picture for European CTV Industry

Producers Of European Televisions in Co-operation (POETIC), a temporary association of producers requested on 21 December 1999 a review, pursuant to Article 11 (2) of the Basic Regulation, of an extension of the anti-dumping measures for imports of colour television sets From Malaysia, the China, Korea, Singapore and Thailand. The argument for an extension of the duties was mainly based on price and production capacity levels. Although various deflections of trade had taken place, attributable to the ineffectiveness of origin rules, or better, an absence of inspection, measures appeared effective, with Thailand as the major exception.

Turkey had become the greatest problem. Almost all European producers were on the verge of succumbing to Turkish inroads. The Turkish market share had increased from 3.7 % in 1995 to 15.3 % in 1999. Most worrying was regarding the difference in price levels in Turkey and the European Community. At retail level they were, as Table 11.10 shows,[46] stupefying.[47]

The grip of Turkish industry on its trade secured these high prices and a low share of foreigners in the Turkish market. The average retail price of Turkish 14-in. sets of €202.84 (value added tax excluded) can be compared with their average retail price in Germany of €107.91, which can be compared with European industry's ex-works selling prices to trade which for 14 in., was €102.63. It can also be compared with the price of all brands together on the German market, including Turkish sales and sales of products from other exporters. This price was

[46] Retail prices and quantities sold are from the German market research firm GfK. The data concern October-November 1999. For Turkey data were available on the period December 1999/ January 2000.

[47] These data were submitted during the proceeding. Before the opening the file contained similar information.

€130.47 and the undercutting by Turkish prices at the retail level was 17.3 %. The dumping at retail level of 14-in. sets was 88 %. These margins were, of course, irrespective of origin of Turkish products. They came from Turkey, were manufactured in Turkey and the dumping and injury came from Turkey.

The European Community authorities were clearly aware that Turkish sales in the European Community were far below cost of production and far below costs of European Community industry and that dumping and undercutting were devastative to the European Community's industry. The European Community industry's market share decreased from 24 %, this small share had been influenced by low duties resulting from previous cases, to 17 % in 1999. The share of all foreign brands, consisting of brands not produced in Turkey, in the Turkish market was only 24 %. The market share of Turkish brands Beko and Arçelik of the Koç conglomerate, brand Profilo Telra (also using Thomson brands), the Vestel brand and Shov, for instance, in the 14-in. segment of the Turkish market was 81 %. Foreign producers' brands were those of Grundig, Panasonic, Philips and Sony: not known as price fighters. Under such conditions, it is not difficult to keep domestic prices at a comfortably high level. The European Commission apparently did not want to take notice of the facts or did not care.

From Tables 11.1, 11.2, and 11.3 it may be clear that added value, in terms of direct labour and other processing, depreciation and selling costs, is not more than 25 %. Taking the resale price level in the European Community of Beko (€88) as an example for the margins of trade in Europe and Turkey, it is clear that the Turkish producers must have incurred huge profits on the domestic market. The difference between retail price in Germany of €107.21 and €88 is 22.6 %. The difference between the Turkish retail price and the resale price of Beko of €88 was 130.4 %. The European Commission must have found the difference, but instead of taking measures for television sets it looked at the content of the sets and stated that televisions dumped from Turkey did not have Turkish origin. It implied that no measures would be taken for products containing tubes from countries that were not subject to the current proceeding. The next Chapter shows that this is very serious discrimination against tube producers in Malaysia, China, Korea and Thailand and irreconcilable with WTO rule.

Not long after this anti-dumping case, the Turkish producers captured more than half of the European television market.[48]

The data of Table 11.10 had been submitted to the European Commission. Nevertheless, the European Commission concluded[49]:

> *Turkey was considered as a reasonable choice of analogue country as it is a competitive market and it has significant production and domestic consumption.*

---

[48] Bob Raikes (2008, p. 12).

[49] Council Regulation (EC) No 1531/2002 of 14 August 2002 imposing a definitive anti-dumping duty on imports of colour television receivers originating in the People's Republic of China, the Republic of Korea, Malaysia and Thailand and terminating the proceeding regarding imports of colour television receivers originating in Singapore Official Journal L 231, 29/08/2002, pp. 1–28, recital 51.

It became clear to the industry that the European Commission mismanaged the case and was trying to decide the case in favour of the Turks and Thomson, which would result in bankruptcies in Europe. The Italian producer Formenti protested to the Italian Ministry of Economic Affairs. The ministry requested President Prodi of the European Commission, who transferred the director of the anti-dumping division to his cabinet. This intervention came too late. Some within the anti-dumping division continued the policy already set out and apparently in accordance with the views of the French trade commissioner. Sacrificing European Community industry to dumping was easier than correcting a mistake in the interpretation of rules. Indeed, two producers, AR Systems and Formenti, went bankrupt during the proceeding and one, Grundig was also bankrupt, but continued, after it had been taken over by Turkish producer Beko (of the Koç group), as a brand only. Philips' secretly prepared subcontracting agreement with Profilo Telra, was one of the reasons (the other was the Chinese pressure on the company by allegedly squeezing its Chinese operations) for Philips to agree with a Chinese proposal for an undertaking.

The Chinese intensively lobbied for an undertaking and Philips strongly endorsed it. Chinese pressure on Philips thus proved a success. A few of the reasons for such rather paradoxical behaviour is that Philips' intention was to put the brunt of the burden caused by Chinese imports on smaller European Community producers. Among those smaller companies was Tecnimagen, a former factory of Philips in Barcelona. This activity was continued by a management buy-out. It produced mainly small and medium sized television sets. Philips envisaged an undertaking in which there would be ample room for the Chinese to export small and medium sets. Philips prepared to purchase these screen sizes from Profilo Telra. If the undertaking offered ample room for total Chinese imports in these segments, Profilo Telra would be put under pressure to sell cheaply to Philips. This was also to the advantage of Philips' wider screen size production, where the undertaking should be stricter. For this manoeuvre, even market figures were manipulated. As an argument for the correctness of the figures, Philips referred to the cost of the market report from the MCI group. Although the cost of the study was high, the quality of the figures supplied by Philips was not.[50] Data contradicted those compiled from GfK, official statistics and data on television production provided by the tube industry. This angered Philips so much that it withdrew from any association with other producers, which was the end of European industry cooperation. It implied that the industry association POETIC had lost the opportunity to

[50] The president of the temporary producers association Producers Of European Televisions in Co-operation (POETIC) had the support of the television cathode ray tube industry and had detailed information at its disposal that was not available to individual members, such as Philips. The Consumer Electronics Division of Philips never accepted the market data of the tube division because the latter estimated the market greater and, consequently, the market share of the television business of Philips lower than management in the CTV business unit preferred to report. People within the television unit systematically served individual interests by overstatement of their market share.

challenge the many mistakes in the proceeding. Fearing that its own interests would be hurt, Philips tried, but could not prevent the submission of evidence on fraud by Thomson and Vestel to the European Commission anti-fraud organisation OLAF. An association need not make such a complaint with OLAF.

The outcome of last proceeding (CTV Asia 3), *inter alia* including Turkey, was Beko's television sets with Korean tubes got a duty of 12.3 %, those with a Malaysian tube 18.2 % and Vestel's sets with a Chinese tube 24.5 % (dumping was 69.2 %). Dumping by Profilo Telra with European tubes was considered 0 % because European Community origin was apparently considered absence of origin and at least products with a European origin could not possibly be dumped in Europe. Thomson had to pay 3 % for its sets with a Thai tube and 0 % for televisions with a Korean or Malaysian tube. No explanation was given for this benevolence, which essentially represented a discriminatory price increase by 7.4 % for tubes from Thai CRT Company Ltd.[51]

Because the Turkish export prices, compared with the tube price, were so low that the exported televisions could not possibly have sufficient Turkish added value, the market share of Turkish producers was assumed to be 0 %. Only were duties applied if the tubes came from Malaysia, China, Korea or Thailand. Consequently, although the origin of the product was Turkish when the televisions were sold in the Turkish market, since the selling price representing Turkish normal value was high, the export price was taken as decisive for the origin of the exported product and, consequently never Turkish. For one company, Beko, two anti-dumping duties became applicable. The cause thereof is intriguing. The large screen 33-in. tube purchased from Korea resulted in an undercutting of 12.3 %, while the dumping margin established was 21.2 %. Beko's television sets of 14 in., containing a Malaysian tube from Samsung, did undercut European Community sets by 18.2 %. The dumping of Beko from Malaysia was 25.1 %. In 1999 Beko had purchased about 50,000 tubes from Malaysia and 650,000 units from Philips in Barcelona.[52] Had Beko purchased all its tubes from the European Community it would, according to the view of the European institutions, not have dumped and not undercut European Community prices. The anti-dumping legislation remained unused, and instead chaos had been created by use of an ill-understood origin rule. In order to show how adverse certain developments may be, it is sensible to scrutinise the television origin rule in more detail. That is done in Chap. 12.

As for the outcome of the proceeding for Chinese exporters, they undertook certain limitation of quantities and minimum prices. Since television sets have various specifications and screen sizes, separation of products into different classes of prices and quantities requires a close inspection of the model variation.

[51] Taking the figures of Table 11.3, the export value is €80.33 ex-works and €81.93 on CIF (2 % CIF) basis. A 3 % anti-dumping duty on a CTV originating in Thailand would imply a price increase by €2.46 over the set, but also over the tube, which is 7.4 % over the value (€33.06) of the tube, by which the Thai tube has become more expensive than the tube of Korean and Malaysian origin resulting in a zero per cent duty for Thomson.

[52] Data from the tube industry's intelligence.

Unfortunately, totally different products were classified in the same category. For instance, 21 in., belonging to what is generally considered the segment of small and medium, 25, 28 and 29 in. sets together was classified in one same category. One European Community producer had 16 completely different models with widely differing prices in one category covered by the undertaking.

11.13 Industry Status and Profile of Courage

Increasing weakness of European industry can be illustrated by the differences in reaction to Chinese pressure on Philips. Responses in the past were quite different from recent reactions. In the springtime of 1989, the president of Philips, Van der Klugt, paid a visit to China. A year before, in 1988, the association of European Community producers lodged a complaint against dumping from China of small screen colour television sets. The president of Philips was received in the Great Hall of the People and the Chinese leader Deng Xiaoping started criticising Philips' trade policy. But Philips' president Van der Klugt was a courageous man, and did not defend Philips' position but calmly explained to the Chinese what quintessentially their problem was. In the Hall of the People, he explained the commercial practice of Philips, which was based on "market minus", i.e. expected market price minus usual selling expenses and margins to trade should at least be the cost of production, as explained before. The Chinese, however, produced televisions without much awareness of market prices and did not sell on the basis of price that could be obtained, but sold volumes for foreign currency. After this lecture, he gave a free course in accounting. Deng Xiaoping listened breathlessly at full attention and the practical accounting tips about "debit and credit" items were welcomed. The Chinese stopped complaining about the issue of the dumping and abstained from further negative comments on Philips' behaviour.

Some 10 years later, Van der Klugt's successors preferred a test of the stamina of their employees to their own display of spine. Cor Boonstra was furious when he, checking the preparations of his trip to China, sensed that Philips had been involved in three anti-dumping proceedings towards China. These three consisted of one for small screen television cathode ray tubes, one for television and one for energy saving lamps. He intended to travel to China triumphantly as glorious business leader, not to be embarrassed by nasty discussions with Chinese authorities about problems he did not understand. These anti-dumping cases were, in any case, a pretext for some people in the Philips organisation for a lack of achievements in the Chinese market. In January 1995, a year before he became president, Boonstra boasted that the target for Philips in China should increase from a turnover of €950 million to €2.3 billion in 1998. Such growth, practically without investments and without dedication of financial means, is an unsound and untenable target. When Philips' results remained far behind schedule, every Philips executive used trade policy troubles – the Chinese attitude towards these anti-dumping cases – as an excuse for disappointing sales and results and industriously looked for perpetrators involved in these anti-dumping complaints who could be blamed. More humane persons pointed at retired former employees, but several careers fell victim to trade policy problems that were perceived as a trouble to Mr. Boonstra or to Philips' business in China.

As a consequence, nobody within Philips had, in any case, the courage to be actively involved in the decision-making in these cases. Instead, Philips ridiculed itself by displaying humility, or better, cowardice. It offered the Chinese legal help in the anti-dumping case concerning compact fluorescence lamps (CFL), discussed in Chap. 15, of which it was one of the initiators. The verbal pressure by the Chinese and, possibly only alleged, active blackmail by means of suspension of all sorts of import and investment licenses were liable for this behaviour, deviating so much from earlier manifestations of determination. Gerard Kleisterlee, successor to Boonstra, demonstrated again the company's loss of clout by his statement that[53]:

> *...Philips had recovered from the fallout in China after it angered Beijing over its involvement in European anti-dumping actions against local manufacturers... 'We are working in a very strong way to help Chinese companies understand how the WTO operates'.*

Philips could not be of much help. It did not have the knowledge about the issues any longer and had practically stopped its trade policy activities. The Chinese probably knew more about the issues at stake. Within a few years, mass electronics would disappear and the company could stop its trade policy activities.

References

Geddes K, Bussey G (1991) Setmakers: a history of the radio and television industry. British Radio and Electronic Equipment Manufacturers' Association, London

Raikes B (2008) The European display market – exciting times for the display industry. German Flat Panel Forum: European Technology: Flat Panel Displays, 6

Rosenthal DE, Nicolaïdes P (1997) Harmonizing antitrust: the less effective way to promote international competition. In: Montgomery G, Richardson D (eds) Global competition policy. Institute for International Economic, Washington, DC, pp 355–383

[53] Financial Times Friday, 3 September, 2004.

Chapter 12
Orientation on Origin Rules: A Digression on Discrimination

Abstract The purpose of origin rules is to achieve the effectiveness of trade policy measures. In their allocation of production, companies take them into account. The origin rule for television sets intended to safeguard the effect of quantitative restrictions (QRs). After the elimination of residual QRs, the origin rules became a nuisance resulting in serious damage to European industry eventually causing its demise. They represent serious barriers to international trade, are highly discriminatory and are in conflict with international agreements. They have also provoked fraud and anti-fraud cases, which may be attributable to bad intentions, as well as a deficient rule. The history of origin rules comprises examples in which they served company trade policy objectives, creating additional, although preferential, trade. The cases are explained.

12.1 Objectives and Functioning of Origin Rules

The objectives of origin rules are, of course, the proper operation of trade measures such as tariffs and other measures. Contracting parties to trade agreements try to reserve benefits granted to contracting parties to an agreement and to exclude others from these advantages. The higher the trade barriers are and greater the benefits of certain concessions, the greater the inclination to restrict the concessions to those who reciprocated with concessions. Accepting the accessions of Japan and some other Asian countries to the General Agreement on Tariffs and Trade (GATT), for instance, was considered a one-sided concession by some countries.[1] In exchange for acceptance, some countries either demanded a special trade agreement with Japan with a safeguard provision, like the Benelux agreement mentioned in Chap. 2, or they be permitted to maintain residual QRs. After the imposition of QRs, rules to make them effective and prevent circumvention were introduced. The origin

[1] "Report on the Accession of Japan" adopted by an ad hoc Committee on agenda and inter-sessional business on 13 February 1953 (GATT, L/76). Also quoted in Chap. 2.

M. van Marion, *International Trade Policy and European Industry*, Contributions to Economics, DOI 10.1007/978-3-319-00392-4_12,

rules, of course, did not precede measures. They certainly did not determine the nature of the measures. More importantly, their objective was to achieve the effectiveness of measures, in this case QRs, not to prevent them. The intention of origin rules is not to supersede measures. The anti-dumping cases of television appeared to be the first in which an origin rule, introduced for the effectiveness of quota, determined the scope of investigations, whether measures should be taken and even the level of anti-dumping measures. In this case, however, the origin rule preceded and dominated establishment and application of anti-dumping measures and had a seriously discriminatory effect, which were opposite to their purpose.

The creation of the single European Community market in 1992 eliminated QRs and was the end of the rationale of the existing television and audio origin rule. This was the momentum for abolishing the existing rule. One restriction, continued on the European Community level for car stereos originating in China, was soon abolished. In the case of car stereos from China, the origin rule was hardly relevant. Chinese consumer electronic products were practically wholly made in China and inevitably had Chinese origin. The protective policy of the Chinese government, aiming at the reduction of imports of components – very similar to the Korean policy until the late 1990s – contributed to added value in the country of production and to fulfilment of the European Community's requirements for origin.

The justification of a high level of added value in the country of last processing had disappeared, anyway. In the 1960s and 1970s, volume of production was the main cost competitive edge. Japanese and other East Asian manufacturers tried to achieve a high volume of production in as few factories as possible. If quotas forced them to break up manufacturing of final products, then the maintenance of volume of production of key components was imperative. Key components, such as tubes and chassis and kits, were sent to assembly sites of the same producer in other countries. In order to circumvent quotas, a small subsidiary processed products as Table 11.2 in Chap. 11 shows. A value requirement, as in the television rule, in an origin rule made sense. The number of producers of tubes and the number of countries of tube production was relatively small. For cost effectiveness, it was almost inevitable that a product from an assembly line for a final product of a Japanese producer, whether or not located in Japan, contained a majority of Japanese components. Since, in the 1990s, the Yen exchange rate forced Japanese producers to move components production abroad, the number of components producers outside Japan, and Koreans in their wake, increased substantially.[2]

[2] Vermulst (1994) states: "In low-cost countries such as South Korea, Thailand, Malaysia, Hong Kong, and China, assembly costs are in most cases far below the percentages assumed for the EC industry, and origin therefore effectively depends, at least for televisions, on the origin of the picture tube, which can easily represent 35 per cent of the ex-works price." And in a footnote: "Color picture tubes are produced in a limited number of countries only, such as Japan, Korea, the European Community, Malaysia, and China." In 1994, when Vermulst's book was published the list of countries was more numerous than the author assumed. Brazil (three producers), Indonesia (two producers), India (four producers), Lithuania (one producer), Mexico (three producers), Singapore (two producers), Thailand (two producers), the USA (seven producers) and Vietnam

Trade policy measures toward Japan and Korea thereby lost much of their effectiveness. Components manufacturing subsidiaries of Korean and Japanese companies could offer the possibility of circumventing the measures by origin diversity. Although there were serious doubts about the benefit of the origin rule for television, in the comprehensive television complaint (Asia 1) such moves of CTV producers with components production had already been taken into account.

12.2 Change in Origin by Dumping

Legal objections against the television and audio origin rule are many: it upsets anti-dumping proceedings, it is discriminatory, it is a barrier to trade with countries that have nothing to do with the dumping, it hurts producers of products not involved in dumping – producers of components. A very simple example is Turkey. On 29 August 2002, definitive duties concerning Turkish producers were published. Before that date, there were no dumping duties imposed on Turkish television sets, irrespective of the origin of the components. There was never a Turkish CTV tube production and, when Turkish exporters dumped, the origin of Turkish exports was non-Turkish by definition, i.e. by the very fact of dumping, as demonstrated in Table 11.3. The Turkish producers had a serious problem. If they indicated that their products did not originate in Turkey but in the country of the tube, then they admitted dumping. They would be admitting a jump from origin as in Tables 11.1, 11.2, and 11.3. The fact of the dumping made a difference in origin of identical sets completely made in Turkey from partly imported components.

The example of origin calculation in Table 11.1, Chap. 11 can be used. From Table 11.10 in Chap. 11, it is clear that undercutting by the Turks of large screen sets (above 21 in.) was more than 100 % rather than 14.2 %. Let it be assumed, however, that the dumping and undercutting by Bekoteknik (Beko) are representative for the issue explained. Figures of Tables 11.1 and 11.3 in the previous Chapter are again used for demonstration of the awkward consequence of dumping for establishing origin.

Dumping is defined as higher sales price in the domestic market than the export price of a similar product. Dumping makes prices unlike, but not the products. The products in Tables 11.1 and 11.3 are identical. The ex-works price in the example of Table 11.1 was €100.49, Beko's normal value. The resale price of Beko's 14-in. sets in the European Community disclosed by the European Commission was €88. Beko's average CIF export price could also be derived from the disclosure: €80.33. That means that to the CIF value an amount of €7.67 (9.7 %) was added as additional cost of distribution incurred before resale. The dumping margin found

(one producer) should have been added to the list. Consequently, the choice and possible confusion concerning possible origin were greater than suggested. Besides, the percentages are not so different and, in any case, European television sets may also have non-European origin, if their content consists mainly of imported tubes. See the adventures of Mr. Grundig in Austria.

by the European Commission for Beko's CTVs originating in Malaysia was 25.1 %. The normal value derived from the export price minus the cost of insurance and freight is equal to cost within the European Community: €100.49. The value of non-originating components including the cathode-ray tube, *inter alia*, does not change by the dumped export price. According to the implementation of the Community Customs Code (CCC), the value of non-originating materials is their value at import.[3] That means that the absolute value of imported materials does not vary, but the absolute value of domestic Turkish materials and domestic added value may vary. The high price on the domestic market, the normal value, results in Turkish origin (Table 11.1). According to the European Commission's interpretation of the origin rule, because the export price in Table 11.3 of €80.33 is €20.16 lower than the domestic price, the origin of the dumped CTVs made in and exported from Turkey are not of Turkish origin, despite the fact that the products are identical.

The European Commission made a distinction between identical television sets on the basis of the very fact of dumping: sales in Turkey were declared originating in Turkey and the sales in the European Community originating, according to the interpretation, in the country of tube origin. The weird phenomenon is that the European Commission initiated an anti-dumping case and started this case not with an investigation of the dumping of similar or identical television sets. It started by declaring products dissimilar, not in appearance or use or according to any criterion, but according to their origin, i.e. the tube. It divided the products according to origin, which as such is irrelevant for the issue of dumping. The product keeps its essential characteristics, regardless the origin.

Besides, Turkey and the European Community were in a customs union. As soon as the products pass customs clearance, origin is irrelevant in a customs union. Rather, the only relevant issue is the existence of distortion of competition resulting in dumping or characterised by dumping. This existence was the legal basis for commercial policy measures.[4] Origin rules are, furthermore, meant, according to Article 22 of the CCC, for the purpose of "applying measures other than tariff measures established by Community provisions governing specific fields relating to trade in goods," not for establishing the existence of dumping. It is for the application of measures and not a requirement for the finding of the necessity of measures.

[3] Article 40 of Commission Regulation (EEC) No 2454/93 of 2 July 1993 laying down provisions for the implementation of Council Regulation (EEC) No 2913/92 establishing the Community Customs Code (OJ L 253, 11.10.1993, p. 1): 'value' means the customs value at the time of import of the non-originating materials used.

[4] Articles 44 and 46 of Decision No 1/95 of the EC-Turkey Association Council of 22 December 1995 on implementing the final phase of the Customs Union, OJ No. L 35, 13/02/1996, pp. 1–47, allowing measures other than free circulation in case of 'acquis communautaire' has not been accomplished by Turkey.

12.3 Like Product and Origin

If products exported and domestically sold are identical, they at least belong to a category called "like product" (French "produits similaires" or similar products). The European Commission's interpretation of how the television origin rule should be applied undermined this logic. To determine whether there was undercutting, the resale prices of imports into the European Community of exporters were compared with prices of European Community industry for the same or like or similar products. The weighted average of the undercutting on a model-by-model of "like products" were then established. The calculation methodology is given in Chap. 16. Prices at resale level of like products on the European Community market of exporters and European Community products are relevant, not their origin. It is quite possible that similar European products have the same origin as the dumped products with which they are compared. A European Community television set may contain a Korean or Malaysian tube. Nevertheless, it is not treated differently from products with a European tube. In all calculations the origin of the European television set, of the tube in the television set, is irrelevant. In the case of Turkey in the case CTV, Asia 3, suddenly the European Commission considers "like products" to be "unlike" or dissimilar in spite of the fact that the origin of the products was as irrelevant as the origin of the CTVs produced in the European Community.

Normally all "like products" are subdivided into categories or classes of products, the prices of which are compared with the prices of European products: dumped 14-in. stereo with European 14 in. stereo, 33-in. Picture in Picture with stereo with similar European sets. The undercutting is calculated per well-defined class or category, as weighted average per category, and the weighted sum of these undercutting margins is the total undercutting. This results in one single rate of undercutting per exporter. Instead of applying one weighted average, the European Commission separated Beko's undercutting of European Community 14-in. sets from the undercutting of European Community 33 in. sets. The 14-in. sets contained a Malaysian tube, whereas some large screen tubes had been purchased in Korea. By separate calculations of undercutting, the European Commission contradicted its own statement that the products were "like products".[5]

> *... it was established that CTVs originating in or exported from the countries concerned and destined for the Community, share the same basic physical and technical characteristics and end-uses as CTVs manufactured and sold by the Community industry on the Community market. It was also found that there were no differences between the CTVs produced and sold in the countries concerned, including Turkey which was used as an analogue country, and those exported to the Community, which were both identical to*

[5] Council Regulation (EC) No 1531/2002 of 14 August 2002 imposing a definitive anti-dumping duty on imports of colour television receivers originating in the People's Republic of China, the Republic of Korea, Malaysia and Thailand and terminating the proceeding regarding imports of colour television receivers originating in Singapore, Official Journal, L 231, 29/08/2002, pp. 1–28, recital 34.

the CTVs manufactured and sold by the Community industry on the Community market. These products are therefore alike within the meaning of Article 1(4) of the basic Regulation.

Apparently the origin puzzled the European Commission so much that they were not even aware that they abandoned the "like product" treatment and that the Council approved a document in which it made contradictory statements, and therefore infringed on its own policy and legislation. Similar products were treated dissimilarly as the consequence of the price of the product in relation to the tube it contained.

Since the complainant, POETIC, had died by bankruptcies (Formenti and AR Systems, or acquisition of the brand name by Beko, or by Philips' decision to stop certain production and purchase from Profilo Telra), there was no possibility to challenge this serious mistake before the European Court of Justice. Generally, complainants do not challenge the decisions of the European institutions because contrary to the exporters, they lack the financial means, and incorrect decisions generally have a lethal effect on industry, as it was the case with POETIC. If the Court decided in favour of European industry, the duties would not be adjusted retroactively, which was useless because the interested parties had disappeared.

12.4 Origin and in- or Exclusion by Confusion

Confusion reached a climax when authorities failed to notice that their statistical registration methods were not in accordance with rules they had chosen to apply. The exclusion of Japan and Hong Kong from the investigation of dumping could not possibly have been based on origin of products concerned[6]:

The complaint was also directed against Japan and Hong Kong. However, in view of the apparently declining or low level of imports concerned, the evidence of material injury in respect of these two countries was considered, at that time, insufficient to initiate a proceeding.

In Chap. 11, it appeared that market share of Turkish television sets in the European Community was absent because Turkish exports to the European Community did not originate in Turkey. Nevertheless, the Turkish share in the European Community market was 15.3 % in 1999. This share was based on Eurostat statistics. This meant that Eurostat statistics did not reflect the origin of dumped products because the products had an origin that differed from the origin of domestic sales. An anti-dumping investigation was not extended to Japan and Hong Kong, even though origin could not possibly have been established[7]:

[6] Commission Regulation (EC) No 2376/94 of 27 September 1994, provisional CTV, Official Journal L 255, 01/10/1994, pp. 50–69, recital (2) (CTV Asia 1).

[7] Commission Regulation (EC) No 2376/94 of 27 September 1994, recital (25).

In particular, import figures concerning Japan and Hong Kong (that is quantities reported as statistics), adjusted to reflect the origin established during the investigation were considered a determining factor to decide the definitive status of those two countries within the framework of the proceeding.

For Turkey, the European Commission needed an investigation in order to find out the origin of products and subsequently came to, as we will see not only from an industrial and trade policy view but also from the view of international trade rule, an unacceptable conclusion. In 1992, the European Commission made statements about import figures adjusted for origin without opening a case. On the contrary, the European Commission alleged that it had adjusted the figures of Eurostat to reflect origin, although it is generally known that it is impossible to do so. It is a mystery how the European Commission can adjust figures as "to reflect origin" without opening an investigation into dumping. The European Commission may have assumed that all exports from Japan were of Japanese origin. Two legal bases for an investigation into origin are available, either in the framework of an anti-dumping proceeding, providing a legal basis for the investigation of origin, or by inspection of television sets arriving at the European Community border. The European Community authorities may inspect the materials content and determine the origin. The latter method is the one in Tables 11.1, 11.2, and 11.3, and the method for finding origin of a Bush television set, manufactured in Turkey, but originating in China, shortly described in Sect. 12.9. The European Commission did not apply these methods. Consequently, the allegation about adjustment of figures "to reflect origin" could not reflect reality. Some Japanese CTVs contained tubes from China, Malaysia, Korea or Thailand. Exports of picture tubes to Japan amounted to more than one million units.[8] These picture tubes conferred a non-Japanese origin, if exported at dumping prices. That was a reason not to exclude Japan or Hong Kong from a proceeding.[9]

Although the volume of imports of CTVs into the European Community registered as Japanese was small, all imports of 14-in. sets must have been of non-Japanese origin. None of the 12,523 units of 14-in. sets could be originating in Japan. Japan had discontinued 14-in. tube production long before the opening of the case. Consequently, the CTVs were originating elsewhere. They had been exported as Japanese television sets and after the imposition of anti-dumping duties, Japanese producers simply continued their exports because there were no measures toward Japan and nobody inspected the origin and content of Japanese sets. The creation of the single market in 1992 and elimination of QRs gave the Japanese a stimulus to declare Japanese origin. The quotas towards Japan had been eliminated. The problem created by the European Commission was, therefore, that it autonomously made a decision in the beginning of a proceeding without warning

---

[8] Global Trade Information Services, Inc. (GTI) from the statistical services of the countries concerned.

[9] The previous Chapter shows how the European Commission accepted inexistent Hong Kong origin as the correct origin and maltreated its own anti-dumping legislation and practice.

interested parties and the decision was based on incorrect knowledge and an erroneous interpretation of European Community law. The decision had an irreversible effect on the proceeding and could only be challenged after a disclosure, i.e. at the final stage of the proceeding, more than a year after the decision.

Exports from Japan did not offer a clue as to origin. Neither was the origin of exports from Malaysia established:

> *The Commission found that approximately 400,000 sets declared to be of Malaysian origin and approximately 285,000 sets declared to be of Singaporean origin could not be investigated due to the non-cooperation of the exporters of those sets from those countries.*
>
> *Information available to the Commission shows that some of these sets are exported by subsidiaries of Japanese producers located in these countries. Accordingly, and in view of the large number of electronic components exported from Japan, the possibility that some of these sets may originate in Japan should not be excluded. However, there was insufficient information to conclude that those sets did originate in Japan.*

Japan was not included in the proceeding and, naturally and consequently, by that fact it could not be obtained. Japanese producers in Malaysia did, of course, not cooperate in the investigation. The European Commission had decided not to investigate Japan, but found that more than 680,000 CTVs of Japanese origin were shipped to the European Community. In 1990, Japan exported one million tubes to Malaysia and 660,000 tubes to Singapore and there was no reason why these tubes would not find their way to Europe in CTVs assembled in and exported from the latter countries as television sets. In 1990, Japanese exports to the European Community amounted to 627,000 units. That means that the European Commission had decided that more than one-fourth of imports should not be taken into consideration. The allegations about the adjustment of imports from Japan to reflect origin were merely a fig leaf. The European Commission cut off the possibility of obtaining necessary information on Japanese origin because of its decision not to open an investigation on Japan. By excluding Japan from the proceeding, Japanese producers in Singapore and Malaysia could export their products as originating in Japan and avoid anti-dumping duties. It eliminated more than 9 % market share from the proceeding.

In 1996, Hitachi, which faced a zero anti-dumping duty, stopped its colour television tube manufacturing in Singapore.[10] From then onwards, not one single television set imported from Singapore had Singapore origin. Therefore, the Council's remark "*it is concluded that Singapore is an appropriate market economy third country*"[11] as a reference country for establishing Chinese normal value defies

[10] USITC: Color Picture Tubes from Canada, Japan, Korea, and Singapore Investigations Nos. 731-TA-367-370 (Review) determinations and views of the European Commission (USITC Publication No. 3291, APRIL 2000): Hitachi Electronic Devices (Singapore) Pte., Ltd. ("Hitachi Singapore") ceased CPT production in Singapore in 1996, leaving Sony Singapore as the only producer in Singapore.

[11] Council Regulation (EC) No 2584/98 of 27 November 1998 amending Regulation (EC) No 710/95 (CTV Asia 2).

reality.[12] The European Commission apparently did not investigate the origin of the television sets made in Singapore. The origin was not Singapore. The conclusion was that from the closure of Hitachi in 1996 onward on all television sets imported from Singapore a duty, the residual duty, of 23.6 % should be imposed, if the European Commission still considered its ludicrous interpretation of the television origin rule applicable. The origin could not be Singapore and that implied that some higher duty was applicable.

In the first case toward Turkey (CTV Asia 1), the origin was considered Turkish when Turkish producers did not cooperate and, as a consequence, no measures were imposed[13]:

> *Exports of non-cooperating exporters were assumed to have the origin of the country from which they had been exported (country of manufacture, declared to the Community customs authorities as country of origin).*

The European Commission concluded:

- In the case of Japan and Hong Kong, the exports were not included because the import data, adjusted to origin, although this was not explained and is impossible, did not show that there was injury, whereby CTVs from Hong Kong, Japan, Malaysia and Singapore with a quantity of 21 % of the market were disregarded (in Asia 1).
- In the case of Hong Kong (small screen television sets), clearly false origin indications were considered to be correct and this lead to extremely low dumping margins for both Hong Kong and China, for which incorrectly calculated Hong Kong values were considered normal value even though not one single set was of Hong Kong origin;
- Singapore was considered an appropriate market economy, the normal value of which could be used for China, even though none of the Singapore CTVs in the case originated in Singapore;
- False origin declarations by Turkish exporters were considered correct, and no measures were taken.

The elimination of exports from Japan, Malaysia, Singapore for Japanese origin, Hong Kong and Turkey represented 21 % of the European Community television market; exports from all of them should have been included as dumped and found to have caused injury. The European Community chose the path of least resistance and of maximum damage to European industry.

If Turkish exporters were involved in false origin indications or, a better description in view of the value attached by the European institutions to applying

[12] Council Regulation (EC) No 2584/98 of 27 November 1998 amending Regulation (EC) No 710/95 OJ L 324, 02/12/1998, pp. 1–13 (CTV Asia 2) had as investigation period from 1 January 1994 to 31 March 1995. The publication of Regulation 2584/98 was more than 3 years after the notice of the opening of the review investigation. In the meantime, the European Commission could have noticed the discontinuation of production in Singapore and loss of Singapore origin of all CTVs. As a consequence, the Singapore origin declarations were false and therefore, fraud.

[13] Commission Regulation (EC) No 2376/94 of 27 September 1994, recital (32).

the origin rule in cases where it should not be held applicable, in fraud, this incident was neither reported to the anti-fraud authorities of the European Anti-Fraud Office (OLAF) nor punished, but rather rewarded by absence of measures. A similar move was made with Thai CTVs with tubes from Korea, Malaysia (the Thomson case) or Japan. Consequently, if producers did not cooperate, no measures were taken against them and no measures were taken against the country from which the tube exports might confer the CTV origin. In the case of Japan and Hong Kong and Japanese exporters from Malaysia and Singapore, there was no need for exporters to cooperate because they were a priori excluded before the investigation started.

In one of the quotes above, the European Commission stated that figures were adjusted to reflect origin. As for Hong Kong, in small screen colour televisions it was established that European Community imports from Hong Kong were not of Hong Kong origin, but rather of Chinese, Korean or Japanese origin (see also Chap. 11). That means that these imports, according to the European Community's authorities' own practice, should not have been excluded from the investigation; but should, in line with any envisaged consistency, be cumulated with China, Korea and Japan. Therefore, these imports should have been investigated during the proceeding according to origin. However, according the European Commission[14]

> *the investigation regarding the origin of CTVs manufactured in the People's Republic of China was less detailed than those conducted in respect of other countries involved in the proceeding.*

Fortunately the European Commission did not reveal which countries it had investigated in detail. The European Commission created the impression that the origin had been investigated meticulously, but in several cases the origin could not be established or was not investigated at all. This omission concerning Chinese CTVs implies that products of Japanese origin – and Japanese exports of tubes to China were one million units – were not excluded from the Chinese figures and were not attributed to Japan. They were neither included as injury figures into the Japanese export figures nor was a proper normal value calculated on basis of a construction with Japanese data. If Thai exports with a Malaysian tube had a Malaysian normal value, then the Chinese CTVs with a tube from Japan should have had a Japanese normal value and not a Singapore normal value. The mistake in the assessment of injury from Japan, caused by disregard of one million units tubes exported from Japan to China, was tragic. Although the investigation in China yielded that

> "*[o]ut of the 10 companies having cooperated with the investigation, seven either acknowledged that their CTVs were of Chinese origin, did not make any comment, or admitted that they were unable to make a proper determination as to origin*", it was decided that "*based*

[14] Commission Regulation (EC) No 2376/94 of 27 September 1994 (Asia 1) imposing a provisional anti-dumping duty on imports of colour television receivers originating in Malaysia, the people's Republic of China, the Republic of Korea, Singapore and Thailand, Official Journal L 255, 01/10/1994, pp. 50–69, recital 33.

on the behaviour of the companies concerned, since their customers declared the origin of the CTVs in question according to the supporting documents and advice they had received from their suppliers",

the CTVs were considered of Chinese origin. Only one independent importer cooperated in the proceeding. That cannot seriously be presented a basis for a decision on origin (see also the paragraph on fraud).

The European Commission found out that its methodology of investigation was incorrect[15]:

The practical consequence of accepting the Korean, Japanese or Taiwanese origin of the CTVs exported by the three [Chinese] companies ... would be that their export transactions would not be computed for purposes of calculating the Chinese dumping margins, that the total exports from China would be reduced by 22.7% and that export figures for Korea, Japan and Taiwan would have to be increased accordingly.

The European Commission described the consequences of its serious mistakes in approach. Exporters tried to avoid duties, and the European Commission excluded clear cases of dumping from the investigation for the reason of origin and attributed injury to exporting countries that did not have anything to do with the dumping of television sets (they exported tubes) also on the basis of origin.

The year 2000 trade statistics of Korea show huge traffic in tubes that are probably all intercompany exchanges.[16] Because tubes were imported, more than 40 % of Korean television production originated in Malaysia (Samsung's factory for all sizes of 21 in. and below) or in China (Samsung 21–34 in.; LGE 21–34 in.). It is, therefore, understandable that Korean producers refused to cooperate because the European Commission's policy made non-cooperation attractive. The duties for Korean producers were lower than the residual duty for Malaysia or China and consequently, there was not the slightest reason to cooperate. Favourable treatment of non-cooperative Turkish – involved in false origin reporting – and Japanese producers stimulated non-cooperation. Cooperation could reveal another origin than Korea, resulting in higher duties. An imposition of higher duties was, of course, undesirable. CTVs, not tubes, were investigated as dumped. According to this awkward European Commission practice regarding origin rules, the outcome was that Malaysian tube content called for higher duties on Korean CTV exports.

The Chinese normal value construction was initially based on data of Singapore. In the last expiry review case, CTV Asia 3, Singaporean firms did not cooperate, which was understandable considering the origin was not Singapore. The normal value was therefore based on Turkish data. In the case of the Asia 1 sets exported to Europe and assembled in one country, and originating in another country in which the tubes were purchased:

... it was considered that the most appropriate approach was to establish duties for these countries according to the origin of the products determined in accordance with Article 39 of and Annex 11 to Regulation (EEC) No 2454/93.

[15] Commission Regulation (EC) No 2376/94 of 27 September 1994 (Asia 1) provisional, recital 34.

[16] Global Trade Information Services, Inc. (GTI) Global Trade Atlas.

Since not one exported Turkish television set was of Turkish origin, it might be wondered why the domestic prices of Turkish television sets not involved in dumping, because of lack of Turkish origin of exported sets, could be used for a determination of normal value for television sets exported from China. The 14-in. sets of Vestel were used for Chinese normal value and a dumping margin of 67.2 % was found. If Turkey was not, according to the logic of the European Commission, involved in dumping, then why could a domestic price be used for normal value? Since the prices in Turkey were awfully high, which enabled huge Turkish dumping, the determination of normal value for China on the basis of Turkish prices was extremely discriminatory. This is clear from Table 12.3.

In view of the chaos caused by the exclusion of some countries such as Japan, it was understandable that one Korean exporter remarked that excluding Japan from the investigation on the basis of, as we have seen, arbitrary assumptions concerning certain data favoured non-cooperation by Japanese subsidiaries in other exporting countries than Japan. This was the case because by excluding Japan from the investigation, Japanese origin would not be affected by anti-dumping duties. If no investigation toward Japan took place and duties not imposed, then the television sets of Japanese origin from Malaysia, Singapore and Thailand would not face anti-dumping duties. The tube origin decisive, Japanese producers abstained from cooperation and declared their CTVs assembled in South East Asian countries to be of Japanese origin as soon as anti-duties were imposed toward the countries in which they were assembled.[17] The European Commission stated that

> *the possibility that some of these sets may originate in Japan should not be excluded. However, there was insufficient information to conclude that those sets did originate in Japan.*

The European Commission was apparently unable to get that information due to its own decision to exclude Japan from the investigation. Amazingly, the European Commission responded to the argument of the Korean exporter:

> *the exporter concerned did not submit any evidence that the CTVs assembled in Malaysia and Singapore by subsidiaries of Japanese companies actually originated in Japan.*

The European Commission did not want to investigate the case properly; it could not, because of its decision to exclude Japan (and Hong Kong) and ensuing non-cooperation by the Japanese, detect the origin of television sets produced by non-cooperating Japanese exporters in South East Asia and stated that exporters did not supply the information. A producer neither has the possibility nor task or entitlement to submit such evidence. A Korean producer could not possibly provide legally acceptable evidence but only business intelligence, which is legally equal to hearsay. Only one party has the competence to obtain such evidence. That is the party with the authority over the investigation of data concerning imports and dumping, and clearly also the origin. That party is the European Commission, if

[17] Council Regulation (EC) No 710/95 of 27 March 1995, CTV definitive, OJ L 73, 1.4.1995, pp. 3–12, recital (9).

it opened an investigation in line with the legal, required proceedings. CTV production in Malaysia amounted to 9.5 million units and Malaysian CTV production by Japanese subsidiaries accounted for 18.6 % of the total global production by Japanese firms.[18] None of the Japanese television producers in Malaysia, including producers such as Matsushita and Sharp, cooperated in the proceeding. The European Commission put the burden of proof of origin of products assembled in Malaysia on a Korean exporter, who made a clever remark. Because Thai producers cooperated, the Malaysian origin of some television sets could be established. Because Japanese subsidiaries in Malaysia did not cooperate, the origin of the sets these exporters shipped could not be established, and were not and could not be considered exports of Japanese origin. Neither direct exports from Japan, whether of Japanese origin or not, nor Japanese exports from subsidiaries in countries concerned were verified. As the Korean producer correctly indicated, the origin rule invites non-cooperation and is discriminatory. It also implied that the measures were completely insufficient and arbitrary.

The registration of Japan's television imports in Eurostat is not based on origin. An adjustment to "reflect origin" is impossible; the means to establish the origin are absent. However, in some cases imports from Japan are undeniably not of Japanese origin. Some screen sizes exported from Japan necessarily contained tubes produced outside Japan because some tube sizes were only produced abroad and therefore, the origin was not Japan.[19] For instance, during the investigation of the first comprehensive television case (CTV Asia 1, investigation period 1 July 1991 to 30 June 1992), Japanese tube production of 14 in. and 20 in. was absent. Nevertheless, television sets with these screen sizes were imported into the European Community from Japan. The production sites for Toshiba's 14-in. tubes were Patrhumthani, Thailand, and Jakarta, Indonesia, where it also produced the 20 in. Matsushita produced 20-in. tubes in Malaysia and 14-in. tubes in China. Until 1996, Hitachi produced 14-in. tubes in Singapore, as did Sony. Exports of small screen television sets from Japan, therefore, were not originating in Japan, but in any of the other small tubes-producing countries. The rejection of Japan as country of export of dumped television sets before the anti-dumping proceeding opened and before the origin was established, implies arbitrariness and a negation of the consequences of the origin rule. It was not explained why the normal value of Korea was not constructed for television sets exported from Singapore with Korean tubes (origin), nor was it explained why domestic Thai origin was assumed for insufficiently cooperating Thai exporters[20]:

> *A small number of the CTVs exported from Singapore actually originated in Korea and Taiwan.*

---

[18] Tanaka, Shoko, and Kenney, Martin: "US and Electronics Industries in Malaysia: A Comparative Analysis"; Journal of International Cooperation Studies, Vol. 4, no 1, pp. 59–72; p. 70.

[19] All Japanese CTV sizes below 25 in. were produced with an imported tube from overseas production and, therefore, not originating in Japan.

[20] Commission Regulation (EC) No 2376/94 of 27 September 1994 (CTV Asia 1), recitals (29) and (30).

Table 12.1 Imports and "originating" imports: misappropriation of injury in Asia 3

Investigation period Half 1999 – Half 2000	Units Eurostat (provenance)	*Originating in country of provenance*	Divergence	Eurostat as % of EU market	*Commission calculation: originating as % of EU market*
Turkey	5,443,408	*0*	−5,443,408	16.8	*0.0*
Thailand	513,685	*0*	−513,685	1.6	*0.0*
Malaysia	23,687	*526,567*	502,880	0.1	*1.6*
China	45,463	*1,259,233*	1,213,770	0.1	*3.9*
South Korea	647,301	*651,366*	4,065	2.0	*2.0*
Singapore	9,049	*5,237*	−3,812	0.0	*0.0*
Total	6,682,593	*2,442,403*	−4,240,190	20.6	*7.5*

A majority of CTVs exported from Thailand originated in the country of export, while some originated either in Malaysia, Korea and Japan or in a country included neither in the complaint nor in the proceeding. Due to the limited information provided by one of the Thai producers, the origin of this company's exports to the Community was based on that declared to the Community customs authorities.

If the proceeding were consistent, then the normal value in the case of Japanese and Korean origin would have been determined in the same way as the normal value of Thai sets originating in Malaysia, i.e. on a construction of Malaysian data. The errors made in the beginning of the proceeding, excluding countries without proper information about the consequences of such a decision, caused absurd evasiveness in later stages of the proceeding and subsequently in all successive television anti-dumping cases. The problem is that European Community institutions never admit mistakes.

The miscalculation finally became apparent after a survey of import statistics and the European Commission's disclosure. Because the European Commission gave priority to the origin rule over the determination of dumping and injury, only for the countries concerned in Table 12.2 at least 4.7 million television sets, or 5.5 % of the market, disappeared from the calculation of the injury. The loss of quantities is even greater with the exclusion of quantities of Japan and Hong Kong from the initial comprehensive CTV proceeding, CTV Asia 1 (Table 12.1).

By applying this methodology in which priority was given to the television origin rule over rules in the Basic Regulation concerning dumping and injury, the European Commission had embezzled 13 % of the European Community market, and thus was directly responsible for serious injury to the European industry. The bankruptcy of various European Community producers is explained by this unfortunate approach of denial of market disruption and by preferential treatment of some exporters. On the other hand, the European Commission allocated exports to some countries that were not those countries' exports at all. These were tube exports. Because of China's tube exports, a share in the European television market of 3.9 % was imputed to China rather than the 0.1 % share actually imported from China. It is incomprehensible that lawyers on behalf of exporting countries did not tackle such a gaffe. It is puzzling why none of the exporting countries challenged this discrimination at the World Trade Organization (WTO).

12.5 Origin Rule as Trade Barrier

The origin agreement of the WTO prescribes that origin rules "*shall not themselves create restrictive, distorting, or disruptive effects on international trade*".[21] The European origin rules for some consumer electronics, however, obviously brought about trade distortions. Because Turkey did not have tube production, the European Community extended measures against countries that lacked noticeable CTV exports to the European Community. Only measures toward Turkey's dumped TV were justifiable, not measures against the countries that exported tubes. An injurious effect was imputed to exports of CTVs from some countries, which was predominantly based on their exports of cathode ray tubes to Turkey. The measures against Thailand and Malaysia, and even possibly against China, were unjustifiable if solely based on data of their exports of television sets. Under application of the origin rule, the greatest number of countries was affected with the smallest degree of effectiveness. International trade was distorted, and the European industry annihilated.

As seen in Chaps. 4 and 5, the WTO assesses protection in terms of duty incidence. Duty incidence is the duty-weighted imports related to a measure. The duties imposed for CTVs in 2002 had a limited effect on the value of the exports of most CTV exporting countries to the European Community. Since 1988, anti-dumping cases have taken place and it is undeniable that the anti-dumping duties had a restrictive effect on imports of CTVs from some countries concerned, with certain exceptions as discussed. The consequence of the origin rule as applied in anti-dumping cases of the European Community has never been calculated. Nevertheless, an approximation can be made of the duty effect of this reprehensible method of origin rule application. If a television set from Turkey (Vestel's) bears an anti-dumping duty of 25.6 % because it contains a Chinese tube, the increase of the price of the set as consequence of the anti-dumping duty is attributable to the fact that the CTV incorporates a Chinese tube. The CIF price of the Vestel sets was €81.53, according to the European Commission's disclosure. A duty of 25.6 % increases the CIF value to €102.40, i.e. a price difference of €20.87, attributable to the use of a Chinese tube. Because Turkish television sets contained Chinese tubes, the price of these sets increased by €20.87 and that made the Chinese tubes more expensive by that amount (the price increase on the set with the Chinese tube due to the duty on Turkish CTVs with Chinese tubes). The average price of these 14-in. tubes on CIF basis, according to statistics available on Turkish imports, was €29.67. Compared with the original price, this is a duty on Chinese 14-in. tubes of 70.3 %. European Community duties on Vestel's 638,628 14-in. television sets exported to the European Community thus implied an additional duty on Chinese tubes of €13.3 million. Since this price increase was prohibitive for sales, the loss to China in trade by this duty was €19 million.

---

[21] PART II Disciplines to Govern the Application of Rules of Origin, Article 2, Disciplines During the Transition Period (c).

Table 12.2 shows calculations for all countries involved.[22] Column (2) gives the anti-dumping duties on CTVs or the equivalence of a duty on the tubes because they are incorporated in a set, which means a duty for the CTV is due. The duty incidence on tubes from China caused by dumping by Vestel is calculated above. In total, China exported only 31,514 television sets. The duty on the television sets from China is 44.6 % over the average price, €108.74, of the set. The amount of incidence was 15,772 × 44.6 % × €108.74 = €764,912 for televisions,[23] i.e. negligible, but the incidence for tubes is 638,628 × 70.3 % × €29.67 = €13,329,092. That is the protection of the European Community against imports of Chinese tubes via Turkish television sets. Similarly, the tubes from Malaysia and Korea were banned from the market by imposition of duties on the sets containing tubes from these countries. Table 12.2 is an approximation of the duty incidence, in which Thomson's data, because they have been kept undisclosed, was not included. Round off

The WTO origin agreement prohibits such trade distortion. The European Community created serious barriers to trade and thereby it created a preferential market for the European Community components industry. The total imports of picture tubes into Turkey in the investigation period (1 July 1999 – 31 June 2000) were 7.7 million units, 4.6 million of which were from the European Community (Matsushita, Philips, Samsung, Thomson, Daewoo/Orion) and one million from at that time from candidates for accession Lithuania (Ekranas) and Poland (Thomson). Tube supplies from the countries involved in the CTV proceeding were 1.8 million (including the Thomson Thai sets with tubes from Korea and Malaysia). By application of the CTV origin rule, these Asian supplies were reduced to zero, in total an amount of €15 million of duties (excluding tubes for Thomson). The tube market for the European Community tube industry increased 39 %. The competition in tubes in the Turkish market was reduced. Some governments, especially the Chinese, protested against the proceeding concerning CTVs, but the Chinese cathode ray tube industry was more gravely affected (a duty incidence of 11 times the duty amount involved with CTV). The tubes from China were indirectly hit by a duty equivalent to 71.86 %. The lawyers of the exporting countries had not noticed this crucial fact.[24] The drop of China's share in the Turkish tube market was from 21.1% to 6.3%. The issue is no longer a hot one as

[22] Note on the Undercutting and Injury Margin Calculations, European Commission, letter of 1 August 2001, number 057867) and Eurostat.

[23] Rounding of numbers has resulted in marginal discrepancies between left and right hand expressions.

[24] The Turkish producers and government protested, the latter heavily in a note "Comments of the Turkish Government regarding Final Disclosure of Anti Dumping Investigation initiated against colour television receivers originating in or exported from Turkey" of 20 August 2001. The Turkish government did not, of course, express the wish that the origin rule be interpreted differently so that television sets manufactured in Turkey and dumped in the European Community would have Turkish origin. That would have eliminated the injury due to dumping and would have saved European television industry.

Table 12.2 Duty incidence on tubes of AD duties on CTVs due to EC origin rule for CTVs

CTV and tube supplies in	AD duty (AD) or duty equivalence (DE)		Units CTV sets or tubes	Avg price of set or tube	Price increase (by AD duty)	Duty incidence
(1)	(2)		(3)	(4)	(5)	(6)
CTV 14-in. Vestel						
14″ CTV Vestel (Disclosure)	AD	25.6 %	638,628	€81.53	€20.87	€13,329,092
Tubes from China 14″ (Commission)	DE	70.3 %	638,628	€29.67	€20.87	€13,329,092
China CIF all CTV to EU (Eurostat, Disclosure)	AD	44.6 %	15,772	€108.74	€48.50	€764,912
CTV 14-in. Beko						
Beko (Disclosure) 14”	AD	18.2 %	10,074	€80.33	€14.62	€147,275
Tubes 14″ from Malaysia (undercutting Beko)	DE	54.2 %	10,074	€26.97	€14.62	€119,274
Malaysia CIF supplies CTV to EU	AD	25.1 %	23,687	€123.87	€31.09	€736,461
CTV 33-in. Beko						
Beko originating in Korea 33-in.	AD	12.3 %	31,514	€316.78	€38.96	€1,227,910
Tubes from Korea for Beko	DE	21.1 %	31,514	€184.86	€38.96	€1,227,909
Korea CIF supplies CTV to EU	AD	15.0 %	647,301	€179.00	€26.85	€17,380,075

Source: Official Turkish import statistics

far as hot cathode ray tubes are concerned; they disappeared. The threat of severe discrimination and distortion remains, however.

It is, therefore, understandable that a tube manufacturer, located in the European Community pursued the continuation of measures for CTV, given the attractive conditions of the CTV origin rule. This was especially attractive because LG Philips Displays, the joint venture of LGE and Philips in Europe was on the verge of bankruptcy and LGE intended to supply customers in Europe from China. It was highly attractive for some remaining tube producers, especially when two other competitors, Ekranas (Lithuania) and Tesla (Czech Republic) went bankrupt, to bar Far Eastern suppliers from the Turkish market. When the "Notice of the impending expiry of certain anti-dumping measures, 2006/C 288/02" was published in OJ C 288/2 of 25.11.2006, the CTV industry was preparing an expiry review file. The origin rule appeared to play a decisive role. The tube producer appropriated the papers already prepared for a CTV review to be announced in the Official Journal and transferred these papers to a law office of its own choice, promising the CTV industry that this tube producing company would pay the bill for the CTV review proceeding on behalf of those few CTV producers that still existed. The review request was never lodged. The ineffective measures expired. Not long after the termination of the anti-dumping measures for CTV, the measures became useless by the simple fact that the flat panel television sets had taken over in the market. The television industry to make these flat panels had practically disappeared.

12.6 Origin, Determination of Normal Value and Discrimination

The increase in the number of competing manufacturers of television sets and tubes, the change in manufacturing technologies and in organisation of companies made existing quotas and the accompanying origin rules superfluous. In addition, the European Community had abolished the quotas, which had induced origin rules for television and audio. The origin rule for some consumer electronics not only reached a stage of obsolescence, but it also appeared fully inadequate. A quota is a quantitative trade defence instrument, the effectiveness of which requires a rule of origin. Dumping is a different commercial issue in which the materials and components content of products is largely irrelevant for the degree of dumping and undercutting. Dumping is an issue of two markets, as indicated in Chap. 8. GATT's Article VI on dumping and the WTO's Agreement on Implementation of Article VI of the General Agreement on Tariffs and Trade (ADA) are clear about the definition: "*if the export price of the product exported from one country to another is less than the comparable price, in the ordinary course of trade, for the like product when destined for consumption in the exporting country*", which is confirmed in the European Community's Basic Regulation.[25]

The ADA definition can not possibly mean that the country of export is the country in which 45 % of the value or 35 % of the materials constituting the like product are produced and exported to the exporting country of the product concerned, the latter of which is the country of export of the like product. Such a definition would create a riot or bring about laughter. Nevertheless, the television origin rule and similar rules for sufficient processing have this effect if applied to dumping in the same ridiculous way. That the origin rule for television is inappropriate is also strikingly clear from the following example. If a country does not export television sets but has a thriving tube industry, its tubes confer origin to television sets that are exported from other countries. Whatever the dumping from these tubes using countries may be, it is impossible to lodge a dumping complaint against them because their products originate somewhere where the like product is not produced. This is only because it is impossible to find dumping of television sets from the tube exporting country, while the countries from where the television sets are dumped do not have sufficient domestic components for domestic origin. This is a Catch-22; in other words, nonsense.

The Regulations concerning small screen colour televisions originating in Korea (SCTV Korea) and in China (SCTV China) did not mention the origin issue, except for Hong Kong and origin in connection with normal value. It was apparently assumed that the CTVs from Korean and China contained domestic tubes. The botch of the normal value construction is another consequence of the false methodology. Although none of the Hong Kong products had Hong Kong origin, the European Commission based normal value for China on Hong Kong sales or on Hong Kong constructed value and not on the construction of a normal value in the country of origin.[26] On the contrary, for Hong Kong normal value it took Chinese prices, promoted to market economy (Hong Kong) values without an investigation whether the producers of these CTVs could be considered market economy producers. If the origin is Chinese, for establishment of the normal value for China the normal value of a reference country should be used. The manufacturing in the reference country confers Chinese origin, but that is a country for which a reference normal value should be used. Again, this is a Catch-22. The normal value both for China and Hong Kong had to be established in another third country.

In a case after the Hong Kong/China small screen TV, in Asia 1, the European Commission established for Thai sets containing a Malaysian tube, and, consequently, of Malaysian origin the normal value on the basis of a Malaysian

[25] Article 1, Principles, 2: "A product is to be considered as being dumped if its export price to the Community is less than a comparable price for the like product, in the ordinary course of trade as established for the exporting country."

[26] Commission Regulation (EEC) No 129/91 of 11 January 1991 imposing a provisional anti-dumping duty on imports of small-screen colour television receivers originating in Hong Kong and the people's Republic of China, OJ L 014, 19/01/1991, pp. 31–45.

constructed value. It is clearly discriminatory compared with Hong Kong, in which the origin of the Hong Kong set was declared Hong Kong, and the normal value was a Hong Kong value even though the product was not of Hong Kong origin and not at all processed in Hong Kong. Another complication in the case of Hong Kong sets with Chinese origin is that the prices of tubes, representing a substantial part of the value of the Hong Kong sets, could not considered market economy prices. The constructed value could accordingly not be representative of the market economy prices. When a complaint was prepared, it was not expected that the European Commission would make such a serious mistake as to establish the normal value of CTVs on the basis of origin of the tube. Normal value shall normally be based on[27]:

(a) "*the prices paid or payable in the ordinary course of trade, by independent customers in the exporting country*"
(b) "*on the basis of prices of other sellers or producers* (where the exporter in the exporting country does not produce or does nor sell the like product)."
(c) "*the cost of production in the country of origin plus a reasonable amount for selling, general and administrative costs and for profits* (where because of the particular market situation such sales do nor permit proper comparison)."

These three possibilities all refer to a situation in the domestic market of the exporter, not to the material and value composition of the product. Nowhere is reference made to the origin as criterion for normal value. In Article 1.3 is stated: "*The exporting country shall normally be the country of origin.*" That does not imply that the country of the origin of the exported product, in this case the country of origin of the tube, should also be the country of normal value. In the description of "like product" the issue of the origin of a product is not mentioned as characteristic. That means that case (b) above is not applicable. As for (c), the market situation in Thailand did not prevent a proper comparison between the domestic sales price and the export price. Besides, for the determination of the dumping margin the origin was not the issue. The issue of origin is only relevant when measures are or have been taken. The non-preferential origin rule is, as far as dumping is concerned, relevant in the case of: "*applying measures other than tariff measures established by Community provisions governing specific fields relating to trade in goods*". The measure had not been applied. It had to be investigated whether measures should be taken. An investigation whether measures must be taken and that is always before the measures have been taken and before the application of the origin rules. The selling price of Thai television sets with a tube from Malaysia is still the commercial price, which is not influenced at all by the origin of the tube. The tube origin may influence the level of cost of production, but not the fact or level of dumping. Therefore, the Thai price, i.e. the price in the

[27] Council Regulation (EC) No 461/2004 of 8 March 2004 amending Regulation (EC) No 384/96 on protection against dumped imports from countries not members of the European Community and Regulation (EC) No 2026/97 on protection against subsidised imports from countries not members of the European Community OJ L 77/12, 13/3/2004, Article 2, Determination of dumping, A. Normal Value, recital 1.

country of export, is the commercial price that may serve as normal value. If measures are taken, the measures can still be toward Thai television sets, not necessarily and not exclusively originating in Thailand.

In two cases, in CTV Asia 1 and in CTV Asia 3, origin of CTVs ***exported*** by Thai producers was Malaysian. The weird and for dumping completely illogical choice was that not the market price in the country of the exporter, but the (constructed) price in the country of the tube exporter to the CTV exporting country was relevant. The question was additionally whether the origin of the domestic sales was also the country of the tube supplies, i.e. were Table 11.1 or 11.3 relevant when the normal value was investigated?

In a number of cases the cooperating producers were exporting CTVs with an origin different from the country in which they were assembled. Accordingly, regard being had to the provisions of Article 2 (6), normal values for those models were determined in accordance with the provisions of Article 2 (3) (b) (ii) by taking the average cost of production, the average SGA costs and the average profit of the producers in the country of origin for a comparable model, provided that the CTVs originated in one of the five market economy countries involved in the proceeding.[28]

Due to the fact that the value of the tube and possibly other materials was either more than 45 % of ex-works value or more than 35 % of the materials value of the exported products, the European Commission chose to construct the normal value on the basis of the data in the country conferring the origin of the exported product, as in Table 11.3, i.e. the normal value in the country of supply of the tube rather than on the basis of the country conferring the origin of the product sold on the domestic market, as in Table 11.1.

The application of a constructed normal value for an exporter on the basis of data relevant for the country from which a tube and other materials were procured does not seem to have support from anti-dumping legislation. Neither is it backed up by customs legislation concerning origin, the CCC[29]:

Articles 23 to 26 define the non-preferential origin of goods for the purposes of:
(a) applying the Customs Tariff of the European Communities with the exception of the measures referred to in Article 20 (3) (d) and (e);
(b) applying measures other than tariff measures established by Community provisions governing specific fields relating to trade in goods;
(c) the preparation and issue of certificates of origin.

Non-preferential origin rules as such are applicable when measures have been established and not as a tool for establishing those measures. On the contrary, the application of the methodology of a constructed value on the basis of data of the production of producers in the country where some components have been procured

[28] Commission Regulation (EC) No 2376/94 of 27 September 1994 imposing a provisional anti-dumping duty on imports of colour television receivers originating in Malaysia, the people's Republic of China, the Republic of Korea, Singapore and Thailand OJ L 255, 01/10/1994, pp. 50–69; Asia 1.

[29] Article 22 of Council Regulation (EEC) No 2913/92 of 12 October 1992 establishing the Community Customs Code, OJ L 302, 19/10/1992, pp. 1–50.

is highly discriminatory against exporters that have fallen victim to this treatment, and appears a violation of the European Community basic regulation as well as the ADA of the WTO.

12.7 Denial of Economics of Dumping and Discrimination Again

Although 22 % of the consolidated text of the treaty establishing the European Community deals with competition policy and state aid and the proper functioning of the market, the priority given by the European Commission to application of an origin rule for determination of normal value and existence of injury denies the economic context of dumping and especially the fact that market conditions are essential. Special rules have been introduced for countries, such as China and Vietnam, which do not have market economy status. Nevertheless, in small screen TV, Hong Kong was the yardstick for Chinese normal value even though the products were originating and even manufactured in China. In the case of Asia 1, and for cases thereafter the European Community has deviated from the principle that the market economy is primordial. For the normal value of one country it created constructed values of or prices of sale in another country because it was the supplier of a totally different product, i.e. the tube. The Malaysian value for television sets from Thailand wherein the like product is domestically sold in Thailand was applied as normal because the tube has been purchased in Malaysia. In Chap. 8, the relationship between domestic market structure and dumping is discussed. Less competition in the domestic market results in higher profit and is a stimulus for dumping. This implies a higher normal value in the country with less competition than in the country with more competition. As far as the normal value is concerned, in an economy with more restrictions to imports and to competition it should, *ceteris paribus*, be higher than in the country with a higher degree of competition. Complete neglect of market circumstances is the corollary of the methodology taking the television and other consumer electronics origin rules not as tool for effectiveness of certain measures, but as guideline for finding of dumping and injury.

In the case of Turkish producer Beko, in CTV Asia 3, two different dumping and injury margins were calculated. One for Malaysia, which resulted in an anti-dumping duty of 21.2 % for its sets exported with Korean origin (a 33 in. tube) and one of 25.1 % for sets with a Malaysian (14-in.) tube. The normal value of Beko was not based on its sales prices in the Turkish market where domestic prices were absurdly high. The artificial construction was repeated; accordingly, the market of the country of origin of the tube was chosen for the construction of normal value. Because none of the producers, including the Koreans, in the East Asian countries involved had cooperated, the normal value for sets originating in Malaysia was based on certain data provided by Korean producers on behalf of sampling.[30] In the case of the Chinese normal value, a market economy country had to be selected, and the Turkish sales data in the Turkish market were used for the determination of the normal value for China, even though none of Turkish television sets had Turkish origin as soon as they were exported and they had Turkish origin when sold in Turkey. How could a normal value of Turkey be used if not one single television set from Turkey was dumped (because of non-Turkish origin of exported sets)? The Turkish origin was used for the normal value of China and not for Turkey. In the case of the Chinese sets, however, the normal value of the Turkish sets was used, whereas in the case Turkish sets of Beko the Malaysian – based on Korean data – and the Korean normal values were applied. If the origin of the Turkish sets were not acceptable for the establishment of the normal value for Turkish sets, they should not have been used for the normal value of the Chinese sets. The Turkish sets of Vestel, because of their tube originating in China, were acceptable as a yardstick for normal value and their selling price in Turkey was utilised for the Chinese normal value and of course, also for the Turkish normal value of Vestel, which was not acceptable for Beko.

> *The dumping margin, expressed as a percentage of the cif price at Community frontier level duty unpaid for Vestel Elektronik Sanayi ve Ticaret AS, Turkey is 69,2 %.*[31]

Since the CIF price of Vestel's 14-in. sets was €81.53, the normal value should have been (1 + 69.2 %) × (€81.53/(1 + 2 %)) = €135.24. This is a pretty and profitable high price compared with the price of the European Community producers' price of €103.19. Since producers quote their price independently of the tube content in the set – the origin of the tube and the tube price can have an effect on the cost level in general, but the television set prices do not vary with the origin of the tube content – this huge dumping margin existed irrespective of whether Vestel sets contained a tube from European Community suppliers Matsushita, Philips or Thomson, or from Lithuanian Ekranas or from Chinese tube supplier Irico. The same applies to sets sold by Beko. This company did not vary its prices with the origin of the tubes. Both the high domestic price, which conferred Turkish origin to the sets and the low export price, which made applicable the low level the origin of the country of the tube and consequently, the origin of the set, were the only criteria for dumping. Origin and dumping did not have any relationship.

How unacceptable the treatment of normal value of various exporters was can be concluded from a survey of 14-in. prices of European producers, with which the Turkish sets of Vestel and Beko are compared for the calculation of undercutting. The average retail prices of Vestel (with the brands Vestel and Watson) and Beko

[30] Sampling takes place when the number of exporters is too great for the European Commission to handle all exporters' data.

[31] Council Regulation (EC) No 1531/2002 of 14 August 2002 (CTV Asia 3), recital (66).

Table 12.3 Origin and false determination of normal value (NV)

	Vestel	Beko
	Turkish NV	Malaysian NV
Average European prices for undercutting calculations 14-in.	€103.19	€102.62
Resale price of Turkish producers in community	€83.30	€88.00
Undercutting amount	€19.89	€14.62
Export price	81.53	80.33
Undercutting margin	24.4 %	18.2 %
Dumping margin	69.2 %	25.1 %
Normal value (from export price and dumping margin)	€137.95	€100.49
Average retail price Turkey minus VAT	€217.60	€218.96

(with the brands Arçelik and Beko) in the Turkish 14 in. market were €217.60 and €218.96, respectively.[32]Taking trade margins as roughly similar, this resulted in the conclusion that the normal value, the selling price, of the two companies is also akin (Table 12.3).

It is, of course, highly questionable whether Vestel's sales in Turkey are representative of China's normal value, and that this normal value is used as indicator for the dumping margin of Vestel only if originating in China. This is the case because the sets contain Irico tubes, whereas the normal value for essentially similar prices for Beko is 17 % lower because a tube has been purchased in Malaysia instead of China. If Beko had purchased tubes in China, then the dumping margin would suddenly have gone up to about 72 % because Turkish domestic sales were used as normal value. A peculiar construction of the normal value based on Korean data for sampling both for the establishment of Korean normal value and for the normal value of Malaysia was applied for Beko without any sensible argumentation. The consequence was that Beko's normal value was lower than Vestels' because Beko's tubes came from Malaysia, to which an artificial Korean normal value was applied,[33] whereas Vestel's normal value was higher, its own normal value, because of its Chinese tubes and origin, used for China. The market circumstances, in Turkey, allowing dumping were in one case completely neglected and in the other case taken as yardstick. Finally, Beko's anti-dumping duties were based on the level of undercutting of European Community prices. Two groups of data were analysed. The television sets with Malaysian origin appeared to represent 14-in. sets, whereas a few sets of 33 in. contained Korean tubes. Normally, as indicated earlier, one calculation is made for the undercutting, taking the product as a "like" product and comparing prices of exporters of similar models in one calculation as given in Chap. 16 on calculation of normal value and injury. Apart from the fact that the principle that a product is one like product was abandoned by

[32] GfK data on the Turkish market in the reference period.

[33] And this normal value was not applicable because Korean 14-in. tubes generally originated in other countries than Korea, with the exception of Orion, which supplied inter alia Thomson in Thailand.

calculating two undercutting percentages, this methodology unjustifiably influenced the level of undercutting and therefore, the level of protection granted to European Community industry. Because the anti-dumping duties are not based on distorted competition conditions but on artificial constructions, it also distorts competition among exporters to the European Community.

Thomson had two levels of dumping, one on the basis of Malaysian origin (25.1 %) and the other on the basis of Korean origin (21.2 %). Thomson's export prices did not differ according to the country of purchase of the tube. Thomson's products must have been exported at the same price, irrespective of the tubes they contained; the export price was indiscriminately similar and an average price based on the average cost of a certain model. This implied that only due to artificial attribution of different origins, normal value differed accordingly. Only because a zero undercutting level was inexplicably granted as gratuity to Thomson (0 % anti-dumping duty), Thomson's identical CTVs were not sold at identical prices because they encountered different anti-dumping duties. If undercutting had been substantial and more than 25.1 % – the authors found more than zero – then duties on identical CTVs would have been different.

Such an origin rule even obstructs the implementation of the Basic Regulation. According to Article 8 of the Basic Regulation, exporters are entitled to offer a price undertaking. However, a price undertaking implies an increase in export price to the level of elimination of either injury or dumping. As we saw in Chap. 11, the selling price changes the origin of the product. This implies that the origin changes from, for instance, the origin in Table 11.3 into the one in Table 11.1. The undertaking would change the origin of the product and could, in principle, be considered invalid. The issue is not theoretical. Although the Chinese exporters did not cooperate and there was not the slightest ground for acceptance of an undertaking, such undertaking was nevertheless agreed upon.[34]

> *According to this undertaking the exporters/producers in question have offered to sell the product concerned directly from the PRC (excluding any independent customs territory) to unrelated customers in the Community at minimum prices. In addition, this undertaking provides for quantitative ceilings in defined periods for sales to the Community of the product concerned. When the relevant ceilings are reached, the anti-dumping duty in force would be levied.*

In the invoices the producers must indicate the origin of the product. If a Chinese producer enclosed an Orion (Daewoo) tube from Vietnam in a set made in China and shipped from China, would the undertaking have no relevance? Would not the Chinese be committed to minimum prices if the tube came from a country not covered by an (residual) anti-dumping duty? The Chinese producer could export the product as originating in Vietnam.

[34] Commission Decision of 29 July 2002 accepting an undertaking offered in connection with the anti-dumping proceeding concerning imports of colour television receivers originating in Malaysia, the People's Republic of China, the Republic of Korea, Singapore and Thailand, O J L 23129.8.2002, recital (4).

Table 12.4 Origin rule, construction of normal value and discrimination

Values/Factors — Countries/Producers	Export Price	Normal Value	Dumping margin	Dumping as % CIF
Malaysia				
Orion	81.94	93.22	11.28	13.5%
Technol Silver	83.76	105.20	21.44	25.1%
Residual	73.74	92.62	18.88	25.1%
Thai with NV Malaysia				
GoldStar Mitr	73.74	88.48	14.74	19.6%
World Electric [Orion]	79.67	93.73	14.06	17.3%
Thailand				
Thomson	87.09	100.15	13.06	14.7%
Teletech	70.31	94.40	24.10	33.6%
Samsung	80.59	105.00	24.41	29.7%
Residual	70.31	94.40	24.10	33.6%

If the Chinese would have had the right to offer an undertaking, in principle the Turks would also have had such a right, but Beko could not possibly sign an agreement in which minimum eliminated either dumping or injury for its sets originating in Malaysia. As soon as the prices increase, they lose their origin. Tables 11.1 and 11.3 clarify the effect of an undertaking. Due to the increase in the export price to a level that eliminates the dumping or injury, the origin changes from the one in Table 11.3 to origin of Table 11.1. If there were duties rather than an undertaking, the origin would remain Malaysian. In this way, the absurd interpretation of the origin rule in connection with anti-dumping is again demonstrated. There is more to it. The Commissioner and some of his officials rendered unique preferential services to foreign producers by granting them unlimited and discriminatory access by dumping: to the Turks, a market from which others were barred and in which European industry was defenceless.

It appears from Table 12.4 that the normal values of sets with a Malaysian tube and based on Malaysian constructed value are lower than the normal values of sets sold on the same Thai market and exported from Thailand. The absolute dumping margin of two Thai exporters with Malaysian origin is lower than of other Thai exporters. However, none of the normal values in Malaysia and Thailand were established on the basis of sales to trade. All were constructed values. That means that the effective protection did not have relevance: Some Thai producers sold on the domestic market and their sales occurred at a loss, but their cost of administration was incorrect. Therefore, Thomson's SGA were taken as correct, but Thomson did not have domestic sales and this data had also to be constructed. Nevertheless, this construction could take the market circumstances in Thailand into account, whereas a constructed Malaysian value could not. Therefore, simply because they had a Malaysian tube encased in their sets, the constructed value in Malaysia was to the advantage of the two Thai producers and to the disadvantage of other producers that competed with the two producers with artificially low normal values.

The European Community institutions must have been confused, to use an understatement, by the origin problem, to which the complaint on behalf of the European Community producers alluded as a complication. Because of that confusion they, opted for a peculiar methodology and for a very innovative and unusual escape: both in the basic regulation and the WTO ADA mention the possibility that

> *when there are no sales of the like product in the ordinary course of trade in the domestic market of the exporting country or when, because of the particular market situation ... the margin of dumping shall be determined by comparison ... (or) with the cost of production in the* ***country of origin*** *plus a reasonable amount for administrative, selling and general costs and for profits.*[35]

But that is only when there are no sales of the product in the ordinary course of trade or in case of a particular market situation. Only when there were problems concerning sales that did not allow a determination of the normal value is there reference to the country of origin. In all cases, at the stage of establishing the normal value the domestically sold product was of domestic origin. The fact that a tube is imported did not mean that the sales of the CTV is not in an ordinary course. This applied both to the market of the exporter and to the European Community market where producers also use imported tubes. Exported television sets had the origin of the country of normal value at the moment of the determination of normal value. It was, therefore, highly discriminatory to use another country that did not have anything to do with the sales (or constructed value derived from the sales) in the domestic market of the producer.

As remarked, the application of this methodology is a violation of the WTO Agreement on Rules of Origin, which states in Article 2 (c): "*rules of origin shall not themselves create restrictive, distorting, or disruptive effects on international trade.*" It is self-evident that the colour television origin rule had an extremely restrictive and discriminatory effect. This is clear from the cases of Thomson and Vestel versus Administration des douanes et droits indirects[36] and from Commission Decision of 7-5-2007 finding that the remission of import duties was not justified in a particular case.[37] For instance, for Thomson's CTVs from Thailand with a tube made in Thailand the anti-dumping duty was 3 %. However, procurement of a tube from Malaysia or Korea changed the origin, and in that case Thomson had to pay either the residual duty for Malaysia of 23.4 % or for Korea of 17.9 %, an increase by more than 14 to even more than 20 %. That is clearly a restriction of international trade: the origin rule for CTVs restricts a Thai producer due to the fact that dumping behaviour of Malaysian and Korean producers results in a higher residual duty and impedes the purchase and use of Malaysian or Korean

[35] Agreement on Implementation of Article VI of the General Agreement on Tariffs and Trade 1994 Article 2.2 Determination of Dumping.

[36] Judgment of the Court (Fourth Chamber) 8 March 2007 in Joined Cases C-447/05 and C-448/05.

[37] REM 03/05 Commission of the European Communities Brussels, 7-5-2007 C(2007)1829.

tubes. As demonstrated above, the two Thai producers with products of Malaysian origin were also curtailed in their procurement policy: the anti-dumping duty on Thai tubes increased by more than 10 %. The Thai tube industry was seriously disadvantaged by such a policy.

The unacceptability of the methodology is especially clear when a further analysis is made of some peculiarities of this anti-dumping proceeding concerning CTV and particularly in connection with the issue of the so-called lesser duty. The European Community's rule and practice of limiting the measures to the elimination of injury attributable to dumping implies that either dumping is eliminated by measures or, if that level is less than the dumping, the injury (see Chap. 16 for the methodology). The injury is measured in terms of price undercutting: the measure for which is the weighted average resale price of the European producer minus the weighted average resale price of the exporter, which difference is expressed in terms of the CIF export price of the exporter. Since the undercutting generally does not leave a profitable price to the European Community producer, the price of the European Community producer is increased until the target profit (the profit that should normally be incurred without the injury) is attained, which for CTVs was in several years kept on 0 % (see Chap. 11). The margin between this profitable price and the exporter's resale price is the underselling margin, which is also expressed as a percentage of the CIF value and normally exceeds the undercutting margin. In that case the lower of the two, dumping or underselling margin, as % of CIF export price is applied as a measure. The use of another country's data for a producer using foreign tubes implies discrimination of producers that use domestic tubes. The level of the normal value in the foreign country supplying the tubes may be lower than in the manufacturer's home country. That may be because competition in the foreign tube producing country is stiffer than at home. One producer using foreign tubes but manufacturing under the same market conditions as the other producers at home would thus be granted a lower normal value and thereby a lower anti-dumping duty than domestic competitors. An example of distortion of competition in this way is Thomson's zero duties for sets originating in Korea or Malaysia, while domestically originating sets are due 3 %. This implies that the Thai tube producer is disadvantaged compared with Malaysian and Korean tube producers.

12.8 License to Kill the European Industry: Preferential Dumping Area

Not only was Thomson inexplicably cleared from paying anti-dumping duties as soon as it used Korean or Malaysian tubes, which implied that from then on Thomson could do as it liked, the European Commission created a preferential area in which the Turkish producers were allowed to dump without any limitation as long as they did not use tubes from China, Korea and Malaysia and perhaps from Thailand. If they used tubes from any of these countries, they had to indicate the origin of the tubes as origin of the sets as long as they continued to dump. In fact, the publication of anti-dumping duties for Vestel and Beko with an indication of the origin did not have any significance. Apart from the anti-fraud unit OLAF, which at least reacted to the information provided by the complainant when it was clear that DG Trade would not take any action against evident fraud, and caught Thomson and Vestel (see the next section), the European Commission did not take any measures to prevent the continuation of illegal practices, which were factually prompted by a highly inappropriate origin rule to which the European Commission stubbornly stuck.

If, for instance, the Turkish producer Profilo Telra, for which no dumping and injury were found (not because there was not dumping and injury, but because under the origin rule the origin was not Turkish or was different from the origin of one of the countries to which already anti-dumping duties were applied) used Chinese, Korean, Malaysian or Thai tubes, nobody in the European Community would check the origin. Profilo Telra purchased practically all its 14- and 20-in. tubes from Ekranas in Lithuania. Since Lithuania was not involved in any dumping case for colour television – as part of the Soviet Union it supplied all its tubes to TV producers in the Soviet Union – its dumped 14- and 20-in. sets were not dumped, according to the European Commission philosophy. Even in the investigation period, 1999 and 2000, Profilo Telra utilised Korean tubes for all its 29-in. real flat television sets. The European Commission did not find these tubes and Profilo Telra escaped anti-dumping duties, even though the duties had no significance. In 2000, Vestel encased Chinese tubes in 40 % of its 20-in. television sets. The European Commission did not find them and limited the calculation of the duty to 14-in. sets.

By applying the television origin rule during the establishment of dumping and injury instead of after measures were taken, the European Commission created a preferential dumping area in which the Turks terminated the European industry in a preferential market from which others were barred. The switch from Korea and Malaysia to other sources of tubes enabled the Turkish producers to continue their dumping policy. An example is Vestel. It shifted its sourcing of 14 in., the origin of which the European Commission did not report as fraud, and on which it based anti-dumping duties, and distributed this sourcing over five producers. Vestel concentrated its purchases of 29-in. real flat tubes on one Korea producer, a fact that remained undetected by the European Commission. It then shifted purchases to the European Community where it chose two European suppliers rather than one. It also spread its 20 in. flat square tube purchases from Korea and the European Community to various sources, including China, Lithuania and India. Apparently Vestel was careful not to improve the competitive positions of one of the suppliers, most of which also had internal supplies, and avoided dependence (Table 12.5).[38]

By a change in purchasing, Vestel could just continue dumping and together with others in the Turkish industry, could finally destroy the European industry when Turkish producers made more than 50 % of televisions sold in Europe.[39]

---

[38] Information on European Community and Turkish CTV production and tube sourcing was supplied by the tube industry during various anti-dumping cases on CTV and cathode ray tubes. The information is, of course, obsolete and since the suppliers went bankrupt and the product has disappeared, is no longer confidential.

[39] Raikes B (2008).

Table 12.5 Shift of tubes purchases by Vestel and change in origin in order to continue dumping

14-in.	China	Malaysia	Korea	EU	India	Lithuania
Vestel (2000)	85 %			15 %		
Vestel (2001)	15 %	6 %		22 %	25 %	25 %
20-in.						
Vestel (2000)	47 %			53 %		
Vestel (2001)				88 %		12 %
29-in. RF						
Vestel (2000)			100 %			
Vestel (2001)				100 %		
51 FS 90						
Vestel (2000)			29 %	71 %		
Vestel (2001)	18 %			64 %	9 %	9 %

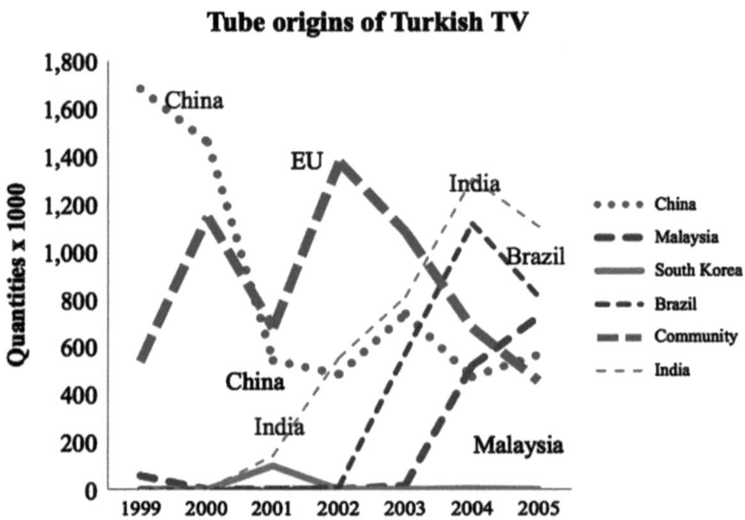

Graph 12.1 Switch in tube origin enables continuation of dumping

The origin rule caused a shift in sourcing of tubes by Turkish producers. During the investigation and immediately after the imposition of measures, European Community sales of tubes – a guarantee against anti-dumping duties – increased. As soon as the Turkish producers were certain that the European Community would not inspect the origin of Turkish television sets, however, the content of sets changed and the proportion of "risky" tubes increased. Nevertheless, the non-dutiable tubes acquired a majority (Graph 12.1).

Thus, both producers of tubes and CTVs in Malaysia, Thailand, Korea and China were disadvantaged by the preferential dumping access created by this extraordinary application of an origin rule.

The European Commission's statement that the "***Community Customs Code... establishes that the non-preferential rules of origin apply to all non-preferential commercial policy instruments, such as anti-dumping***" is alarmingly wrong.[40] With this disastrous mistake Commissioner Pascal Lamy and some of his officials sealed the fate of the European CTV, and as a corollary the consumer electronics industry. It is evidently a false interpretation of non-preferential origin rules in general. The non-preferential origin rules clearly do not apply to all non-preferential commercial policy instruments. The purpose of non-preferential origin rules is "***(a) applying the Customs Tariff of the European Communities...; (b) applying measures other than tariff measures established by Community provisions governing specific fields relating to trade in goods***". The purpose is applying of anti-dumping measures, and they certainly do not apply to all trade policy instruments, including investigations and the establishment of facts that might result in such measures. The non-preferential origin rules cannot be used as pretext for not applying measures. In investigations of dumping and injury, the European Commission must apply the rule of the anti-dumping legislation and the origin rule must follow when the use of the trade policy instruments results in measures. Before measures are taken there is no non-preferential origin issue. Establishing dumping and injury is clearly not an application of measures, but it can result in such measures, which subsequently can legally and administratively be applied in accordance with applicable non-preferential origin rules. The utilisation of the origin rule for CTVs from the Community Customs Code (CCC) would imply that the origin of "like" products, i.e. inputs like tubes, is considered decisive. Absurdities and incompetence have destroyed the European consumer electronics industry.

The Basic (AD) Regulation states that the "*exporting country shall normally be the country of origin.*" This does imply that the CTV origin should be applied to the exports of this country in the stage of investigation, whether measures should be taken. The dumping can be established in the exporting country or country of origin, i.e. in practice, the country of production and domestic sales in the ordinary course of trade and the country of export of the television sets imported into the European Community, for which the establishment of origin the origin rule exists. As soon as dumping is established, imports count as dumped imports. The Basic Regulation does not require that while dumping is being established, it must be based on the origin rules. And if so, it certainly must not be based on origin rules applicable to measures. The CCC is clear about it. If measures have been taken, i.e. do exist, the non-preferential origin rule is applicable. Article 1 of the CCC establishes that customs rules shall apply to trade. It does not apply to trade policy instruments. During investigations concerning dumping and injury caused by dumping CTVs, the European Commission applied rules with which the measures

---

[40] Commission Decision of 28 September 2001 terminating the anti dumping proceeding concerning imports of colour television receivers originating in Turkey (noted under document number C(2001) 2916), O J L 272/37 of 13.10.2001 (2001/725/EC), recital (9).

resulting from investigations should comply. The finding of dumping is, however, sufficient to consider the products as being dumped and if they are imported into the European Community they are dumped imports into the European Community. Subsequently measures can be taken and the origin rules will have to be applied. The way in which this application takes place is a matter of deliberation when a decision has been made on measures With respect to establishing injury cause by dumped CTVS, it cannot possibly be attributed to countries of exporting dissimilar products, i.e. tubes. The fact that in some cases countries exporting dumped CTVs to the European Community also exported tubes does not imply that the exports of these dissimilar products should be imputed to the injury inflicted by dumping CTVs from the countries that exported tubes because of the fact that the tubes were exported to third countries. These tubes were incorporated in the CTVs made in the third countries and dumped imports from these third countries cannot possibly be allocated to the tube exporting countries. The dumping from countries where the CTVs were produced and sold in the ordinary course of trade should be the countries of determination of normal value. As final measures toward Turkey or other countries, the European Commission could simply have deemed the products as "products of which the last processing has taken place in ... and either originating in that country of another country."

The disastrous consequence of the origin rule is, of course, that some European Community officials destroyed the European television industry, but also that exporters and importers were punished by this false interpretation of a rule.

12.9 Origin Rules and Fraud in Television Trade

From previous sections it may be clear that prior to the lodging of a dumping complaint the origin rule for television had the attention of European industry. During the proceedings described above, the attention of the complaining industry was drawn to the possibility that the complaint might result in discovery of fraud attributable to deceptive reporting of origin. The European Commission was informed by a complaint lodged on 5 October 1988, by the European Association of Consumer Electronics Manufacturers (EACEM) that the provisions of the Association Agreement and the Additional Protocol were apparently not being respected in connection with exports of colour television sets from Turkey.[41] An analysis of television sets Turkish producers exported to the European Community revealed that Turkish television sets did not have, according to the European Community origin rule, Turkish origin and that duties on imports of components into Turkey had not been paid, even though the final products, the CTVs, had been

[41] Judgment of the Court of First Instance (Third Chamber) of 10 May 2001, in Joined Cases T-186/97, T-187/97, T-190/97 to T-192/97, T-210/97, T-211/97, T-216/97 to T-218/97, T-279/97, T-280/97, T-293/97 and T-147/99, recital 264.

exported duty-free to the European Community. The European Commission did not react. In view of the value attached on the origin rule in the subsequent proceeding, this lack of response was striking. If application of the rule had implications for exporters, the rule was neglected.

During the preparation of the CTV case (Asia 1) against China, Malaysia, Singapore and Thailand (and Hong Kong and Japan, excluded by the European Commission), the European Community industry member of a temporary association SCAN (Society for Coherent Anti-Dumping Norms) was by the management of that association about problems with duty payments by Turkish producers and about the origin issue. If duties were to be imposed on colour televisions originating in China, Hong Kong, Malaysia, Singapore and Thailand, sets from Turkey might become dutiable because the components conferred the origin of the countries concerned to CTVs assembled in Turkey. It was, of course, nonsensical that the purchase of tubes would result in dumping duties for CTVs, but the risk was that the European Commission would, although not consistently, take this erroneous course. Irregularities were found in the case of the Turkish producers, but the European Commission seemingly decided that the Turks should be treated favourably and that Turkish promises about changes in behaviour should be believed. The market share of Turkish imports on the basis of Eurostat into the European Community was 5.5 %. The European Commission found only 1.5 % however. The non-cooperating Turkish producers represented 0.7 % of the European Community market, but the exports of these exporters were of unknown origin and therefore, assumed to be Turkish. The producers that exported with a known origin represented, according to the European Commission, the rest, and by subtraction from 1.5 % this was 0.8 %. The case was closed: the Turkish imports into the European Community were not considered as injurious, i.e. should not be considered in connection with the other imports or, technically, should not be cumulated. A discovery of Turkish export subsidies was neglected and the European Commission remained blind to the fraud of non-payment of import duties on components.[42] Nevertheless, the customs officials of the European Commission wanted European Community importers to pay duties due on imports of components by Turkish manufacturers that were not paid by the Turkish exporters. The European Court of Justice acquitted the importers, however.[43]

Later, new evidence concerning "fraudulent" Turkish (Vestel) and Thai (Thomson) origin reporting was brought to the attention of the directorate-general of trade, *inter alia*, in a later proceeding (Asia 3) including Turkish imports. This

[42] Commission Regulation (EC) No 2376/94 of 27 September 1994 imposing a provisional anti-dumping duty on imports of colour television receivers originating in Malaysia, the people's Republic of China, the Republic of Korea, Singapore and Thailand Official Journal L 255, 01/10/1994, pp. 0050–0069, recitals (98) and (99).

[43] Judgment of the Court of First Instance (Third Chamber) of 10 May 2001.

Table 12.6 Estimate of Turkish fraud

		1998	1999	IP[a]
A	China (originating, Commission)	*984,205*	*1,054,200*	*1,259,233*
B	Minus Eurostat imports China	119,776	246,885	51,599
C = A − B	Fraud from Turkey	***864,429***	***807,315***	***1,207,634***

[a]IP (investigation period) is from 1 July 1999 and 30 June 2000

fraud was neglected and, although the information was not confidential and, consequently, not essential for the cooperation of exporters,[44] OLAF was not informed about the existence deception by false origin declaration.[45] Various forms of fraud are discussed in Chap. 15. Some brief remarks, however, are made in this Chapter.

Although the European Commission had stated it was convinced during the CTV case Asia 1 that Turkish producers and government would comply with the rules, Turkish honesty appeared soon overestimated and fraud remained common Turkish practice. Vestel's Bluesky branded (Carrefour hypermarkets) sets or the Universum (Quelle, a mail-order company in Germany) contained tubes imported from Korea (Daewoo Orion) and China (Irico). Vestel even sold television sets with tubes identified as from Daewoo Orion, to which a sticker was attached with the indication that the tube was a Philips Display Components tube from Spain. Most of this information was submitted to the trade directorate general of the European Commission, but it did not report the fraud to OLAF neither did it inform the complainant that OLAF would remain uninformed. Vestel's was a weird practice because in a customs union, origin rules are in principle irrelevant and after customs clearance the origin of products does not matter.

Bush CTVs were marked "Made in Turkey", but after opening of the set it appeared of Chinese origin: the tube was from Irico. Since Vestel knew the origin rules and knew the Community's weird interpretation of the origin rule, it knew that on its supplies to Bush anti-dumping duties should have been paid, if the Community would indeed verify the effectiveness of its origin rule interpretation (see footnote 48).

The European Commission reported in disclosures concerning CTV (Asia 3) that part of the imports into the European Community from Turkey originated in China.[46] If the Eurostat data on imports from China are subtracted from all "originating imports" data provided by the European Commission, the imports from Turkey – allegedly originating in China – can be found. The figures are reproduced in Table 12.6.

[44] For the sake of the cooperation of exporting producers, the data provided confidentially in a proceeding are, of course, kept as confidential information to the investigating authorities. If information is non-confidential, there is no reason not to inform the European Anti-Fraud Office (OLAF).

[45] It is normal that the European Commission not report fraud if the information was obtained from confidential information provided by cooperating exporters. Reporting to OLAF would inhibit exporters' cooperation in anti-dumping proceeding. This does not apply to evidence that is provided by other parties in non-confidential material.

[46] General Disclosure Document AD No 433, R No 232, 1 August 2001.

If the average price of a Turkish set in that period is taken at €85, the amount of the fraud in the period 1998 to the Investigation Period (1 July 1999 and 30 June 2000) concerns 2,879,378 units and a total amount of €244,747,130. The residual duty for China of 25.6 % implies a total customs fraud of roughly €63 million. As may be concluded from the preceding paragraphs, this fraud was wholly incidental, because it was detected in connexion with an anti-dumping proceeding. If the CTV origin rule was as sacrosanct as the European Commission pretended during the investigations into dumping and injury in anti-dumping proceedings, it is amazing that no investigation had ever been initiated before the complainant drew attention to the matter. If the rule had been taken seriously, continuous, at least frequent inspections should have taken place of the correct origin indication by exporters. No investigations were undertaken and when fraud was found, no measures were taken. It was even taken for granted that the fraud did not exist, although it was discovered.

Fraud by Turkish manufacturers (in this case Vestel), worth in unpaid duties estimated at about €63 million, was the consequence of a peculiar origin rule. European Community legislation is applicable to European Community citizens and enterprises. Turkey is a part of a customs union with the European Community, and although the Turks have all the benefits of a customs union, the burden of conformity to European Community law is not upon them, but on importers into the European Community. Importers were liable, but how could they possibly know the content of a television set manufactured by their suppliers? They were not obliged to open television sets purchased or to calculate the number of tubes imported into Turkey from any provenance or origin. The Turkish domestic market for sets with those tubes and the share of their Turkish supplier in tube imports and in sales to the European Community should have been calculated. Competing European Community CTV manufacturers may make importers aware of the problem, and are safe as long as they pretend not to know the origin. It means that infringements of European Community law, like non-payment of duties and false origin indications, are without consequences to Turkish exporters and, as a corollary, to independent European Community importers. Turks are not supposed to read the Official Journal of the European Communities and nevertheless enjoy all the benefits of the customs union.[47] Vestel did not hesitate to tell stories revealing that he knew the European Community origin rules quite well[48]:

[47] Although the importer might have the knowledge that tubes imported from China into Turkey are used for exports to the European Community, it is not liable. The Judgment of the Court of First Instance opined that before it is reported: "To encourage the export of Turkish products to the European Community and to third countries, the Turkish authorities set up an export aid programme (the export incentive scheme) providing for exemption from customs duties on importation of components from third countries on condition that they were used in the manufacture of products which were then exported to the European Community or third countries." That implies that it is self-evident that Vestel exported all its tubes imported from China in sets to the European Community.

[48] Anti Dumping proceeding concerning imports of colour television receivers originating in or being exported from Turkey; Comments submitted by: Vestel Group of Companies, 15 September 2000, p. 80.

Table 12.7 Thomson's "fraud" due to a perverse origin rule

	1995	1995	1997	1998	1999	2000	Total
Imports of 14-in. sets from Thailand (€ × 1,000)	87,251	67,257	48,551	44,319	34,640	34,190	316,208
Anti-dumping duty difference with Thai duty (best case)	15.9 %	15.9 %	15.9 %	15.9 %	15.9 %	15.9 %	
Amount payable if all sets are non-Thai (€ × 1,000)	13,873	10,694	7,720	7,047	5,508	5,436	50,278

The large majority of CTVs produced in Turkey are of Community origin. This is because a high proportion of the products total value is due to components supplied by the Community component industry.

And:

Given that Vestel's CTVs are of Community origin it would manifestly not be in the Community's interest to impose antidumping measures.

The European Commission seemed to agree with this point of view. As soon as customs found out, which was after signals from European industry that tubes from China conferred Chinese origin, Vestel challenged this before the European Court of Justice, escorted by Thomson.[49] Although the application of the origin rule was in their advantage in the anti-dumping case, Vestel nevertheless challenged it as soon as this interpretational benefit granted by the European Commission in the form of preferential dumping access to the European Community was collected.

When the importer in the European Community is related to the exporter declaring false origin, it is liable. That is one of the reasons why both Vestel (its sales organisation in France) and Thomson Multimedia Sales Europe challenged the payment of duties and penalties. Because it is only an estimate, an indication of the amount of fraud as calculated above for Vestel is probably not the amount that customs tried to recuperate. As for Thomson, the false indication of origin of its three million sets imported from Thailand between 1995 and 2000 may have saved the company about €50 million. The amount of duties that would have been claimed by customs authorities is considerably less. The level is certainly the indication of loss of duties by the European Community and additional injury to European Community industry. This is a rather assailable discrimination between importers; if they are multinationals, they have to pay.

Thomson was involved in a non-payment of about the same amount. After 1994, it changed its procurement policy and purchased tubes from Korea and Malaysia. It did not pay the residual duties due to the Korean and Malaysian origin. The amount of duties due to this fact was about €50 million (Table 12.7).

In order to prove that they were not responsible for the mistakes, Thomson's customs lawyers drove their company into all sorts of useless legal proceedings.

[49] Judgment of the Court of Justice Vestel Thomson Joined Cases C-447/05 and C-448/05 Thomson Multimedia Sales Europe and Vestel France.

Unfortunately, they challenged the correctness of the collection of duties and they blamed the complexity of the origin rule as cause of their violation of customs law, even though they knew the rules well. The duties undoubtedly were in line with the law, or at least in line with its awkward interpretation. They could have challenged the European Community institutions' interpretation of the origin rule. The origin rule violates the agreements on origin of the WTO and even contradicts the CCC, but it may be wondered whether the Court would have accepted this logical argument. The Court normally investigates whether the rules were applied correctly. The rule was not applied correctly as far as the application in the establishing of dumping and injury was concerned. But when this procedural mistake had taken place and had resulted in wrong measures, the exports from Thailand and Turkey were covered by anti-dumping duties, even although the origin rule is nonsensically applied. In 2007, Thomson still appeared reluctant to pay the duties, which according to re-assessment notices received were considerably less than calculated above. It was an aggregate amount of around €16.1 million.[50]

> *Thomson still firmly believes that it has correctly declared and paid duty on the imported televisions concerned, accordingly strongly disputes the grounds of these re-assessments and booked the appropriate postings.*

Thomson may have believed this, but its corporate trade lawyer knew the rules quite well. Using Korean tubes and declaring ASEAN origin, by which the Generalised System of Preferences (GSP) treatment (0 % instead of 14 % customs tariff) was claimed, was clearly swindle. The product did not have preferential ASEAN origin and, because of the Korean origin, Thomson had to pay an additional residual anti-dumping duty, although the latter rule is assailable from the WTO point of view. In fact, all Korean tubes used outside of Korea conferred Korean origin and antidumping duties were due. If it had been up to some officials in DG Trade, Thomson would have had to pay anything.

12.10 Origin and Definition of European Industry

In the case of integrated compact fluorescence lamps (electronic energy savers), the complainant detected that one "Community producer" imported main components, the electronic ballast and the burner, from China. The value added to the parts brought in, during the assembly or completion operation, was less than 10 % of the manufacturing cost. In the case of anti-circumvention, the product would be found to circumvent the duties. Objections were made against including this assembler

[50] Notes to the unaudited interim condensed consolidated financial statements, 2008, p. 35.

into the definition of European Community industry. The European Commission, however, decided otherwise[51]:

> *The investigation showed that the product concerned has a different customs classification than the imported components. This reclassification results from a substantial transformation of the components. On these grounds, and based on the information gathered in this investigation it can therefore be concluded that the products concerned manufactured by Company A are of Community origin.*

Here the general non-preferential origin rule must have served as basis for the response. As in the explanation about the purpose of non-preferential origin rules, when it was considered to apply to trade policy instruments, the interpretation is not precise and therefore, not correct. The CCC does not refer to "a substantial transformation". The relevant text is[52]:

> *Goods whose production involved more than one country shall be deemed to originate in the country where they underwent their last, substantial, economically justified processing or working in an undertaking equipped for that purpose and resulting in the manufacture of a new product or representing an important stage of manufacture.*

The issue was not what the origin of the products assembled by Philips was. It was quite well known what the origin rule meant. The question was whether a company adding so little value could be considered part of Community industry, apart from the fact that the company imported the major share of its turnover from the dumping country. Besides, a substantial transformation is inadequate an expression. The last, substantial, economically justified processing is originating or the manufacture of a new product, which in this case was the lamp, made from two main components. The European Commission's conclusion about the "substantial transformation" raised two problems:

- Are producers excluded from the definition of European Community industry if their products, although manufactured in the European Community, do not originate in the European Community according to the European Community origin rules? That would be a surprising conclusion, but the opposite is also amazing. A negligible added value could apparently be sufficient to render the status of part of European Community industry.
- If an anti-circumvention proceeding must be opened, is the production found to be circumventing the measures counted as European Community production or not and is the company thus circumventing the duty part of European industry or not?

[51] Council Regulation (EC) No 1205/2007 of 15 October 2007, OJ L 272 of 17.10.2007, Annex Company A.

[52] Council Regulation (EEC) No 2913/92 of 12 October 1992 establishing the Community Customs Code, Official Journal L 302, 19/10/1992, pp. 1–50, Article 24. Even the Internet site of the Taxation and Customs Union directorate general refers at "products having undergone a last substantial transformation."

These issues are not without consequence. For instance, if there were dumping of LCD television sets, none of the European Community manufacturers produces television sets originating in the European Community. All LCD and plasma screens are imported and components constitute more than 50 % – and in any case more than 45 % – of the value of the flat screen colour television set and the product is originating in a third country. This implies that there is no European Community industry to which injury could be inflicted. A dumping complaint would be impossible.

The second question shows the Catch-22 nature of the philosophy that in anti-dumping the customs law should determine whether a producer is part of European Community industry. According to the anti-dumping legislation, it is possible that assembly in the European Community circumvents the measures. If circumvention is found, the conclusion by the European Commission could, nevertheless, be that the products are originating in the European Community. Therefore, the circumvention would count as production by European Community industry. In principle, circumventing assembly could block the continuation of measures.

It is clear that both the anti-dumping and origin legislation need review and revision. This problem should be sorted out fundamentally and should be settled and should not remain a free style wrestling game.

12.11 Origin and Other Fraud

Various forms of fraud exist.[53] The most spectacular was fraud that could hardly be considered to represent fraud. This is the case of the examples of fraud found in the field of television sets. Although the exporters like Vestel and Thomson knew quite well the risks of purchasing tubes conferring origin of countries for which anti-dumping duties existed, most cases represented sound practices of cheap components procurement. However, in some cases fraud was intentional fraud for the sake of circumventing the duties. Cases of inadvertent fraud are foreign television makers exporting CTVs to the European Community that are unaware that the products originate in a country with an anti-dumping duty. European citizens are supposed to know European Community law, but foreigners are not.

An interesting case of intentional fraud was car radio. Car radio is sold in two separate markets. One is the automotive producers' market. Auto radio producers sell their equipment to car manufacturers who install the radios into the automobiles. The other is the after sales market. Customers purchase car radios in specialised shops. ALARM, the temporary Association for Legal Auto-Radio Measures representing practically all European car radio producers, lodged a

[53] Vermulst and Rovetta (2006) have written a comprehensive and illustrative article about the subject. It gives information on origin and fraud, sometimes deliberate and sometimes attributable to false legislation.

complaint about dumping by Korean manufacturers in the after sales market. It was not easy to find the normal value for car radios in the Korean market because practically all of Korean sales were to car producers Daewoo, Hyundai and Kia. The policy of these car manufacturers was, of course, to wrest as low prices from the many producers in the market as possible, but the prices were sufficiently high to keep them alive. The export market served for most producers as means to obtain scale of production and low costs, which made their sales in Korea more competitive. In 1992, the European Community imposed duties.[54] Soon it became apparent that imports of car radios into the European Community from other sources increased very quickly. Eurostat data on imports from Indonesia challenged information from Indonesia about the absence of car radio industry in the country and certainly of car radio production meant for exports. In 1992, Indonesian car radio exports suddenly increased within a few months from 2,000 a year to 60,000. In the surveys of GfK, the German market research company, it was apparent that sales of some Korean brands had decreased after the measures were imposed but one brand was particularly thriving, despite the measures in place. The combination of the two data gave rise to suspicion that a Korean producer used Indonesian trade documents, origin certificates, for Korean exports to the European Community.[55] The non-preferential origin rule for car radio is the same as the television origin rule.

The matter was reported to OLAF, which had also received indications from member states. An investigation supplied a colourful picture of fraud. The story is that an investigation team visited a kampung, an Indonesian village, where women from the fields, the desa, were present in a sort of factory building imitating production. In one part of the building, which created the image of a factory, parts and components were inserted into a printed circuit board, but not soldered, and the boards were placed into car radios, while in the other corner of the building components were in turn taken out from the radios and from the boards and put into baskets. These parts were again put onto the boards and so on. This does not constitute “an important stage of manufacture”. A team of OLAF – at that time UCLAF, Unité de la Coordination de la Lutte Anti-Fraude – visited these premises and found the building not exactly “an undertaking equipped for that purpose”, as Article 24 of the CCC prescribes. The following day, the team revisited the place and found it deserted. Some papers that had been left offered additional evidence of fraud. The total amount of duties involved was €3,671,299, relatively modest compared with the television examples in this Chapter. Even without the special origin rule of 45 % of value or 35 % of materials, this activity could be seen as fraud. In a later Chapter some fraud strategies supported by evidence show how some exporters tried to mislead customs.

[54] Commission Regulation (EEC) No 313/92 of 4 February 1992, OJ L 34, 11.2.1992, p. 8–20 and Council Regulation (EEC) No 2306/92 of 4 August 1992, O J L 222, 07/08/1992, p. 0008–0015.

[55] Report from the Commission Report on the follow-up of traditional own resources in cases of fraud and irregularities, Brussels, 4.2.2005, COM (2004) 850 final/2, p. 30.

12.12 Example of Other Origin Rules: Integrated Circuits

Philips Semiconductors complained that their customers wanted integrated circuits (ICs) with European Community origin certificates. These customers were mainly Japanese producers in the United Kingdom who wanted to fulfil the 45 % value or 35 % materials conditions in the television origin rule. There was hardly a reason for them to demand this European Community origin because they already purchased picture tubes from Philips or Thomson – and after the acquisition of Nokia's tube factory in Eslingen – Matsushita made tubes in the European Community and thus acquired European Community origin. The argument was likely used to obtain the chips at a lower price.

The change in origin rule from the last stage – the assembly operation – to an earlier stage – diffusion – as criterion for origin of integrated circuits seemed logical. The diffusion process grants the essential character to the integrated circuit. From the economic point of view, there was hardly an advantage in changing the rule. In the period in which the Philips' Semiconductor Division wanted this change, there was hardly a reason for it except the French, Italian and Spanish quota with the need for television, radio and radio cassette recorder origin rules. The value of the chips in these products was, however, of minor importance. Even if the European Community changed the non-preferential origin rule, the change would not have affected trade with EFTA countries, which at that time included Austria with various electronics producers. It would take a huge effort and time to get the preferential origin rules of EFTA and European Community changed.

Nevertheless, Philips' Semiconductor Division demanded a change in origin rule. Representatives in the Origin Committee and European Commission officials visited the factory for a demonstration of the importance of diffusion and the necessity that the origin rule should be adjusted accordingly. The diffusion process is not very interesting for a visitor to a wafer factory. The factory must be dust-free and people are in white clothes. The delegation wanted also to have a look in a room where some chips were encased with a few machines. Because there were machines with many moving parts, this process enthused them. This encasing was the last process and, unfortunately, the delegates were so impressed by it that new initiatives to change the origin rule had to wait for some years. Finally the change took place, but did not offer any advantage. In Annex 11 to the Commission Regulation (EEC) No 2454/93 of 2 July 1993 laying down provisions for the implementation of Council Regulation (EEC) No 2913/92 establishing the CCC a "list of working or processing operations conferring or non-conferring originating status to manufactured products when they are carried out on non-originating materials" was given containing a definition for the processing conferring origin to integrated circuits. For the item ex 8542, integrated circuits, the "operation of diffusion (where integrated circuits are formed on a semi-conductor substrate by the selective introduction of an appropriate dopant)" conferred the origin. After this change the semiconductor industry did not wonder what the point and advantage of the new rule was, but demanded extension of this rule to all semiconductors.

Because the origin rule was a European Community rule not recognised by Taiwan, the weird consequence of this new origin rule was that the customer received chips in a package indicating "Made in Taiwan" with a certificate of origin indicating EEC origin.

When the Information Technology Agreement had reduced all duties on semiconductors to zero per cent, all efforts to change the origin rule appeared pointless.

12.13 Accession of Spain and Portugal to the European Community: Temporary Preferential Origin

Chapter 5 referred to the possibilities presented by Spain and Portugal's accession to the European Community. This accession could have given the opportunity to use the higher protection of Spain and Portugal and the decrease thereof by accession to the European Community as exchange for increases of European Community duties on consumer electronics. The effort to use this case failed. On 12 June 1985 the European Community, Spain and Portugal signed the accession treaty to the European Community, which became effective on 1 January 1986. The European Community granted the two countries a transitional period in which they could maintain some protection as an Iberian preferential area. This preferential area implied that, for instance, for television there was a preferential market with Iberian rules of preferential origin. Some producers had an assembly basis in Spain, among which Sharp, Sanyo and Philips in Spain and Samsung had recently invested in a small subsidiary in Portugal. Philips had small screen picture tube production in Barcelona and, consequently, it had a preferential market.

Before accession of Portugal to the European Community, Philips transferred its small-screen monochrome television production from Lowestoft in the United Kingdom to lower cost Ovar, south of Porto. A factory in the North of the Netherlands, in Stadskanaal, manufactured the tubes for the sake of employment in a depressed area. This monochrome cathode ray tube factory was the only one in the European Community. Competition in monochrome TV came from Korea and Taiwan. It was, therefore, useful to adjust origin rules of the Iberian preferential area so that the Portuguese plant could use European Community tubes without duty on monochrome tubes and without duties on exports of monochrome television sets to Spain and the European Community. Access of products originating in the Iberian Peninsula gave preferential access to Spain and Portugal. In the case of monochrome cathode ray tubes the Dutch origin was allowed to be counted as Iberian origin and could take part in the Iberian free trade. By adjusting the preferential origin rules, the industrial activities in both Ovár and Stadskanaal were served.

The chairman of Philips Spain complained heavily about the price behaviour of Sanyo and Samsung in the Spanish market, but he did not mention the preferential industrial position in Barcelona, where Philips produced both small screen television sets and tubes. This small change in origin rules for black and white television had, indeed, occurred unnoticed by most of the European Community member states. It was introduced without much fuss and served the interests of the producer of tubes and of television sets quite substantially. Therefore, a close look at origin rules is of importance.[56]

References

Raikes B (2008) The European display market – exciting times for the display industry. German Flat Panel Forum: European Technology: Flat Panel Displays, Leaflet 6

Vermulst EA (1994) Rules of origin as commercial policy instruments? In: Vermulst EA, Bourgeos J, Waer P (eds) Antidumping Law and Practice: A Comparative Study (Studies in International Economics), University of Michigan Press, Ann Arbor

Vermulst EA, Rovetta D (2006) Origin rules in EU anti-dumping law and practice: an update. GTCJ 3(10):337–348

Vermulst EA (2010) EC anti-dumping law and practice. Sweet and Maxwell, London

[56] See Vermulst (2010).

Chapter 13
Inter and Intra European Company Politics

Abstract External factors, such as peculiar interpretations of rules by officials or even their personal interventions, can complicate the conduct of trade policy. Interests of competing European industry can interfere with objectives. Conflicting policies within a company, or bureaucratic politics within the industry, can cause confusion and are elements for a risk analysis. Internal company conflicts and interests sometimes overshadow external problems. This Chapter gives various examples of internal barriers to use of trade policy instruments. These internal obstacles interacted with challenges posed by external factors, such as lobby by exporters, industrial European opponents, member states and European institutions and their handling of rules or sometimes their unpredictable policies. Many internal complications prevent trade policy from being successfully conducted, and contribute to the downfall of an industry in distress. Negative consequences are generally unnoticed because they do not belong to the management repertoire that is popular in such a period. Management books generally discuss conditions for success and rarely the causes of distress and failure. Some of them are accounted for in this Chapter.

13.1 The Workers' Council Courageous Chairman

In the autumn of 1990, the chairman of the Philips large aluminium capacitors factory's workers' council in Zwolle, the Netherlands, wrote two letters, one to Mr. Frans Andriessen and the other to Mr. Koos Andriessen, both of which used the Christian democrat political party as background. Koos Andriessen, a Protestant, was the Dutch Minister of Economic Affairs; Frans Andriessen, a Catholic, was the External Relations Commissioner, which is now *inter alia* the task description of a Trade Commissioner. Both were highly capable and integer politicians. In response to the letter from the workers' council chairman, both referred to the Bureau for International Economic Relations at Philips headquarters. The fact that the chairman received a response in this affair was a new experience. He was in an isolated position

M. van Marion, *International Trade Policy and European Industry*, Contributions to Economics, DOI 10.1007/978-3-319-00392-4_13,

at Philips due to three problems: lack of care, lack of courage and lack of communication. The main customer of large capacitors was the Consumer Electronics division of Philips. It had switched to cheaper Japanese supplies. Due to the switch, the business unit of large aluminium capacitors ran into serious overcapacity and cost problems. The total procurement for television and other consumer electronics applications by Philips Consumer Electronics exceeded four million units and represented about 50–60 % of the Philips capacitor factory's output and sales. The consumer electronics division did not care that its switch decreased capacitors factory load by about 27 %. The director of the capacitor factory did not have the courage to officially advance the matter to corporate headquarters. He discussed the issue with the management of the components division, but the chairman of that division's vision was that every business unit had to sort out its own problems. He either did not care or did not have the courage to tackle the issue. The chairman of the workers council sensed that management preferred to sacrifice employment rather than take the matter to the next highest corporate level. His advantage was that, as chairman of the workers council, he could not be dismissed and at 59 years old was at the end of his career. He wrote letters to the chairman of Philips' components division and to the president of the company. He did not receive an answer. In desperation he finally wrote letters to the Dutch minister and European Community commissioner explaining the situation.

The situation required a quick and resolute action. A recently emergent heroic mood at Philips held that all problems could be solved, predominantly by dismissal of personnel and closure of factories. Scrutiny of data threw light on the cause of the problems. If the management of Philips' components division and corporate centre had taken the issue more to heart, a temporary solution could have been achieved. The Consumer Electronics division could have ordered its normal quantity, thus reducing the additional costs incurred by underutilisation of capacity in the components factory. Simultaneously, an anti-dumping complaint could have been prepared. By underutilisation of capacitor production capacity, the total corporate losses exceeded the gains from a price difference between the Japanese and Philips capacitors. The Consumer Electronics division was confronted with dumping of compact disc, VCR and television, but suddenly denied the existence of dumping when its in-house supplier was involved. According to the Consumer Electronics division, the capacitor factory was less efficient than the Japanese. As evidence for this allegation, only the Japanese export selling price was the yardstick. Factual evidence of the opposite, Japanese inefficiency, was rejected. Cooperation in supply of evidence was refused. The purchasing department of the Consumer Electronics division was clearly proud of its purchasing activities. Later, disbelief in these abilities appeared correct, when purchasing prices of Philips and of competitors were compared in an anti-dumping case (Asia 3). Competitors purchased components sometimes considerably cheaper.[1] There was a deep mutual mistrust

[1] The Barcelona factory purchased from Philips in a Spanish management buy-out and baptised Technimagén involved in a dumping complaint with Philips appeared to pay less for its components.

between supplier and client within the same company. Apparently the Consumer Electronics division did not believe that the components unit was able to write a complaint. Additionally, shopping in Japan and purchasing from polite salesmen in Japan was more interesting than procuring from the Philips factory in boring Zwolle (the Netherlands).

The situation was severe. Drafting an anti-dumping file in a very short period of time available to collect data was imperative. Other producers' support of the complaint was required. Roederstein and BH Components were invited for a meeting at Amsterdam Schiphol Airport and an association was founded, the Federation of Appropriate Remedial Anti-Dumping (FARAD, a name that coincided with the unit of measuring capacitance). Philips' Bureau for International Economic Relations assumed project management of this temporary federation. The cooperation among these producers resulted in a realistic market picture. Since the purchasers of Philips Consumer Electronics used price information of Japanese offers in negotiations with the in-house Philips capacitor supplier, the European import price was known. A constructed normal value was calculated from data on offers by Japanese producers of foil and other capacitor parts, such as anode, paper, cathode, tabs, tape, can, cover, sleeve, disc and electrolyte and the cost of production. The materials content of an aluminium capacitor is a cylinder or can, and within this can is a winding construction of the materials, to which an acid liquid, electrolyte, is added. On the basis of offers of parts and components from independent Japanese suppliers, a construction of Japanese cost of production determined the normal value.

European Commission officials understood the reasons for the bizarre conflict within the same company. The Cabinet of Commissioner Andriessen was aware that the matter was urgent and prompted the services to act swiftly and effectively. Peace between the two parties, Philips capacitors unit and Consumer Electronics purchasing department, would not be restored, however. In view of the many services rendered by corporate centre to the Consumer Electronics division, not all cooperation was denied. Non-cooperation was an embarrassment.

Relations among competing European capacitor producers had become more cordial. The creation of temporary association FARAD was the starting point of communication among producers about market size and the behaviour of global competitors. Before this anti-dumping case, European producers did not have a common platform. Existing producer associations, such as the European Electronic Components Manufacturers Association (EECA), were too distant from this particular industry. The actual European Passive Components Industry Association (EPCIA), now also comprising former enemies, in the framework of EECA is the successor to the temporary association FARAD.

The composition of the capacitor market was rather diverse. Philips, Roederstein and BH Components sold respectively 7.8 million, 4.7 million and 3.0 million large aluminium electrolytic capacitors. Their combined share in European Community market was 27 %. BH Components focused on dedicated solutions to the market segment of smaller specialised customers. Its prices were considerably higher than those of Philips Passive Components and Roederstein, which concentrated on mass production customers for general-purpose applications in the television, computer, monitor and major domestic appliances industry. Japanese manufacturers of mass general-purpose applications capacitors created the major problems in the European market. Among those Japanese were giants Matsushita, Elna, Nichicon, Nippon Chemi-con and Rubycon. The Japanese had a broader range of products than individual European Community producers. These producers were particularly active in the same mass application product range as Philips, Roederstein and Siemens/Matsushita. Matsushita's role was remarkable. Its joint venture with Siemens, later transformed into a stand-alone company, EPCOS, had a market share of 27 % in 1990. Matsushita nevertheless clearly dumped from Japan into the European Community market, thereby causing losses and incapacitating the capacitor joint venture with Siemens. This policy of damaging interests of a joint venture partner implied that Siemens beared half the burden in Europe and Matsushita had the full advantage of the increase of market share, production volume and profit.

Matsushita obviously tried to conceal its destructive role in the European Community market. It would not cooperate in the proceeding. It was not expected that the Japanese would dump their way into the European Community. The capacitor market is highly volatile and, although growing in the long run, showed a cyclical pattern. Over-booking takes place when equipment markets are booming, and massive order annulments follow when equipment demand falls. The distance from Japan to the European Community market was also disadvantageous for European customers of Japanese producers. A short reaction time to a change in demand is an essential asset. For that reason, the Japanese attack came as a surprise. If cycles are geographically unevenly distributed, dumping may also have a cyclical cause, i.e. the dumping in Europe is consequence of depressed demand in Japan. The information from Japan was that its market was not depressed. There was no reason for Japanese companies to dump away domestic overcapacity.

Excluding Japan, there seemed to be a battle for global market share. The European industry felt that the Japanese rush was an effort to obtain volume of production, foreshadowing worldwide restructuring of the industry. Domestic peace in the Japanese market was not affected by the prospect of the necessary consolidation of global market positions. Matsushita's participation in dumping, at the cost of the joint venture with Siemens in Europe, showed the violent struggle between the Japanese and other competitors for volume on markets outside Japan. As quoted before with the microwave oven example, Matsushita went for market share in order to improve its overall competitive position that could not be challenged in Japan.

Within 2 months, the letters of the chairman of Philips' factory in Zwolle to the Minister and Commissioner had a follow-up by the compiling of an anti-dumping file, which surprised Japanese exporters. The dumping exporters are normally quite well informed about impending cases due to active lawyers and information leaked by European Commission officials.[2] The investigation opened within a few months,

[2] Complaints were lodged without clamour. Lawyers were usually well informed about complaints. It is not clear how and why European Commission officials inform lawyers, but this practice is almost ineradicable. It results in excessive political and commercial pressure on complainants in the period prior to formal submission of a complaint.

but it took almost 1½ year before anti-dumping measures were in force. In the meantime, a major industry reorganisation took place. Some outstanding producers were taken over by others. Vishay acquired Sprague and Roederstein. Matsushita, Nippon-Chemi-con, Nichicon and Rubycon inflicted also injury on the United States market. The acquisitions of some firms, such as Toshiba's subsidiary Marcon by Nippon Chemi-Con, gave them easier access to the United States market and this market rather than to the European market. In the meantime, Taiwanese and Korean capacitor producers saw an opportunity in the European market where the Japanese experienced difficulty selling their products at lower prices. The temporary association FARAD also dealt with this problem of the Koreans and Taiwanese.

The proceeding resulted in anti-dumping duties, which improved the results of Philips' capacitors business and also saved the life of others. The situation in the capacitor market had changed in the meantime. There was still not a change in anti-dumping legislation to counter the circumvention of Japanese producers. In Thailand, Japanese ELNA had started a subsidiary, which mainly used Japanese materials for final production. Nippon Chemi-Con had established a subsidiary in Singapore, and Matsushita exported from Malaysia using materials and production technology from Japan. The activities only benefited from lower labour costs, which are not essential in this line of business. Material costs are predominant (69 % of costs of manufacturing) and fixed cost constitutes another 24 %. Therefore, there was no reason for an anti-circumvention complaint. A capacitor factory established outside of Japan by a Japanese producer was a relatively rigid asset; therefore a normal anti-dumping proceeding was suitable.

13.2 Dutch Disbelief of a Japanese Cartel in the United States: The Council's Draw

By a practically complete conquest of the United States capacitor market by takeovers, *inter alia*, the Japanese created an excellent position for resumption of dumping to the European Community from a new base. Their position was dominant in the United States. Their behaviour in the United States market finally enabled re-entry of Vishay, which had taken over the remnants of Sprague and Roederstein. The United States branch of Philips Passive Components in Columbia, South Carolina, United States, tried in vain to sell capacitors in the United States market. Where efforts were made to offer to major customers, one of the Japanese producers, either Matsushita or United Chemi-Con offered a lower price. Japanese suppliers never competed among themselves with price offers to United States customers in competition with non-Japanese suppliers. Consequently, the price in the United States was normally relatively high, except when a non-Japanese producer tried to gain customers and market share at the cost of non-Japanese. This targeted pricing policy was clearly cartel-like behaviour, which was cause for worry, but did not offer a clue for action against these producers.

When, however, these two Japanese producers started dumping again, this time from the profitable and almost uncontested United States market and went for market share in the European Community, thereby doing what they did from Japan in the earlier years of the decade, there was an opportunity to tackle the problem. An internal fight again preceded the action of one of the two complaining producers. Philips Consumer Electronics purchased Japanese capacitors again, this time from the United States. Although the share of Philips CE in Philips Components' capacitor production volume had decreased from 60 % to 40 % of production, the reduction of internal purchases again had an extremely negative effect on cost of production of Philips' components producer. Relations between the two remained fragile and when there was again an opportunity abroad rather than in dull Zwolle for Philips' Consumer Electronics Division's for procurement, they risked a trip overseas to the United States this time.

A new president had taken office at Philips. His business experience was limited to the milk and grocery delivery (SRV in the Netherlands), selling shoe polish (Erdal of Sara Lee) and to coffee roasting (Douwe Egberts of Sara Lee). These products are neither particularly characterised by business cycles nor by trade policy issues. He saw his lack of knowledge of the business as an asset, and cherished innovative ideas about strategy in electronics, accounting and general business strategy. Without consulting some colleagues, brilliant technology and marketing experts in the board of management, he devised a strategy he called "high volume electronics", based on the luminous idea that if one produces mass electronics and is able to earn €0.01 more per kilogram, one makes a handsome profit. By advertising and creating brand awareness, there would be a boost in sales and profit of products with high volume. It implied that initially small innovative activities did not get a chance; they were killed because they were not consistent with the high volume strategy. He imposed his vision on accounting and introduced the "new" notion of Economic Profit Realised as a novelty, which he thought superior to mere profit. As for the business strategy, he first sold some profitable parts of Philips that his predecessor had valued so much. He – apparently because he disliked his predecessor, who had appointed him as Board member and recommended him as Chairman of the Board as successor – sold Polygram. His predecessor had made this company one of the highest-ranking music publishers, which was also successful in the film business. He also had ideas about the business structure of the company. His second luminous idea was that bleeders, the business units incurring losses, should be turned around, but preferably sold or closed. Since he was not acquainted to the phenomenon of business cycles, all professional and components units of the company were doomed. Because people during a recession brush their shoes with shoe tan rather than buy new ones, more shoe polish is sold during a slump. The coffee business is highly open to cycles, but the cycles are of a nature that depends on the vicissitudes of the weather or of nature and not business cycles. It was bad luck for some business parts of Philips when Mr. Boonstra paid attention to them; their ill fortune of temporary unprofitability got even worse. If he focused his attention on a particular business unit, he did so during a period of economic downturn and losses. He inevitably smelled blood, concluded that they were bleeders and had to be sold. In this way he disposed of various businesses, including extremely promising activities, little interested in the technological coherence of activities with strategic opportunities in other product areas.

He sold passive components, which was quite understandable in view of the limited connection with other product fields, although such considerations were scarce in his frame of mind. He wanted to do so in secrecy. His threat was simple: everybody in the unit's management who revealed the possibility of negotiations on a divestment would immediately be dismissed. Consequently, while the European Commission investigated a dumping case and assessed European Community interest, the company involved as complainant in the case was not allowed to inform the authorities about the possibility of change in ownership. Even the management of the Philips department that drafted the complaint and was involved in the lobby on behalf of the complainant was not supposed to be informed. This phenomenon occurred three times. Three business units of Philips involved in anti-dumping proceedings were secretly sold. Boonstra did not know what dumping or anti-dumping was, and did not take the time to acquire knowledge on this or any other subject. He considered a business in anti-dumping cases to be bleeders. The passive components, the car systems and the television broadcast equipment businesses were sold after the start of an anti-dumping proceeding and during investigations and decision-making by the European Community institutions and he finally also killed the fax business. The moves were conceived as efforts to sell business activities involved in an anti-dumping proceeding as an additional asset. This impression overestimated his comprehension of trade policy issues, however.

The Dutch government authorities were eager to show their independence from Philips, especially when they acted in relation to a business that no longer belonged to Philips but to an investment company Compass Partners, and decided to refrain from supporting a European Commission proposal for measures against Japanese dumping from the United States, Thailand and continuation of measures towards Japan.[3] The chief executive of BC Components (Beyschlag Centralab Components, property of the investment company) and former general manager of Philips Passive Components was suddenly confronted with opposition from authorities he had never heard about. His knowledge of state institutions and their complex role in European decision making was – after more than 25 years at Philips – rather weakly developed. He tried to get the support from the liberal mayor of the city of Zwolle. He phoned the city hall of Zwolle and asked for Frans Janssen, although the mayor's name was Jan Franssen. He finally got a hold of him and explained that some female civil servant in The Hague, Jorritsen, blocked positive support to this case of anti-dumping. He meant the minister of economic affairs, Annemarie Jorritsma-Lebbink, a party and former parliamentarian colleague of the mayor. The components manager was exhausted by tough and complex negotiations with

[3] The responsible director general held the opinion that the competition policy in the United States did not allow for high normal values and dumping by subsidiaries of Japanese firms in the United States.

the investors, and details of Dutch politics were alien to him. He certainly did not understand the rejection by some Dutch civil servant, a Director General, of the possibility that Japanese dumped from the United States.

Secrecy of sales of the business did not leave time for a lobby in member states. The Dutch abstention of support finally resulted in a non-decision by the Council caused by a draw: there was neither a majority in favour of the measures toward the United States and Thailand nor against. As a consequence, and because of the principle of non-discrimination, the measures toward Japan, Taiwan and Korean could not be prolonged.

13.3 A Japanese Camera Cartel and European Community Politics

In the 1980s, a struggle started about the standard for a high definition television broadcasting system. Since 1968 the Japanese industry, lead by broadcaster NHK, had been busy developing the MUSE system of High Definition TV (HDTV), which used digital techniques for an analogue system of 1,125 lines. Europeans feared that the Japanese were trying to impose their system on a global scale. They started cooperation, the Eureka HDTV Directorate, which coordinated research and development with support of the European Commission in order to arrive at a common standard for HDTV at least on a European scale. The objective was a common European broadcast system, imposed in the European Community, based on the D2 MAC system. In 1991, the impossibility of imposing a European system was clear. Thomson and Philips had hoped that the European Community was capable of a mandatory system. Thomson practically had a monopoly in France for camera systems, and believed in the possible compulsory introduction of the system. Although Philips was more accustomed to market conditions, there was a deep belief in a salutary effect of compulsion. Expectedly, private broadcasters, supported by Mrs Thatcher and the Luxemburg government, opposed the introduction of D2 MAC.

Before the final collapse of the European high definition project, Japanese television broadcast equipment producers started an attack on the European broadcast equipment market. They had divided among themselves the European Community market in exclusive territories. Their offers were spread over Europe according to a scheme, the objective of which was apparently the destruction of the European Community broadcast camera industry. The demise of this industry would doom the HDTV project, anyway. Germany was apparently allotted to Ikegami Tsushinki, which offered equipment to the West German Broadcast Corporation WDR. Prices were far below the level that Dutch-German joint venture of Philips and Bosch, BTS (Broadcast Television Systems) could afford. Sony's hunting ground were the Netherlands and Belgian broadcast markets, and it offered to the Nederlandse Omroep Stichting (NOS) at about half the price of long-time supplier BTS. Hitachi dedicated its attention to Radio Audizioni Italiane (RAI) and offered far below the prices of both

European contestants, Thomson and BTS. In September 1991, the Ministry of Research and Technology (Bundesministerium für Forschung und Technologie, BMFT) sent a letter to the WDR both indicating the price in Japan of the equipment and the offer price to WDR. The price in Germany was, according to the ministry, 46 % below the domestic Japanese price. With corrections for differences between the European PAL and the United States and Japanese NTSC system, the margin was even greater. The domestic price of an Ikegami HK 355 camera head was DM 123,000, according to the ministry, whereas the German export price was DM 78,000. The ministry appeared well informed. Information from Philips' national sales organisation in Japan confirmed domestic prices of the equipment sold by Ikegami. Philips had acquired experience in the Japanese market during the period that Philips' plumbicon tube camera LDK 5 was globally leading, even in Japan. Philips only led until Japanese producers had developed their own cameras, even though they were not competitively priced. After the Japanese industry acquired camera technology, the Bosch-Philips combination BTS hardly stood a chance, although its prices were substantially below Japanese prices in Japan. The European Commission would, after an investigation in the proceeding, find a difference between the Japanese domestic and export price, or a dumping margin, of up to 86.4 % over the CIF value for the smallest Japanese producer.

BTS protested with German broadcaster West Deutsche Rundfunk. The technical director of WDR condescendingly denied, immediately and without investigation, the existence of dumping, and claimed that WDR obviously selected from competitive offers only. Most broadcasters had narrow relations with the state. Purchasing officers felt upset by allegations that their cheap purchases were due to dumping instead of their own expertise and negotiation abilities. They lobbied strongly against anti-dumping actions. The closer the relations of customers of broadcast equipment to the state, the more lenient the attitude of member states towards dumping. The lodging of a dumping complaint raised anger, certainly in Japan, but also unjustifiably in some European Community member states. Luxemburg normally had a benevolent attitude toward justifiable and well-documented anti-dumping actions, but as centre of private broadcast activities, now raised serious objections against measures. Investments in hardware by broadcasting companies are a minor part, far less than 3 %, of their budget.[4] Investments in camera systems are less than 0.5 %. The effect of duties on those budgets was marginal and did not justify such fierce opposition. In view of the fact that all broadcasters would equally be affected by measures, their relative competitive stance would not be influenced. Italian broadcasters were also furious. Of course, the company of the later Prime Minister Berlusconi protested, and also RAI management

[4] For instance, total broadcast and technical equipment (Rundfunktechnische Anlagen und Geräte) was only 2.8 % of total assets of the WDR in 1999. Camera equipment was, therefore, a minor issue in the total economy of the broadcasters and total investments in all assets were only 3.3 % of the WDR's expenditures. The figures of the ZDF are similar. Camera systems were negligible items, except for purchasing officers.

raised serious objections with the Italian government. Later it was apparent that some – as it appeared – personal financial motives in the form of secondary income flows – were against barriers to imports from Japan.

Broadcast Television Systems (BTS) was created in 1986 as a joint venture between Robert Bosch GmbH's Fernseh Division and Philips Broadcast. Bosch was leading in recording and Philips' camera technology enjoyed worldwide recognition. The company made remarkable contributions to the development of High Definition Television. It had a tremendous problem, however. The failure of HDTV inflicted serious losses. This was an extreme, but normal business risk, however. The main issue was that the Japanese started a dumping offensive. The second problem was that BTS had not properly identified specific items that caused these losses. The Japanese undercutting of prices and BTS' stagnation of sales were clear, but how much exactly should be allocated to television camera systems was not clear. Two accounting systems, of Bosch and Philips, had to be united. The chairman of the company was Dutch (from Philips), whereas the finance and accounting officer came from Bosch. Both insisted on acceptance of an accounting system of their own background. The result was that considerable losses by about €42 million compared to a total turnover of slightly more than €210 million were not allotted unambiguously. Desperately, the BTS Chief Executive Officer requested Philips headquarters to take action against dumping. When an anti-dumping complaint had to be prepared, it was not difficult to get the data on production costs and on shipments. The results in the factory were clear, but it was impossible to obtain company-wide data on sales turnover, specific prices and a profit and loss account on studio camera systems. Projects were offered at lump sum. Initially an offer was based on an aggregation of costs, but during negotiations the link between overall price and specific costs was lost. In the stage of the draft of the dumping complaint it appeared impossible, in view of the comprehensive offers and sales, to report specifically selling prices of studio camera systems.

Thomson's bad relations with Philips did not prevent Thomson Broadcast's readiness to join the complaint and to join a temporary association CAMERA (Committee for Appropriate Measures to Establish Remedial Anti-dumping). Although Thomson, as a French company benefiting from French preferential purchasing and as a state owned company, was less bothered by market considerations, it was also worried about the Japanese attacks. Fortunately, Thomson Broadcast had excellent management and staff who were well prepared to support a case. The fact that there were only two European Community producers created a problem, and also offered a solution.

If two producers represented the total European production, then aggregate information on production, sales and sales prices, and profit and loss is sensitive by definition from the point of view of competition policy. That was a problem on one hand, but a relief on the other. The two individual companies provided all data in indices, even in the confidential annex for the European Commission. BTS indexed data were preliminarily provided in the complaint on the basis of a reasonable approximation based on the data of the factory. The European Commission did not ask for the actual sales volumes and prices, rather it accepted the indexation. In the preparation stage of an anti-dumping complaint, it was the experience of those involved at Philips' anti-dumping activities to not supply data on the truth: their abysmal results. Management was predisposed to clamour triumphs. If possible, bad results were hidden. When a proceeding was opened, they were compelled to cooperate in the investigation and produced the figures, provided they remained confidential, which they normally do. In the case of BTS it was different. It appeared that, since the accounting system was in a mess, data on proceeds and costs of individual products were not in a centralised database. Therefore, some creativeness concerning BTS' sales data on cameras was unavoidable in the period before the opening. After opening of the case, however, the situation concerning business data appeared worse than expected. All data were declared present in "der Kartei", the database in Darmstadt, but it remained in "der Kartei" and nobody was capable to draw the data from it. Losses had been incurred on lump sum projects comprising a multitude of equipment, the costs of which could not directly be allocated. The company's interest payments, for instance, were huge. When asked, the director of finance and accounting explained that these costs came from the banks. It had escaped him that these payments did not come from banks, but were paid to banks. There was not the slightest idea where actual costs came from and what had caused the debts and interest payments.

Consequently, shocked by absence of an accurate accounting system, the international economic relations department at Philips headquarters developed a suitable reporting of the accounts of BTS, with the objective of providing a proper response to the questionnaire normally circulated immediately after the opening of the investigation by the European Commission. The sales organisations of BTS in European Community countries received floppy discs with data on the quantitative sales they had made and they were requested to report the selling prices of these projects and when possible, the selling costs related to the projects allocated to equipment, but at least total cost of the projects. On the basis of the responses and a comprehensive product catalogue with prices of all sorts of studio equipment items, even including reporting vans and mixing tables, monitors, routers, recorders and imported products, data on sales to broadcast studios and other camera users and of ex-works costs of cameras and on overall loss data, selling costs were imputed to camera systems, the ex-factory prices of which had been reported by the factory in the Netherlands. The cost of sales was allocated in accordance with price lists and results were derived from the losses on total projects. Loss as a percentage of turnover was about 37 %.

Creating reliable accounts was not easy. When the European Commission verified the data, improvisation was vital. Fortunately, before the European Commission made its definitive verification, it sent a small group of accounting experts who explained some principles of accounting. Questionnaires of the European Commissions have a structure that tries to conceal the embedded check of data consistency. A reconstruction of accounts must take that method of control into consideration. The respondent to the questionnaire is supposed to report costs, sales and results of the product concerned and other products, but the format allows the European Commission to trace inconsistencies. The set-up of the accounts should have followed the same pattern. All entrees in a novel accounting system had to take the European Commission's testing methodology of coherence and correctness in mind. Some parts of such a coherent response should not have been presented in the response itself, however, because these parts contain the data used for a check and were not requested in the format. Since the questionnaire response of BTS was the result of a re-construction of the accounts and the accounting system, it was not possible to respond in time in accordance with the format demanded by European Commission. The response was coherent, but the time was insufficient to adapt all data to requirements of the questionnaire structure. The team of the European Commission tried to explain how the response should have been calculated. This gave time to adjust the data in accordance with the format.

When the European Commission verification team first visited the factory in Breda, the Netherlands, where data were based on the old Philips accounting system with which the officials were acquainted, some essentials of the injury in the production stage were verified. Manufacturing cost data of the factory showed tremendous undercutting by the Japanese. Subsequently, the officials visited the headquarter premises of BTS Darmstadt (Germany) and asked for evidence by documentary data. The director of the BTS accounting department, a former Philips employee, was frequently missing because he was searching data in the "Kartei", BTS' chaotic database. His bad luck was that his boss in the board of management, a Bosch man, had been dismissed and that he had hoped to succeed him, which was impossible because he did not come from Bosch. He was also blamed for absence of a proper accounting system, and had been informed that he would also be dismissed. He was, however, not allowed to seek another job within Philips or Bosch before his replacement and a replacement for his boss were found. It was not amazing that he lacked zeal for his job. Even if he passionately wished to contribute, however, the database remained inaccessible. When the European Commission's verification team asked for a document, they were either informed that it was shown last time during the visit of a previous team in Darmstadt, or that it was in the database, knowing that it would remain hidden in the data base. At the end of the day the European Commission verification officials were satisfied, as were some people at BTS. The accounting director was still lost.

The system's approach, in which a range of products together constitute a system and are considered "like product", was unprecedented in European Community anti-dumping proceedings. The reason for including the equipment of the whole camera system was that measures would be completely ineffective if cameras had been singled out as a "like product". Exporters could easily circumvent duties by artificial pricing of cameras and other parts of studio systems. Each camera can be offered either as complete camera stand-alone or in a systems setup of a camera head, a studio viewfinder, a camera control unit and an operational control panel. Of course, the studio also contains other equipment. Regrettably BTS produced some of these, like vision mixers, routers and monitors, in the United States and these could not be covered by a complaint.[5] Therefore, a comprehensive broadcast studio system could

[5] The United States government could have requested for measures against dumping and injury caused by Japan in the European Community market, but the chance of success was minimal.

not be covered. After all, the definition of like product was sufficiently comprehensive for excited discussions and weird practices. All producers had a problem with allocation of costs. If the product definition of the product concerned was limited to cameras only, exporters could rather readily use the argument that the price of cameras was low because they were subsidised by other products sold at higher costs, dependent as these products commercially were on the camera sales. Ikegami had a subsidiary in Switzerland, which seemed to pay certain costs for the related importers; therefore the low export price was justified by low costs of cameras in relation to the peripherals, the costs of which were hidden in Switzerland.

The greatest fight was not about system peripherals to the camera, but about so-called "professional cameras", claimed to be distinct from broadcast studio cameras. Sony argued that part of its camera sales were not broadcast, but professional cameras. It was the bulk of their sales and essential for its industrial position, especially in charge-coupled devices or sensors. The only good reason for this special treatment was exactly why a complaint had been lodged: it was the low price of the equipment. Sony fabricated the existence of a difference between "professional" and studio cameras and finally fooled the European Community officials. Traders offered equipment as studio equipment cameras that Sony and later the European Commission treated as "professional cameras" not covered by measures. In trade the cameras proposed by Sony for exclusion from the "like product" or the product concerned were normally considered studio cameras. "Sony DXC D30 WSP Triax SDI 16:9 studio camera chain", for instance was excluded from application of duties.[6] The problem was that only one single European Commission official, amply wined and dined by Sony England, finally decided on the matter. He personally contributed to the misfortune of European camera production. A simple verification of the use of this camera would have saved European Community industry.

Sony's resolve to safeguard its interests and to exempt these dumped cheap cameras from the definition of the product concerned was so tough that it let its lawyer Jean-François Bellis of the Van Bael and Bellis law office organise a secret meeting in a building opposite Frankfurt Airport, which specialised in hosting the meetings of business people aiming at mutual understanding, if not price arrangements. The meeting took place in the late autumn of 1993. Sony arranged a heavy delegation. Sony's director of the global camera business came from Tokyo and directors of Sony Europe and Sony's camera sales organisation in the European Community were present. On the side of BTS, the president of the company and the president of the Philips division, to which the BTS activities belonged, and the vice-president of the Philips' international economic relations department were present. Sony's lawyer, Mr. Jean-François Bellis, demanded on behalf of Sony that the vice-president of the Philips international economic relations department be prohibited from visiting Brussels for 1 month. Non-compliance therefore implied that Sony would interpret such a visit to Brussels as an act of hostility toward Sony, and Sony would discontinue

[6] http://www.tv-bay.com/FORSALE/Cameras/Studio/SONY/DXC_D30_WSP_TRIAX/134579.html

supplies of Betacam camera recorders to BTS. This threat, especially non-delivery of the Betacam, seriously shocked the president of BTS. Unfortunately, he did not know his sales figures. Fortunately, BTS's sales of Betacam camera recorders had been limited to two units only. Sony had a dominant market position of 75 % global market share in camera recorders. These two camcorders sold under the BTS brand name and supplied by Sony were sold at a loss because Sony's prices to OEM customers such as BTS and Thomson were higher than to its own independent customers. Thomson was also customer of Sony, both for sensors and camcorders. Sony's threat of non-delivery of sensors to Thomson was more effective than a refusal to sell Betacam. Like BTS, Thomson also incurred losses on sales of Betamax camcorders. Philips was the only non-Japanese producer of CCD camera sensors. Their specification deviated from the Japanese and Thomson preferred the Japanese sensors and had become dependent on Japanese supplies and could not easily switch. Indications of a Japanese sensor cartel forced it to kindness and indulgence towards Sony's claim. Sony's threats to Philips were less impressive. Its lawyer obtained the promise, however, that the Philips manager would not visit Brussels for that month prior to the European Commission decision on the dumping and the products that would be exempted. He was to abstain from taking part in the camera proceeding during that month.

The concession weakened resistance against manoeuvres of Sony and its lawyer. Sony's special position had already become apparent during the compact disc anti-dumping case. This time a considerable range and volume of cameras, allegedly professional cameras, were exempted from anti-dumping duties and thus gave Sony a huge volume and cost advantage in camera electronics and particularly charge-coupled devices. There had not been any reason to surrender to Sony's demands. Sony's threats to BTS were meaningless and void, but towards Thomson they were more consequential. Ultimately, a complaint about anti-competitive behaviour of Sony with its Betacamcorders would have been an option. Sony did its utmost to frustrate cooperation in the field of development of competing recorder systems by price undercutting in its OEM sales as soon as cooperation could be successful. After a switch to Betacam, Sony increased its prices for the OEM customer. Evidence of such abusive practices was present. Philips' absence during the last month in the proceeding did not make much difference: Sony had already convinced one European Commission official, who subsequently deprived the industry from restoring its presence in the camera business.

The final anti-dumping duties on camera systems were: 82.9 % for Ikegami (the undercutting was 98.9 %), 62.6 % for Sony (undercutting was 81.3 %) and 52.7 % for Hitachi (with an undercutting of 89.2 %). Most important was the long list of exceptions, which allegedly concerned "professional cameras". The lowest duties, based on its dumping margin, were imposed on Hitachi. This exporter's main customer was Italian RAI. The dumping and undercutting were less because part of the higher price covered payments to purchasing officers outside the formal tender. Such practices were, as other fraud, generally not reported to the authorities and as with television fraud the exporter received the benefit of lower duties.

Soon after imposition of the anti-dumping duties, it became evident that exporters were involved in circumvention or even fraud. Ikegami used its premises in Neuss,

Germany for circumvention, and angered the customs police by customs manoeuvres. It shipped major components from Japan to Neuss where they cleared customs and were forwarded to Switzerland. In Switzerland, cameras were assembled practically without added value – they were just clicked and screwed together – and re-exported to Neuss. No anti-dumping duties were paid. When German authorities were informed about the practices of Ikegami, they acted appropriately.

The response of the United Kingdom officials was quite different. The United Kingdom seemed pleased that Sony circumvented duties by sending components to Basingstoke and thus provided some employment to a few people. A file was prepared to tackle this circumvention, which had also been facilitated by the fact that "professional cameras" were exempted. Some parts of professional cameras were similar to those of studio cameras and it was impossible for careful customs officials to find out whether the anti-dumping duties were legally circumvented. There were indications, however, that exporters had initially, immediately after imposition, also absorbed anti-dumping duties on studio cameras and peripheral equipment. Resale prices did not reflect the duties imposed. Absorption of duties is factually an increase of the dumping. It was concluded that it was preferable to increase duties first by means of an anti-absorption case. Subsequently, a file on circumvention could be submitted. There were not many illusions about the effectiveness of such measures. The duty on Ikegami cameras indeed went up to 200.3 % and on Sony's cameras to 108.3 %. The European Commission in the meantime started to grant exemptions for "professional cameras" to a degree hardly reconcilable with a policy objective of an anti-dumping instrument to eliminate injury caused by dumping. Whatever might be said about usefulness of the anti-dumping instrument, it was clear that uninterrupted continuation of these anti-dumping actions was more expensive to the dumping exporters, even if they did not have the effect that they should have. In the first place, the costs of lawyers to the exporters were considerable and much higher than of Philips' staff to BTS. Secondly, anti-dumping proceedings require time and attention. One of the advantages of the absorption complaint was that the exporters necessarily had to provide some data on their sales in the European Community. Although these data were often in index form, the combination of figures provided information on market and market positions and on huge circumvention of duties. Besides, the anti-circumvention actions forced the exporters to devise new practices of avoidance.

Due to the arbitrary distinction between professional and broadcast cameras – all essentially similar products – it was impossible to lodge a new complaint covering all products. The Japanese would argue that European producers did not manufacture professional equipment: a repetition of arguments. This would become a useless debate. The European Commission would never admit its mistakes. The Japanese had already eliminated competition in the low price segment of the camera market. Community industry had only one option and that was obstruction of some of their movements.

Nuisance value was, therefore, considered main value of new trade actions and each effort yielded information on the market behaviour of the exporters enabling a next step, which because their lawyers were incapable of providing the right and coherent figures, created coordination problems for the exporters. The exporters, mainly Sony and Ikegami, had to use staff for response to the questionnaires and for providing adequate information for their legal representatives in Brussels. The European Commission had already bartered real effects away by exempting a majority of studio cameras as professional cameras, but the idea was that the dumpers would not get rest. The next steps were tackling of circumvention of anti-dumping duties on those cameras that were not exempted and keeping Sony and Ikegami busy in new proceedings and creating uncertainty for their customers. It was wondered what the next step by the Japanese would be in response. It was evident that they would try to find new ways of circumvention, apart from the route allowed to them with respect to professional cameras by benevolence of one official. A preference to absorption was also related to the expectation on information that could be gained from the proceeding. Proof of circumvention is not easy. Afraid that the Japanese would not supply sensors, Thomson was not prepared to participate in a complaint against circumvention. The threat that no CCD sensors would be supplied from Japan to Thomson bent the knees of those in Thomson who feared that this would terminate its business. BTS, which became Philips BTS because of Bosch's departure, had to pursue the policies against the Japanese dumping alone. The courageous chairman of the Philips camera business in the Netherlands knew that the expedition had its risks, but he was an entrepreneurial executive who also succeeded in improving the effectiveness and promptness of his organisation and enhancing its competiveness.

If more than 60 % of the components in the product are originating in the country of export of dumped goods and that less than 25 % value is added in the European Community, imports are circumvention of duties. Major parts of a television camera are the camera head, optical block including sensors and optics (prisms and filters) and rear adaptor. These can be imported and supplied as one or as separate units. In Table 13.1, camera and main subassemblies are listed. Each subassembly has its own subassemblies. Consequently, an extremely complex exercise of demonstration that the products meet the criteria of 60 % and 25 % requires information on composition of the product, precedes a complaint.

These subassemblies have their subassemblies. The analysis of the equipment went into four levels of assembly. Although the materials content of a camera may vary according to concept of the construction, the composition of costs was roughly the one given in Table 13.2.

The complexity of the product made extension of the complaint to other elements of the system unfeasible. The European Commission would not be capable to handle the case with so many customs intricacies properly. Motive for an absorption complaint was inter alia that an increase anti-dumping duties might compensate for the fact that anti-circumvention measures restricted to cameras instead of complete systems would not have too small an effect. The European Commission opened a case on circumvention, but serious problems could not be solved. The most serious obstacle was how measures should be applied. It was therefore better to apply duties to camera systems and certain components thereof as such rather than to start a highly controversial and politically sensitive application of the anti-circumvention rules. The European Commission promised to replace an investigation concerning

Table 13.1 Main television camera parts

Assemblies	Subassemblies
Camera house	House assembly Triax back panel
Front module	Basic house assembly
	Filter wheel holder
	Filter wheel assembly
	House assembly
	Optical module
	Peltier assembly
	Sensor unit
Additional supplies	Shoulder pad

Table 13.2 Cost composition of a television camera

Materials totals	Euro	%
Mechanical parts	€2,562.16	22.7
Optical parts	805.70	7.1
Sensors	4,537.76	40.2
Service manual	207.87	1.8
Printed circuit boards (PCB's)[a]	607.97	5.4
Electronics on PCB's	2,560.10	22.7
Total	€11,281.55	100

[a]Printed circuit boards

circumvention, and possibly measures, if any, resulting from such an investigation, with measures concerning main components. This would not cope, however, with a new phenomenon. Sony had transferred assembly operations from Basingstoke, England to Florida, United States, whereby it evaded measures concerning circumvention in Europe. Therefore, Philips, advised by the European Commission, withdrew the circumvention complaint. In exchange, it got an investigation into the dumping of components. The European Commission would investigate dumping of components, a phenomenon equal to circumvention, and Philips would launch a complaint concerning dumping from Florida. Philips guessed that Sony would be able to deceive the European Commission again. And indeed it succeeded.

Sony promised to close the activities in Florida and to transfer them to the European Community. The European Commission seemed to believe it.[7]

> *It was confirmed in the course of that verification visit that Sony was phasing out its production of TCS* [Television Camera Systems] *in the USA with a view of closing down its manufacturing facilities for TCS in the USA as from September 1999 and transferring them to the Community. The company made an official announcement to this effect on 27th September 1999 stating that this transfer would be concluded by December 1999.*

It could be conjectured that Sony would not transfer production, but that it would circumvent measures again. In view of the flexibility of production, the only restraint could take place by anti-circumvention measures. The Japanese Ministry

[7] Commission Decision of 31 January 2000 terminating the anti-dumping proceeding concerning imports of television camera systems originating in the United States of America (notified under document number (2000) 208) (2000/73/EC), OJ L 25 of 1.2.2000, p. 24.

of International Trade and Industry protested vigorously and apparently successfully.[8]

> *In June, 1998, an anti-circumvention investigation was initiated for Japanese television camera systems. Japan has protested this to the EU, as there is nothing in the WTO that justifies current anti-circumvention measures (including circumvention investigations), and arguing that the investigations are therefore illegal. As a result, the EU terminated its investigations in February 1999, but is currently conducting an antidumping investigation of Japanese television camera system parts. We consider this case to be extremely problematic in terms of the Anti-Dumping Agreement, especially with regard to whether there is sufficient evidence for the authorities to decide to initiate a case of their own initiative. We will need to continue to monitor developments to ensure that investigation procedures comply with the rules in the Anti-Dumping Agreement.*

The European Commission had made many promises. The measures had been eroded by an exemption of a substantial volume of products relevant for mass production. Consequently, only in the market for the big broadcasters measures may have had some significance.

Again, the divestment of a business was prepared without pre-notice to those involved. President Boonstra perceived that the camera business, although improving, was involved in anti-dumping and concluded that it was a bleeder he should dispose of. From cost and technical abilities point of view there was not the slightest reason for Philips, Bosch or Thomson to leave the camera business. The gap between Japanese domestic market and export market prices, i.e. the dumping, and destruction of non-Japanese competitors remained overwhelming. The many reorganisations and sell-offs of business parts by Philips' president Boonstra curtailed the technological spin-offs of broadcast activities on other parts of Philips' activities. The demolition of Philips' professional and consumer electronics resulted in the abandonment of the broadcast activities business. Philips camera systems business was finally sold to Thomson and after the breakdown of Thomson all broadcast activities went to Grass Valley, a company Thomson had acquired. The LDK cameras in Grass Valley's product range are a splendid witness of its heritage. In 2001, Hitachi's anti-dumping duties were repealed and in 2007 all duties were repealed. Grass Valley had submitted a new complaint, which was withdrawn later.

13.4 Internal Inhibitions to Trade Policy: The CD Car Radio and Changers Case

Philips' president Boonstra had a new and innovative definition of leadership and made it his habit to threaten people with dismissal. Every time he saw losses, he decided to dismiss the culprits and sell the business. In some cases profits lay ahead, but his focus was on shareholder value, i.e. his bonus, and he wanted to eliminate

[8] Ministry of Economy, International Trade and Industry of Japan: "2000 Report on the WTO Consistency of Trade Policies by Major Trading Partners" Chap. 5, p. 75.

even the chance of losses. He focused on a business when and because it incurred losses. To him, if they were involved in anti-dumping cases, businesses must be bleeders. Unfortunately for Philips Car Systems, it got involved in an anti-dumping case. The profitability of the in-car information and entertainment industry was strongly hampered by the behaviour of Japanese producers of compact-disc changers and players. It appeared that Korean Haitai, supplier to Blaupunkt, and Japanese Alpine, which supplied changers to Philips, increased their prices on occasion and decreased them as soon as these Europeans considered their own production. The intention of production became immediately obvious when Europeans showed interest in price quotes from Japanese components makers, which were instantaneously heralded in Japan. In the United States and Europe, such behaviour or components suppliers is rare. In Japan it was different.[9] Most worrying, however, was that the price of the Korean and Japanese to Blaupunkt and Philips far exceeded prices to car manufacturers and other customers in Europe. Table 13.3 presents a selection of the data supplied by the exporters in their royalty statements on their sales of compact disc equipment.

It is apparent that the dumping of CD combinations exceeded the dumping level of changers. Europeans produced combinations and did not manufacture changers. The competition among changer producers was less fierce than in combinations of radios with CD players. Therefore, the level of dumping on combinations had to be higher in order to gain market share, both at the cost of European and non-European competitors. In changers, Europeans did not pose a similar problem.

Japanese (and Korean) producers with obligation to pay royalties for CD technology revealed domestic and export prices in their royalty statements. Domestic Japanese prices exceeded those of their exports to Europe of identical models by more than 30 % to even more than 120 %. It was, as in the case of CD players and in the Tosoh example in Chap. 8, an amazing phenomenon that the accounting departments of the Japanese producers reported their sales so meticulously and provided such reliable information on severe dumping. It is not surprising that they immediately after the lodging of the dumping complaint, stopped reporting on model-by-model and country-by-country basis. The information on pricing behaviour they provided was too embarrassing. A dumping case for combinations of car radio and a disc player could be made relatively easily. It was insensible to tackle CD changers without inclusion of the car radio. A car radio (head) unit is used for the operation – for instance selection of discs and tracks – of the changer. The problem was not very different from camera systems. If only dumping of changers stopped, this would be insufficient. The dumping of head units or radios also had to be terminated. If these head units, which could also be sold as standalone car radios, were not included in the proceeding, the exporters could shift the dumping of packages of changers and head units by increasing the dumping of head

[9] During the VCR self-restraint and during the microwave anti-dumping proceeding Japanese components producers reported their sales of components to the Ministry of International Trade and Industry. Such behaviour is uncommon in the west.

Table 13.3 Dumping margins found for CD combinations and changers

Combinations	
Alpine CDM 7983 R	56.4 %
Kenwood KDC7040 RL	72.2 %
Kenwood KDC5040 RL	81.9 %
GoldStar TCH-880	72.2 %
Pioneer DEH-P825 RDS	126.48 %
Changers	
Alpine S 604	42.6 %
Kenwood KDC C504	40.3 %
Pioneer CDX-P1210	38.2 %
Pioneer CDX-P610EW	33.9 %
GoldStar TCH-C61	41.9 %

units. Several Japanese producers produced their head units in factories in South East Asia. These head units were not in the license statements because they did not contain a CD mechanism. Three complications arose. Firstly, the normal value in the countries of production had to be found, which was, of course, lower than the resale price by these Japanese companies in Japan. Secondly, countries other than Japan and Korea had to be added. Thirdly, the explanation why head units had to be included would have to occur in intensive information campaigns to member states.

The data the Japanese exporters supplied shed light on another issue. Mitsubishi Electric, for instance, had become preferred supplier to Volvo. Volvo Japan had to pay more than Volvo Europe, anyway. On the other hand, Volvo Europe had to pay substantially more than Renault in Europe for the same CD changers. Philips France was a long time preferred supplier to carmaker Renault. Mitsubishi clearly wanted to undercut Philips, either in order to make Philips' deals with Renault unprofitable, or to take over Renault as a customer. The volume of Mitsubishi's supplies to Renault was still limited. Although there certainly was overall dumping by Mitsubishi, the dumping margins of sales to Volvo Europe were considerably less than dumping margins on supplies to Renault. In the case, should the calculation of dumping include all export prices and should the average dumping margin be less or should only the dumping margins of supplies to Renault be preponderant? Here the issue of "zeroing" emerges.

If there is low or no dumping or even a negative dumping, such prices may, according to European Community and United States practice, be excluded from the calculation. The idea is that establishment of dumping margins is not just an algebraic or arithmetic exercise, i.e. a calculation of the weighted average prices on the domestic market minus the weighted average prices on the export market, but a commercial activity. The dumping exporter may aim at obtaining market share and volume of sales, in which it inflicts injury to the producing party in the export market on one hand. If it, on the other hand, gained a customer by the dumping the exporter can increase its prices. Dumping margins can consequently become smaller, zero or even negative. This practice of exclusion of low or negative dumping margins from the dumping calculation is called "zeroing".

Several authors have criticised this zeroing practice. Zeroing aims at elimination of "targeted dumping". Targeted dumping is selective dumping. After the exporter has eliminated competitors and gained a customer, it raises prices (a form of the predation discussed in Chap. 8). Customers already gained need not obtain benefits of dumping, which are discontinued as soon as the exporter has become preferred supplier. A price increase to the level of producers in the export market is sufficient to remain the preferred supplier. Dumping margins can decrease and dumping and undercutting can even disappear, as far this customer is concerned. If the higher export prices are included into the calculation of dumping, it is clear that the average export price to both Renault and Volvo decrease by inclusion of the prices to Volvo. The dumping in the past, by which Volvo became Mitsubishi's customer, would be advantageous to Mitsubishi if the exclusion of Volvo's relatively high purchasing prices were not allowed. Focusing on the arithmetic peculiarities of zeroing may prevent one from seeing that sales at different points of time can cause differences in economic significance of sales.[10] Authorities must limit the period of investigation to a reasonable time frame. This cannot possibly imply that all sales in that period should be considered of equal economic significance. The major problem of dumping is that the practice of price differentiation is not necessarily confined to one fixed investigation period. It is procedurally and practically impossible to test sales before the investigation period and to find out whether these were dumped by the exporters and undercut sales of producers in export markets. If dumped deliveries to Volvo in Europe at lower price than selling prices in Japan took place in the period before the investigation period the dumping was, according to some authors, non-existent in the investigation period, then the deliveries should equally contribute to the calculation of the dumping margin as the new dumping. It would be unjustifiable, however, to accuse authors criticising the zeroing practices of theorising and of statistical tunnel vision. Discrimination is a danger indeed. More attention is dedicated to this subject in Chap. 16 on the methodology of dumping, Sect. 16.9 (c).

Attractive prices may have convinced European car manufacturers to choose Japanese preferred suppliers. Whether offers are a manifestation of dumping and price undercutting is irrelevant to them. In the case of car CD changers, it was administratively not possible to establish whether the exporters' prices had been dumped for a longer period. Their license statements clearly indicated, however, structural dumping combined with targeting, but the European Community cannot investigate more than a limited investigation period and cannot even accept information from license statements, if provided to the authorities.[11] The dumping by Japanese and also Koreans caused "material retardation of the establishment of such an industry"[12] by European producers and, therefore, price undercutting did not exist.

[10] Hindley and Vermulst (2001); Ikenson (2004).

[11] Some data was disregarded. If authorities have own data, they prefer it to evidence that may be superior, but has not been verified by the authorities.

[12] Article 3 Determination of injury (1), the definition of injury in the Basic Regulation, Council Regulation (EC) No 384/96 of 22 December 1995 on protection against dumped imports from countries not members of the European Community, (OJ L 56, 6.3.1996).

European production was simply absent. At the times that bashing Japan was fashionable, conspiracy was alleged. There was no evidence on such a practice. It was, however, striking that other Japanese producers were hardly competing with Alpine for Philips Car Systems as a customer. Companies in Japan approached as alternative sources suddenly, without explanation, terminated negotiations.

Before a complaint was submitted, both Blaupunkt and Philips promised to start production of changers within the European Community. These promises did not materialise. They went to Hungary, not member of the European Community yet. This made a complaint rather feeble. It meant that the whole burden for a successful proceeding was borne by an argumentation that the car radio with CD player and a car radio with a link to a changer were the same or similar products. Initially this argumentation was accepted, but inclusion of separate car radios with a head unit for the operation of the changer without changer production in the European Community appeared too far-fetched for various member states. Again a secret sale of a business had been engineered, accompanied with the famous threat with dismissals. The sale of Philips Car Systems to Mannesmann appeared a decisive blow to the project. The fate of the proceeding was attributable to several factors. The first was the impression on member states that Philips was not interested in the good result of an anti-dumping complaint at all. That may have been the case. As soon as an anti-dumping proceeding was initiated, the president of Philips looked at the business, and that was more fatal than dumping.

References

Hindley B, Vermulst EA (2001) Zeroing in on zeroing, anti-dumping in WTO dispute settlement. Wall Street J 6 (9 Aug 2001)

Ikenson DJ (2004) Zeroing in: antidumping's flawed methodology under fire. Cato Institute

Chapter 14
Trade Policy and Pressure Politics: Fax Machines

Abstract Before preparation and submission in December 1996 of a complaint on dumping of "personal or consumer faxes" from Japan, China, Korea, Malaysia, Singapore, Taiwan and Thailand, lobby groups, lead by Japanese governmental institutions and industrial associations, almost succeeded in preventing the opening of a dumping investigation. Their zeal in the political arena was greater than their inclination to cooperation in a proceeding. The story on consumer faxes describes a struggle only partly in a legal arena. Member states gave priority to the purchasing interests of their telecom companies over industrial interests and appeared able to reduce the period of applicability of measures from five to six years. In addition, a European Commission official succeeded in forcing the complainant to reduce the scope of the product for which measures would be applied to technologies that had the least impact on the lobbying exporter. The threat was that the official would fail to collaborate if the complainant did not adjust the product and exclude the printing technologies that were important for the future. Lobbying by the Japanese made customers insecure, because the Japanese alleged that the case would not be opened and when it was opened they declared that measures would not be taken, but customers did not take the risk. The complainant finally disappeared by some coincidences.

14.1 Fax Machine and Facsimile Markets

The Scotsman Alexander Bain invented the fax machine in 1846. All other additions to this invention came from Europe. The scanning technology was also developed in Europe. Siemens produced the first working fax machines.[1] Western written communication does not require handwriting. Fax was not much easier or

[1] Communications Industry Association of Japan (CIAJ) "Position Paper –2- for the EU with regard to the anti-dumping complaint against facsimile machine imports", September 27, 1996, Annex 2.

M. van Marion, *International Trade Policy and European Industry*,
Contributions to Economics, DOI 10.1007/978-3-319-00392-4_14,

cheaper than telex or later, than e-mails, but fax is extremely helpful for communication in Japanese Kanji characters. Therefore, Japan had a public interest in development of fax machines: [2]

> *The Ministry of Posts and Telegraphs, unlike its more telex-oriented counterpart agencies elsewhere, encouraged fax research and development through research contracts and purchases of machines. Thus it is not surprising that Nippon Telegraph and Telephone had the largest fax R&D lab in the world in the 1970s. This Ministry interest also assured that fax technology was given attention as the Japanese government and large Japanese corporations collaborated in shifting the national economy towards exploitation of the microelectronic revolution in the mid-1970s. This paid off in the 1980s in the form of a commanding lead in reliable and lowest cost manufacturing that pushed most of the remaining U.S. competitors out of the market and permitted maintaining market share even against South Korean newcomers.*

The claim of cost effectiveness was beside the point. A comparison of the Japanese costs with the Koreans, Taiwanese and even with Europeans is disappointing. That the remaining United States competitors had been pushed from the market, as has been shown, was not necessarily dependent on low cost, but rather on dumping. Between 1945 and 1970, about 50,000 fax machines were sold in Japan and about 15,000 in the United States.[3] In 1977 sales of fax machines in Japan amounted $160 million, $40 million more than sales in the United States (including Japanese sales). This shows the attractiveness of fax machines to Japan. The first compact fax machine standards were specified in 1978 by NTT to its main suppliers Matsushita, NEC, Toshiba, Hitachi, Fujitsu and Murata. It was the thermal paper fax machine.[4] In Japan, about twenty producers were involved in the production of facsimile. Some were particularly specialised in fax technology and had leading positions. Murata Data Equipment Corp. was one of them. The strongest was Matsushita Graphic Communications Systems, known in Japan as Matsushita Denso. It was clearly the market leader with a market share in Japan of about 60 % and world wide of roughly 40 % in 1985.[5] Its position as a market leader eroded outside Japan where the many Japanese producers tried to obtain market share in order to improve their volume of production and cost effectiveness. In order to meet this declining market share and profit erosion, Matsushita transferred production of its cheaper consumer fax range to Singapore. Such a relatively big number of Japanese producers were possible because the fax machine was a product for which the distribution was spread over various distribution segments. Sales were, for instance, channelled via telecommunication shops such as NTT's, office and consumer distribution.

Initially, technology applied was limited to thermo sensitive paper (TSP). Later thermal transfer (TT) plain paper fax (PPF) technology was introduced. This

---

[2] Peterson (1995, p. 477).

[3] Quotation from "Moving Images a Japanese Way," Business Week (August 29, 1970) p. 30, by Peterson (1995, p. 477).

[4] Gregory (1985, p. 369).

[5] Gregory (1985).

Table 14.1 Printing device and technology background of fax suppliers to European Community (Calculated on basis of the GfK market surveys on June/July 1996 and August/September 1997)

		Technology emphasis				
		Plain paper faxes (PPF)				Thermo-sensitive
Producer/brand (rank order in market)	Technology background[a]	Laser	LED	Ink jet	Thermo-transfer	Thermal
Matsushita Panasonic **(1)**	General	3		1		2
Canon **(2)**	Business	2		1		3
Brother **(3)**	Business	2			1	3
Sharp **(4)**	General	2		3		1
Hewlett-Packard **(5)**	Printer			1		
Toshiba (6)	General	1	3	4	2	5
Samsung **(7)**	General		2			1
Ricoh **(8)**	Business	1		2		
Olivetti **(9)**	Business			1		2
Sanyo **(10)**	Home	3		1		2
Oki **(11)**	Business		1		2	
Philips **(12)**	Home					1
Minolta **(13)**	Business	1		2	3	

[a]The bold figures between parentheses in the brand column are the pick-order of manufacturers in the German market for faxes based on GfK surveys. The figures in the columns of the technologies present the technology rank order per brand: Panasonic's most important was inkjet, followed by thermo-sensitive and laser as number 3

technology is in principle identical to the thermo sensitive paper technology. A heated ink foil prints on the plain paper where the printing is done directly on the thermo sensitive paper with the other technology, which is the original and more perfected miniaturised technology. Advanced memory technology made other printing devices gradually more economically acceptable. Unlike TSP and TT, other printing devices like inkjet, laser and light emitting diode devices need a considerable buffer memory for storage of signals received. Fax producers with printer production background specialised in some printing technology. Technological specialisation of the various companies is sketched in the survey of Table 14.1.[6] Table 14.1 is based on turnover of the companies under their own brand in the German fax market. Ranking is according to proportion of technologies in total turnover. Behind the name of the producer the ranking in the German electrical retail market of 1996 is given, i.e. before imposition of anti-dumping measures.[7] Brands of European or foreign distributors are excluded. The producers with a background in general or consumer products were present in thermal technology, the professional market specialists limited their products to plain paper laser, LED and ink jet.

[6] See note before for Japanese backgrounds, the others are not difficult to be added.

[7] GfK (Geselsschaft für Konsumforschung), June/July 1996 retail survey including all fax technologies.

Matsushita Panasonic was number one in the German market and its share amounted to about 16 % in 1996. The majority of the machines were ink jet faxes. Uncertainty about the question whether a dumping investigation would be opened and measures would be taken reduced its share to almost 5 % 1 year later. Matsushita was mainly present in those two technology segments in which the impact of dumping and fierce competition had been toughest, in the thermo sensitive paper (TSP) and inkjet technologies, as the Table 14.1 shows. Stiff competition from extremely price competitive Hewlett Packard, Olivetti as well as from Canon served this market leader a severe blow in the German office market, and its share in the consumer market also fell considerably. Uncertainty in the market of TSP, due to an unexpected initiation of a dumping investigation and harsh competition in the TSP market, especially the consumer fax machines, affected Panasonic's position severely.[8] The company is not present in TT PPF and in laser. Laser technology especially yielded a more favourable position. The direction of technology in Table 14.1 is clear. TSP lost position, and TT did win strongly as compact printing technology.

Prior to the opening of the investigation, two product technologies were especially applicable to personal or consumer faxes, and other technologies quickly advanced in the same direction of smaller home appliances. TSP was still the core of home fax market, but the advantage of plain over thermal paper was decisive. Thermo transfer gradually gained the upper hand in personal fax. Table 14.2 shows the quantities sold in Germany in 2 months of 1996 and 1997.

Thermo transfer (TT) PPF would soon overtake the other thermal technology TSP. In terms of price and volume involved, the trend was clearly toward TT, inkjet and laser PPF. A definite shift took place from TSP and LED faxes towards other technologies. Table 14.3 lists the relation between volume increase and price decrease (elasticities). If the quantity increase in response to the price decrease is more one, demand is neither elastic nor inelastic. If it is less than one, demand is inelastic, and if it is more than one, demand is elastic. Cross-effects of price movements pose a problem. Prices of technologies and inherent advantages of the technologies have mutual effects. Prices of the consumables are also extremely important. Consumables are the products needed for operation of the printer: thermo-sensitive paper, foil for TT PPF, ink, toner etc.

Total demand in Table 14.3 increased less than 1 % in reaction to a price decrease by 1 %, i.e. the elasticity is 0.77, but electronics prices decreased anyway. The decrease by 18.3 % of thermal paper fax prices decreased rather than increased demand. That is partly due to the greater decline of prices of the more expensive segment of TT PPF machines. Price reduction by 17.8 % of light emitting diode (LED) technology did not stop the dip in demand. Since LED and laser are like technologies, the price decrease of LED should have attracted some of the growth

[8] The exporters assured their customers that their political intervention would prevent an opening of a dumping investigation. Indeed, some member states voted against the opening of the investigation, which is to the knowledge of the author, a rare phenomenon in anti-dumping.

Table 14.2 Sales and share in sales per fax printing technology (Table 14.2 shares the same basis as the source referenced in the previous note)

Technology	Sales in units in month			Share in total sales		
	1996[a]	1997[b]	Change (%)	1996[a] (%)	1997[b] (%)	Change (%)
Thermo sensitive paper	84,670	78,076	−7.8	60.5	51.0	−15.8
Thermo transfer PPF	12,086	22,198	83.7	8.6	14.5	67.7
Laser PPF	11,480	16,648	45.0	8.2	10.9	32.6
LED PPF	3,490	1,346	−61.4	2.5	0.9	−64.7
Ink jet PPF	28,309	34,885	23.2	20.2	22.8	12.7
Total in units	140,035	153,153	9.4			

[a]June/July
[b]August/September

Table 14.3 Price elasticities of fax printing technologies (1996–1997) (Table 14.3 is based off of the same source as the preceding table)

Technology	Price decrease (%)	Volume-price reaction
Thermo sensitive paper	18.3	−0.40
Thermo transfer PPF	26.4	3.17
Laser PPF	13.1	3.45
LED PPF	17.8	−3.46
Ink jet PPF	22.3	1.04
Total faxes	**12.7**	**0.77**

from laser technology applications. It did not. The choice by Toshiba, Oki and Samsung for LED technology appeared not highly attractive and profitable. The overall price decrease was less than the price decrease of individual technologies. An autonomous shift towards more expensive categories of printing device must have caused this. The move towards TT PPF and laser is the most important for the anti-dumping case of home fax machines.

14.2 Technologies and Markets: European Producers, Market and Distribution

Philips specialised in consumer faxes. French SAGEM produced various ranges and was extremely advanced in the TT PPF. The main European Community producers were SAGEM, Philips and Olivetti, which also produced in Taiwan and partly purchased from Cal-Comp and others in East Asia. Siemens, Alcatel, DETEWE were small-scale producers of heavy professional equipment. The market was unclear because of the great number of Original Equipment Manufacturers (OEM) suppliers and customers. Table 14.4 below shows this phenomenon.

Table 14.4 Examples of OEM and stencil branded fax supplies

Supplier	Brand and OEM/stencil brand customer
D and B El. Corp. (Taiwan)	DBFax, Doro
Cal-Comp Electr. (Thailand)	Olivetti, Triumph-Adler, Xerox
Daewoo Tel. Ltd. (Korea)/ITO	Daewoo, Olympia, Triumph-Adler, Deutsche Telekom
Double Kingdom Ltd (Hong Kong/ China)	Alcatel, Amstrad, Cresta, Loewe, SIP
Kinpo Electronics Inc., Taiwan	Bosch, Kinpo, Olivetti, PTT Telecom, SIP, Triumph Adler
Murata Machinery Co Ltd. (Japan/ China)	Facit, Mita, Murata
Philips	Philips, Grundig, Ricoh, Schneider, ITO
SAGEM	Sage, France Telecom, Deutsche Telecom, Siemens
Sindo Ricoh (Korea)	Lanier, OKI, Olympia, Ricoh
Tokyo Electric Co. (TEC) (Japan/ Malaysia)	TEC, Telia, Vocofax, Xerox
Toshiba (Japan/Malaysia)	Alcatel, ITT, Lanier, TEC, Toshiba, Xerox

From the brands involved in Table 14.4, the conclusion that OEM supplies took place in all segments is obvious. Customers of Taiwanese and Korean suppliers are particularly telecom companies and small office distribution customers, like Triumph Adler and Olympia.

1. *Big office*. SAGEM, Olivetti, Siemens and DETEWE were the main Europeans in this field. Various office distributors sold in their distribution channels both own made or purchased products: Xerox, Facit, Gestetner, Bosch and various Japanese producers specialised in this segment in which they also sell their copiers and printers: Canon, Ricoh, Toshiba, Minolta and Konica. Xerox, for instance, sold fax machines it purchased from ten different suppliers. The document processing and management company Lanier, related to Ricoh, distributed fax machines from Oki, Sindo Ricoh, Sanyo, Sharp, and Toshiba. This segment of major office distribution represented about 35 % of the market in money terms and 8 % in volume. Various producers supplemented their range with products from other producers, often the cheaper range.
2. *Small office and home office* (SOHO). Former typewriter firms like Triumph Adler, Olympia, and Olivetti were active in this market segment, but not necessarily as producer. Triumph Adler, for instance purchased from Cal-Comp Electr. (Thailand), Daewoo Tel. Ltd. (Korea), Funai Electric (China), Kinpo Electronics Inc. (Taiwan), Olivetti (Taiwan) and Olivetti-Lexikon, Italy. All of this business was OEM business or stencil brand supplies.[9] The need to survive forced their presence in various technologies. Olivetti produced certain components in Italy, which it shipped to Asia and

[9] OEM equipment has both the brand and the specifications of the distributing customer. The stencil brand fax is a standard machine purchased the customer's brand name marked on it. The difference between the two is generally small.

re-imported after assembly, i.e. the outward processing regime described in Chap. 6, Sect. 6.3. Brother, Sharp and Hitachi specialised in SOHO equipment. Matsushita was, of course, also strongly represented in this part of the market. This market represented in 1996 15–20 % of the total market, but declined quickly.

3. *Telecom distribution*, covering mainly small business and the consumer market. Telecom companies have their own distribution networks and sell telephone equipment under their brand. Telecom companies purchased relatively a lot from Taiwan and Korea. However, Matsushita was also strong supplier of telecom-branded equipment. Kinpo's supplies from Taiwan, for instance, were found in the shops of the Italian, Belgian and Dutch telecom companies under telecom brands. Alcatel distributed fax machines it had purchased from Double Kingdom (Hong Kong with factory in China) and Toshiba. Double Kingdom also supplied Amstrad, Loewe and Cresta. French SAGEM supplied Dutch, British and French telecom. Some telecom companies purchased European-made fax machines using a Japanese firm as intermediary and leaving these intermediaries a handsome trade margin. The intermediaries were, for instance, ITO Communications and Funai, which were also producers. Telia and Deutsche Telekom purchased from ITO, instead of making purchasing efforts themselves. Serving both the small business and the consumer markets, the telecom companies originally had a reasonably strong and comfortable position without much competition from consumer distribution. The share of the telecom firms in the market increased steadily until 1995. In Germany, the share rose to 10 %, in Italy to more than 20 % and the United Kingdom and France to about 30 %. The estimates for Belgian, Dutch, Swedish and Spanish telecom firms are in the same range. Gradually the market share of these telecom firms declined. It was, therefore, understandable that they protested heavily to their governments, with which they still in spite of some privatisations had excellent relations, blaming an anti-dumping proceeding for this misfortune instead of the competition by the consumer distribution.
4. *Consumer distribution*. Stagnating sales of audio and video equipment and domestic appliances forced this distribution segment into computer and related products and fax. Increasingly big chains took over the consumer electronics distribution. Examples are Media Markt in Germany and some other countries, Dixons and Currys in the United Kingdom and Darty in France. Companies such as Panasonic (Matsushita), Sanyo, Sharp, Samsung and Philips, offering a wide range of consumer products and therefore having distribution strength, were strongly present in the consumer segment. Philips was the first to effectively target the consumer market with its three-in-one Message Machine: telephone, fax, and answering machine with comfort and size of a telephone, soon copied by others. The size of this part of the market was 20–30 % of the total fax market, but increased quickly.

14.3 Trade and Distribution in Exporting Countries: The Competitiveness Issue Again

Distribution in Asia is similar. Economic organisation in Europe and Asia differs and so does the volume differentiation over market segments. Typical for Japanese industrial organisation are a relatively limited number of very big corporations, and a mass of small ancillary supply and distribution enterprises. Fax production was differentiated accordingly. It comprised bulky machines for big international companies. On the other hand there is the mass of dependent ancillary suppliers and traders, dependent on big business. They use SOHO equipment. When Korea and Taiwan, Japan's main Asian competitors, offered small fax machines on export markets in the West at prices that Japanese producers could not meet, Japanese manufacturers transferred production to low cost locations, mainly in South East Asia and China. The initial loss of competitiveness did not result in additional imports from those countries that had been accused by the Communication Industry Association of Japan to be the main cause of the problems in the European Community, i.e. Korea and Taiwan.

In addition to SOHO equipment, specific consumer fax machines had been developed in Japan, Korea, Taiwan and China in accordance with consumers' need for handwritten communication. The characters required handwriting, and the fax machine was an excellent medium for handwritten communication. That implied a booming consumer market, but as made clear in previous Chapters, the consumer market in Japan is not very attractive for both Japanese consumers and prospective non-Japanese exporters to Japan. The distribution networks directly related to manufacturers enabled oligopolistic pricing in the way described in Chaps. 7 and 8, leaving the Chinese and Taiwanese produces not have much chance in this market with its extremely attractive high prices.

The gap between Japanese domestic and export prices had taken preposterous proportions. Import and export statistics are illustrative. Japan's imports from Southeast and East Asia are imports from relocations of cheap fax machine production. These products find their way to Japan, but competitive products from Taiwan, Korea and the United States face uncommon barriers. The exports in 1996 from the various countries to Japan were low and to the European Community were high, as the Eurostat and the Japanese customs reveal in Table 14.5. A highly competitive country, Korea, supplied only 18,170 units or 1.6 % of Japanese imports and 0.7 % of the Japanese market. The machines imported in Japan were cheaper than those imported into the European Community. This difference of 19.5 % is attributable to the fact that imports by Ricoh and Oki from Korea were limited to low specification machines, whereas the high-end faxes were produced in Japan. The machines imported were mainly low-end consumer and SOHO thermo sensitive paper faxes made by the Korean-Japanese joint venture Sindo-Ricoh for distribution in Japan by Ricoh and Oki.

Prices in Japan and the European Community in Table 14.5 show a clear difference. In Table 14.6, a comparison is made on a model-by-model basis

Table 14.5 Fax imports into Japan and the EU-15 (1996, prices in ECU = €)

Imports of facsimile machines in Japan 1996	Japan units	Share Japanese market (%)	EEC units	Share EEC market (%)	Japan average price imports	EEC average price imports
China (Funai, Murata, Sanyo)	256,117	9.8	171,647	4.1	€146.18	€276.15
Hong Kong (Sanyo/ Murata)	8,198	0.3	128,718	3.1	439.11	195.39
Japanese production	1,500,000	57.4	623,292	14.9		319.81
Korea (Ricoh, Oki)	18,170	0.7	768,544	18.4	153.54	183.55
Malaysia (Brother, TEC-Toshiba)	515,024	19.7	70,468	1.7	190.35	189.74
Singapore (Panasonic)	61,884	2.4	71,408	1.7	179.13	329.29
Taiwan	36,681		189,161	4.5	167.28	210.86
Thailand (Canon, Oki, Fujitsu, Sharp)	254,742	9.7	242,461	5.8	192.50	187.20
Total Japanese subsidiaries/ Asia excl. Japan	**1,114,135**	42.6	**1,453,246**	34.8	181.30	
United States	511	0.0	53,721	1.3	420.10	288.93
Total imports	1,151,327	44.0	**2,352,479**	56.3	180.96	241.78
Total market (including domestic production)	**2,614,135**		**4,175,000**			

between the Panasonic fax Panafax UF-P1 sold in Japan and the similar Panafax UF-S1 sold in Germany, both made in Singapore. The survey of imports and import prices in Japan and Europe in Table 14.5 shows that Korea and Taiwan did not have the slightest opportunity on the Japanese market. Only the countries with substantial Japanese presence export to Japan.

As Table 14.6 shows, similar fax machines, UF-P1 and UF-S1, were shipped from Singapore and sold in Japan at a huge profit margin and in the European Community at disruptive prices. The price gap was 61 %. The actual dumping margin found during the investigation for Matsushita Panasonic Singapore was considerably lower at 30.1 %. The normal value was based on sales in Singapore instead of Japan where the selling price was substantially higher. Initially the complainant thought that the UF-S1 was produced in Japan and it calculated normal value for Japan. The price discrimination between the Japanese and European sales cannot, according to the World Trade Organization's (WTO) agreement on anti-dumping, serve as basis for dumping calculations. For products originating in

Table 14.6 Panasonic's Singaporean home faxes dumping: Japan and Europe compared (ECU rate = €)

Panasonic UF -P1 (made in Singapore) sold in retail in Japan			
Listed retail price (in Japan)		¥64,800	
Rebate	45.73 %		20,334
Net actual retail price (in Japan)			44,466
Dealer's margin (in Japan)	25 %		8,893
Price to retail trade (in Japan)			35,573
Wholesaler's margin (in Japan)	15 %		4,640
Net wholesale price (in Japan)			30,933
Consumption tax	3 %		901
Price in Japan of Singapore fax machine		¥30,032	
1 ECU is Yen	75.589		€397.31
Panasonic UF- S1 (Singapore) price in Germany's retail			
Actual retail average price in Germany of Singapore Panasonic fax		DM 508.00	
Value added tax (in Germany)	17.5 %		66.26
Net retail price			441.74
Dealer's margin (in Germany)	25 %		88.35
Price to retail trade			353.39
Wholesaler's margin (in Germany)	15 %		46.09
Landed price (in Germany)			307.30
Import duty	7.5 %		21.44
CIF export price from Singapore			285.86
Shipment costs	0 %		5.61
FOB ex-works price from Singapore		DM 280.25	
DM is	0.5455	ECU	€152.88
Sales price in Japan			€327.14
Export price to Germany from Singapore			152.88
Margin between sales price in Japan and Germany			174.26
CIF value			€285.86
Margin as % of CIF value			61 %

Singapore,[10] the Singapore normal value applies. The Japanese market can still serve as profit centre, while the products are dumped for the sake of cost cutting, but if based on dumping margins, duties are lower. Japanese undercutting of Philips' prices, with products from within or outside Japan, was substantially less than undercutting by Koreans or Taiwanese. Dumping margins of the latter were far less than Japanese dumping. The conclusion is, as it was from the cases on microwave ovens, VCR and television sets, that the Japanese efficiency was far below the level of the their Asian competitors and also below the level of the European competitors, which were not able to dump.

[10] In this case the simplest assembly is originating. All inputs are of a different customs heading than the final product.

Another conclusion is that Japan has always been a cul-de-sac for non-Japanese exporters. The Japanese price level shows lack of competition, but non-Japanese producers do not succeed in entering that market. The United States and Europe had to bear the burden of the economic growth in Asia. Producers in Taiwan and Korea are highly competitive in small office and home equipment and their competitive products would easily sell in Japan if there were free distribution. Like the Japanese, Taiwanese and Korean producers also enjoyed relatively inaccessible markets that allowed them to dump at prices that undercut European prices. Their dumping was substantially less, however, indicating greater relative competitiveness compared with the Japanese. They also undercut Japanese prices in Western markets when Japanese competitors still produced in Japan. Japanese producers were thereby forced to cut costs and to relocate their small business equipment production to South East Asia. From these low-cost countries they were not only capable to dump on the European Community market and to undercut the complainant's prices, but also to resist competition from other Asian producers better. Table 14.7 shows the price fight between the Japanese and their other Asian competitors. This mutual competitive strife damaged their own positions, and certainly those of the Europeans.

The move of Japanese producers to locations in China and South-East Asia had an advantage of formidable profits on their sales in Japan, similar to those depicted in Table 14.6, and lower costs for low price exports to the United States and Europe. Nevertheless, Japanese producers had higher individual dumping margins wherever they were located. Dumping margins on exports from Japan were higher than from elsewhere, but their undercutting was less. The situation confirms the conclusions from the Tosoh case and the experience in the compact disc player dumping case: the Japanese were not efficient, not even when they produced in low cost countries.[11]

Table 14.7 illustrates the phenomenon of Japanese lack of competitiveness. By a dumping margin of 49.2 % on its exports from Japan, shown in Table 14.7, Brother Industries appeared capable of undercutting prices of Philips by only 7 %. Sanyo needed a dumping margin of more than 100 % for undercutting Philips' prices of similar models by 28.1 %. All Japanese firms dumped more than other Asian competitors. Again, the competitiveness of the Japanese was much applauded, but highly overestimated and, the facts indicate, non-existent. The biggest producer in Korea, Samsung, with the biggest home market, was capable of dumping to a considerable extent, but not as much as the Japanese. All other Korean price undercutting was more than the dumping and that points to competitiveness compared with the Japanese.

[11] If all duties are classified according to the lesser duty, i.e. if the dumping margin is less than the injury margin, or vice versa, the Japanese (in Japan or abroad) show a higher dumping than injury margin. The exception is Murata (China/Hong Kong), with a definitive dumping margin of 21.2 % and injury margin of 23.5 %.

Table 14.7 Fax dumping and undercutting: Japan and the competitiveness gap

	Definitive dumping margin (%)	Provisional injury threshold (%)	Definitive duty[a] (%)	Lesser duty
China				
Murata Machinery (HK) Ltd (Hong Kong)	21.2	23.5	21.2	Dumping
Highsonic Industrial Ltd (Hong Kong)	23.2	59.3	23.2	Dumping
Others	51.6	74.2	51.6	Dumping
Japan				
Brother Industries Ltd	49.2	7.0	7.0	Injury
Tottori Sanyo electric Co., Ltd	124.2	28.1	28.1	Injury
Others	130.2	34.9	34.9	Injury
Korea				
Daewoo Telecom Ltd	11.6	61.6	11.6	Dumping
Tae Il Media Co., Ltd	9.2	50.8	9.2	Dumping
Samsung Electronics Co., Ltd	19.8	17.4	17.4	Injury
Nixxo Co., Ltd	7.5	54.8	7.5	Dumping
Others	25.1	73.1	25.1	Dumping
Singapore				
Matsushita Graphic Communication Systems (S) Pte Ltd	30.1	7.7	7.7	Injury
Others				
Malaysia				
Others (Tottori Sanyo's dumping margin)	124.2	89.9	89.8	Injury
Taiwan				
Kinpo electronic, Inc	6.0	32.4	6.0	Dumping
Sampo Corporation	56.2	35.8	35.8	Injury
Others	60.8	36.6	36.6	Injury
Thailand				
Cal-Comp Electronics (Thailand) Co., Ltd (Kinpo Thailand)	10.4	40.7	10.4	Dumping
Others	22.6	47.3	22.6	Dumping

[a]If the duty is lower than the dumping margin, the duty is based on the injury margin or threshold

Some manufacturers appeared to have gone for price only, trying to save market share at the cost of price-cutting. Japanese manufacturers voiced the view that others were more to blame for price decreases. As Table 14.8 shows, that is incorrect. Admittedly, the price level of Samsung's SF 30 was absurdly low (€191.54, compared with Philips' €512.34). A further price decrease was hardly possible. Sharp's price, however, was not much higher and Murata showed a price level of its Muratec machines verging to charity (initially €159,09, but ending with €118.55). These machines must have been sold at marginal cost or even below.

Table 14.8 Price destruction in the German thermo sensitive market (Philips €512.34 = 100)

Thermo sensitive paper producers/brands (1)	Models: T = Telephone; TAM = Telephone Answering machine (2)	1996[b] AVG (3)	1997[b] AVG (4)	1997/1998[b] AVG (5)	Change in price 1998/1996 (6) (%)
Muratec (China)	M 700 Thermo sensitive + T	31	23	23	−5.8
Samsung (Korea)	SF 30 Thermo sensitive + T	37	32	33	−4.8
Samsung (Korea)	SF 100 Thermo sensitive + T	40	37	36	−4.9
Sharp (Thailand)	UX 70 Thermo sensitive + T	40	32	32	−10.4
Triumph Adler (Taiwan) (S)[a]	FX 505 Thermo sensitive + T	41	31	31	−9.0
Olympia (Korea, Daewoo) (S)	OF 620 Thermo sensitive + T	42	40	40	−1.9
Philips	HFC 4/21 Thermo sensitive + T	45	39	39	−9.1
Amstrad (China, Double Kingdom) (S)	FX 8400 AT Thermo sensitive + T	46	39	38	−4.7
Sanyo (China)	SFX 33 Thermo sensitive + T	54	33	33	−5.7
Brother (Malaysia)	FAX 570 Thermo sensitive + T	55	47	47	−6.2
Bosch (Taiwan, Kinpo) (S)	FAX-TEL 216 Thermo sensitive + T	60	44	44	−10.0
Panasonic (Singapore)	UF-S1 Thermo sensitive + TAM	65	51	51	−10.6
Brother (Malaysia)	FAX 470 Thermo sensitive + T	65	51	51	−5.7
Toshiba (Malaysia)	TFP 25/55/71 Thermo sensitive + T	66	42	60	−15.3
Alcatel (S) (China)	FAX 130 Thermo sensitive + T	71	52	52	−11.4
Panasonic (Singapore)	UF-V 60 Thermo sensitive + TAM	77	61	60	−6.9
Philips	HFC 12 Thermo sensitive + TAM	100	75	75	−7.1
Total above average prices		46	39	37	−9.3

[a](S) is stencil or OEM brand supplied to customer/distributor with latter's brand
[b]Periods: 1996 (June/July), 1997 August/September, 1997/1998 (December/January)

Price behaviour of some of the players in the German market is shown in Table 14.8. In columns (3)–(5) the average retail market prices, including VAT, in June/July 1996 – half a year before the Investigation Period (IP) of the proceeding, August/September 1997 in the IP and December 1997/January 1998 are given in index for certain models. The period of December 1997/January 1998 was chosen because it was just before the formal opening of the proceeding, which the exporters expected for a long time and against which they had launched a fierce lobby. In column (6), the average price change in these periods is reported. Finally, the percentage level of discrepancy between the minimum and average prices is given in column (7). If the sum of sales in the three periods is more than the sum of the stocks, it may be concluded that the price decreases are not a sign of stock clearance by retail trade, but indicate the aggressiveness of the producer or the distributor. Where stocks were higher than sales level, the minimum price is treated as sign of stock clearance and the space was left blank.

Apparently, Japanese exporters expected that the investigations would not be opened. They communicated their expectations in this respect to European customers and they must have expected that their lobby was successful, for they continued to cut prices, which influenced their dumping margins found in the investigation. In any case they defied their own statistics, by which they tried to prove that other countries especially were responsible for the price decay in Europe. This – as Table 14.7 shows – proved incorrect.

14.4 Fax Market Volume and Trends

In 1991, Japan's production amounted to $3,089 million. In 1994, this amount had decreased by about 8 % to $2,855 million. The Japanese market was $1,052 million in 1991, but it decreased in value by 16 %. Only 45 % of production was for Japanese consumption. Europe's market rapidly exceeded Japan's, both in size and growth.[12] While Japan's market remained at a $900 million level, the EC market showed healthy growth, with a market of $1,200 million in 1992 and $ 1,400 million 4 years later. Various aspects of the Japanese market would give Japanese producers a volume advantage, which could easily be translated into a natural competitive edge. Europeans had to cope with a fragmented home market with divergent national communication standards and this influenced their production process and costs.[13] This did not point toward higher European cost, but to a disadvantage.

Market estimates of European market of all fax machines diverged, as Table 14.9 shows.

Differences between various fax market estimates in Table 14.9 seem striking. The figures commonly indicate a growth trend in the market. InfoSource, a market

[12] Yearbook of World Electronic Data, several editions.

[13] The statement that the same applies to Japanese exporters is a truism, which denies the problems in the production process itself. If products have to fit national European requirements, the production process is not one big flow with some adjustments to national standards, as it is for Japanese with a big homogenous home market and with the need to adjust to some export markets.

Table 14.9 Estimated European total European fax market

Fax market estimate by	1993	1994	1995
InfoSource	2,270,470	2,971,910	3,372,450
BIS	2,192,140	2,805,820	3,123,370
Dataquest	2,233,128	2,521,662	2,771,308

research institute most generally relied upon in the fax business, had the most comprehensive surveys on the fax machine market. In its position paper distributed among member states and the European Commission services the Communications Industry Association of Japan (CIAJ) mainly used InfoSource figures.[14]

Quantitative growth in the European fax market was mainly attributable to home, personal or consumer faxes. The European Commission found that the market had risen from 1,173,416 units in 1993 to 2,583,587 in 1996, or by 120 %. It was clearly a growth market, particularly in units. This was a trend in contrast with developments in the professional segment where volume stagnation prevailed. Market growth differed per technology segment. The German market is generally considered a representative market for the total European Community. In the 1996 (June-July) German market, thermo sensitive paper represented 61 % of total sales in units. Slightly more than 1 year later the share of thermo sensitive paper technology in total sales had declined to 51.0 % (August-September 1997).[15] Its share in money sales in 1996 was 34 % of total sales. One-year later money sales had been reduced to 26.5 % of total sales. Price erosion was significantly stronger in this segment than in segments in which competition was practically limited to Japanese producers (laser and LED). From these data, some background of the strategy of Japanese exporters can be explained. The change in composition of the market explains why Japanese manufacturers lobbied so intensively against a case involving other technologies than thermo sensitive paper faxes. They hoped to get a free play with non-TSP technology after measures were imposed.

The shift to higher the end, like thermo-transfer and other plain paper technology, did not stop the Japanese exporters from dumping and undercutting with respect to those machines in less direct competition with Korean and Taiwanese technologies. Exporters from these countries were blamed for the price decay, however.[16] The shift of certain productions to other Asian locations concealed the

[14] On 8 July 1996 the Communications Industry Association of Japan (CIAJ) and the Machinery Exporters' Association of Japan (JMEA, a private branch of the Japanese Ministry of Trade and Industry (MITI)) submitted a "Position Paper for the EU with regard to the anti-dumping problem concerning facsimile machines" to member states and European Commission.

[15] These data come from representative market studies on price developments in the consumer market, Gesellschaft für Konsumforschung, GfK.

[16] The CIAJ "Position Paper for EU with regard to the anti-dumping problem concerning facsimile machines" states that the "Japanese manufacturers' prices do not constitute a threat to EU producers." The thesis is clarified by the index of the average import prices from Japan, which developed from 100 in 1993 to 111 in 1995, whereas the price of others' decreased from 100 to 67. Others were unjustifiably blamed for the situation. CIAJ did not mention the fact that most producers had transferred production to these other countries.

fact that the Japanese were mainly involved in practices, of which they accused others. Although generally the weight of electronic products decreased, the average weight of faxes exported to the European Community went up from 8.35 kg in 1993 to 9.8 kg in 1995, indicating specialisation in heavier machines in Japan and transfer of production of lower segments to other Asia. A survey of the average price in the German market shows a pattern that differed from Japanese allegations; these price studies are based on brands rather than on provenance or origin of products. The issue was not one of low prices, but of dumping, and as Table 14.7 shows, the dumping margin of the Japanese was more than of others, although, as Tables 14.7 and 14.8 suggest.

14.5 Procedure: Politics, Pressure and Product Definition

14.5.1 Pressure and Product

Two European producers Philips and SAGEM prepared, originally together, a complaint on dumping. They represented more than 50 % of European production volume in units of all fax machines types, without differentiation according to application. In the middle of 1996 Japanese producers were aware of the preparation of a complaint. Exporters and their governmental interest protectors launched an offensive. They tried to pre-empt a complaint by massive intervention with European Commission and member states.[17] The trump card was pressure on SAGEM, which was technologically dependent on supplies of components and technology by Japanese competitors. The other producer, Philips, limited its vulnerability in this respect by purchasing policies aiming at supplies from component suppliers instead of dependence on direct competitors. SAGEM surrendered and abstained from open support. Successful blackmail of this European producer brought "standing" to the fore. The issue of standing included whether Philips represented sufficient production, the definition of "like product", which product should be the subject of the complaint and of the proceeding and measures would be in the interest of the European Community. In another position paper, the European Community was confronted with the successful result of Japanese pressure[18]:

[17] On 8 July 1996 the Communications Industry Association of Japan (CIAJ) and the Machinery Exporters' Association of Japan (JMEA, a private branch of the Japanese Ministry of Trade and Industry, MITI) approached member states and European Commission. They submitted a "Position Paper for the EU with regard to the anti-dumping problem concerning facsimile machines". Soon to be followed by another, more jubilant, one. Their triumph was that they had been capable to reduce the number of complainants.

[18] The "Position paper –2- for the EU with regard to the anti-dumping problem concerning facsimile machines." The CIAJ circulated this paper 3 months before submission of the complaint, but shortly after its pressures on the other producer, SAGEM, appeared successful.

We understand that the complaint is reportedly being prepared by only one manufacturer. There is a serious doubt if the manufacturer could truly present Community industry in terms of production share, etc. Would it be in the best interest of the European Community if such a complaint was allowed to be accepted which might lead to protective measures only that one manufacturer had requested?

Thus the Japanese wanted to harvest its intimidation tactics.

The strategy of the Japanese intervention was keen. First the number of complainants was restricted, which reduced the scope of the product definition. Similarly, to the method of Sony when it had convinced Thomson to abstain from opposing the inclusion of cheap broadcast cameras in the scope of measures against Japanese dumping of camera systems, the threat to SAGEM of a technological boycott resulted in abstinence from the complaint. Although a big fax producer, Philips did not produce big machines. The question remained to what extent this would have a consequence for the product definition in the complaint. The inclusion of all faxes in the complaint would create a precedent and an opening for free rider behaviour, in this case by SAGEM.

It was specifically the market of the small size personal consumer or home fax machines Philips had in mind when it started production in 1991. The objective of cooperation with Ricoh was to obtain the technology, especially printing. Before this cooperation, Philips had in-house knowledge of printer and telephone technology. It lost printer technology in the 1980s, when dumping from Japan forced it to close its factory in Germany. When it started again in the field of this combination of printing devices and telephones, it found a partner in Ricoh for printing technology. Ricoh specialised in up-market professional copiers, printers and fax machines. It did not seek the consumer market. Philips offered mass volume distribution possibilities and a suitable product design. Philips had neither much presence in the professional market nor the ambition to be there. Buy its launch of the message machine in 1993 as combination of fax, copier and answering machine in a telephone set it had clearly limited its production scope to distribution via the consumer electronics outlets.

SAGEM's abstention of support did not necessitate a change in definition of "like product", i.e. the product to be covered by a proceeding. The pressure by Japanese producers seemed impressively successful, but the definition of "like product" could still have covered all fax machines. The intervention of the Japanese industry associations and MITI raised several issues:

- From the procedural point of view: Should the remaining complainant Philips revise the product definition, the definition of "like product", i.e. the product to which the investigation should be limited in order to ascertain sufficient status as a complainant? By the revision of the parameters of "like product" and by a more tailored definition of the product concerned the remaining complainant, Philips represented a higher proportion of collective European Community output.[19]

[19] Article 5.4 of Council Regulation (EC) No 384/96 of 22 December 1995 (the Basic Regulation) is based on Article 4.1 of the WTO Agreement on Implementation of Article VI of the General

- From the view of general trade policy principle: A full-scale war on fax machines was considered, which implied inclusion of all fax machines in order to punish Japanese producers for the ruthlessness of their intervention.
- From the political point of view the question was whether the European Community would consider measures for a broad range of fax products reconcilable with the "Community interest", a concept so open to political manoeuvring.[20] If not, a narrower product scope, limited to consumer fax, was preferable.
- Also from a more general political point of view: Would, in view of the lobbying power of the telecom companies and their close relations with governments, the majority of the member states approve measures covering all products?

If all faxes were included, the standing of one producer was sufficient for a complaint that would fulfil representation requirements of the WTO agreement on anti-dumping and the Basic Regulation of the European Community. A single producer remaining as a complainant represented more than 25 % of non-related European production of total fax production. It was wondered whether SAGEM would oppose the opening. The response to a question in this respect was that it was not the intention. Olivetti could raise objections to the opening of the investigation. It was importer of small fax machines. It could have been excluded as related company but this would possibly result in opposition from this company, which could politically be important during and after the proceeding. The complaint could have covered all fax machines from China, Japan, Korea, Malaysia, Taiwan and Thailand and there was not any legal inhibition as to the expansion of the scope to all fax segments. This was due to the fact that al fax machines, regardless price and specifications, would be treated equal and the volume of Philips' small fax machines production exceeded total combined production of other European producers. Although it was tempting to retaliate against Japanese pressure, the

---

Agreement on Tariffs and Trade. It defines "domestic industry"; in this case, the industry under the definition was the European Community industry. Therefore, according to the Article, a complaint shall be considered to have been made by or on behalf of the European Community industry if it is supported by those European Community producers whose collective output constitutes more than 50 % of the total production of the like product produced by that portion of the European Community industry expressing either support for or opposition to the complaint. However, no investigation shall be initiated when European Community producers expressly supporting the complaint account for less than 25 % of total production of the like product produced by the European Community industry.

[20] Article 21 of the Basic Regulation concerning European Community interest states that a determination as to whether the European Community interest calls for intervention shall be based on an appreciation of all the various interests taken as a whole, including the interests of the domestic industry and users and consumers; and a determination pursuant to this Article shall only be made where all parties have been given the opportunity to make their views known pursuant to paragraph 2. In such an examination, the need to eliminate the trade distorting effects of injurious dumping and to restore effective competition shall be given special consideration. Measures, as determined on the basis of the dumping and injury found, may not be applied where the authorities, on the basis of all the information submitted, can clearly conclude that it is not in the European Community interest to apply such measures. No such article exists in the WTO agreement on anti-dumping.

objective of anti-dumping is elimination of injury due to dumping, not realisation of general trade policy objectives.

Limitation of the scope of the product to consumer fax machines seemed economically and legally and certainly also politically the most suitable course.[21] The objective was limited to eliminating injury to the producers' own production and to goals politically feasible. A limitation by means of size and weight could achieve an adequate restriction to personal faxes.[22]

The redraft of a complaint was preceded by an investigation into the specifications of products. 227 Models were analysed for a proper and more precise product definition. The main function was the telephone function, to which the fax function is added. Professional fax machines often were fax machines only, with some additional telephone possibilities. Additional features such as dialling memory, hands-free telephoning, answering machine, cordless telephone functions were analysed. It was found that if the home, personal or consumer fax had to be distinguished from professional equipment, the size was a decisive parameter. But in view of the necessary solidity and bulk of professional equipment, the combination of size and weight appeared to offer the best distinction for the home fax. Products with relatively small dimensions were the appropriate selection. In terms of price brackets, the products should also distinguish themselves from office equipment. The latter condition could not be applied strictly, of course. Price is not a characteristic and possibly indication of dumping. Some products offer an abundance of features and others are without more facilities than telephone and fax functions, but all were consumer faxes. The borderline was roughly DM 600 (€309) for TSP (thermo sensitive paper) fax machines. The upper limit for plain paper was DM 1200 (€619). Below these limits, products were acceptable as simple personal or consumer fax machines. SAGEM and its OEM customers had a price level for plain paper consumer faxes with thermo transfer technology of about DM 1140 (€587). Because of the marginal presence of such plain paper personal faxes in the market at that time, these prices were still premium prices, but undoubtedly they would drop more rapidly than any other technology as soon as dumping exporters acquired the technological ability to produce them. This was partly due to technical issues and the patent situation in printer technologies.

The other characteristics of the 227 models were analysed for the definition of consumer fax machines. Printing technology, features, dimensions and weight were parameters. With a few exceptions, the dimensions of inkjet products were below

---

[21] The situation is comparable with plain paper copiers, in which the Japanese exporters stated that their products were dissimilar from the products made by European copier producers. Small personal copiers had to be exempted from the procedure. In the case of fax machines, the approach of a narrowing down the product definition was also met with dissatisfaction.

[22] Machines with a facsimile function with a weight not exceeding 5 kg, excluding the paper load and the set for the cordless hand-held telephone, and with a size (width × depth × height) of the main body not exceeding 470 mm × 450 mm × 170 mm. A study in depth of 60 different machines resulted in the conclusion that a gap exists between professional and consumer faxes of several kilograms and that the borderline of 5 kg was the best and would not cause confusion.

470 mm, 450 mm and 170 mm width, depth and height respectively. Their weight was 5.7 kg or above. The dimensions of laser machines, with exception of three, exceeded the assumed maximum of 470 mm × 450 mm × 170 mm. Their lowest weight was 6.8 kg. A distinction could not be made between personal and professional thermo transfer machines. SAGEM of France was capable of producing a very light thermo sensitive paper machine of 1.5 k only. It appeared also capable of production of a TT PPF with a weight with a weight of 2.7 kg. During preparations of a complaint it was clear that these products should also to be covered by the product definition. Philips was also developing a TT consumer PPF. Calculations indicated that all plain paper fax exports from Japan were dumped.[23] The relevant point was whether dumping procedures should be limited to existing technologies and whether measures should include technologies that are in developmental stage. It was clear that in the near future also ink jet and laser technology would be introduced in personal fax machines. Panasonic advertised sine laser machines as consumer fax equipment.

Dimension and weight offered a sharp and satisfactory delineation between professional and consumer fax machines. The product definition is fair to exporters incapable of offering small and light machines. As for the size of the equipment, almost all laser fax machines exceeded the volume of 470 × 450 × 170 mm. A few models were smaller, the Toshiba TF-501 and TF-505, the Sharp F0-2600 and the Minolta Fax 2500. The latter had a weight of only 2 kg superior to the limit of 5 kg. Almost all ink jet machines were inferior to the maximum dimensions for the personal faxes, but the weight criterion showed that the minimum discrepancy was 700 g, which is substantial. The heavy equipment appeared not applicable as consumer fax, although inkjet applications in personal fax machines were expected soon.

Without offering an alternative other than that the product concerned should be limited to thermo sensitive paper technology, the Japanese strongly attacked the criteria of size dimensions and weight prior to and during the procedure. The Japanese had convinced various members of the Anti-Dumping Committee of the European Community that these distinction criteria were inappropriate. That was not because they knew better criteria, but because they did not want measures at all and if there were measures they should be limited to one technology that would disappear in a few years. Technically, however, there were no serious disadvantages to the criteria proposed. The Japanese devised only one serious objection against the weight criterion. They claimed that electronic products tend to decrease in weight and that in the long run all products would be covered by the definition. Apart from the fact that because of massive non-cooperation, it was impossible for the European Commission to establish the undercutting of European prices with adjustments for the more expensive construction of plain paper faxes, this thesis does not hold. Electronics are a minor part of fax machine. The printing device and some non-electronic options determine the weight. Few Japanese were

[23] Van Marion (1993), gives an explanation for this phenomenon.

capable of making a thermo-transfer plain paper fax as light as SAGEM. Europeans appeared superior in personal fax technology. Their only problem was the price undercutting by dumping exporters.

14.5.2 Politics and Proceeding

The lobby effort of the Japanese CIAJ and MITI was almost successful. By rejecting the opening of the investigation, some member states appeared to embrace Japanese lobby interventions. The strong relation between telecommunication firms and member states contributed to this opposition. Japanese lobbying would in the first place have an impact on the product definition and later on the procedure itself and the acceptance of the measures by member states in the Council of Ministers.

Only a few per cent of total Japanese production cooperated with the procedure. In spite of the allegation that it represented all Japanese production, their association, CIAJ, was not very successful in convincing its members to loyally cooperate in the proceeding, if it ever even tried. Instead, the Japanese efforts by the CIAJ cartel and the Japan Machinery Exporters Association, a private branch of and funded by MITI, consisted, apart from the coercion on SAGEM, of frequent propagandistic and lobby interventions with European Commission and member states. Several papers were distributed to member states and European telecommunication enterprises before the opening of the investigation. In these papers and leaflets, CIAJ alleged that it acted on the behalf of all Japanese producers. Which companies it actually represented it did not disclose. Of 19 major Japanese producers, only two producing in Japan cooperated and only two Japanese subsidiaries abroad cooperated, Matsushita Graphics in Singapore and Murata in Hong Kong/China.[24] All others opted for lobbying and economic and political pressure. The procedure even stimulated cooperation between the Electronic Industry Association of Korea and CIAJ.[25]

It goes without saying that the Japanese political lobby pressed very hard for exclusion of all plain paper fax machines from the "like product" definition, i.e. from proceeding and measures. Japanese associations CIAJ and the MITI's organisation JMEA lobbied almost continuously with member states instead of cooperating in the procedure. They were almost fully rewarded. The European Commission finally decided to exclude the inkjet, laser and LED technologies, the background of which is sketched below. Japanese exporters believed, however, that the case could politically completely be crushed. Since Japan was the major

[24] Brother Industries, Ltd. and Tottori Sanyo cooperated for their Japanese operations. They did not cooperate for the bulk of their production elsewhere. Funai Electric, Matsushita Panasonic and Murata Machinery, Ltd. (Muratec) cooperated as non-Japanese exporters, i.e. exporters from Singapore and China. Japanese producers in Malaysia, Toshiba TEC and Brother, abstained from cooperation.

[25] Annual Report of EIAK on 1997 reports the first cooperative talks between the two associations.

production place of promising plain paper thermo transfer, the Japanese trade and exporters' associations renewed lobbying with member states. The extent to which this was successful remains unknown. Some member states never voiced an opinion, voted even against opening of a case, rallying behind their telecom companies; other member states voted traditionally against interests other than their own and against European Community trade policy in general.[26]

The intervention by a French Commission official, head of the injury department and deputy director, responsible for the relations between the anti-dumping division and the member states, later director of the Anti-Dumping Division, about whom the Chapters on television and about origin reported, presented a blow to the position of European industry and to proper proceedings. He said, in his office without presence of other officials, that the proceeding would not have the slightest chance without his collaboration. He was responsible for relations with the member states. This hidden threat was serious. If Philips did not exclude plain paper printer technology from the product concerned in the proceeding, he would not support the case with the European Commission and the member states and the case would fail. He demanded that all plain paper fax technologies be excluded from the complaint. Later, it appeared that he did not speak on behalf of the European Commission. In a dispute within the European Commission services he defended himself by the allegation that the change in product definition was the complainant's choice. The idea was that Philips did not do anything it did not want to do. Philips certainly did not want, however, to exclude the thermo transfer plain paper printing technology. It changed the product definition by omitting ink jet, laser and LED printing, but the thermo transfer fax was kept in. Since the French official did not take the trouble to look closely into the definition on the basis of some expertise, it escaped his attention that the changes were not completely in accordance with his own wishes or with, possibly, his promises to others. It was too late by the time he became aware of this omission. SAGEM had already launched the thermo transfer plain paper faxes and had a strong interest in inclusion of this technology in the "like product" definition. Philips was also on the verge of launching the product. SAGEM had been informed about the behaviour of their compatriot in the European Commission and it intervened with the French government with the result that the ambitions of the French Commission official were tamed and more in harmony with specific French economic interest.

Although there were no tenable arguments for the exclusion of any printing device or technology from the procedure on personal faxes – the personal nature of fax machines does not depend on printing devices -, the definition of product concerned was restricted to thermo sensitive paper (TSP) and thermo transfer (TT)

[26] The British department of Trade and Industry, now United Kingdom Department for Business, Innovation and Skills, leaked practically all confidential information distributed by the European Commission to interested exporters and importers and advised Japanese exporters how to lobby against measures. The Swedish representative in the anti-dumping committee was not allowed to vote in favour of measures proposed by the European Commission, unless he had asked permission from his minister. He rarely saw the minister.

printing devices. Use on the desktop or in the home was decisive, rather than the question how data transferred by telephone was finally printed. Part of the injury that the European Community industry incurred after the proceeding was attributable to unjustifiable further restriction of the product definition. The dumping continued in the personal fax segment with plain paper printing technology: mainly ink jet fax machines. The product definition had already been limited by the reduction of the scope to a certain weight and maximum sizes. Philips's estimate was that a small part of the home faxes contained the heavier printing technologies of ink jet or laser and that the criterion for home faxes based on weight and size would, although only provisionally, be sufficient to offer some relief from dumping and injury. Nevertheless, the play by this European Commission official was highly injurious and gave Japanese and some communication companies, supported by member states, new audacity.

14.6 From "Victims" to Customers: Anti-Dumping and Commerce

Fierce opposition from the communications companies Belgacom, Telia in Sweden, KPN in the Netherlands, Deutsche, France and British Telecom, and Telefónica could be perceived in the attitudes of representatives of member states in the Anti-Dumping Committee. Countries that were otherwise supportive of corrective measures against market disruptive dumping were reluctant to oppose dumping by Far Eastern producers. The vehemence of the communications industry was not very understandable. Their profitability would not be negatively affected by anti-dumping measures. The consumers would pay the bill of corrections for prices attributable to dumping. They acted, however, as if their profits would be reduced to abysmal levels. It seemed that their primary was that they prided themselves in their capability to purchase cheaply, and suddenly they had to find alternative sources.

A fruitful step of Bernard Donners, director of the fax unit, was that he paid visits to the protesters among the communications suppliers against the anti-dumping proceeding. The purchasing officers of communication firms especially became victims of his unprecedented move. The first was the purchasing and logistics director of Telia in Sweden. The company had recently been privatised. It founded Telia Asia Ltd in 1994 in order to purchase equipment in Asia, mainly in China. The visit to Telia near Stockholm began with a surprise. Ringing the doorbell did not have the desired effect. Much hilarity could be heard, but the door was not opened. The ring did not disturb people, loudly and cheerfully talking in the office. After the third ring the door was opened and the sight of a lively crowd in the coffee corner was offered. The director of purchasing emerged and led the way to his room. Bernard Donners explained the goal of his visit, marginally different from what he had promised. Formally, he wanted to explain the anti-dumping case of fax machines to the purchasing director of Telia. This person was also Chairman of the powerful Alliance Purchasing of Unisource, four telecom operators (Swedish Telia, Dutch KPN, Swiss PTT Telecom and Spanish Telefónica), a combination *inter alia* to keep purchasing prices low and profit margins high, and was a key person for additional sales. Proud that he was an employee of a company that now had to compete in the market instead of a state company's bureaucratic official, he stated that Philips should be more competitive. His face grimaced and became red as Telia's results account bottom-line, when his attention, by a gesture to the door, was drawn to the noisy hilarity in the hall near the coffee-corner, where Telia's staff still enjoyed their morning coffee and joyously faced the scourge of the market.

He understood that – with the roaring laughter outside his room – he should not talk too much about competition and market forces and developed a keen and vivid interest in the photographs of new Philips fax machines Bernard Donners showed him and that offered an alternative to the fax machines he still imported from the Far East, but about which he had started to develop some nervousness. In view of Telia's membership of the powerful purchasing syndicate of telecommunication companies and Telia's purchaser's chairmanship of this association, some interest from this purchasing league might be profitable.

A visit to the Dutch telecom provider and distributor of fax machines, KPN had the same goal during. The main personal fax machines distributed by this provider were Panasonic fax machines assembled in Singapore and Taiwanese equipment, mainly from Kinpo. KPN was extremely active in its opposition to the proceeding and to measures, which were depicted as highly negative for this company. During the proceeding it became apparent that Panasonic was wavering in decision-making and its sales in the European Community fell. Personnel and management of Panasonic in Singapore did not need to invent a pretext for mal-functioning; they just received it from Brussels in the form of an anti-dumping proceeding. The meeting with KPN was like attendance of a mass meeting in a Soviet ministry. The meeting room was more luxurious, but similarly overcrowded with KPN officials, all proud that they were at least equals of their visitors and now business people, who also had also to get used to the market torment rather than act as civil servants. There were only two Philips representatives and eight KPN people in the meeting room. In spite of the efforts of some of the KPN people to demonstrate how much they knew about the anti-dumping case, the director of the Philips fax business drew the attention of the meeting to his fine fax machines rather than the boring subject of anti-dumping and succeeded in convincing the purchasing people that measures against dumping would certainly – in contradiction to assurances by Japanese exporters, CIAJ, JMEA and diplomatic sources – be taken and in that case telecom distributors were too late for finding alternatives. They better make up their minds soon. Philips offered some beautiful fax machines as option. And, indeed, during the proceeding KPN took the risk that measures might be taken and switched to Philips for stencil brand supplies.

14.7 Original Equipment Manufacturers: A New and Original Concept

In the second VCR case, against Korea and two Japanese producers, the European Commission came across OEM supplies,[27] as it had done in various cases afterwards. In Chap. 8, it is demonstrated that profits on the domestic market increase by volume supplies abroad. OEM supplies are essentially volume supplies and are made at export prices far below normal market conditions. The European Commission's innovation of the reduction of Normal Value by application of a lower profit margin was besides economic rationale. The European Commission had gone astray by absence of domestic OEM sales, which phenomenon was attributable to the restriction of competition on the domestic market. Characteristic for OEM are extremely low export prices and, generally, absence of domestic OEM sales, at least a lower prices than the main producers' branded products.

The fax machines of Daewoo, Tae Il Media, Nixxo (Korea) or Kinpo and Sampo (Taiwan) or Cal-Comp Electronics (Kinpo in Thailand) were completely unknown to European consumers. These producers supplied to distributors as Deutsche Telecom, Olympia and Triumph-Adler and many other brands. These distributors – with the exception of Olivetti with its own production and distribution of fax machines – did not care very much about consequences of low pricing. They did not have production and did not care about the effects of price decay. This is an indication that OEM supplies generally undercut the prices of producers on the export market substantially.

All exporters selling under their own brands, with exception of Murata (China/ Hong Kong), of which the injury margin was somewhat higher had a higher dumping margin than injury margin.[28] This might be attributable to the fact that these companies were mainly Japanese. All Japanese had extremely high dumping margins. If they did not dump so much, they would probably have not been able to sell at all. The difference between the dumping and underselling is quite clear. With the exception of Sampo, all companies supplying only on OEM basis had a lesser dumping than injury margin. Since OEM normally contributes to profitability of domestic sales, there is no reason for another approach to the calculation of profits of OEM suppliers than for domestic sales in traditional channels. Since the VCR case, this had become practice. One Korean manufacturer exported only OEM fax machines. He requested a special treatment, i.e. a lower normal value for adjustment to level of trade. However the European Commission rejected the claim because "the investigation in Korea showed that there were no consistent nor distinct differences in prices on the Korean market between sales to OEM and

[27] Commission Regulation (EEC) No 2684/88 of 26 August 1988 imposing a provisional anti-dumping duty on certain imports of video cassette recorders originating in Japan and the Republic of Korea, OJ L 240, 31.8.1988, pp. 5–17.

[28] Injury margin is in this case underselling: which is undercutting of a price constructed from weighted average cost plus compensation for losses plus a target profit, of, in this case, 12 %.

own sales."[29] Consequently, if there are not any domestic OEM sales, as with VCR, the normal value is adjusted downward. If there are domestic OEM sales, the special treatment is denied to the exporter. That means that exporters from an oligopolistic domestic market where only a few exporters sell, the European Commission grants benefits of a lower normal value. How the small producers with no domestic sales are discriminated against, is shown in Chap. 16, Sect. 16.13.

14.8 Politics and Defeat of Principles: Playing the Rules

The impact of anti-dumping measures for fax machines on total trade was marginal. Imports of fax machines from the countries involved represented less than 0.2 % of the European Community's imports of office and telecommunication equipment and less than 0.1 % of the exports of such equipment from the countries concerned.[30] The Japanese industry association CIAJ referred in its papers to the Information Technology Agreement (ITA). Its argument was that measures would violate the spirit of the ITA. The spirit of the ITA and dumping do not coincide, however. This spirit would not be very strong if anti-dumping measures covering such a marginal volume of trade would damage it. The ITA covered tariff concessions and did not deal with non-tariff barriers in the form of restriction of competition in distribution nor with anti-dumping, which is part of WTO rules. Nevertheless, for some member states – the Netherlands among them – this was again an argument for voting against measures, reflecting the proud, but riskless, "principled" free-trade attitude, while favouring the national telecom provider.

Unprecedented economic pressure, political lobbying and even personal interventions of a European Community official and ensuing changes to product definitions, which would economically and legally have been unnecessary, preceded the proceeding. The product definition made a clear distinction between products for consumer, home or personal use. That distinction by means of size had been sufficient, but the weight limitation was added. Exclusion of certain technologies that had a strong impact on the price level of products covered by the procedure meant that recovery was less and slower than envisaged by measures. Even the distinction between fax machines above and below 5 kg had the disadvantage that recovery by European producers of the injury incurred would be retarded by exports of dumped equipment that is just above 5 kg. That is the gain the Japanese booked by their interventions, which was a loss to European Community respectable procedure.

---

[29] Commission Regulation (EC) No 2140/97 of 30 October 1997 imposing a provisional anti dumping duty on imports of personal fax machines originating in the People's Republic of China, Japan, Republic of Korea, Malaysia, Singapore, Taiwan and Thailand, OJ L 797/61, 31. 10. 97.

[30] Imports of fax machines (source Eurostat) divided by the imports and exports of this equipment (source WTO Annual Report 1997, Vol. II, p. 95).

Dumping and injury should determine the definition of a "like product". Only the product that is dumped is defined as "like product". In the case of fax machines all faxes were dumped, but the injury was mainly in the field of a certain application. The product definition was manipulated and had become an instrument of granting favours to exporters and importers of certain products. Olivetti behaved differently from the trend in this case. It imported its home faxes partly from Cal-Comp in Thailand and from its subsidiary on Taiwan. But Olivetti did not take a one-sided position and helped convince the Italian government to adopt a positive attitude toward measures. The influence of such distributors as British Telecom and Belgacom and some other telecom operators had as a consequence that some member states, normally prepared to support measures for the full period of 5 years, not only wanted some technologies to be excluded, but also demanded a limited period of application. They demanded the European Commission to limit the duration of the measures to 2 years instead of the normal 5 years. This implied that the European Commission would start a new procedure after 2 years. Belgium especially demanded such a review in exchange for a positive vote. In addition, the blatant discrimination on the side of some member states was a striking element in the decision-making.[31] The European Commission appeared to have violated the principle of non-discrimination by its concession to the interests of some telecommunication companies and claims by member states. In a decision of termination of an interim review for Japan and Singapore mentioned existence of:

> *In a declaration made by the Commission and annexed to the Minutes of the Council session of 27 April 1998, the Commission has agreed to re-examine the existing measures concerning Japan and Singapore if the producers/exporters concerned would submit sufficient evidence showing that the volume of the imports concerned into the Community is not such as to contribute substantially to the injury suffered by the Community industry. The reason for the declaration was that the investigation showed zero or low levels of price undercutting for Japan and Singapore (respectively), and that the market shares of the two countries had to be assessed on the basis of estimates, due to the absence of sufficient cooperation.*[32]

It meant that Brother and Matsushita Panasonic in Japan and Singapore as well possibly some other Japanese were designated as beneficiaries of a potentially shorter period of application of duties not intended for other exporters. The European industry was kept in the dark about these concessions. It did not receive any information about a shorter period of applicability of measures. Consequently, the industry did not have certainty about the time allowed for revival of its activities. As Table 14.7 shows, the European Commission's allegations about Panasonic and Brother were false. The undercutting was not marginal or zero. The undercutting had caused serious injury and losses to Philips and the level of injury was

[31] Again, an initiative of the official already mentioned in the Chap. 11 on television and origin and in this Chapter at other occasions.

[32] Notice of initiation of a review of the anti dumping measures applicable to imports into the European Community of personal fax machines originating in Japan and Singapore, 1999/C64/10, OJ 6.3. 1999.

substantial. Brother and Panasonic had the greatest market share in the European Community and obtained this market share before the opening of the investigation and before the investigation period. Nevertheless, they still maintained prices that were far – more than 30 % – below their own domestic market prices (and more than 60 % difference between Panasonic's price of imported products compared with export prices to Europe). Besides, the concession to the member states was a flagrant neglect of the European Community's own rule of the "lesser duty". The Korean exporter Nixxo and Taiwanese Kinpo had dumping margins of 7.5 % and 6 % respectively. The European Community discriminated in order to satisfy some member states. Thereby its damaged its image of an institution impartially and carefully implementing the law.

During the investigation, a revolution took place. All parties except Philips lost market share. More impressive was that Philips' share in the German market increased from 3.2 % in the middle of the Investigation Period (1 January 1996 to 31 December 1996) to more than 20 % a year later, but still during the investigation. Its average price decreased by 40 %, while the general average price decreased by 23 %. A striking phenomenon was that all Japanese and Korean producers with a brand name decreased their prices more than market average and, of course, more than distributors of OEM products. Not only did Philips' market share increase, it started to incur profits. Volume and learning curve effects improved quality and cost effectiveness. Before the initiation of the dumping investigation, losses per unit had decreased with increase of production, but this stopped in 1994 and the situation had worsened since. As soon as the dumping exporters, and especially their customers, started to become uncertain as to whether measures could be expected, they lost market share. When, however, it became increasingly probable that measures were to be expected, the exporters with brand names tried to defend or increase their market share before the measures were imposed.

Final measures were imposed on 27 April 1998 and the review was announced on 1 July 2000. The disreputable aspect of these measures were that they included a non-published decision that measures would not be applied for the full period normally applicable to such measures, i.e. 5 years, but that a confidential deal had been made in writing in the minutes of the Council. The same civil servant who intervened in order to limit the product scope had once again brokered some deal in favour of exporters. Some other performances have been sketched in the television case. The European Community industry had merely been granted 2 years of uninterrupted relief from vicious dumping. That relief period was even shorter. As soon as they mastered the thermo transfer technology sufficiently for the introduction of personal faxes with this technology, the exporters, especially the Japanese, shipped thermo transfer personal fax machines with a paper tray for plain paper and indicated as sizes of the equipment a height of more than 170 mm, which exceeded the minimum sizes of the personal faxes and the duties were circumvented. The minimum size – according to the Regulation – of the main body was 470 mm × 450 mm × 170 mm and the maximum weight was 5 kg. Some exporters adjusted quickly. Panasonic exported machines from China with a large paper tray that it thought or pretended the size of the main body exceeded the maximum. Brother launched its Thermo Transfer Fax models of the 900 series with a higher paper tray by which the machine exceeded the maximum height by 12 mm. Thus, it circumvented the duties.

Already on 6 March 1999, the European Commission announced opening of a review concerning Japan and Singapore. But the exporters did not cooperate. Nevertheless, the European Commission allowed the non-cooperative exporters a "further opportunity to the companies to provide a minimum of data on exports concerning the year 1996 and a statement of their willingness to receive an on-the-spot verification. This second attempt was equally unsuccessful".[33] The European Commission showed ample benevolence to the member states, awarding the telecom companies and their suppliers their benefits, but the exporters chose not to reveal the actual situation. Some had found their solutions.

More cooperation than before could not be expected from exporters. The European Commission felt compelled to conclude about cooperation in the initial proceeding[34]:

> *The level of cooperation by the producer/exporters in this proceeding was particularly low in Malaysia, Thailand, Taiwan, Japan and China, since the export volume to the Community covered by the cooperating exporting producers represented only a small fraction of the total exports from the countries concerned.*

There were no signs of moderation in undercutting, however. The machines both of Brother and Panasonic undercut the prices of Philips as apparent from the surveys of GfK in the period April/May 1999, i.e. after duties had been imposed and Brother had newly introduced its first 910 Thermo Transfer fax machine, which undercut the Philips' machine.

April/May 1999	Average price
Brother 910 thermo transfer	€231
Philips Magic Primo thermo transfer	€250
Undercutting at retail level	€19.00
As per cent of Philips price	7.6 %

The duties were not yet imposed in the period in which the made in Singapore Panasonic was compared with the Philips thermo sensitive paper fax. There was no Japanese moderation and the side-promise in the Council minutes was based on illusion or was deception.

[33] Commission Decision of 10 September 1999 terminating the anti-dumping review concerning imports of personal fax machines originating in Japan and Singapore (notified under document number C (1999) 2888), 1999/607/EC, Official Journal L 241, 11/09/1999, pp. 19–20.

[34] Commission Regulation (EC) No 2140/97 of 30 October 1997 imposing a provisional anti dumping duty on imports of personal fax machines originating in the Peoples Republic of China, Japan, Republic of Korea, Malaysia, Singapore, Taiwan and Thailand, OJ L 797/61, 31. 10. 97.

December 1997/January 1998	Average price
Panasonic UF-S1 thermo sensitive	€120.61
Philips HFC 21 thermo sensitive	€165.46
Undercutting at retail level	€44.84
As per cent of Philips price	27.1 %

14.9 Reorganisation and Relocation: End of a Business

When he took over the director of the fax business, Bernard Donners cleared the Philips organisation. Staff in marketing and market research, partly appointed because his predecessor wondered what the cause of the misfortune of the business unit was, tried to take part in the management strategies rather than fulfilment of their tasks. Serious price undercutting had inflicted havoc. The problem of necessary drastic cost cuts had been tackled by volume increases. The new director reduced staff and general expenses, which amounted to 15 % of the cost of production ex-works. He did not need the staff. He took responsibility for business decisions instead of relying on staff as a sort of insurance against failure. The result of the dismissal of staff was that now those remaining in marketing and market research paid attention to their actual jobs instead of would-be management. The new technical director Manfred Halbe drastically reduced technical problems, especially quality problems that were the consequence of rushed production changes applied under pressure of the havoc in the market. His policy created stability and restored quality. When anti-dumping measures were imposed the business was in shape for normal competition. It quickly gained market share. After the departure of these two directors, the situation soon deteriorated as the consequence of uncertainty about the continuation of measures, *inter alia*. This uncertainty at Philips led to an increase in the marketing and market research staff at the fax business as an insurance against wrong decisions. Overhead costs went up again. Instead of cutting staff cost, production was moved to Hungary. The reason was that costs had increased too much and president Boonstra of Philips had demanded measures. That was the argument for a decision in the course of 2001 to move the factory to Hungary. Transfer of manufacturing to Hungary an absurd decision, which was totally beside the point, as Table 14.10 shows.

Production labour represented 4 % of cost of production only. Manufacturing overheads were also relatively low and would not change much. Some cost items in SG&A were out of proportion. A transfer of manufacturing to Hungary would not reduce these general expenses of 12 %. The argument "we have to do something" out of fear for dismissal was the ground for this transfer of production by which the president of Philips could be satisfied. Slightly more than 2 years after imposition of

Table 14.10 Fax machines: Philips' cost composition and blind decision-making

Costs items	Composition (%)
Materials (including parts)	65
Direct labour	4
Manufacturing overheads	5
(1) Total manufacturing costs	***74***
General expenses	12
Administrative expenses	4
Selling expenses (excluding transport and freight)	11
(2)Total SGA	***26***

the definitive duties The European Commission opened again an investigation. [35] Philips had to inform the Commission of the awkward decision to move to Hungary. Since Hungary was not in the European Community yet, the move implied that there was no European Community production interests involved in the continuation of measures.

Brother Industries had started assembly operations in the United Kingdom and tried to convince Philips that it should try to delay an abolition of the measures or even try to ensure their continuation. Even SAGEM should be convinced – Brother advised – to support measures. Philips could not request continuation and SAGEM did not dare. The measures were discontinued and Philips returned into unprofitability. The measures could have been continued if Philips stayed in Vienna. The new management of the Fax Business Unit, however, decided that it had to do something and moved the factory rather than removing staff. Philips' CEO Mr. Boonstra already wondered whether involvement in anti-dumping was not a sign of bleeding. During the anti-dumping proceeding he had already considered to get rid of this business. Divestment might bring in cash and, consequently, profit and bonus.

He sold the fax activity to SAGEM. This sale broke the chain of consumer communications business that was already weakened. Mr. Boonstra's loud-mouthed target that Philips would become number 3 worldwide in mobile phones could not be met. Production problems impeded it and the huge sales force created for this grand performance made the activity a huge bleeder before it came to life. The fax business did not get a chance to develop as part of a larger consumer communication branch and Philips' professional activities had, as explained, died long before. Finally all communications business disappeared.

Price and volume attacks by mainly Japanese dumping meant that the business did not have a future as a stand-alone business, particularly after European institutions adjusted interpretation and implementation of the law to fit political

[35] Notice of initiation of a review of the anti-dumping measures applicable to imports into the Community of personal fax machines originating in the People's Republic of China, Japan, the Republic of Korea, Malaysia, Singapore, Taiwan and Thailand (2000/C 184/10), C 184/26, OJ 1 July 2000.

requirements. It became clear that a sound legal basis for measures against disruptions from protected markets was illusory and dependent on the character of politicians and civil servants involved.

References

Gregory G (1985) Japanese electronics technology: enterprise and innovation. The Japan Times, Tokyo

Peterson MJ (1995) The emergence of a mass market for fax machines. Technol Soc 17 (4):469–482

Van Marion MF (1993) Liberal trade and Japan, the incompatibility issue. Springer, Heidelberg

Chapter 15
Dark Practices in Lighting

Abstract This Chapter is about dumping from China. It shows the peculiarities of dealing with a non-market economy and the problems an industry incurs when it tries to tackle the serious economic and political problems encountered in trade with China. China is treated as non-market economy, which from its perspective implies a worse treatment. (Non-market economies are Azerbaijan, Belarus, North Korea, Tajikistan, Turkmenistan, and Uzbekistan; and countries considered as economies in transition include Albania, Armenia, China, Georgia, Kazakhstan, Kyrgyzstan, Moldova, Mongolia and Vietnam. In terms of economic performance, but with less clout, Vietnam is copying China.) This is not necessarily correct. Criminal behaviour and fraud by Chinese exporters appeared matchless. The dumping affair of Chinese energy saving lamps was one of the most bizarre examples of political blackmail, interference, irregularities, European producers discord, European Commission arbitrariness, biased decision making and internal European Commission competence struggles ever, resulting in a weird compromise giving the idea to the Chinese that, henceforth, they had a free rein in trade policy.

15.1 European Manufacturers' Manoeuvres

Chinese infringements on certain European Community producers' patents concerning electronic integrated compact fluorescence lamps (CFL-i's) or energy saving lamps (ESLs) were subject of regular meetings in the European lighting industry. Since it was practically impossible to sue flouting Chinese producers under Chinese law, discussions about the issue may have been lengthy and therefore, costly; they were also fruitless. By 1997, most patents concerning CFL had expired and Chinese producers, knowing that there would be no means for patent holders to act against imports, started dumping exports. The lawyers at Philips did not have the slightest notion how to act. They thought they should solve the issue by means of intellectual property legislation, which was a blind alley.

M. van Marion, *International Trade Policy and European Industry*,
Contributions to Economics, DOI 10.1007/978-3-319-00392-4_15,

It was a serious trade policy problem and a profit issue rather than a theoretical legal intellectual property matter. The recommendation to consider the anti-dumping instrument was accepted at Philips after lengthy discussions. Subsequently, it was even more firmly debated in the European Lamp Companies Federation, ELC. All European producers suffered, they stated, and were seriously shocked by Chinese prices. Indeed, Chinese prices did not have much relationship with normal business practice or even with costs. The cause of the extremely low export prices was clearly a different issue than the Japanese cases of dumping.

After a demonstration of the existence of dumping, an explanation of the various aspects of a proceeding induced the European industry association to come to a mutual agreement. One company insisted on the inclusion of a range of other products also dumped from China, but these products would, it was commonly decided, be included in future proceedings. These cases would finally disappear behind the horizon. Collection of data could start, if General Electric (GE) had not suddenly demanded that a notary deal with individual company data, which the notary should then aggregate to European industry figures. GE demanded that the notary supply data in a sealed envelope to the European Commission separately from the rest of the complaint. In this way, GE hoped to get a guarantee of confidentiality of individual data. All others wondered why the counsel for the case could not do this work. This detour would consume time, verification of the injury inflicted to the industry would be impossible and the proceeding would be hampered. The notary appeared to struggle with economic data and needed an extremely long time and frequent explanations about the methods to aggregate the data. The draft file was finally submitted without data on individual producers' production, results and other essential information on injury. The European Commission official responsible for the "Office of Complaints" opened the notary's envelope with figures and in one glance was clear that GE had fooled the other producers. It was easily visible that the lines on GE's European Community production and related data were either blank or filled in with zeroes. It did not produce in the European Community, but in Hungary, which was not yet a member. Consequently, another two costly months had been lost. It has remained unclear whether GE frustrated the proceeding on purpose or from ignorance. In view of later occurrences, it was probably the former.

15.2 Chinese Environment: Energy Saving Lamp Production and Sales

The Chinese government interfered heavily in domestic compact fluorescence production. It bolstered Chinese companies' refusal to pay for technical know-how in the patents issue. It had financially boosted domestic production of integrated CFLs by means of subsidies. It wanted CFLs to replace normal bulbs, but also subsidised electricity. The main effect was overcapacity. This overcapacity resulted in dumping. In Table 15.1 a sample of subsidies is given compiled from various studies.

Table 15.1 Production subsidies on energy saving lamps in China

Subsidies to Chinese industry	Total amount US$	Annual effect of subsidies per annum 1996–2000
Low interest loans	60,000,000	12,000,000
Subsidies found in ACEEE study	26,500,000	5,300,000
ACEEE study, per producer	0.5	35
UNDP subsidies	950,000	190,000
Total amount per year		17,490,035
Lamps units produced		200,000,000
Subsidized amount per lamp		0.087
Average price of exported lamp		0.75
As per cent of price of lamp		11.7 %

Demand-pull programs were absent. Artificially low electricity prices distorted competition and this was an additional cause of surplus production. The Chinese authorities blew their own trumpet about their energy saving policies, which failed and had a vicious effect on production elsewhere in the world. Frequently CFL consumption targets were set, but never met. It resulted in dumping.[1]

> *Lighting accounts for 12 percent of China's total electricity use. In its latest five-year plan, which concludes in 2015, China said it would reduce energy consumption per unit of gross domestic product by 16 percent and cut carbon emissions 17 percent. The plan to phase out incandescent light bulbs, NDRC estimates, will save China 48 billion kilowatt hours of power annually. China is the world's largest producer of both energy-saving and incandescent light bulbs, NDRC says. In 2010, production of standard bulbs totalled 3.85 billion units, with domestic sales accounting for 1.07 billion units.*

Implementation did not follow determination. As soon as fear of trade retaliations for infringements of patents disappeared, Chinese producers started to export rather than sell on the domestic market. Their sales in China were about 35 million units in 1999.[2] Sales to the European Community were more than double this volume, and China's second destination, the United States, absorbed about 40 million units in 1999. Graph 15.1 depicts the explosive development of Chinese exports.

This flashing influx of energy saving lamps resulted in a drop in European Community sales, a steep fall in market share, huge overcapacity and a catastrophic drop in prices of European producers, as Graph 15.2 indicates.

European prices of sales to trade dropped from €7.20 in 1995 to €5.10 in 1999 and Philips' prices from its production in Poland from slightly below €5.00 to €4.00 in 1999. Resale prices of Chinese lamps decreased from €1.20 to less than €1.00.

---

[1] UPI.com, 7 November 2011, http://www.upi.com/Business_News/Energy-Resources/2011/11/07/China-plans-switch-to-energy-saving-lights/UPI-10351320683681/#ixzz1eKOM2wqD. This coercive policy does not differ from the European Community policy, which also – in response to the lobby of some major producers – imposed energy saving lamps on the population, violating market freedom principles and consumer choice.

[2] IAEEL News letter February 2000.

Graph 15.1 EU sales and imports of integrated CFLs from China

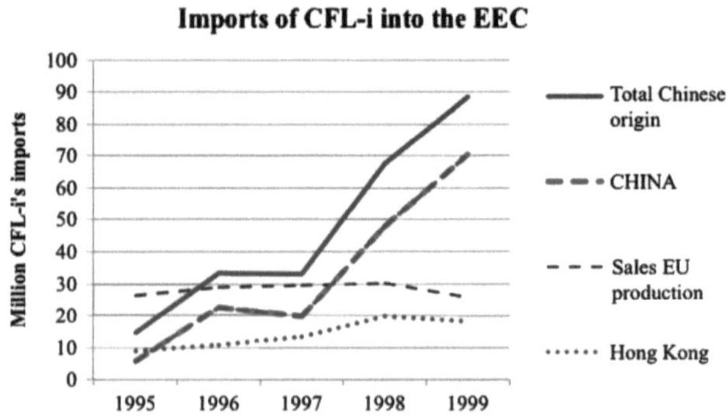

Graph 15.2 Falling average CFL selling prices in Europe

Table 15.2 shows cost data of two companies in China and of a European Community producer. One Chinese producer is related to a European manufacturer. The other Chinese producer supplied simple lamps.[3] The third, a European producer, is related to the producer in the first column.

The European producer could not cover costs of 138 because of the dumping. The European in China (Column 1) made a handsome profit on its lamps sold in China.[4] The sales of the lamp of the Chinese producer in Table 15.2 column (2) in China also occurred at a profit. The product of the Chinese producer, 15.2 column (2), was a simple stick lamp, whereas the European's products, both those made in Europe and in China (columns (1) and (3)) contained higher quality components. The lamps were more complex and had a longer lifetime. What was striking was the difference in energy cost of the two producers in China. Chinese producer, in B(2) paid one-tenth

[3] These real data in indices are from legal practice in various anti-dumping cases. One of the companies in this Table received Market Economy Status in the European Community case and the other received Market Economy Status in a third country proceeding concerning energy saving lamps toward China.

[4] The prices of 137 and 130 in China and the European Community respectively concern similar lamps with similar quality. The three companies had market economy status in different anti-dumping cases.

Table 15.2 Cost composition and comparison Chinese, Chinese European and European producers (ex-works) (in indices: European materials are 100)

	Cost items	European producer's subsidiary's cost in China (1)	Chinese producer's cost in China (2)	European producer's cost in Europe (3)
A	Direct materials	45	31	**Index base: 100**
B	Direct energy	2	0.2	B included in E
C	Direct other costs	7		
D	Direct labour	4	2	1
E	Indirect cost of manufacturing	19		12
F	SG&A	24	2	24
G	Total cost of production	101	36	138
H	Profit	36	4	−8
I	Average selling price	137	39	130

The index is made in order to protect confidential data and to give a better awareness of cost relations. Index base is direct materials cost A(3) of the European producer

the cost than the cost paid by the European in China: B(1). Since the Sino-European producer had a more machine intensive production, this was not amazing. What was amazing, however was that labour cost of the Chinese producer was half the level of the Sino-European's and only 6 % of its total costs, compared with the 4 % of the Sino-European's. This was in spite of the fact that the Chinese apparently did not incur any other direct costs, such as machinery. The Chinese producer did not depreciate or have financing cost. The Chinese producer's selling, general and administrative costs were only 9 % of those of the European producer in China, i.e. in column (1) SG&A is 24 and column (2) only 2. Due to such differences, the Chinese cost account showed an inexplicable cost advantage by 64 %.

Zero capital cost, an absence of other direct costs than materials, labour cost at only 6 % of total and a negligible electricity bill, as well as an absence of indirect costs of manufacturing resulted in pricing by the Chinese producer without relation to the economic reality. GE, Osram and Philips with their joint ventures in China were confronted with economic reality and the costs that Chinese did not incur. It is alleged that European industry first complained about Japan, thereafter about Korea and now about China. The China case of dumping is different. It does not share similarities with the domestic market structures explained in Chaps. 7 and 8. The major problem with exports is that Chinese producers do not have serious accounting systems, and do not allocate costs properly to their operations, do not incur costs other producers normally incur and do not take costs into account in their production for export that are normally part of cost of production. Positive cash flow seems often confused with profits on proper selling prices and costing. Chinese producers seem to consider positive cash flow profits. As a consequence of such accounting practices, a slow-down in sales results in diminishing cash flows, and bankruptcy is inevitable. Chinese authorities did not blame their excessive stimulation of production in China nor on the accounting errors in China for problems in the Chinese lighting industry. They blamed European industry and anti-dumping measures for insolvencies in China's energy lamp industry after measures were imposed.

15.3 European Industry: Errors and Omissions

European Community producers often assume that acceptance of an anti-dumping file is a political gesture. They suppose that its acceptance implies that Chinese firms are covered by a proceeding and not their own exports from China. An example is a change in construction of the ballast – from magnetic to electronic – of Philips' famous prismatic SL lamps. These lamps were first produced in the Netherlands until production was transferred to China. The magnetic ballast was too heavy and too expensive. Only about 60,000 lamps with the new electronic ballast were exported from China to the Netherlands in the last quarter of the Investigation Period (IP) – 1 January 1999 to 31 March 2000. This was sufficient for the highest dumping margin (61.8 %) found during the investigation. Nobody was aware that the delay by a few months of this switch could prevent this duty. In that case, a newcomer review could have been requested, which is usual for producers not involved in exports of the product concerned during the investigation period or before the start of the proceeding.

The second error is also comprehensible. It is a slip that any Western producers with investments in a non-market economy like China normally would make. Some multinationals think that they are automatically considered a market economy company and will receive market economy treatment (MET). Before they obtain that treatment they must fulfil normal procedural requirements, i.e. fill in a questionnaire. Pride and ignorance compel other multinationals to go, without proper advice and calculation, for market economy status (MES) or MET. Of course, they must be seen as market economy party, they think. A side expectation may be that such MES is advantageous and preferable to non-market economy status. When it enjoys MES, real sales prices and costs, instead of a price in an analogue country, are used as yardstick for normal value. Lawyer Jean-François Bellis was lucky to obtain a zero-duty for Lisheng Neonlite. He claimed that his special competence was a decisive factor in obtaining this special duty for one of his Chinese clients, to which (MES) was granted. He probably aimed at more Chinese clients, who were also convinced that MES was advantageous by definition. This was a fallacy. Section 15.4 explains the case. Had Philips & Yaming chosen to be a non-market economy company, its normal value would have been 9 % lower and its dumping margin 47.9 instead of actual MES normal value resulting in 61.8 %.[5] The case of

[5] This subsidiary in China, Philips & Yaming, made a mistake to its advantage. It reported about its SL prismatic lamps that it had a lifetime of between 6,000 and 10,000 h instead of 10,000 h or more. This mistake caused that the undercutting found was less than the undercutting applied if the lifetime had correctly been applied. The undercutting, which was its anti-dumping duty, of 32.3 %.

MES or MET and the level of normal value is dealt with in Chap. 16. The issue of the related exporter and the treatment of its prices is also mentioned in Chap. 16. It is advisable that, before the opening of a proceeding and in any case before request for MES treatment, a calculation is made whether MES is indeed advantageous. That is preferable to ill-founded contentions by lawyers.

Also highly understandable was the idea at multinational companies that dumping concerns ex-factory supply prices. Transfer or supply prices from a multinational's subsidiary factory in China to the Chinese sales organisation and to the European sales organisation may be identical, but such a transfer price is irrelevant in anti-dumping. Of course, all European companies with investments abroad should and generally do act in accordance with the Organisation for Economic Co-operation and Development (OECD) guidelines concerning multinational enterprises and in particular the transfer pricing clauses. The sales from the factory should and often do occur, although some examples given from the TV sector challenge this assumption, at arm's length. Indiscriminate transfer pricing does not safeguard such companies from anti-dumping duties. "We don't dump," an industry representative proudly announced. Indeed, ex-factory supply prices to sales organisations in China and Europe were identical. Average resale prices of products sold in China were 71 % higher than the supply price and the European Commission found a gap of 61.8 %, the dumping margin, between resale prices of the Chinese and European sales organisations. An additional problem is that the European Commission applies a special methodology for the calculation of the dumping margin in case of related companies. The calculation is based on the assumption of compensatory financial transactions between related parties. By such a construction the export price is artificially decreased and the dumping margin increased. Chapter 16, Sects. 16.9 and 16.10 deal with the issue. For a European Community company with a joint venture in the exporting country there is hardly a reason for a compensatory scheme. On the contrary, in the case of Philips there was a strong incentive to ship products at a transfer price as low as possible for as much as profit by Philips' sales companies in Europe as possible. The assumption that the transfer price was artificially high may have been applicable for producers with offensive intentions, which they try to hide by higher transfer prices. A joint venture in China implied that part of the profits earned in China accrues to the Chinese shareholder. A low transfer price can transfer profit to the European Community. Especially when the Chinese production was supplementary to European production, a low transfer price and a high resale price were advantageous for the transfer of profits to the European Community. Reconstruction of the export price resulted, however, in a decrease of the CIF value by 11 % compared with the actual CIF price. Table 16.7 shows the difference in treatment of assumption of compensatory finance compared with an unrelated company.

Philips' sales were treated on the assumption of compensatory finance, which was disadvantageous. The existence of compensation should not be ruled out. The loss of subsidiaries of Thomson in Thailand (for CTV) and in Malaysia (CD players) may well have been concealed by high transfer prices. In this way, Thomson in France, which received state aid, could subsidise its subsidiaries and compensate losses in the counties of export by higher transfer prices to Europe. In view of its treatment in general, it is doubtful whether Thomson's prices were treated part of a compensatory arrangement. It would have been an improvement in proceedings if anti-dumping authorities at least gave a justification for the assumption of compensatory arrangement. Companies with subsidiaries in exporting countries must be aware that under present circumstances, dumping and undercutting is almost always found by the mere existence of a relationship with the subsidiary in the exporting country.

The errors mentioned above show that it is imperative that producers be made aware of such issues during the stage of preparation of a complaint.

15.4 Proceeding, Chinese and European Political Actions and Outcome

The Chinese government and regional authorities energetically supported energy saving lamp production. This made Chinese fury about initiation of a proceeding against exports by an industry, so buoyantly shored up with state finance and propaganda, understandable. The Chinese state lost money and face. The Chinese authorities were to blame, but this may have increased their anger. Export of excess capacity at any price could not possibly be conceived as cause of their own deficient demand-pull policy. Chinese pressure on European industry and governments was therefore severe. Some European governments became unsteady. Danish and Swedish authorities showed adamant opposition to measures before the case was opened. The principled Scandinavian opposition was considerably moderated when the main supplier of IKEA, Lisheng Electronic & Lighting (Xiamen) Co., Ltd. owned by Neonlite Electronic & Lighting (HK) Ltd., finally obtained a zero duty and had a free play. This improvement in the competitive position of IKEA as an importer silenced Scandinavian resistance. IKEA had a purchasing office in Hong Kong, IKEA Trading (Hong Kong) Ltd. Until the year 2000, Lisheng had seemingly invoiced to IKEA in Hong Kong for further global distribution. Consequently, Lisheng's pricing of IKEA lamps to Europe was not part of a normal proceeding. IKEA's European purchases were about eight million units in 1997 and jumped to about 20 million 5 years later. Since IKEA's prices were exceptionally low, IKEA's Hong Kong purchasing operations may have hidden Lisheng's dumping. Lisheng's prices other than those to IKEA, in sales via specialised traders with a solid brand name, such as Megaman, were relatively high and may have contributed to the zero duty.

Shortly after the proceeding opened, Philips announced its withdrawal of support from the complaint. The decision had several reasons. The first was the outrageous anger of its president, Mr. Boonstra, who thought his glorious trip to China would become cumbersome. He disliked trouble for himself. Several Philips executives blamed bad business results in China to forceful Chinese reactions against Philips

Table 15.3 Consequences of transfer of CFL production from Netherlands to Poland

Sales in European Community of products made in	**1996**	**1997**	**1998**	**1999**	**IP**
Netherlands (Terneuzen)	81	78	61	24	29
Poland (Pila)	19	15	31	54	70
Total (1996 is 100)	**100**	93	92	78	98
Results on sales of products from					
Netherlands	32	23	−11	−176	−165
Poland	−132	−121	−1	−21	5
Total	−100	−98	−12	−198	−160

Because it may be considered confidential material, the information is indexed

products. Section 11.13 of Chap. 11 describes these events. The second argument, also a pretext, was the closure of the factory for CFL production in Terneuzen, the Netherlands, where production of the famous first SL energy saving lamp started. Philips had already moved a substantial part of its production to Poland, at that time outside the European Community, and with nearing termination of European Community production, participation in the proceeding was no longer required or desired; Philips' Lighting division was off the hook. The usual phenomenon had popped up. When some production is transferred, certain overheads remain a burden on the old production site, which inevitably becomes increasingly uncompetitive because of a loss of volume of production. That was also cause of the final step, total closure of the CFL production plant in Terneuzen. Transfer of some production, final transfer of production and closure of the factory were clearly attributable to dumping. The first decision to transfer production to Poland was taken in 1995, when the first surge in Chinese exports started (see Graph 15.1). The first defensive action of transferring production did not solve the problems, as Table 15.3 demonstrates.

Indisputably, the Chinese jump of exports and dumping prices triggered this transfer of production to Poland. It was induced and characterised by losses. There was a clear relationship between results and the transfer of production to Poland: the correlation was 0.9917. The decision to transfer was clearly directly instigated by the import influx from China. The correlation between Chinese imports and Philips' results in the Netherlands was −0.91496. The withdrawal of support by Philips created particular problems. It was, *inter alia*, the result of Chinese pressure, as described in the Chinese press[6]:

> *The EU's anti-dumping investigation and the pressure from the Chinese media have cost Philips about 40 million yuan worth of sales in China. Sales by Philips Yaming accounted for 15% - 17% of the Philips total. Philips' total sales in 1999 were US$31.5 billion.*
>
> *Philips global R&D center for energy-saving bulbs will be relocated from the Netherlands to Shanghai, where a new development center will be established and R&D personnel will be tripled to 50 persons, including three to four expatriates.*
>
> *Philips has also decided to close its Dutch CFL plants and relocate most of CFL part production to countries outside the EU, including Poland and China.*

[6] Beijing Youth Daily 23 December 2000: "Philips draws out all of a sudden?"

Rewarding Chinese pressure, the European Commission concluded in recital 49 of the regulation concerning provisional duties[7]:

> *In the course of the proceeding Philips Lighting BV informed the Commission that it* ***no longer wished to be treated as a member of the group of complainants****. Therefore,* ***data relating to Philips*** *Lighting BV* ***were not taken into account for the purpose of determining*** *the Community industry and* ***injury*** *to the Community industry. It should be noted that the provisional conclusions concerning injury and causal link would not have been different had the data relating to Philips Lighting BV been taken into consideration.* [Emphasis added]

This was a remarkable procedural twist. The data of Philips in Holland were eliminated from the proceeding, although this was, since Philips' losses were also excluded from the injury calculation, clearly disadvantageous to European industry. When exporters stated that injury was inflicted by Poland, the European Commission admitted that the move to Poland was a consequence of injury inflicted by the Chinese[8]:

> *The investigation showed that, at least for one of the two companies that fully cooperated in the proceeding this decision was partly due to the aggressive price policy of the Chinese exporting producers.*

The transfer was recognised as injury, but injury figures were eliminated from the data. The grant of Philips' wish had serious consequences. A few of these consequences can be spelled out. The first is that a company can inflict serious damage to others by support and subsequent withdrawal. The Chinese government could focus on remaining supporters of the complaint and become more vicious after its successful pressure. This was the actual effect of this move. The remaining producers had to bear the brunt of the burden of Chinese pressure, even blackmail. The withdrawal of support also influenced the injury figures. The Commission's conclusions were incorrect.

Another consequence of granting Philips' wish was an apparent change in the figures used for determination of injury inflicted by dumping. By exclusion of data from the range of injury figures, the injury margin changed. By the elimination of Philips' data, the injury inflicted to European Community industry was reduced by about 3 %. Such elimination would be meaningless if for all exporters the dumping margin would have been lower than the injury margin and the lesser duty rule would have implied that all anti-dumping duties would be based on the dumping margin. However, in the case of CFL, the only exporter whose anti-dumping duty was based on the injury margin was Philips & Yaming, as appears from Table 15.4. Philips' withdrawal from the complaint appeared beneficial to this company's related exporter. It resulted in a reduction of the duty on Philips' imports from Philips & Yaming. The duty was reduced from about 35.3 % to 32.3 %. This was detrimental

---

[7] Commission Regulation (EC) No 255/2001 of 7 February 2001 imposing a provisional anti dumping duty on imports of integrated electronic compact fluorescent lamps (CFL i) originating in the People's Republic of China, Official Journal of the European Communities, L 38/8, 8.2.2001.

[8] Commission Regulation (EC) No 255/2001, recital 89.

Table 15.4 Dumping margins, anti-dumping duties and the lesser duty: dumping or injury of CFL

Individual dumping margins	Dumping margins (%)	Duties (%)	Lesser duty rule
Changzhou Hailong Electronics & Light Fixtures Co. Ltd	59.5	59.5	Dumping
City Bright Lighting (Shenzhen) Ltd	17.1	17.1	Dumping
Deluxe Well Enterprises Ltd	37.1	37.1	Dumping
Lisheng Electronic & Lighting (Xiamen) Co. Ltd,	0.0	0.0	De Minimis
Philips & Yaming Lighting Co. Ltd	61.8	32.3	**Injury**
Sanex Electronics Co. Ltd	20.2	20.2	Dumping
Shenzhen Zuoming Electronic Co. Ltd	8.4	8.4	Dumping
Zhejiang Yankon Group Co., Ltd	35.3	35.3	Dumping
All other companies		66.1	

to Chinese competitors and to European Community industry. The European Commission stated: "conclusions concerning injury and causal link would not have been different". That may have been incorrect. It remained a fact that injury had been inflicted and that there was a causal link between dumping and injury, which a withdrawal did not change. The withdrawal affected the injury threshold. The withdrawal resulted exclusively in a lower anti-dumping duty for the exporter related to the withdrawing party. Such practice seems unacceptable.

15.5 Dumping Duties and Criminal Commerce

Some relatively high duties, reported in Table 15.4, triggered a range of impressive manoeuvres. The duties were a starting signal for Chinese exporters and European importers to get involved in massive absorption, fraud and circumvention of duties. Most prices did not move in accordance with the duties imposed. According to Article 12 of the Basic Regulation, a complaint may be lodged if it is demonstrated that "export prices have decreased or that there has been no movement, or insufficient movement in the resale prices or subsequent selling prices", and therefore a reinvestigation can take place.[9]

[9] Council Regulation (EC) No 384/96 of 22 December 1995 on protection against dumped imports from countries not members of the European Community; Revision with Council Regulation (EC) No 461/2004 of 8 March 2004 amending Regulation (EC) No 384/96 on protection against dumped imports from countries not members of the European Community and Regulation (EC) No 2026/97 on protection against subsidised imports from countries not members of the European Community Official Journal of the European Union 13.3.2004, L 77/12 or OJ L 343/51 of 22.12.2009 09113002 Council Regulation (EC) No 1225/2009 of 30 November 2009 codified AD Council Regulation (EC) No 1225/2009 of 30 November 2009 on protection against dumped imports from countries not members of the European Community (codified version).

Several prices were indicative for absorption of duties, or increased dumping. A temporary association "Establishing Legal Lighting Competition (E 2 L C) Federation" prepared a complaint. The original complainant was the ELC (European Lamp Companies Federation). GE's veto prevented ELC's support for the complaint. That was a reason to call the new association E 2 L C. The association lodged an anti-absorption complaint on 26 August 2002. That was 1½ year after definitive duties had been imposed. The proceeding was opened on 10 October 2002,[10] but was closed by Commission Decision of 9 March 2004[11] because the complainant withdrew the complaint. The European Commission stated in recital 7 of its decision:

> *In its withdrawal letter the applicant stressed, inter alia, that emphasis and priority should be given to those imports of CFL-i that have illegally taken place by violating the Community customs law, the international trade law and are otherwise in conflict with acceptable trade practices rather than on imports for which normal customs procedures have been fulfilled, on which antidumping duties have been paid and which apparently represent a minority of imports of Chinese CFL-i entering the Community.*

During and immediately after the anti-dumping proceeding, European energy saving lamps importers and other traders were contacted for exchange of information. Due to these good relations with trade, information was acquired on a variety of fraudulent practices. Very soon a first striking irregularity was found when an energy saving lamp distributed by the German trade company Sacom Außenhandel GmbH (its name could be found by its Global Trade Item Number (GTIN) 4010206880784 on the package) was sold by a do-it-yourself retail chain at a price of €1.02. This price could not, of course, reflect the costs of production, transport cost plus anti-dumping duties and, consequently, was likely the result of fraud. Underneath the article Number and the Global Location Number with the bar code the name of the importer was printed: "importiert durch Hendrik Trading Putten NL". Companies involved in resale of such products were well informed about prices and could guess that the price did not reflect normal import practices. Further research yielded the conclusion that the lamps were imported as normal general lighting services bulbs (GLS) and not as energy saving lamps. Eurostat statistics revealed a sudden rise in imports of normal bulbs or GLS lamps from China into the Netherlands. The matter was reported to the anti-fraud authorities and the importer finally went bankrupt. It appeared that this trader imported between 2.5 and three million energy saving lamps between January 2002 and October 2003.[12] The trader had also implied a forwarder in Rotterdam whom it blamed for this "error".

Traders provided documentary evidence that two Chinese companies and companions in crime, Changzhou Hailong Electronics and Light Fixtures with a duty of 59.5 %, and Changzhou Red Sun with a duty of 66.1 %, supplied a Danish

---

[10] Notice of Initiation OJ C 244 of 10.10.2002.

[11] Commission Decision of 9 March 2004 terminating the reinvestigation pursuant to Article 12 of Council Regulation (EC) No 384/96 (the Basic Regulation).

[12] Reformatorisch Dagblad, 30 June 2006. The prosecutor demanded an unconditional prison sentence of two years. The court sentenced him to 240 h community service.

Table 15.5 Deflection of trade and average CIF prices to the European Community

European Community				United States average import prices		
Average import prices	2001	2002	2003	2001	2002	2003
China	€1.41	€1.34	€1.34	€4.26	€3.11	€1.73
Pakistan	€1.61	€1.51	€1.29	No imports		
Philippines	€1.98	€1.86	€2.00			
Vietnam	€1.52	€1.36	€0.95			

Source: Eurostat and ITA of the United States

import trader via a trading company in Dubai. Evidence of about two shipments of 150,000 units each was submitted to the Organisation pour La Lutte Anti-Fraud of the European Community (OLAF). The papers of the bank cooperating with these deals were also copied and supplied as evidence. In Denmark's statistics, the lamps could not be traced. The products cleared customs in Hamburg. Another Danish company traded in bamboo furniture, and was also a clandestine importer of lamps. The containers were closely followed up to customs clearance in Hamburg. When Danish customs inspected the truck, it appeared empty because it was unloaded between Hamburg and the Danish border.

Since some countries on the route from China to Europe did not have energy saving lamps production or, in the case of Vietnam, the lamps did not qualify for any certification or compatibility marking, imports as indicated in Table 15.5 and in the first years of Table 15.7 aroused some suspicion. For instance, Pakistan's requirements for energy saving lamps were served from imports and suddenly the country turned up as an exporter that did not sell its products in the United States, but in the European Community only. The same applied to some other countries, like the Philippines. The embassy of the Philippines, for instance, was consulted and the response from the country's lighting industry federation was that there were no energy saving lamp production sites known in the Philippines.

Nevertheless, China Zhongshan Wecan Lighting Co. Ltd. announced that prices should be adjusted in case of shipment of products from the Philippines with a certificate of origin:

> *Now I should check my cost then I can provide you our best price, I hope you can wait one more day. About the anti-dumping duty you questioned, I just checked, it's very high. So I hope you can accept S.K.D. term so that you can avoid the unfair duty. Another, if you are interested, we can transfer our goods from PHILIPINES, then we can get the original certificate from PHILIPINES.*

And CE Lighting (with the brand name Landlite) also offered to ship from the Philippines:

> *...we have Energy Saving lamps plant in Philippines. Attached please kindly find the pictures of our plant there. At the moment, the engergy saving lamps that we are selling into EU are all delivered from Philippines. And of course, we can supply CFL to you from there.*

The pictures from the factory, again, showed arrangements that created the impression that some production took place in the Philippine premises. In the

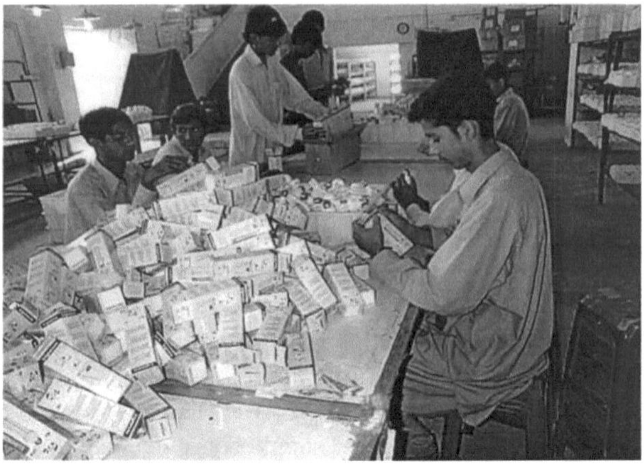

Picture 15.1 A "production process" in Pakistan (under the chaotic circumstances as illustrated in this picture of Ecopak's "factory", a production of some million units a year is impossible and the picture was a strong indication of fraud)

photograph, two Philippine women simulated assembling lamps, and a few men, probably their supervisors, seemed to be discussing their labour conditions. A comparison of pictures of CE's own factory in Shenzhen, China, and of the Philippine imitation showed a radical difference.

As for Pakistan, in the IMPORT GENERAL MANIFEST (IMG) customs authorities report shipments to Pakistani ports. For instance, it was reported that the ship Marivia on 4 May 2004 carried a cargo with among others a 40 ft container with 1959 cartons of energy saving lamps in SKD (semi-knock-down) consisting of ballast and fluorescent tubes, with Ecopak Lighting as importer and Firefly Lighting Co., Ltd. as consigner. A carton contains about 30 lamps and the load of a full container is about 63,000 lamps. Thirteen days later the vessel Iris had 1,254 cartons of the same product on board. The shipments to Pakistan matched exports from Pakistan to the European Community. Not surprisingly, the lamps with the brand Ecopak had exactly the specifications of lamps of the Chinese company Firefly Lighting Co., Ltd. The electronic ballast and the tube (the burner) of Ecopak and Firefly lamps were identical. European importers received a set of photographs that should have convinced them of the reality of Pakistani production. It was clear that production of 700,000 lamps or even 1.3 million units a year was impossible to achieve using the manufacturing process in Picture 15.1. The information was provided to OLAF, which inspected the production site, and the conclusion was easy. Picture 15.1 shows that this "producer" could not possibly manufacture energy saving lamps at a price of €1.51, as the statistics of Eurostat in Table 15.5 suggests.

Picture 15.1 hid rather simple and pitiable criminal operations, which were overshadowed both in terms of wickedness and in injury to the industry by "circumvention" of duties by other Chinese "operations" outside China. The circumventions finally stimulated an anti-circumvention complaint, which would be more effective than a hunt for individual companies that tried to avoid the duties by illegal operations.

After a request for quotations, Firefly, which had used Pakistan as an intermediary of its fraud, explored other possibilities and sent the following response to a request for information:

> *In the past few days, I was check your matter with other factories, but seems not find the suitable one for you now. The Tunisia factory only produce 3000hrs lamps. The Pakistan factory can supply 5000hrs lamps, but the situation there is very serious now, they almost stop the producing for safety problem. Now, I will check again for you with the Indonesia factory.*

Three different locations and origin certificates were offered for the sake of circumvention or – the more adequate term – fraud. The factory in Tunisia had, in the meanwhile, already been traced. Some investigation indicated that this was the same factory where one of the "European" producers, Sylvania Lighting International, had its "competence centre". Indonesia was previously not known as a location for transhipment. Imports to the European Community from Indonesia also appeared to increase.

As a neighbouring country, Vietnam, with its badly paid and consequently corrupt officials, was an exquisite site for fraud and circumvention. The fraud that took place via a government company in Vietnam was spectacular. A European trader provided documentary evidence on this ingenious fraud. Because he had imported energy saving lamps from the Philippines, although as the Philippines industry association could confirm there was no CFL production in that country, this trader in spite of the services rendered to arrest other evildoers, was later seized for fraud. The documents he provided concerning the Vietnam case showed how, again, Changzhou Hailong Electronics and Light Fixtures, inventively shipped energy saving lamps to the Vietnamese state-owned company Construction Installation and Building Materials Co. No. 5, Hai Phong City, owned by the Ministry of Trade of Vietnam. The Vietnamese company's invoices were printed by Changzhou Hailong, and these new invoices had the heading of the ministry printed with the same lamps description and with a mark-up from, for instance, US $0.14 per lamp – margin for the Vietnamese government institution – on the price of the Chinese manufacturers accompanied the shipment with destination Transworld Exports HK Co., LTD., in Hong Kong. The Hong Kong company, with its main seat in Thailand, shipped them under a false Combined Nomenclature (CN) Code (8539 22 90 of certain other filament or GLS bulb lamps, instead of the code for CFL 8539 31 90) and shipped the products as filament lamps with the same type and same Wattage indication. This should have aroused suspicion at customs because a filament or general lighting services lamp of 11 W was rather unusual in Europe. Nevertheless, imports of filaments from Vietnam increased of the lowest wattage increased from 35,000 in 2000 to 1.8 million in 2002, but it remained unobserved.

Zhejiang Yankon (previously Sunlight) Lighting – the main supplier to and a joint venture partner of Philips – had created an even trickier case of circumvention and fraud than Firefly. In January 2001, Yankon signed a joint-venture agreement with Philips, "Zhejiang Yankon Lighting Co., Ltd." Either this new producer of

Philips and Yankon or Yankon group itself supplied Philips from China.[13] In 2001, Yankon created a subsidiary in Vietnam, Kimsung VietNam Co Ltd near Hanoi. This subsidiary simulated production. Some assembly of lamps initially occurred, but thereafter Yankon shipped its Chinese products via Haiphong to Europe with documents indicating that the origin was Kimsung VietNam. It supplied extremely cheap lamps from Vietnam without payment of anti-dumping duties to competitors of Philips – like 4MBO International Electronic AG and Energy Research 2000. Average prices in Europe were clearly below any reasonable level and far below the normal value for an 11 W stick lamps (the simplest uncovered lamp with the shortest lifetime) at €2.04. The dumping margins had increased. With this fraud and circumvention it competed on the European market with its joint venture partner Philips, which probably had to pay a full duty.

Ningbo New Oriental Electric Industrial Development Co. surpassed even Yankon's methods. This company approached a Vietnamese company for creation of a joint operation, Halong-New Oriental Electric Factory. Originally the firm Ha Long Service and Import Export joint stock Company – Ha Long Simexco – was involved in processing of fish and fish products and distributing them. In the joint venture, the Vietnamese provided tools, workers and premises and the Chinese partner sent the components and brought know-how as input. As soon as the joint venture had been created, some lamps were assembled. Even industry and safety compliance certificates were produced. Soon, the joint venture produced certificates rather than lamps. The Vietnamese were highly disappointed that their investments were fruitless. Ningbo New Oriental Electric Industrial Development Co. proudly announced that it could supply 0-duty lamps from Vietnam, just as it stated that a subsidiary in China had lower duties, which represented an advantage to Ningbo's customers in Europe (for this method of fraud see below).

The anti-dumping duty of one of the Chinese exporters was more than 40 % lower than the residual duty. That was an attractive advantage, which was employed by some others. One company, Ningbo New Oriental Electric Industrial Development Co., distributed a leaflet with the allegation that the company with the lower duties was a subsidiary and that European customers received the lamps at the lower duties. A comparison was made between the lamps made by the "subsidiary" and the other imported "Ningbo" lamps allegedly made by the subsidiary. The lamps were completely different. The European temporary industry association Lighting Industry and Trade in Europe (LITE) e-mailed the result of the analysis to the Chinese company with the low duty. The response of the president of the company to the temporary association LITE was full of anger. He alleged that his company made a broad range of products of different quality and different construction. Whatever he alleged, the tubes of the lamps and the electronic ballasts – starter components on a small printed circuit board – were completely different. Normally producers have a

[13] Nobody investigated or verified whether this Joint Venture or Yankon produced the lamps imported by Philips. If it were the joint venture, Philips should pay the residual duty for this new company of 66.1 % instead of the duty for Yankon of 35.3 %.

sort of fingerprint in the construction of the ballast, which may vary, but does not change completely from one model to the other and does not contain completely different components from different suppliers. An abuse of the low duty and a margin to the producer with the low duty was apparent. Ningbo New Oriental Electric Industrial Development Co. openly referred in a leaflet to the possibility of low duties via this route.

A cooperative European Community trader sent a copy of an offer he received from a Chinese manufacturer concerning delivery from China through Thailand to Rotterdam on CFR (cost and freight) basis. The producer quoted following prices, which represented dumping as per cent of CIF value:

Type of lamp	FOB US$	Dumping margin as % of (2 %) CIF
2U 5–9 W	$0.58	209.8
2U 11–15 W	0.60	236.0
3U 15–20 W	0.80	152.5
3U 24 W	0.83	195.2
GLOBE 15 W	1.25	115.9
GLOBE 20 W	1.30	124.2
CANDLE 7 W	0.80	166.9

The message from the Chinese exporter stated that it could also send the products without the 66.1 % anti-dumping duty, but in that case an uplift of 20 % would be applied to the price:

It means that 120% of above price can be CFR from China through Thailand to Rotterdam. Compare with 67% Anti-dumping duty, 20% tranship from Thailand can save 47%. It is a large amount.

Indications about imports by a major European producer via Thailand were a shocking experience. Some customs authorities had become curious about shipments from Thailand with the brand name of this major producer on the packing. When information was requested from this major European company whether there was presence of certified lamp producers in that country fulfilling the specifications of that company, a response was promised. When, however, no answer came and the anti-fraud authorities collected the first pieces of evidence, the law department of this company was warned that the company ran severe risks. The company decided that all communications with the messenger of this information were forbidden. It was even forbidden to inform him that he was held incommunicado from the company. Such practices were more dangerous for European producers than for exporters. If there is proof of direct involvement and knowledge of the activity, a European importer is completely liable for fraud. As is clear from the television case, the importer may be involved in fraud, but as long as he supposedly does not know that the exporter was involved in the fraud, the importer is safeguarded. Some cases of fraud, however, are more obvious than those of televisions with a tube that renders a certain origin, which one cannot detect neither from the outside of the product nor from the documents. A European producer has minimum quality requirements and knows the origin of the lamps.

A lamp sold under the brand name "Kepeng" by a Dutch trader/distributor in Amsterdam had been imported from Dubai. After removal of a sticker on the package a bar code became visible. The sticker on the Kepeng box had hidden a bar code, indicating the Global Trade Item Number 6291050105485, which is, as http://gepir.gs1.org/ indicates, associated with Gulf Advanced Lighting Co. Ltd. in Dubai, United Arab Emirates, which is known as a supplier, *inter alia*, of sensor lamps to Philips. When the package was opened, a carton protecting the glass burner was exposed. It had the printing Yaxing 5,000 h and a telephone number. The address of Yaxing Lighting Co., Ltd is in Xiaolan Town, Zhongshan City, Guangdong Province. The factory had started its activities in 1998. Closer inspection showed that the lamp is similar to the Yaxing Lighting energy saving lamp 2U model 6,542. Apparently, all preparations for the fraud were already made in the factory in China, but not very carefully.

The Chinese exporter, "Luxram", offered an opportunity to avoid anti-dumping duties by importing lamps via Indonesia. A CD-ROM with pictures from a factory in Indonesia should convince prospective buyers that activities in Indonesia did not violate European Community customs law. The pictures on the CD-ROM were of the premises of PT. Sentra Solusi Elektrindo in Surabaya. There was indeed a superficial impression of production, but there was not the slightest tinge of organised and full-scale manufacturing. It might be that there was some production, but this could not possibly have a scale of 600,000 to one million units, which represented the imports from Indonesia into the European Community and certainly could not be as cost effective as the offer price indicated.

Another Chinese exporter proudly announced that it could provide also from Iran at preferential (generalised system of preferences) rate – a lower rate of zero per cent for developing countries, provided that special origin rules are fulfilled:

> We can provide Full shipping documents from Iran. Shipment could be made from Iran with G.S. P. FORM A. You only need to Pay "0" Tax to custom. Pls check and give me comments by return. So that I can see that you've got this email.

This showed that any port between China and Europe could serve as intermediate for transhipment and circumvention. The cost of transhipment paid by the customer was about $0.15 per lamp.

Preparation of an anti-circumvention case was required if this massive fraud should be countered. Before an anti-circumvention file was constructed, the industry contacted the Organisation pour la Lutte Anti-Fraud, OLAF, national authorities like the Zollkriminalamt (ZKA, Germany's Customs Criminal Investigations Office), the Dutch fiscal and economic crime investigation authorities FIOD/ECD and the Belgian Customs and Excise Administration and other customs offices of member states. Some of the cases illustrated above were submitted to the excellent staff of these governmental institutions. OLAF's investigators appreciated factual information and not simply suspicions. On 4 December 2006 OLAF announced successful actions.[14] Several investigations led to administrative and criminal proceedings to recover an amount of €30 million. The background of some of these cases is presented in this Chapter.

15.6 Anti-circumvention: Fraud in the Floodlight

Countering fraud on such massive a scale can never solve economic problems that an industry incurs. The complete immorality of exporters made an anti-circumvention complaint and investigation the only alternative legally open to industry. OLAF had qualified personnel, but not the means and manpower to hunt for all the Chinese cases of fraud. The Chinese had for decades believed that capitalism was evil and earning money was bad. Their apparent conclusion was that since the introduction of capitalism, pursuit of profits allowed all imaginable practices. A file was made on the circumvention via Vietnam, the Philippines and Pakistan. Factually, all countries on the route between China and Europe could have been included: Malaysia, Thailand, Indonesia, Sri Lanka, Dubai, Iran and Tunisia – and indeed evidence on all these countries was available – but evidence indicated irregular trade flows. The fraud was so widespread that it was too much for OLAF, but too little for an anti-circumvention proceeding covering all these countries.

It was without precedent that traders supported a complaint on circumvention. A temporary association, Lighting Industry and Trade in Europe (LITE), lodged a complaint and some traders importing from exporters with low or no anti-dumping duties supported the complaint. The advantage of cooperation with trade was the information supplied. The industry had different sources of information. Electronics companies are often multinationals and the information acquired was fragmentary and spread over various departments and countries. Traders have more information about their competitors than industry.

A complainant should be aware of the possibility of circumvention in the stage before an initial anti-dumping procedure is started. If the product is professional equipment, for instance, (these are products with small production runs and limited production capacity) then possibility of circumvention is abundant. It might even be wondered whether the anti-dumping instrument was a waste of time. An example is electron microscopes, which are sold at high prices per unit in a professional market with small production runs. The product can be shipped in modules and assembled by a team of technicians. The example of television camera systems, already discussed, is similar. It was practically impossible to catch the wrongdoers.

[14] OLAF/06/21 Brussels, 4 December 2006; Cologne: Press release, Zollkriminalamt, 4 December 2006.

The definition of circumvention is[15]:

- A change in the pattern of trade between third countries and the European Community or between individual companies in the country subject to measures and the European Community;
- Which stems from a practice, process or work;
- For which there is insufficient due cause or economic justification other than the imposition of the duty; and
- Where there is evidence of injury or that the remedial effects of the duty are being undermined in terms of the prices and/or quantities of the like product; and
- Where there is evidence of dumping in relation to the normal values previously established for the like product, if necessary in accordance with the provisions of Article 2.

Practice, process or work may consist of a slight modification, not changing the essential characteristics, of the product, by which the measures do not cover the products any longer. Practices as demonstrated in the previous paragraph all belong to a practice or process constituting or resulting in a change in the pattern of trade. It is also possible that measures are evaded by circumvention by use of the documents of the producer with low duties. The previous Sect. 15.5 includes examples.

Because a pattern of trade in professional equipment is statistically hardly noticeable, it is extremely difficult to show a change in pattern of trade. Market research studies may offer help, however. The definition for circumvention is that a change of pattern of trade between third countries and the European Community takes place. The main characteristics of changes in pattern of trade to be demonstrated are the exports from the country of dumping decrease and are substituted by imports from other third countries. In the combined nomenclature, studio cameras are classified in the same group as high volume consumer cameras (8525 80 19) and statistics do not provide any clues. Market studies, however, might give information on the change in market shares. GfK is a market research institute that might be of help. If it can be demonstrated that the duties have not had any impact on the market price, volume and market share of the dumping exporters, there is either absorption or circumvention.

Section 15.5 gave various examples of immoral business behaviour. The imports from China decreased by 45 % between 2000 and 2001 and by another 11 % a year later. The increase of imports of CFL-i from other third countries is also manifest. The Basic Regulation, Article 13 requires fulfilment of other conditions, however.

---

[15] Article 13 of the Basic Regulation, Council Regulation (EC) No 384/96 of 22 December 1995 on protection against dumped imports from countries not members of the European Community; Revision with Council Regulation (EC) No 461/2004 of 8 March 2004 amending Regulation (EC) No 384/96 on protection against dumped imports from countries not members of the European Community and Regulation (EC) No 2026/97 on protection against subsidised imports from countries not members of the European Community Official Journal of the European Union 13.3.2004, L 77/12 or OJ L 343/51 of 22.12.2009 09113002 Council Regulation (EC) No 1225/2009 of 30 November 2009 codified AD Council Regulation (EC) No 1225/2009 of 30 November 2009 on protection against dumped imports from countries not members of the European Community (codified version).

The World Trade Atlas of the Global Trade Information Services (GTIS) can help to construct a reliable set of data concerning imports and exports in volumes and values. *Inter alia* it should be demonstrated that the circumvention is the consequence of the practice or process in the third country. This condition requires that practices and processes be discovered, described and documented. The practices and processes can be discovered by analysis of trade flows of certain products to third countries. OLAF uses all sorts of information on shipping and cargo often unavailable to European complainants. The use of statistics of GTIS may be of help for the detection of regular trade flows, in the case of circumvention, trade data often does not provide a clue. There was not much correlation between exports of certain components – like ballasts and glass components, i.e. burners, from China to certain countries and their exports to the European Community. Most circumvention was just fraud. It may also be that the lamp exporters had hidden their exports of parts and components for assembly by false nomenclature when the products were exported.

The other criterion is that for the practice, process or works there must be insufficient due cause or economic justification. That means that it must be demonstrated that there are additional costs to the circumvention and that these costs are lower than the value of the duty. The simplest example is the transhipment of manufactured products via a third country or such an assembly that the value added in the third country is less than the added value in the country of dumping.[16]

Assembly in the European Community or in a third country circumvents the measures in force if

(a) It started or increased after or just before initiation of an anti-dumping investigation and the parts used in the assembly operation are from the country towards which the duties are applied;
(b) The parts from this country constitute more than 60 % of the total value of the parts of the assembled products, unless more than 25 % value is added in the third country.

Additionally, the remedial effects should be undermined by this circumvention.

The example in Table 15.6 shows a calculation in practice, as submitted to the European Community authorities.

If ballast materials are made in China, the materials value of these ballast materials is 68.5 % of the materials bill. However, when the ballast is ready-made imported and processed in assembly, the value of the ballast is 74.1 % of the materials bill. Generally, the Chinese producer also ships the burner ready-made to the assembly site abroad. In that case, materials from China are 91 % of total materials, assuming that the plastic upper part of the burner and the housing are from the third country of assembly.

[16] The adventures of various exporters are sketched. Cooperation of governmental institutions and Chamber of Commerce with fraudulent exporters was in some cases found. Section 15.5 shows the cost of the cooperation of a company of the Vietnamese Ministry of Trade. The higher cost of Thai origin is attributable to the cost of bribing some employees of Chambers of Commerce in third countries for false origin certificates.

Table 15.6 Materials bill and added value of energy saving lamps

Items	% of ex-works value	% of materials bill
Printed circuit board of ballast	5	8
Various small components	25	38
Transistors	7	11
Ballast choke (inductor)	7	11
Total cost of ballast materials	**45**	**69**
Plastic housing (lower part)	3.7	5.6
Assembly of ballast and plastic housing	6.6	
Total cost ballast assembly and housing	10.2	
Material for burner	11.0	16.9
Plastic part (upper part)	2.9	4.5
Assembly of lamp tube, plastic part + ballast	15.3	
Total cost burner assembly and lamp assembly	**29.2**	
Packing incl. packing material	2.9	4.5
Total material	**65**	**100**
Factory added value of assembly and indirect costs	22	
SG&A and profit (not to be included into the calculation)	13	
Ex-works price	100	

The factory added value in assembly is at its maximum, 22 %. Since ballasts are imported as assembled components, the maximum added value is about 21.9 % – 6.6 % = 15.3 %. Since there are normally no selling or administrative costs and no profits made in the third country of assembly or fake-assembly, the added value is in the case of energy saving lamps always under 25 %. When the products from the third country were found, their analysis did not pose too many problems and it was relatively easy to demonstrate that they were basically Chinese by analysis of the ballast content and comparison with ballasts of Chinese producers. Therefore, it was advisable to purchase products of the exporters in the country of import before a complaint was lodged for the sake of later analysis after the imposition of duties.

A comparison of Ecopak and Firefly lamp ballasts revealed that Ecopak lamps had principally or completely been made in China, which Picture 15.1 indicates, and Picture 15.2 provides further evidence. The two lamps in Picture 15.2 appeared to have identical ballasts (electronic driver devices) and burners (the glass pipe). Only the shells differed to make the appearance different. The investigations by OLAF revealed that only a few lamps were assembled in accordance with Picture 15.2. The majority of Firefly lamps were transhipped in the Port of Karachi.

The definitive anti-dumping measures were imposed in July 2001. The European Commission opened an anti-absorption case in October 2002 and, because the circumvention was so evident that the effect of absorption was relatively minor, the complainant – at that time one producer only – withdrew the absorption complaint in March 2004. The temporary association of trade and industry (LITE) lodged a complaint on circumvention in August 2004 and the results

Picture 15.2 Housing and ballasts of Firefly and Ecopak lamps: circumvention and fraud (practically all components were identical. In a Firefly lamp, an identical electrolytic capacitor was found with a name "Ecopak" printed on it, however. Apparently, Firefly ordered capacitors that bore the name of the company of circumvention on it. Apparently, some errors had been made. The structure of the printed circuit boards and the indications where the components should be inserted and mounted were identical. In documents, Ecopak admitted that the burner (the coated glass part) was obtained from Firefly)

appeared on 6 June 2005 with extension of the duties. Although the extension of duties would stop fraud and exports from Vietnam, Pakistan and the Philippines, the complainants did not have the illusion that this would bring an end to similar practices via other countries. Massive fraud via Malaysia and Thailand could hardly be stopped. As for Tunisia, the evidence that Firefly also used the same intermediate station that SLI used for its international competence centre was embarrassing. Afterwards, it appeared that imports from Tunisia as a country had increased from 0.4 in 2004 to 1.8 million a year later and it may be wondered whether the SLI was not also a customer of supplies from Firefly via Tunisia. However, SLI was in serious trouble. An extension of the measures meant that SLI would run into aggravated losses if duties were to be extended to Tunisia. It must have known, however, that its own "competence centre" was involved in intolerable practices. In the United Arab Emirates, the company Gulf Advanced Lighting had real production and the small fraud via this route was relatively endurable. Taiwan seemed to shelter some companies involved in circumvention, but the Taiwanese had also lost substantial market share to the Chinese. Their production was limited to high specification lamps. There were some shipments via Taiwan on which documentary evidence also existed. The statistical evidence of circumvention via

Taiwan was absent or weak, however. The same applied to some other countries of circumvention. In 2010, after the measures were discontinued, the imports from Iran, Malaysia and Sri Lanka disappeared and the imports from Indonesia, Thailand and some other countries contracted to a few hundred thousand. Consequently, these countries must have been involved in circumvention. Since the Chinese resumed their dumping after expiry of the measures on 19 April 2008, it might have also been that they could no longer compete on the European Community market.

The problem with fraud and circumvention is that there is hardly a limit to the number of countries involved in such practices. A country like Sri Lanka had clearly been involved in circumvention and fraud and there was sufficient evidence for the inclusion of the country in a file. However, the maximum of imports of lamps from Sri Lanka was one million in 2007. In this country, two producers had since long been involved in contract manufacturing, including for European Community producers. This contract manufacturing started before the investigation of Chinese dumping and before measures toward China became effective. Quantities from Thailand were already 1.3 million in 1997. Thailand had some industry, but hardly qualified for exports. Nevertheless, the existence of some CFL production was a complication. Later, during the preparation of a circumvention complaint that was never lodged, Indonesia, Malaysia, Sri Lanka, Taiwan, Thailand, Tunisia and the United Arab Emirates were included. The documentary evidence on Tunisia was sufficient to include this country as route for circumvention by Firefly, but the fact that SLI's outward processing in Tunisia in the same factory where the "circumvention assembly" took place complicated matters. The Chinese company Firefly could have easily chosen a new route for its practices and such inclusion implied more work than effectiveness.

The major advantage of an anti-circumvention case was that it could be demonstrated that the measures had not been fully effective and that in case of an expiry review, the industry was entitled to a continuation of measures.

Table 15.7 shows the anti-circumvention proceeding was effective. Imports from Pakistan, the Philippines and Vietnam had disappeared. The other countries, with the exception of Indonesia, Malaysia and Thailand, were of marginal significance. After 2008, imports from Thailand reduced to 28 % of its peak level. If the measures toward China had not discontinued, a file toward these countries would certainly have been effective.

15.7 The Politics of Definition of "Community Industry"

Not long after the extension of measures to Pakistan, the Philippines and Vietnam, an expiry proceeding took place. The intention of this investigation was whether discontinuation of measures after 5 years would lead to a continuation or recurrence

Table 15.7 CFL imports from China and circumvention (in million units)

Into European Community-15												
China and countries of circumvention	1997	1998	1999	2000	2001[a]	2002	2003	2004	2005[b]	2006	2007	2008[c]
PR China	20	48	71	85	47	38	55	73	112	147	265	415
Hong Kong	13.07	19.55	17.89	25.00	5.09	5.14	2.48	1.26	1.39	1.43	4.75	6.80
Indonesia	0.11	0.20	0.94	0.67	0.74	1.65	0.63	1.08	1.42	2.39	2.41	1.83
Iran								0.17	0.23	0.20	0.41	0.45
Malaysia			0.23			0.12	0.62	2.05	5.97	4.80	8.95	3.31
Pakistan					0.20	0.58	0.67	1.38				
Philippines		0.44	0.77		1.49	3.00	3.25	4.38	0.57			
Sri Lanka						0.13	0.49	0.74	0.89	0.74	1.05	1.07
Taiwan	8.40	13.93	10.62	9.69	2.21	1.32	8.12	2.01	2.43	4.16	7.87	3.88
Thailand	1.33	1.74	2.05	1.78	0.58	0.93	1.22	1.96	3.51	4.70	3.84	4.28
Tunisia					0.25	0.36	0.37	0.36	1.73	1.10	2.21	1.85
Un. Arab Emirates	0.11	0.18	0.33	0.91	0.47	0.77	0.99	1.20	1.88	1.30	2.92	4.04
Vietnam					0.93	1.92	5.45	8.50	1.24	0.12		
Total excl China & Taiwan	1.55	2.57	4.32	3.37	4.65	9.47	13.70	21.82	17.45	15.35	21.80	16.82

[a]February 2001: provisional measures
[b]June 2005: anti-circumvention measures
[c]April 2008: expiry measures

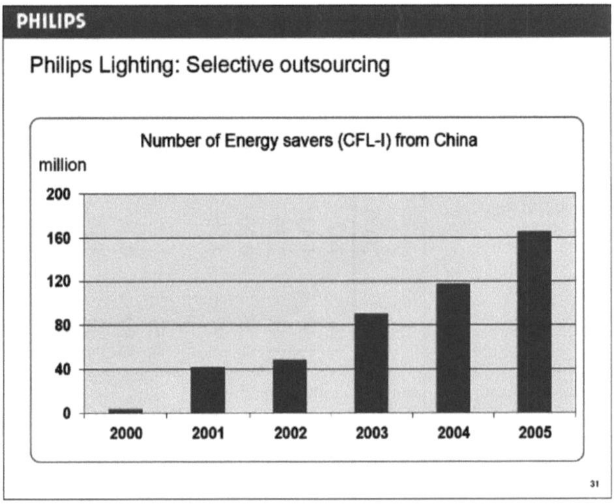

Graph 15.3 Philips' declared import priorities as carrier of dumping of CFLs

of dumping and injury.[17] All European producers had benefited from anti-circumvention, although some apparently had themselves tried to circumvent the measures by fraud or otherwise. Some, however, were bothered by the mere existence of duties. They had reached the conclusion that investments were needed for a serious competitive presence in the European Community. Philips had closed its factory in Terneuzen and shifted production to Poland, which had entered the European Community in 2004 again making Philips a European Community producer. The move to Poland was because it hoped that labour costs would be sufficiently low to meet Chinese competition. However, in Poland the machinery that had been moved from the Netherlands was still an impediment to high-speed mass production. Therefore, Philips changed its policy and decided to import products from China in mass volume and to continue production of certain long life products in Poland. This had even become a declared policy.

In 2007, Philips expressed its policy to use dumped imports, which it called outsourcing, as essential element in its marketing, as Graph 15.3 indicates.[18]

Philips confirmed its policy in a hearing by the European Commission in the review case on CFL in January 2007.[19]

---

[17] The Basic Regulation: Council Regulation (EC) No 1225/2009 of 30 November 2009 on protection against dumped imports, OJ L 343/51 of 22 December 2009 (codified), Article 11, Duration, reviews and refunds, of Council Regulation. In Chap. 14 is reported that, because the European Commission had made a compromise and a promise, the duration for fax machines was 2 years only. Expiry and interim reviews were mixed up.

[18] Power point presentation of Kai den Daas, COO of Philips Lighting, Financial Analysts Meeting, 7 December 2005: "Building on strength in existing businesses. - Shaping the future in new business areas."

[19] Philips Lighting: Follow-Up Submission to the Hearing on 11 January 2007, Version for Inspection by Interested Parties.

Philips reiterates its argument that imports of mid-segment CFL-i from China are a necessary strategic complement to EU produced CFL-i. As explained in Philips' responses to the Commission questionnaires and Philips' submission of 10 January 2007 on injury and Community interest, CFL-i imported by Philips are mid-segment consumer, in contrast to Philips' EU produced CFL-i which are high-segment consumer and professional.

Since Chinese exports cover all segments, as shown below, it remains in the dark what is understood under "mid-segment consumer". Apparently Philips gambled on the intervention by Trade Commissioner Mandelson, who was not particularly a non-judgmental Commissioner. Specification of this term "mid-segment consumer" was not offered. The exporters Lisheng and Supertrend exported lamps with the same and higher specifications, which Philips called "professional". So did Yankon, and at present Philips sells lamps from China with specifications identical to those it made in Poland.

During the whole process, Philips' position was underestimated and there was insufficient awareness that it pursed the elimination of its main competitor in all lighting segments, OSRAM, *inter alia* by means of dumped imports. It hoped to do so by using its distribution clout in the consumer market and using imported Chinese lamps from its related party Yankon and some others, thereby undercutting prices of OSRAM and gaining market share. Its distribution force, it hoped, enabled it to resist competitive Chinese imports by its own low priced imports accompanied with its brand name. Many problems would have been avoided if Philips had been excluded from the definition of European Community industry. For this exclusion ample arguments were present and presented.

Since GE's General Manager of Lighting & Appliances, GE Consumer & Industrial, EMEA, had informed the complainant: "I reviewed the GE Lighting position on Anti dumping Duties for CFL internally, and I would like to inform you that we would prefer that the AD duties will remain in force indefinitely", a majority of the European Community production appeared to support the request for an expiry review. GE was located in Hungary and this company had, like Philips in Poland, become a European Community producer by the accession of this country in 2004.

Before opening the investigation, the European Commission had investigated whether a majority of production was in favour of continuation of the measures. This appeared to be the case. The European Commission initiated the investigation[20]:

The request was lodged on 18 April 2006 by the Community Federation of Lighting Industry of Compact Fluorescent Lamps Integrated (2 CFL-i) ('the applicant') on behalf of producers representing a major proportion, in this case more than 25 %, of the total Community production of integrated electronic compact fluorescent lamps (CFL-i).

Before the initiation of an investigation the European Commission must establish that the complaint was made on behalf of the industry[21]:

[20] Notice of initiation of an expiry review of the antidumping measures applicable to imports of integrated electronic compact fluorescent lamps (CFL-i) originating in the People's Republic of China (2006/C 167/04), OJ C 167/13 of 19.7.2006.

[21] The Basic Regulation: Council Regulation (EC) No 1225/2009 of 30 November 2009 on protection against dumped imports, OJ L 343/51 of 22 December 2009 (codified), Article, 5 Initiation of proceedings, 4.

An investigation shall not be initiated pursuant to paragraph 1 unless it has been determined, on the basis of an examination as to the degree of support for, or opposition to, the complaint expressed by Community producers of the like product, that the complaint has been made by or on behalf of the Community industry. The complaint shall be considered to have been made by or on behalf of the Community industry if it is supported by those Community producers whose collective output constitutes more than 50 % of the total production of the like product produced by that portion of the Community industry expressing either support for or opposition to the complaint.

It had been established that the majority supported the Request. This appeared also to be the case, when data from the producers in the questionnaire responses had arrived at the Commission's. In the Expiry Request the complainant emphasised "Of at least one company imports from China represent a substantial, increasing and injurious part of sales of the product concerned in the Community. The imports cover such a great portion that imports cannot be considered defensive…" and urged the exclusion of Philips from the definition of European Community industry, but the European Commission did not respond and hid its intentions.

The definition of industry is not a positive description of characteristics, but based on exceptions and exclusions. The reasons for exclusion of Philips and even of GE appeared ample and the Request presented these arguments, but data and arguments were disregarded after some time. Some of the aspects of the definition of European Community industry and the conditions for exclusion from the definition needed attention.

According to Article 4, Definition of European Community industry, paragraph 1, the European Community industry refers "to the Community producers as a whole of the like products or to those of them whose collective output of the products constitutes a major proportion, as defined in Article 5(4),[22] of the total Community production of those products, except that…" And the exceptions are normally[23]:

(a) *"when producers are related to the exporters or importers or*
(b) *are themselves importers of the allegedly dumped product*".

The relationship is taken to exist if:

(a) "*one of them directly or indirectly controls the other; or*
(b) *both of them are directly or indirectly controlled by a third person; or*
(c) *together they directly or indirectly control a third person provided that there are grounds for believing or suspecting that the effect of the relationship is such as to cause the producer concerned to behave differently from non-related producers.*"

[22] If it is supported by 25 % or more of the volume of production of the "like product" and not more than 50 % opposes the complaint.

[23] Article 4.1.a. of the Basic Regulation. According to Article 4.1.b exceptions do also exist in the case of regional markets, which need not be discussed here, exceptional as they are.

In this respect, the analysis of the text of the Basic Regulation and of European Community policy given by Müller, Khan and Neumann, and the cases to which they refer, is worthwhile[24]:

> *The institutions have, on several occasions, concluded that exclusion is justified where the producers in the Community either:*
>
> 1. *participated in the dumping practices,*
> 2. *are shielded from their effects, or*
> 3. *where they benefited unduly from them.*[25]
>
> *With regard to the first category, i.e. the participation in dumping practices several typical situations may be distinguished. On the one hand, the exclusion is indeed appropriate where the injury of a Community producer is self-inflicted because imports of dumped products:*
>
> (a) *provoked or contributed to a fall in prices on the market,*[26] *or*
> (b) *reduced the use of Community producers' own capacity,*[27] *or*
> (c) *resulted in the abandonment of Community producers' projects designed to increase their own production.*[28]

All criteria point at excluding Philips. A critical inspection of the criteria for exclusion is not excessive in this respect[29]:

- With a share of 25–35 % of total dumped imports from China, Philips was Europe's main importer of dumped energy saving lamps from China. Philips' imports constituted about 60 % or more of its own total volume of sales. According to GfK January/February 2003, 2005 and 2006, stick lamps imported from China constituted an overwhelming 67 % of Philips' sales. The share of stick lamps made in Poland of the PLE-T and PLE-C type finally dropped from 48 % and constituted only 3 % of its sales in 2006, while the rest of other Polish made lamps constitute 31 %. The share of Polish lamps, which is European Community production, dropped from 79 % to 34 %. During the proceeding, Table 15.8 was presented as evidence of Philips' was shielded by imports of dumped products from injury and contributed to reduction of own and others' production.
- As for the relationship, the main exporter Yankon had a relationship with Philips. On its Internet site Yankon proudly announced: "*2001: Yankon, by joining hands with Philips, established 'Zhejiang Yankon Lighting Co. Ltd'. Endeavoring to the R&D of energy saving products.*" Philips and Yankon had a joint venture, already described earlier at the occasion of circumvention of duties via Vietnam by Yankon.

---

[24] Müller et al. (1998), pp. 243–244. In following footnotes, their references are given.

[25] OJ No L 80, 24.3.94, p. 1 (recital 22) – potassium chloride from Belarus, Russia and Ukraine/review; OJ No L 157, 29.6.93, p. 76 (recital 12) – electronic typewriters from Japan/review; OJ No L 95, 21 .4.93, p. 5 (recital 40) – magnetic disks from Japan, Taiwan and P.R. China/provisional.

[26] OJ No L 54, 24.2.87, p. 12 (recital 62) – plain paper photocopiers from Japan/definitive.

[27] Case C-69/89 Nakajima All Precision Co. Ltd. v. Council [1991] ECR 1–2069 (paragraphs 81 and 82).

[28] Same source as previous footnote.

[29] See also Müller et al. (1998), pp. 237–254.

Table 15.8 Role of Chinese imports in sales of Philips

Share in Philips sales in Germany[a]	2003 (%)	2005 (%)	2006 (%)
Stick lamps from China	20.5	66	67
Stick lamps from Poland (PLE-C/PLE-T)	48.9	2.3	2.5
Other (from Poland) (softone, bulb, etc.)	30.6	32	30.5

[a]Source GfK on first 2 months of 2003, 2005 and 2006

- The request presented several examples of increased dumping – 93.5 %, 105 % under the Philips brand and more than 300 % under the Pila brand – of lamps from Yankon and other Chinese lamp producers via Philips.
- There was a demonstration of undercutting of Philips' prices of European Community manufactured lamps by Philips' imports from China, i.e. Table 15.9.
- In a later submission the information was reiterated that, under pressure from China, Philips Lighting's senior vice president in China Mark K. Hu announced in 2000: "…that Philips Lighting would shift its CFL-i R&D centre from the Netherlands to Shanghai (China), and would close its Dutch plant while moving the production line off European Community, to countries including Poland and China."[30] The interest of Philips was clearly not the elimination of dumping and concentration of interests in the European Community.
- Philips' imports could have been defensive; the company did not consider its imports defensive, but part of an aggressive strategy.

In view of initial support by GE to the opening of the investigation, the exclusion of Philips from the definition of European Community industry did not initially seem, although urged in the file, urgent or essential. However, in view of the European Commission's silence and ambiguity on this subject, this appeared a mistake. These considerations did not take Commissioner Mandelson's contempt of European Community rule and practice into account, which were not in conformity with his own imagination. The definition of European Community industry became an essential issue, though. As we shall see, this Commissioner even made Article 5.4 about the opening of a proceeding (quoted above) poly-interpretable.

At the beginning of the review, Philips opposed continuation of duties and alleged that the complainant did not have sufficient support. Since a GE executive had expressed the opinion that GE did not oppose the review, a majority of production had in any case expressed support to the initiation of the investigation. Three months after opening of the investigation, however, the European Commission approached GE to review its opinion. Suddenly and stunningly the definition of European Community industry had become an essential issue by this surprising initiative of the European Commission. Although prior to the opening, a sufficient amount of support was established, unexpectedly the European Commission raised the question

[30] Quoted in Antidumping and Competition: The Case of China by Hang Zeng, August 2005, from a press release of Philips China on 22 December 2000, in "Philips turan chechu oumeng fanqingxiao diaocha (Philips Withdraws from The E.U. Antidumping Investigation)", Beijing qingnian bao (Beijing Youth), 23 December 2000.

Table 15.9 Self-destruction: undercutting of Philips' production by its own Chinese imports

Philips' undercutting of its own products[a]	1998	2003	2005
Philips PLE-T stick lamp 15 W made in Poland (>10,000 h) C15AA	€13.92	€12.93	€10.98
Philips PLE-T adjusted to 3,000 h lamp (A15AA)	€8.20	€7.62	€6.47
Philips/Yankon lamp 18 W made in China, 3 years lifetime		€6.04	€4.47
Undercutting at retail level		€1.58	€1.99
As per cent of CIF value		**68 %**	**150 %**

whether the investigation could continue. It appeared that the European Commission had again assumed a questionable role. Because of the Philips' wish, the European Commission excluded Philips and its injury data from the investigation. Now it wished Philips to be included, although all parameters pointed to exclusion. Besides, this time the European Commission provided even false information. In a letter of 19 January 2007 a European Commission official wrote[31]:

> *As you are aware, the known Community producers that have explicitly stated opposition to the application are Philips Lighting, GE Hungary and Sylvania Lighting Ltd. According to Article 5(4) of the Basic Regulation, the application must be supported by at least 50 % of those Community producers that either expresses support for or opposition to the application.*

This statement was deceptive. According to Article 5 (4) an investigation shall not *be initiated*, unless it has been determined, on the basis of an examination as to the degree of support for, or opposition to, the complaint expressed by European Community producers of the like product, that the complaint has been made by or on behalf of the European Community industry. The investigation was already initiated. Consequently, the European Commission had found a majority of production expressing support to the investigation and subsequently the investigation was opened. By a highly awkward move the European Commission created confusion by a false presentation of the rules. The Basic Regulation explicitly refers in Article 5.4 to initiation of the investigation and support that has to be given to a complaint. It does not state that the investigation should or can be terminated when one or more producers would change their minds.

> *The complaint shall be considered to have been made by or on behalf of the Community industry if it is supported by those Community producers whose collective output constitutes more than 50 % of the total production of the like product produced by that portion of the Community industry expressing either support for or opposition to the complaint. However, no investigation shall be initiated when Community producers expressly supporting the complaint account for less than 25 % of total production of the like product produced by the Community industry.*

It does not state that during the investigation the parties should be re-interviewed about whether they continue their support. Such behaviour would produce great uncertainty about the proceeding and its outcome, as it was by the exclusion of

[31] Letter H.6/TO D (2007) 602 of 19 January 2007 from the Commission to the industry association.

Philips in the original case. The European Commission had apparently approached GE. This company responded, but it did not oppose the investigation.[32] Either the European Commission had not, if it had not scrutinised the support, legally opened the investigation or its second enquiry was groundless.

> *Reference is made to your earlier email, in response to which I confirm that GE is* ***now not interested*** *in the continuation of the anti-dumping duties.*
>
> *Since the Commission's review was initiated, GE has undertaken its own review of market developments and trends.* ***GE does not believe*** *that the Community industry would be injured by Chinese imports if there were no measures and all players were competing under the same import duty treatment. ... We are confident that* ***your investigation*** *will come to the same conclusions and look forward to discussing these issues with you further* [Emphasis added.]

Without prior notice to participants, the European Commission approached GE, which had supported the review, and the European Commission drew misleading conclusions because the letter apparently did not contain opposition to the investigation. It expressed belief and confidence that the investigation would result in some and the same conclusions as GE. This implies that GE did not oppose the continuation of the investigation. That was not sufficient for the European Commissioner, apparently.

Although indicators pointed at the exclusion of Philips from the definition of the European Community industry, the complainant did not get any decisive answer about this subject. Instead, suddenly, on 26 November 2006 – more than 4 months after the opening of the investigation and in response to e-mail from the European Commission for which there was neither a cause nor legal ground – GE was "now not interested" in a continuation of duties. It did not oppose the investigation and did not express that it wanted the investigation to be stopped. GE did not believe that the industry would be injured. The European Commission tried to stop an investigation into facts on the basis of a belief of GE.

Since GE did not expressly state that it did not want the investigation to be terminated, the European Commission again took the initiative, insisted and wanted a more articulate expression of opposition against the measures. On 13 February 2007, GE responded to a European Commission e-mail of the European Commission:

> *With reference to your e-mail below we confirm that our position paper of 26 November, 2006 (which you referred to in your e-mail below) was meant to confirm our opposition to the continuation of the measures (within the meaning of Article 5(4) of the basic Anti-dumping Regulation), therefore the Commissions understanding is correct.*

This GE response was to an e-mail sent by a European Commission official, with a suggestion concerning the content of the response that should be negative for the complainant, inviting GE to oppose the case:

> *It is the understanding of the Commission services that GE Hungary Zrt now (as expressed during the on the spot visit on 7 November 2007 and made available to other interested parties by your position paper of 26 November 2006) opposes continuation of measures*

[32] Letter of 26 November 2006, signed by Csaba Kuhne, Product Line Manager GE Hungary."

(within the meaning of Article 5(4) of the basic Antidumping Regulation). Could you confirm that the understanding of opposition to continuation of measures is correct? Could I have this confirmation asap?

It remains a secret whether GE's thoughts had changed and if so, what the official of the European Commission had done to change the thoughts of GE during the on-the-spot verification in the beginning of November and whether he was instructed by the Commissioner. This is the more amazing because exactly 1 week after the official's 7 November 2007 visit to GE Hungary Zrt a meeting took place between the same official and the complainant, prior to a verification visit of the European Commission to Philips in Eindhoven. The European Commission official did not say a word about GE's inhibitions or change of mind, if any and instead gave some rather superfluous instructions to the complainant how to make the complainant's case even more successful.

Sylvania Lighting International, although it knew how some Chinese producers circumvented duties by intermediary assembly in the same Tunisian factory where it had its own assembly, did not fear these imports, but rather feared European competitors with Chinese production[33]:

SLI Lighting Ltd ("SLI") is a European manufacturer and supplier of CFL-i lamps which sources some products from the People's Republic of China. SLI does not consider that dumping is occurring as it appears that input costs are comparable for Chinese manufacturers and European suppliers manufacturing in the People's Republic of China. SLI does not, therefore, consider that the European market would be harmed if anti-dumping measures were discontinued.

Further, SLI considers that, if the anti-dumping measures are maintained, they will result in a distortion of competition on the European market as European suppliers manufacturing in the People's Republic of China will enjoy a competitive advantage over European competitors which import products from the People's Republic of China. Ultimately, SLI believes that this distortion of competition will lead to higher prices on the European market to the detriment of consumers.

This still did not reveal clearly whether SLI, with this confusing letter with inconsistent statements, opposed the complaint and continuation of measures or not. Apart from this uncertainty, it was obvious that its allegations were untrue. European suppliers did not enjoy a competitive advantage. The European Commission drew the conclusion from these statements that Sylvania was against the continuation of the investigation and wanted to stop it. There is not any clue in the Basic Regulation to stop without measures on other grounds than those mentioned in the regulation, in particular Article 9. Sylvania's fear, however, was specifically directed against advantages from which some European producers benefited. These benefits were attributable to duties for Chinese exporters that were lower than others'. But on 13 February 2007, almost 5 month after the opening, prior to which the European Commission had already verified the support, the company finally revealed some "considerations" but not an opposition to the investigation.

[33] SLI Lighting Ltd Position Paper – European Commission Expiry Review of anti-dumping measures applicable to integrated electronic compact fluorescent lamps (CFL-i) originating in the People's Republic of China, of 19 December 2006.

Apparently, Philips had convinced somebody at the European Commission, probably the Commissioner, that its imports were not injurious and even salutary to the European Community and that the Commission should not apply the law. Its sales of dumped Chinese lamps amounted to 25–30 % of total imports from China, and exceeded sales from own production. Philips indicated that dumping imports had become its normal practice. Most of imports of stick lamps, in total about 40 million units, came from Yankon, its related party in a joint venture. All of this would have been a sufficient condition of exclusion of the company as "related" party and as a major importer. The Commissioner was not bound by logic or rules, however. Due to the opinions of the Commissioner, it was probably the first time that, although it imported more dumped products than it produced in the European Community, a company successfully claimed to be European Community industry.

The position of Philips and GE fit into a vagary of Commissioner Peter Mandelson's mind. He brought one of his ideas, which had already vigorously been rejected by both industry associations and most member states in a discussion about his Green Book, in practice, without prior consent. This idea is summarised in a statement in the Green Book.[34]

> *Many more EU companies now produce goods outside the EU for import into the EU, or operate supply chains that stretch beyond the EU market. These changes challenge familiar understanding of what constitutes EU production.*

It may be wondered what familiar understanding of what constitutes EU production is. The sentence does not have a meaning. Although it is undoubtedly the case that companies with headquarters in Europe have production overseas, this fact does not imply that the European Community should allow dumping of these products. The use of foreign markets as carriers for dumping and dumped imports should not be a main argument for denial or negligence of existence of dumping by a Commissioner, who is supposed to foster international trade on the basis of sound and normal competition. Price differences should be based on (relative) competitive advantage and not on dumping. Since he failed to make any contribution to world trade liberalisation in the Doha Development Agenda (DDA), the round of world trade negotiations, he apparently tried to leave marks in the international trade history. The Commissioner tried to bring into practice in this review case his exotic, even bizarre idea about changes, challenging familiar understanding, which had sensibly been rejected in the discussions about the Green Book. The European Commission services under his command brought forward the following simple thesis: all producers import from China. Not even an attempt was made to distinguish between a company that imported from China three times its own production and covered all its needs for stick lamps with a lifetime of less than 10,000 h from China, and a company that sold four times more from European production than it imported. The latter imported products that were specialities requiring much manual labour, whereas the first imported all its needs for less than 10,000 h

[34] GLOBAL EUROPE, European Commission External Trade Europe's Trade Defence Instruments in a Changing Global Economy, A Green Paper.

lifetime stick and some other models of lamps from China. Because all producers imported from China, they apparently should be treated as identical cases. The conclusions of the European Commission were wrapped in obscure phraseology, which ultimately is proven to be nonsense:

> *However, while the imports are considerable in quantity, they are far less so if the value is taken into consideration. The value-based analysis clearly shows that they are keeping high value production in the Community while outsourcing low value production. All of them also continue provide considerable employment in the Community. This shows that they clearly have kept their "centre of interest" of production in the Community. For these reasons, none of them are being considered for exclusion from the definition of the Community production.*

These remarks are not only *prima facie* stunning; they are, after some analysis, stupefying and "challenge familiar understanding" of any kind. Due to low prices of these imports, characteristic of dumped import prices and price undercutting, the value of these imports is so low that European production has a relatively high value, which is allegedly "kept" in the European Community. As long as there is dumping and undercutting, there remains of course relatively higher value of the remaining production in the European Community until the undercutting results in zero European production. When this stage is achieved, the average price of European production kept in Europe is infinite (a price divided by zero volume).

It might be expected that a producer is considered not to belong to European Community industry if it makes the following statement: "Philips produces high-segment and professional CFL-i in the EU (Poland and the Netherlands) and imports mid-segment CFL-i from China." Since all CFL-i is one "like product" in a proceeding, the distinction is nonsense and irrelevant. The imports from China appear to represent the major part (60 %) of Philips' sales volume, but due to the low prices and the high volumes, the average value of these imports is by definition relatively low. This inspired the European Commission to one of the weirdest manoeuvres ever, apparently inspired by a Commissioner with "new ideas" challenging familiar understanding. In a letter of 19 January 2007, the European Commission services used the following terms about resale of dumped imports:

> *The value-based analysis clearly shows that they are keeping high value production in the Community while outsourcing low value production.*

The European Commission presented as "*value-based analysis*" some list with percentages in the stunning Table 15.10 that does not deserve the connotation of "analysis".

There would not be the slightest reason to present such a lengthy and detailed case in this book were it not a warning of highly peculiar steps that can impossibly be expected, but took place with the authority of a Commissioner. If the Commissioner was unable to conduct a trade policy, he swifted to whims. It is an instructive example of surprises caused by blind ambition of a Commissioner wishing to impose his preconceived ideas in proceedings, not in accordance with European Community rule and practice. He made anti-dumping a political instrument in

Table 15.10 Commissioner Mandelson's new ideas: untenable thesis as basis for a new policy

Company (1)	European Community sales (volumes) sourced from community production as % of total volume sales (2)	European Community sales (values) sourced from community production as % of total value of sales (3)
A	60	80
B	20	50
C	70	70
D	40	60

which he intervened arbitrarily, according to his own high-handedness. Table 15.10 is supposed to be a reflection of the Commissioner's Green Book thesis and demonstrates the fallacies in opinions of Commissioner Mandelson.[35]

Before the content of Table 15.10 is criticised, some remarks should be made about such a table in general. Table 15.10 can be represented by some simple equations. Column (2) of Table 15.10 gives the share of the volume of sales of European Community sourced products in total sales volume in the European Community of each producer A to D, i.e. share of these sales in the totality of European Community-sourced and Chinese-sourced products. For instance, in the second cell of the first row the fraction of 60 % is the share of European sourced volume (Q_E) in total volume $Q_E + Q_C$, where Q_E and Q_C are respectively sales volumes sourced from European production and sourced by means of imports from China:

$$a = \frac{Q_E}{Q_E + Q_C} \tag{15.1}$$

Where a is, for instance, the coefficient 60 % in the first row in column (2) for Company A, i.e. the share of A's European sales in total sales volume.

Similarly, column (3) of Table 15.10 can be expressed in a very simple equation:

$$b = \frac{P_E \cdot Q_E}{P_E \cdot Q_E + P_C \cdot Q_C} \tag{15.2}$$

P_E and P_C are the average resale prices of the European and Chinese sourced products. The coefficient b is the 80 % value share of European Community sourced lamps in the sales of Company A.

[35] It is incomprehensible that a politician, who was transferred from London to Brussels after the conduct of his financial affairs was criticised, can so deliberately cross lines of law without any check and balances. Even the threat to challenge such practices in Parliament or in court would not have had the slightest effect on the acts of a Commissioner for whom rules of European Community law were apparently irrelevant.

Table 15.11 Challenging familiar understanding: Mandelson's "value based" analysis

Company		Relationship	Relationship P_E/P_C
A		a = 60 %; b = 80 %	Factor is **2.67**
B	$\frac{b.(1-a)}{a.(1-b)} =$	a = 20 %; b = 50 %	Factor is **4.0**
C (= OSRAM)		a = 70 %; b = 70 %	Factor is **1.00**
D (= Philips)		a = 40 %; b = 60 %	Factor is **2.25**

The substitution of 15.1 in 15.2 results in 15.3:

$$\frac{P_E}{P_C} = \frac{b.(1-a)}{a.(1-b)} \tag{15.3}$$

If the Table produced by the European Commission is converted in some simple algebraic expressions, it merely states that there is a price relationship between the European sourced products and Chinese products sold by these European Community producers, which are also importers. There is no greater wisdom in it than the fact that there is a relationship between average selling or resale prices of European and Chinese sourced products. That is, of course, not a "value-based analysis". It is nothing at all (Table 15.11).

The only evidence that Table 15.10 presents is that on the average, resale prices of all imports from China – with the exception of the prices of OSRAM – undercut European Community prices, i.e. $P_C < P_E$. The average prices are irrelevant, however. They do not supply any information on the products involved nor about the value of the production kept or imported. As stated in Chap. 2, the only permissible price comparison in anti-dumping is between individual and similar models. Conclusively, the European Commission presented the fruits of a meaningless operation, undermining its own legislation. The truism is that all products sourced in the European Community have some price relationship with the China-sourced products. That is, of course, not a secret. The conclusion can also be drawn that all resale prices of Chinese lamps are below those of European lamps, with the exception of Company C, the complainant OSRAM. The conclusion that the company with the lowest share of Chinese imports does not keep "value" in the European Community is the absurd corollary of this "value-analysis". It is, furthermore, essential to anti-dumping investigations that price differences, indicating injury by undercutting average European Community resale prices, are found and this is certainly not a reason for the termination of an investigation. Rather, it is a reason for perseverance and for conclusions on dumping and undercutting. More frequent presentation of tables such as Table 15.10 would undoubtedly have had a lasting negative impact on the reputation of the European Commission in anti-dumping. Commissioner Mandelson did not very long after this proceeding return to the United Kingdom to challenge familiar understanding there.

Table 15.12 Thinking in anti-thesis: increase in dumping is value creation in the European Community

Company C (in Table 15.10)	Community sales (volumes)	Community sales (values)	Average prices[a] and fraction
Resale European Community production in index	**100**	297	€2.97
Resale Chinese imports in index	43	127	€2.97
Producer % as in Table 15.10	70 %	70 %	1.00
Resale European Community production in index	**100**	297	€2.97
Resale Chinese imports (price change – 20 %)	43	106	€2.48
Producer % as in Table 15.10	70 %	74 %	1.05

[a]Actual data for C could have been presented, but since the data provided by the European Commission in Table 15.10 were incorrect and differed from those given in the official confidential disclosure, volume figures had to be revised to those of Table 15.10

Some other conclusions are:

1. The Basic Regulation prescribes that the European Commission investigate whether the expiry of the measures would likely result in a continuation or recurrence of dumping and injury, not whether companies – on the basis of undefined and even senseless criteria – keep some or "high" value in the European Community. The European Commission neglected its assignment as prescribed in the Basic Regulation and presented an "analysis" without relationship with the basic anti-dumping regulation.
2. The higher the level of injury, i.e. the higher European prices are in relation to the Chinese, or vice versa, the more Chinese prices undercut European prices, the "higher" – according to this absurd theory – the value kept in the European Community. The conclusion of the European Commission contradicts common sense and familiar understanding. See Table 15.12.
3. The word "keeping" was used. "Keeping" requires a comparison of data at least at two points in time. A comparison of data over time by the European Commission was absent, however. From Table 15.11 it is clear that OSRAM, which kept production and value in the European Community, did not keep value according to the Commission's "value analysis", but kept the highest level of value when an intertemporary comparison was made (Table 15.13).
4. Only by neglect of the differences between products that are essential in the proper calculation of dumping and injury, the European Commission arrived at untenable theses about "high value". It is easily demonstrable that neglect of the difference between product characteristics resulted in an unfounded confirmation of prejudices.
5. The data presented in Table 15.10 appeared wrong and the European Commission presented different figures in the formal disclosure.

Intervention by Commissioner Mandelson or his Cabinet must have caused such errors. When a Commissioner keeps his distance from the procedure, European

Table 15.13 "Keeping value" in the European Community and Chinese import share

	European volume (%)	European value (%)	Ratio	Volume share Chinese imports (%)
Philips **2002**	64	78	1.22	36
Philips **2006**	36	52	1.44	64
OSRAM **2002**	77	91	1.18	21
OSRAM **2006**	68	68	1.00	32
GE **2002**	24	37	1.54	76
GE **2006**	10	36	3.60	90
Sylvania **2002**	31	60	1.94	54
Sylvania **2006**	62	75	1.21	38
All 4 **2002**	65	83	1.28	35
All 4 **2006**	52	61	1.17	48

Commission services normally do not demonstrate such a lack of common sense or know-how. The attempt to close the case on other grounds than the question whether continuation of dumping and injury would take place if the measures were discontinued was clearly an infringement of European Community law. The question whether producers keep high value in the European Community is irrelevant, particularly if the answer to that question is based on irrelevant relations between some percentages.

It is an apparent error that the data demonstrated that high value is kept in the European Community. Table 15.12, shows that, if dumping increased (Chinese import prices decreased), the "value kept" in the European Community would, according to this excentric argumentation, "increase", although the value remains exactly the same. The European volume and value, as given in Table 15.11, do not change, but the import price of Chinese lamps is decreased by 20 %. The conclusion is that European Community share in total sales value increased from 70 % to 74 % by an increase in dumping margin of 20 %.

Clearly, European resales as a share of total resales in volume and value do not give an indication of value kept in the European Community. The only conclusion is that Chinese prices were lower than European prices. When the dumping margin increased by a decrease in the export price of the Chinese product, the value kept in the European Community, according to this weird European Commission theory, increased! Such argumentation defies familiar and any understanding and, more importantly, the basics of anti-dumping law and agreed practice and of logic.

The other point of critique was that "keeping value" implies that at least data at two points in time should be provided and compared. Philips' European share in its sales decreased substantially. The volume of its sales of European products decreased by 29 % points and the value by 25 % points. According to the way of thinking of the European Commission, the value kept in the European Community would "increase".

Between 2002 and 2006, the European Community (in this case the German retail) market increased in volume by 17 % and in value by 15 %. This low decrease in average price did not mean that prices decreased so little. The decrease per lamp model was substantial. The composition of product range changed by which the total average remained relatively stable. Between 2002 and 2006 the share of the simplest lamps, stick lamps, in total volume of sales decreased from 73 % to 60 %. The market share of Philips' resales of imports from China, mainly stick lamps, in the total market, comprising all models, increased from 2.8 % to 12.7 %. The share of its European-made products also increased by 2 % points. Philips stopped production of its own technology stick lamps other than long-life lamps, which Philips called "professional", although OSRAM, GE and SLI sold the same type of lamps, but as consumer products. In 2002, Philips' European "professional" stick lamps had a share in the stick market of 3.7 %. This dropped to 1.2 % in 2006. Its Chinese stick lamps increased their share in the German stick market from 3.7 % in 2002 to 22.7 % in 2006. By an increase in imports of cheap stick lamps, Philips was allegedly "keeping high value production in the Community", as the European Commission services were felt compelled to state, although it lost value in terms of volume and value market share. By its imports of dumped Chinese products, Philips' market share in the German market increased from 7.8 % in 2002 to 19.8 %. In 2006, Philips' Chinese products obtained a share of 12.7 % in the total German CFL market.

The European Commission neglected differences between behaviour of the manufacturers in Europe and the objectives of these companies. Table 15.13 shows sales of CFL-i in January and February 2003 and 2006. From type indications and market research, provenance of products can be derived. Philips, for instance, purchased all its less than 10,000 h lifetime lamps in China, from Yankon, Librite, Feihua and some others. It purchased its sensor lamps from Gulf Advanced Lighting in Dubai. That Philips purchased its stick lamps from China was, *inter alia*, the consequence of the deplorable construction of its burner, the fluorescent tube, which is too weak for sticks and needs a cover. Philips produced bulb, candle and globe lamps with this frail burner in Poland. Its "professional", i.e. highly – because of the costly burner production, which is produced in low volume – expensive stick lamps were also produced in Poland after the closure of the factory in the Netherlands. Osram imported from its subsidiaries in China or purchased lamps in the beginning of a product cycle, when automated production was not yet not suitable. GE and Sylvania rather completed their product range with some products that they presented as "economy" mainly because of the low price.

The ratios between European value to volume sales shares did not offer a clue to value kept in the European Community. Philips "keeps value" by importing a larger volume of Chinese lamps than any other manufacturer in the European Community at a lower price than any other producer. The "value kept in the Community" by Osram decreased from 118 to 100. This phenomenon was attributable to the fact that the average resale price of imports from China increased by 23 %. As a consequence the ratio between Osram's sales of European products sales, as share in total value and total volume decreased. Because it did not resell its imports from China cheaply, i.e. did not undercut its own prices and those of others, the only producer who did not "keep value", according to this innovative and inimitable methodology was, although the European Commission did not dare to draw such a

Table 15.14 Movement of average CFL prices (January/February 2002–2006) in the German market

	Sticks	Bulbs (%)	Candles (%)	Globes (%)	All products (%)
Philips' European products prices	**54 %**	−20	−29	−10	
Philips' European products volume	**−71 %**	321	137	112	67
OSRAM's European products prices	−42 %	−29	−40	−22	
OSRAM's European products volume	36 %	−7	1,052	−28	35

conclusion and allege it openly, complainant OSRAM.[36] OSRAM's Chinese imports represented a lower share in its total sales, but the very fact that resales from China were not cheap awkwardly implied that, according to the European Commission's amazing approach of "value analysis", OSRAM did not keep value in the European Community as others did. Table 15.13 gives information on the policy of Philips that demonstrates the absurdity of the "value creation" thesis advanced by the European Commission on instruction from Commissioner Mandelson.

Table 15.14 shows that the prices of Philips' stick lamps of European make went up because of a huge reduction of production and sales of its stick lamps from China in the lower price ranges, which it started to import mainly after 2002. In relation to the Chinese lamps the European value, of course, increased.

There was a clear difference among European Community companies for levels of imports and characteristics of imported products. OSRAM imported Chinese products, but the proportion of Chinese products was far inferior to sales from domestic European Community production, as may be clear from the graphs. It also presented its production plans, showing that its imports would be replaced by production in the European Community. From Graph 15.4 is clear that Chinese imports represented a small minority in OSRAM's sales. The company already had idle capacity in 2003 and the situation worsened in 2003. The lamps imported from China were those for which much manual labour was required. These were especially "twist lamps" and certain reflector lamps. The capacity remained stable, but capacity utilisation – already below 75 % in 2003 – fell substantially. The other producers increased their capacity moderately, but Philips' utilisation of capacity fell by 23 %, mainly attributable to the fact that its imports increased to more than 25 % of total imports from China.

[36] The illogical methodology of the European Commission is repeated in these allegations. If the comparisons are not made on the basis of model per model, statements on keeping value are meaningless. If heavily dumped products are imported and these did heavily undercut European prices, the value is destroyed on the side of the European producers, but is presented as value creation because the prices of remaining European products are relatively higher than those of Chinese imported product.

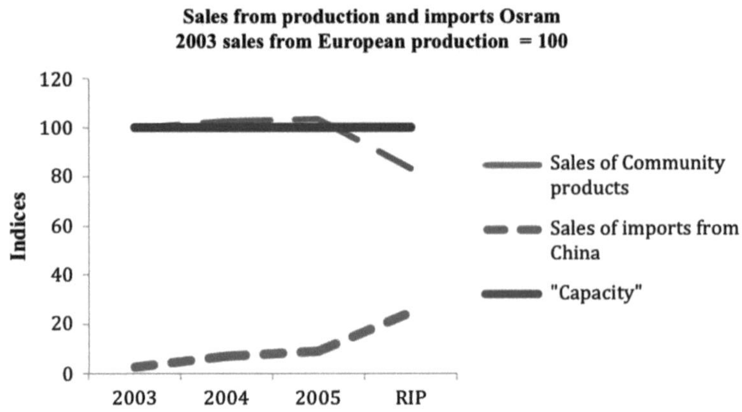

Graph 15.4 Composition of CFL sales by OSRAM in the European Community (sales from European Community production is 100; European production capacity in 2003 is 100)

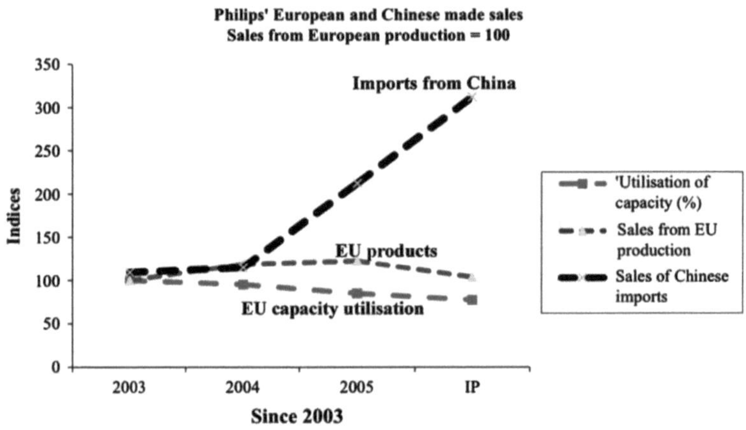

Graph 15.5 Composition of CFL sales by Philips and development of capacity (sales from European Community production in 2003 is 100; European production capacity in 2003 = 100)

OSRAM revealed its production plans to the European Commission. Most imports from China would be replaced by investments in the European Community. A new factory had been installed in Slovakia and the first production runs had been started.

As Graph 15.5 shows, in 2002 Philips' sales from China still balanced its sales from European Community production. Thereafter, Philips became the European Community's greatest importer. Its import volume had become three times its sales from European production. Imports from China represented about 75 % of its volume sales, the prices of which were relatively so low that the European prices were necessarily relatively high and the European Commission labelled this "value

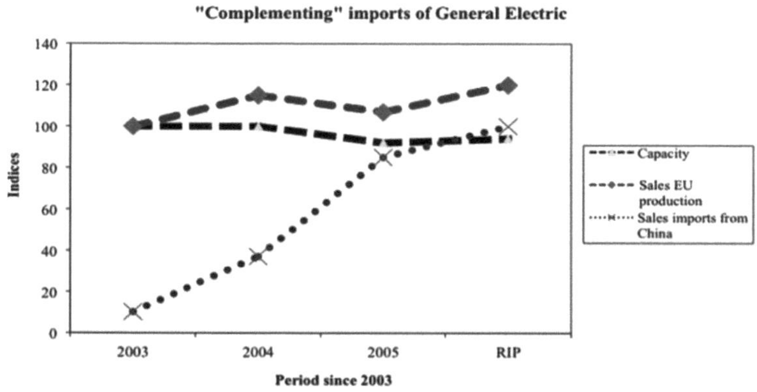

Graph 15.6 Composition of GE's CFL sales (sales from European production in 2003 = 100; European production capacity 2003 is 100)

creation". Normally, the decrease in sales of European production and decreasing capacity utilisation and imports that caused injury to own and others' production would have been sufficient condition for the exclusion of companies from the definition of "Community industry". This time it was not. Mandelson had his own ideas.

Finally, GE's sales from Chinese imports also heavily increased to a level almost equal to its European production. The capacity of GE was underutilised in 2003 and utilisation increased in the next year, but rather than increasing capacity, GE decided to import from China a quantity approaching the European production volume. Graph 15.6 is witness of developments.

Price setting reflected fundamental differences in policies. Philips' evident policy was the elimination of its main competitors in Europe, Osram and GE when possible with help of Chinese products. Sylvania was practically dead. Philips underestimated Chinese possibilities to gain market in Europe outside its own distribution channels. The market share of all importers other than the four major manufacturers' imports in the European Community from China was more than 50 %. The selling prices of some importers were far below those of European Community production and even below Philips' resale price of Chinese lamps. Philips' Chinese imports had a market share of 13 % in 2006. In the German market, three major importers, other than Megaman (a subsidiary of Lisheng with zero anti-dumping duty) with lower prices, Isotronic, LUXXX and Sacom, together had a market share of about 19 %. There was clearly a difference between the conduct of price policy, as Graph 15.7 shows. It was Philips' clear intention to use stick lamps imports from China in order to capture market share at the cost of its main competitor OSRAM.

Since OSRAM's record in cost efficiency was superior to Philips', stick imports from China must have subsidised Philips' prices of non-imported lamps, especially bulb and candle models. Undercutting of OSRAM's prices was persistent until 2006. Graph 15.8 depicts the situation. The information was that both production

Graph 15.7 Stick lamp price competition between the big four

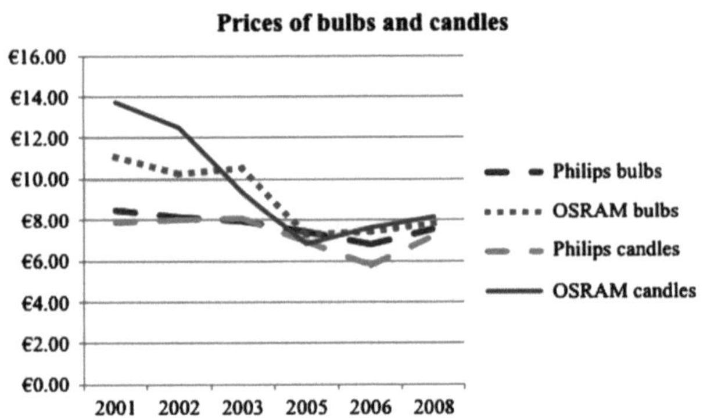

Graph 15.8 The struggle between the major two in bulb and candle CFL

and selling costs of Philips were higher than OSRAM's but nevertheless, apparently hoping for decisive market shares, Philips undercut the prices of its competitors, apparently subsidising its prices with the profit incurred on the lamps imported from China. Such a situation cannot last long, of course. This must have been attributable to the price level of its lamps made in the European Community, the cost of which showed a temporary improvement, but could not offset the price decreases in the market.

Table 15.15 shows that Yankon's prices and Philips' profit, as concluded from offers from Yankon and resale prices of Philips, clarify the fear by Sylvania of distortion of competition. Philips sold stick lamps of the type depicted in Picture 15.3, but in the investigation period practically all were imported from Philips' joint-venture partner in China. Yankon offered its lamps at prices as given in Table 15.16. SLI, complaining about benefits to other producers, must have been aware of Philips' formidable profits on its Philips-branded Yankon lamps. As a basis for the calculations in Table 15.15, it is assumed that Yankon's offer prices to

Table 15.15 Yankon's selling prices and Philips' assumed profit (in Euro)

Level of trade	%	Yankon values	Philips values
11 W 2 tubes lamp 6,000 h ($0.75) purchasing price FOB		€0.82	€0.82
Insurance and freight	2	€0.02	€0.02
CIF value		€0.84	€0.84
Customs duty	2.7	€0.02	€0.02
Landed price before anti-dumping duty		€0.86	€0.86
Anti-dumping duty Zhejiang Sunlight (Yankon)	35.3	€0.31	€0.31
Landed value duties paid		€1.17	€1.17
Level of trade adjustment (distribution margin and costs importer)	27	€0.32	€0.32
Sales to trade; price of Philips to trade (excluding profit)		€1.48	€1.48
Profit to Philips			**€0.90**
Price of Philips to trade (including profit)			€2.39
Trade margins and value added tax	63	€0.94	€1.50
Retail value: derived and real average GfK retail of stick lamps		€2.42	€3.89

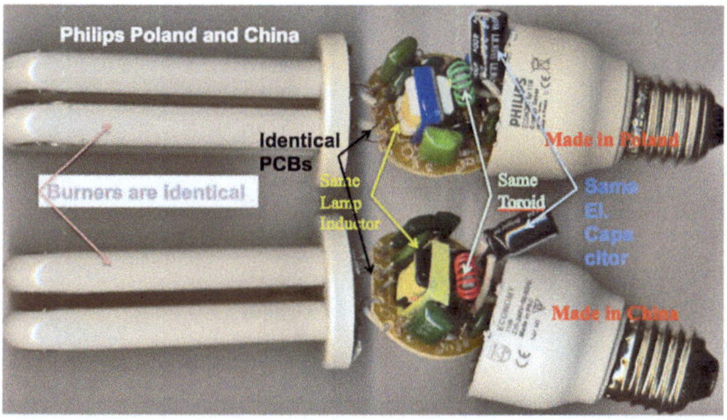

Picture 15.3 European and Chinese lamps compared: "circumvention" or "originating" (the two economy 11 W stick lamps of the Philips brand have different plastic housings. One, the *upper* lamp, bears an indication "Made in Poland"; the other is "Made in PRC" by Yankon. The construction of both lamps is identical, the burners are identical and the components on the ballast are identical. Philips claimed to be European Community producer and its production volume on which it based this claim included clear circumvention of duties. Total added value including the plastic housing and mounting of the burner and ballast to one lamp was less than 20 %. Although it is circumvention, because the ballast has a Combined Nomenclature (CN) Code 8504 10 10 and the burner the CN 7011 10 00, whereas the complete lamp has the CN code 8539 31 90, the product was under the European Commission's interpretation and, according to Community Customs Law, considered of European Community origin)

any third European importer in Table 15.16 were also Philips' purchasing prices. In that case, Philips made a handsome profit. The average Philips price of the 11 W 6,000 h lamp price in the German market was €3.89. The offer price of Yankon of $0.75 (€0.82) with all usual margins and costs incurred up to the shop price is normally €2.42. Philips' price was €3.89 and that implies a profit of €0.90 accruing to Philips. No wonder that Philips began to cherish dumping.

Table 15.16 Yankon's price offer FOB in 2002 in US$

		Unit price		
Lamps	Wattage	CE/230 V/3,000 h	CE/230 V/6,000 h	UL/120 V/6,000 h
2 tube T4	5–11 W	0.65	0.70	
	13–15 W	0.70	0.75	
	18–20 W	0.75	0.80	
3 tube T4	13–15 W	0.90	0.95	
	18–20 W	0.95	1.00	
	22–25 W	1.10	1.20	
Spiral T3	9–11 W		0.95	1.00
	13–15 W		1.00	1.05
	20 W			1.85
	24 W			1.95
Spiral T4	15–18 W		1.10	1.20
	20–22 W		1.30	1.40
	24–26 W		1.40	1.50
A-line	7–11 W	–	1.05	
	14 W	–	1.15	
Reflector	5 W 2 tube	–	1.05	
	7 W 2 tube	–	1.10	
	9 W 2 tube	–	1.10	
	11 W 3 tube	–	1.20	
	18 W 3 tube	–	–	
Candle	3–5 W	–	0.95	
	7 W	–	1.00	
	9–11 W	–	1.10	
Globe	15 W	–	1.50	
	20 W	–	1.65	
	25 W	–	1.80	

Philips made a better profit on its lamps than if it had invested in efficient mass production in the same way OSRAM had, but with its fallible or weak lamp design of its lamps it could not compete in the mass market. The conclusion from Table 15.15 is that Philips made a huge profit with which it subsidised its other lamps made in Poland that were also sold extraordinarily cheaply.

If an increase in production would have reduced the cost of Philips, this import policy would have been a rational choice. But Philips' European production and sales from European production decreased, and cost again increased. This import policy was, therefore, self-destructive. Commissioner Mandelson did not want his staff to discover such simple facts, however. He wanted to stick to his newly developed notion and that was irreconcilable with continuation of an thorough investigation and proper findings as result.

15.8 Circumvention, Origin and Definition of Industry

The question which company can be included into the category of European Community production is in Chap. 12 in relation with the origin issue. This issue was – even though the complainant repeatedly emphasised the desirability of a decision on such an important matter – kept pending in the CFL-i case. Circumvention was even reported, but not a ground for exclusion from the definition of European Community industry. Legally, a company involved in the circumvention of measures can be considered part of European Community industry. The European Commission expressed it as follows with regard to some fake activities of Philips in Poland: "the product concerned has a different customs classification than the imported components. This reclassification results from a substantial transformation of the components." The transformation was clearly not substantial. Customs legislation does not require a substantial, but sufficient transformation for a product to be originating: if a product is produced in more than one country, the product "shall be deemed to originate in the country where they underwent their last, substantial, economically justified processing or working in an undertaking equipped for that purpose and resulting in the manufacture of a new product or representing an important stage of manufacture".[37] The phrasing by the anti-dumping division of the European Commission was misleading. The issue was not what the origin of the product was. After importation of parts and components and the assembly of them into a new product confers, of course, origin. That is the basic rule of the Community Customs Code (CCC). And simple assembly did take place in the case of the assembly of parts as given in Picture 15.3. Not the product, but the status of the producer is the issue. If a product originates in the European Community, according to the CCC, but circumvents anti-dumping measures according to the criteria of the Basic Regulation (see also Sect. 15.6) is the producer of such a product considered part of European Community industry, in spite of the possibility that it can be hit by anti-dumping measures because of circumvention (see also Sect. 12.10). Of course, such contradictory interpretation of the rules is not tenable. A solution to this problem will have to be devised. A product that circumvents measures and inflicts injury under Article 13 of the Basic Regulation cannot simultaneously be included as a product of European industry that is possibly injured by dumping and by this very circumvention. Picture 15.3 shows that there was not a substantial transformation of the components. The question becomes whether the "producer" could oppose and even block a complaint on circumvention if the producer circumvents duties as in conditions of Sect. 15.6.

The complainant's components from China in European production represented only 3 % of its total components and materials. In some cases of Philips stick lamps, the product was merely an assembly of two Chinese major parts – burner and ballast in Picture 15.3 – in a plastic housing, which was the only European material.

[37] Article 24 of Council Regulation (EEC) No 2913/92 of 12 October 1992 establishing the Community Customs Code, OJ L 302, 19/10/1992 pp. 1–50, Document 392R2913.

Negligible added value did not have relevance for the inclusion or exclusion of both Philips and GE from the definition of European Community industry. The new product was, indeed, originating in the European Community, regardless of the insignificance of the value – although the European Commission dubbed it "substantial" – added in the European Community and regardless of the fact that such production circumvented anti-dumping duties. The fact that the assembled lamp contained components with product codes that differed from the code of the lamp did not imply that the company adds 25 % and processes less than 60 % of the components in the European Community. Combined Nomenclature Codes different from the codes of the inputs – burner and ballast – was a sufficient condition for European Community origin. If a complaint had been lodged on circumvention, circumvention would have been found. A draft complaint that clearly demonstrated circumvention had already been prepared. If circumvention had been found, circumventing products would attract a duty, but the company involved in such a practice could still be considered a "Community producer" and possibly be entitled to reject an opening of an investigation into the circumvention in which it is involved. Such a situation should, of course, be clarified. It cannot possibly be accepted that a producer is accepted as "Community producer" if its products circumvent the duties. The response by the European Commission in the CFL i-case led the parties astray about the status of industry in such cases. The reference to the Community Customs Code has added to the confusion.

Commissioner Peter Mandelson had built a reputation by his inventiveness and intervention in anti-dumping, rather than by steady maintenance of the law. He considered his personal opinions and his interference so important and impressive that legal consequences of his behaviour were of minor importance. His interventions forced his staff to invoke illogical arguments and to violate the law. Since these interpretations could not be arrived at from standard enquiry forms, normally sent to producers in the framework of the usual investigations, new phenomena of mini- or interim-enquiry forms were devised that provided the basis for a confirmation of the Commissioner's prejudices. European Commission officials were forced to pop up with new approaches and even with fabrications.[38]

[38] In colour television picture tubes from the People's Republic of China (PRC), the Republic of Korea, Malaysia and Thailand, the case was closed on the basis of arguments found in the Financial Times of 20 January 2006. The Commission alleged to have conducted market research, but the data were those from a newspaper and some arguments advanced by LGPhilips Displays (LGPD), which this company borrowed from the same newspaper article. This joint venture of LG and Philips for cathode ray tubes wanted to close all its factories in Europe and move to China, a move that would be difficult if the dumping from China was countered with measures. The Financial Times referred in the article on which both LGPD and the European Commission based their wisdom to a study made by GfK. But GfK denied existence of this study. The European Commission concluded in recital 108 of its disclosure document that it had obtained information from market intelligence: "As an example, flat panel TV sets accounted for 63 % of the total value of all retail TVs bought in the UK in 2005, compared with just 37 % for 2004. Both the result of this investigation and information obtained from market intelligence suggest that the sales volume of CPT TVs peaked in the EU in 2004, and that the drop in demand is sustained since then." It was

15.9 Politics, Competence, Competency and Environment

When dealing with environmental problems, the first impulse is to think that cheap is preferable to more expensive energy saving products. Consequently, the argument, even used by organisations such as the World Wild Life Fund (it is unclear what this organisation had to do with energy saving lamps),[39] was that the anti-dumping duty should be abolished. However, the cause of the problem was not known to most of these fervent adherents to action without knowledge of the factual background. The cause of the problems was that China, for the sake of reduction of electricity consumption, stimulated and subsidised growth of CFL-i production, but maintained subsidised electricity prices. Accordingly, a surplus of lamps had been created that could only be sold on foreign markets. It should be noted that China is one of the most polluting countries in the world and that particularly its electricity production is polluting. Energy saving in China has been imperative, but neglected or made impossible by counterproductive policies.

Since imports from China mainly consisted of lamps with a lifetime shorter than 6,000 and in any case shorter than 10,000 h and had a content of about double the level of mercury, the degree of mercury waste in the European Community environment from Chinese imports is substantially higher than waste from European lamps. However, the production of coal-fired electricity in Europe is essentially less polluting than in China.[40] Chinese coal fired electricity production emits 600 t, accounting for nearly a quarter of the world's non-natural emissions, about seven times as much mercury into the air each year as Europe. It implies that European CFLs have a more positive effect on the environment in Europe and that consumption of Chinese lamps in China contributes relatively substantially more to the restriction of global pollution than when such Chinese lamps are used in Europe,

deception by the Commission and, consequently, the institutions. LG. Philips wrote on 21 March 2006 a submission in which it referred to the same inexistent piece of market research: "Flat screen CTVs accounted for 63 % of the total value of all retail TVs bought in the UK in 2005, compared with just 37 % for 2004 [footnote 7: GfK, reported in the Financial Times 20 January 2006.]". Commissioner Mandelson appeared to have read a newspaper and forced his officials to violate normal anti-dumping practice and the truth and pretend to conduct market research for the sake of closing a case. The European Commission did not even check the information nor did it pay any attention to correct information from GfK studies.

[39] http://www.wwf.eu/climate/news_climate/?112120/EU-keeps-unfair-market-barriers-on-energy-saving-lamp: "EU keeps unfair market barriers on energy-saving lamps", Posted on 29 August 2007.

[40] Matt Pottinger, Steve Stecklow, John J. Fialka in The Wall Street Journal, 20 December 2004: "China is already believed to be the world's largest source of non-natural emissions of mercury. Jozef Pacyna, director of the Center for Ecological Economics at the Norwegian Institute for Air Research, calculates that China, largely because of its coal combustion, spews 600 t of mercury into the air each year, accounting for nearly a quarter of the world's non-natural emissions. And the volume is rising at a time when North American and European mercury pollution is dropping. The U.S. emitted about 120 t of mercury into the air in 1999 from manmade sources. Chinese power plants currently under construction – the majority fuelled by coal – will alone have more than twice the entire electricity-generating capacity of the U.K."

whereas the consumption in China is kept low. As soon as the Chinese international trade and financial systems and Chinese electricity prices would become more in line with normal market conditions, dumping of CFL-i's would probably disappear. Under such conditions, CFL consumption in China could fully absorb Chinese production, a situation salutary for worldwide environmental policies. The situation of exports of about 450 million units to Europe – apart from those imported into the European Community by means of circumvention – is an expression of lack of normal market conditions in China rather than of sound environmental policies and market conditions in Europe. If market conditions would, in the future, be restored, European production would in the meantime have disappeared by destruction as the consequence of dumping, and a lack of production capabilities would highly impair European Community environmental policies. At present, electricity prices in China are so artificially low that application of energy by lamps or other devices of energy saving is economically hardly attractive. It implies that the programmes for the stimulation of Chinese production, which were based on artificial increase of production, resulted in a tremendous supply excess over demand in China. China's plan to prohibit normal lamps in 2015 implied that 1.07 billion GLS lamps consumption[41] would be replaced by CFLs, whereas its CFL production in 2006 was estimated at 2.4 billion units and its total exports at 1.7 billion units in 2006.[42] This implies that European production is highly welcome, and should not be eliminated by Chinese production.

Europe's CO_2 emissions are below China's and China's emission of mercury represents 25 % of world emissions.[43] An approximation of China's electricity prices, which are about 1/4 of the lower range of European Community price rates, to European levels would automatically have tremendously boosted demand for energy saving lamps in China (under the prevailing rate in China economically not very interesting to consumers), and this would have offered a major contribution to global environmental objectives. European Community made lamps appear to contribute more to European Community environmental savings programs than Chinese lamps. In this respect, a law of comparative advantage is also applicable in an environmental issue with the opposite conclusion: For an approach of both the local and global pollution problem, European lamps are more effective than Chinese in Europe. This is because, although more polluting than European lamps, Chinese lamps are more effective in China – because of the huge pollution there – than when they are exported to Europe. As will be seen, most European decision makers neglected such arguments. They preferred a more convenient and extremely simple view that is easier to sell to the public: low prices in Europe were good for the environment, regardless the waste and regardless the effects on the environment in China and the global environment.

---

[41] United Press International, 7 November 2011: "China plans switch to energy-saving lights".

[42] du Pont (2006); US AID: "Quality Control and Market Supervision of CFLs in China". Figures on production and exports are from the industry federation CALI.

[43] Frederick Weston (2007).

Table 15.17 The environment and European or Chinese energy saving lamps

	15,000 h European (average)	10,000 h European (average)	10,000 h China	6,000 h European (average)	6,000 h China
3 glass tubes	1×	1.5×	1.5×	2.5×	2.5×
Circuit board	1×	1.5×	1.5×	2.5×	2.5×
Ca. 40 other components	1×	1.5×	1.5×	2.5×	2.5×
Mercury	1 × 2.5 mg	1.5 × 2.5 mg	2.5 × 5 mg	2.5 × 2.5 mg	2.5 × 5 mg
Waste	1×	1.5×	1.5×	2.5×	2.5×

In the course of the on-going and necessary discussion about energy saving and reduction of CO_2, arguments were raised that anti-dumping duties are contrary to environment protection targets. This is incorrect: Anti-dumping duties do restore normal competition both in the European Community market and worldwide. It is not protection, as often assumed, but restoration of normal competitive relations. Furthermore, they do not hinder importation of products into the European Community, but only counter distortions in competition. Moreover, to verify the degree of environmental friendly products, not only the effects during the use-phase have to be taken into account but also effects during the production and end-of-life-phase. CFL-i's are produced in the EU in conformity with highest standards and are a contribution to the environment protection:

- Regarding components (e.g. mercury) and production processes: Chinese CFL-i needs double the amount of mercury compared to European CFL-i to achieve 50 % of the European CFL-i's lifetimes.
- With production in Europe, long and high energy-consuming transportation to Europe is avoided.
- Beside generation of energy/CO_2 saving, less harmful waste due to less hazardous components also protects the environment.

An example is a CFL-i with a three-tube burner. In order to achieve 15,000 burning hours, the following materials are needed and used, as given in Table 15.17.

The environment is worse off with Chinese lamps. The cheapest Chinese lamp, the first one, represents five times 5 mg or 25 mg mercury, while the European lamp is 1/10 this amount (one lamp for 15,000 h at 2.5 mg). The Chinese lamps cause five times as much electronic waste and five times as much glass waste (in the Chinese case with lead content).

Although the price of the Chinese lamp is lower in all cases, it is more expensive compared with a European lamp over the whole lifetime of the lamp, especially in terms of environmental costs.

15.10 Politics, Pressure and Profitability

Philips made a presentation with Power Point at the occasion of a visit by the Dutch Environmental minister and tried to convince the minister that normal light bulbs should be banned, that energy saving lamps should be promoted and that this, of course, implied that the anti-dumping measures toward China should be lifted. The naïve minister was highly impressed by the Power Point presentation and wanted general lighting services lamps to be banned immediately and convinced the minister of Economic Affairs that he should vote against the extension of anti-dumping measures toward China.

This approach of the imposition of a production on the consumer was, as shown before in the television case with the HDTV escapade, not unique. Together with "statist" Thomson, Philips had tried to impose analogue High Definition Television. Philips hoped that more profitable energy savers and light emitting diode lamps would replace the low margin bulbs. Philips' profitability could be enhanced, it thought, by abolishing anti-dumping duties. It almost had success. It wrote letters to all member states declaring that Chinese lamps were good for the environment and that the majority of production in the European Community was against the anti-dumping measures. Philips failed to succeed, because its efforts were too evident and the opposition of other European Commission members against the arbitrary and condescending behaviour of Commissioner Mandelson was, after a fierce lobbying battle, sufficient to prolong the measures for 1 year. But it became clear that the simple idea that cheap energy saving lamps should replace normal bulbs gained popularity. The decision-making also became too cumbersome because of the number of member states that could influence the voting. Twenty-seven countries with a voting right on the imposition of duties is a questionable structure and certainly in a highly complex case such a number of member states that can decide on measures with such an impact without proper democratic control is clearly too much.

Philips' lawyer, Lourdes Catrain, made an amazing claim and presented a defeat as an asset in representative experience[44]:

> *Representing Philips in the highly complex expiry review investigation of anti-dumping duties on energy-saving lamps from China, and obtaining an unprecedented limited one-year extension of duties (as opposed to the normal five-year duration).*

The review investigation may have been complex to her, but it was not. The case had hardly a legal aspect; the case was a political one. The Commissioner violated the rules and the case was not legally determined. It was a political decision and the result of a trade-off within the European Commission and between member states. The conviction that there was dumping was balanced by the impression that low prices of energy savers contributed to the environmental objectives of member states. Philips' legal representation was immaterial to the outcome. It was not

[44] http://www.hoganlovells.com/lourdes-catrain/

unprecedented in limitation, but unprecedented an extension, where the Commissioner wanted politically to terminate the case. The compromise was to limit the prolongation of duties, against intentions of Commissioner Mandelson who wanted to abolish them immediately, to 1 year. It was the opposition against Mandelson that should be credited for this outcome, if any credit can be given. It was certainly not a victory of anyone, but rather a defeat of European Community law.

The issue whether the three producers with more imported products than their own European production and with the clear intent to use the dumped imports as aggressive rather than defensive instruments of market share gain could actually be considered to belong to "Community industry" remained unsolved. A file was prepared with evidence of huge circumvention of duties by both "Community producers" via Poland (Philips). Hungary (GE) and the United Kingdom and by Chinese exporters via new third countries Indonesia, Malaysia, Sri Lanka, Taiwan, Thailand, Tunisia and United Arab Emirates. A sticker on a package of Philips lamps, for instance, indicated that the origin was the United Arab Emirates. When the sticker was removed a printed indication "made in PRC" became visible. Lamps of the brand Attralux, with indication "Made in Poland" and those "Made in PRC" were compared and appeared identical. The European Commission had already indicated about GE: "Company C's production in the Community mainly consists of assembling components from several sources. Less than half of these components are sourced from within the Community." An analysis gave rise to the expectation that circumvention would, indeed, be found, if investigated. Regarding Sylvania Lighting International (SLI), the European Council of Ministers established in the Annex to its regulation: "The investigation showed that the product concerned has a different customs classification than the imported components. This reclassification results from a substantial transformation of the components." The adjective "substantial" in the Council's Regulation is a subjective simplifying judgment and inappropriate. In the case of lamps, transformation is sufficient for origin if two parts like ballast and burner are assembled into a lamp. It was not substantial, but legally sufficient for European Community origin. An insignificant processing can result in a change in customs classification and in change of origin. By combining the burner (the tube), in the Combined Nomenclature of the European Community (7011 10 00, glass envelopes for electric lighting) and the electronic ballasts for discharge lamps (8504 10 80) and possibly lamp bases (8539 31 90) and some soldering these three different components are made into for energy saving lamps (8539 31 90). Picture 15.3 show how little is needed to confer origin. This is not a "substantial processing" as the Council innocently alleged. In an investigation of circumvention of duties the product would be considered circumvented. The important problem is how the industry in the European Community involved in such operations is considered: part of European industry or not. The question was not investigated in practice, but the problem remains. It was doubted whether the European Commission would open such a case in which its error not to exclude three producers from the definition of European Community industry in the expiry proceeding would become too apparent. The predictability and legal security demand a solution.

A new interim Expiry Review file was also prepared, which showed increased dumping margins. Suspicion, if not conviction, that Commissioner Mandelson would let down European Community producers who were confronted with rough Chinese political pressure on complainant, was sufficient not to submit these files and to let the Chinese resume their dumping. When this Commissioner had returned to the United Kingdom, it was too late to file the documents for further anti-dumping actions.

References

du Pont P (2006) Reducing barriers to market transformation: from low quality to high performance and high efficiency. Efficient lighting initiative, US AID: "quality control and market supervision of CFLs in China"

Müller W, Khan N, Neumann HA (1998) EC anti-dumping law – a commentary on regulation 384/96. Wiley, Chichester

Weston F (2007) China's energy challenges. In: Symposium China in Transition Environmental Challenges in the Far East, The Regulatory Assistance Project, Montpelier

Chapter 16
Methodology of Dumping

Abstract The examples from trade policy practice presented in this book are a demonstration that a guide, as supplied by the European Commission, though useful, is inadequate. In order to give some ideas to the interested reader on several aspects of a dumping proceeding and the techniques used in calculations of dumping and injury, as well as other technical information, methodological Chap. 16 is presented. Some formulae are used, which look more complex than they are. The examples given in Chap. 16 are rarely found in textbooks on dumping; thus, they offer methodological tools for those interested in practical aspects of anti-dumping proceedings. Various complications in anti-dumping are elucidated with data not offered elsewhere. Quantitative examples on the differences between market economy status (MES) and non-market economy (NME) treatment show that serious mistakes can be made by the assumption that MES is always preferable. The treatment of related companies and their actual data show that multinationals are sometimes seriously disadvantaged. The differences between OEM and branded supplies are quantified. Practically all of the issues involved in anti-dumping are quantified.

16.1 Demonstration of Dumping: Product Concerned

The European Commission's website, http://ec.europa.eu/trade/tackling-unfair-trade/trade-defence/anti-dumping/complaints/, contains a link: "Guide on how to draft an anti-dumping complaint". This guide gives examples how a potential complainant can demonstrate dumping and provides information on the framework of a complaint. Before a complaint is lodged, consultation of profound legal analysis is advisable.[1] The issue of product choice or definition of "like product" is discussed in previous chapters. Sometimes it may be attractive to include all

[1] Vermulst (2010) EC Anti-Dumping Law & Practice. Sweet & Maxwell offers such a comprehensive study.

M. van Marion, *International Trade Policy and European Industry*, Contributions to Economics, DOI 10.1007/978-3-319-00392-4_16,

similar products in a file. For instance, in the case of fax machines it was attractive to include all fax machines. It was simple and did not require special market research and statistical calculations. From various computations, it was apparent that especially the Japanese producers' dumping margins (the ex-works domestic price minus the ex-works export price) on all fax machines and especially the professional fax machines were substantially higher than margins found for smaller, home faxes. But when all faxes were included, it required Olivetti and SAGEM's participation as complainants. Olivetti was an importer of home faxes from Thailand and Taiwan. That made the choice of the scope of the products in the definition of "like product" dependent on producers' interests, level of dumping and injury and on the market concerned.

In "small screen television sets" and "small television tubes", the exporters' share in the market and the injury was more than if the whole product range of televisions or tubes was covered. One should, however, keep in mind that such a narrow definition may have repercussions in the future. New market conditions must subsequently be put forward in arguments for the creation of a broader coverage in which the formerly separated products are included together. In colour televisions from Asia, the volume of small screen sets contributed sufficiently to the injury caused in the European television market so that Chinese and Korean television sets of the large screen format could be covered, while in the past only their small screen sets were involved. This could only be achieved by a redefinition of the market and consequently of the definition of "like product" or product concerned.

An example of a mistake due to too narrow a definition of a product was the case of cameras. The cameras were defined in such a way that the impression was created that only cameras in a broadcast studio setting were the objective of measures. Sony grabbed the opportunity to abuse the situation and claimed an exception for its cheap cameras, which although the low price was mainly attributable to dumping, it called "professional" cameras. A European Commission official had developed an sympathy toward Sony, partly attributable to the excellent wining and dining by the English Sony organisation. He finally agreed with this costly exception. The threats by Sony stemming opposition by European industry against exclusion of "professional" cameras have already been mentioned. Therefore, a careful examination of the product concerned and all eventualities should be analysed.

16.2 Product Concerned, Injury and the European Community Industry

A complaint must be supported by sufficient production, at least 25 % of total volume, provided that not more than 50 % opposes the opening of an investigation. This condition may also influence the choice of definition of the product concerned.

The question how producers are treated when their main activity is importation of dumped products remained an unsolved problem in the case of energy saving lamps in Chap. 15. Normally, "related" producers are excluded from the definition of European Community industry, unless some conditions are fulfilled. If the imports are defensive, for instance, the relation is generally allowed. In the case of compact fluorescence lamps, the clemency towards certain producers/importers who imported more than they produced created a serious precedent. A method for the elimination of opposition to a complaint is inclusion of an exporting country from which an opposing producer imported substantial quantities. In the case of compact fluorescence lamps, for instance, the inclusion of Poland as dumping exporting country could exclude Philips as complainant in this case. After accession of Poland and Hungary the two former outsiders became factor of importance. In the case of Philips and GE, it was insufficiently secured that these companies would be excluded from the definition of European Community industry.

Sometimes it was sufficient to convince an opposing European Community producer to refrain from opposing by the mere threat of the inclusion of an exporting country from which it imported. The case of VCR against Korea (Samsung, LGE and Daewoo) and Singapore (Thomson) is an example. There was sufficient evidence of Japanese dumping, but the injury element was a weak spot. Japanese producers in Europe abstained from opposition, not only because of this threat, but also because the case was in their advantage. When the European Commission made an inquiry before the opening of the investigation, they finally appeared to endorse the anti-dumping investigation. In view of the unique position of the complainant, the product covered in the case of VCR was the VCR including scanner and heads; the complaint did not need such support. Since the Japanese were highly indulgent, this move afterwards appeared unnecessary.

A study of the product in detail and scrutiny of the interests of European producers in countries of export is inevitable. The manufacturing of the product is also worth some study. Can the product easily be assembled? In that case, one should beware of the possibility of circumvention and prepare the information required for such a case. A European Community producer of ironing boards searched a lawyer for a dumping file against China. Before compilation of a file was agreed upon, a visit to the boards factory in order to get acquainted with product and production method was suggested. The manufacturer rejected this proposal and a potential working relation was aborted. Suspicion that the producer just assembled boards from Chinese components was supported by European Commission observations after measures had been imposed[2]:

Indeed, certain complainant Community producers supply customers in the Community that also source their products from the PRC and Ukraine, thus benefiting directly from these imports. Those complainants argued that they were therefore in a particularly

[2] Commission Regulation (EC) No 1620/2006 of 30 October 2006 imposing a provisional anti-dumping duty on imports of ironing boards originating in the People's Republic of China and Ukraine, 31.10.2006. OJ L 300/13, recital 9.

sensitive position since they had good reasons to believe that some of their suppliers and customers would not be satisfied with their lodging or supporting a complaint against alleged injurious dumping and would react to such action. Indeed, they alleged that they risk retaliation from these suppliers and customers, including the possible termination of their business relationship.

The situation was not dissimilar from the lamp assembly described in Sect. 15.8 (Picture 15.3) in Chap. 15. In this case of ironing boards it was evident that angry Chinese suppliers could, either without or with instigation of the Chinese authorities, punish European producers by the termination of supplies. The European shoe industry used similar arguments as the iron board maker, but they were especially afraid of retaliation by their customers, big retail chains, which are common in the shoe sector. Although such a worry is comprehensible, retaliation by customers is rare. Serious harm inflicted by exporting countries to subsidiaries of complainants is far more obvious, such as the intimidation by China. Nevertheless, in such cases stamina helps more than indulgence.

As for the collection of data, the inclusion of and cooperation with a major producer, preferably a multinational with detailed information on the exporting countries is helpful. Such a company should assume ownership of the dumping problem. It is a question of selection of the company with the greatest interest and the highest experience in foreign markets, and especially a company that is not complacent. Sometimes big producers have contacts in the country of export and can obtain certain necessary documents or can provide information on trade margins in the country of export, but their self-righteousness creates frustration because of lack of initiative. On the other hand, they are more susceptible to pressure from the exporting country. The China example is again illustrative.

16.3 The Problem of the Origin of Products Concerned

In an anti-dumping complaint evidence must be presented on dumping and consequently, a comparison between the domestic market price (or an alternative to this price to be discussed below) and the export price of the same or similar product. Many distributors sell their products without indication of origin of the product. Sometimes the box in which the product is sold indicates the origin, but generally the true origin is concealed by the distributor, requiring the need to analyse the product. This might become an expensive exercise. An analysis of origin of a video recorder would require a purchase of a set and an analysis of its components. Such exercises were done in cases of VCR from Japan (Orion and Funai), and also in the case of CTV toward Turkey. The purchase served two purposes: cost analysis and anti-dumping. In the latter case of Turkey, it was evident that fraud – the declaration of Turkish origin instead of application of the weird CTV origin rule – was pervasive. The origin of various Turkish television sets was Chinese, Korean or Malaysian. It is not easy to find the origin of products, but normally it is easier to detect the origin before the measure is imposed rather than after. Sometimes a bar code may help to find the producer. Using the bar code, the producer or distributor can be found on the Internet site http://gepir.gs1.org/v32/xx/. On this site, a search by barcode (GTIN) can reveal the producer. Some Turkish producers, for instance, shipped their television sets with a tube from China. The interior of the set showed that the tube, and therefore the set were of Chinese origin, according to the CTV origin rule, so often criticised in the book.

After the imposition of anti-dumping duties, dubious traders become active. It is, therefore, advised to acquire detailed information on products from the dumping country, the essential characters of which may remain the same after imposition of measures, but the brand names and origin indication may change. This makes it easier to check the characteristics and origin of products after measures are imposed. A collection of Chinese compact fluorescence lamps before opening of the investigation helped to detect cases of fraud and circumvention more easily than in a later stage. It is also worthwhile to seek contacts with traders after opening and during the investigation. These contacts may also produce valuable information producers generally do not have. After the imposition, an exchange of information will contribute to the interests of importers of products with relatively low duties and of European Community producers.

16.4 Product Definition: Similar or Like Product

For a finding of dumping and undercutting a precise product definition is required; only similar products must be compared. In an anti-dumping complaint, the complainant labels the product in question, but a definition in a complaint is often broad: videocassette recorders, colour television sets with a certain screen size, CD-players, energy saving lamps (compact electronic fluorescent discharge lamps with all lighting elements, all electronic components and cap in the same housing). However, if the normal value must be compared with the export price, prices of identical or similar types and models must be compared. Products sold in the domestic market and exported should either closely resemble or preferably be identical. Features of a VCR are, for instance, the number of recording heads affects quality of sound (stereo or mono) and picture, single or multiple recording and playback speeds, "pause" and "slow-motion" features, one-touch recording and programming features. These features should be taken into account when the price of the domestic and exported set is compared. The prices of dumping exporters undercutting complainant's in the complainants market should be compared on basis of the same, identical or similar models with such features.

Sometimes complex tables of products with their specifications and features or characteristics must be constructed. To each of the characteristics a code figure or letter is attached and a product code represents a group of products with identical characteristics. The exporters cooperating in an investigation proceeding of dumping (defendants) and producers in the country of dumped imports (complainants) are obliged to report their costs and sales according to product codes containing the relevant features affecting the value of the product. An example concerning energy saving or compact fluorescent lamps is given here. An energy saving lamp with a lifetime of 6,000 h (6 years) or more, but less than 10,000 h, with a cover (a bulb) of 11 W without special, sensor or dimmer, devices has the code B11BA. Is the lifetime 10,000 h or more, the code is C11BA. A prismatic lamp (with prismatic cover) of 15 W with 6,000 h lifetime and without a sensor for light and dark or a dimmer has the code B15FA. Lamps with magnetic ballast, Philips' original SL lamps, were excluded from the proceeding, but when the joint venture in China switched its prismatic (code F after the Watt indication) SL lamps to SL lamps with electronic ballast – respectively 11, 15 and 20 W lamps – during the investigation period, the company ran into bad luck: it ran unexpectedly into a duty. The products of Philips & Yaming were, for instance, reported as B11FA, B15FA and B20FA. The dumping margin found was 61.8 %, and the prices of these lamps were 32.3 % – in our treatment in this Chapter it is, as consequence of difference in foreign exchange rates, 31.4 % – as percentage of CIF value below the European prices minus losses and plus some profit mark-up of European Community producers' prices.

Lamps with product code number B11FA, the 11 W 6,000–10,000 h prismatic lamps, sold domestically (the producer Philips & Yaming[3] was one of the two producers in China to which market economy treatment (MET) was granted and, therefore, its Chinese prices were relevant) had to be compared with lamps sold on the export market with the same characteristics, covered by an identical product code, reflecting these specifications and for the sake of injury calculation, the weighted average selling or resale price of this (dumped) model was compared with the weighted average of prices of the product with that same code sold by European Community producers in the European Community. Of course, such an elaborate product code requires knowledge of the product, to be acquired before the opening of the investigation, 45 days after the formal submission of a complaint. Normally, the product code number (PCN) can be linked to internal reporting systems of the industry, exporters and industry in the country of dumped imports, cooperating in an investigation. Sensible complainants have prepared a suitable system of product characteristics that can underlie the product codes and the product comparison. The European Commission personnel's intellectual gifts generally guarantee competent investigations.[4] Sometimes exporters – Sony in the CD

[3] The author had the data of a few exporters and some European producers at his disposal. For the sake of demonstration, the data of these companies have been used, but are indexed and made unidentifiable by indexation. Some of the data such as the overall dumping and undercutting margins, however, have been maintained in order to make clear that the case is borrowed from practice of dumping proceedings.

[4] A mistake may be made and insufficiently detailed product characteristics may be listed. When this becomes apparent during the investigation, the results are chaos and disaster. One European Commission official temporarily placed by a member state at the disposal of the European Commission described how he frustrated an investigation concerning certain shoes, the product specification of which had been insufficient. The member state from which he came opposed

player case – do not appreciate these efforts. Sometimes the definition of the product concerned was arbitrarily changed – as has been demonstrated – and in the complainant's disadvantage.

16.5 Choice of Market Economy

Countries like China and Vietnam are considered non-market economies. This implies that the normal values of the exporters that have not received MES are established on the basis of values in a representative third country economy. It means that the choice of a country that is representative for the Chinese or Vietnamese situation should be presented. A list of eligible countries should be drafted and their characteristics compared. A problem is often that producers in a third country do not cooperate and do not provide required information.[5] Assistance by companies with international links to the selection of the reference or analogue country is helpful. In any case, it is urgent that proper argumentation concerning the economic characteristics is presented in the complaint. Weakness in such a presentation causes serious and unnecessary delays.

16.6 Elements in the Determination of the Level of Measures

Several times it is indicated that measures are imposed at the level of dumping or injury, whichever is lower. This is called the "lesser duty rule". In the determination of the level of the measures, i.e. the establishment of dumping and injury, there are several complications that need attention. Scrutiny by industry representatives of the methods applied by the anti-dumping authorities is rare. Mostly they are satisfied that measures will be taken and often authorities act as if measures are a gift rather than a right. Legal cases before the European Court of Justice commenced by exporters exceeds by far the number of cases started by European producers. The number or legal cases brought before the Court of Justice by the European industry is negligible. The complaining industry generally does not have the financial means for lengthy court cases, which, after all would not result in retroactive increases in anti-dumping duties, whereas exporters expect restitutions

anti-dumping and this objectionable conduct of a proceeding did, consequently, not obstruct his career after return to his home country. It was considered a feat of resistance.

[5] This is highly understandable. If the complaint is successful and the European Community takes measures, a third country may be confronted with additional imports from the country to which the duties are applied.

of duties when they win a case.[6] False decisions by European Community institutions at the disadvantage of European producers are, therefore, never corrected.

(A) **The First of the Lesser Rule: Dumping: the gap between normal value and export price**

16.7 Determination of Normal Value

(a) Ordinary course of trade.

Domestic sales of the exporter are taken into consideration for the establishment of normal value when in the "Ordinary Course of Trade" (OCT). Not all sales are in the OCT. If they are not in the OCT, an alternative calculation will take place.

In following cases, sales are not in the ordinary course of trade (OCT):

– If parties appear associated or have compensatory arrangements, the normal value and export prices may be constructed. Several examples of dumping by Japanese exporters have been given. The existence of captive trade with producers' ownership of wholesalers and special relations with retailers is clear from Chaps. 7 and 8; these facts prevent the selling price to wholesaler and retailer from being considered in the OCT. The most impressive example given was Matsushita, which had only one independent wholesale customer in the case of audio, video and domestic appliances distribution. The sales of the joint venture Philips & Yaming to the Philips sales organisation in China were transfer prices, but not normal value. The sales prices of Philips' sales company in China were taken as basis for establishment – taking certain conditions, to be mentioned below, into consideration – of normal value. These sales prices were compared with the selling prices of the European sales organisations of Philips to independent customers. However, in the calculation of the export price, the existence of a compensatory finance generally, and was also in this case of Philips assumed, results in a constructed and lower export price. This was a serious disappointment to employees of this multinational company. As revealed in Chap. 15, a representative of Philips' lighting division declared confidently: "we do not dump. All our prices ex factory to all sales organisations are the same". Although Organisation for Economic Co-operation and Development (OECD) guidelines for multinationals prescribe equality of ex-factory prices, in dumping it is irrelevant. Sales organisations' resale prices in the domestic and export country are vital and domestic and export price are generally not identical. If resale prices in the domestic market of the dumping exporters are identical

[6] The number of court cases was rather high in the 1980s and 1990s. Many Japanese producers, ill advised by their legal counsels, were eager to make a bet, but they were rather unsuccessful and the number of cases dropped thereafter.

to the resale prices in the country of export, the authorities may still treat them differently because of the assumption of a compensatory relationship.

- If the domestic sales volume constitutes less than 5 % of the sales volume of the product to the European Community, the products are domestically not in the OCT. If these sales are less than 5 %, the cost of production plus a reasonable amount of profit is applied in order to establish the normal value. The normal value is in that case based on prices of other producers in that country.
- If sales at a profit are less than 80 % (or those at a loss are 20 % or > 20 %) of total sales volume (per product type or per PCN, see above), sales are considered not to be in the OCT. If they are less than 80 %, a constructed value is applied, which is normally the cost of production plus the profit made on the products sold at a profit.[7] Consequently, the unprofitable sales are put at zero and only the profitable sales are selected.
- If the exporter in a NME country – for instance, in China and Vietnam – has not obtained MES, its products are not in the OCT.[8]

If the products are not in the OCT, a constructed value is applied. In the case of NME countries, including China and Vietnam, *inter alia*, the normal value is generally the price in the OCT of a comparable market economy or a constructed value. The issue of normal value in case of NME treatment of producers, for instance in China, is dealt with in this methodological chapter.

(b) General representativeness of domestic sales.

Authorities investigating dumping (in the European Community it is the European Commission) establish domestic sales prices on the basis of prices actually paid or payable by independent customers in the domestic market to the dumping exporter. This is done on the basis of transaction-by-transaction reporting by the exporters per product category (according to the PCN code: an example is a less than 6,000 h stick lamp of 11 W without special features (A11AA)). Equally, export sales have to be reported on transaction-by-transaction basis. This transaction-by-transaction reporting of quantities and values enables the authorities to compare domestic and

---

[7] Council Regulation (EC) No 384/96 of 22 December 1995 (Basic Regulation) on protection against dumped imports from countries not members of the European Community OJ No L 56 of 6.3.96; Revision with COUNCIL REGULATION (EC) No 461/2004 of 8 March 2004 amending Regulation (EC) No 384/96 OJ L77 of 13.3.2004, (Basic Regulation) Article 2.4: if "the volume of sales below cost is not less than 20 % of sales being used to determine normal value" the current net market prices may be used as normal value.

[8] Council Regulation (EC) No 905/98 of 27 April 1998 amending Regulation (EC) No 384/96 on protection against dumped imports from countries not members of the European Community, Official Journal of the European Communities, 30. 4. 98, L 128 creates the possibility that a producer in Vietnam and China make a properly substantiated claim that market economy conditions prevail for the producer in respect of the manufacture and sale of the like product concerned. If certain conditions mentioned in that regulation are met, the producer's sales may be considered suitable for the check whether products are sold in the ordinary course of trade (OCT) on the basis of the other criteria mentioned in a. Ordinary course of trade.

export prices made at the same time with due allowances for exchange rate changes. If domestic sales of the product concerned account for more than 5 % of the total export sales quantities to the European Community, they are representative. Thus, the sales are considered and accepted as made in the OCT. If they are not more than 5 %, they are not in the OCT and the constructed value (the cost of production plus reasonable profit) is applied. Transactions that are profitable define, however, what is reasonable. If they are more than 5 % of exports, the normal value can be based on domestic sales. After this acceptance of domestic sales, the rules are applied to those domestic sales for those products not considered in the OCT (like the 80 % or more rule, see above).

(c) Domestic distribution and normal value.

Many Japanese and Korean producers have applied in the Court of Justice for annulment or change of calculations because the European Community institutions made adjustments to the domestic price when the normal value was established. Producers and their domestic distribution system are related, and this requires a recalculation of the sales price. Normally, United States or European producer sells in its domestic market to independent distribution, but in Japan and Korea it is different. The Japanese pressured their partners in the General Agreement on Tariffs and Trade (GATT) to accept that the ex-factory prices should be taken as the normal value and as the export price. In this way the trade distortion attributable to the captive distribution would be disregarded. In various cases, Japanese exporters challenged the inclusion of data of distributors into the normal value.

(d) Type specific representativeness of sales.

If a limited share of product types (in PCN) is exported to the European Community, the authorities determine whether more than 5 % of these types are sold in the domestic market. During the proceeding or after disclosure of findings, exporters may challenge similarity of the product range sold in the domestic market and the range exported. They could, therefore, challenge whether the 5 % criterion has been met. For this case, the general 5 % test is also made. This test safeguards the proceeding. It is, therefore, often also established whether more than 5 % of the models or product ranges per PCN exported are also sold in the domestic market compared with the exported models.

(e) Profitable sales.

For the establishment of normal value, the exporter must report the net price to third independent customers, which is the gross turnover per transaction minus rebates and minus allowances for payment terms, delivery terms (credit), warranty and other costs incurred. In order to establish sales below cost the cost of production (COP), including the cost of manufacturing, selling, general and administrative costs, are compared with the net unit sales price per transaction. After the establishment of detailed cost of production for each product type (PCN category), a profitability analysis is carried out by comparing the sales prices of transactions of products sold to independent customers in the domestic market with cost of production (including selling, general and administrative costs; or, together with cost of manufacturing, also called the cost of sales) for each product type. On this basis, and according to the Basic Anti-Dumping regulation of the European Community,[9] the profitable domestic direct sales turnover (rebates excluded) of the product concerned during the investigation period expressed as a percentage of the cost of production is established. The first move is that it is established whether sufficient transactions are profitable.

The formal expression is:

$$\text{Quantity to be selected} = \text{IF (Net Price} \leq \text{COP, Quantity} = 0\text{, Quantity)}$$

This expression means that if the net price is equal to or below cost of production, this quantity is to be neglected (put on zero); if the net price is above cost of production, the quantity and its related price and cost factors are included.

The European Community creates a special column in the matrix of information reported by the exporters concerning the sales and costs dedicated to the quantities of profitable sales. If sales occur at a loss, the quantity of profitable sales is zero. For the calculation of normal value, quantities of profitable sales are established. The sum of the profitable (when the net price is >COP) quantities is compared with the total sales per PCN. If more than 80 % of sales volume of a certain product category (PCN) is profitable, the net ex-works market price is taken as representing 100 % of sales and as starting point for the normal value. If 80 % or less is sold at profit, an alternative is applied. That alternative excludes the unprofitable sales and selects sales having occurred at a profit.

Table 16.1 is an example showing how normal value is established in cases of acceptance of domestic sales as normal value, i.e. when domestic sales of the like product present more than 5 % of total sales and the company has MET of MES. In Table 16.1, two products (B11AA and B11FA) of an amount of 187 out of 1,000 and 86 out of 113 units (or 18.7 % and 76.1 %, i.e. less than 80 %) have been sold at a profit. That means that they are not treated as in the OCT and the alternative method is applied.

In row 1 of Table 16.1 column J (cell J1) for product B11AA presents the quantity of cell F1, which is the quantity of profitable sales (187) only, instead of all sales (1,000). The normal value is in that case based on the COP plus the profit on the profitable sales of that product group B11AA. The profit applied is not average price 10.00 – COP 9.88. Since the profitable quantity is less than 80 %, it is applied to the average price of profitable sales only. The same applies to the second row for B11FA. However, this product is also exported and appears in the survey on

[9] Called the Basic Regulation. Council Regulation (EC) No 384/96 of 22 December 1995 on protection against dumped imports from countries not members of the European Community; Revision with Council Regulation (EC) No 61/2004 of 8 March 2004 OJ of 13 March 2004, L 77. Codification in Council Regulation (EC) No. 1225/2009 of 30 November 2009 on protection against dumped imports from countries not members of the European Community (codified version), OJ L 343/51 of 22.12.2009.

Table 16.1 Profitability analysis with exclusion of unprofitable sales (indexation of real case)[a]

	A	B	C	D	E	F	G	H	I	J	K	L[a]
	PCN	QTY sold on domestic market	Net sales value	Net unit sales value	Unit COP in domestic market	Profitable sales quantity	Profitable sales value	Unit price of profitable sales	% of profitable sales	Profitable sales quantity in OCT	Profitable quantity (amount of profit) in OCT	Profit = K/J (%)
1	B11AA	1,000	10,000	10.00	9.88	187	2,080	11.10	**18.7**	F1 = 187	23	12.33
2	B11FA	113	1,308	11.63	10.72	86	1,055	12.32	**76.1**	F2 = 86	13	14.86
3	B15AA	608	6,838	11.24	9.90	595	6,712	11.24	97.7	B3 = 608	82	13.47
4	B15EA	19	257	13.76	11.21	19	257	13.76	100.0	B4 = 19	4	22.76
5	B15FA	176	2,151	12.19	10.63	167	2,054	12.19	94.5	B5 = 176	26	14.69
6	B20AA	142	1,720	12.15	10.66	137	1,672	12.15	96.7	B6 = 142	20	13.96
7	B20EA	31	447	14.36	11.26	31	447	14.36	100.0	B7 = 31	9	27.61
8	B20FA	188	2,463	13.11	11.14	188	2,463	13.11	100.0	B8 = 188	33	17.76
9	**Total**	**2,277**	**25,184**	**11.06**	**10.17**	**1,409**	**16,740**	**11.88**	**61.9**	**1,437**	**210**	
If > 20 % unprofitable transactions per group are excluded, is profit margin: K9:J9 ⇒											**14.59 %**	

[a]Small deviations are caused by round offs

Table 16.2 Example of a disclosure (in indexes) on dumping (with market economy status)

PCN	Sum of quantity	Sum of CIF value (CURR)	Sum of total ex-works price	Normal value at ex-works	Ex-works export price per unit	Absolute dumping	Abs. dumping quantity	% Dumping
1	2	3	4	5	6	7	8	9
B20FA	167	1,462	1,253	12.96[a]	7.49	5.47	916	62.6
B11FA	14	114	100	12.13[b]	7.11	5.02	70	61.8
B15FA	57	467	415	12.01[c]	7.21	4.80	276	59.1
	239	2,043	1,767				1,262	61.8

Cost of production plus profit: [a]From Table 16.1: E8 × (1 + K8/J8) = 11.14 × (1 + 17.76 %); [b]10.72 × (1 + 14.86%); [c]10.63 × (1 + 14.69 %)

dumping in Table 16.2. The profit for this product applied is not average price 11.63 – COP 10.72, but average price of profitable sales 12.32 – COP 10.72 = 1.59 or 14.86 % over COP. The normal value is in those cases is not COP plus average profit. It is COP plus the profit on profitable sales. If profitable sales are more than 80 % of total sales, the normal value is COP plus the profit on all sales on that product group. The formal expression for determination of profit is:

$$\text{Profit} = \text{IF}(\%\text{ of profitable sales} > 80\%,\ \text{Unit price} - \text{Unit COP},$$
$$\text{Unit price of profitable sales} - \text{Unit COP})$$

Or in Table 16.1, where the columns are alphabetically and rows digitally represented:

$$\text{Profit} = \text{If}(\text{I1} > 80\%,\ \text{D1} - \text{E1},\ \text{H1} - \text{E1})$$

Therefore, if the profitable sales are more than 80 % of total sales of a product class (PCN), the unit price of all sales minus the unit COP is taken as profit representing the whole group or PCN and if profitable sales are 80 % or less, only the profitable sales are selected. The exclusion of unprofitable sales and the establishment of the normal value on the basis of profitable sales only results in a normal value that is higher than a weighted average of all sales. If sales are 80 % or less of the total quantity of sales of a similar group (for instance the group of 11 W stick lamps of 6,000–10,000 h, B11AA), it results in a higher normal value than if all sales were included. In this case, the normal value of B11AA and B11FA increases by 13 % compared with the simple average of all sales. The line of reasoning of the Court of Justice in various cases is that sales at a loss are not an OCT. However, some products do not sell in one country, even in a buoyant market, and they are easily sold elsewhere. Failures in marketing in the domestic market are thus punished by a higher normal value and dumping margin.

The exclusion of non-profitable sales, if these are more than 20 % of the volume of a PCN class, has as a consequence increases in the profit presented in Table 16.1 from 8.58 % (J9 ÷ G9) to the level of 14.59 % (K9 ÷ J9). During the Uruguay

Round of GATT negotiations, resulting in the Agreement on Implementation of Article VI of the General Agreement on Tariffs and Trade 1994, often referred to as the Anti-Dumping Agreement, pleas were made in favour of sales at a loss and their complete inclusion into the calculation of normal value. Three cases were presented, which should be treated as normal business practices:

- *Forward pricing*, i.e. sales at a loss in anticipation of future profits.
- *Trade cycles*, in which sales at a loss were normal characteristic of a highly cyclical industry where profits in the boom compensated losses in the downturn.
- *Start-up production operations*. This argument is similar to the first one: a minimum sales volume is planned and initially the cost is not covered.

Japan especially was in favour of treating losses as normal phenomenon or ordinary course of trade. Japan claimed the right that its companies dump and inflict injury immediately when a product was put onto the market. The start-up losses were finally, under strict conditions concerning quantities (>20 % at a loss) and time limits (principally extended period, part of the investigation period), accepted into the Anti-Dumping Agreement[10] and European Community legislation.

(f) Example of calculation of dumping.

From the CFL-i case an actual example is given on calculation of dumping. This is Table 16.2. Values and quantities are given in index.

The data from Table 16.1 was reduced in Table 16.2 to those products that were actually exported. A formal presentation of a calculation by the European Commission, as given in formal disclosures, is mostly absent in studies on dumping and readers rarely get a presentation on the quantitative aspects of anti-dumping in the legal context. Such a calculation is, for this reason, presented in this chapter.

(g) Non-market economy and normal value.

Since prices in the OCT are market prices, the prices of sales in non-market economies can, by definition, not be in the OCT.[11] Companies may, as already remarked obtain MET. The criteria for MES or MET are[12]:

- The decisions of firms regarding prices, costs and inputs, including for instance raw materials, cost of technology and labour, output, sales and investment, are made in response to market signals reflecting supply and demand, and without significant State interference in this regard, and costs of major inputs substantially reflect market values.

[10] Agreement on Implementation of Article VI of the General Agreement on Tariffs and Trade 1994, 2.2.2.1.

[11] Countries considered to be non-market economies include: Albania, Armenia, Azerbaijan, Belarus, China, Georgia, North Korea, Kazakhstan, Kyrgyzstan, Moldova, Mongolia, Tajikistan, Turkmenistan, Uzbekistan and Vietnam.

[12] Basic Regulation, Article 1 (c).

- Firms have one clear set of basic accounting records that are independently audited in line with international accounting standards and are applied for all purposes.
- The production costs and financial situation of firms are not subject to significant distortions carried over from the former NME system, in particular in relation to depreciation of assets, other write-offs, barter trade and payment via compensation of debts.
- The firms concerned are subject to bankruptcy and property laws that guarantee legal certainty and stability for the operation of firms.
- Exchange rate conversions are carried out at the market rate.

In the case of China, input prices of raw materials, technology, etc., are highly dependent on the overall environment, which is not a market economy. The Chinese exchange rate is anyhow not a market rate. Consequently, as long as the government's and party members' interference plays an important role in the economy, there is no rationale for granting MES to indigenous Chinese producers.[13] The situation results in extremely weird cost structures as demonstrated in Table 15.2 in Chap. 15, "Cost composition and comparison Chinese, Chinese European and European producers in indices". Some multinationals have implanted their accounting and other business systems in their Chinese operations. This does not imply that the business environment is one of a market economy. Nevertheless, some companies, especially foreign non-Chinese, cannot practice the methods that some Chinese producers use in terms of employment policy, wages, tax evasion and similar practices. Their transactions are more or less reflecting a normal price level of inputs and outputs.

If MES is not granted, the normal value of the NME is, instead, generally the normal value in an analogue country. This analogue country is preferably selected prior to the draft of a complaint covering a NME. The demonstration of dumping must be the comparison between the price in the ordinary course of trade in an analogue country and the export price of the NME exporters. It is a myth that MET is preferable to NME status. Any conclusion in this respect is dependent on prices in the NME and the analogue market economy. In the case of CTVs and compact fluorescence lamps (CFLs) from China the analogue countries Singapore and Mexico had very low prices, which in the case of Mexico (CFL-i) had been seriously depressed by Chinese dumped imports. The analogue country normal value was lower than the price in China.

As indicated in Chap. 15, if Philips & Yaming had not opted for MET, its normal value would have been lower. This latter fact must have been unknown to two other Chinese exporters. Before the European Court of Justice, Changzhou Hailong

[13] A very striking example is the case of a company in which the director was a general in the People's Army and high-ranking party member. Multinationals have to obey a set of stiff rules concerning labour relations and financial transactions, whereas the general could neglect such rules. The general became a major supplier of a multinational, which had substantially higher costs in China.

(anti-dumping duty 59.5 %) and Zhejiang Yankon (Sunlight, anti-dumping duty 35.3 %) claimed that they should have received the same treatment as Philips & Yaming.[14] They wanted the normal value of Philips & Yaming to be applied as their normal value. It should be noted in this respect that the anti-dumping duty for these two was based on their dumping margin, which was lower than the undercutting margin. Consequently, if they wished that their dumping margin be calculated on the basis of Philips & Yaming's, they should have been certain that this would be beneficial to them. Their demand was amazing and even stupid. They should have looked at Mexican selling prices. These prices were used for the calculation of the Chinese normal value. Changzhou Hailong and Yankon, apparently instigated by the Chinese government, made a serious mistake. Their normal values would have been more than 40 % higher than those actually calculated and the anti-dumping duty for Yankon would have been 53 % instead of 35.4 %.

If the Court had found that granting MET to an exporter in an NME would require the normal value of this exporter with MET to be the basis for the normal value of the companies without MET in that country, the Chinese exporters of energy saving lamps would have been worse off.

The calculation in Table 16.3 is Table 16.2, but with normal values applied to the NME exporters in China. NME treatment appears to offer an advantage.

A similar calculation as the calculation for compact fluorescence lamps can be made for CTVs from China. Because of cartels within China, the Chinese CTV price level was considerably higher than the price in the analogue country Singapore.[15] As indicated in the CTV case Asia 1 Singapore normal value was applied to China, but, without any justification, at a lower level than the Singapore normal values.

16.8 Determination of Export Price

(a) Export Price (sales to independent customers in the European Community)

If exports take place to independent customers who resell the imported product, the export price is simply the weighted average of CIF value minus insurance and

[14] In Case T-255/01, Changzhou Hailong Electronics & Light Fixtures Co. Ltd, and Zhejiang Yankon v. Council wanted to have the normal value of Philips & Yaming applied as their normal value. The Court rejected this claim. The circumstances by which a company is eligible for MET are special to that company and the fact that its operations are recognised as market-oriented does not imply that the values applied to that company are applicable to other companies in the NME. Judgment of the Court of First Instance (Fifth Chamber, Extended Composition), 23 October 2003.

[15] The South China Morning Post reported in its issue of 16 August 1999 that a cartel of colour television tube makers had increased the prices of tubes and therefore, the cost of Chinese CTV makers. A confidential calculation indicated that the CTVs from China were necessarily more expensive than producers outside China. Nevertheless, analogue country prices were applied as normal value.

Table 16.3 (Non-MET) normal value (analogue country) applied to MET exporter in Table 16.2

R-PCN	Sum of QTY	Sum of CIF value (CURR)	Sum of total ex-works price	Normal value at works	Ex-works export price per unit	Absolute dumping	Abs. dumping quantity	% Dumping
1	2	3	4	5	6	7	8	9
B20FA	167	1,462	1,253	12.55	7.49	5.06	847	57.9
B11FA	14	114	100	9.20	7.11	2.09	29	25.7
B15FA	57	467	415	9.01	7.21	1.80	103	22.1
	239	2,043	1,767				979	47.9

ocean and land freight in the country of export and inland transport and handling costs. The European Commission subtracts these costs from the CIF value and arrives at the ex-works export price. For the establishment of injury, among which price undercutting, the CIF value plus the usual trade margins and costs between CIF import value and sales price to the first independent customer at the same level of trade or stage of transaction as the sales of European Community industry is used. This resale price minus CIF value is the Level of Trade (LoT) adjustment, to be discussed below.

(b) Export Price (individual treatment of exporters from Non-Market Economy)

Exporters from NMEs (and in case of sampling of exporters, when the number of exporters does require so) may request individual treatment, and their individual export prices are compared with the normal values per product group (PCN).

Individual treatment requests are granted if

1. In the case of wholly or partly foreign owned firms or joint ventures, they are free to repatriate capital and profits;
2. Export prices and terms of sale are freely determined;
3. The majority of the shares belong to private persons;
4. Exchange rate conversions are carried out at the market rate; and
5. State interference will not permit the circumvention of the measures if individual exporters are given different rates of duty.

If producers do not cooperate in a proceeding, the export prices for all exporters are applied to them using the best available evidence. It is the result of risk assessment whether companies may request such preferable treatment. As is clear from the issue of the request of MES, a request should be based on the calculation of alternative strategies. That is more difficult in the case of individual treatment because the best available evidence is generally not available prior to the opening of the proceeding, whereas a calculation of prices of the analogue country, on which the complaint provides information, and comparison thereof with the exporter's own domestic prices can more easily result in a quantified decision.

(c) Export Price (sales to related customers in the European Community)

If export sales are made through a related importer, which subsequently resells to independent customers, the export price is constructed on the basis of the price at which the imported products are resold to the first independent buyer and adjustments are made – with the goal of establishing a reliable export price – for all costs, including duties and taxes, incurred between importation and resale, and profits accruing, at the European Community frontier level. Such adjustments can result in surprises for multinational companies. In preceding chapters, various examples are mentioned of multinationals both complainant and also victim in anti-dumping proceedings because of the special treatment of their export prices. Thomson and Philips consumer electronics are mentioned in the CTV cases, but Philips & Yaming is a similar case. There is a strong difference, however, because Philips & Yaming is a joint venture and profits cannot freely be transferred as part of the price level. The issue is dealt with below.

16.9 Comparison of Normal Value and Export Price

(a) Level of trade (stage of transaction)

There are various distribution channels all with their own level of prices and gross trade margins. In electrical and electronic products there are the traditional wholesalers who sell to retailers, but also retail chains (such as Media Markt, Dixons, Currys and Darty), cooperative purchasing organisations (Expert in various European Community member states), supermarkets and department stores (such as French Carrefour or the German Kaufhof) with their own brands, do-it-yourself chains and finally producers or would-be producers (Original Equipment Manufacturers, OEM). It is, of course, imperative that the normal values are compared with export prices at the same level of distribution. In some cases the same levels of distribution cannot be found. Captive distribution is an example of a system that is only existent in the domestic market of the dumper but not in the export market. Another striking example is the OEM. OEM transactions are referred to in various chapters and more about them is discussed below. A salient feature of OEM is that it generally does not occur in the domestic market of the dumping exporter, entailing surprising consequences for the determination of normal value. The treatment of OEM producers appears highly discriminatory.

(b) Related companies: normal value and (re-) construction of the export price

Unless they conduct active dumping policies from a secure home market, like the VCR, CD player and various other cases in which Japan and Korea were involved, multinationals do not expect to be found dumping. They produce for the market in the country that is source of dumping and ship certain products to their main market. A different case is Thomson's CTV production in Thailand and audio production in Malaysia. It produced in these countries for the sake of low cost and any intention of dumping was absent. Thomson did not even have domestic CTV sales in Thailand. Unfortunately for Thomson the company was incapable of avoiding losses and that implied dumping and another bad luck was that a constructed normal value was applied to Thomson Thailand. If the multinational produces in the dumping country for various markets, pricing is commonly in accordance with the OECD guidelines for multinationals: non-discriminatory prices for all destinations. If the factory supplies both the sales organisation in the country exporting dumped products and in the country of imports at the same price, dumping may nevertheless be found. The basis for the export price is not an ex-factory invoice value, as Japan preferred, but a construction is made of the export price. This construction takes the resale price in the market of the complainant as a given basis and subsequently selling, general and administrative costs and other distribution costs of the sales company are subtracted. These are not necessarily those actually incurred and reported. They are adjusted and a profit is allocated, regardless whether a profit was made.

The fact that the company is related and compensatory financing is assumed results in finding of an export price that is substantially below the invoiced export price and in a dumping margin that is in the case at hand about 11 % higher. Table 16.4 shows the data – in indexed form, but in relative values in an identical case –as constructed by the European Commission and the data as reported by the related company. Due to the adjustment of certain items, the related company is worse off. The constructed export price is substantially lower than the actual price.

In the calculation of the export price, the dumping margin is inflated by a construction as applied in Table 16.4. In the calculation of injury, again a constructed resale price rather than the actual price is applied, resulting in an undercutting level, which is also inflated, as shown in Table 16.8.

(c) Excluding non-dumped export transactions: zeroing.

A heavily criticized practice in anti-dumping is zeroing. Zeroing is, as we have seen, a calculation methodology ignoring cases of "negative" dumping in which the export price is higher than normal value. A margin of absolute dumping (see column 7 in Tables 16.2 and 16.3) is taken into consideration if normal value > export price, in which case the export price is subtracted from the normal value to arrive at the absolute dumping margin, but if normal value < export price, the dumping margin is treated as being zero and is not taken into consideration. This method increases the weighted average dumping margin.

The issue of zeroing has frequently been discussed. Edwin Vermulst and Daniel Ikenson (2007), *inter alia*, have dedicated a profound contribution to this issue. Some practices of selective dumping and undercutting in the case of car CD changers, *inter alia*, have been mentioned. The example was given of Mitsubishi supplying Volvo in Sweden at prices substantially higher than prices to Volvo in Japan, but far higher than to Renault in France, for which Philips was the preferred supplier. Price discrimination between the domestic and export price appeared to decrease as soon as the exporter obtained the preferred supplier status. The effect of zeroing is demonstrated in Table 16.5 with some modified data of Table 16.2. First the non-zeroing case is demonstrated. It is assumed that there are two quantities and

Table 16.4 Related companies' data and constructed export price: inflating the dumping margin

Dumping margin calculation		Commission data construction	Data reported by company
Resale price as reported by related company and verified		12.04	12.04
Profit allocated	5 %	0.60	n.a.
Rebate	9.6 %	1.15	1.15
Commissions	2.9 %	0.35	0.35
Inland freight over number	0.010	0.01	0.01
Freight over units	0.169	0.17	0.17
Insurance over units	0.001	0.00	0.00
EC freight over units	0.061	0.06	0.06
Charges	0.081	0.08	0.08
Package		0.00	0.00
Credit	0.798 %	0.10	0.10
Total allowances		1.91	1.56
Average selling, general and administrative costs	16 %	1.93	1.93
CIF price constructed respectively invoiced		8.20	8.55
Transport cost China-Europe		0.18	0.18
Allowances in China for EU		0.01	0.01
Ex-works export price reconstructed respectively invoiced		7.40	8.36
Normal value (MES or MET) used in calculation		12.68	12.68
Ex-works export price (constructed respectively invoiced)		7.40	8.36
CIF value for AD duty calculation		8.55	8.55
Dumping margin		5.28	4.33
Dumping margin as % of CIF value		61.7 %	50.6 %

two export prices of product B20FA. The total quantity is the quantity of Table 16.2, which has been divided in one quantity of 85 at a price of 14.08 instead of the export price of 7.49 in Table 16.2. The dumping margin is −1.12, instead of 5.47 as in Table 16.2. The other quantity of B20FA is 82 and the export price is the 7.49 resulting in a dumping margin of 5.47.

Exports of the article B20FA take place at two different prices in different transactions. One customer gets the product at the price that is higher than normal value, i.e. at 14.08. The dumping is negative (−1.12 per unit) and the value of the negative dumping is 95. On the other hand there is a dumping margin of 5.47 per unit of a volume of 82 units of B20FA. The total dumping value (quantity) is 451. The result is that total dumping is 34.3 % instead of the 61.8 % dumping margin as percentage of CIF if all products had been dumped as in Table 16.2. The methodology of zeroing neglects negative dumping margins, which is considered a phenomenon of tactics by the dumping party to be separated from the real dumping. Zeroing of the transactions with a negative dumping margin neglects export prices with a higher than normal value, thus decreasing the export price and increasing the dumping margin (Table 16.6).

Table 16.5 Negative dumping margins with non-zeroing

R-PCN	Sum of QTY	Sum of CIF value (CURR)	Sum of total ex-works price	Normal value ex-works	Ex-works export price per unit	Absolute dumping	Absolute dumping quantity	% Dumping
B20FA	85	1,397	1,197	12.96	14.08	−1.12	−95	−6.8
B20FA	82	719	616	12.96	7.49	5.47	451	62.6
B11FA	14	100	100	12.13	7.11	5.02	70	70.5
B15FA	57	467	415	12.01	7.21	4.80	276	59.1
	239	2,043	1,767				701	34.3

Table 16.6 Zeroing negative dumping margins

R-PCN	Sum of QTY	Sum of CIF value (CURR)	Sum of total ex-works price	Normal value ex-works	Ex-works export price per unit	Absolute dumping	Abs. dumping quantity	% Dumping
B20FA	85	1,397	1,197	12.96	14.08	−1.12	0	0.0
B20FA	82	719	616	12.96	7.49	5.47	451	62.6
B11FA	14	100	100	12.13	7.11	5.02	70	70.5
B15FA	57	467	415	12.01	7.21	4.80	276	59.1
	239	2,043	1,767				701	39.0

If zeroing eliminates negative dumping margins, the dumping margin increases. Excluding transactions with a negative dumping margin does, of course, result in a lower export price than if negative dumping margins were not excluded. The problem here is the one of Mitsubishi, enjoying the results of dumping by having Volvo as a fixed customer, attacking Philips' position with Renault with heavy dumping. The zeroing practice may be utterly unfair, but so is non-zeroing. There are some logical economic arguments for zeroing. A fair solution to this problem is difficult to find. As stated before, the time restrictions of an investigation period limits the possibilities to analyse whether the tactic of selective dumping has effectively taken place.

16.10 OEM, Normal Value and Non-market Economy

The European Commission and the Court of Justice accept OEM as a special phenomenon. The Court states that[16]

[16] An ample number of cases have been dealt with in the Court of Justice, including: Case C-172/87 Mita Industrial Ltd. v. Council [1992] ECR 1–1301; Joined Cases C-133/87 and C-150/87 Nashua Corporation v. Commission and Council [1990] ECR 1–719; Goldstar v. Council, Judgment of the Court (Sixth Chamber) 13 February 1992 in Case C-105/90 ECR 1–677.

The essential difference between the two types of sale is at the marketing stage. The two types of sale are aimed at different customers, who generally operate at different marketing stages, but the product sold to the final consumer by an OEM is similar to that sold under the manufacturer's brand. Production costs are therefore comparable for the two types of sale.

There are generally no sales of similar OEM products on the domestic market in any stage. Domestically, an OEM producer/supplier sells either under its own brand or not at all. Bizarre legal cases are mentioned below (Nakajima All Precision). But also in the personal fax case a great injustice was done to a Thai OEM producer. The producer did not have any domestic sales and could economically not dump. Nevertheless, the Commission applied a normal value to this company and this normal value was constructed using the average SG& A and profit of the Taiwanese market.[17] If domestic sales were found of OEM products, the prices were similar to or higher than sales by the OEM producer under own brand. These cases should have tempted the European Commission to review the OEM phenomenon. Japanese and Korean exporters with powerful domestic market positions did not sell on the domestic market under OEM, but on the export market they did so massively. Examples of producers with OEM exports are mentioned: Matsushita and its daughter JVC in television and VCR cases. The Sanyo offer to Grundig is mentioned in Chap. 2. In these cases, the export prices were so low that it was attractive for the customer to purchase the product from the exporter and distribute it via its distribution channels and even to make some extraordinary profits on it rather than produce the product itself. This means that the export price should be a guideline for the calculation of dumping. It is not an issue of the normal value. In the case of OEM supplies, the export price is just lower than the price to any other reseller in the country of import. It implies that the dumping margin should not be less, but rather be higher than in the case of supplies to resellers in the stage of distribution in which the OEM customer sells. This form of OEM should be distinguished sharply from the case in which the exporter does not sell in the domestic market at all.

In the case of plain paper copiers, several producers did not sell domestically at all. Nevertheless, a normal value had to be or, at least had been, calculated. This was done on the basis of the selling, general and administrative costs of the producers with "captive" sales in their domestic market. That means that the companies with the advantage of access to the domestic market by means of a distribution system that does not permit sales by others are used as yardstick for the establishment of normal value of those that had the bad luck or weakness of lacking that opportunity. The weak are compared with the powerful and punished by their lack of power. Correctly, Nakajima holds the view that the method taking into account[18]:

[17] Council Regulation (EC) No 904/98 of 27 April 1998 imposing definitive anti-dumping duties on imports into the Community of personal fax machines originating in the People's Republic of China, Japan, the Republic of Korea, Malaysia, Singapore, Taiwan and Thailand, OJ L 128 of 30 April1998, 1–17, recital (42).

[18] Nakajima v Council Case C-69/89, ECR 1991, 1–02069 Plea of Nakajima, paragraph 13.

expenses incurred and the profits realized by other producers and exporters in the exporting country or country of origin on profitable sales of the like product, is likely to lead to unreasonable and discriminatory results in a case such as this in which the structure of the reference undertakings is in no respect comparable to that of the undertaking concerned.

Nakajima, rightly, refers to the existence of vertical integration in Japan[19]:

Nakajima stresses that it does not have any marketing structure for its products as its entire production output is sold at the "ex-factory" stage to independent distributors, whereas all of the reference undertakings have a vertically-integrated structure designed to ensure distribution of their products within Japan.

The Court of Justice did not care and drew economically and, consequently legally, untenable conclusions, underlying jurisprudence in subsequent cases. Especially the fact that normal value was inflated by accepting the selling, general and administrative cost of those producers dominating the Japanese market, including their costs incurred for the maintenance of their dominating position results in a form of discrimination, which has always been endorsed by the Japanese Ministry of International Trade and Industry (currently the Ministry of Economy, Trade and Industry) in the practical conduct of its trade policy that benefits the strong. It is bizarre that the European Court of Justice supported the anti-competitive system in Japan and considers it a normal system and yardstick for normal value of those that, such as Nakajima, suffer under the system. These companies are, consequently, twice victims of the system. First they are secluded from profitable sales in Japan and subsequently they are discriminated and treated as if they would incur the same cost if they did have such sales in Japan, of which the costs become yardstick for their normal value, which is thereby artificially increased.

The Court agreed with the view that the small should be treated equally to the dominating major producers in the country of export of dumped products and came to the peculiar conclusion that economically unequal operations should be treated equally: [20]

Undertakings which sell only for the purposes of exportation and those which market a product – if only similar – on the domestic market must be treated in the same way. If the producer for whom a normal value is constructed sold his products on the domestic market he would inevitably have to adapt to the conditions imposed on other undertakings operating on that market. There would therefore be discrimination between undertakings if the normal value for a producer operating on the domestic market were to be calculated on the basis of all expenses and profits included in the price of the product in question whilst in the case of an OEM exporter the normal value were to be calculated without having regard to those accounting data.

---

[19] Nakajima v Council Case C-69/89, ECR 1991, 1–02069 Plea of Nakajima, paragraph 36.

[20] Case C 69/89 Nakajima All Precision Co. Ltd. v. Council [1991] ECR I-2069 (paragraphs 65 to 67). The details are set out in the opinion of Advocate General Lenz, [1991] ECR I-2112 (paragraph 173 to 177). It should be noted that the European Community institutions took to a certain extent account 01 Nakajima's particular structure by making some adjustments which were, however, restricted the selling costs represented by commissions and salaries paid to sales staff.

Totally unequal situations of enterprises should apparently, in the view of the Court, be disregarded for the sake of "non-discrimination". If a producer does not sell on the domestic market because it cannot, it does not have any benefit from domestic sales. The domestic sales do not enable it to dump and to increase domestic profits by this dumping. Such a producer is disadvantaged. Nevertheless, the Court neglects such simple economic arguments and argues that if such a company would sell in Japan, it would have the same cost, and normal value, as those that bar them from the sales in that market. Therefore, Chap. 7 of this book may probably be highly instructive to European Court of Justice members. It may be assumed that in the case of Nakajima All Precision Group, prices reflect the relative competitive advantage of the country or, more precisely, of the company. It may be that a Japanese infrastructure has been created by destruction of foreign competition by dumping from Japan. In this case, competition may have been distorted in the way shown in Diagram 8.5 in Chap. 8. It would suggest that the division of labour has the reverse direction. There is no *prima facie* evidence, however, that this is the case with Nakajima or similar companies and reasons for assumption of its presence are absent. Authorities and the Court should not treat producers without access to the market of the country from where dumping took place in the same way as those who created the obstructions to market access.

It seems imperative that the European Commission explain in such anti-dumping cases of OEM exports without domestic sales why it uses the selling, general and administrative costs and profits of other companies with domestic sales, on grounds other than legal arguments based on a European Court of Justice case, for the normal value of a company without domestic sales of the like product. It is not the task of the European Commission to stimulate competition in the country of exports, but a simple application of the selling, general and administrative costs incurred by producers with domestic sales to producers without such domestic sales is economically not defensible and even reinforces restrictive practices in that market.

There is clearly a serious inconsistency in treatment of OEM. Producers of OEM products with domestic sales, like Korean and Japanese VCR and Compact Disc player producers, claimed a reduction of the normal value, which was, without justification, granted on some occasions. However, the COP of all products, both domestically sold and exported, decreases by addition of OEM quantities to production volume normally sold under the producer's own brand and as a result domestic profits increase. At least this is the outcome for the major industrial enterprises in Japan. The decrease in normal value granted on the basis of some assumptions concerning OEM is in the advantage of the dumpers. Smaller producers without sales in Japan or Korea are discriminated by the use of the selling, general and administrative costs of these very dominating majors for establishment of normal value of the small OEM producers. As seen in Chap. 8, dumped exports may contribute to profitability by the volume effect. Nevertheless, a more favourable treatment, by inexplicable adjustment of normal value has been applied where the OEM has nothing to do with the domestic market but with export distribution. As the Court correctly remarked, OEM is an issue of distribution, but on the export market, and this does not have any relationship with normal value.

As Chap. 8 tries to make clear, the COP of oligopolistic producers decreases by increase in volume sales and domestic profits increase thanks to OEM. It is self-evident and economically natural that OEM does not exist in the domestic market of exporters. OEM creates its own competitors in an oligopolistic market. An OEM policy that created competitors with the same products under others' brands would be insane in such a market. The OEM policy by Philips' VCR joint venture with Grundig, iR3, was a mechanism of self-defence vis-à-vis Japanese and Korean OEM practices. Normally OEM is for export markets only and especially for the increase of volume and the improvement of cost. By OEM, iR3 created volume of production and thus defended its cost position. OEM policies on the domestic market require price discipline of OEM customers competing with similar products from the same supplier in the same market as the supplier. As Chap. 10 sketches, price discipline was a main issue. In all cases, the dilemma is between own branded sales and OEM sales. Generally dumping exporters of OEM grant large rebates to OEM customers and this phenomenon is injurious to the profitability of own branded sales. Gradually, exporters try to reduce the sales of OEM in favour of their own brands as soon as total production volume is satisfactory. This means that the level of undercutting of European industry prices decreases over time when the dumping is successful.

Korean exporters, and before them, Japanese exporters, *inter alia*, of plain paper copiers, convinced the European Commission that adjustments to the production according to specifications required special efforts. As a consequence the European Commission applied:

> *5 %, instead of the profit level for the exporters' sales of VCRs on the domestic market applied in other constructed values*

If B20FA had been exported as OEM, it would have implied that the normal value of this product would have been 11.54 instead of 12.96, as in Table 16.2, and the dumping margin of Philips & Yaming as percentage of CIF were 50.1 % instead of the actual 61.8 %, at identical ex-works export prices. Had all Philips and Yaming products been exported as OEM and the profit were held at 5 % instead of the actual profit incurred in China, the decrease of the normal value would have caused a decrease of the dumping margin to 35.8 %. However, the price to OEM customers, i.e. to those lamp producers not making the specific lamps exported by Philips & Yaming, is normally below the price to independent wholesalers and distributors. In some cases, the institutions of the European Community have applied other calculations in the case of OEM. In Goldstar versus Council the issue was discussed[21]:

> *Profits... were estimated for OEM sales at 30% of the profits realized on Goldstar's own-brand sales.*

[21] Judgment of the Court (Sixth Chamber) 13 February 1992 in Case C-105/90 ECR 1–677 paragraph 41.

In the case of Philips & Yaming, the dumping margin would have been substantially reduced if 30 % of domestic profits had been applied. The problem of dumping was not caused by the normal value, however. The problem is one of allocations of cost and the level of trade in the export market. The main issue is the stage of trade in the export market. The OEM supplier could save on cost of distribution in the export country.

The European institutions have clearly been misinformed. Such sales of products with "special specifications" to OEM customers do not increase cost of production but rather lower them, as Philips' iR3 VCR practice taught. The "special adjustments of products to wishes of the customers" did not cost more, but less. Mostly the customer draws up specifications and some components that have to be adjusted, but such changes do not increase the COP. The adjustment required a switch in the factory to another design in the printed circuit boards in computer software, but the additional volume decreases the COP. The production of sets supplied by iR3 to Blaupunkt, Dual, Melchiori, Metz, Nokia, Quelle, RFT, Schneider, Siemens, Synudine, Grundig or to B&O was not more expensive than similar sets supplied to Philips. The prices to these customers were the same, depending on specifications. Some of these customers never made VCRs or did not even have activities in the consumer electronics business. An example of the latter is Siemens. Companies other than Grundig and Philips had never made VCRs. Nevertheless, the prices were the same. As shown in Table 10.4 of Chap. 10, there were differences between the margins from their purchasing to retail prices to consumers, which may have been expression of their effort to gain market share at the cost of other customers. The prices to these customers were the same and further distribution is similar to the distribution by a trader with the same margins. Therefore, there has never been a single reason to make a distinction between a producer's branded sales and OEM. The latter is merely the easiest way for realisation of rapid increase in volume and decrease in cost per unit.

However, since the European Commission is still on the track of neglect of economic reality of OEM, this special benevolent treatment still exists. It would create an issue, however, in the case of China, which has neither been brought up by the Chinese exporters nor by their lawyers. Most, but not exclusively, electronic and other consumer products made in China and sold in the European Community with a brand name are OEM or stencil brand products, i.e. the products are supplied to European Community producers or traders with brand names of producers and traders and not infrequently in accordance with some specifications of customers. A special problem is that their operations are generally of the OEM type, requiring special attention and treatment because of the special beneficial treatment granted by the European Community to this phenomenon. In the case of Chinese television producers, they practically always sold their product under a brand of the importer, but the Chinese did not claim OEM treatment. Very often the sets were just Chinese sets with a brand name sticker. But, even in cases in which other exporters claimed OEM treatment, the Chinese did not.

A striking example is the case of *Bicycles*.[22] Taiwanese producers requested OEM adjustments. Since there was no difference between the domestic market and exports, the European Commission rejected the claim. The dumping found for Taiwan was negligible and the European Community did not impose duties on imports from Taiwan. The Chinese requested adjustments for differences in quality. The Chinese exporters did not ask for OEM adjustments, in spite of the fact that their bicycles exported to the European Community were quite different from those for the domestic market, as emphasised by the European Commission in Recital 20 of the quoted regulation: "The fact that the Chinese production sold domestically consists mainly of 'city bicycles' is irrelevant as these models are not exported to the Community." These bicycles were only sold in China, whereas special export bicycles were made for the European Community and resold under European Community customers' brand names. This implied that Chinese exporters seem to have been entitled to some adjustments to their normal value, if such an adjustment is (remarked above it is not) justifiable.

A serious problem would arise in case of recognition of OEM status of Chinese exporters. In that case, the normal value might, although the thesis here is that there is no valid argument for adjustment of the normal value, be adjusted by a reduction of the selling, general administrative costs or of profit. If exporters enjoy MET, this would ensue a reduction of normal value. If prices in an analogue country are the basis for normal value calculations, an adjustment should be applied to the analogue country normal values, which were Taiwanese prices. The request by Taiwanese bicycle makers for special OEM treatment was rejected, "...since prices, costs and profits for OEM sales on the Taiwanese market were found to be comparable to those for own-brand sales." This may be the case for the Taiwanese market, but Chinese products sold domestically were mainly "city bicycles". This means that the European Commission should have constructed some normal value for OEM on the basis of an inexistent market in Taiwan.

16.11 Summary of Various Approaches of Normal Value and Export Price

The discussion on treatment of normal value and export price boils down to following issues:

- Sales at a loss may be eliminated from calculations if they constitute more than 20 % of transactions. Bad marketing may result in an increase of normal value.

[22] Commission Regulation (EEC) No 550/93 of 5 March 1993 imposing a provisional anti-dumping duty on imports of bicycles originating in the People's Republic of China, Official Journal L 058, 11/03/1993, 12–21, recital (27).

Table 16.7 Different circumstances, diverging duties

		Traditional (%)	OEM (%)
Market economy	Related	61.8	50.1
	Unrelated	50.6	38.9
Non-market economy		47.9	37.0

- MET may result in a higher or lower normal value than when analogue country values are applied. This is not a matter a fairness, but of market conditions in the country of non-MET and in the analogue country.
- OEM sales may result in a different, lower normal value, which has a considerable injurious impact and for which there is no reasonable basis.
- Zeroing, the elimination of negative dumping margins, may result in a lower average export price and, consequently, higher dumping margin.

A simple matrix resumes the various outcomes in one specific case, Table 16.7.[23]

The matrix in Table 16.7 gives an example how differences in dumping margin may arise from various methods applied in investigations. It does not imply that Table 16.7 gives the precise differences between the outcomes of various methods, but that differences may be substantial. It is, therefore, worthwhile for a party in a proceeding to scrutinise the disclosures. There are some caveats. Generally, a related party in an exporting country does not send OEM products to the related party in the European Community, but branded products. If the dumping margin would be 61.8 %, however, the OEM products, provided the European Commission recognises them as OEM, would bear about 11 % less. The normal value of the Chinese CFL-i lamps based on the analogue country prices are known to the author, but the selling, general and administrative costs, of the producer in the analogue country are not. It is assumed that they are comparable with the selling, general and administrative costs in China, but profit in China was considerably higher than in Mexico, so that the normal value of the company with MET was considerably higher. In the case of CFL-i the exporters with NME treatment could have asked for OEM treatment, which would have given them a better perspective than a request for the allowance of a normal value of the company with MET, which was highly disadvantageous and resulted in 11 % higher normal value. Finally the survey shows that related parties are worse off when they quote identical prices as non-related parties. The thesis that NME treatment is unfair is based, again, on lack of proper analysis of specific situations, i.e. on prejudice.

(B) The Second of the Lesser Rule: The injury margin

[23] The turmoil made in this case, Case T-255/01, Changzhou Hailong Electronics & Light Fixtures Co. Ltd, and Zhejiang Yankon v. Council, inter alia about market economy treatment (MET), appears unjustifiable. Lawyers could have paid attention, instead, to more rewarding issues than MET.

16.12 Injury: The gap Between industry's Price and Import Price

Although various indicators are applied for discovery of a relationship between dumping and injury incurred by producers in the market where exporters dumped,[24] one indicator plays a leading role in the determination of the level of injury. As for the total of injury factors, the European Commission must make an[25]

> *evaluation of all relevant economic factors and indices having a bearing on the state of the industry, including the fact that an industry is still in the process of recovering from the effects of past dumping or subsidisation, the magnitude of the actual margin of dumping, actual and potential decline in sales, profits, output, market share, productivity, return on investments, utilisation of capacity; factors affecting Community prices; actual and potential negative effects on cash flow, inventories, employment, wages, growth, ability to raise capital or investments. This list is not exhaustive, nor can any one or more of these factors necessarily give decisive guidance.*

It appears that all these factors should, indeed, be analysed.[26] The principal indicator for the determination of the level or amount of injury is price undercutting, which might be supplemented by the price underselling, which latter is the positive amount of price undercutting, minus losses attributable to the dumping, plus a target profit deemed necessary for the industry without injury attributable to dumping.

---

[24] In European Communities – Anti-Dumping Duties on Imports of Cotton-Type Bed Linen from India, Report of the Panel, World Trade Organization, WT/DS141/R, 30 October 2000 (00–4407) it was made clear: "The Anti-Dumping agreement requires that examination of the impact of the dumped imports on the domestic industry concerned shall include an evaluation of all relevant economic factors and indices having a bearing on the state of the industry, including actual and potential decline in sales, profits, output, market share, productivity, return on investments, or utilization of capacity; factors affecting domestic prices; the magnitude of the margin of dumping; actual and potential negative effects on cash flow, inventories, employment, wages, growth, ability to raise capital or investments."

[25] Council Regulation (EC) No 1225/2009 of 30 November 2009 on protection against dumped imports from countries not members of the European Community, Article 3.5.

[26] In European Communities – Anti-Dumping duties on imports of cotton-type bed linen from India the WTO, Panel report WT/DS141/R of 30 October 2000, Appellate Body report WT/DS141/AB/R of 1 March 2001 and report of Appellate Body WT/DS141/AB/RW of 8 April 2003 report discussions in detail the way in which the European Community had conducted its investigations. The Community should indeed investigate all relevant economic factors and indices having a bearing on the state of the industry, as it is prescribed in the anti-Dumping Agreement. India infringed on the very rules emphasised by the WTO appellate body – whose opinion was seen as a victory for India – and promptly, but almost necessarily, exempted two exporters from China from draconic measures, when these referred to failures in the Indian proceeding and to contradictions between India's own methods in the case and the outcomes, victorious for India, of the panels in the WTO in this case.

Since the lesser duty rule is applicable or, since the

> *anti-dumping duty shall not exceed the margin of dumping as provisionally established, but it should be less than the margin if such lesser duty would be adequate to remove the injury to the Community industry,*[27]

determination of the level of injury by the European Commission is as essential for the level of duty as the dumping margin. The calculation of the level of injury starts with a comparison of resale prices at the same level of trade (the same stage of transactions) and whether these resale prices of imports do undercut selling prices of EU industry at that level of trade.

1. Resale price

A determination of the resale price of complainant seems relatively easy. It is the ex-works price to the first independent customer. This ex-works price is a price in which rebates and certain supply costs, like transport and insurance, paid for by the seller are subtracted. Other costs subtracted are packaging and credit. At multinationals, the superficial opinion on resale prices is often the same as the opinion on dumping. Resale prices are not as clear as they seem.

The resale price has to be compared with the selling prices of importers from the country of dumped exports at the same level of trade. This comparison poses a problem. The exporters sell normally at CIF price to importers, but that price is not the resale price at the same level as complainant's sales. Provisions must be made for costs and profits of importers/wholesalers. Such information on importers' costs and margins is dependent on the cooperation of traders. Are cooperative traders those with highest profit margins and lowest costs? This may be doubted. Consequently, the margin of "Level of Trade Adjustment" (LoT) is not necessarily based on the highest turnover, generally related to a low price level, but based on data of a cooperative trader, which may distort the total picture. This level of trade adjustment found is thus applied to all resale prices of products from independent defendants.

For the related party, the resale price is the basis for the calculation of the ex-works price. This price is the price used for the dumping calculation and is generally lower than the ex-works price reported by the related exporter and lower than its reported CIF value minus cost of land freight, sea freight and insurance and handling. The CIF value as reported by the related party is used for the determination of the resale price rather than the actual resale price as established as basis for the calculation of the ex-works export price. The resale price of the related importer is the CIF value reported by the related exporter plus the LoT applied to all imported products from the country of dumping. Consequently the ex-works export price is not the price reported by the related exporter, but constructed value calculated from the resale price with all sorts of deductions of imputed profits

[27] Council Regulation (EC) No 1225/2009 of 30 November 2009 on protection against dumped imports from countries not members of the European Community (codified version), Article 7. 2.

and costs, whereas the actual CIF price is the starting point for the application of the LoT generally resulting in a lower resale price than the actual resale price of the related sales company.

2. CIF value

The CIF value is the ex-works export price plus costs of inland freight in the country of export, handling and insurance and sea freight. Often this is also the value of the invoice to the importer. The CIF value of the related exporter is not his ex-works price plus costs incurred up to European Community frontier, but the reported CIF. The first (from ex-works) is 8.20 and the second (reported and used for the construction of the resale price) is 8.55 (see Table 16.4). Consequently, there are two CIF values of a related exporter, one used for the determination of the ex-works price and the other as basis for the calculation of undercutting.

3. Injury: Undercutting

The principal measure for determination of injury is undercutting, which is the difference between the resale price of the injured (complainant) and the resale price of the dumper (defendant) as a percentage of the resale price of complainant. The following formula is a simple representation of undercutting (***UC***). The undercutting is the negative weighted sum of CIF value of the transactions of each model (quantity times price of each product category) plus the cost of trade (the ***LoT***) of each group, which total is the representation of the resale value of the defendant minus the quantities of European industry for each of the product groups or models times the quantity of the sales of the defendant attributable to each product group as part of the constructed European resale value.

$$UC = -\frac{\sum_{i=1}^{n} Q_{iE}.P_{iECIF} \times (1 + LoT) - \sum_{i=1}^{n} Q_{iE}.P_{iEUR}}{\sum_{i=1}^{n} Q_{iE}.P_{iEUR}} \tag{16.1}$$

In other words, the undercutting level ***UC*** is the weighted average selling price of European Community industry minus the weighted constructed resale price of similar products of the importers as a percentage of the weighted constructed average selling price of European Community industry, where the importers' resale level is CIF plus a ***LoT*** adjustment.

However, the undercutting is the start of the calculation of injury. It is generally understood that the dumping and undercutting have depressed the European industry's prices and that these prices have been pushed below a level of a reasonable profitable level, except as seen previously in the television cases, where the European Commission arbitrarily juggled with profit targets.

4. Underselling and the injury margin

(a) General formulae and practice.

Underselling is the undercutting of European profitable industry prices, i.e. actual industry prices have been augmented with an amount to eliminate losses and to include a target profit that the European industry is supposed to make under normal competitive circumstances. This price is the profitable or target price, which is the prevailing weighted average price of the European Community industry times a factor ***t***, which, in principle, eliminates the losses and includes a reasonable profit. The underselling rate is expressed as a percentage of CIF value of the imports from the dumping exporter.

$$US_{CIF} = -\frac{\sum_{i=1}^{n} Q_{iE}.P_{iECIF} \times (1 + LoT) - \sum_{i=1}^{n} Q_{iE}.P_{iEUR} \times (1 + t)}{\sum_{i=1}^{n} Q_{iE}.P_{iECIF}} \quad (16.2)$$

Formulae 16.1 and 16.2 may seem impressively complex and even appalling to some readers. It is the difference between value of the resale by the importer and the quantity of imports times the profitable European price as a percentage of CIF value. An example of a disclosure of undercutting and underselling is given in the next Table 16.8.

Table 16.8 gives a survey of an injury calculation, i.e. price undercutting and underselling or the calculation of the injury margin. The data the European Commission constructed are compared with those multinational company with exports to the related importer reported. The injury margin is based on the (negative) price of the exporter's price minus the European Community industry price excluding losses and including profits (a correction by 8.37 %) divided by the CIF export price. If this value – in Table 16.8 row 33.1 % – is lower than the dumping margin, the underselling, as % of CIF value will be applied as anti-dumping duty. Since the dumping margin was 61.8 %, the injury margin was the anti-dumping duty. The two cases are presented parallel: the European Commission method and the erroneous idea of a multinational about the treatment it would get.

(b) Injury and related company

The error of multinationals is the idea that resale prices of the related party are the yardstick for a calculation of injury. Suspicion is that the undercutting by Thomson has not been based on such a reconstruction (see Chap. 11), but this is not the general approach. Most European companies are not aware that resale prices of their imports from the country of dumped exports will be based on a LoT adjustment, i.e. the cost of importation, including duty payment and handling, and of distribution and allocated profit (of 5 %) of independent exporters/importers, often without cost of brand support and marketing. These independent exporters/importers certainly do not

Table 16.8 Calculation of undercutting and injury margin

	Undercutting calculation		Commission method	Related company reporting
			A	B
1	CIF price of exporter (invoiced)		8.55	8.55
2	Level of Trade (LoT) adjustment (Commission)	27%	2.31	
3 = 40.7 % × B1	Value added (LoT) to CIF by multinational as reported	40.7%		3.48
4 = 1 + LoT	Resale price for undercutting		10.86	12.04
5	Community industry weighted average price			12.64
6 = 5 − 4	Undercutting		−1.77	−0.60
7 = 6 ÷ 5	Undercutting as % of EU industry price		14.0 %	4.7 %
8 = 8.37 % × 5	Target allowance for European industry	8.37%	1.06	1.06
9 = 5 + 8	Average resale price EU industry (incl. profit)		13.69	13.69
10 = 9 − 4	Underselling		−2.83	−1.66
11 = (−) 10 ÷ 1	Underselling as % of CIF value		**33.1 %**	19.4 %

have market research and marketing departments and a range of other indefinite staff, which multinationals have available, and which inflate the gross margins of such companies.

The assumption of a compensatory relationship between related companies inevitably results in both an inflation of the dumping margin and in an increase of the undercutting and underselling or injury margin. The dumping margin increases because of an ex-works export price that is lower than the invoice price. The lower Level of Trade adjustment than the actual gross margin of the related sales company results in undercutting and an injury margin, which in this case is about 14 % higher by the application of the LoT to CIF instead of application of the actual resale price.

(c) Undercutting and target profit margin

The undercutting figure reflects market price phenomena. Undercutting is not an essential characteristic of injury. It may be that dumping happens over an extended period and that initially price undercutting took place. Defence of market share and protection of the cost position may induce an industry to decrease its prices to levels such that the undercutting is reduced to zero or is even negative. The calculation of the undercutting is the first step in the process of calculation of injury. The underselling margin, i.e. the undercutting of the profitable price, is the injury margin, which is the level at which the European is damaged. If the injury margin is higher than the dumping margin (both as percentage of CIF value), the dumping margin as per cent of CIF export price is applied as anti-dumping duty. If the reverse is the case, the injury margin as percentage of CIF export price is the anti-dumping duty.

From the calculations above, it may be apparent that a demonstration by the industry of the level of profit needed for European industry is crucial for the level of anti-dumping duties. The case of colour television makes clear what consequences were of a target profit of 0 %, which level did not have a serious factual basis, but did serve Thomson. In the case presented in Table 16.8, the duty fell from 33.1 % to 20.7 %, which is the (negative) undercutting margin divided by the CIF price or (−) $-1.77 \div 8.55$. Another essential phenomenon is that if the undercutting is zero, possibly because of the defensive price behaviour by the European industry, the underselling margin is also zero. Defence of the market share is not appreciated.

The target profit is generally between 5 % and 10 %. In the case of CD players, a comprehensive demonstration was produced of total capital employed in European CD production. From a reasonable return on capital and the velocity of turnover over capital required, the profit was derived. Statistical methods demonstrated which price trends would have prevailed, and what the profits would have been, if dumping had not taken place. Furthermore, a calculation on the investments delayed and additional costs to be re-earned under normal circumstances were presented and the amounts to be earned in the period of 5 years in order to cover these outlays. A profit of 12–15 % was required. The European Commission, however, neglected these calculations and instead took a target profit from a Table and allocated 10 %. It appears that this percentage was equal to the various other products in the sphere of electronics. This amount would never be earned as the consequence of absorption and circumvention. But exporters made a substantially higher profit in their home market.

The choice of a target profit by the European Community authorities is rather arbitrary. In the case of colour television, there was no evidence for a zero profit rate granted to European Community industry. No proof of low profitability on a global scale was offered. Evidence on the opposite was neglected. Indeed, the profits of the exporting countries could have been taken as a starting point for the calculation of profit. In the case of plain paper copiers, the profit rate of Matsushita's domestic sales found was to be 14.6 %,[28] while the rather high target profit rate granted to European Community industry was 12 %.

(d) Alternatives to the present methodology.

Various authors on economics have considered the determination of injury by the institutions insufficient. A weakness, indeed, is that the price undercutting may not only be attributable to dumping, but can also be the consequence of a relative competitive advantage of the exporter. Alternatives have been proposed. Various authors recommend as an alternative a model called Comparative Analysis of the Domestic Industry Condition (CADIC). This model requires the presentation of

[28] Judgment of the Court (Fifth Chamber) of 10 March 1992. – Matsushita Electric Industrial Co. Ltd and Matsushita Electric Trading Co. Ltd v Council of the European Communities. – Anti-dumping duties on plain paper photocopiers originating in Japan. – Case C-175/87, European Court reports 1992 Page I-01409, recital 27.

data such as elasticity of supply and of demand both of exporters and of the complainant in respective markets and of elasticity of demand in respective markets and even cross-price elasticity, which is the percentage change in the quantity demanded of the domestic product of the complainant given a one per cent change in the price of the dumped import. Unfortunately, models such as CADIC or an alternative, COMPAS, are presented after a flawed analysis of the actual practice of the anti-dumping authorities.[29] The same has been done by the Danish Business Authority, which bases its decision, authorised by the Government for anti-dumping decisions, on a vague model, which it defends with the following statement[30]:

Elasticities are never complete unknowns. They merely reflect the behaviour of a market, and an analyst with sufficient insight into a market can easily pin down realistic elasticities.

Crystal ball economists pretend that they have sufficient insight in the market, which comprehension participants in the market themselves lack. These authors, however, hide their data and only claim insights.

The major problem for the European Commission and any other investigating authority is that only a limited period is investigated in detail. Reference has been made to the demonstration of injury by means of a trend analysis of prices of Compact Disc players with and without dumping. The Consultants in Quantitative Methods could do this on the basis of many years of data available from GfK retail trade studies. It was assumed, however, that in some years there was no dumping and on the basis of this assumption a price trend was calculated, which was assumed to be the "normal price" trend. The dumping price trend was the trend in the year prior to the complaint. This almost coincided with the investigation period of the European Commission. Because only in an investigation period of one or one and a half years, the domestic market prices and export prices are available and compared, there is no information available about a situation without dumping. There are no supply and demand schemes and certainly no elasticities, on which only the Danish Business Authority and some CADIC diviners seem to have a clairvoyant vision.

The point of criticism is that a model such as CADIC requires data nobody has available. It requires demand and supply functions, which do not exist. All literature in which models are used with supply and demand characteristics is useless. These data are unavailable. Besides, some allege that they have information such as market share of the dumping party (defendant) in the domestic market. That

---

[29] Tharakan et al. (2006), is a striking example. The authors present a model after a representation of the European Union practice that does not have a relationship with reality. They even pretended that they analysed cases of the European Union and did: "calculate, for 233 cases, the parameter α', i.e. the share of the respondent in his combined home and EU sales". The data they used for it is inexistent. The information is not available and the data must have been devised.

[30] 1321 National Agency for Enterprise and Construction: "Economic Assessment of the Community interest in EU Anti-dumping Cases", 22 August 2005. The paper contains disastrous misinformation about CTVs.

information is not available and certainly the elasticity of supply and demand is not available. In one particular case, in an article recommending a "counterfactual analysis", an author presented data that is clearly counterfeit. It concerns one of the most unknown and difficult markets, the DRAM market. Producers do not know their supply curves and certainly not the reaction of their supplies to a price change. They determine their quantities to be produced and set prices and pray. The latter issue is especially significant when prices continuously decrease, both because of product innovation and because of cost cuts. There is not a demand curve, but a continuously shifting and increasing demand.[31]

(C) **The lesser duty rule: elimination of injury caused by dumping and some consequences**

Discussions on the lesser duty rule of the European Community are abundant in international literature. Some minor remarks are made here below.

16.13 The Lesser Duty Rule in General

An anti-dumping duty should eliminate the injury caused by dumping, i.e. the price undercutting of the complainant's price augmented with a certain amount of elimination of loss and with profit. If an exporter dumps a product by 61.8 % but the effect on the price is that its underselling is only 33.1 %, the exporter is clearly not very efficient and it needs a substantial difference between his home market price and the export price in order to be able to undersell prices of European Community producers by 33.1 %. This is the rationale for a limitation of an anti-dumping duty to the lower of two margins. In this case it is restricted to the lesser duty of 33.1 %. If the underselling were 75 %, the exporter is assumed to be so efficient that only 61.8 % of that underselling is attributable to dumping.

This is economically an assailable point of view. Chapter 8 demonstrates that the existence of dumping influences the dumper's competitiveness. The positive influence of dumping on the cost of production of the dumping exporter is included in

[31] Tharakan (1997) presented results of calculations, on the basis of "trade sources" – kept anonymous – and also used an expert opinion: "Although the elasticity of demand (N_d) and the elasticity of supply (E_d) of the EC like-product are also based on available expert opinion, same disparity between them and reality is not impossible." Some trade sources have reported spot DRAM market prices without quantities involved, but long-term contracts between suppliers and customers and internal supplies with their prices and quantities involved – covering the major part of trade flows in semiconductors – are secret and not available to trade sources or experts and opinions of undisclosed experts are, therefore, useless. As for the volumes and prices on the Japanese domestic market, these are only known to the Japanese ministry of trade and are kept secret. Even the ministry would not be capable of computing "elasticity" of demand and supply. The conclusion is that Tharakan's article attacking the European Union institutions contains devised data.

the normal value in terms of increased profit. But the price in the domestic market of the dumper does not necessarily change. The composition of cost and profit in that price changes. The improvement in profit in the country of dumped exports due to the loss of sales volume by the complainant in the country of imports is a factor that is not taken into account. In Chap. 8 demonstrates that in the case of two equivalent competitors, one of which is the dumping exporter, the dumping causes a decrease in the dumper's cost and an increase in the victim's cost. The injurious effect of the dumping on volume of production of the victim and via this volume on its cost position has not been taken into account. The elimination of injury up to the level of undercutting of the victim's price or of underselling of the victim's profitable price (price plus target profit) does not eliminate the injury inflicted by the quantitative effect of dumping, but restricts it to a price difference. The decay in cost position of the victim has not been compensated and the elimination of injury is too small. That was in any case very strikingly the situation of the CTV industry, which was characterised by continuous drops in market share and even absolute sales and which was strangled by dumpers and the European Commission with its zero percent profit and origin mismanagement.

16.14 Tenability of the Lesser Duty Rule

It has been shown that the view of the European institutions concerning the lesser duty does not hold. The opinion that the lesser duty is a desirable rule is based on a static view of the economy and on the unacceptable assumption that dumping does not contribute to improvement of efficiency. This is mainly attributable to the idea that dumping is related to a protection of the domestic market of the dumper. Although this may be the case, dumping may improve the competitive position of the dumper substantially, as the Tosoh case in Chap. 8 shows. This treatment of injury is sufficient reason for the industry to continuously challenge the level of the target profit determined by the authorities in actual cases. In the case of CTV, for instance, it was demonstrated that the dumpers were profitable, but the European Commission denied profits to European industry, in spite of the fact that the dumping almost continuously took place, and thus saved the face of continuously loss incurring state-owned Thomson and contributed to the destruction of European Community industry.

As made clear in Chap. 8 the concept of Community interest is not tenable if the investigation is restricted to the effect of the product concerned and other sectors, paying for the dumped imports by exports, are unjustifiably disregarded.

16.15 European Community Interest

The development of argumentation in an early stage of a proceeding for measures is an urgent issue. Experience shows that the organisation of support by the ancillary suppliers and arguments concerning the importance of measures on their behalf is highly useful. In the case of the energy saving lamps, for instance, the industry had ample support from the suppliers of components. Although enthusiasm on their part is not generally expected, customers of complainants may also help to support measures. Consumer organisations are tempted to react to the invitation to express their views by unresponsive reactions, generally lacking sound material argumentation. Nevertheless, it is always useful to make estimates on the effects of measures on the consumer. Generally, such effects tend to be overstated. Strong opposition often comes from traders and customers or potential buyers of dumping exporters. An example was the computer industry in the case of DRAMs. They showed a rather overstated impact of measures on their bill of materials and their competitive position. The bill of materials is of minor importance in relation to the total value of a computer. Preparation of argumentation by calculations is essential. Since economic theory also points at negative effects of measures on the competitive position of users, it is always valuable to give a factual insight into the situation. Calculations concerning the cost effects are a valuable contribution to the presentation of a solid case.

16.16 Disclosure

When a disclosure is presented to complainant and defendants, the documents are often extremely vague as far as the data of the export side of the proceeding is concerned. These figures are often aggregates or hidden. Undercutting, for instance, is only given in terms of exporter A, B, etc. or even an aggregate and the amounts of undercutting. The amounts of hypothetical turnover of European industry (quantity of the exporters times the aggregate average price of European producers) and amounts of data on the CIF value of the exports of the dumping exporters A, B etc. do not offer much insight. This implies that the opportunity to act against the level of the undercutting and underselling is small or even completely negligible. Keen attention to the content of the disclosure and a strong attitude toward insufficiencies in the disclosure is valuable and even essential. Anti-dumping measures are not a favour granted to, but a right of the complaining industry, if dumping and injury take place. Too easily complaining industry accepts outcomes of anti-dumping cases in disclosures as gestures by magnanimous European Commission officials. Too many examples have been given of results in which data appeared engineered.

16.17 Conclusions on Methodology

There are sufficient reasons for industry to pay careful attention to the interpretation of rules and the methodology of the establishment of dumping and injury. Only a few points are emphasised in these conclusions. It is unavoidable to check whether the "like product" definition resulted in the correct injury calculations. Details concerning the establishment of normal value and export price should be kept in mind and the complainant should not wait until the disclosure of information on results of the proceeding to make its statements on the tenability of OEM treatment if there are indications that exporters request such treatment. During the investigation, the complainant should have its recommendations concerning the target profit with necessary underlying calculations on return on investment and on turnover and necessary cost improvement. Chapter 16 is intended to lend support to prospective complainants.

References

Tharakan PKM (1997) The Japan-EC DRAMs anti-dumping undertaking: was it justified? What purpose did it serve? De Econ 145:1–28

Tharakan PKM, Greenaway D, Kerstens B (2006) Anti-dumping and excess injury margins in the European Community: a counterfactual analysis. Eur J Polit Econ 22:653–674

Vermulst EA (2010) EC anti-dumping law & practice. Sweet & Maxwell, London

Vermulst E, Ikenson D (2007) Zeroing under the WTO anti-dumping agreement: where do we stand? Global Trade Cust J 2(6):231–242

Chapter 17
After All

Abstract Active use of trade policy instruments that are legally open to industry did not prevent the decay of electronics business. On the contrary, the conclusion is that negligence in application of the rules, certain personal political ambitions that did not aim at proper application of the law and even prejudices against application of internationally agreed law has created an unreliable trade environment. Serious, but unchecked and even unnoticed errors in the conduct of trade policy, have caused havoc. The book and this chapter mention some cases. The result has been catastrophic for European electronic industry. Industry is entitled to a reliable trade policy. Predictability of trade policy would be improved if it would be removed from the back rooms of member states' ministries and would be transferred to a European level, partly to a specialised European court for recourse in cases of procedural errors. Since trade policy is the European competence, already established in the Treaty of Rome, democratic supervision could be enhanced by transferral of legislative powers to the European Parliament. This could also prevent that member states are played off against each other by foreign powers and the sometimes unfathomable but unchecked individual trade policy routes of some Community Commissioners.

17.1 Trade Policy and the Decline of an Industry

The preceding pages sketch the decay of the European electronics industry, which was subjected to practically continuous attacks from abroad by trade practices condemned under the GATT and WTO Agreements. An outline has been given of the various methods to counter these troublesome practices. Although the remedies were not self-evident, they might have been effective if the trade instruments would have been applied properly and without other ambitions than proper application of the rules.

M. van Marion, *International Trade Policy and European Industry*,
Contributions to Economics, DOI 10.1007/978-3-319-00392-4_17,

Not only governmental impulses and even mistakes but also circumstances in businesses and certain business doctrines appear to upset proper application of trade rules or to disrupt the lobby pursuing the acceptance of trade measures.

How trade rules are applied and should be applied in practice has been explained in varying degrees of detail. The crucifixion of the European industry were acceptable if it had been the result normal of competitive relations. Trade rules were often abused and not or insufficiently applied, because the rules were considered a favour rather than a right, and officials sometimes perceived their function in trade policy as a fief, from which they could grant benefits.

17.2 Trade Policy and Business

Evidently, a multitude of possibilities to change the trade environment by the application of trade rules or by bending the rules is open to industry. Historical facts have been presented about trade policy as conducted in practice. Interactions with governments and other authorities are essential and often decisive, however. Because they did not fit in the sequence of narration, many cases have been left out. The description of various other trade policy actions, including anti-dumping cases, might have been of interest but unless this book was a treatise on trade policy law, these were mainly of anecdotal significance. Many of the cases presented show that a scrutiny of World Trade Organization (WTO) trade rules in connection with business trade practice are worthwhile. Rules are instruments. It is important for any business to be knowledgeable about the framework in which it must work and the areas in which it may invoke the rules. A strictly legalistic approach to trade rules has disappointing results. The rules give ample opportunity to find ways for the representation of industrial interests. Such an approach also appears to leave room for subjective interpretation of the rules and the implementation of trade policy in practice for those who regard the rules as means to build a fief and who behave as if the application of the rule is a favour to business. It is not a favour, but a right. A major mistake is to have too much confidence in politicians and officials. The problem is that some expect gratitude if they apply the rule and some pursue their own interest, hoping it will foster their career. They often are successful in silencing industrial criticism with threats by means revealed in this book. Fortunately they are a slim minority, however, who have a negative effect on the image in general of the authorities. As shown, exporters may also suffer under unintelligible implementation or explanation of rules. The case of differential treatment of Original Equipment Manufacturer (OEM), and the application of origin rules with almost inevitable fraud as a consequence in the case of CTV are examples. The advantage of exporters is that they can seek justice in court, although this may sometimes not help them. Careful attention to the all details of implementation of the rules appears vital.

17.3 Trade Policy, Politicians and Officials

The book described the conduct of some Commissioners and other politicians. Of course, some Commissioners cherished views that were not always welcomed by the European industry or even by lawyers of foreign dumping exporters. Sir Leon Brittan, who was extremely critical towards certain trade policy actions and towards dumping complaints, has been mentioned as an example. The velocity of the European Commission's acceptance of complaints slowed down drastically. But Sir Leon did not push his ideas beyond the limits of the law, and he was not a person driven by vanity who considered the rules inferior to his whims. Some Commissioners had other motivations than merely application of the rules, as the famous VCR case and the format battle and the case of energy saving lamps demonstrated.[1] However, most Commissioners carefully respect and guard the rules, and take care that their organisation is not wrecked by an image of unprofessionalism or arbitrariness.

Most European Commission officials in the trade policy directorates displayed high moral, professional and intellectual standards. Sometimes the general image of the institution was negatively affected by inexplicable acts. These occasions have been described. They are exceptions which must, however, always be taken into account. These exceptions undermine predictability, which is the essence of legal security.

17.4 State and Business

Some of occurrences depicted in this book and recommendations made have been fervently rejected as dangerously protectionist. Academics especially pay ample attention to practices of trade defence and deem them objectionable by definition. Economists agree that liberal trade, aiming at gains of and allowing comparative advantage, is a carrier of welfare. It has also been demonstrated in Chap. 8 that some unofficial barriers to trade may result in a reverse or uphill division of labour, where the trade is in a direction opposite the relative competitive advantage. The injury inflicted by trade distortions are in the field of the product markets in which distortions take place, but they have also a negative influence on other products. Measures against injury to industry in the countries of imports are often depicted as protectionist and as injurious to consumers of those imported products. It may be wondered, however, why such benefits not based on relative economic advantage but on distortion of competition should continue, whereas consumers of other products are disadvantaged because payments have to be made by means of exports for importation of those products that inflict injury on the import markets. This general wisdom is amply applied in the discussion on the Common Agricultural

[1] See also picture tubes mentioned in a footnote 39 of Chap. 15.

Policy (CAP) of the European Community, but not if third countries' industrial products are exported to the European Community as consequence of systems causing trade distortions. The European Community CAP has protected European farmers and disadvantaged farmers and processing industry in countries of imports of European agricultural products, but also the European industry by relatively higher European food prices and extra-concessions in international trade rounds as payment for the maintenance of the CAP restriction. The CAP has often firmly been challenged, but measures against the dumping of third countries' industrial products are rejected by often the same authors. The CAP has a similar influence on foreign consumers as the dumping by third countries in the European Community. CAP also has an effect on the European industry because the relative competitive position is distorted in the same way as dumping distorts relative competition in Diagram 8.5 of Chap. 8.

It is, however, not the task of business to defend itself or to weigh interests involved in trade measures. If there are negative consequences, and there are always some negative aspects, of claims for measures, it is up to the political machinery to balance interests involved and to make a decision. The problem in the European Community is that 27 countries decide on the desirability of measures that have an effect on a few member states only. Often, decisions are made in the backrooms of ministries, and in some cases the disclosures of the European Commission remain closed: officials of member states do not want to look at the facts. Policies are regularly based on presumptions. In the case of energy saving lamps, a Dutch civil servant confessed that the facts on dumping and injury, the level of environmental benefits of European or Chinese CFL lamps and the effects on the environment in Europe and China were not relevant at all. There was a policy and the facts were immaterial. Since 27 member states voted on unknown basis, the outcome of trade policy deliberations was highly arbitrary. Some governments are not interested at all in the wellbeing of industry and disregard the distortion of competition as long as this distortion is superficially in favour of the country. Alternatively, they give in to pressure from an exporting country. Even Commissioners of the European Community left the industry in the lurch and betrayed it by abusing their power over officials, taking a course marked by infringing on the rules and leaving industry with the damage of both insufficient measures and disturbed relations with the exporting country. The energy saving lamps is an example. If measures are taken, the effect can be disappointing. Trust in even-handed and scrupulous application of the rules, without political surprises, is not advisable. Sometimes specific interests play a stronger role than an industry can expect from application of rules. The problem is that a minority of negative experiences have more influence than the more frequent, almost general phenomenon of firm compliance with the rules. Therefore, continuous awareness that some politicians or officials may try to take the results of a proceeding away is imperative.

17.5 Business and Protectionism

Since states – or, in Europe, the European institutions and even 27 member states – are responsible for trade measures, they are responsible for "protectionism"; not the industry that requests protection against market disruptions or complains about trade distortion by third countries. Some member states consider trade defence instruments a priori objectionable and were suspected of trying to do the opposite of what the industry felt needed. The consequence was that industry tried to represent its interests directly with the European Community and its representatives in trade negotiations. In the European Community, the one member state tried to demonstrate that the European Commission was involved in trickery in anti-dumping. Symposia were organised in which the European Commission's anti-dumping policy was attacked. The problem was that these attacks were not based on facts but on suspicions about proceedings. Factual evidence was absent.

The attitude of some member states is not quite understandable. The instructions to the Swedish representative of the anti-dumping committee were to vote against any proposal by the European Commission for measures, unless he convinced his minister of the Swedish interest that a vote against the European Commission is another sign of impaired relations in the European Community decision-making. A European Community of 27 countries can neither be protectionist nor liberal. It cannot properly decide. Definitive anti-dumping and anti-subsidy duties are imposed by the European Community Council of Ministers with a simple majority after the European Commission consults the member states in the Anti-dumping Committee. Denmark is advised by "crystal ball" economists, knowing parameters hidden for anybody else, and, consequently, in principle against anti-dumping. It is clear that both for exporters and European Community industry, an intolerable situation has arisen, in which 27 member states must be informed about the pros and cons of certain cases and all sorts of parties influence their decisions. Complainants are generally poorer than exporters and the interference by these interested parties are often made at diplomatic levels, not infrequently in the shape of pressure. The outcome of decision-making by 27 member states is completely unpredictable, and protectionist and free-trade prejudices may play a free role. A change in the decision-making framework is inevitable. A reduction of arbitrariness and juridification is imperative. A special chamber of the Court of First Instance should be charged with supervision on the correctness of procedural details, correct application of the rules and acceptability of dumping and injury calculations. A transfer of certain decision-making on trade policy from ministerial backrooms and coteries of member states to the European parliament would both improve transparency and democratic accountability.

17.6 The Law as a Non-tradable

In various chapters, intervention by trade officials in proceedings has been sketched. Too frequently the power of individual Commissioners or officials or member states' "principles" – often equal to prejudice – played a role in trade policy. Trade policy should be independent from individual and particular political sentiments and be based on the law. The European Community should act as a Community of Law and not of personal ambitions and arbitrariness.

This does not only apply to the European Community. Fortunately, the WTO plays a supervisory role. The famous case won by India against the European Community concerning bed linen had effects on another case, i.e. of energy saving lamps into India from China.[2] The victory of India had a mitigating effect on India's own conduct of proceedings. It certainly also had its effect on the European Community and that is positive contribution to legal certainty

The issue of a Korean proceeding on shavers has been mentioned. It was another case in which the existence of international rules and supervision contributed to a moderate outcome. In 1995, Samsung's trade policy department designed a complaint on behalf of Korean electric shavers of the Kaiser brand by the Korean producer Ulim Electronics Co., Ltd. against Braun (Germany), Panasonic and Hitachi (Japan) and Philips (the Netherlands and China). The Kaiser shavers were of inferior quality and consumers needed a first aid kit. Samsung's department store Shinsegae preferred to sell imported high quality shavers that did not injure people. Samsung therefore rendered services to Ulim, but the complaint and the proceeding had so many flaws that the Korean authorities suggested that the exporters should offer undertakings. The flaws were that, as concluded from the file, the complaint did not have sufficient support and the calculations of the support were not based on production, but on capacity. The flaws had been exposed and the case was, as reported, settled by price undertakings. Again, WTO supervision offered some legal certainty, but the room for arbitrariness was ample.

Gradually, trade rules have become increasingly reliable. Nevertheless, as may be concluded from the present book, there are still factors that affect certainties that industry and exporters might expect. Self-restraint agreements seem to be history. However, the greater the legal certainty by means of WTO surveillance, the greater the temptation to innovatively develop trade policy instruments. This is especially the case in times of economic decline.

[2] World Trade Organization, WT/DS141/R, 30 October 2000, (00–4407) European Communities – Anti-Dumping Duties on Imports of Cotton-Type Bed Linen from India, Report of the Panel.

17.7 Abuse of Trade Policy and the Demise of Electronics Industry

The gradual demise of European industry, and in particular the electronics business, has been sketched in this book. Many other electronics activities have suffered and succumbed due to an ineptitude for those charged with application of the rules to do so in accordance with the reason the rules were conceived. The United Kingdom television industry thought to recue itself by pulling itself out of a swamp by its hair, i.e. by voluntary restraints, and failed. Philips chose the same method and was deceived. Rather than applying existing anti-dumping legislation for VCRs, Vice President Davignon carried away this instrument for some political issues like relations with France and Japan and concluded a VRA, which inevitably resulted in a disaster for the European producers. European industry never recovered from this catastrophe. It lost hundreds of millions Euros and the necessary switch to VHS required development capacity that could not be dedicated to other technologies. The time period of investigation and indulgence toward exporters dumping of CD players and subsequent circumvention of the duties resulted in triumph for producers, exporters from Japan and Korea that were clearly inferior in efficiency, in the same way that the case of Tosoh was an indication of inefficiency and low export pricing.

European television industry has demonstrably been sacrificed by application of zero profit rates for the benefit of Thomson's face and by preposterous interpretation of origin rules enabling a dumping Turkish industry to continue their dumping freely in the European Community until the remnants of European industry were crushed. Measures were insufficient because the face of state-owned producer Thomson had to be saved. Commissioner Peter Mandelson challenged familiar thinking and high-handedly decided that the dumping of energy saving lamps by the Chinese was favourable to European Community producers. Such interference bereaves industry from confidence that the rules prevail in anti-dumping. If companies have demonstrated the courage to go ahead in an anti-dumping case and to withstand the pressure from the government of the exporters, even at the cost of some business in that country, they cannot be sure that some Commissioner will not aggravate the situation.

17.8 Trade Policy in the Future

An awareness of the trade policy environment is essential for business. This book has tried to clarify the importance of knowledge on the trade policy instruments available. It has also warned for illusions. It has pointed at the importance of effects of foreign economic structures for trade and possible need of trade policy instruments. The issue of China and in its slipstream, some other countries like Vietnam, is a special case. The fundamental distortions in the economy as consequence of governmental intervention in key sectors of the economy will not disappear soon, if ever. That also implies that distortions will take place in China's external economic relations. Apart from massive overproduction as consequence of government promotion of certain production, as was the case with compact fluorescence lamps, a lack of knowledge on cost calculation and pricing policy is a second characteristic of Chinese production and exports. This problem may be solved in the long run, but as John Maynard Keynes explained, in the long run we are all dead.

MIX
Papier aus verantwortungsvollen Quellen
Paper from responsible sources
FSC® C105338

If you have any concerns about our products,
you can contact us on
ProductSafety@springernature.com

In case Publisher is established outside the EU,
the EU authorized representative is:
Springer Nature Customer Service Center GmbH
Europaplatz 3, 69115 Heidelberg, Germany

Printed by Libri Plureos GmbH
in Hamburg, Germany